Gandhi

The Man, His People and the Empire

RAJMOHAN GANDHI

HAUS BOOKS
London

Copyright © 2007 Rajmohan Gandhi

First published in Great Britain in 2007 by Haus Publishing,
26 Cadogan Court, Draycott Avenue, London SW3 3BX
www.hauspublishing.co.uk

The moral rights of the author have been asserted

A CIP catalogue record for this book is available from the British Library

ISBN 978–1-905791-24-8

Typeset in Garamond 3 by MacGuru Ltd
info@macguru.org.uk
Printed in Dubai by Oriental Press
Jacket illustrations: Front image courtesy of the National Portrait Gallery, London; back image
author collection.

Contents

In Bombay – 1944 (Original photo: D R D Wadia)

In Madras – 1946

To U, who (a bit like a key character in this story)
is fearless by nature, independent, and always giving

Mohandas Karamchand Gandhi in Rajkot – 1883

Preface

Begun as an exercise to delineate the 'true' Gandhi, this project turned naturally and swiftly into a retelling of a modern-day epic involving an unusual hero, a complex people and a powerful empire.

With its sweep, its oscillations between glory and tragedy, the profusion of its characters, the richness (in infirmity and strength) of its (several) principal characters and the valiant persistence of the chief among them, the story I have sought to relate is without doubt a classic. I only hope my retelling does not hopelessly undersell it. In some ways it is an unbelievable story. Einstein thought that 'generations to come will scarce believe' that Gandhi actually did what he did.

This is also an attempt to identify the 'true' Gandhi – to convey the truth about him. Though a popular metaphor, 60 years after his death, for innocence, ingenuity or courage, he is not clearly known as a person.

The Good Boatman, an earlier study of Gandhi I wrote, attempted to answer some important questions, including why the subcontinent saw so much violence despite Gandhi's non-violence, and why Partition occurred despite his opposition. But it was not a biography. This one is.

The metaphor has shrouded the man. A courageous, selfless and non-violent foe of oppression anywhere may be dubbed a Gandhi, even in places far from India, while a tormentor of the innocent may be called Gandhi's new assailant, as happened in India during massacres in 1984, 1992 and 2002.

But what was Gandhi like as a human being? Despite his fame, or perhaps because of it, Mohandas Gandhi the individual is not sufficiently felt, or seen, or understood.

In India we think we know him. No face is more familiar. He looks at us from banknotes, postage stamps and billboards. We feel we can sketch the spectacles, the bald head, the loincloth, the pocket watch. But familiarity is not knowledge. We think we also know what he stood for. Yet the obvious and predictable Gandhi may be very misleading, and the beliefs of the real man may have been quite different from what we think.

Who was he, this timid lad who became the conscience of a century and led India to liberty? This discoverer of satyagraha, the one wanting to remove every tear from every eye, this pioneer of religious pluralism and dissenter from modernity, what was he like in his daily life, in his close relationships? What was he like in his confrontations, his face-offs with the Empire, with his own bitterly divided people, with his adversaries – and with himself, perhaps his greatest confrontation? What was he like in his relationships with his parents, his wife and sons, with women in general and with his young female associates, and with political and non-political colleagues?

Was he a politician or a saint? If both, how did these two Gandhis combine, and in what proportions? Or was he, as critics have alleged, someone who broke a pledge that he would rather die than accept Partition? Was he not an unfeeling husband and father? A man who did strange things in the name of chastity? Or emasculated India in the name of non-violence? Or patronized Dalits without empowering them?

This study is a bid to free Gandhi the person from his image or images, and to present his life fully and honestly. Many have presented their versions of Gandhi, often power-fully. Assisted by his sister Sushila Nayar, Gandhi's faithful secretary Pyarelal provided a remarkable multi-volume biography that began with Gandhi's last phase, turned to his childhood and boyhood, and then covered the 'middle' decades. Earlier, D G Tendulkar had produced his eight-volume biography. B R Nanda, Louis Fischer and Geoffrey Ashe have each given us memorable and popular volumes, and they are not the only ones to have done so.

Erik Erikson's *Gandhi's Truth* analyzed his subject's tension-filled psychology and his often peculiar practices, and Martin Green has presented Gandhi as a New Age revo-lutionary. In 1909 Joseph Doke wrote the first Gandhi biography, while in the 1920s Gandhi wrote his own account in *My Experiments with Truth*. Dozens of other biographies followed, and more will be written.

In the 1990s, Yogesh Chadha wrote a widely welcomed life of Gandhi. Recently, Narayan Desai, the son of Mahadev Desai, Gandhi's secretary from 1917 to 1942, has published a significant four-volume Gandhi biography in Gujarati. An English trans-lation is to follow. The numerous diaries into which Mahadev Desai entered many an enlightening detail were published earlier.

Yet there seemed a need for the chronological, complete and candid portrayal attempted here. Studies written shortly after his assassination naturally focused on

Gandhi's final decade and on some aspects of his personality, inevitably excluding others. Moreover, the early biographers produced their works without access to the vast amount of illuminating material now available to scholars. Perhaps time was needed before the whole of his life could be looked at as one piece, and a touchable, seeable, comprehensible Gandhi brought out.

It was a tall order. I went for it in fear and trembling, praying that I might do some justice to the man and also to truth. God only knows how far I have succeeded or failed.

This is the story of someone who was neither simple to understand, nor easy to live with, nor a stranger to error or to defeat, but who continues to inspire many and interest many more. It seeks to unravel Gandhi's complexity, looks at his quirks, failures and weaknesses, and looks too for the secret behind the power of a frail man who renounced wealth, comfort and rank.

This man, a metaphor for innocence, was in fact an exceedingly shrewd tactician and strategist. How he made his decisions, and recruited allies, are exercises portrayed here, as also his moves regarding India's future leadership.

In the epic I seek to retell, several stories intertwine with the story of Gandhi's life. The stories of India's freedom movement and the 1947 Partition and violence. The story of caste and untouchability. The story of Hindu-Muslim relations and of India's princely states. The origins of modern Indian democracy. The story of modern Hinduism. Aspects of all these stories will be found in the pages that follow, as well as the story of a youth, a man, and an old man hungry to change history.

For full disclosure, let me state that I am a grandson of Mohandas Gandhi, one of the 15 grandchildren born to his four children, who were all sons. Nine grandchildren (four granddaughters and five grandsons) are living as of the time of writing, as well as a large number of great-grandchildren and their offspring, plus many Gandhis descending from his siblings and cousins. My father, Devadas, was Gandhi's youngest son. I was twelve-and-a-half, a schoolboy in New Delhi, when the Mahatma was killed. But I am also, I hope, a scholar committed to facts and their discovery.

The Gandhi portrayed in these pages emerges from a mass of material: letters, memoirs, diary jottings, records of conversations, talks, interviews, articles, books. A series of talented aides recorded his remarks and moods. Newspapers recorded his public statements. His own journals carried Gandhi's articles. He wrote an autobiography as well as a history of his South African satyagrahas. Foes, critics and psychoanalysts have exposed to view aspects of Gandhi missed by admirers. Several companions, and critical allies, have offered glimpses and interpretations.

An important item from family archives has been used here for the first time (in Chapter 7). This study benefits also from material recently brought into the public domain by Nilam Parikh and Uma Dhupelia-Mesthrie, granddaughters, respectively, of Harilal Gandhi and Manilal Gandhi, the Mahatma's first and second sons.

A biographer hoping to construct the 'real' Gandhi suffers not from a paucity of material but from its abundance. His task is to weigh and select, to decide what is significant, and discern true and perhaps hidden meanings. Furthermore, a Gandhi biographer does not start from scratch. He owes large debts to (among others) numerous diarists, other biographers and autobiographers, libraries and librarians, archives and archivists, and to the compilers of the *Collected Works of Mahatma Gandhi*.

I acknowledge these debts as well as what I owe to the University of Illinois at Urbana-Champaign, which allowed me to write this biography while discharging my responsibilities as a visiting professor and as the academic director of one of its living and learning communities. I also thank the Navajivan Trust for permission to quote from Gandhi's writings and speeches.

This book has been written over a 30-month period, but it has been thought about, and its questions wrestled with, for much longer. May it inform and interest the reader and, God willing, speak to today's questions.

Rajmohan Gandhi

References in the text

References to certain frequently-cited works appear in the text, not in the notes:

A = The 'Autobiography': M K Gandhi, *My Experiments with Truth* (New York: Dover Publications, 1983).

K = Krishnadas, *Seven Months with Mahatma Gandhi* (Ahmedabad: Navajivan, 1951).

S = M K Gandhi, *Satyagraha in South Africa* (Ahmedabad: Navajivan, 1928, 1993 edition).

All other references are to the digitized edition of the *Collected Works of Mahatma Gandhi* (New Dehli: Publications Division).

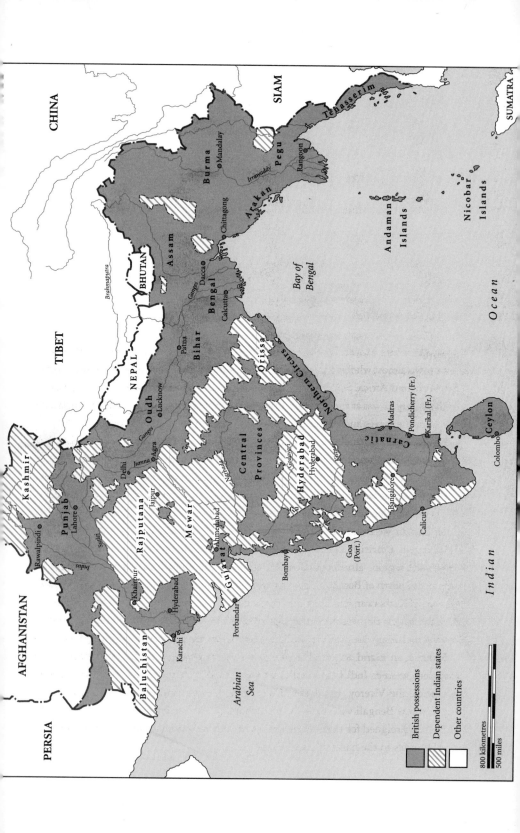

CHINA

PERSIA

AFGHANISTAN

TIBET

SIAM

NEPAL

BHUTAN

SUMATRA

Kashmir

Rawalpindi

Punjab

Lahore

Indus

Sutlej

Baluchistan

Khairpur

Hyderabad

Karachi

Rajputana

Jaipur

Delhi

Agra

Jumna

Ganges

Oudh

Lucknow

Assam

Brahmaputra

Burma

Mandalay

Pegu

Rangoon

Irrawaddy

Arakan

Chittagong

Bengal

Dacca

Calcutta

Bihar

Patna

Ganges

Mewar

Gujarat

Ahmedabad

Porbandar

Bombay

Narbada

Central
Provinces

Orissa

Northern Circars

Godavari

Hyderabad

Hyderabad

Krishna

Nagpur

Goa
(Port.)

Bangalore

Calicut

Carnatic

Madras

Pondicherry (Fr.)

Karikal (Fr.)

Ceylon

Colombo

Tenasserim

Andaman
Islands

Nicobar
Islands

Bay of
Bengal

Arabian
Sea

Indian

Ocean

British possessions

Dependent Indian states

Other countries

800 kilometres

500 miles

1

Boyhood

Kathiawar, 1869–88

Porbandar, where Mohandas Karamchand Gandhi was born on 2 October 1869, was a coastal town almost wholly encircled by the Arabian Sea and long engaged in trade with the Arab world and Africa. Since legend held that Krishna's friend from childhood, Sudama, had lived there, it was at times called Sudamapuri. A wall of white limestone protected the town from the waves and reflected the sun into the eyes of approaching sailors.

The state of Porbandar (of which the town, with a population of about 15,000 in 1869, was a part) was ruled by an Indian prince on whom a British Resident kept a watchful eye. The India of the British Raj contained more than 500 'princely' states of this sort, some larger than Porbandar, which had an area of about 600 square miles, and others smaller, all shown in yellow on the Raj's maps. Territories ruled directly by the British were shown in red. From Rajkot, an inland city 120 miles to the east of Porbandar, a British agent supervised all the princely states of the Kathiawar (or Kathiawad) region, also known as Saurashtra – the conspicuous peninsula south of Karachi and north of Bombay that juts westward into the Arabian Sea. Gujarati was the language of Kathiawar, as also of the adjacent region (largely 'red' on the map) to its east, where the largest city was Ahmedabad, and of the coastal lands (also 'red') to the north of Bombay, including the port city of Surat, one of Britain's earliest Indian outposts.

Bombay, an island acquired by the British from Portugal in the 17th century, had grown into western India's greatest city (where a majority spoke Marathi), but the Raj's top official, the Viceroy, ruled from Calcutta in the subcontinent's east, on the Bay of Bengal (where Bengali was the principal language). The ancient city of Delhi, where the Mughals had reigned for three centuries (and where the populace spoke Hindustani), lay over 600 miles to the north of Ahmedabad.

In 1857, only 12 years before Mohandas's birth, Delhi and several places to the east, including some yellow 'princely' states, had witnessed a violent rebellion that nearly overthrew British rule in India, which had begun a century before. Learning that the new cartridges they were biting into were greased not only with beef fat, which was forbidden to Hindus, but also pork fat, which was anathema to Muslims, the Raj's sepoys, Hindus and Muslims, mutinied. But the rising was crushed, and British power in India had acquired an air of permanency by 1869, which was also the year in which the Suez Canal was built, shortening the journey between London and India. Songs, including one in Gujarati that Mohandas learnt as a boy, praised the peace the English had brought, yet resentment at alien rule was not far from the surface.

The hierarchy of cities, with London at the top of the heap and, among the cities named, Porbandar at the bottom – below Rajkot, which ranked below Ahmedabad – was matched by other hierarchies in India. Villages were subservient to towns, women to men, the young to the old, the unarmed to the armed, low castes to high castes, the untouchables to everyone else, Indian languages to English, and Indians to the white man.

But between the deeply religious Hindus (a majority in most parts of India, including in Porbandar) and the less numerous yet equally religious followers of Islam, who had memories of pre-British Muslim hegemony, the question was of walls, not levels. Hindus and Muslims lived separate lives, often harbouring strong if uninformed feelings about those on the other side of the divide.

❦

For five generations or more, Mohandas's forebears had served Kathiawar's princes as administrators. Uttamchand or Ota Gandhi, Mohandas's grandfather, was the most successful among them. The ruler of Porbandar made him a diwan or first minister of his territory, and Ota Gandhi, who enhanced the state's irrigation and revenues, obtained for his master a Class One status from the British. Two of Ota's sons – Karamchand, Mohandas's father, and his younger brother Tulsidas – also became diwans of Porbandar.

The Gandhis belonged to what was called the 'Modh' branch of the commercial caste of Vanias (or Banias). While ranked third in the Hindu hierarchy after Brahmins and Kshatriyas, Vanias were seen, and saw themselves, as a 'high' caste.

The three-storey house in Porbandar in which Mohandas was born, and in which numerous Gandhis, young and old, lived as an extended family, had been built about 100 years earlier. It bore marks from shelling ordered by a Porbandar princess serving as regent, Rani Rupaliba, who was angered by Ota Gandhi's support of a state treasurer she disliked.

That an Arab bodyguard had defended Ota Gandhi on that occasion was one of the stories on which his children and grandchildren were raised. We may mark this early link of the Gandhis with the Muslim world, which lay not far across the Arabian Sea and was also connected to a expansive desert that began near Porbandar and extended across Kutch and Sindh into West Asia.

Possessing a meagre knowledge of written Gujarati and none of English, Karamchand, also known as Kaba, had, however, a keen grasp of practical affairs. Putlibai, Mohandas's mother, was his fourth wife. Mohandas, her youngest child, had been preceded by a girl, Raliat, and two boys, Laxmidas and Karsandas. Kaba's first two wives had each delivered a girl; each wife had died soon after giving birth. The third wife, childless, died early. Muli and Pankunwar were the names of Mohan's half-sisters.

When Mohan, or Monia as his parents called him, was four, Kaba moved as diwan to the thakore or ruler of Rajkot and then became diwan in another of Kathiawar's princely states, Wankaner. Putlibai, other relatives, and a loving nurse named Rambha reared Mohan in the Porbandar house. Terrified of ghosts and spirits, he was told by Rambha that the divine name of Rama would drive his fears away. Having 'more faith in her than in her remedy', Mohan recited the name but the terrors did not disappear (Autobiography, hereafter 'A', p 28).[1]

As the favourite child, which he was, of an influential father and of a mother who 'had strong common sense', 'was well informed about all matters of state' and of whose intelligence 'the ladies of the court thought highly' (A 3), Mohan was petted inside and outside his home and probably also in the Dhool Shala ('School in the dust') to which he was sent. Among those offering affection to him were Khushalchand, a cousin 18 years older who had been raised by Kaba and Putlibai and lived in their house, and his wife Deva, who found it hard not to pick up the child, whose partly curly hair and broad face she found attractive.[2]

In about 1876, Kaba Gandhi returned from Wankaner to Rajkot to join the Rajas-thanik court which addressed disputes involving members of Kathiawar's ruling families. Putlibai moved to Rajkot with her children. Her youngest son, now seven, took his fears with him to Rajkot, yet much love, too, had been caressed and whispered into the child.

In Rajkot Mohan first went to a primary school and soon thereafter to a taluka or suburban school. In his Autobiography, written when he was in his mid-fifties, he claimed that he could 'well recollect' not merely the names but also 'other particulars' of the teachers who taught him in the primary school when he was seven or eight (A 4). Because of this

Mohandas with (left) brother Laxmidas – 1886

capacity to observe and remember, and perhaps some other signs as well, Kaba Gandhi said, when Mohan was ten, that the boy would some day be sent to London for higher education.[3]

'When I was an urchin of ten,' Gandhi would recall in his Autobiography, 'I envied the Brahman lads sporting bunches of keys tied to their sacred threads, and I wished I could do likewise' (A 351–2). His wish was met, for at this time the Banias of Kathiawar were asserting the right to wear the shoulder-to-waist thread. Mohan wore it and also flaunted a bunch of keys tied to the thread, though he did not need them.

Lacking the sea that in Porbandar evoked a wider world, Rajkot had a parochial air. But it had a larger population (about 23,000 in 1879) and was the seat of the Raj's political agent in Kathiawar. By 1880, Kaba had built a large house there for his extended family, with high walls around the compound and a prominent gateway. At the age of 11 or 12, after passing an entrance examination where he was placed ninth out of 70 boys, Mohan was enrolled in Rajkot's Alfred High School, where English was the medium of instruction.

At about this time the governor of Bombay visited Rajkot, and Kaba Gandhi was required by the Resident of Rajkot to appear in European-style stockings and boots at a durbar in the governor's honour. The 'disgust and torture' on Kaba's face while 'he was putting his legs into his stockings and his feet into ill-fitting and inflexible boots' was seen by his youngest boy and lastingly remembered.[4] On another occasion Kaba Gandhi objected openly when an assistant political agent, a Briton, spoke discourteously of the Rajkot thakore. Asked to apologize, Kaba Gandhi refused, whereupon he was detained under a tree for some hours.

In 1947 Gandhi would provide a glimpse of the climate in Rajkot (and the rest of India) in the 1880s: 'The [1857] Sepoy War was quelled by means of superior force. Outwardly, things quieted down but the hatred against an imposed rule went deep underground ... The British established schools and law courts and Indians took to these with enthusiasm ... but in spite of this they could not bear the insult or the degradation involved in political subjugation' (94: 111).[5] In his teenage years in Rajkot, Mohan shared both this enthusiasm and the humiliation.

The Raj's cultural and political impositions were matched by rules laid down for their children by parents like Kaba and Putlibai. These rules had a religious or cultural basis. Kaba Gandhi was faithful to the Vaishnava tradition he had inherited, which called for ceremonies at temples of Rama and Krishna. More liberal than some other Modh Banias of his time, Kaba and his wife also went to the 'rival' Shiva temple, and their home was often visited by Jain monks. At times Muslim and Zoroastrian friends visited Kaba in his home and talked about their faiths – Mohan thought that Kaba listened 'with respect and often with interest' (A 29). The worldly-wise Putlibai was also strongly

religious and fasted frequently. The Pranami sect to which her parents belonged was
said to bear an Islamic influence and did not worship idols, but Putlibai seemed entirely
comfortable with the images of Krishna, Rama and Shiva honoured by the Gandhis; and
she respected Jain monks.

When Mohan was 'hardly yet twelve,' Putlibai told her children that they were not
to touch Uka, the 'untouchable' boy who cleaned the lavatories in the Gandhi house
in Rajkot. Apparently, Mohan had 'tussles' with her on the question and smiled at her
reasoning, yet he tried to obey the injunction. Any accidental contact with Uka or any
other 'untouchable' called for a cleansing bath. If a bath could not be easily had, Mohan
was to cancel the 'unholy touch', his mother told him, by touching any Muslim passing
by (23: 42). The second pollution would remove the first. This sense of Muslims as
unclean coexisted with Kaba's willingness to hear about Islam; we do not know what
steps, if any, were taken to purify the house after a Muslim's visit.

Another firm injunction was against touching or eating meat, from which it followed,
and Kaba made this plain, that a medical career was not open to Mohan: it required the
dissection of animals. Smoking, too, was forbidden. And like other 'high-caste' boys
including his brothers, Mohan tied his hair in a shikha or knot at the back of his head.

Mohan and brother Karsan, two or three years Mohan's senior but only a year ahead in
high school, chafed violently at the rules and secretly broke them. To be 'unable to do
anything without the elders' permission' was 'unbearable' for Mohan and his brother.
They smoked cigarette ends thrown away by an uncle and pilfered a servant's coppers
to buy bidis.* Frustrated by the limited supply of tobacco and coppers, and hating
the secrecy they were forced to maintain, they thought of suicide. Fetching poisonous
dhatura seeds from a jungle, they sought blessings at a temple and walked to a lonely
corner. But their courage failed them and they chose 'to put up with the lack of independence' (A 22–3).

Though this account was provided decades after the incident, the lines hint that
even at the time that Mohan contemplated suicide, he was observing himself, and was
amused. Yet it is clear that, conscious of his parents' great love for him, Mohan was
experiencing intense emotional conflict. An 'agonized lament' of an old blind couple
over the death of their caring boy, Shravana, sung by itinerant showmen, and a picture
the showmen displayed of Shravana with a pole on his shoulder, with baskets in which
his parents sat hanging at its ends, had gripped Mohan.

---

* Handmade cigarettes.

The melting tune moved me deeply, and I played it on a concertina which my father had purchased for me (A 5).

Remembered by relatives as a hyper-active child, Mohan was stirred, too, by a play which he had 'secured [his] father's permission to see'. It told the story of Harishchandra, who clung to the truth even when all his loved ones, and he himself, suffered greatly as a result. The play haunted the 12-year-old boy, who evidently 'acted Harishchandra to [himself] times without number' and wept (A 5). Yet the boy who wanted to be like Shravana and Harishchandra was also the boy longing for independence and stealing coppers to experience it. Moreover, his schooling in the English language was isolating him from others in the family, including his father, who knew no English.

If he argued when not quite 12 with his mother over touching the scavenging boy Uka, he rebelled also against the notion of pollution from contact with Muslims. In 1947 he would assert that his belief in 'complete brotherhood' among Hindus, Muslims and Parsis dated back to 'before 1885' to 'before the Congress was born'. 'At the time that communal unity possessed me, I was a lad twelve years old,' he added (96: 330). That was his age when he joined the Alfred High School, which had Hindu, Muslim and Parsi pupils and Hindu and non-Hindu teachers. A 78-year-old man looking back may of course imagine thoughts in his boyhood that did not exist, yet one has to be impressed by the number of times the older Gandhi spoke of his dreams at the age of 12.

When in January 1948, at the start of what would prove to be his last fast for Hindu-Muslim reconciliation, he again recalled his boyhood 'dream' of 'amity' between Hindus, Muslims and Parsis, he dated that dream to Rajkot and to a time when he 'never even read the newspapers, could read English with difficulty, and my Gujarati was not satisfactory' (98: 235). The description fits his opening year in Alfred High School.

This boy-rebel was also the one, we should note, who 'would not be prompted' when his teacher tried, 'with the point of his boot', to urge him to copy a word from a neighbour's slate, an incident occurring during Mohan's first year in high school, when an educational officer called Mr Giles, obviously a Briton, was visiting the school on an inspection (A 4).

In 1882, before Mohan was quite 13 years old, he was married to Kastur Makanji Kapadia, a Porbandar girl (with relatives in Rajkot) who was a few months older than him. Karsan and a cousin were also married at the same time. Bunched together for economy, the three weddings took place in Porbandar. The thakore of Rajkot detained Kaba until the last minute but offered stage-coaches that enabled the marriage party to reach Porbandar in three days instead of the usual five. However, the coach carrying Kaba Gandhi rolled over on the final day, and it was a badly injured and heavily bandaged Kaba who went through the ceremonies.

Excited as the 12-year-old groom was at his wedding, he did not fail to observe his father's 'brave face in spite of his injuries' and 'the places where he sat as he went through the different details of the ceremony' (A 8). Mohan would also remember how he and Kastur sat on the wedding dais, took their seven steps, put sweets into each other's mouths, and held each other's hands 'lovingly and for long'.[6] Putlibai took him and Kastur to several Hindu temples in Porbandar, including the Vaishnava haveli and a Shiva temple and also to the shrine of a Muslim fakir.[7] The older Gandhi would blame his father for his 'Child Marriage' (the title of the chapter in the Autobiography about the wedding), which cost him a year of school. In 1882, however, Mohan thought only of 'the prospect of good clothes to wear, drum-beating, processions, rich dinners, and a strange girl to play with' (A 7).

But the boy had entered a tempest. Though Kastur was often at her parents' home – for three years, in all, out of the first five years after marriage (A 11) – Mohan felt desire for her and could gratify it. Yet Kastur, a beautiful and uneducated Modh Bania girl with a will of her own, offered resistance. She also asserted her independence, running without Mohan's permission to friends and relatives in the neighborhood, refusing to be taught English and arithmetic by Mohan, and shaming him by her natural courage. For his terrors had continued. Haunted by fears of thieves, ghosts, serpents and robbers, the boy-husband 'did not dare to stir out of doors at night' and could not sleep without a light near him. 'Sleeping by [his] side' was the lovely but resisting Kastur who 'knew no fear of serpents and ghosts' and 'could go out anywhere in the dark'. Mohan felt ashamed of himself (A 17). He had read –'from cover to cover' (A 9) – booklets, presumably in Gujarati, that discussed subjects like conjugal love, thrift, child marriages and the advantages of long walks in the fresh air. The Autobiography does not tell us how he obtained the booklets or who wrote them. Perhaps they were supplied by a high school teacher.

Implementing the advice on walking, Mohan also seems to have accepted the norm of 'lifelong faithfulness' – and watched Kastur to ensure that she too observed it. But 'she made it a point to go out whenever and wherever she liked'. The more Mohan tried to restrain her, the greater the liberty she took. 'Refusal to speak to one another became the order of the day with us, married children' (A 9), but Mohan's male pride also received a blow, though he remained 'passionately fond' of his bride and could not get her out of his mind even at school.

The boy faced other storms. One day, at 'a corner near the high school,' he heard a white evangelist pour 'abuse on Hindus and their gods'. Mohan 'could not endure' what he heard and refused to go near the man again, and he was also angered by a rumour that a local Hindu converting to Christianity had been forced to eat beef and drink liquor (A 30).

Another storm came in the shape of Sheikh Mehtab, who was a year older than Karsan and thus three or four years older than Mohan. The son of a jailer employed by the British in the Kathiawar town of Gondal, Mehtab evidently lived only 'paces away' from the Gandhis' Rajkot home. Martin Green's research tells us that Mehtab's father, probably a Meman Muslim, earned about 20 rupees a month, compared with the 300 rupees that Kaba Gandhi had been making.[8]

A friend and classmate of Karsan in the high school and attracting a ring of admirers, Mehtab was a rakish youth of strength, speed and daring – he ran fast, ran long distances, did the high and long jumps, swam swiftly and 'could put up with any amount of corporal punishment' (A 17).[9] In all this he provided a complete contrast to Mohan, who did not play either cricket or football in school, partly because he was needed at home to nurse an increasingly sick father, and also because he shrank from, or was not drawn to, competitive games.

Nonetheless, in 1883 or 1884, shortly after Mohan's (and Karsan's) marriage, Mehtab seems to have selected Mohan as a lad to be won over. We have Mohan's account of the start and course of his relationship with Mehtab but not the latter's version. Yet we may guess that Mehtab had heard from Karsan of the ex-diwan's expectations of, and plans for, Mohan, and also that Mehtab had noticed something a little different in Karsan's young brother. It is more than likely, for instance, that in school Mehtab had heard of Mohan's peculiar behaviour during Mr Giles's visit. To Mehtab, Mohan was strange in a deplorable way but also strong. He was worth capturing. To this end Mehtab (joined by Karsan, who had left school after his marriage) mounted a campaign that played on Mohan's eagerness to repair his male pride. Mehtab knew from Karsan of Mohan's cowardly fears and of his frustration at Kastur's independence, and also of Mohan's annoyance at white rule.

'You have to take meat and wine,' Mohan was told by Mehtab. That was the only way to drive out the British. Also, meat would toughen Mohan, dissolve his terrors and, even if this last argument was not explicit, help in putting Kastur in her place. Didn't Mohan know Narmad's verse, Mehtab asked?

Behold the mighty Englishman/ He rules the Indian small/ Because being a meat-eater/ He is five cubits tall.

Mohan admitted he knew the Gujarati verse, which was in vogue in the school. Mohan should also know, Mehtab added, that distinguished Rajkot figures were eating meat. Karsan, physically much stronger than Mohan, revealed that he agreed with Mehtab and had indeed eaten meat himself. 'You know how hardy I am,' Mehtab went on, 'and how great a runner too. It is because I am a meat-eater.' Finally, Mohan was asked whether or not he had the courage to try.

These conversations, punctuated with assurances of faithful friendship from Mehtab, took place over a period of weeks, during which Mehtab also displayed his swimming and athletic skills to Mohan, who was 'dazzled' by Mehtab's 'exploits'. In the end Mohan convinced himself that meat would make him and other Indians strong, enabling them to 'defeat the English and make India free' (A 16–18), and probably also, though he does not admit it in the Autobiography, help him in his relationship with Kastur.

'A day was fixed for beginning the experiment' and a lonely spot by the river was chosen. The anticipated thrill overcame 'the shame of hiding like a thief', and Mohan went with Karsan to the tryst. The goat's meat brought by Mehtab was 'tough as leather' and Mohan could not finish his portion. That night he had a nightmare in which he imagined a live goat bleating inside him. But he had committed himself to Mehtab, who on subsequent occasions cooked other delicacies along with meat, and also found access to 'a State house, with dining hall, tables and chairs, in collusion with the chief cook there'. Mohan started relishing dishes with meat in them. But after about half-a-dozen feasts spread over a year or so, Mehtab (who paid for them in unknown ways) ran out of funds; and in his home Mohan found it increasingly hard to explain to his mother why he was not eating his dinner. Deciding that lying to his parents was worse than not eating meat, he told Mehtab that the experiment was over; but he told himself that he would resume meat-eating once the parents 'are no more and I have found my freedom'. This meat-eating phase probably lasted from some point early in 1884, when Mohan was a few months over 14, to early 1885 (A 17–20).

Here we may note Gandhi's report in the Autobiography that another high school friend of his (a Parsi boy, some think),[10] with whom Mohan had formed a close friendship, forsook Mohan, 'though I never forsook my friend', after Mohan had 'made friends' with Mehtab (A 16).

Two texts he read at about this time affected Mohan. The creation story in the *Manusmriti*, which he found among his father's religious books, not only 'did not impress him very much', it made him 'incline somewhat towards atheism' (A 30). Given his parents' uncompromising vegetarianism, he was also puzzled by positive references to meat in the *Manusmriti*.

But a stanza by the Gujarati poet Shamal Bhatt in a schoolbook gripped his imagination and lodged itself in his memory:

For a bowl of water give a goodly meal;
For a kindly greeting bow thou down with zeal;
For a simple penny pay thou back with gold;
If thy life be rescued, life do not withhold …
And return with gladness good for evil done (A 31).

Soon, help was needed by Karsan, who had notched up a debt of 24 rupees. On his arm Karsan wore an armlet of solid gold. Mohan clipped a bit of metal out of it, and the debt was cleared. Whether it was that he could not live with the knowledge that he had cheated his parents on more than one front, or because something unusual had been stirring inside him for a while, Mohan now (in about the middle of 1885) did another peculiar thing: he confessed his theft of the gold.

Mohan did not dare to speak to the former diwan of Porbandar, Rajkot and Wankaner. What he did was to write out a confession and tremblingly hand it to his father while Kaba, suffering from a fistula, lay on a plain wooden plank. According to the Autobiography, Mohan did not fear being beaten, for evidently Kaba had never beaten any of his sons. The Autobiography claims that Mohan's chief fear was that a shocked Kaba would hit himself.

The confession said that his father would now know that his much-loved son was merely a common thief. But the son would steal no more and was asking for forgiveness and also for adequate punishment. The note closed with a request that the father should not punish himself.

I was trembling as I handed the confession … He read it through, and pearl-drops trickled down his cheeks, wetting the paper. For a moment he closed his eyes in thought and then tore up the note. He had sat up to read it. He again lay down. I also cried. I could see my father's agony. If I were a painter, I could draw a picture of the whole scene today. Those pearl-drops of love cleansed my heart and washed my sin away (A 23).

Biographical or autobiographical literature from 19th-century Kathiawar, or India as a whole, contains few accounts of a similar confession, which was remembered in the family for a long time, including by Mohan's sister Raliat, later a critic of some of her brother's attitudes.

Very few spaces, and very few incidents, in an extended family like that of the Gandhis, were private. Certainly, Mohan's confession was not, and we can only speculate on how Karsan reported the confession to Mehtab, or on what Kastur made of it. It was a brave deed, and yet (as Erikson points out) the Mohan of this confession seems to be in control. Any anxiety in his mind relates not to what might happen to him, but to what might happen to his father.

We should note, too, what this confession was not – it did not admit his very recent meat-eating. As the Autobiography acknowledges, 'My parents never knew that two of their sons had become meat-eaters' (A 20). Mohan did not confess that sin because it would have been too much of a shock to his parents, and also because he fully intended to resume meat-eating in the future.

Which, then, is the real 15-year-old? The boy-husband afraid of the dark? The timid-looking youth on whom Mehtab's exploits cast a spell? The penitent and brave son who can decide what he will admit and what he will not, and who can calmly study the impact of his apology on his father? A person is many persons. The third Mohan was the reason for Mehtab's pursuit of him, while the first offered hope that Mohan could be caught.

From the time of his wedding until Kaba's death at the end of 1885, i.e. from the age of about 13 to when he was 16, Mohan seems to have spent some time each day attending on his increasingly sick father, who had given up his position with the Rajasthanik court shortly before the triple wedding, and who never fully recovered from the injuries he sustained in the stage-coach accident.

Mohan's caring and nursing tasks – massaging his father's legs and feet, dressing the fistula that had grown on Kaba's neck, compounding and administering drugs, and so on – cut into, or cut out, walks, games with school-friends, the possibility of going out to see a play, or reading something he liked. 'As soon as the school closed, I would hurry home and begin nursing him' (A 13). Obtaining, on one occasion, his father's permission to go to a play, Mohan heeded an instinct and left for home before the play started. He found that Kaba had needed him. Similar permission was never sought again.

Despite the price he paid, Gandhi would claim in the Autobiography and elsewhere that he 'loved to do this service [of nursing his father]' (A 25). There has to be some truth in the claim, for the lad performing these chores continued in later life to take every chance to nurse people, including political opponents. (Erikson suggests that Mohan got the upper hand over the one he nursed, his father in Rajkot and others later.)

Yet this three-year period included the phase of Mohan's adventure with meat. During that phase of about 12 months, and even after the adventure was suspended, the devoted yet independent son at the father's bedside was carrying the weight of a big secret. Some lightness of heart doubtless followed the confession episode, and Mohan would have been moved by Kaba's words, uttered not long before his death, that 'Mohan here will keep up my reputation. He will increase the fame of our lineage.'[11]

Yet we should recognize the multiplicity of feelings about the father – not all loyal or kind – within a son-nurse who is also acknowledged, though the youngest, as the father's heir. Mohan liked going to a play but could not go; he liked to read interesting books but where was the time? Recalling his boyhood in a letter he would write from prison (25 Mar. 1909) to his second son Manilal, Gandhi would say: 'Of amusement after I was twelve, I had little or none' (9: 318). In this letter he would claim that nursing his father gave him joy, but that joy was surely joined by unexpressed disappointment. Our inwardly 'amused' boy was also, in another layer of himself, a sad boy.

One draw away from his father would be memorably and frankly recorded by Gandhi: 'Every night whilst my hands were busy massaging my father's legs, my mind was hovering about [my] bedroom. I was always glad to be relieved from my duty, and went straight to the bedroom after doing obeisance to my father' (A 25). An unsurprising outcome was that when he and Kastur were sixteen, she became pregnant.

Kaba's health worsened. 'Ayurvedic physicians ... tried all their ointments, hakims their plasters, and local quacks their nostrums.' Finally, a British physician suggested surgery in Bombay, but the family physician ruled that at his age Kaba would not survive it.

Shortly before eleven o'clock on the fateful night, Tulsidas, Kaba's brother, who had come from Porbandar to be of support, offered to relieve Mohan, who was massaging his father. Accepting the offer, Mohan 'went straight to the bedroom' and roused the pregnant Kastur, who was fast asleep. In five or six minutes there was a knock on the door, and a servant told Mohan that his father was no more. Running to his father's room, and wringing his hands in wretched shame, Mohan told himself that '[Father] would have died in my arms' had his carnal desire not cheated him of the privilege, which Tulsidas had faithfully earned. Mohan's devotion to his parents had been 'weighed and found unpardonably wanting' (A 26). These circumstances of his father's death, and the fact that 'the poor mite' to which Kastur in due course gave birth died in three or four days, would leave a permanent mark on Mohan's attitude to sex.

Almost from the very start of their child marriage, Mohan tried to educate Kastur and to help her become a life-partner in a 'modern' sense. The sexual or carnal element, as he calls it, was of course there, strongly so. He underlines that fact, calling himself a 'lustful' husband (A 10). But there was also a longing for mutual strengthening, a wish for a beloved who would also be a lover, not merely in a sexual sense but also in the psychological one, a partner who would help him become what he longs to be, even as he tries to 'develop' her.

'I wanted to *make* my wife an ideal wife,' Gandhi says in the Autobiography, referring to his early years with Kastur. 'My ambition was to *make* her ... learn what I learnt and identify her life and thought with mine.' (Emphases in the original.) But she was 'illiterate' and 'not impatient of her ignorance'. Also, the 'ambition was all one-sided'.

> My passion was entirely centred on one woman, and I wanted it to be reciprocated. But even if there was no reciprocity, it could not be all unrelieved misery because there was active love on one side at least (A 10–11).

These are strong statements, acknowledging the pressure in young Mohan's attempts to turn Kastur into an active sharer of his life and goals, and breathing disappointment that the passion, which here clearly includes but goes beyond sexual passion, was not reciprocated.

He tried hard to teach her, but time and opportunity were hard to find, for in that family household in Rajkot elders were always around, and in their presence there was no question of his even talking to her, let alone teaching her (A 11). Moreover, 'the teaching had to be done against her will'. She resisted him uncompromisingly, and he totally failed. Later, he blamed his carnal desire, arguing that without it he would at least have had more time, in the privacy of their bedroom, to teach her.

We are speaking of a boy in his teens who, while given to unmanly fears, is still conscious of some deep inner stirrings. We may speculate that he senses longings going beyond his extended family and thinks that this pretty wife that has come to him can help realize them if he can but educate her. After long and difficult years, and in ways he might not have thought of in Rajkot, she would indeed become a valuable ally; but in Rajkot in the mid-1880s she resisted strongly, and Mohan reacted with an even stronger effort on his part. It would have been wiser to accept Kastur as she was, and let her be, but with Kastur in Rajkot Mohan was not wise. He was only a disappointed, frustrated and overeager teenager.

This reality was well understood by Mehtab, who persisted with his approaches to Mohan despite the end of the experiments with meat. His closeness to Mohan was not liked by Putlibai, or by his brother Laxmidas, or by Kastur. All three, the Autobiography tells us, warned Mohan that Mehtab (who is not named in the Autobiography) was bad company. Writes Gandhi:

> This companion was originally [Karsan's] friend. They were classmates. I knew his weakness, but I regarded him as a faithful friend. My mother, my eldest brother

(Laxmidas), and my wife warned me that I was in bad company. I was too proud to heed my wife's warning. But I dared not go against the opinion of my mother and my eldest brother.

Nevertheless I pleaded with them saying, 'I know he has the weakness you attribute to him, but you do not know his virtues. He cannot lead me astray, as my association with him is meant to reform him. For I am sure that if he reforms his ways, he will be a splendid man. I beg you not to be anxious on my account.' I do not think this satisfied them, but ... they let me go my way.

The fact that Kaba Gandhi is not mentioned suggests that the discussion took place either when he was quite ill or after his death. We can be fairly certain, given family customs in Kathiawar at the time, that the three family members talked separately to Mohan, rather than in one session. As for the 'weakness', mentioned in the singular, the meaning seems plain. The Gandhis viewed Mehtab as a loose character who might corrupt Mohan. It is of interest, nonetheless, and indicative of Mohan's standing, that the 16-year-old is allowed by his mother and a much older brother to 'go his own way'. Older relatives are deferring to this lad. Challenged by his mother, Laxmidas and Kastur, Mohan claimed that the friendship was meant to reform Mehtab. He would seek to turn Mehtab into a 'splendid man' by his own standards, different from Mehtab's, even though Mohan clearly envied Mehtab's capabilities.

As to what 'really' motivated Mohan in this relationship, Gandhi offers one clue: 'As one is always dazzled when he sees in others the qualities he lacks himself, I was dazzled by this friend's exploits. This was also followed by a strong desire to be like him ... Why should not I also be as strong as he?' (A 17) Another clue is presented in a glimpse provided by the older Gandhi in 1927: 'I have a vivid recollection,' he said, referring to his school days, 'of boys who put on an air because they had athletic skill and had physical power'. But 'their pride went before destruction, because weaker ones, realizing their haughtiness, segregated them ... and so they really dug their own graves' (40: 70). This is clearly a description of Mehtab, who was struck off the rolls of Alfred High School in 1884, and suggests that sympathy for a 'segregated' Mehtab may also have entered Mohan's mind. In 1942 he would recall another motivation: 'I believed even at [a] tender age that ... it did not matter if I made no special effort to cultivate friendship with Hindus, but I must make friends with at least a few Muslims' (83: 190).

Other factors, too, may have been at work. Apart from hoping, in Mehtab's company, to become 'as strong' as him, Mohan may have received from Mehtab an affirmation he did not receive from Kastur. For all his mischief, Mehtab had some virtues, to which Mohan referred in those discussions with his mother and Laxmidas. Though these virtues are not named in the Autobiography, an ability to affirm faith in Mohan's future role may have been one. In addition, we shall soon see, Mehtab provided some amusement for Mohan.

Moreover, some of Mehtab's progressive views were to Mohan's liking, who had reacted against his family's acceptance of untouchability, accepted the principle, if no longer the practice, of meat-eating, and was increasingly critical of his and Karsan's early marriages. Mehtab's stand for the new against the old appealed to Mohan. Both boys wanted 'reform' in Indian customs; the two disliked the hierarchies in the India around them, except for the one between men and women; and no matter how vaguely, both dreamt of Indian freedom.

In the Autobiography Gandhi writes of how his relationship with Kastur was undermined by Mehtab, who 'fanned the flame' (A 21) in Mohan of unfounded suspicions about Kastur, causing the husband to level cruel accusations at her. As for Mehtab's well-known success (related in the Autobiography) in taking Mohan to a Rajkot brothel, it relied on two simple arguments: you will prove your manliness, and your wife will come running after you if she knows you can go elsewhere. This brothel incident probably occurred in 1886, perhaps when Kastur was at her parents' home. Mehtab took his friend to the house of ill repute, paid the money and sent Mohan in. The woman was all prepared, but Mohan froze, sitting tongue-tied 'near the woman on her bed'. She showed him the door with abuses and insults. Mohan felt 'as though my manhood had been injured, and wished to sink into the ground for shame'. Later he would thank God for this escape from the 'jaws of sin', while admitting that 'the carnal desire was there, and it was as good as the act' (A 20). But at the time he was ashamed of failing a test of manhood, not of visiting the brothel.

The warnings of his mother and Laxmidas had been vindicated, but Mohan did not shake Mehtab off. Upset by his 'failure' with the prostitute, he failed also to perceive Mehtab's mischief. And he continued to imagine qualities in Mehtab, enjoy his friendship, and fancy that he might reform him.

The Mohan emerging from this reading, entering his late teens with prestige in his circle, curiosity about the world around him, a peculiar strength, a weakness for a questionable character, and surprising fears, is different from the popular image of a timid, unimpressive, pious boy awaiting a life-enhancing experience.

Much of the blame for this other image must go to Gandhi himself, for in the Autobiography he mixes frank recollections of his boyhood and youth with the contrition of a later period. ('Autobiography' is a misleading description; what Gandhi wrote was a chronological account, ending in 1920, of his ethical and spiritual experiments.) The contrition of an older Gandhi, and descriptions of lessons learnt long after the events described, surround the candid recollections and can conceal them, just as accounts of his early fears envelop the revelations of his strength as a lad.

Unless it is carefully read, the self-deprecating Autobiography can also incorrectly suggest that Mohan was a mediocre student. He was one of only two reaching matriculation out of the 38 who had passed the high school entrance examination with him, though when in 1887 he cleared the matriculation, journeying for the first time to Ahmedabad in order to do so, he was placed 404th out of about 3,000 in western India, a decent though not outstanding rank. But in Ahmedabad he was deprived of the emotional and logistical support of his family.

'Sure, I was the leader of the boys in my class,' an older Gandhi said to a close colleague, D B or 'Kaka' Kalelkar, who wanted to know more about his Rajkot boyhood than the Autobiography conveyed.[12] The reference was to his all-round standing in his class, not to his academic performance.

A term in Samaldas College in Bhavnagar, another of Kathiawar's 'princely' towns 90 miles south-east of Rajkot, followed. Mohan would have liked to go to a college in Bombay, but the family's fortunes had taken a dive after Kaba's illness and death, and Bhavnagar it had to be. But he was unhappy and homesick there. When, after the first term at Samaldas College, he returned to Rajkot for the break, an old family friend, 'a shrewd and learned Brahmin' called Mavji Dave, told Mohan, Laxmidas and their mother that the only way to restore the family's prestige was to implement Kaba's old idea: Mohan should go to London (A 32).

In the Autobiography Gandhi says that 'nothing could have been more welcome to me' and that he 'jumped at the proposal'. But he said even more in the Diary he wrote soon after arriving in London: 'Before the intention of coming to London was actually formed, I had a secret design in my mind of coming here to satisfy my curiosity of knowing what London was' (Diary entry, 12 Nov. 1888; 1: 2). Before Dave had spoken, Mohan had imagined London (as he would recall in an interview in England in 1891) as 'the home of philosophers and poets, the very centre of civilization'. Mavji Dave had only 'fanned the fire that was burning in me'.[13] So this timid son of conservative parents had been 'secretly designing' a journey to England. It was Jayshankar Buch, a student in the Bhavnagar college, who first put the thought into his mind (Diary; 1: 3).

Erikson has speculated that curiosity regarding London, the exciting metropolis, was not surprising in a young man in a conservative corner of the Empire. We may speculate in addition that it was not surprising in an Indian youth resenting if also admiring

British rule. What history books he read at Alfred High School and Samaldas College we do not know, but much later (while in England in 1931) he would recall that

> as a schoolboy I had to pass a paper in history also, and I read that the page of history is soiled red with the blood of those who have fought for freedom ... (1 Dec. 1931; 54: 221)

In school he had also read (he would say in 1943[14]) Byron's line that 'freedom's battle once begun' is 'bequeathed from bleeding sire to son'.

Mohan's curiosity was not casual, it was earnest; it was a curiosity about a foe that had humiliated Indians but that could not merely be hated, for it formed 'the very centre of civilization'. He said to Dave, his mother and Laxmidas that he wanted to go to England as soon as possible, and qualify for the medical profession. Laxmidas interjected that a Vaishnava could not do that. 'Father never liked it ... He intended you for the bar.'

'I want you to be diwan,' Dave said to Mohan, 'or if possible something better' (A 33). Unlike a doctor, a barrister could become a diwan. (Dave's phrase, 'or something better', is indicative of the potential the 18-year-old Mohan conveyed to at least some observers.) Law was acceptable to him, Mohan said, and Dave ended his visit with a strong exhortation to Putlibai and Laxmidas to send the lad to London, adding that 5,000 rupees, or about £400, would cover the passage, studies and three years of stay in England.

Mohan 'began building castles in the air' (A 33). In fact, to use his own words, whether 'sleeping, walking, drinking, eating, walking, running, reading,' he was now 'dreaming and thinking of England'.[15]

However, Putlibai asked Mohan to travel to Porbandar and seek the consent of his uncle Tulsidas, who was now the head of the wider Gandhi clan. Putlibai thought though that Tulsidas – like her late husband a former diwan of Porbandar – would withhold permission. Supporting the England plan, Laxmidas said that in Porbandar Mohan should also try to meet Frederick Lely, the Political Resident, and ask for aid. Lely had a good opinion of Tulsidas Kaka, Laxmidas added, and in any case the Gandhis were entitled to help from the state of Porbandar.

Mohan set off for Porbandar, a five-day bullock-cart journey across unsafe territory inhabited by supposedly dangerous tribes. Mohan should have felt frightened, 'but my cowardice vanished before the desire to go to England'. On the way, in Dhoraji, the young man in a hurry switched to a seat on the back of a camel. Arriving in Porbandar, he did obeisance to his uncle (that was the custom), described the Dave proposal and sought permission. Tulsidas said that at his age, when he was 'at the threshold of death', he could not support an irreligious act. Indians returning from England knew no scruples regarding food, 'cigars were never out their mouths', and 'dressed shamelessly'. Yet if Mohan's mother let him go, that was up to her.

Mohan's request for a letter of introduction to Lely was also turned down by Tulsidas, though he said that Mohan could mention their kinship to Lely. A letter from Mohan elicited an appointment at Lely's home. When Mohan turned up there, Lely was climbing the stairs. Having practised carefully for this first meeting with a British official and nursing high expectations (he had his dream and was moreover the grandson of Ota Gandhi), Mohan 'bowed low ... saluted Lely with both hands' and spoke the Gujarati sentences he had rehearsed. From where he stood Lely curtly replied that Porbandar state was poor. Adding, 'Pass your BA first and then see me,' Lely hurried up the stairs (A 33–4).

Returning to Rajkot, a bitterly disappointed Mohan next tried his luck with the thakore and with Colonel J W Watson, the Raj's political agent in Kathiawar. While the thakore donated a photograph of himself, Watson gave 'a trivial note of introduction which he said ... was worth one lac of rupees' (1: 7). In his London diary Mohan would soon write that these responses made him laugh, and also that the memory of 'the fulsome flattery which I had to practise about this time made me quite angry' (1: 8).

Not all Indians in their late teens would have reacted thus in 1888, when British supremacy was a given. That was the year when John Strachey, a senior servant of the Raj who once acted as Viceroy, declared:

> This is the first and most essential thing to learn about India – that there is not, and never was, an Indian, or even any country of India, possessing according to European ideas, any sort of unity, physical, political, social or religious.[16]

Strachey was responding to, among other things, the creation three years earlier of the Indian National Congress. A group of lawyers, doctors and other intellectuals from different parts of India had formed the body, thanks to the goading of a Scotsman called Allan Octavian Hume, who had experienced the 1857 Revolt in Etawah in the United Provinces. The Congress, of which Mohan was evidently aware, sought greater rights for Queen Victoria's Indian subjects and also hoped for Indian unity.

We do not know what Mehtab was doing all this time, except that the Diary written in London tells us that before Mohan left Rajkot for Porbandar, the two had an argument, it is not clear over what. 'I was always quarrelling with my friend Sheikh Mehtab,' Mohan would write (1: 4).

'Quite engrossed in thinking about the quarrel,' Mohan tripped while walking down a Rajkot lane and 'banged [my] head against a carriage'. A little later Mohan fainted and lay unconscious for about five minutes; companions thought he had even died. Perhaps Rajkot's oven-like summer contributed to the incident, yet the tiff had clearly weighed heavily on Mohan's mind.

While Mohan was in Porbandar, Mehtab performed, in his own style, some money-related errands for Mohan in Rajkot. As Mohan would soon note down in his London Diary,

> My friend Sheikh Mehtab who, I should say, is full of tricks, reminded Meghjibhai of his promise and forged a letter with my signature in which he wrote that I stood in need of Rs 5,000 and so on … (1: 4–6)

Though Meghjibhai, a relative of the Gandhis who had indicated that he might help, was taken in at first, the ploy failed. Astute as always, Putlibai had told Mohan that he would 'never get any money from [Meghjibhai]' (1: 3–4). According to the Diary, Mohan managed to see the funny side of these obstacles to his dream, and also to make his mother laugh heartily, including at Mehtab's tricks – an ability to be amused was joined to the resolute chase of a dream.

Though many questioned the London project, including some in the Kathiawar press, Dave did not let up, and neither did Mohan. The options of taking a loan or selling his wife's jewellery were considered. The second was also an accepted course, especially if the ornaments had come from the husband's family.

Laxmidas said 'he would find the money somehow' (A 34). This proved hard, however, and at one point in the summer of 1888, Laxmidas (possibly also influenced by the public criticism) asked Mohan to give up the London project. Coming from one who was not only 'generous to a fault and loved me as a son' but also, after Kaba's death, the head of the immediate family, this advice should have been demoralizing (A 34). But Mohan rejected it. Revising his stance, Laxmidas scraped together some funds.

Yet Putlibai, who had made careful inquiries, was troubled. She asked Mohan – with good reason, as we know, even if she did not – whether he could live in England without meat and without liquor. He would swear, Mohan said, that he would. 'In a distant land?' the practical Putlibai asked. It was only when Becharji Swami, a Modh Bania who had become a Jain monk and who, like Dave, was an adviser to the family, said that he would 'get the boy solemnly to take … three vows' that Putlibai relented.

With Becharji Swami administering the oath, Mohan vowed not to touch wine, women or meat, and Putlibai voiced, or gestured, her permission. She also tied a string of tulsi beads round her son's neck, a token of her plea to Providence for his protection. The vow could not have been pleasant for Mohan, who at this point seemed convinced, in his own mind, of the benefits of meat, was yet to feel really guilty about his visit to the brothel, and, despite an early acceptance of 'lifelong faithfulness to the wife', might well have been curious about the charms that London might offer. Yet this lad who remembered not only his secrets but perhaps also his response to the tale of Harishchandra, knew that the unwelcome vow had bound him.

Kastur, to whom a boy, Harilal, was born in the spring of 1888, did not feature in these discussions about her husband's plans, even though they would make a large difference to her. Like most other Indian wives of her time and of later times, she was expected to accept what her husband (and her mother-in-law) decided. We have no evidence that Mohan asked for Kastur's views on his plans. Another name, too, is absent from these accounts: Karsan. Discontinuing school after his marriage and drifting steadily downward, he seemed in no position to offer his younger brother counsel.

'It was an uncommon thing,' Gandhi would later record, 'for a young man from Rajkot to go to England' (A 35). His friends and presumably his teachers presented an address to him at the high school. Mohan 'stammered out' a reply in Gujarati. His 'head reeled' and his 'whole frame shook' (A 35).

This reaction in a youth who did not lose his poise at his first-ever encounters with men like Lely, Watson and the Rajkot prince, calls for examination, especially as the quaking Mohandas reappears at times during the next dozen or so years, trembling before gatherings in England, a courtroom in Bombay and before larger meetings in Bombay and Calcutta. Alternating with this shaking Mohan is the resolute young man. Where he faces a hurdle or a foe, or is one-on-one with another, Mohan seems fearless. However, before a group of people, whether peers, friends or strangers, he often seems terrified – often, but not always. Shyness is a considerable element in this fear, and he is afraid of being laughed at. Behind the shyness may be detected an awareness that he cannot impress or please and also that impressing or pleasing an audience will not satisfy him. Even in his late teens he seems to sense that his surroundings – his peers, his people – are asking something more of him.

The timid Mohan is also the seeing and listening Mohan who after his arrival in England would sketch in words scenes from Kathiawar, including: 'the shepherd trotting onward in his milk-white suit, worn for the first time, with his long beard turned up beside his face and fastened under his turban, singing some broken verses', 'a herd of cows, with their horns painted red and green and mounted with silver', 'a crowd of little maids, with small earthen vessels resting on cushions placed on their heads', including one 'spilling some milk from her vessel', 'the great banker' with 'white whiskers and a big white turban, with a long reed pen thrust into his turban [and] a long scarf wound round his waist with a silver inkstand adjusted in the scarf', as well as – let us take note – people who 'have only one meal per day, and that consists of stale bread and salt'.[17]

This witness of hardship around him and of other street scenes was also, we notice, observing his father and teachers (as also his fellow students) and watching caste and religious divides. Referring, two months before his death, to his early years in Porbandar and Rajkot, Gandhi would claim, 'I saw everything that happened there' (97: 428). Not obviously to be taken literally, this large claim should nonetheless enter our reconstruction of Mohan's teenage years. Perhaps the trembling and aware Mohans are inter-related.

The send-off at Rajkot (for Bombay *en route* to London) was portrayed by Mohan in the Diary he wrote after arrival in London:

> Many had come to bid me farewell on the night. Messrs. Kevalram, Chhaganlal Patwari, Vrajlal, Harishankar, Amolakh, Manekchand, Latib, Popat, Bhanji, Khimji, Ramji, Damodar, Meghji, Ramji Kalidas, Naranji, Ranchhoddass, Manilal were among those who came. Jatashankar, Vishvanath and others may be added (1: 8).

Actually, therefore, the now-timid-now-audacious teenager observing his surroundings is also a leader in his small world. That many should see him off is not surprising in itself – departures for London were not everyday affairs in Rajkot in 1888. What is striking is Mohan's lack of surprise about the send-off. He takes it for granted, and the way he reels off the names of persons who 'were among those who came' certainly suggests a leader in the making, if not one already made.

The Kathiawar Times published (on 12 July 1888) an English translation of what Mohan had said in the high school: 'I hope that some of you will follow in my footsteps, and after your return from England you will work wholeheartedly for big reforms in India' (1: 1). Though he has solemnly taken the triple vow, on the eve of his departure for England Mohan still wants 'big reforms'.

After arriving in London, Mohan would describe his parting from his wife, son and mother. Putlibai cried, but the son successfully fought back his tears. Kastur 'had begun sobbing long before'. 'I went to her and stood like a dumb statue for a moment. I kissed her, and she said, "Don't go." What followed I need not describe' (Interview in *The Vegetarian* of London, 13 June 1891; 1: 45).

The Mohan who copes next with old and new obstacles in Bombay is unrecognizable from the uncertain teenager. He had arrived in Bombay along with Laxmidas (who carried the money that he had put together), Mehtab and a couple of others. Learning that it would be weeks before a ship left for England, Laxmidas returned to Rajkot, entrusting the money to Kastur's brother, who lived in Bombay.

Also living in Bombay were a number of other Modh Banias, most of whom disliked the idea of someone from their community going overseas and living and eating in the company of impure whites – thus far no Modh Bania had committed that sin. When Mohan, waiting for news of a sailing, showed up in their district, they jeered at him. A community meeting was convened and Mohan summoned before it. 'Nothing daunted and without the slightest hesitation,' Mohan went. The Sheth who presided was a distant relative and had been close to Kaba Gandhi. In front of a large audience he addressed Mohan:

> In the opinion of the caste, your proposal to go to England is not proper. Our religion forbids voyages abroad … One is obliged there to eat and drink with Europeans!

Answering that he did not agree that going to England was against their religion, Mohan also mentioned his vow, taken before Putlibai, 'to abstain from three things you fear most'. 'We tell you,' the Sheth rejoined, 'that it is *not* possible to keep our religion there.'

'I am helpless,' the 18-year-old replied. 'I cannot alter my resolve.'

'Will you disregard the orders of the caste?'

'I am really helpless. I think the caste should not interfere.'

'Incensed', the Sheth 'swore' at Mohan, who sat unmoved. The Sheth then pronounced his order that Mohan was henceforth an outcast and anyone helping him or seeing him off at the dock would be fined a rupee and a quarter (A 36–7).

To Laxmidas's credit, he sent word from Rajkot that despite the Sheth's order Mohan still had his permission to go, but Kastur's brother lost his nerve and refused to hand over the money. At this Mohan asked Ranchhoddas Patwari, a Modh Bania friend living in Bombay, for a loan to cover his 'passage and sundries' and requested Patwari to recover the loan from Laxmidas.

Patwari agreed (another indication of Mohan's standing), and Mohan bought his passage, Western-style clothes (including a short jacket and a necktie) and foodstuffs. In the Autobiography he writes of an unnamed 'friend who had experience in the matter' who 'got clothes and other things ready'. This may be a reference to Mehtab, who was in Bombay and was, we know, the one who could get 'things ready' for Mohan. From what we know of Mehtab, he could very well have claimed 'experience in the matter' of clothes for England.

Mohan took care, also, to get rid of his shikha or hair-knot, fearing that it would 'expose [him] to ridicule' in England (A 352). After writing letters to his family that he asked Mehtab to carry to Rajkot, Mohandas sailed from Bombay on 4 September 1888 on the P & O liner, *Clyde*. He was carrying four letters himself. Introducing Mohandas, the letters were addressed to Pranjivan Mehta and Dalpatram Shukla, Kathiawaris in London at the time, Ranjitsinhji, a prince from Jamnagar (another 'yellow' tract in Kathiawar) who had acquired fame in England as a cricketer, and Dadabhai Naoroji, a founder of the Congress who was in London to promote awareness of India.

Mohandas's cabin-mate was Tryambakrai Mazmudar, a vakil or pleader from Junagadh (another princely state near but larger than Porbandar). 'An experienced man of mature age', as the Autobiography describes him, Mazmudar hoped, like Mohan, to become a barrister. Learning that Mazmudar was travelling on this ship, Mohan had asked for a berth in his cabin. Twenty-two years later, speaking of the youth, one month shy of 19, whom he had met on the *Clyde*, Mazmudar would recall that young Mohan (Mazmudar called him a 'child') was 'obstinate' and had untypical 'strength'.[18] 'There is no one more truthful,' added Mazmudar. 'But along with truth he has a lot of ego. Only what he says is the truth.'[19]

Both qualities, strength and obstinacy, were claimed by Mohan in his London Diary:

I must write that had it been some other man in the same position which I was in, I dare say he would not have been able to see England (1: 9).

But I am not a man who would, after having formed any intention, leave it easily (1: 4).

2

London and Identity

1888–92

On the voyage to England Mohandas struggled to speak in English – 'I had to frame every sentence in my mind before I could bring it out' (A 38) – and to eat with a knife and fork. Not knowing what on the ship's menus was meat-free, and too shy to ask, he survived on the sweets and fruits he had brought with him until Mazmudar coaxed some Indians on the crew to cook dal for him and Mohandas.

Despite Mazmudar's advice that he should move around and get to know people, Mohandas avoided the dining room and the deck, staying in his cabin except when it was safe to 'venture up' to a more or less empty deck. One night he thought diamonds were dancing in the waves below him. Since diamonds could not float, perhaps they were shiny sea creatures? Realizing that a clear night's stars were being reflected in the water, he 'laughed at [his] folly' (Diary; 1: 10).

The London Diary would record this little experience and also his occasional attempts with the piano on board, his admiration of the efficiency with which life was organized on the ship, and his sense of marvel and curiosity at the construction of the Suez Canal through which the *Clyde* passed – the Canal's engineers had competed with nature, he felt, and he wanted to figure out just how they had built it.

Word of his vows spread quickly through the vessel, and Indian and European passengers warned that ahead of him lay a climate where no one could live without meat and liquor – certainly not without meat. He would find this out, he was told, if not in the Red Sea then in the Mediterranean, and without question in the Bay of Biscay and the English Channel. But the different seas came and went, and Mohandas survived.

At a halt in Brindisi a man accosted 'black' men like Mohandas and said, 'Sir, there is a beautiful girl of fourteen, follow me, sir, I will take you there, the charge is not high, sir.' Though 'puzzled', Mohandas seems to have answered 'calmly and boldly' that he did not want the girl and asked the man 'to go away' (Diary; 1: 13). In Malta, the next port of call, he saw tapestries for the first time, 'very old paintings that were not paintings'.

Towards the end of the voyage an English passenger called Jeffreys wrote out a note that Mohandas had not eaten meat: he had been advised in Bombay to obtain such a testimonial. But since such certificates were also offered to those who had eaten meat, the piece of paper lost 'all its charm' for Mohandas (A 39).

Having worn a black suit while on board, Mohandas emerged, on landing, in white flannels and found that he was 'the only person wearing such clothes'. Whether in choosing what to wear he was following his own instincts or the (mischievous?) advice of the friend who helped him obtain the suits (Mehtab?) is not known.

From Tilbury, where the ship docked on 29 September 1888, Mohandas, Mazmudar and another passenger named Abdul Majid (who had travelled first-class) took a train to London, and from there a cab (a horse-drawn four-wheeler) to the Victoria Hotel. Noticing others leave their bags with a travel agent at Tilbury, Mohandas had done likewise, but at the hotel a Mohandas impatient to get at his black suit was told that it would take two nights for his bags to reach him.

The Victoria Hotel, one of London's grandest hotels at the time, 'dazzled' him. He was bowled over by the rows of lights, by the lift – he was seeing one for the first time – and by the room to which he was taken. 'I thought I could pass a lifetime in that room,' he would write before long (1: 16 & 83). But he also noticed 'the dignified air' i 1 which Abdul Majid, whose dress 'was perhaps worse than that of the porter', had asked 'the porter of the Victoria Hotel to give our cabman the proper fare'. The manager asked Majid, who appointed himself the leader of the trio of visiting Indians, whether they wanted rooms on the second floor. 'Mr Majid,' Mohandas would soon write in his Diary, 'thinking it below his dignity to inquire about the daily rent said yes. The manager at once gave us a bill of six shillings each per day and a boy was sent with us.'

Not sure that his words fully conveyed his amusement (at Majid and at his own white flannels), Mohandas would add in the Diary: 'I was all the time smiling within myself' (Diary; 1: 16). Amusement was not, of course, his only emotion; he felt overwhelmed, as we have seen, by the hotel's splendour, the Bania in him was troubled by the size of the bill, and he was annoyed, if also amused, by his white clothes. Yet we should note this evidence of the inwardly smiling Mohandas arriving in London.

A telegram that Mohandas had sent from Southampton brought a London-based Kathiawari to the hotel on the evening of Mohandas's arrival in London. Pranjivan

Mehta, one of the four to whom Mohandas had been given letters of introduction, was a Jain who had graduated from Grant Medical College in Bombay. Older than Mohandas by a few years, he was studying both law and higher medicine in London. This meeting would lead to a lifelong friendship, but its start was not very propitious. After laughing at Mohandas's white clothes, Mehta showed irritation when, without asking for permission, Mohandas picked up Mehta's top hat and stroked its fur the wrong way. Mohandas put the hat down and received a warning about English etiquette. Breaching one of its rules, though not legally a crime, was worse. Anyone hoping to do well in England had to observe the rules, and the way to learn them, Mehta said, was to move as a paying guest into an English home. But since Mohandas was too raw for such a move, he should first apprentice under an Indian already placed with a British family.

This other Indian was quickly found: Dalpatram Shukla, another of the four for whom Mohandas had letters. A Brahmin Kathiawari, and also hoping to become a barrister, Shukla was willing to accept Gandhi, and so, evidently, was Shukla's English 'family'. After a couple of days in the Victoria Hotel, and some more days in cheaper rooms that he and Mazmudar had jointly rented, Mohandas moved into the house in Richmond where Shukla was living.

In those 'cheaper rooms', where Mohandas passed his 19th birthday, he had overcome a torrential attack of homesickness.

> I would continually think of my home and country. My mother's love always haunted me. At night the tears would stream down my cheeks, and home memories of all sorts [*including, we may surmise, of Kastur and Harilal*] made sleep out of the question. It was impossible to share my misery with anyone ... I knew of nothing that would soothe me. Everything was strange – the people, their ways, and even their dwellings. I was a complete novice in the matter of English etiquette ... There was the additional inconvenience of the vegetarian vow. Even the dishes that I could eat were tasteless and insipid. England I could not bear, but to return to India was not to be thought of. Now that I had come, I must finish the three years, said the inner voice (A 40).

This is from the Autobiography, written 37 years later. Yet the recollection has the ring of reality: his London Diary too makes several mentions of his 'bold and dearest mother', his 'dear, dear mother' and so forth (1: 6–8). However, the 19-year-old rejected the homeward pull.

Like Mehta, Shukla was keen to break the newcomer into English ways. The youth who in Rajkot had never read newspapers started enjoying, from his days in Richmond, the hour he spent every day in reading three – the conservative *Daily Telegraph,* the liberal *Daily News* and the audacious *Pall Mall Gazette,* the editor of which, William T Stead, was sent to jail (within months of Gandhi's arrival) for his role in exposing how child prostitutes were being recruited. With their stories, and differing perspectives, on Victorian England's tensions between workers and employers and between England and Ireland, the newspapers, introduced to him by Shukla, nurtured Mohandas's political side. They also quickly improved his English.

Shukla strove also, 'day in and day out', to rescue his new friend from the vegetarian vow. A pledge made before an illiterate mother, and in ignorance of the conditions Mohandas was now facing, was valueless, he argued. 'You confess to having eaten and relished meat,' Shukla added. 'You took it where it was absolutely unnecessary, and will not where it is quite essential' (A 42).

Daily realities supported Shukla's reasoning. While the oatmeal porridge that Mohandas was given for breakfast felt adequate, the unvarying, unappealing contents of lunch and dinner (spinach and two or three slices of bread) left him hungry. Though 'a good eater' and possessing 'a capacious stomach', he felt it would go against etiquette to ask for additional slices (A 41).

Yet the 19-year-old resisted Shukla's pressure. 'The more [Shukla] argued, the more uncompromising I became.' Confronting Shukla with 'an eternal negative', Mohandas at this time also turned, so he says in the Autobiography, to some kind of prayer. 'Not that I had any idea of God,' but 'daily I would pray for God's protection and get it' (A 42). He remembered his maid Rambha and recited the name of Rama. His ability to survive those difficult weeks without meat seemed to give Mohandas a sense that a higher power was helping him, starting a process whereby, he would later say, he 'crossed the Sahara of atheism' while a student in London (A 61).

In another bid to save Gandhi, Shukla read aloud passages from Bentham's *Theory of Utility,* but Mohandas asked him to stop. 'Pray excuse me,' he said. 'I admit it is necessary to eat meat. But I cannot break my vow. Give me up as foolish or obstinate. A vow is a vow.' After this Shukla, who had no problems himself with drinking, smoking or eating meat, seemed to cease his efforts, though his anxiety about Gandhi in England remained.

Richmond being far from the centre of London, in November 1888 Mohandas moved to 20 Baron's Court Road, West Kensington. This was the four-storey home, in a long row of terraced houses, of a widow and her two daughters. Behind the row roared the trains of the District Line. In this house, located for him by Shukla and Mehta, Mohandas spent several months. Informed by Mohandas of his vow, the landlady, who had spent a few years in India, tried out some vegetarian cooking but could satisfy neither the palate nor the stomach of her lodger. At times the daughters would serve Mohandas an extra slice or two of bread, 'but little did they know that nothing less than a loaf would have filled me' (A 42). Mohandas was too shy to ask for more.

But the youth from Rajkot was enjoying his walks, often doing several miles a day, eating his fill of bread in cheap restaurants, looking forward to his legal studies, observing and perhaps smiling more than we may know, and feeling fairly confident in the Empire's capital. He was enjoying the newspapers, and also Alfred Harmsworth's *Answers to Correspondents,* finding it 'smutty but witty and very readable always', as he seems, decades later, to have told Pyarelal.[1]

The London he had come to was alive with ideas and movements. From here Victoria reigned over an expanding Empire. That Anglo-Saxons were the world's supreme race, and Christianity the greatest religion, was assumed in London, and also, at the time, in much of Europe and in America, but browns and blacks were not disliked in England, partly because there were so few of them.

There was also, in some circles, an interest in Asian thought and religions, in part inspired from across the Atlantic by Ralph Waldo Emerson. Other groups espoused socialism, or women's rights, or Irish rights, or atheism, or a universal religion of one form or another, or a return from a problematic industrialization to a simpler life on the land, or prescribed a variety of vegetarian diets for sound health. These ideas and debates touched Gandhi, who also followed a controversy sparked off by some of Oscar Wilde's writings published at this time.[2]

The Inner Temple, where Gandhi had enrolled, was one of four Inns of Court (all situated close to the western edge of the City of London) with a history that went back to the 13th century. Mehta, who would become Mohandas's closest Indian friend in London, and Shukla had joined the somewhat less expensive Middle Temple. Those desirous of being called to the bar had to pass two sets of written-and-oral examinations, one in Roman law and the other in Common law, and attend six dinners a term for 12 terms spread over three years.

The course was prestigious and advanced but not arduous. Almost everything depended on personal study – there was no such thing as campus life, and there were not many classes or lectures to attend. Because time was needed to find one's feet, an Indian aspirant for the bar usually waited several months after arrival in England to begin this personal study in earnest. This was certainly the case with Mohandas.

In most probably November or December 1888, on one of his wanderings on foot far from West Kensington, Mohandas hit upon the Central, a vegetarian restaurant off

Farringdon Street. It was a sight that filled him with the 'joy that a child feels on getting
a thing after its own heart'. Before entering the dining room, however, he bought – 'for
a shilling' – Henry Salt's *Plea for Vegetarianism* that was on display at the entrance. At
the Central he ate his 'first hearty meal since ... arrival in England', and his feeling was
that 'God had come to my aid' (A 43). Reading Salt's book 'from cover to cover', Gandhi
became a vegetarian by choice. Once more a text had pointed a path to him. Mohandas's
wish that all Indians should become meat-eaters, and his hope that one day, freely and
openly, he himself would resume eating meat were now fully behind him. His appetite
whetted by Salt's book, he 'went in for all books available on vegetarianism and read
them', including studies by William Howard, Anna Kingsford and Thomas Allinson,
and thought of dietetic experiments he would make himself.

Learning of his fellow-Kathiawari's new enthusiasm, Shukla was well and truly perturbed.
This bright youth brought to London to study for the bar – lightly built, thick-lipped,
big-eared, broad-cheeked and eager-faced, charming in his peculiar stubborn way – was
reading irrelevant, muddle-headed stuff, speaking of pointless experiments, and giving
every sign of turning into a crank.

Another effort to save him, an imaginative one, had to be made. Shukla asked
Mohandas to join him for an evening at the theatre (he knew that Mohandas liked
London's plays), to be preceded by dinner at the Holborn Restaurant. Perhaps glitter
and culture, mixed with a straight talking-to, would pull the young man back from the
brink. After all, as Shukla surely knew, Mohandas had been 'dazzled' by the Victoria
Hotel. The first big restaurant in which he found himself, the Holborn seemed 'palatial'
to Mohandas. Moreover, it was 'a very big company of diners in the midst of which my
friend and I sat sharing a table between us' (A 44). After the first course, soup, had been
placed on the table, Gandhi summoned the waiter, whereupon Shukla asked Gandhi
what the matter was. 'I want to know whether the soup is vegetarian,' said Gandhi.

Shukla exploded. 'You are too clumsy for decent society,' he exclaimed. 'If you cannot
behave yourself, you had better go. Eat in some other restaurant and await me outside.'
Out Mohandas went. Walking to a vegetarian restaurant close by, Gandhi found it
closed. He waited for Shukla and went with him to the play (we do not know its title)
on an empty stomach, and neither he nor Shukla said a word about what, in the Autobiography, Gandhi characteristically calls 'the scene *I* had created' (A 45).

According to the Autobiography, Gandhi's relations with Shukla were unaffected
by this 'last friendly tussle we had'. Yet the accusation of 'clumsiness' had needled
Mohandas, who reacted by wanting to demonstrate his refinement not only to Shukla but

also to himself. As the Autobiography puts it, he informed Shukla of a resolve 'to become polished and make up for my vegetarianism by cultivating other accomplishments which fitted one for polite society' (A 45). He would become 'an English gentleman'! New clothes bought at the Army and Navy Stores and a £10 evening suit from Bond Street replaced the 'unsuitable' outfits brought from Bombay. A stovepipe hat was obtained for 19 shillings. The ready-made tie was discarded, and the art of tying a tie was learnt. A letter went to Laxmidas in Rajkot for a double gold watch-chain. And Mohandas spent ten minutes every day 'before a huge mirror' arranging his tie and parting his hair 'in the correct fashion' (A 45).

Since looks alone did not make an English gentleman, Gandhi also engaged tutors for dancing, French, the violin and elocution. Four years after ending his 'reform' experiment with meat in Rajkot, he seemed engaged in a wider, more dramatic experiment in London. (We may note, in connection with the violin, that the young man *was* interested in music: apart from playing that haunting lament on a concertina, he had been attracted by bhajans sung while, nursed by him, his father lay ill.) He paid £3 for a term's dancing lessons, another £3 for a violin, unstated fees for French and violin lessons, a preliminary fee of a guinea to a man teaching elocution, who began with a speech by Pitt, and another unknown sum to buy Bell's *Standard Elocutionist.*

'But Mr Bell rang the bell of alarm in my ear and I awoke.' Something in the book – we do not know quite what, but once more in a book – triggered a chain of thought. How would English elocution help in India? Could dancing make one a gentleman? As for the violin, it could be learnt even in India. He was in England to study, not to become an English gentleman.

The 'infatuation', as the Autobiography calls it, lasted roughly three months. After about six dancing and two or three elocution lessons, Mohandas ended his pursuit. Letters announcing his inability to continue with the lessons and, also, spelling out the thoughts that Mr Bell had triggered, went to the dancing and elocution tutors. The truncated elocution course left a lasting benefit: Mohandas learnt to articulate his consonants, enabling future audiences to hear him distinctly. Calling on the violin teacher, Gandhi requested her to 'dispose of the violin for any price it might fetch' and confessed that he had been 'pursuing a false idea'. Apparently, the teacher encouraged Mohandas 'to make a complete change' (A 46).

Ending the 'infatuation' was a sort of milestone. Mohandas was sensing that not a personality but an inner firmness was what he needed to develop; not a power to charm or impress with figure or voice, but an internal spirit that holds on to a goal. Begun in November 1888, his London Diary, of which sadly only the opening portion has survived, indicates a wish to reflect, and also to write. The Diary's second sentence – 'The scene opens about the end of April' – could have been the start of anyone's writing life.

Its author enjoys the written word and is aware that he has an interesting story to relate and a feat to record – his making it to England despite all obstacles. Yet the writer seems secondary to a man examining himself.

By April 1889 or so, he had resolved to focus on his studies and given up chasing the identity of an English gentleman, but he admits in the Autobiography that he retained 'punctiliousness in dress' (A 46). As James Hunt points out in *Gandhi in London*, those hoping to become barristers were 'expected to conform to a certain standard of dress', and Gandhi, who 'had a fine appreciation of the social drama', knew 'the value of fitting his costume to his role'.[3]

In any case, the 'infatuation' had been well controlled. The dancing lessons were that and no more. Monitoring himself, Mohandas had kept a sharp eye, in particular, on his expenses. 'I kept account of every farthing I spent, and my expenses were carefully calculated.' Every item, an omnibus fare, a postage stamp, coppers spent on newspapers, or whatever, was entered into a notebook, 'and the balance struck every evening before going to bed' (A 47). 'The thought of my struggling brother, who nobly responded to my regular calls for monetary help' (A 49), sharpened Mohandas's effort to economize.

The loss of much of the diary and of almost all the long letters that Mohandas wrote to Laxmidas and his mother has removed valuable evidence of Gandhi's London life. Messages to Kastur, who was still unable to read, and to his little boy, were sent via Laxmidas.

Mehtab not only remained in touch with Gandhi; he seems to have asked from time to time for money, which Mohandas occasionally sent, out of Laxmidas's remittances to him, but, we must assume, without Laxmidas's knowledge, at least at the time. Our awareness of this help from London to Mehtab is derived from Pyarelal, who presumably learnt of it from Gandhi himself.[4]

To return to Gandhi's budget in London, he soon saw that he could cut his expenses by moving out of his West Kensington lodgings, where he paid for all meals even though he often ate elsewhere. Besides, an important part of etiquette was courtesy, which in practice meant taking the landlady's daughters out to dinner at times. It also meant paying for their transport while courteously attending parties with them. Moreover, the West Kensington family was not likely to offer many new lessons in etiquette.

In the summer or autumn of 1889, he moved to a bedroom/living room suite on Store Street. He decided, also, to walk instead of using a conveyance. 'This habit of long walks [*eight to ten miles a day*] kept me practically free from illness throughout my stay in England and gave me a fairly strong body' (A 48). If during some of these walks he thought of Mehtab, we may assume that he smiled at his friend's thesis about what made a person strong.

Soon discovering that London had ten vegetarian restaurants apart from the Central,

Gandhi walked to them all and sampled their fare. The walking Gandhi would become a familiar image to his London friends, though some also remembered his top hat and expensive clothes. Encountering Gandhi in Piccadilly Circus, another Indian student, Sachchidananda Sinha of Bihar, thought him 'more interested in fashion and frivolities than in his studies'.[5] Perhaps this occurred when Gandhi was trying out dancing, the violin and elocution, and he may have spoken of these interests to Sinha. But the move to Store Street, which brought him closer to the Inner Temple and to the University of London, had been preceded by a commitment to his legal studies, and by a decision also to sit in January 1890 for the University of London's matriculation examination.

Oxford and Cambridge, too, had entered his thoughts, but the time and fees required for a course at either of these universities seemed unaffordable. He was eligible to sit for his Roman law examination in November 1889 but chose to wait until March 1890, a timing influenced by the demands of the matriculation exam, which called for some proficiency in languages totally new to him, Latin and French, as well as in English, history, mathematics, physics or chemistry and geography. Studying chiefly by himself but also attending some preparatory classes for matriculation, and framing a timetable 'to the minute', Mohandas, at 19 one of the youngest of the roughly 200 Indians then studying in England,[6] bought all the costly textbooks prescribed, rejecting the option of memorizing inexpensive 'Notes'. He found Latin hard, and the textbooks in law called for a lot of perseverance, although some were 'full of interest' and at least one, Joshua Williams's volume on the principles of real estate, 'read like a novel' (A 71).

While enjoying, on the whole, his demanding studies – 'Nothing like self-preparation,' he would soon write[7] – he failed the Latin paper in December 1889. He therefore had to repeat the matriculation exam in June 1890, when he passed in all subjects including Latin. By this time he had also passed his Roman law exam, for which a student could read either a summary or the full text of Justinian's code.

Gandhi had opted for the latter, reading a book by Thomas Sandars containing a Latin text and an English translation.[8] Out of 46 students, of whom 40 passed, Gandhi was placed sixth. In December 1890, the earliest time possible for him, he sat for his four-day bar finals. A month later he heard that he had passed – out of 109 who took the finals, 77 had done so. Now 21 years old, Mohandas was ranked 34th.

To return, however, to 1889. In probably May of that year, before his move to Store Street, Mohandas went to Paris for the World Exhibition of 1889–90. (Whether Gandhi's visit to France occurred in 1890 or 1889 is not entirely clear; but it may be doubted that he spent a week in Paris immediately prior to writing the matriculation exam of June 1890.)

We know that he lived in a vegetarian boarding house in Paris, walked with a map to wherever he wanted to go, climbed the newly built Eiffel Tower two or three times, and 'threw away seven shillings' for 'the satisfaction of being able to say that [he] had had lunch at a great height'. The Eiffel Tower seemed 'unique' and 'novel' to him, but he was also, or more, impressed by the grandeur, peace and sculptures of Paris's ancient churches, including the cathedral of Notre Dame. He noticed, too, that 'the fashions and frivolity of Paris', about which he had 'read a lot', 'were in evidence in every street' (A 68–9).

This 'reading' by him is of interest. It was wide, going beyond his textbooks and newspapers, and resulted in his becoming 'completely fascinated by English literature', as he would inform Kaka Kalelkar in 1915.[9] But we do not know what he read. Nor do we know of the plays he saw, though he clearly went to several. On a 1931 visit to London he would recall that he had 'worshipped' the 'incomparable' Ellen Terry (53: 348).

Mohandas also found time to visit (perhaps for a meeting of vegetarians) the resort town of Brighton. There, in a hotel, he sat at the same table with 'an old widow of moderate means', as he remembers her in the Autobiography. (We do not know her name.) The menu being in French, which Mohandas could not as yet read, the lady helped him identify vegetarian items. The 'acquaintance ripened into friendship'. She invited him to dine on Sundays at her house in London.

To help Mohandas 'conquer his bashfulness', the old lady introduced him to young ladies and encouraged him to converse with them. 'Particularly marked out for these conversations was a young lady who stayed with her, and often we would be left entirely alone together.' At first Gandhi 'found all this very trying', but soon he 'looked forward to every Sunday and came to like the conversations with the young friend'.

What he did not tell her was that he had a wife and a son back in India.

Evidently he did not tell that, either, to the family with whom he had stayed in West Kensington. The Autobiography admits that Indian youths in England concealed their marriage, and gives reasons. Embarrassment at their early marriage was one. Another was the wish not to be deprived of opportunities 'to go about or flirt with the young girls of the family in which they lived', and, possibly, a related gallant desire not to deny the girls similar opportunities. Apparently the girls' parents 'encouraged' the 'more or less innocent' flirting, which seemed required by a culture where 'every young man has to choose his mate'. 'I too caught the contagion,' Gandhi confesses in the Autobiography. 'I did not hesitate to pass myself off as a bachelor' (A 56).

But he had to reveal the truth when it appeared (to him at any rate) that the lady befriended in Brighton 'had her own plans' for him and her ward. According to the Autobiography, after several attempts at drafting and redrafting a letter, he wrote to the lady 'somewhat to this effect':

> Ever since we met at Brighton you have been kind to me ... You also think that I should get married and with that in view you have been introducing me to young ladies ... I should have told you when I began my visits to you that I was married ... while yet a boy and am the father of a son. I am pained that I have kept this knowledge from you so long. But I am glad God has now given me the courage to speak out the truth. Will you forgive me? I assure you I have taken no improper liberties with the young lady ...

The Autobiography says that the reply, which came 'almost by return post', was 'somewhat as follows':

> I have your frank letter. We were both very glad and had a hearty laugh over it. The untruth you say you have been guilty of is pardonable. But it is well that you have acquainted us with the real state of things. My invitation still stands and we shall certainly expect you next Sunday and look forward to hearing about your child-marriage and laughing at your expense (A 58).

Whether the 'more or less innocent' companionship (A 56) lasted weeks or months is not stated in the Autobiography, which relates the story in a chapter called 'The Canker of Untruth', where he adds that he 'never thenceforward hesitated to talk of [his] married state' (A 58). We do not know the story from the other side, and may guess that 'a hearty laugh' was not the only reaction from the young woman.

Also told in that chapter is an amusing story of an outing with an unnamed young lady in Ventnor on the Isle of Wight, later identified by researchers as the daughter of a Mr Shelton, who owned a vegetarian hotel on Madeira Road in Ventnor. Evidently five years or so older than Mohandas, the young lady, who 'took me one day to the lovely hills round Ventnor', was 'flying like a bird'. 'No slow walker' himself, Gandhi was nonetheless left far behind, and when it came to descending from a cliff, Miss Shelton, despite her 'high-heeled boots', 'darted down like an arrow' while Mohandas could only 'scramble to the bottom, crawling at intervals'. Having 'stood at the foot smiling and cheering me and offering to come and drag me', Miss Shelton offered a 'loudly laughed bravo' when Mohandas finally reached level ground. It seems plain that the amusement provided (and felt by the author) in the Autobiography was also felt, along with embarrassment, at the time – perhaps January 1890.[10]

The story's inclusion in the 'Canker of Untruth' chapter suggests that Miss Shelton did not at this time know of Gandhi's marriage. It is obvious that young Gandhi enjoyed these meetings with members of the opposite sex, even if one part of him was insecure about his way with them, and another part guilty at concealing his marriage.

The Autobiography mentions Gandhi coming across, in London, 'two unmarried theosophists', whom he calls 'brothers'. James Hunt's research indicates that in fact the two were an uncle and nephew, Bertram and Archibald Keightley. Probably in August or September 1889, they took Mohandas to meet Annie Besant, the Irishwoman who had just moved from radicalism to theosophy and was very much in the news, and Helena Blavatsky, a co-founder of the theosophical movement. The Keightleys had told Gandhi that Mme Blavatsky felt great joy at the 'capture' of Annie Besant.

Intrigued, he says, about the thinking of a 'former atheist', Gandhi went to hear a public speech by Annie Besant and was struck by her remark, made in answer to a charge of inconsistency, that she would be content with an epitaph that she lived and died for truth.[11] Mohandas also read Blavatsky's book *Key to Theosophy*, which was sympathetic to Hinduism and was pleased with its rejection of the notion entertained by several Englishmen he had run into that 'Hinduism was rife with superstition' (A 60).

He also attended meetings of the London Indian Society, founded by two men who had presided over the Indian National Congress, Naoroji (for whom Gandhi was carrying a letter of introduction) and W C Bonnerjee. We may note, too, that within months of his arrival in England he had started cutting out and keeping items from newspapers that interested him. Saying this to his future secretary, Pyarelal, Gandhi would add that during his student days in London he 'closely followed' newspaper reports of criminal trials as also the proceedings of the Commission on Irish Crimes and Lord Russell's brilliant cross-examination that exposed forgeries and vindicated the Irish nationalist leader, Parnell.[12]

After passing the matriculation exam in June 1890, and thereby gaining a sense of accomplishment, he spent a four-week holiday in Brighton, where, among other things, he learnt to cook. Keener than ever to economize, he now moved from his two-room apartment on Store Street to a single room in Tavistock Street, at eight shillings a week. However, as Hunt points out, both Store and Tavistock Streets were areas of middle-class or well-to-do housing; and Gandhi admits in the Autobiography that he could not compete in frugality with some other Indian students in London, one of whom stayed 'in the slums in a room at two shillings a week', eating a two-penny meal of cocoa and bread (A 49).

While living in his Tavistock Street room, Gandhi invested in a stove, cooked oatmeal porridge for breakfast, ate lunch out, and had bread and cocoa at home for dinner. The meals cost him a total of a shilling and three pence a day. (Despite the economies, the London project would cost the Gandhis a total of 13,000 rupees, or about £1,000, two-and-a-half times the estimate given by Dave, the family friend.)

The bar finals of December 1890 were only a few months away, but the Gandhi of the second half of 1890, and of the less tense first half of 1891 (he left for India in June 1891) was very active socially and intellectually. The vegetarian movement absorbed a good deal of his time, and he also explored religious avenues.

Another diversion was provided by a visit to London (probably in the summer of 1890) by the Gujarati poet, Narayan Hemchandra, to whom Gandhi offered companionship and practical help. Because of his unusual appearance, Hemchandra, a light, short man in 'a clumsy pair of trousers, a wrinkled, dirty, brown coat ... a tasselled woollen cap, and a long beard', his 'round face scarred with small-pox' – to quote from the sketch Gandhi drew years later in the Autobiography – 'was bound to be singled out in fashionable society', as Gandhi would put it (A 64). Mohandas taught Hemchandra English and at times cooked for him.

Discussing with Hemchandra a famous dock strike that had ended in September 1889 through the efforts of Cardinal Manning, Gandhi recalled a tribute once paid to Manning by the Prime Minister, Benjamin Disraeli (who had died eight years earlier), whereupon Hemchandra decided that the Cardinal was a man he had to meet. A note Gandhi wrote produced an appointment, and at a short interview Mohandas translated the poet's Gujarati for the Cardinal. It was his custom, Hemchandra said, 'to visit the sages of the world' (A 66).

But Hemchandra did something for Gandhi too. Demonstrating to Mohandas that earnestness was as effective as social polish, Hemchandra stayed in Gandhi's mind, eliciting, 36 years later, a whole chapter in the Autobiography.

At some point in the autumn of 1890, the two theosophists, the Keightleys, sought Gandhi's help with the *Bhagavad Gita*. They were reading Edwin Arnold's translation, *The Song Celestial,* and wanted, with Gandhi's aid, to understand the Sanskrit original. Though Mohandas had studied some Sanskrit at Alfred High School, his knowledge of the language was meagre. As for the *Gita*, he had not read it, not even in Gujarati. He conveyed this to the Keightleys but read the *Gita* with them nonetheless, in English and

Sanskrit, and developed an interest in the text. (For the rest of his life, he would speak of Arnold's as the best English version of the *Gita*.)

The Keightleys next told Gandhi of Arnold's book on the Buddha, *The Light of Asia*, which Mohandas read with 'even greater interest'. At the suggestion of a 'good Christian from Manchester', whom Gandhi had met in a vegetarian boarding house, he also read the Bible, buying it, 'along with maps, concordance, and other aids', from the same man. He found the Old Testament heavy going, especially the Book of Genesis, but the Sermon on the Mount in the New Testament 'went straight to [his] heart' (A 60).

At least some of his prejudice against Christianity evaporated in London. The Christians he was meeting seemed likeable, and he attended church services a number of times. Charles Spurgeon, who preached at the Metropolitan Tabernacle, the Congregationalist Joseph Parker, and Frederick William Farrar, the Bombay-born temperance advocate who would become Dean of Canterbury after Gandhi's return to India, were some of the famous preachers he heard while in London. He took something from them. In 1907 or 1908 he would tell Joseph Doke, the Baptist minister in South Africa who became his first biographer, that Parker, whose midday sermons on Thursdays he went many times to hear, helped him in his rejection of atheism.

Part of the London Gandhi, independent and curious, was clearly looking for the right religion to follow. Though not his central pursuit in London, this was a question on his mind. Most of his Christian encounters were outside England's mainstream Anglican or Roman Catholic churches, and, men like Joseph Parker apart, with Britons who combined their Christianity with vegetarianism. The man from Manchester from whom Gandhi bought the Bible was a vegetarian, as was Josiah Oldfield, an eloquent theology graduate from Oxford (and a future barrister and doctor) who moved to London while Gandhi was studying law.

Possibly the 'only Englishman with whom the young Gandhi lived on a basis of friendship and equality',[13] Oldfield, who was six years older, had heard of Gandhi from Dr Pranjivan Mehta, and sought him out. The two met in the summer of 1890, which is when Oldfield became the editor of *The Vegetarian*, published by the London Vegetarian Society (LVS). In September 1890 Oldfield invited Gandhi to attend 'the greatest event of organized vegetarianism, the International Vegetarian Congress'.[14]

Right after this conference Gandhi was elected to the executive committee of the London Vegetarian Society. And from March 1891 until his departure for India three months later, Gandhi and Oldfield 'took rooms together' at 52 St Stephen's Gardens, Bayswater, as Oldfield would later recall.[15] When Gandhi confessed to Oldfield that he was wondering which religion to follow, the Englishman said, 'Why not Christianity?'[16] But the searching Gandhi was in no hurry and seemed also to be looking for Christians who would acknowledge that truth was not necessarily confined to their faith.

As for the theosophists he had met, they did not seem to favour one religion over another, and they respected aspects of Hinduism. This he liked, but he could not share the theosophists' interest in occult powers. From Carlyle's *Heroes and Hero-Worship*, recommended by an unnamed friend, he learnt something about the Prophet of Islam. This reading should be seen together with Mohandas's participation in meetings in London of the Anjuman-e-Islam, founded in 1886 for Muslim students by an Indian barrister, Abdullah Sohrawardy.[17] We know, of course, that even in Rajkot Gandhi was interested in Hindu-Muslim friendship.

The name of at least one Muslim student he befriended in London is known: Mazharul Haq from Bihar, a future president of the Muslim League.[18] In London Gandhi noticed that some Muslim students were attracted by ideas of Pan-Islamism.[19] Among other Indian students he got to know were Keshavrao Deshpande, a Maharashtrian Brahmin and Pestonji Padshah, a Parsi, both studying law.

Towards Hinduism at this stage he was tentatively loyal. People who were likeable and seemed to have a standing in British society valued the culture he had inherited. Hinduism was respected by the theosophists, and vegetarianism was embraced by them and other Britons he was meeting. Men like Oldfield, while openly committed to Christianity, were strongly supportive of his vow against meat. All this raised the standing of Hinduism in his mind, yet the London Gandhi, like the Rajkot Mohan, was too rational to accept all that went under the name of Hinduism.

The one clear religious conclusion he had come to was that God existed. He recognized, and rejected, his atheistic side. Mohandas had indeed admired the pro-India views of Charles Bradlaugh, Britain's famous advocate of atheism, and on 30 January 1891 he went to Bradlaugh's funeral, as, he thought, 'every Indian residing in London did' (A 63). But what Mohandas had experienced, heard, read and thought in London produced a verdict against atheism (A 60–1).

In 1947, when he was 77, Gandhi would say that 'at the age of twenty or twenty-one it became a dream of mine to attain … a state of mind [which] cannot be affected even in dire circumstances or at the moment of death' (93: 228). Gandhi does not tell us what triggered the desire, whether it was an incident like the ejection from the Holborn restaurant by Shukla, or a religious text read or heard in London, or something else.

He had passed his bar finals by the time of Bradlaugh's funeral. Having sat for these from 15 to 20 December 1890, he learnt on 12 January that he had passed. All he now needed to do to be called to the bar was to pay for and attend 12 more dinners at the Inner Temple. Otherwise, the five months that lay ahead were entirely free. Because he did not drink, Mohandas was in demand at the dinners, where each table for four was given two bottles of port or sherry or, at times, champagne.

Told on the voyage to England that life there was dependent on meat, Gandhi saw instead that Britain's vegetarians had given him new life. Through them he found friendship, a field of activity and a platform for writing and speaking. As we will see, they also linked him to politics.

In other ways, too, the vegetarians were useful to him. In Paris, Brighton, the Isle of Wight, and for a time also, it would seem, in London, he had stayed in vegetarian hotels or boarding houses; and in London he became, for the rest of his life, something of a food scientist, experimenting with different varieties of vegetarian food. Soups that he had at first despised for their apparent dullness were later seen as nutritious and even tasty – he learnt from his experiments that 'the real seat of taste was not the tongue but the mind' (A 50).

The pickles and sweets from Rajkot that he had sent for no longer seemed indispensable. He tried out a starch-free diet, strongly recommended by some of his vegetarian friends, of milk, cheese and eggs, but stopped eating eggs after a few weeks because he was certain his mother's 'definition of meat included eggs' (A 51). He also rejected tea and coffee as non-nutritious and possibly harmful, and substituted cocoa for them. Food, in a variety of aspects, was a major part of his life in England.

But the English vegetarians, whose interest in diet was linked to a wider idealistic concern, were also an important part of his social and intellectual world. Apart from the friendship with Oldfield, Mohandas also valued the chance to get to know a wealthy industrialist who provided much of the funding for the LVS and *The Vegetarian,* Alfred Hills, chairman of the Thames Iron Works, a shipyard that built warships and other vessels.

A devout Christian, Hills wanted *The Vegetarian* to be a 'radical yet rational reformer' that would address England's 'national vices and sorrows', including 'the congestion of our great cities, with its attendant curses of debauchery and disease' and 'the housing and feeding of our starving poor'.[20] Another friend Gandhi found through the vegetarian movement was Thomas Allinson, a doctor who had invented a breakfast cereal and a wholemeal bread. From these and other friends, and from the literature to which they introduced him, he learnt of Tolstoy, John Ruskin, Thoreau, Emerson and Edward Carpenter, though it does not seem that in London he read any of their writings.

It was Hills who first persuaded Mohandas to write for *The Vegetarian.* Between February and April 1891 Gandhi would write nine articles for the journal, with the encouragement, no doubt, of its editor, Oldfield. It is in these articles, and in talks and interviews he gave in 1891 to vegetarian groups and journals, that we glimpse what we have failed so far to see in the London Gandhi – his political and philosophical side.

The subjects for these articles and talks were strictly non-political – 'Indian

Vegetarians', 'Some Indian Festivals', 'The Foods of India', and so forth – but he made suggestive forays into the broader field of life in India under British rule. In the first part of 'Indian Vegetarians' he speaks of 'salt, a heavily-taxed article' (*The Vegetarian*, 7 Feb. 1891) and in a later part, saying that 'those who have learnt a little bit of English have picked up English ideas here and here', he adds, 'Whether this is for the worse or the better must be left to the reader to judge.'

In this article he also says that 'one of the most greatly-felt evils of the British rule is the importation of alcohol – that enemy of mankind, that curse of civilization', and takes care to point out that both Hindus and Muslims are unhappy that 'the Government, it seems, instead of stopping, are aiding and abetting the spread of alcohol'. Also indicative are references in the article to '*so-called* educated Indians' and to 'the poor' who are 'the greatest sufferers' (*The Vegetarian*, 14 Mar. 1891; emphasis added.).

A piece by him on Divali and Holi claims that during such festivals 'a serious attempt is made' to patch up 'old family quarrels', 'old debts are paid up' where possible, and 'alms are freely given'. 'It will be easily seen that good and far-reaching consequences cannot fail to flow from such holidays, which some cry down as a relic of superstition and tomfoolery, though in reality they ... tend to relieve a great deal the dull monotony of life among the toiling millions' (*The Vegetarian*, 4 Apr. 1891).

In his talk on 'The Foods of India', given on 2 May 1891, he wants his British audience to realize that they are listening to one from India as a whole, not a part thereof. So he says something about the foods of Bengal and of 'the southern and northern provinces' in addition to what is eaten in western India. And he informs British vegetarians that whereas their vegetarianism was a question of choice, that of many in India was a matter of necessity. Stating that the poor in India were 'compelled to live on vegetable foods because they cannot afford to pay for meat', Gandhi adds:

There are millions in India who live upon one pice – i.e. one-third of a penny – a day ... These people have only one meal per day, and that consists of stale bread and [*repeating a phrase previously used*] salt, a heavily-taxed article.

The end of this talk is also of interest:

In conclusion, I further hope that the time will come when the great difference now existing between the food habits of meat-eating in England and grain-eating in India will disappear, and *with it some other differences which, in some quarters, mar the unity of sympathy that ought to exist between the two countries*. In the future, I hope we shall tend towards unity of customs, and also unity of hearts (*The Vegetarian Messenger*, 6 May 1891; 1: 35–8; emphasis added).

If the vegetarian movement gave him opportunities to make political points, he also felt confident enough to assert, on the basis of 'my personal experience', that 'English Vegetarians will more readily sympathize with the Indian aspirations' and indeed that 'the vegetarian movement will indirectly aid India politically also …' (*The Vegetarian*, 28 Apr. 1894; 1: 125ff.). Contained in 'a letter to Indian students' published in *The Vegetarian* three years after he left London, this was an assessment Gandhi had made while in London. It suggests that young Gandhi kept an interested eye on the attitudes to India held by different kinds of Britons. His own political stance in London was of one who aspired steadily, if quietly and indirectly, for Indian rights but also valued India's British connection.

Revealing the political strand in Mohandas in London, his involvement in the vegetarian movement also trained him in the basics of politics – organizing meetings, enlisting allies and patrons, raising resources, getting the word out. The London of 1890–1, when Gandhi joined in 'lecturing at clubs and public meetings' and arranging suppers of 'lentil soup, boiled rice and large raisins', was, as Oldfield would later point out, 'a fine training ground' for Gandhi.[21] On his part, Gandhi would acknowledge Oldfield's role in encouraging him towards a public life.[22]

Though nervousness while addressing an audience remained a problem for Mohandas, he was willing to step forward. When Oldfield asked him to stand for a place in the executive committee of the LVS, Gandhi agreed and was elected. And he took an initiative of his own.

'Full of the neophyte's zeal,' as he puts it in the Autobiography, he started 'a vegetarian club' in the London neighbourhood where he and Oldfield had taken rooms. Oldfield would remember the new body as 'the West London Reform Society'. At the instance, it would seem, of Gandhi, who became the secretary, Oldfield became the president, and Sir Edwin Arnold, who apparently lived in the vicinity, the vice-president (A 52).

If initiative is integral to public life, so is conflict. Two of Gandhi's esteemed friends, Hills and Dr Allinson, differed sharply over a publication by Allinson, *A Book for Married Women*, propagating artificial birth control. Opposed to Allinson's ideas, Hills asked the executive committee to expel the doctor from the LVS. Though Gandhi supported Hills's viewpoint, he opposed Allinson's expulsion, arguing that 'the exclusion of anti-puritans' was not part of the declared objects of the LVS. Another committee member read out Gandhi's statement after a nervous Mohandas had failed to do so himself. However, 'Dr Allinson lost the day', and 'in the very first battle' of this kind Gandhi found himself 'siding with the losing party' (A 54).

Connecting him to politics, London's vegetarian movement was yet greater than politics. Joining the religious to the political dimension, and the ethical to the dietary, it satisfied an inner need in Mohandas and strengthened him. He was aware, though, that mainstream England thought of vegetarians as faddists.

Anxieties assailed him as his departure neared. He was no longer the person who had left Rajkot in 1888. One part of him was very English now. After three years in a great city he had grown to like, how would he cope in provincial Rajkot? How would he reconnect with his mother, wife, son, siblings, the wider family and caste, his friends?

He worried also about his professional prospects. He had heard that Sir Pherozeshah Mehta, who was said to dominate the Bombay bar, 'roared like a lion' in the courtroom, but Gandhi could not picture himself roaring anywhere (A 73). Could a timid man like him who knew virtually nothing of law in India succeed there?

On 21 April he read the paper mentioned earlier, 'The Foods of India', at the Waverley restaurant. *The Vegetarian* reported: 'After congratulating the previous speaker [*a Mrs Harrison*] and apologizing for his paper ... [Mr M K Gandhi] began to read it. He was rather nervous in the beginning' (1: 35).

By now Tryambak Mazmudar had reappeared. On 5 and 6 May he and Gandhi attended a vegetarian conference in Portsmouth where, on 6 May, Gandhi was scheduled to present his paper again. In the Autobiography Gandhi says that the house in which he and Mazmudar were billeted in the port town was of dubious reputation, though the conference organizers 'did not know anything about it'. Returning to this lodging after the opening day's conference, Gandhi and Mazmudar had dinner. What followed is in the Autobiography:

> After dinner we sat down to play a rubber of bridge, in which our landlady joined, as is customary in England, even in respectable households. Every player indulges in innocent jokes as a matter of course, but here my companion and our hostess began to make indecent ones as well. It captured me and I also joined in.
>
> Just when I was about to go beyond the limit, leaving the cards and the game to themselves ... [my] good companion uttered the ... warning: 'Whence this devil in you, my boy? Be off, quick!' ...
>
> I fled from the scene. To my room I went quaking, trembling, and with beating heart, like a quarry escaped from the pursuer (A 62–3).

In the Autobiography, where he refers to the incident as 'the first occasion when a woman other than my wife moved me to lust', Gandhi calls Mazmudar's warning 'blessed', adds that it was God who sent it through Mazmudar, and adds also that while fleeing ashamed from the scene, he 'expressed gratefulness within myself to my friend'.

That night he did not sleep. He doubtless remembered his mother and his vow to her, and Kastur. There were other thoughts:

> Should I leave this house? Should I run away from the place? What would happen to me if I had not my wits about me? I decided to act thenceforth with great caution; not to leave the house, but somehow leave Portsmouth (A 63).

He seems to have reckoned that an abrupt departure from the house might invite suspicion. He would go through with the second day of the conference, read his paper, and then, quietly and quickly, leave Portsmouth. This is just what he did. On 6 May he gave his talk and left for Ventnor, where he was also scheduled to speak, on 11 May. There were other talks in the London area – he had after all become a celebrity in the world of English vegetarians.

Though harbouring guilt over what had happened in Portsmouth, he tackled his engagements better than is suggested in the Autobiography, which claims that extreme nervousness silenced him at Ventnor and again at a farewell occasion he organized in London. Contemporary accounts unearthed by researchers do not fully corroborate the version in the Autobiography.[23] Recalling the Portsmouth surge of lust in the Autobiography, Gandhi says that at the time he only 'vaguely understood that God had saved me'. Neither then nor in the Autobiography did he explore a link between it and his anxieties.

Aware of Mohandas's fears about practising law in India, a friend (not named in the Autobiography) advised him to seek the counsel of Dadabhai Naoroji, the London-based ex-president of the Indian National Congress. Gandhi had respectfully heard Naoroji at meetings of Indian students and, after much diffidence, handed to the old man the introduction he had been carrying from September 1888. But he could not bring himself to trouble Naoroji over his personal worries.

He did, however, approach the jurist and orientalist Frederick Pincott (again on the advice of a friend), described in the Autobiography as 'a Conservative but [with a] pure and unselfish affection' for Indian students. Pincott 'laughed' Gandhi's 'pessimism away' and said that everyone did not have to have the dominance and brilliance of 'a Pherozeshah Mehta'. Honesty and industry would suffice. Pincott's 'smiling open face' entered Gandhi's memory, and he felt reassured (A 74). Though a celebrity in a certain circle, and admired there for his commitment, Gandhi was in need of encouragement. He was fortunate to receive it from Pincott.

Pincott also recommended books by Lavater and Shemmelpennick that would help

Gandhi in 'reading a man' from his face, an ability that he said lawyers should have (which was also an ability Gandhi was interested in), as well as the volumes by Kaye and Malleson on the 1857 Rebellion: an Indian lawyer should know India's history, Pincott said. Buying the Lavater book, Gandhi also studied Shakespeare's physiognomy, but 'did not acquire the knack of finding out the Shakespeares walking up and down the streets of London' (A 74). His anxieties had not banished his ability to be amused.

Shortly before his departure, Gandhi was interviewed for *The Vegetarian* by its editor, Josiah Oldfield. The interview, referred to previously, is revealing, urbane, honest and appealingly modest. In it Gandhi describes the reason for coming to England – 'In a word, ambition'; how he 'exacted' the consent of some relatives – the exercise was 'nothing else'; how he showed to his mother, of whom he was 'the pet', 'the exaggerated advantages of coming to England'; and how 'an old friend of my father … fanned the fire that was burning within me'.

Gandhi recalled his thinking before leaving India: 'If I go to England not only shall I become a barrister (of whom I used to think a great deal), but I shall be able to see England, the land of philosophers and poets, the very centre of civilization.'

Three years on, he frankly admits that it was 'ambition' that brought him to England, but now he seems to smile at that drive, and also at barristers. Added Gandhi, 'You will perhaps be astonished to hear that I am married. The marriage took place at the age of twelve' (1:42–44; *The Vegetarian*, 13 Jun. 1891).

> In conclusion [*Gandhi went on*], I am bound to say that during my nearly three years' stay in England, I have left many things undone, and have done many things which I perhaps might have left undone, yet I carry one great consolation with me, that I shall go back without having taken meat or wine … (*The Vegetarian*, 20 Jun. 1891)

Apart from the fact that the Portsmouth episode was fresh in the young man's mind, it would have been indelicate to claim in a newspaper interview that he had also managed – a close shave notwithstanding – to keep the vow about women.

He had done more. He had enjoyed living in London, observed (with a fairly sharp eye, we must assume) its personalities and crosscurrents, studied the British mind, dipped into English literature, and mingled with some gifted (if also unusual) individuals. Gaining skills that could help him in law and public life, yet retaining much of his shyness, he had also reflected on his goals and embraced interests larger than himself. While experiencing embarrassments and a jolt, he had also nurtured an earlier ability to be amused by himself and the world, built promising connections, and could count some solid achievements.

On 5 June 1891 Gandhi hosted a private farewell dinner for his friends in Room XIX of the luxurious Holborn Restaurant, at the south-west corner of Holborn and Kingsway,[24] the very place from which, about three years previously, Shukla had ordered him out for wanting to ask a waiter if the soup was vegetarian. What is more, Gandhi got the Holborn to serve, for the first time, a wholly vegetarian meal. The attendees, Hills, Oldfield and other pillars of vegetarianism, were delighted with 'the new experiment' (A 54). Mohandas liked the taste of his little coup.

Music, too, had been arranged by him, and there were speeches. In the Autobiography Gandhi thinks that because of nervousness he could only utter the first sentence of a short speech he had rehearsed, but on 13 June 1891, *The Vegetarian* published a slightly different report:

> At the close, Mr Gandhi, in a very graceful though somewhat nervous speech, welcomed all present, spoke of the pleasure it gave him to see the habit of abstention of flesh progressing in England, related the manner in which his connection with the LVS arose, and in so doing took occasion to speak in a touching way of what he owed to Dr Oldfield.

Oldfield said at the dinner that Gandhi had provided a lesson of 'patient, persistent overcoming of difficulties, in pursuit of an aim'.[25] On 10 June Mohandas was called to the bar. Two days later, he boarded first a train at Liverpool Street and then, at Tilbury Docks, a ship going east.

> I could not make myself believe [*he would soon write*] that I was going to India until I stepped into the steamship *Oceana,* of the P & O Company. So much attached was I to London and its environments, for who would not be? London with its teaching institutions, public galleries, vegetarian restaurants, is a fit place for a student and a traveller, a trader and a 'faddist' – as a vegetarian would be called by his opponents. Thus it was not without regret that I left dear London (1: 50–1).

The suave tone evident during Gandhi's final weeks in England also permeates the two short articles that he wrote about (and probably during) the voyage back to India. Their author (perhaps hoping to develop his writing skill) affects a (very British) mocking, snobbish and understated style. His articles refer to 'a crowd of dirty-looking beggars'

who 'pester' passengers in Malta, 'rogues and rascals' encountered in Port Said, and waiters who 'murder the Queen's English' and 'are the reverse of clean'.

Gandhi describes the meals in a day of 'an average passenger': the pre-breakfast tea and biscuits, a huge breakfast, its elements detailed, an 'easily digestible' lunch ('dinner') with 'plenty of mutton and vegetables, rice and curry, pastry and what not ... fruit and nuts', followed by 'a "refreshing" cup of tea and biscuits at 4 p.m.' and 'a "high tea" at 6.30 p.m. – bread and butter, jam or marmalade, or both, salad, chops, tea, coffee, etc.' Thereafter, since the sea air was 'so very salubrious', 'the passengers could not retire to bed before taking a few, a very few – only eight or ten, fifteen at the most – biscuits, a little cheese and some wine or beer'.

> Some very nice ladies and gentlemen [travelled] in the first saloon. But it would not do to have all play and no quarrel, so some of the passengers thought fit to get drunk almost every evening (beg your pardon, Mr Editor, they got drunk almost every evening, but this particular evening they got drunk and disorderly).

He also wrote of a speech that he was all set to make on board (on vegetarianism, of course) but did not because the evening 'devoted to speeches and concerts' never came off. Asked to be humorous in his speech, Gandhi replied (he wrote) that he 'might be nervous but humorous I could not be'. But the man writing this knew that he was being funny.

This time mingling freely with others and helping to organize some common activities, Gandhi persuaded the crew to provide vegetable curry, rice or brown bread, and fruit for the two vegetarians, including himself, on board. The other passengers, British and Indian, seemed to like and respect him. He was, in his own words, a student, traveller, trader and 'faddist', but also, now, an Indo-Anglian. Trader meant a Bania, an element of his never-forgotten Indian identity, while the 'fads' he had acquired were at least partly of British origin. And the style he was employing, in his life on board and in the articles, was of a sophisticated young man aware of a modernizing world. (In the summer of 1891, a new century was not too far off.) His comments, while again revealing an interest in what was going on around him, ended on a serious note:

> What a human cargo was on the *Oceana* and the *Assam*! [*Bombay-bound passengers were transferred to the* Assam *in Aden.*] Some were going to make fortunes in Australia ... some, having finished their studies in England, were going to India to earn a decent living. Some were called away by a sense of duty, some were going to meet their husbands in Australia or India ... and some were adventurers who, being disappointed at home, were going to pursue their adventures, God knows where (1: 50–6).

During the journey, he says in the Autobiography, he was 'taxing' himself, being 'a reformer', 'as to how best to begin certain reforms', starting no doubt with the Rajkot household. But underneath a nonchalant exterior he was aware of two troubling questions: how would his caste receive him (he had heard in letters of continuing objections), and how would he begin a career?

The sea was rough as the *Assam* approached Bombay. 'Almost every passenger was sick; I alone was in perfect form, staying on deck to see the stormy surge, and enjoying the splash of the waves' (A 75). In Mohandas, an inner storm matched the outer one, but he says he felt ready to face both.

There was indeed something to face on landing, which occurred in pelting rain. After initial prevarications, Laxmidas, who met his younger brother off the boat, revealed that Putlibai was no more. She had died, aged around 41, not long after hearing that her son had passed his bar finals, but the family spared Mohandas 'the blow in a foreign land'.

'Most of my cherished hopes were shattered,' Gandhi says in the Autobiography (75), without spelling out these hopes. Perhaps he had wished to become a diwan in her lifetime, or dreamt of even more; he certainly wanted to tell her that he had kept the vows.

'My grief was even greater than over my father's death ... But ... I did not give myself up to any wild expression of grief. I could even check the tears, and took to life just as though nothing had happened.' We have seen that while in England he had wished to cultivate an ability to endure shock or danger.

ஂ

Rajchandra. Laxmidas took his brother to the home of Dr Pranjivan Mehta, whose return to India had preceded Gandhi's, and who introduced Mohandas to his relatives. One of these was Rajchandra, who had just married a daughter of Dr Mehta's older brother. Two years older than Gandhi, Rajchandra, who had a Bania father and a Jain mother, was a Kathiawari soon to win fame as a Jain scholar-saint.

In 1891, at the age of 23 or 24, he was already known as a poet, as a jeweller of unimpeachable integrity and for feats of memory. Vain about his English, and about what he knew of Latin and French, Mohandas wrote out a series of European words and technical terms, read them aloud, and challenged Rajchandra to repeat them. Rajchandra did so faultlessly. The experience brought the barrister back down to earth. As Gandhi would later confess, 'Having been to England made a man feel that he was heaven-born.' The 'binding spell' of England was broken 'a little' by Rajchandra's performance.[26]

At Laxmidas's urging and also because of his late mother's wish, Mohandas went through a ritual of 'cleansing' himself of the sin of crossing the seas. Performed in Nasik in Maharashtra, the ritual bridged a divide between the Gandhis and much of the Modh Bania community, though the leaders of one group were not appeased. They demanded a fine that Mohandas refused to pay. The result was that his sister Raliat and her husband, and the parents of Kastur, who belonged to the minority group, were not allowed to offer Mohandas even a glass of water in their homes.

To suit the home-coming barrister, Laxmidas had had the Rajkot home whitewashed. A ceiling had been installed under its tiled roof. Chairs and tables and china had been bought. Tea and coffee were already being used. It was expected that increased expenses would be more than offset by the large income that Mohandas would bring in. Though doubtful about some of the spending, the reformer added his own innovations such as cocoa, oatmeal and European clothes.

There is no suggestion in the Autobiography or elsewhere of an ecstatic reunion with Kastur in 1891. He renewed the attempt to educate her and again met with resistance. Mohandas's response was less than patient, and his 'jealousy', 'squeamishness' and 'suspiciousness' (to use his words in the Autobiography) were revived. Whether Mehtab again had a role in inciting these feelings is not known. The Autobiography is silent on the subject; in fact Mehtab is not mentioned in the short account Gandhi gives of experiences between his return from England in 1891 and his 1893 departure for South Africa. But we should assume that Mehtab, who reenters the narrative in South Africa, was around, and interacting with Gandhi, in Rajkot in 1891. What we know (from the Autobiography) is that Mohandas was indeed harsh to Kastur. On one occasion he sent 'her away to her father's house, and consented to receive her back only after I had made her thoroughly miserable' (A 79). His attitude was 'pure folly', says the Autobiography, but there was no sign of this realization in the early 1890s.

He had a more satisfying reunion with his son Harilal, now over three, and enjoyed 'playing and joking' with the boy and with the children of Laxmidas, carrying them on his shoulders and teaching them physical exercise 'to make them hardy' (A 79). In 1935 he would also say:

In 1891, after my return from England, I virtually took charge of the children of the family and introduced the habit of walking with them – boys and girls – putting my hands on their shoulders. These were my brothers' children (*Harijan,* 21 Sep. 1935; 67: 434–6).

This is the tactile Mohandas, who found it natural, like many of his people in Kathiawar and other parts of India, to touch or hug intimates, even as he was careful and reserved with others.

Expenses were mounting – 'new things were added every day' – but there was no income. Why would anyone in Rajkot pay ten times the fees of a local vakil to a barrister who knew nothing of Kathiawar's laws? It was decided, presumably between Laxmidas and Mohandas, that the barrister should try his luck in Bombay and at least familiarize himself with the High Court there and with Indian law.

Renting, from November 1891, an apartment in Girgaum in the heart of Bombay, he hired a Brahmin cook whose culinary skills were inferior to his own, but at least Gandhi had some company. European vegetarian dishes were also cooked in the kitchen of the modernizing Indian. Treating Ravishankar 'as a member of the family rather than a servant', Gandhi became his teacher. To reduce expenses, but also because he had acquired the habit, Mohandas walked about three miles daily to the High Court and back, instead of using a tramcar or a carriage. (He thought the walking helpful even when the sun was hot, and the reason for his remaining fit.)

In the High Court, he met Sir Pherozeshah Mehta and other lawyers and made friends among them, but attracted no clients. The awe of men like Mehta that appears in Gandhi's autobiographical recollections masks a desire to match those he calls the 'stalwarts'. In Bombay he was unnerved, he claims, to be reminded of Mehta's 'prodigious memory' and Badruddin Tyabji's 'wonderful power of argument' (A 81), but the remark betrays a wish to compete in their league.

When at last he was engaged at the Small Causes court by a defendant called Mamibai, for a fee of 30 rupees, a wave of fear hit him and he could not cross-examine the plaintiff's witnesses. 'My head was reeling and I felt as though the whole court was doing likewise.' He sat down, returned his fee and made his exit. But when another client, a poor Muslim from Porbandar whose land had been confiscated, wanted a memorial drafted, Gandhi drew up a text that his friends praised. It fetched no fee, but he felt he was competent at something.

Urged to pay a commission to touts for bringing clients, Gandhi refused. 'Even that great criminal lawyer, Mr So-and-So, who makes three to four thousand a month, pays commission,' he was told. Mohandas answered that he would be content with 300 rupees a month. 'Father did not get more.'

He looked for a part-time job, if possible of a literary kind. Seeing an advertisement by 'a famous high school' (we do not know its name) for someone who would teach English for an hour a day, he applied for the 75-rupees-a-month post. Certain that his skills were more than adequate, he went 'in high spirits' when called for an interview but was rejected because he did not possess a BA degree. 'But I have passed the London matriculation with Latin as my second language,' he pointed out. A 'graduate' was wanted, he was told, not just anyone who could teach English (A 82). His discontent in Bombay was not assuaged by stories that barristers had to 'vegetate five or seven years' before enjoying a decent practice. After six frustrating and money-losing months, he wound up the Girgaum establishment and returned to Rajkot.

Yet his time in Bombay in 1891–2 was not a total waste. For one thing, he had read, liked and digested the Evidence Act and Mayne's *Hindu Law.* Secondly, he had deepened his friendship with Pranjivan Mehta's family and in particular with Rajchandra. The poet-jeweller and the lawyer discussed ethics and philosophy, and Gandhi liked the Jain doctrine that 'maybe' was a valid position and that reality had many sides. But he was struck most by Rajchandra's 'equipoise' and by the fact that 'the centre round which his life revolved' was 'the passion to see God face to face'.

'The moment he finished his business,' Gandhi would later recall, this shrewd 'connoisseur of pearls and diamonds' would open a religious book or start entering reflections of an ethical or spiritual nature into his diary. On his part Rajchandra also responded to Gandhi, who would say in the Autobiography:

> There was no business or other selfish tie that bound him to me, and yet I enjoyed the closest association with him. I was but a briefless barrister then, and yet whenever I saw him he would engage me in conversation of a seriously religious nature (A 76).

Always ready, in amiable and irreverent fashion, to challenge the eminent, which the young Rajchandra was even in 1891–2, Gandhi on one occasion asked him, after the two had voiced agreement against the use of leather, to remove the cap he was wearing. A strip of leather was found in it, which Rajchandra promptly and quietly tore off.

One outcome of the friendship was that Gandhi was asked to speak at a public celebration in Ahmedabad of Rajchandra's birthday. We do not know what Gandhi said on that occasion, or with what confidence he said it, but we will see the relationship grow.

In Rajkot, where he drafted applications and memorials, Gandhi found some satisfaction and a steady if modest income ('on an average, Rs 300 a month' – A 84). A few clients came directly to Mohandas, the rest through Laxmidas, now a small-time pleader himself, and through Laxmidas's partner, a senior pleader with a larger practice. The partner expected a commission from each job given to Mohandas, and Laxmidas pressed his brother to pay it. ('All barristers do it.') Despite his dislike of it, Gandhi went along.

Helped by his new sense of security and stability, the relationship with Kastur improved. Mohandas's 'love', while by no means 'free from lust', was, to quote the Auto-biography's view of this period, 'getting gradually purer' (A 89). The couple seemed happy together, with Kastur consenting to being taught (we are not told what) by her husband and to 'certain reforms' (also unspecified). In October 1892 their second son, Manilal, was born. Acting on a thought that had been with him for a while, Gandhi started to write a handbook or guide for Indians planning to study in London.

But he would be denied a life of calm.

3

South Africa and a Purpose

1893–1901

An insistent plea from Laxmidas, and Mohandas's inability to resist it, led to what he called 'the first shock of my life' (A 84). The plea was in respect of a charge hanging over his eldest brother's head. Previously having served as secretary and adviser to the young heir to the Porbandar throne, Laxmidas was alleged to have winked at an apparent theft of some state jewels by the heir. The Raj's political agent (PA) in Kathiawar, a young man called E C K (later Sir Charles) Ollivant, was examining the allegation.

Learning with some excitement that Mohandas had met Ollivant in England and found him friendly, Laxmidas pressed his brother to intervene. At first Mohandas declined and asked his brother to 'submit a petition in the proper course'. It did not seem right, Mohandas added, to try to take advantage of a chance acquaintance in England. Laxmidas, who had helped finance his brother's time in England, answered:

> You do not know Kathiawar, and you have yet to know the world. Only influence counts here. It is not proper for you, a brother, to shirk your duty, when you can clearly put in a good word about me to an officer you know.

Giving in, Mohandas sought an appointment 'much against [his] will' and got it. The Autobiography relates what happened next:

> I reminded [Ollivant] of the old acquaintance ... The political agent owned the acquaintance, but the reminder seemed to stiffen him. 'Surely you have not come here to abuse that acquaintance, have you?' appeared to be ... written on his brow. Nevertheless, I opened my case. The sahib was impatient. 'Your brother is an intriguer. I

want to hear nothing more from you. I have no time. If your brother has anything to say, let him apply through the proper channel.'

The answer was enough, was perhaps deserved. But selfishness is blind. I went on with my story. The sahib got up and said, 'I must go now.' 'But please hear me out,' said I. That made him more angry. He called his peon to show me the door. I was still hesitating when the peon came in, placed his hands on my shoulders and put me out of the room.

From, it would seem, the foyer of the PA's imposing office, an enraged Gandhi

at once wrote out and sent over a note to this effect: 'You have insulted me. You have assaulted me through your peon. If you make no amends, I shall have to proceed against you.' Quick came the answer through a sowar. 'You were rude to me. I asked you to go and you would not. I had no option but to order my peon to show you the door ... He therefore had to use just enough force to send you out. You are at liberty to proceed as you wish.'

The Autobiography reproduces Ollivant's answer without qualifying it as being 'in essence' or 'more or less' what was said. Gandhi had either preserved or memorized its contents.

Pherozeshah Mehta happened to be in Rajkot at this time, for a case. Sending Mehta an account of what had happened, along with copies of his note to Ollivant and Ollivant's reply, Gandhi sought the great lawyer's advice.

Tell Gandhi [*Mehta said to the intermediary*], such things are [a] common experience ... He is still fresh from England, and hot-blooded. He does not know British officers ... Let him tear up the note and pocket the insult. He will gain nothing by proceeding against the sahib and will very likely ruin himself (A 84–6).

The Gandhi who had to 'swallow' this advice, as 'bitter as poison', a proud, Westernized Indian who thought he was bringing reforms to his homeland, was now attacked by three crippling emotions: guilt (he had gone to Ollivant for a wrong purpose), humiliation (he, a barrister and son to a prime minister of Rajkot, had been ejected in Rajkot by a 'friend' of his days in 'dear London') and impotence (he could not carry out a threat he had made in black and white).

Yet the shock proved useful. Gandhi had seen the face of racial arrogance, something he had not encountered during three years in England, and he had realized the folly of standing on weak ground while confronting it. Three decisions constituted his response.

Firstly, henceforth he would be alert to racial or white arrogance, though refusing as yet to call it imperial arrogance. Secondly, in facing it he would 'never again' place himself 'in a false position' (A 86). And, thirdly, he would focus his anger on the arrogance rather than on the person displaying it.

This last decision could not have been easy. He was 'no doubt at fault in having gone to that officer', yet Ollivant's 'impatience and anger were out of all proportion'. Gandhi had been with him for five minutes or less. Ollivant 'could have politely asked me to go', but 'power had intoxicated him to an inordinate extent' (A 87). This is Gandhi writing in 1926. In 1892–3 his reaction must have been even stronger.

Three decades after the Ollivant episode, Gandhi would speak of his interest as a young man in writing, and of what overrode it: '[A]t at the earliest period of my life it became one of storm and stress. It commenced with a fight against the then political agent of Kathiawar. I had therefore not much time for literary pursuits' (*Young India,* 4 Sep. 1924).

Yet Ollivant's ejection of Mohandas had set off a creative turmoil that would lead, 50 years later, to Quit India.

❧

The practice of law in Rajkot lost any charm it may have had for Gandhi. The thought of having to salute Ollivant, the ultimate authority for all the courts of Kathiawar, was unbearable for Kaba Gandhi's son and Ota Gandhi's grandson. 'It was beyond me to conciliate him. I had no desire to curry favour with him.' A ministership or judgeship in a Kathiawar state seemed an acceptable alternative to Mohandas and his brother, but obtaining such a post 'without intrigue ... was out of the question' (A 87). The 'petty politics' of Kathiawar – intrigue by prince against prince, sycophancy towards British or Indian political officers, and bribing the minions of these officers – now seemed more 'poisonous' than ever to Gandhi. This was not the idyllic Kathiawar he had presented to readers of *The Vegetarian* in England.

For a few weeks in Porbandar he breathed nicer air. The state's throne was vacant at the time, and the young heir was Gandhi's client. From Frederick Lely, whose aid he had vainly sought before leaving for England, Gandhi secured privileges for the heir; and Lely permitted Mohandas to live for some days with the heir as his tutor, presumably in the palace. However, an Indian political officer turned down Gandhi's plea for relief on behalf of the Mers, a warrior tribe in Porbandar state.

Back in Rajkot, Gandhi was again feeling 'thoroughly depressed' and 'exasperated' when a letter arrived from Dada Abdullah & Co., a firm of Meman Muslims in Porbandar. Addressed to Laxmidas, the letter asked whether his brother would be willing to go to

South Africa, where the firm had a large business, and assist with a lawsuit for a claim of £40,000.

Discussing this proposal with Abdul Karim Jhaveri, a partner in the Dada Abdullah company, Mohandas learnt that he was envisaged as a link between the firm and its European lawyers. The firm's head in South Africa, Jhaveri's brother Abdullah Sheth, was not proficient in English, and his lawyers knew no Gujarati. Gandhi's help would enable Abdullah to instruct and understand his lawyers.

'You can be useful to us,' Jhaveri added, 'in our shop.' When he asked for the terms, Mohandas was told that he would be wanted for 'not more than a year'. 'We will pay you a first class return fare and a sum of 105 pounds, all found.'

Gandhi promptly 'closed with the offer'. Though fully realizing that he was being asked to go not as a barrister but 'as a servant of the firm', he wanted 'somehow to leave India'. Also, he tells us, he welcomed the idea of returning £105 to his brother (A 88). He was tempted in addition, he says, by the prospect of 'fresh fields and pastures new'.[1]

There was more in this than fascination with a new country. Mohandas seemed to think – or hope – that the opening would be an outlet for his hunger for reform; and perhaps, though he does not say so, he wished to take a closer look at racial arrogance.

He 'felt the pang of parting from my wife'. For some months, and in some ways for the first time, he and Kastur had 'both felt the necessity of being more together'. For him the separation was 'rendered bearable' by the 'attraction of South Africa'.

'"We are bound to meet again in a year," I said to her, by way of consolation, and left Rajkot for Bombay' (A 89).

The Autobiography does not tell us how much Gandhi knew about the country he was going to. Nor does *Satyagraha in South Africa* (hereafter S), Gandhi's account, written in the early 1920s, of his political battles in a land where, notwithstanding his agreement and expectations, he would end up living for almost 21 years.

The lands and resources of the Africa of 1893 had been 'possessed' by European powers and, following the Berlin Congress of 1885, parcelled out among them. South Africa was not yet a single political entity. Natal, on the east coast, was a Crown Colony, and the Cape, in the south-west, a self-governing colony of the British (with Cecil Rhodes as Premier), while the interior territories of the Transvaal and Orange Free State were Boer or Afrikaner republics, their culture influenced by the Dutch and by French Huguenots. Paul Kruger was President in the Transvaal.

After the varied blacks (Zulus, Xhosas and others) and the varied whites, South Africa's third largest group (living mostly in the Cape) were the 'coloured': mixed descendants of Indonesians, Malays, whites, blacks, and the indigenous Khoi and San. The Indians were next in number.

Because Natal's Zulus were thought unreliable for working the sugar plantations (first introduced in Natal in 1850), Indians were brought in as indentured workers from 1860, mostly Tamil or Telugu speakers from south India or Hindi-speakers from Bihar and east UP. In their wake came Indian merchants and traders, to sell things to Indian labourers and also to the whites and the Africans. A majority of the Indian merchants, and all the most successful ones, were Muslims, often from Gujarat. In 1893, Durban had a population of close to 30,000. About half were whites. The other half was made up, in roughly equal numbers, by blacks and Indians: to make it difficult for blacks to live in cities was settled policy in Natal and elsewhere in South Africa.

Gandhi's watchfulness from the moment he would land in Durban suggests that whatever else he knew or did not know about South Africa, he was aware of anti-Indian sentiments among that region's whites.

Nonetheless 'full of zest' about South Africa, Gandhi boarded the *Safari* in Bombay on 19 April 1893. Told that all space in first class had been booked for the Governor General of Mozambique and his party, Gandhi had coolly gone up to the chief officer and asked to be 'squeezed in' somehow. After being surveyed 'from top to toe', Gandhi was given a spare berth in the chief officer's cabin, not normally offered to passengers. The ship's captain also befriended Gandhi, playing chess with him.

After halts at Lamu Island and in Mombasa, the *Safari* reached Zanzibar, where the captain invited Gandhi and an English passenger on an 'outing'. Gandhi found out what this meant when a tout took the party to a native brothel. Each in the party was shown into a room. Gandhi 'stood dumb with shame' and 'came out just as I had gone in'. As in Rajkot seven years or so earlier, he wondered about 'what the poor woman must have thought of me', but this time shame quickly 'wore away'. The woman 'had not moved him in the least', but he blamed himself for not having refused to enter the room (A 89–91). He thought that a merciful God had again saved him, and that the shame he had briefly experienced was false.

At Zanzibar, where passengers bound for South Africa waited eight or ten days before boarding the *Admiral* of the German East Africa Line on 14 May, Gandhi obtained a few glimpses of life in Africa (he noticed that Africa's trees and fruits could be 'gigantic'), went to a law court to observe its proceedings, and had time to reflect on what South Africa had in store for him (A 81).

After cruising across a wide harbour and offering passengers a view of forested hills and seaside boulevards, the *Admiral* berthed in Port Durban on 23 May. Gandhi emerged wearing a frock coat, striped trousers, a black turban, a watch and a chain – a modernized yet Indian barrister. As he would later recall, 'I was well dressed according to my lights and landed at Durban with a due sense of my importance' (S 38).

He was met on the ship by Abdullah Sheth. Glancing around him with eyes sharpened by the Ollivant episode, Gandhi noticed that the whites boarding the *Admiral* to welcome passengers seemed scornful towards Indians. Many of them greeted Abdullah Sheth, whom they seemed to know, in a 'snobbish' manner, Gandhi thought. Gandhi also noticed that he himself was looked at with curiosity. Durban's whites had not seen an Indian dressed like him. Muslim merchants, including Abdullah, wore loose clothes, large white turbans, and thick beards. They called themselves, and were often called, Arabs. Parsis who had come from India, traders or clerks, were referred to as Persians. Hindus and Christians were called 'coolies' or, simply, 'Sami', from the suffix of many a south Indian name in Natal, derived from the Sanskrit 'Swami' (master). If an Indian had the cheek to answer, 'You call me master when you say Sami,' whites would 'wince', 'swear' or threaten violence. [2]

In any case, an Indian in elegant European clothes *and* a turban puzzled Durban's whites. Also puzzled was Abdullah. He knew of Christian Indians who wore cheap European clothes and perhaps a hat but never a turban. Recent converts born in Natal to indentured workers from south India, these Christian Indians often worked as waiters, of whom Abdullah did not think highly.

A shrewd if 'practically unlettered' man from Porbandar, owning ships and running several businesses in Natal as well as the Transvaal, Abdullah had amassed a fortune in the late 1880s by selling newly discovered South African gold to India. He wonder:d (Gandhi thought) how this Anglicized barrister would help him and how much his upkeep would cost, and feared that his brother in Porbandar had 'sent him a white elephant' (A 92). However, after a few days of scrutiny and discussions, Abdullah felt reassured.

By this time Gandhi had met some of Durban's leading Indians (Muslims, Hindus, Christians and Parsis) and learnt of the racial prejudice they daily faced. He had also featured in the newspapers. Taking him, on the second or third day of his arrival, to the Durban court, Abdullah had asked Gandhi to sit next to Abdullah's white attorney. After staring at Gandhi a few times, the magistrate asked Gandhi to remove his turban. (Men like Abdullah could keep their turbans on – they were 'Arabs'. But 'Indians' like Gandhi were expected to remove their headgear in court, the more so if they hoped to speak to it.) Yet, for an Indian, removing a turban was a humiliation, not a mark of courtesy. Indian lawyers in the Bombay High Court did not take their turbans off. Refusing to remove his, Gandhi left the Durban court. The next day the *Natal Advertiser* ran a story, headed

'An Unwelcome Visitor', criticizing Gandhi for not taking off his turban. In a spirited if also courteous answer, Gandhi defended the Indian attitude to turbans. Written with the support of Abdullah, who had long smarted under offensive racial behaviour, Gandhi's reply appeared in the *Advertiser* on 29 May, giving the young barrister 'an unexpected advertisement in South Africa' within days of arriving there. Though 'severely criticized' by some for his 'temerity', he felt no remorse (A 94).

Was this a new Gandhi, transformed from the man who a few months earlier had collapsed, head reeling, in a Bombay courtroom? Or was he the same person who five years earlier had stood up, when not yet 19, to his caste leaders, and who now felt, following the Ollivant incident, that he had to stand up to white officials?

Certainly he felt more at ease in Durban, far from Rajkot and Bombay, where he had often allowed himself to be intimidated. He also immediately felt needed by the Indians of Durban, and Abdullah seemed to trust him. But going by his determination from the moment of arrival in Port Durban, and the swiftness with which he met the leaders of Durban's Indian community, we must conclude that the Ollivant shock and the invitation from Dada Abdullah & Co. had already done something to his soul.

By now he had gone into the details of the case for which he had come – the claim of Abdullah and his firm for £40,000 against a relative, Tyeb Sheth, who lived in Pretoria, the capital of the Transvaal. That was where the case was being fought, and where Gandhi was to go.

For Indians, Gandhi was informed, the Transvaal was worse than Natal. Europeans there apparently thought that Indians had no sense of human decency, suffered from loathsome diseases, considered every woman as their prey, and believed that women did not have souls. 'Four lies,' Gandhi would soon comment (S 30). A Transvaal law, Act 3 of 1885, specified small locations away from the cities where Indians could own land; the law also severely restricted their right to trade. When the republic's leading Indians tried to complain to President Kruger, he did not admit them to his house. Addressing them in his courtyard, Kruger, like many Afrikaners a devotee of the Old Testament, apparently said:

> You are the descendants of Ishmael and therefore from your very birth bound to slave for the descendants of Esau. As the descendants of Esau, we cannot give you rights placing you on an equality with ourselves. You must rest content with what rights we grant to you (S 30–1).

Learning of ever-increasing sums that Abdullah was paying his lawyers, matched no doubt by Tyeb Sheth's payments to *his* lawyers, Gandhi expressed to Abdullah a wish to 'try, if possible, to settle the case out of court'. After all, said Gandhi, Tyeb was 'a relative of yours'. Though 'startled' at the suggestion, Abdullah authorized Gandhi to explore that path, while asking him to remain wary of Tyeb's cleverness.

On 31 May 1893, in the southern hemisphere's winter, Abdullah escorted Gandhi to a first-class compartment in the train to Charlestown in Natal, close to the Transvaal border, from where a stage-coach would carry him to Standerton in eastern Transvaal and, after an overnight halt, to Johannesburg, a road trip of about 150 miles in all; from Johannesburg another train would take him to Pretoria. Gandhi did his homework for the complicated journey, and collected information that might prove useful, but the journey proved more difficult than he had anticipated.

At 9 p.m. the train stopped at Pietermaritzburg, which was on a plateau and colder than Durban. A passenger entered Gandhi's compartment, looked him 'up and down', left, and returned with one or two railway officials. Another official then arrived and ordered Gandhi to go to the van compartment.

'But I have a first class ticket,' said Gandhi.

'That doesn't matter. I tell you, you must go to the van compartment.'

'I tell you, I was permitted to travel in this compartment at Durban, and I insist on going on in it.'

'No you won't.'

'I refuse to move.'

A police constable was called, and Gandhi was pushed out. So was his luggage. The train steamed away. Gandhi walked to a dark waiting room, leaving the luggage where it was. It was bitterly cold but Gandhi's overcoat was inside his luggage. Unwilling to invite another insult, Gandhi did not ask anyone about it, and shivered through the black night. At one point a man entered the room and 'possibly wanted to talk' but Gandhi was 'in no mood' for that. A storm raged inside him, and he also felt afraid of the stranger (A 97–8).[3]

Returning to India entered his mind but was rejected as a cowardly option. He would stay and fight, and for more than his personal rights, for a shapeless spectre had assaulted a belief deep inside of him – the insight, nurtured from childhood and confirmed by his three years in England, that all human beings, creations of the same God, were of equal value. When the Ollivant incident occurred in Rajkot, Gandhi had not quite known how to apportion the blame between Ollivant and himself. Now, in Pietermaritzburg, he had committed no impropriety, yet he had been tossed out by a monster, not the man who threw him off the train, but a spirit in which the arrogance of power joined the arrogance of race.

Emerging from the depths of his soul, young Gandhi's decision to stay and fight was both political and spiritual. The two impulses had fused and spoken to him as one. If he had moved as ordered, he would have accepted that souls covered by brown and black skins were of lower value than the souls of white folk. But he knew that all souls had equal value. Yes, even Ollivant's soul, and the soul of the man who had tossed him off the train, carried the worth of Gandhi's soul; but, by God, his own soul was not cheaper.

He did not realize it at once, but the dilemma of his life-goal, whether it should be political or spiritual, had been resolved. The humiliation was a turning-point for him, for he had found a task 'in which his will to God and his will to politics could flow together as one force'.[4]

In that unlit waiting room, Gandhi also seems to have decided to set aside any interest in personal redress. It was risky, Mehta had warned in Rajkot, to proceed against white officers. In Pietermaritzburg Gandhi figured it would be a waste of energy and time, for these were now needed to fight the shapeless monster that had violated his virgin faith (A 97).

In the morning (1 June) he sent telegrams telling what had happened to Abdullah and to the general manager of the railway. Abdullah met the manager and also wired Indian merchants at every halt on the way to Pretoria, asking them to help Gandhi.

That night the Charlestown train stopping at Pietermaritzburg offered Gandhi a reserved berth in the first class. On the morning of 2 June he reached Charlestown, where, however, he was told that his ticket for the stage-coach (run by George Heys & Co.[5]) was no longer valid: 'You should have come yesterday.' But Gandhi pointed out the rules, which he knew were in his favour.

Though allowing him to board the coach, the conductor or 'leader', as he was called, asked Gandhi to sit away from the other passengers, who were all accommodated inside. The 'leader' offered Gandhi his own seat, on one side of the driver's box. (A Khoi helper sat in a similar seat on the other side of the driver.)

Though aware that he was being humiliated, Gandhi swallowed the insult. He had lost 24 hours already and there was no assurance that things would improve if he waited another day. As the vehicle chugged along in the Transvaal country, the 'leader' sat inside the coach, along with the other passengers, while Gandhi sat in the conductor's outer seat.

However, at a stop in Pardekoph, reached at about 3 p.m., the 'leader' decided that for the next leg he would use his own seat, where he could comfortably smoke. He spread 'a piece of dirty sack-cloth' on the footboard and, addressing Gandhi, said: 'Sami, you sit on this. I want to sit near the driver.' This was too much, and Gandhi replied:

It was you who seated me here, though I should have been accommodated inside. I put up with the insult. Now that you want to sit outside and smoke, you would have me sit at your feet. I will not do so, but I am prepared to sit inside.

Enraged, the 'leader' boxed Gandhi's ears and, seizing his arm, tried to force him down. Gandhi 'clung to the brass rails of the coachbox and was determined to keep [his] hold even at the risk of breaking [his] wrist-bones'. After a while some of the passengers spoke up for Gandhi: 'Man, let him alone. Don't beat him. He is right. If he can't stay there, let him come and sit with us.'

'No fear,' the 'leader' cried. But he let go of Gandhi's arm, swore some more at Gandhi, asked the Khoi servant to sit on the footboard, took the seat the servant vacated, and gave the whistle for starting. As the coach rattled away, Gandhi, his heart beating fast, wondered whether he would reach his destination alive, while from time to time the 'leader' shook his finger at Gandhi and growled threats of what he would do 'once we get to Standerton'.

Thanks to messages from Abdullah, several Indians were waiting for Gandhi at Standerton, and a Muslim businessman called Isa Sheth put him up for the night. Gandhi sought (in writing) an assurance from the coach company that the problems he had faced would not be repeated on the leg to Johannesburg, but he made no attempt to proceed against the man who had assaulted him. The assurance was given.

On the evening of 3 June, the coach carrying Gandhi in 'a good seat' reached Johannesburg. Abdullah's friends had been alerted here as well, but the man sent to meet Gandhi's coach missed him. Gandhi took a cab to the Grand National Hotel ('I knew the names of several hotels,' Gandhi writes in the Autobiography) and asked the manager for a room. After being 'eyed for a moment', Gandhi was told that the hotel had no space. He went next to the firm of Muhammad Kassim Kamruddin (he had the address), where Abdul Ghani Sheth had 'a hearty laugh' over Gandhi's expectation of a room at the Grand National. Abdul Ghani went on to speak, as Isa Sheth had done in Standerton, of the insults borne by Indians in South Africa.

As for the train journey to Pretoria that lay ahead, Abdul Ghani assured Gandhi that he would *have* to travel third class. First-class or second-class tickets were *never* issued to Indians in the Transvaal. Rules existed to that effect, said Abdul Ghani. Gandhi replied that he would make an attempt to go first class, failing which he would take a cab for the 37-mile journey.

The attempt was executed with finesse. At the station in Johannesburg, Gandhi left a note for the stationmaster in which he identified himself as a barrister, always travelling first class, who needed to reach Pretoria as soon as possible. Since there was no time to receive a written response (added Gandhi), he would present himself at the station and hear the reply the next day. The plan was to impress the stationmaster with his appearance.

In the morning Gandhi 'went to the station in a frock-coat and necktie, placed a sovereign on the counter, and asked for a first-class ticket'. He got it (from a friendly stationmaster who explained that he was a Hollander and not a Transvaaler), but only after Gandhi had given his word that he would not sue the railway if problems arose on the way to Pretoria.

Later that day, a surprised Ghani saw Gandhi enter a first-class carriage at Johannesburg station but warned him of likely trouble ahead. Sure enough, at Germiston the guard asked Gandhi to move to third class. Gandhi showed him his first-class ticket. When the guard repeated his instruction, the only other passenger in the compartment, an Englishman, said, 'Don't you see he has a first-class ticket? I don't mind in the least his travelling with me.' Muttering, 'If you wish to travel with a coolie, what do I care?' the guard went away.

At eight in the evening of Sunday 4 June the train reached Pretoria. The station was quite dark, and nobody was there to meet him. (Later Gandhi learnt that Sunday evening was not a good time for Albert Baker, Abdullah's lawyer in Pretoria.) After waiting for other passengers to make their exit, Gandhi surrendered his ticket at the gate and (afraid of being insulted again) cautiously asked if the ticket-collector could suggest a small hotel for the night. (If he could not, Gandhi was ready to spend the night at the station.) The ticket-collector was courteous but at a loss. However, an African-American 'who was standing nearby' took matters in hand and offered to take Gandhi to Johnston's Hotel. 'I know Mr Johnston very well. I think he will accept you,' the unnamed African-American said. Johnston, also an American, accepted Gandhi but with the stipulation that this guest would have meals in his room. If he went to the dining room, other guests 'might be offended and even go away'. Gandhi agreed to this and was shown to his room, where he was awaiting his dinner when Johnston appeared and invited Gandhi to the dining room. His guests, he said, had no objection to Gandhi eating there. Thanking Johnston, Gandhi 'went to the dining room and had a hearty dinner' (A 99–104).

We may pause to assess Gandhi after his 12 days thus far in South Africa. Quickly taking in the world around him, he also appears to be in control. Physically shaken but mentally and morally firm, he has reacted to ejection, assault and rejection – needles of South Africa's racism – with dignified defiance and prudence, and also by recording the wrongs in letters and telegrams. (His interest in writing has not left him.)

One sign of his control is having a second string to his bow: in Johannesburg he retained the option of the Kamruddin firm even as he first went to the Grand National Hotel, and of the coach to Pretoria even as he sought the first-class ticket; and in Pretoria he had settled on the station as fall-back accommodation for the night.

Secondly, this 23-year-old has won not just the trust but also the respect and affection of a man like Abdullah, who takes pains for Gandhi's safety and comfort. In young Gandhi, Abdullah and his friends seem to have found the sort of person they have hoped for. One of his qualities, not yet fully noticed by Abdullah, is a grasp of the power of a symbolic act, revealed at Johannesburg station when Gandhi, conspicuous in a frock coat and tie, dramatically placed a sovereign on the counter.

Thirdly, and this is related to the second point, there is a hint of the newcomer quickly becoming known and noticed, among fellow Indians and also among the whites of South Africa.

Fourthly, while he grasps opportunities (the London idea, the invitation to South Africa) swiftly, he is able also to clear obstacles (opposition to the London trip, assaults in South Africa). And whether facing a window or a wall, he maximizes his response by doing his homework and enlisting allies. True, Ollivant's blow stymied him. But he drew lessons from it.

Finally, he seems to have found both purpose and confidence: vulnerable Indians in South Africa need his help, and maybe he can help. It may have also occurred to him that the same might be true one day of Indians in India.

₰

Christianity. On the morning of 5 June Gandhi met Albert Baker in his office and found that Abdullah's attorney, 13 years older than him and a second-generation South African, was above all a warm-hearted and committed Christian. Baker arranged lodgings for Gandhi, at 35 shillings a week, with 'a poor woman', the wife of a baker. She was willing to cook vegetarian food, and Gandhi soon 'made himself quite at home with the family', which was free of prejudice.

After briefly discussing with Gandhi the case against Tyeb, for which, said Baker, 'we have engaged the best counsel', and expressing happiness that Gandhi would make communicating with Abdullah 'easy for me', Baker asked Gandhi, 'during the very first interview', about his religious views. Gandhi answered that he was a Hindu by birth but unclear about where he stood and what he believed, and keen to make a careful study of Hinduism and other religions.

To help Gandhi come to a decision, Baker invited him, 'from tomorrow', to a daily prayer of about five minutes during the lunch hour. Gandhi agreed to do this, and over the next months may have attended over a hundred of these five-minute prayer sessions when participants, including Gandhi, knelt down while one or more of them petitioned either for a peaceful day or for a special event or, at times, for God to open and speak to Gandhi's heart.

On the first night in his Pretoria lodgings, 'absorbed in deep thought' as he lay on his bed, Gandhi asked himself questions that are recalled in the Autobiography. Why was Baker interested in him? How far should he go in studying Christianity? Should he not study Hinduism just as deeply? After concluding that he should 'dispassionately' study all that Baker and his friends supplied but not think of 'embracing another religion before I had fully understood my own', he fell asleep, he writes (A 105). The decision became a compass for the uncertain religious voyage that lay ahead.

Baker's colleagues in his daily prayers, coming from different Christian backgrounds but united in a missionary purpose, included Michael Coates, an English-born Quaker, and two ladies who had learnt the Zulu language, Clara Harris and Georgina Gabb, who would later serve in Swaziland. Living in the same house, Misses Harris and Gabb asked Gandhi to join them for tea on Sundays, when Coates, too, was often present.

Older than him by about seven years, Coates became one of Gandhi's closest friends in Pretoria, in some ways taking the place that Josiah Oldfield had occupied in London. Coates plied Gandhi with one religious book after another until Gandhi's 'shelf was filled with them', read a weekly religious diary that Gandhi wrote, took Gandhi to church services, and had long walks and talks with him.

Gandhi told Coates that he liked and agreed with some things he was given to read, but not others, and that he had difficulty accepting Jesus as God's only incarnation or the only mediator between God and man. However, Coates and Baker did not weaken either in their warmth toward Gandhi or in their prayer, and sometimes made a more direct effort for his enlightenment. One day Coates told Gandhi that a rational man like him should not be wearing a necklace of tulsi beads. 'This superstition does not become you. Come, let me break the necklace.'

'No, you will not,' Gandhi replied. 'It is a sacred gift from my mother.' Asked by Coates whether he believed that the necklace had spiritual powers, Gandhi answered that he did not think so, and added that he was unlikely to replace the necklace when it wore off. But it was 'put round my neck out of love' and he would not break it (A 107–8).

A member of the Plymouth Brethren introduced by Coates to Gandhi told him that human attempts at improvement and atonement were futile. The burden of sin could only be thrown at Jesus, whose death at the cross took care of believers' sins. The Brother predicted a life of restlessness if Gandhi strove to conquer sin by his own effort. According to Gandhi, who answered that in that case he would be 'content to be restless', this Brother 'knowingly committed transgressions' in the faith that Christ would redeem him and other believing sinners.

This version of redemption did not appeal to Gandhi, who was aware that other Christians did not believe in it either. As he saw it, Coates and Misses Harris and Gabb acknowledged the value of efforts at self-purification, and that Coates himself 'walked in the fear of God' and had a 'pure heart' (A 108).

Gandhi was once walking by himself on a sidewalk close to the modest home of Paul Kruger, the Transvaal President, a sidewalk he had frequently used before, when, without 'the slightest warning' or prior word, a guard on duty 'pushed and kicked' Gandhi 'into the street'. Happening to be riding by at the time, Michael Coates saw the assault. Going up to Gandhi, he said: 'I have seen everything. I shall be your witness in court if you proceed against the man. I am very sorry you have been so rudely assaulted.'

According to the Autobiography, Gandhi replied that he had no intention to proceed against the guard, who 'no doubt treats Negroes just as he has treated me'. He had chosen, Gandhi said, not to go to court over personal grievances. Coates then reprimanded the guard, who apologized to Gandhi. 'I had already forgiven him,' says Gandhi in the Autobiography. But he stopped using the sidewalk. 'Why should I unnecessarily court another kick?' (A 114)

Blacks were banned from Pretoria's sidewalks and could be flogged if found defying the ban. Indians too were shooed away, though successful Muslim traders, the 'Arabs', were permitted to use them. After 9 p.m., a black man could not be on the streets without a pass from his employer.

To enable Gandhi to go out after 9 p.m., an Afrikaner public prosecutor, F E T Krause, like Gandhi a barrister from the Inner Temple, gave Gandhi a letter authorizing him to be out of doors at all hours without police interference. Perhaps because he was often recognized, Gandhi never had to produce this letter, but he always carried it with him while out walking. He owed the letter to Coates, who had taken him to Krause.

'The climax of the campaign for Gandhi's soul,' to quote James Hunt,[6] came in October 1893, when Baker invited Gandhi to a great Christian convention in Huguenot College in Wellington, 40 miles from Cape Town. Accepting the invitation, Gandhi travelled for the first time to Cape Town and the Cape Colony. It was a long journey, but, persuading officials to relax racial rules, Baker ensured that Gandhi travelled with him in the same compartment, and at the convention he and Gandhi shared the same hotel room.

Rev. Andrew Murray, one of the biggest names in South Africa's Dutch Reformed Church, addressed the convention, as did others including Baker, but Baker's prayer that Gandhi would 'embrace Christianity in the atmosphere of religious exaltation' was not answered.[7]

Gandhi was impressed by the faith of the devout assemblage. He met Rev. Murray, liked some of the hymns, and saw that many were praying for him. But he saw no reason to change his religion, and said so to his 'good Christian friends'. They were disappointed and some were 'shocked'. But Gandhi could not help it. That by his death and blood Jesus had redeemed the sins of the world was something that Gandhi was ready to accept metaphorically but not literally. That Jesus was the only incarnate son of God was 'more than I could believe'. 'If God could have sons, all of us were His sons' (A 119).

But his reading in Pretoria brought him close to two thinkers connected to Christianity who in some ways reduced the differences between Gandhi and his Christian friends. Edward Maitland of England, to whose works Gandhi was introduced by Oldfield (with whom he was continuing to correspond), and Russia's Leo Tolstoy provided versions of Christianity (dissenting versions to be sure) to which Gandhi could respond in quite a wholehearted way.

Leo Tolstoy. Maitland, who spoke of God in both genders, also referred to 'the Finding of Christ' and suggested that a Christ was to be found within a person, a mystical Christ different from the unique historical Son of God, and not very far from Hindu notions of the Self. And Tolstoy, whose *The Kingdom of God is Within You* was sent by Maitland,[8] gripped Gandhi in Pretoria in 1894, offered a Christ who was not the son of God atoning for the world's sins but the powerful author of the Sermon on the Mount. The five commandments selected by Tolstoy from the Sermon – do not hate, do not lust, do not hoard, do not kill, love your enemies – went directly to Gandhi's heart, answering important questions that occupied it.[9]

Tolstoy's book 'overwhelmed me', the Autobiography says, referring also to the book's 'independent thinking, profound morality, and truthfulness' (A 120). Elsewhere, Gandhi would say that reading Tolstoy saved him from violence. 'When I went to England I was a votary of violence. I had faith in it and none in non-violence.'[10]

After returning from England, too, the experience with Ollivant in Rajkot and, later, the ordeals in the journey from Durban to Pretoria probably engendered violent thoughts in Gandhi's mind, even though he was unwilling, after arriving in South Africa, to proceed against those assaulting him. There was a clash in his mind between violence and forgiveness, and Tolstoy resolved it against violence.

Another encounter of a Christian kind he had in the mid-1890s was in a Trappist monastery at Mariann Hill in Natal. Gandhi was struck by the skills taught there to Africans, by the practice of silence in the monastery, and by the ascetic life of the monks and nuns, who did not eat meat, which is how he had first heard of them.

Abdullah Sheth, meanwhile, was speaking of the beauty of Islam and suggesting its study to Gandhi, who read Sale's translation of the Koran and obtained other Islamic books. Unconvinced that he should embrace Christianity or Islam, and not certain either that Hinduism with its untouchability and 'a multitude of sects and castes' (A 119) was a perfect religion, Gandhi remembered the Jain thought that doubt should accompany every certainty.

To his friend Rajchandra, a Jain who was also a scholar of Hinduism, Gandhi sent 26 questions about God, Christ, Rama, Krishna, Brahma, Vishnu, Shiva and more. In October 1894, Rajchandra sent careful answers and books on Hinduism and recommended patience. Gandhi was 'somewhat pacified' (A 120).

Though disappointing Baker, Coates and other Christian friends, Gandhi acknowledged a permanent debt to them 'for the religious quest that they awakened in me' (A 120). His relations with them remained warm, and until the 1940s Baker, for one, continued to write to Gandhi, and no doubt to pray for him.

❦

At their first meeting Baker had told Gandhi that the case for which he had come would not get under way for a while. Gandhi's task was to understand all its points of fact and law, all its intricacies of accounting and promissory notes, and explain it to Baker, who in turn would brief the most eminent counsel available.

Studying the case requiring only a part of his time, Gandhi decided, in his very first week in Pretoria, to study also 'the condition of Indians there' – the political life was attracting him. The man who could help him reach Pretoria's Indians, perhaps the city's most influential Indian, was Abdullah's adversary and relative, Tyeb Sheth. Gandhi made his acquaintance within days of arrival in Pretoria. This, too, was a sign of self-confidence. Someone comfortably approaching a powerful opponent of his employer had to have a good deal of faith in his relationship with the employer, or in himself, and in what he was doing. Gandhi told Tyeb of 'his intention to get in touch with every Indian in Pretoria'. This again is worth noting. Gandhi does not seek Tyeb's approval, he merely informs Tyeb of his intentions. We must conclude that within days of his arrival in South Africa, Indians there saw young Gandhi as a leader. (This no doubt contributed to the persistence with which Gandhi's Christian friends tried to win him over.)

With Tyeb's help, Gandhi called a meeting of Pretoria's Indians, held in the house of another Meman Muslim merchant, Joosab Sheth. It was a largely Muslim gathering with 'a sprinkling of Hindus'. Most were traders. To them Gandhi made what he would call 'the first public speech of my life'. Contesting the view that truthfulness was not possible in business, he asked the traders to realize that their conduct in Pretoria determined how 'millions of their fellow-countrymen' were being judged. 'Insanitary habits' that incurred unpopularity were referred to. He wanted his audience to remember what united them – their Indian origin – not their differences of religion, sect, and language. Asking them, finally, to form an association to ventilate their hardships, he 'offered to place at its disposal as much of my time and service as was possible' (A 109–10).

Already, then, in the first half of June 1893, Gandhi also saw himself as a leader. In the Autobiography he says that he 'made a considerable impression on the meeting'. An ensuing discussion produced a consensus on two points: they would meet regularly, and Gandhi would teach some of them English.

Several more meetings were held, but only three men present agreed to be taught

English by Gandhi: a Muslim barber, a Muslim clerk and a Hindu who kept a small shop. For about eight months, Gandhi went to their places to teach them, often waiting while they were busy. Two of the three learnt enough English to keep accounts and write ordinary business letters, while the barber was satisfied with a few sentences to use with his customers.

Not very surprisingly, 'an English hair-cutter in Pretoria ... contemptuously refused' to cut Gandhi's hair. Though he 'certainly felt hurt', Gandhi purchased a pair of clippers and cut his hair himself, with the help of a mirror (A 187). The results were not flattering, and amused friends asked whether rats had chewed his hair. Gandhi replied that the white barber would not condescend to touch his black hair.

In the Autobiography he would claim that the conviction that such humiliations were 'the reward' for untouchability in India 'saved me from becoming angry' (A 187). Following long talks with Gandhi, Doke would write in 1908 that in Pretoria the young man proud of his birth and education had 'learned self-restraint' and 'to bear the insults which attached to his race and colour until ... he almost gloried in them'.[11]

After some months of interactions, 'there was ... in Pretoria no Indian I did not know, or whose condition I was not acquainted with' (A 110). Some of the Indians were wealthy – traders who sold goods and provisions in a Transvaal hungry for supplies. For them Gandhi won a tangible, if small, advance. A letter from him to the Transvaal's railway authorities brought the response that stationmasters could issue first- and second-class tickets to 'properly dressed' Indians.

But from Tyeb, and from Jacobus de Wet, the British Agent in Pretoria, whom Gandhi met several times, he also learnt the bitter story of the hounding out of Indians from the other Boer republic, Orange Free State.

We must assume that interacting with the Indians of Pretoria reminded Gandhi of India and its politics, and of the nine-year-old Indian National Congress. South Africa was an absorbing stage in his life but not his permanent home.

In Pretoria in 1893–4 Gandhi honed his religious, political and legal understanding and, until the case summoned almost all his time, also read close to a hundred volumes that included writings by Tolstoy, religious books that Coates, Baker, Abdullah and others supplied or suggested, and books sent by Rajchandra. Fulfilling a promise made in London to Pincott, he also read the volumes by Kaye and Malleson detailing the horrific course of India's 1857 Rebellion.

In Pretoria he was also able to complete a work interrupted by the Ollivant episode – the *Guide to London*. Written in a relaxed style but not destined to be published in his lifetime, the short *Guide* claimed, in 1893, to 'attempt that which has not yet been attempted', a portrayal of the life and needs of an Indian in London. Space is given in the *Guide* to food, its purchase and cooking, to how one can live in London on £1 a week, and to clothes an Indian should wear in England. Any Indian who can, he says, should go to England, where he would be 'alone, no wife to tease and flatter him, no parents to indulge, no children to look after, no company to disturb'. He would be 'the master of his time', which is what Gandhi was in Pretoria while writing the *Guide* (1: 71).

Continuing to experiment with food, Gandhi lived for some weeks only on uncooked cereals, vegetables, fruits and nuts, managing thereby to damage his health and his teeth. Dutifully he reported the experiment's failure to *The Vegetarian* in London.

Coming across plainly in *Satyagraha* and in later references, his fondness for the landscape, climate and fruits of South Africa was probably engendered during this period in Pretoria, when he had the leisure to walk on the terrain and absorb its charms.

The case. Yet the case against Tyeb was his primary commitment in Pretoria. He read the law on the points in dispute, and all the cases with a possible bearing on it, and examined every fact that Abdullah, who 'reposed absolute confidence' in Gandhi, had presented.

Gandhi's conclusion was that the facts made Abdullah's case strong indeed, and also that Abdullah as well as Tyeb would be ruined if they fought in the courts to the bitter and distant end. The parties, too, realized this, but much money, time and feeling had been expended on the dispute, and Gandhi had to 'strain every nerve' before the two sides agreed to arbitration. The case was argued before an arbitrator, and Abdullah was awarded £37,000 plus costs.

Tyeb 'meant to pay not a pie less than the amount' but it was impossible for him to 'pay down the whole sum'. Since Memans like Tyeb seemed to prefer death to bankruptcy, the only solution was for Abdullah to accept payment in moderate instalments. Abdullah fiercely resisted this, but in the end Gandhi persuaded him, and Abdullah allowed Tyeb's instalments 'to be spread over a very long period'. 'Both were happy over the result, and both rose in the public estimation.' Gandhi's satisfaction was 'boundless' and he felt convinced that 'the true function of a lawyer was to unite parties riven asunder' (A 117).

Change in plans. His job in South Africa had been completed. To bid farewell to Gandhi, Abdullah invited prominent Indians to spend a day with him in Sydenham on the Natal coast. There Gandhi's attention was caught by a small item in a newspaper. Headed 'Indian Franchise', it mentioned a Bill before the Natal legislature to bar Indians from the right to vote.

Asked about it by Gandhi, Abdullah explained that Natal's attorney-general, Harry Escombe, who was also a legal adviser to Abdullah's firm, had helped several Indians to register as voters when Escombe was fighting an election against a popular wharf engineer, and the Indians had voted for Escombe. Now, obviously, the franchise was being resented. Gandhi commented that the Bill would worsen the position of Natal's Indians – it was 'the first nail into our coffin'. When Abdullah asked for Gandhi's advice on what should be done, one of his guests butted in and said that Gandhi should postpone his departure by a month. Others took up the cry and said that Abdullah should detain Gandhi. Gandhi himself was clearly open to the idea. The question of South Africa's Indians had captured his imagination, and no business awaited him in India. Moreover, he swiftly saw a chance to organize Natal's Indians.

'You should all detain Gandhi,' Abdullah told his guests, adding that a barrister had his fees. He would not take any fees for public work, Gandhi clarified, but were they willing, he asked, to pay for a campaign – for telegrams, printing, some law books ('I am ignorant of your laws'), and any travelling? Were they willing to give their time?

'Allah is great and merciful,' several shouted. (Most of those gathered in Sydenham were Muslims.) 'Money will come in, and men there are, as many as you may need. You please consent to stay, and all will be well.'

Gandhi agreed, 'worked out in [his] mind the outline of a campaign', and turned the party into a working committee. Recalling the occasion later, he would see in it the hand of God, which 'laid the foundations of my life in South Africa'. Once more an invitation had found Gandhi ready (A 121–2).

From Durban he organized a brilliant campaign. The targets were multiple: the Natal Assembly, which had all but passed the Bill; the Europeans of Natal; leaders of the Empire in London; and public opinion in India. His means were petitions to the Assembly and a monster petition to Lord Ripon, Secretary of State for the Colonies in London – with copies to the press in Natal, England and India.

At the opening meeting, held in Abdullah's house, telegrams were sent to the speaker of the Assembly, the Premier of Natal, and Harry Escombe, and a petition to the Assembly was drafted. An old Indian with a neat hand, Arthur, sat up much of the night writing the master copy. Others made five copies by hand.

That the Bill would be passed was a foregone conclusion, and it was. But the campaign 'infused new life into the community'. In fact it helped redefine the community, for Gandhi secured the participation of all sections, traders and clerks, Muslims, Hindus, Parsis and Christians, the small and the great. Several volunteers were young Natal-born

Christian Indians. Indian merchants had tended to disdain this Christianized section of the Indian community, but to Gandhi they did not 'cease to be Indians because they had become Christians'.

In the petition to Ripon, Gandhi argued that as Indians enjoyed 'a kind of franchise in India', they were entitled to the franchise in Natal, and also that Indians with the property and educational qualifications required by the Natal franchise in any case amounted only to a small number. Taking off in carriages from Abdullah's house, volunteers scurried across the colony and obtained about 10,000 signatures in a fortnight. No one asked to be reimbursed for expenses.

Newspapers in Natal commented favourably on the Indian petition, an editorial in *The Times of India* strongly backed the Natal Indians' demands, and in London *The Times* voiced support. Another consequence was that Indians in Durban surrounded Gandhi on all sides and asked him to 'remain there permanently'.

Gandhi was ready with his answer. He was prepared to stay on but not at the community's expense. He would live in an independent house in a good locality and in a style that brought credit to the community. This would cost not less than £300 a year. Were members of the community willing to guarantee him legal work to that extent?

They would easily raise that sum for his public work, he was told, 'apart from the fees you must charge for private legal work'. Gandhi did not agree. His public work would mainly be 'to make you work', for which he could not charge them. But it could be done out of a barrister's income.

He clearly wanted his independence, and said so to Durban's Indian merchants: 'I should occasionally have to say hard things to you.' His terms were accepted, and about 20 of the merchants gave him retainers for a year, despite a warning by him that a brown barrister might not sit well with Natal's judges (A 124–6). The 24-year-old Gandhi of early 1894 put his cards on the table, but he also knew how to play them.

The house he rented, Beach Grove Villa, was a two-storey building on the beach in Durban. Escombe, Natal's attorney-general, lived next door. Gandhi took the house 'for the sake of prestige' (A 142) and to refute white charges that successful Indians were stingy.

The Law Society of Natal opposed Gandhi's application for admission as an advocate to the Supreme Court, but the Court rejected the opposition, saying that the law made no distinction between whites and non-whites. Then, shortly after Gandhi took the oath, the Chief Justice asked Gandhi to take off his turban. Advocates in court, the Chief Justice added, had to remove their headgear.

Telling himself that he should conserve energies for bigger battles, Gandhi acceded. A year earlier he had insisted on keeping his turban in the magistrate's court. Now, in the Supreme Court, he removed it. Abdullah was not pleased, but Gandhi replied that in Rome it was often necessary to do as Romans did. Meanwhile, the Law Society's opposition had given Gandhi 'another advertisement in South Africa' (A 127–9).

Launching a party. Practice in the law courts was but a means for addressing the court of public opinion. On 22 May 1894 Gandhi, Abdullah and a number of friends met in Abdullah's house and launched the Natal Indian Congress (NIC). Believing that the ten-year-old Indian National Congress (INC) was 'the very life of India', Gandhi, who became the NIC secretary, wanted a name that would also 'popularize the Congress in Natal'.

The constitution of the NIC was simple but its monthly subscription was a solid five shillings. A few like Abdullah committed themselves to £2 a month, several others, including Gandhi, to £1 a month, and many more to ten shillings a month.

Apart from collecting subscriptions, for which he and some others journeyed to different parts of the colony, Gandhi taught members of the NIC the elements of democratic politics he had learnt in London: how resolutions are moved, amended, voted on, spoken for, opposed and publicized; how minutes and accounts are kept, and receipts given. In the Autobiography he would claim: 'Every pie was thus accounted for, and I dare say the account books for the year 1894 can be found intact even today' (A 132).

Two pamphlets written for the NIC by Gandhi were soon published: *An Appeal to Every Briton in South Africa* and *The Indian Franchise – An Appeal.* Requesting support from Dadabhai Naoroji in London, Gandhi wrote to him, 'The responsibility undertaken is quite out of proportion to my ability.' Yet confidence matched a sense of duty, and the 25-year-old added: 'I am the only available person who can handle the question' (Letter of 5 July 1894; 1: 155).

x

The five-shilling fee kept many Indians out, but for some of these an Indian Educational Association (IEA) was formed under the aegis of the NIC. Overseen by Gandhi, the IEA enabled its members, mostly Natal-born educated youths, to discuss issues and approach the merchants. This still left untouched the large number of unskilled wage-earners and indentured workers of Indian origin, but Gandhi was soon connected to them.

An indentured labourer in tattered clothes, two front teeth broken and his mouth bleeding, turned up trembling and weeping before Gandhi. In his hands he carried his headscarf, which he had removed from his head, a practice that seemed required of every indentured labourer meeting a European or an important Indian. Humiliated at being 'respected' in this fashion, Gandhi asked the man to don his scarf again, and saw the pleasure on his face as he did so.

It was a mystery, Gandhi thought, that 'men can feel themselves honoured by the humiliation of their fellow-beings' (A 135). The labourer, Balasundaram, was a Tamil-speaking Hindu. Translating his remarks, Gandhi's clerk, a Tamil Christian, explained that the master under whom Balasundaram was serving his indenture had beaten him.

After securing from a white doctor a certificate about the nature of Balasundar-am's injuries, Gandhi took the labourer to a magistrate, who obtained Balasundaram's affidavit, issued a summons against the master and convicted him. Gandhi also found a new European master for Balasundaram, and other indentured workers heard of the relief that one of their number had received.

That some of the indentured had become growers of vegetables and fruits and owners of land after completing their terms alarmed Natal's Europeans. In order to send them back to India, the Europeans proposed, in 1894, an annual tax of £25 on a labourer who stayed on in Natal after the expiry of his indenture, and similar taxes on his wife and grown children. Even £1 a year per person would have been harsh on families that earned no more than 15 shillings a month but often contained four taxable individuals. The NIC organized a fierce campaign against the tax, but the Viceroy of India agreed to a yearly levy of £3 on every ex-indentured Indian in Natal. That is what was imposed, a crushing racial burden that for years would torment the Indians of South Africa and challenge the NIC.

According to Martin Green, Beach Grove Villa had a drawing room, a lounge, a dining room, and five bedrooms.[12] Gandhi kept photographs of Kaba Gandhi and Laxmidas in his bedroom, and biographies and religious books, including the works of Tolstoy, Maitland and Blavatsky, on a bookshelf. The Autobiography says that some of the furniture was given by Abdullah 'in lieu of a purse he had intended to give' on Gandhi's departure for India (A 126).

Gandhi walked to his office (14 Mercury Lane) every working day, wearing a lounge suit, a turban, a wing collar, a striped tie and polished shoes. 'English friends and Indian co-workers' were constantly invited to the house for meals and discussions, and some of Gandhi's clerks, usually Tamil Christians, 'boarded and lodged' with him. Though Gandhi offered 'simple food' to his guests, cooked by a servant 'who had become a member of the family', he also needed someone to manage the cook and the household generally, a task for which he himself had neither time nor ability.

Mehtab again. For performing the task he selected Sheikh Mehtab, who had turned up in South Africa. Mehtab may have pursued Gandhi into South Africa, or, as Green speculates, 'the reputation of South Africa as the site of a gold rush' may have attracted Mehtab.[13] Gandhi took him in as 'companion and help', as the Autobiography describes his role.

We do not know whether it was for a few weeks or a few months that Mehtab functioned as 'manager' at Beach Grove Villa. In the Autobiography Gandhi does not tell us. Nor does he name Mehtab (he similarly avoids naming some others), but the person's identity is not in doubt. The context also suggests that the year is 1895 or 1896.

Still adept at plausible talk, and 'jealous of an office clerk staying with [Gandhi]', Mehtab 'wove a tangled web' and poisoned Gandhi's ears against the clerk. The moment he felt suspicion from Gandhi, the clerk left 'both the house and the office'.

Gandhi felt that he may have been unjust to the clerk, but it took a more serious incident to open his eyes. At about noon one day, the temporary cook in Beach Grove Villa (the regular cook was on leave) 'came panting' to Gandhi's office and said to him, 'Please come home at once. There is a surprise for you.'

Gandhi asked what the matter was but the cook merely said, 'You will regret it if you don't come.' Accompanied by Vincent Lawrence, a clerk in his office, Gandhi walked quickly to his home, preceded by the cook, who took Gandhi to the upper floor and asked him to open Mehtab's door. The Autobiography records:

I saw it all. I knocked at the door. No reply! I knocked heavily so as to make the very walls shake. The door was opened. I saw a prostitute inside.

Gandhi told Mehtab and the woman to leave at once, 'never to return'. He told Mehtab, 'From this moment I cease to have anything to do with you.' Mehtab threatened to 'expose' Gandhi, who said, 'I have nothing to conceal. Expose whatever I may have done. But you must leave me this moment' (A 143).

When Mehtab resisted, Gandhi asked Lawrence to go and tell the police superintendent that someone had misbehaved in Gandhi's house and was refusing to leave. An unnerved Mehtab apologized, begged Gandhi not to inform the police and left.

Gandhi's fierce knocks on the door on the upper floor of his house were rebukes to himself as well. He had known what Mehtab was like but had been beguiled by the man's promises of faithfulness and by imagining that he was reforming Mehtab.

He tried to make amends to the clerk who had left but could not satisfy him fully. As also happened ten years or so earlier, his relationship with Mehtab had deprived him of a more reliable friend. The conclusions he drew are spelt out in the Autobiography:

[Only rarely and] only between like natures, can friendship be altogether worthy and

enduring ... [I]n friendship there is very little scope for reform ... [A]ll exclusive
intimacies are to be avoided. He who would be friends with God must remain alone,
or make the whole world his friend (A 16).

But he and the Indians of Natal had formed a good relationship. He liked them and they
seemed to need him. His practice was flourishing. His reading, including of a religious
kind, was continuing. He had made a number of new friends, including Spencer Walton
of the South Africa General Mission and his wife, devout Christians who never asked
Gandhi to convert.

Realizing that he was 'in for a long stay' in South Africa, Gandhi decided to go home
for a while and return with his wife and children. He would also inform people in India
of conditions in South Africa. At Gandhi's suggestion, Adamji Miyakhan was named to
substitute for him as the NIC secretary. A dedicated and well-liked Muslim from the
merchant community, Miyakhan spoke English and also Zulu.

Since no ship to Bombay was due for some time, Gandhi boarded (in the middle
of 1896) the *Pongola,* which was bound for Calcutta to pick up a new lot of indentured
labourers. During 24 days at sea he learnt something of two languages he could use with
Indians in South Africa: Urdu, taught to him by a Muslim passenger, and Tamil, which
he studied from a *Tamil Self-Teacher*. An hour of chess a day with an English officer of the
ship was also part of Gandhi's life on the *Pongola*, as was interacting with her friendly
captain, another member of the Plymouth Brethren.

From Calcutta, the capital of British India, Gandhi took a train for Bombay but
was left stranded *en route* in Allahabad, thanks to an impulse, during a 45-minute halt,
to see the city and buy some medicine. The train steamed away as Gandhi returned to
the station. Luckily, a thoughtful stationmaster had removed Gandhi's luggage from it,
and Gandhi decided that Allahabad was a good place to commence talking about South
Africa. The British editor of *The Pioneer* gave him an appointment, heard him patiently,
and promised 'to notice in his paper' anything that Gandhi wrote, adding that he would
also 'give due weight to the viewpoint of the Colonials'. That was fine by him, Gandhi
said.

What Gandhi produced in response to the editor's remark soon became known,
because of the colour on its cover, as the Green Pamphlet. The writing and printing, done
in Rajkot, took about a month. Gandhi claims in the Autobiography that the pamphlet
'drew a purposely subdued picture of the condition of Indians in South Africa'.

Five thousand copies were printed and sent 'to all the papers and leaders of every
party in India'. To save money, children and youths related or known to Gandhi wrapped

the pamphlets and stuck stamps. Gandhi rewarded them with used postage stamps he had collected and brought.

The Pioneer was the first to write an editorial on the questions raised in the pamphlet. Soon 'every paper of note' in India commented on it, a summary was cabled by Reuters to England, and a summary of that summary was cabled from London to Natal.

💠

The Autobiography does not describe Gandhi's reunion in Rajkot with Kastur and the two boys. Once more there had been a separation of three years during which Kastur could not have had an easy time. As the wife of a younger brother, she was the 'junior' housekeeper in an extended family with several children apart from her own, and had lots of chores. Her husband's absence had made Kastur's position weaker still. We can glimpse some eagerness in Gandhi's remark: 'I went straight to Rajkot without halting in Bombay' (A 148).

Queen Victoria's Diamond Jubilee was only a few months away, and Gandhi taught 'God Save the Queen' to his boys – eight-year-old Harilal and four-year-old Manilal – and to other youngsters in the joint family. He had learnt the anthem 'with careful perseverance' in South Africa, where, at NIC meetings and other occasions, it was frequently sung. The 27-year-old Gandhi was still a believer in the Empire, and thought that South Africa's colour prejudice was a 'temporary and local' flaw (A 151). We know that his picture of Empire included images of British bravery, of opposition to slavery, and of at least a verbal commitment to protect the weak.[14]

While in Gujarat he met up again with Rajchandra and was struck by the latter's views on the beauty and effectiveness of brahmacharya, or celibacy, even for a married person, a Hindu and Jain concept (similar in some ways to the quality of the pure in heart celebrated in the Bible's Sermon on the Mount) that went far beyond Mohandas's 1888 vow to his mother (A 179–80).

Plague, meanwhile, had hit Bombay and threatened Rajkot. Gandhi offered to help with the city's sanitation – we can see this as a social-cum-political initiative – and was taken on a committee to inspect latrines and suggest improvements. Gandhi and the committee found that rich citizens resisted scrutiny far more than poorer ones. The untouchables' quarters were discovered to be the cleanest, but only one other committee member had joined Gandhi in visiting them. The rest thought such a visit 'preposterous' (A 150).

His sister Raliat's husband, who belonged to the Modh Bania branch that continued to ostracize Gandhi, lay seriously ill in Bombay. Gandhi brought him to Rajkot, installed him in his own room, 'and remained with him night and day' for many days, no doubt remembering an earlier nursing, in the same house, of his father. He could not, however, save the brother-in-law (A 153).

Gandhi went with copies of his Green Pamphlet to Bombay, Poona, Madras and Calcutta. In Bombay he met Pherozeshah Mehta, Justices Ranade and Tyabji, and Mehta's 'right-hand man', Dinshaw Wacha; in Poona he met Bal Gangadhar Tilak and Tilak's political rival Gopal Krishna Gokhale. These influential figures arranged meetings for Gandhi to address.

In Bombay, however, Gandhi's voice did not reach all who filled a large hall, and his speech, fortunately written down, was read out first by Keshavrao Deshpande, known to Gandhi from their days together in London, and then, on popular demand, by Wacha. Its contents made an impact, Mehta liked them, and Deshpande and another barrister, an unnamed Parsi, said they would accompany Gandhi on his return to South Africa.

In Poona, both Tilak and Gokhale took part in the meeting, which at Tilak's suggestion was chaired by a non-political personality, Dr Bhandarkar. But it was to Gokhale, only three years older than him, that Gandhi felt instinctively and compellingly drawn, a sentiment apparently reciprocated by Gokhale.

A public meeting in Madras 'was wild with enthusiasm', not least because of Gandhi's references to the labourer Balasundaram, a native of the Tamil country. In Madras Gandhi printed 10,000 more copies of the Green Pamphlet, the newspapers, including *The Hindu*, covered his speech at length, and one of them, *The Madras Standard,* asked Gandhi to contribute to its columns, which he did.

Calcutta was slower to respond. Surendranath Banerji, known as 'the idol of Bengal', told Gandhi that Bengalis faced too many local problems to be interested in South Africa, an assessment confirmed by the indifference of the editors of *Amrita Bazar Patrika* and *Bangabasi,* on whom Gandhi called. But the editors of two British-owned papers in Calcutta, *The Statesman* and *The Englishman,* published long interviews with Gandhi. After finding in 'a searching cross-examination' that Gandhi was unwilling to exaggerate, Saunders, the editor of *The Englishman,* wrote an editorial on Indians in South Africa and asked Gandhi to make 'whatever changes' he liked in it. A public meeting in Calcutta too now seemed likely, but a cable arriving from Durban asked Gandhi to 'return soon', in time for the January opening of the Natal Parliament. Abdullah, who had just purchased the *Courland,* said that Gandhi and his family could travel free on it to Durban.

Accepting the offer, Gandhi went to Rajkot, collected Kastur, Harilal, Manilal, and Gokuldas, the only son of the recently widowed Raliat, and, in early December, boarded the *Courland* in Bombay. (The barristers who were to accompany Gandhi to South Africa, Deshpande and the unnamed Parsi, pleaded difficulties and did not join him.)

Kastur and the boys were excited at the prospect of the voyage, but it was Gandhi who decided every detail for it, including their shoes, stockings and clothes, the food they should eat and their manners. His family had to approximate to 'the European standard' without quite copying it. Gandhi ruled that Kastur's sari and the boys' coat and trousers would be worn in the style of the most Westernized Indians of the time, the Parsis, and that the family should wear stockings and shoes and eat with knives and forks.

Recalling in the Autobiography these aspects of the journey to Durban, 'my first voyage with my wife and children', as he terms it, Gandhi is both amused and contrite. He smiles at the hybrid identity he had prescribed for his family and regrets 'the force of authority' that lay behind his prescriptions, which were not easy for Kastur and the boys to carry out. But in 1896 he was not amused or contrite and thought that a 'practically unlettered' wife required teaching from her husband (A 162).

Accompanying the *Courland* on the non-stop voyage to Durban was the *Naderi,* for which Dada Abdullah & Co. were the agents. The two ships together carried about 800 passengers, half of whom were bound for the Boer republic, the Transvaal, and the other half for Natal, many of them, like Gandhi, returning to the colony.

Storms. Four days from the coast of Natal, a violent gale struck the ships. Though the *Courland*'s captain said that 'a well-built ship could stand almost any weather', the passengers became 'inconsolable'. The ships rocked and rolled, and 'every minute were heard sounds and crashes which foreboded breaches and leaks'. In different languages and ways, all prayed, including the captain, to 'the one and only God'. 'His will be done' was the only cry on every lip.

Always a good sailor, Gandhi took hourly reports from the captain to the *Courland*'s passengers and sought to calm them. (The Autobiography makes no mention of the reactions to the tempest of Kastur and the boys, who are subsumed among 'the passengers'.) After 24 hours the storm cleared, but just ahead was a gale of another sort, and Gandhi's bonding with the passengers was put to good use.

A number of Durban's whites were planning to prevent the Indians from landing. Angered by the summary they had received, via London, of Gandhi's Green Pamphlet, they felt defamed by him in India – and alarmed by a rumour that Gandhi was bringing 800 Indians to settle in Natal. Harry Escombe, the attorney-general who lived next to Gandhi's house, had joined in exciting them. At one public meeting after another, the whites were warned of a Gandhi-led 'invasion' of Natal by 'free' or non-indentured Indians. There was, as yet, no law in Natal to deny entry to people like the passengers on the *Courland* and the *Naderi*, which reached Port Durban on 18 or 19 December. But the plague that had broken out in Bombay came in handy to a Committee of Europeans formed to prevent the Indians from landing. The ships were placed in quarantine, and messages were sent to the passengers trapped in them that if they valued their lives they should return to India.

The 'quarantine' lasted 23 long days during which the Committee's warnings were repeated. Dada Abdullah & Co. was also warned, and offered inducements for sending the ships back, but the firm stood by the passengers it had brought, as did the captains of the ships. And Gandhi rallied the passengers, very few of whom he had known before departure in Bombay and all of whom declared their readiness to wait, and arranged games for their entertainment while they waited. Following a speech by Gandhi on Christmas Day, he was asked by Milne, the *Courland*'s captain, how he would respond if Durban's whites assaulted him. Gandhi reply was that he prayed that he would be given courage and good sense.

The 'quarantine' could not be extended indefinitely, and on 13 January 1897 the Indians were finally allowed to land. Before leaving the ship, Gandhi was interviewed by a reporter from the *Natal Advertiser* about the Green Pamphlet, his speeches in India and his future plans. Also, Escombe sent word through Milne that since the whites were 'highly enraged' against Gandhi, he and his family should land at dusk, when Mr Tatum, the port superintendent, would escort them to their home.

Gandhi seemed willing to do this but readily changed his mind when F A Laughton, lawyer for Dada Abdullah & Co. and a friend of many of Durban's Indians, came on board and told Gandhi that he should not enter the city 'like a thief in the night'. Laughton and Gandhi had Kastur and the boys driven to the home, two miles from the dock, of Parsi Rustomji (where Gandhi and his family would stay for a few days before moving to Beach Grove Villa), and the two of them walked.

But Gandhi was quickly recognized by some white youths who shouted, 'Gandhi! Gandhi!' and 'Thrash him! Thrash him!' When several others joined the shouting, a worried Laughton hailed a rickshaw and asked Gandhi to get inside. Gandhi had never sat in a rickshaw before – the idea of being pulled by another human had seemed 'thoroughly disgusting' to him. But now, after Laughton's urging, he was willing. However, the shouters, whose ranks were swelling, frightened the African rickshaw-puller, who said '*Kha*!' ('No') and disappeared.

The crowd was 'enormous' by the time Gandhi and Laughton reached West Street, where a man 'of powerful build' dragged Laughton away while others pulled down Gandhi's turban, pelted him with stones and eggs, and slapped and kicked him. About to pass out, he staggered to a fence and held on to it.

After recovering his breath and balance, he started to walk again when Mrs Alexander, the wife of Durban's police superintendent, who knew Gandhi and was walking in the opposite direction, saw him. Spreading her umbrella over Gandhi, she kept in step with

him. Though Gandhi received some more blows, the presence at his side of a well-known white woman saved his bones, and he made it to Rustomji's home. Decades later he would write:

> God has always come to my rescue ... My courage was put to the severest test on 13th January 1897 when ... I went ashore and faced the howling crowd determined on lynching me. I was surrounded by thousands of them ... but my courage did not fail me. I really cannot say how the courage came to me. But it did. God is great (*Harijan*, 1 Sep. 1940; 79: 129).

Gandhi's later surprise at his courage is of interest, but so is a comment that Laughton made in 1897: 'Intimidation is out of the question because, if he knew the Town Hall were going to be thrown at him, I believe from what I saw that he would not quail.'[15]

But 13 January 1897 held another test for him. A large crowd surrounded the Sorabji house (where the *Courland*'s medical officer, Dr Dadiburjor, a Parsi like Sorabji, was treating Gandhi's wounds) and shouted, 'We want Gandhi!' Alexander, the police chief, arrived on the scene and found it ugly indeed. His advice was that Gandhi should leave the house in the disguise of a south Indian constable. That was the only way to save his family and that of Rustomji, and Rustomji's property. 'I am afraid the crowd will raze Rustomji's house to the ground.'

The advice was at once implemented. Changing quickly into a constable's uniform provided by one of Alexander's men, Gandhi also wore a protective 'helmet' that consisted of a metal plate wrapped inside a headscarf, and slipped out of the rear entrance of the Rustomji compound. He was quietly taken to the police station. Alexander, meanwhile, had been leading the crowd in singing, 'Hang Old Gandhi/ On the Sour Apple Tree.' On being informed that Gandhi had reached the police station, Alexander announced to the crowd that their quarry had escaped, a claim confirmed by a delegation that inspected the house. Outwitted, the crowd dispersed.

Within a few days the climate improved, for two reasons. The *Natal Advertiser* published its interview with Gandhi in which he had managed 'to refute every one of the charges levelled against' him (A 171). Even more importantly, a Gandhi blessed with good sense in addition to courage chose not to prosecute his assailants.

From London the Secretary of State for the Colonies, Joseph Chamberlain, had indeed cabled the government of Natal asking for prosecution, but Gandhi told Harry Escombe that he did not want it. When Escombe indicated that he would like to have this in writing, Gandhi at once 'obtained some blank paper from him, wrote out the desired note, and handed it over to him' (S 52–61; A 164–70).

As Escombe admitted to Gandhi, the government of Natal had been saved the 'most awkward' task of proceeding against its supporters, but the Indian community too benefited. Declaring that Gandhi was innocent, Natal's newspapers condemned the mob. Later Gandhi could write:

> In three or four days I went to my house, and it was not long before I settled down again. The incident added also to my professional practice (A 171).

Family life. But for Kastur and the boys it had been a turbulent start to life in Durban, and they were not destined to find peace. The boys' schooling was a dilemma. Gandhi's contacts would have secured them places in the best European schools, but other Indian children were not admitted there, and Gandhi rejected a 'favour and exception' for his family. He also decided against the schools for Indian children run by missionaries, which were of indifferent quality, taught no Gujarati, and seemed likely to indoctrinate pupils in Christianity.

The boys were therefore schooled at home, a decision strengthened by Gandhi's belief, no doubt born of his years away from his sons, that 'young children should not be separated from their parents' (A 174). However, Gandhi's public life restricted his teaching at home, even if it was enthusiastic and creative whenever it occurred.

Though he also engaged an English governess at £7 a month, the schooling of Harilal and Manilal and their cousin Gokul was overall a dismal affair. Harilal and Gokul showed a flair for soccer, and no doubt all three saw life at Beach Grove Villa as an exciting change from Rajkot, but their education was not Gandhi's primary goal, and it suffered.

Harilal, however, would later view this early part of his life, when his father seemed to ride what the Autobiography calls a path of 'ease and comfort', as its best period (A 174–6). Though Gandhi was beginning to simplify his lifestyle (among other things he was washing, starching and ironing his numerous shirts and collars and had taught Kastur these skills), what nine-year-old Harilal found, for the first time, was the company, in a large comfortable home, of a father who was engaging, rich and influential.

In 1898 he and Manilal were joined by a new brother, Ramdas, and in 1900 there was a fourth boy, Devadas. Kastur and Gandhi 'had decided to have the best medical aid at the time of her delivery', but it was just as well that Gandhi had also studied childbirth. When Devadas was due, 'the travail came on suddenly' and neither the doctor nor the midwife was immediately available. Gandhi saw through the baby's safe delivery and apparently 'was not nervous' during the exercise (A 177–8).

Gandhi had profited from a Gujarati book and also from the time he was spending at a dispensary funded by Parsi Rustomji and supervised by Dr Booth, the head of St

Aidan's Mission. (The Autobiography hints that Gandhi helped set up the dispensary.[16]) For an hour or more each day, Gandhi ascertained patients' complaints, laid the facts before a doctor, and compounded medicines. The work brought 'some peace' to one 'ill at ease' with his prosperity and also a closer contact with the indentured, most of whom came from India's Hindi, Tamil and Telugu regions (A 177–8).

Gandhi's joy at the arrival of Ramdas and Devadas was joined by some awkwardness, for it proved his inability to practise brahmacharya to the full. He had wished to do so following the talk with Rajchandra in Gujarat, and he and Kastur were sleeping in separate beds, but there were nights when he failed to resist the physical urge.

The dispensary and Gandhi's work there had been triggered by the arrival in Beach Grove Villa of an indentured labourer suffering from leprosy. Unable 'to dismiss him with a meal', Gandhi offered him shelter, dressed his wounds and looked after him. But this could not go on forever, and after some days Gandhi sent the man to a government hospital for indentured labourers (A 177).

The leper was hardly the only outsider in Beach Grove Villa, which as before also accommodated Gandhi's clerks, one of whom was indirectly responsible for a bitter exchange between Gandhi and Kastur recounted in the Autobiography and elsewhere. This clerk, a Christian born of 'untouchable' parents, was a newcomer who had not yet started cleaning the chamber-pot kept in his room, and in his reformist zeal Gandhi decided that it was up to him or Kastur to take it down, empty and clean it, and bring it back to the clerk's bedroom. Kastur had acceded to cleaning the chamber-pots of some other lodgers, but carrying an 'untouchable's' urine, or letting her husband carry it, was too much. 'Her eyes red with anger, and pearl drops streaming down her cheeks', she chided her husband as, pot in hand, she descended the outer stairway.

He answered by shouting, 'I will not stand this nonsense in my house.' 'Keep your house to yourself and let me go,' said the spirited wife. Her husband 'caught her by the hand, dragged the helpless woman to the gate, which was just opposite the ladder, and proceeded to open it with the intention of pushing her out'.

The tears ran down Kastur's cheeks in torrents, and she cried: 'Have you no sense of shame? ... Where am I to go? I have no parents or relatives here to harbour me. Being your wife, you think I must put up with your cuffs and kicks? For heaven's sake behave yourself and shut the gate.'

Coming back to his senses, Gandhi shut the gate, but Kastur had seen, not for the first time, her husband's domineering side. At such moments, mercifully short-lived, he was master, teacher, husband, and she servant, pupil, wife, indeed a piece of property he owned and could dispose of as he pleased. Moreover, his success (as lawyer, leader, reformer) had swollen his pride, and Kastur's resistance to his moral certitude had turned the reformist spirit into a knife.

We owe *our* glimpse of this unpleasant face entirely to Gandhi's own candid recollections. Yet these recollections, along with his acknowledgment of a domineering and pitiless side to his nature, and the contrite envisioning of Kastur as 'a helpmate, a comrade and a partner in the husband's joys and sorrows', rather than one 'born to do her husband's behest', came many years after the incident, which occurred in 1897 or 1898. (He gives both dates in different accounts.) At the time, while no doubt 'really ashamed' (as he puts it in the Autobiography) at his behaviour, Gandhi did not seem to comprehend the forces inside him that made him act or react the way he did (A 243–5).

Here we may mention a French tale that Gandhi heard in South Africa and never forgot. It was translated for him (we do not know exactly when) by 'an Anglo-French philosopher', as Gandhi would later describe him, 'an unselfish man who always sided with the minorities', whose 'mother was a Frenchwoman and his father an Englishman'. The story was about a scientist who journeyed to India before Mughal times 'in search of truth'. He saw many so-called high-caste people, men and women, but was not satisfied. Finally the scientist went to the humble cottage of an untouchable in a humble village and 'found the truth that he was in search of'.[17]

We can see why the story made such an impression on Gandhi, who disliked untouchability but belonged to a high caste, an Indian seen as an untouchable by some South African whites, and one who sensed that he might some day have truths to share.

On the public front there were gains and losses. Thanks to the NIC's lobbying, London ruled that Natal could not discriminate against Indians on the ground of race. But Natal nullified London's ruling through 'non-racial' laws aimed at Indians that imposed stringent conditions on traders and made immigration virtually impossible for those not proficient in English, unless they were indentured labourers, who were still wanted. Despite an appeal by the NIC, the Colonial Secretary in England refused to block the new laws.

Useful work was nonetheless done in England by Mansukhlal Nazar, another of Gandhi's Beach Grove Villa lodgers, a public-spirited Gujarati fluent in English who had moved in 1896 from Surat to Natal. In 1897, when the premiers of self-governing colonies and dominions assembled in England for the Diamond Jubilee, Gandhi sent Nazar to London, to be guided there by three men whom Gandhi had cultivated through correspondence: Dadabhai Naoroji, Sir William Hunter, the 'India' editor of *The Times*, and Sir Muncherjee Bhownugree, a Parsi Member of Parliament whose politics were milder than Naoroji's. With their help Nazar was able to brief several influential Britons on the situation of Indians in South Africa.

Continuing an old friendship, Pranjivan Mehta showed up briefly in Durban in 1899, but opposition, too, surfaced, especially when Gandhi persisted in asking Natal's Indians 'to keep their surroundings clean'. Running into 'polite indifference' and even 'insults', Gandhi concluded that 'it is the reformer who is anxious for reform, not society', and that society may offer 'opposition, abhorrence, and even mortal persecution' to a reformer (A 190).

The Boer War and Sergeant-Major Gandhi. The Boer War, which broke out in 1899, also divided the Indian community. The gold of the Transvaal was a factor in this war between the British and the Afrikaners or Boers, and though Indians were shabbily treated in the Transvaal and had been forced out of the other Boer republic, the Orange Free State, Gandhi admired the Afrikaners' independent spirit. In this historic battle between the Boers and the British, where, on both sides, 'lawyers gave up their practice, farmers their farms, traders their trade, and servants their service' (to use Gandhi's sentence), his 'personal sympathies were all with the Boers'.

Yet he raised an ambulance corps of 1,100 Indians for the British side, reasoning that failure to support the British would invite fresh hostility and probably expulsion. On the other hand, supporting the British would strengthen their right to live in South Africa, gain the whites' respect, and perhaps improve their lot – the poor treatment of Indians in Boer lands was in fact a ground the British cited for the war. But should victims help oppressors? And what if the other side won? Gandhi answered that soldiers facing a battle never asked the second question, but we must assume also that his finger on the pulse of events, and his awareness of Britain's naval power and the Empire's resources, indicated to Gandhi a British victory.

Allegations that Indians were cowardly and stayed at home to make money were common in Natal, and Gandhi's offer of an ambulance corps (for which his work in the dispensary had to some extent prepared him) was not immediately accepted by the authorities. But men like Laughton and Escombe, and the Bishop of Natal, on whom Gandhi called, championed the offer, as did Dr Booth, who also trained the Indian volunteers in ambulance work.

In the end, about 300 'free' Indians and 800 indentured Indians were permitted to serve in the Boer War as an ambulance corps. Thirty-seven Indians were listed as 'leaders'. Gandhi saw to it that different sections of the Indian community – Hindus, Muslims and Christians, the well-off and the poor, south Indians and north Indians – were represented in the corps and among the leaders. In fact Gandhi seemed to sense in the ambulance corps a chance to develop Indian solidarity. He was there himself, of course, with the rank of a sergeant-major, as was Dr Booth.

The corps served only for six weeks, and during a phase in the war that saw British attacks repulsed by the Boers. When the commander-in-chief decided to postpone further forays until reinforcements arrived from Britain and India, the corps was disbanded. But it had achieved something. Though asked at first to remain outside the firing line, the corps was requested by General Buller, after a repulse at Spion Kop, to fetch the wounded from the front. On some days Gandhi and his fellows on the corps carried the wounded on stretchers for 20 miles or more; among those carried was General Woodgate.

Camaraderie quickly replaced colour prejudice. On a hot and exhausting day, Gandhi and some other Indians marched toward Chievely Camp, where Lieutenant Roberts, son of Lord Roberts, had received a mortal wound. When, trudging together, thirsty Indians and whites eventually reached a tiny brook, the Indians asked the whites to drink first, while the whites asked the Indians to do the same. Vere Stent, editor of the *Pretoria News,* who ran into Gandhi early one morning after the latter had completed 'a night's work' and British soldiers were 'heartily invoking damnation on everybody', found Gandhi 'stoical in his bearing, cheerful and confident in his conversation', and possessing 'a kindly eye'. 'He did me good,' Stent would record.[18]

Gandhi had in fact turned a difficult dilemma for the Indians into an opportunity. In Natal and in England, the press lauded the Indians' work. 'We are sons of Empire after all,' ran the refrain in a poem in *Punch.*[19] General Buller mentioned the Indian corps in his dispatch, the 'leaders' received medals and the Indians sensed a unity they had not felt before (A 188–90; S 62–73).

Gandhi was near the entrance of his Mercury Lane office when, on a day in December 1899, Harry Escombe crossed over from across the street to have a word with him. Saying that he was really sorry about the attack of January 1897, Escombe added that he had not realized that 'so much Christian charity was locked up in the Indian heart'. Three hours later, within minutes of Gandhi returning home, a servant from Escombe's house hurried in to report that Escombe had just dropped dead.[20]

Return to India. Boer defiance could not prevent a British victory, which seemed to brighten the Indians' prospects. Fluttering over the Transvaal and Orange Free State, the Union Jack was expected to bring rights to Indians there. That and the goodwill won in Natal signalled to Gandhi that he could return to India, a decision apparently buttressed by a fear that 'merely money-making' might become his 'main business' in South Africa (A 192), and also, we may assume, by the appeal of law and politics in India. India had responded well to him in 1896, and his Durban time had made him confident in the law.

Arguing that Miyakhan, Nazar and others would look after the work in Natal, Gandhi obtained in 1901 the community's conditional consent to his departure. The rider was that if in a year's time the community needed him, he would return. He accepted the proviso. 'The thread of love that bound me to the community was too strong to break' (A 192).

This love was expressed in a series of farewell events and in costly presents: a gold necklace for Kastur, other gold chains, gold watches, diamond rings. Most were from the community, some from clients. After an evening occasion when the bulk of the gifts were given, a 'deeply agitated' Gandhi spent a sleepless night, walking up and down his room and debating the gifts. Should a public servant accept gifts? Since his clients were also helpers in public work, should he even take what they had given? The Autobiography is frank: 'It was difficult for me to forego gifts worth hundreds [of pounds].'

But he found it more difficult to keep the gifts. After all he was trying to simplify his life, and telling his children and wife that service was its own reward, and in fact urging the community 'to conquer the infatuation for jewellery'. That night he drafted a letter placing the presents in a trust for the community, and naming trustees led by Parsi Rustomji.

We can see this renunciation, as Gandhi may also have done, as both an ethical and political step, and capable of adding to his influence, whether in South Africa or India.

In the morning he held a 'consultation' with Kastur, but only after securing (unfairly, it must be said) the boys' agreement. Apparently, Harilal and Gokul (who were now 13) and Manilal, nine, not only said to their father that they did not need the presents; they also agreed to persuade their mother.

This did not prove easy. Kastur fought with both passion and logic. The boys might dance to his tune, she told Gandhi, but 'what about my daughters-in-law?' The future was unknown, and she would be 'the last person to part with gifts so lovingly given'. She cried, too.

But the boys and the husband would not budge. Gandhi said that the boys would not marry young. When they did marry, their wives would be free from the lure of ornaments; if, however, ornaments were needed, Kastur could ask him.

'Ask you? I know you by this time. You deprived me of my ornaments … Fancy you offering to get ornaments for my daughters-in-law! You who are trying to make sadhus of my boys from today!'

Erikson's translation of the last remark is, 'You want them to be saints before they are men.'[21] Saying, 'No, the ornaments will not be returned,' Kastur asked a proper legal question: 'And pray what right have you to my necklace?'

In a pitiless legal reply, Gandhi asked if the necklace was given for her service or his.

'I agree,' Kastur said. 'But,' she added, 'service rendered by you is as good as rendered by me. I have toiled and moiled for you day and night. Is that no service? You force all and sundry on me, making me weep bitter tears, and I slaved for them.'

'These were pointed thrusts, and some of them went home,' Gandhi would acknowledge. But his mind was made up. In his own words, he 'somehow succeeded in extorting' her consent (A 192–4). The gifts received in 1896 and 1901 were all returned. In the Autobiography (the sole source for this discussion and our knowledge of it) Gandhi would claim that as the years went by Kastur saw the wisdom of the step, but the 1901 'consultation' over the presents was not between equals.

In October 1901, Gandhi, Kastur and the boys sailed for Bombay.

With (seated) *Sonja Schlesin and Henry Polak in Johannesburg* – *1905*

4

Satyagraha

India and South Africa, 1901–6

The voyage to India was via the island colony of Mauritius, where the Gandhis spent a night as guests of Sir Charles Bruce, the governor. From Bombay, where Kastur and the boys were lodged with friends, Gandhi proceeded to the Indian capital, Calcutta, for the annual session of the Indian National Congress at the end of 1901, boarding the train taken by the leaders – Dinshaw Wacha, who was to preside at the Calcutta session, Pherozeshah Mehta, 'the lion of Bombay', Chimanlal Setalvad, the renowned lawyer, and others. He wanted to interest the leaders in South Africa and also to get to know them. At a designated station *en route* Gandhi entered the special saloon that Mehta had booked and talked with the leaders assembled in it; at the next halt he returned to his compartment. Mehta's response that 'nothing can be done' for South Africa's Indians as long as 'we have no power in our own land' disappointed Gandhi (A 195).

At the Calcutta session Gandhi played two roles. He sponsored, with Gokhale's help, a resolution on South Africa, which was passed without discussion; during a five-minute speech, Gandhi managed to challenge Mehta's view. Secondly, he tried to introduce some order at the session venue. Picking up a broom, he started cleaning a verandah where delegates had answered 'the call of nature at night'. It was, however, an example that no one else followed. Gandhi also dealt with a pile of correspondence that was overwhelming one of the Congress secretaries, Janakinath Ghosal. Still, Gandhi met most of the leaders and 'came to know the working of the Congress', a useful acquisition (A 199).

But he also wanted to get to know Bengal and was glad when Gokhale, the Congress stalwart from Poona who was also a member of the Imperial Council that periodically met in Calcutta, asked him to stay on in his Calcutta residence. Invited by Gokhale to join all the discussions in his home, Gandhi was struck by his host's commitment and civility, and Gokhale on his part came to esteem his eager, disciplined and persevering guest.

During his weeks in Calcutta Gandhi met many of Bengal's intellectual and political leaders and found a love for Bengali music. Eager to call on Swami Vivekananda, he walked 'with great enthusiasm' the long path to Belur Math, only to be told that the Swami was 'in his Calcutta house, lying ill, and could not be seen' (A 209). Yet this disappointment was nothing compared with Gandhi's horror at the 'rivers of blood' beside Calcutta's Temple of Kali where goats were sacrificed. The sight was unbearable and unforgettable, and he was again shocked later that evening when a Bengali friend argued that the animals felt no pain since loud drumbeating accompanied their slaughter (A 208).

After a quick trip down the Bay of Bengal to Rangoon, where the irrepressible Pranjivan Mehta had now transferred himself, Gandhi decided to visit Benares, Agra, Jaipur and Palanpur before rejoining his family in Rajkot. He had to know the India he intended to engage, and would educate himself by travelling by train in third class.

It was winter, so in Calcutta Gandhi bought a long woollen coat that had been made in Porbandar. He also bought, for 12 annas, a canvas bag that would hold the coat, a shirt, a dhoti and a towel. Armed with the bag, a blanket and a water-jug that he already possessed, and a metal tiffin box presented by Gokhale, Gandhi left Calcutta. Gokhale, who had quite taken to Gandhi, insisted on seeing him off at the station, as did Sir Prafulla Chandra Ray, the scientist, whom Gandhi had befriended at Gokhale's, an indication of their regard for the young 'South African' leader.

Gandhi found the third-class compartments littered with trash and packed with people, many of whom shouted and spat at all hours of day and night. In Benares (Varanasi) he called on Annie Besant, who had made the holy city her home, took a dip in the Ganga, and was shaken by the din and dirt at the Kashi Vishwanath and Gyan Vapi temples. Engaging India was going to be no picnic.

Bombay, 1902. Desiring Gandhi's assistance with Congress work, Gokhale wanted him to join the bar in Bombay, but, cautioned by memories of past failure in that city, Gandhi set up his practice in Rajkot. When Gandhi quickly won cases in Kathiawar against reputed lawyers, his friend and successful advocate Kevalram Dave (whose father had urged Mohandas to go to England) insisted that Bombay was the place for Gandhi. 'You are destined for public work,' Dave said. 'We will not allow you to be buried in Kathiawar' (A 218).

Agreeing, Gandhi rented chambers in the offices of Payne, Gilbert and Sayani in the Fort and a house in Girgaum, but just when it looked as though he and his family were settling down, ten-year-old Manilal came down with a severe attack of typhoid combined with pneumonia. The doctor, 'a very good Parsi', said that while medicine would have little effect, eggs and chicken broth were likely to help the boy.

Gandhi's vow would not permit the use of these foods, and for a few days he went through great torment while nursing his boy and giving him the Kuhne hip baths that he had studied and had some faith in. When the high temperature persisted late one night, and Manilal grew delirious, Gandhi wondered whether he had any right to inflict his fads on his children.

Torn between conflicting thoughts, Gandhi decided to give his boy a moist sheet pack. Wetting a sheet and wringing the water out of it, he wrapped it around Manilal, sparing only his head, and then covered him with two blankets. To the head he applied a wet towel.

The boy's whole body was burning like a hot iron, and there was absolutely no perspiration. Sorely tired, Gandhi left Manilal in charge of Kastur and stepped out for some minutes by the sea at Chowpatty. Plunged in anxiety and prayer – scarcely looking at the few pedestrians who were about at that hour – he soon returned, his heart beating fast, to the Girgaum home.

'You have returned, Bapu?' the boy asked.

'Yes darling.'

'Please pull me out. I am burning.'

'Are you perspiring, my boy?'

'I am simply soaked. Please take me out.'

Gandhi thanked God, for the temperature was clearly coming down. After managing to divert his suffering son for some more minutes, Gandhi undid the pack and dried Manilal's body. Then father and son fell asleep in the same bed, and each slept like a log. Forty days of recuperation and nursing and a diet of diluted milk and fruit juices were to follow, but the boy had turned a corner (A 219–21).

Settling down? Since the Girgaum house lacked enough light and air, Gandhi searched for a house in the suburbs to the north. With the help of Pranjivan Mehta's brother, Revashankar Jagjivan, he eventually hit upon a 'fine bungalow' (at an unknown address) in Santa Cruz.

He also prospered better than he expected in his profession. Twice or three times a week Gokhale would drop in at Gandhi's chambers, often with friends he wished Gandhi to cultivate. A first-class season ticket eased Gandhi's commute between Santa Cruz and the Fort. Frequently, Gandhi walked to Bandra to take the direct train to Churchgate. Later he would confess to an occasional feeling of 'a certain pride in being the only first-class passenger' in his compartment (A 222).

His aims at this time were to do 'public work under the advice and guidance of Gokhale' and, 'side by side with public work', to make a living for himself and the family

(S 74). Appearing to 'settle down' in 'normal' and admirable fashion, and flourishing, he even took out an insurance policy for 10,000 rupees. An American insurance agent – 'a man with a pleasant countenance and a sweet tongue' – convinced barrister Gandhi that it was almost a religious obligation to get insured. Thinking of Kastur and the children, Gandhi told himself, 'Man, you have sold almost all the ornaments of your wife. If something were to happen to you, the burden of supporting her and the children would fall on your poor brother. How would that become you?' (A 230).

This comfortable period in their Santa Cruz home was probably the one to which, years later, Kastur was referring when, in response to a remark from Gandhi about spiced food that women in his ashram seemed to enjoy, she hit back, saying:

> You had better keep quiet on the subject. Remember when every Sunday you would ask me to prepare some delicacies for you and you would gulp them down lustily?[1]

But Gandhi's life was not intended for comfort or pleasure. A cable arrived from South Africa: 'Chamberlain expected here. Please return immediately.' Soon, funds for his fare also arrived. Remembering the promise he had given, Gandhi gave up his Fort chambers and in November 1902 went again to South Africa, even though Pherozeshah Mehta 'strongly advised' him 'not to go to South Africa', as he would be able to do nothing there (S 258).

In the belief that he would be back in some months, he retained the Santa Cruz house and left Kastur and his children there, under the care of a 22-year-old relative who in 1896 had helped Gandhi with the Green Pamphlet, Chhaganlal (son of Khushalchand Gandhi) and Chhaganlal's wife Kashi. Chhaganlal's effort was supported by Revashankar in Bombay and supervised, from Rajkot, by Laxmidas.

Accompanying Gandhi to South Africa were four or five young men from his clan, including Chhaganlal's younger brother Maganlal: for all its harshness to Indians, South Africa was still a land of opportunity. On Gandhi's part it was not an easy decision to leave again, terminating a rare spell of stability and security:

> The separation from wife and children, the breaking up of a settled establishment, and the going from the certain to the uncertain – all this was for a moment painful, but I had inured myself to an uncertain life (A 223).

Rebuff and response. It was in the Transvaal, now under the British flag, that Gandhi's help was most needed. Though the maltreatment of Indians in the Transvaal and the Orange Free State had been cited as a reason for Britain's war against the Boers, British victory had in fact worsened the Indians' position in the two states. Many of their hardships were connected to a new Asiatic Department in the Transvaal, largely staffed by British officials who had migrated from India and Ceylon during the Boer War.

Indians who had left the Transvaal during the war were required to apply to this department for permits to return to their homes, jobs or trade; and bribing seemed necessary to obtain the permits. Also, unlike South African officials who had acquired 'a certain courtesy of manner' while serving a European public – a courtesy also extended at times to Indians – white officers imported from Asia, used to lording over dark-skinned subjects, thought it beneath their dignity to be courteous with Indians (A 225).

Gandhi led the delegation of Indians in Natal that called on Joseph Chamberlain, Secretary of State for the Colonies, and found him polite, but Chamberlain's mission was to win South Africa's white hearts, Boer and non-Boer, and to collect £35 million that South Africa had promised to Britain, not to satisfy the Indians of Natal. From Natal Chamberlain hastened to the Transvaal. Gandhi, who had prepared the case of the Transvaal's Indians and had earlier lived for a year in Pretoria, was asked to lead a deputation there as well. But Indians in Pretoria and Johannesburg were unable to procure a permit for Gandhi's entry. However, an hour before Gandhi's train was to start from Durban, his old friend Alexander, still the police chief, secured a permit for him from a Transvaal representative.

The men at the Transvaal's Asiatic Department were furious. Thinking at first that Gandhi had arrived without a permit, they planned to arrest him. On realizing that he carried a permit, they resolved to prevent him from leading the deputation. Tyeb Sheth, who explained to the assistant colonial secretary, a man called W H Moor, formerly of the Ceylon Civil Service, that he and other Indians in the Transvaal had sought Gandhi's assistance, was ordered by Moor to fetch Gandhi. When Gandhi, Tyeb and some others arrived at Moor's office, no seats were offered.

'What brings you here?' Moor asked a standing Gandhi, who replied that his presence and advice had been asked for. 'The permit you hold was given you by mistake,' Gandhi was told. 'You shall not wait on Mr Chamberlain. You may go. Goodbye.'

The rudeness seemed too much for Tyeb, who said that no Indians would go to Chamberlain. Gandhi too 'smarted under the insult' but asked Tyeb and the others to swallow it. George Godfrey, an Indian barrister, went in Gandhi's place, but the deputation heard nothing encouraging from Chamberlain.

Following his exclusion from the meeting with Chamberlain, Gandhi chose not to return to India. Later he would write that he rejected 'the vain fancy of serving on a larger field in India' in favour of dealing with 'the great danger which stared the South African Indians in the face' (S 78), but we can assume that the personal rebuff made him keener to address the danger. Once more a crisis had changed his, and his family's, life. Gandhi told Tyeb and the others that not only would he stay on in South Africa, he would live in the Transvaal, practising in Pretoria or Johannesburg, deal with the Asiatic Department, and strive to prevent the hounding-out of the Indians.

Johannesburg, 1903–4. Delighted, the Transvaal Indians backed Gandhi in starting the Transvaal British Indian Association (TBIA or BIA), a counterpart of the Natal Indian Congress, and adopted him as their leader. And to everyone's surprise the Law Society did not oppose Gandhi's application to be enrolled in the Transvaal Supreme Court.

Again unexpectedly, Gandhi found rooms in mid-1903 at Rissik Street in Johannesburg's legal district, with the help of a European friend called Louis Walter Ritch, a manager in a commercial firm. 'A modest room behind his chambers' was where he lived.[2] He did not send for Kastur and the boys right away; he would wait and see.

Gandhi's practice in Johannesburg blossomed. Before long he had four Indian clerks and a secretary, a Miss Dick (we do not know her first name), who had come fresh from Scotland. Gandhi soon felt he could place complete confidence in Miss Dick, who managed his funds and account books. Trusting Gandhi fully on her part, she sought his advice in her choice of husband, and eventually it was Gandhi who gave her away to become Mrs Macdonald. Gandhi's burden was lightened further when Ritch left his firm and got himself articled under Gandhi.

In Johannesburg Gandhi resumed his contacts with the theosophists (many of them vegetarians frequenting a restaurant, run by a German, that Gandhi often went to), not to join their society but to read religious, mostly Hindu, books with them, including Patanjali's *Yoga Sutra,* which espoused vows of non-violence, truth, non-stealing and chastity. His two years in India had taught Gandhi that he had to steep himself in Hinduism if he wished to affect India – if, for instance, he intended to challenge untouchability and animal-sacrifice. Accordingly, in Johannesburg, he studied the *Bhagavad Gita*, in English and also, with the aid of an English translation, in Sanskrit.

It hit him with unexpected force. Gripped by the *Gita*'s notion of aparigraha or non-possession, Gandhi accepted that he could not follow God without giving up all he had. How, in practice, was this to be done? To Gandhi the answer lay in what he remembered, from his London days, of Snell's law book. If an owner of considerable possessions regarded not an iota of them as his own, but saw himself as a trustee, he had in effect given up his possessions. Once again Gandhi was being moulded by a combination of East and West, not by one or the other. We should note that it was in Johannesburg, the city of gold, where, as he would say, citizens did not walk but ran, where 'no one has the leisure to look at anyone else', that Gandhi was impelled to reject the god of money (S 4). He sought also – in line with Hindu tradition – to memorize the *Gita*'s Sanskrit verses. Pasting verses on his bathroom wall, he recited them while he bathed. In three years he would memorize 13 of the *Gita*'s 18 chapters.

Continuing to experiment with food, he found that skipping breakfast stopped headaches he was experiencing, and also that applying 'a bandage of clean earth moistened with cold water and spread like a poultice on fine linen' to the abdomen did wonders for his constipation (A 238).

One experiment linked to vegetarianism proved a disaster. Ada Bissicks, an 'enterprising lady' with a large circle of friends, came to him with a plan for turning a small vegetarian restaurant she was running into something 'on a grand scale' to promote vegetarianism, and asked for help. She knew that some of Gandhi's clients kept large sums with him. With the approval of Badri, a client who had risen from the ranks of the indentured, Gandhi lent £1,000 of his money to the lady. But her project failed, and Gandhi had to reimburse Badri's account from his savings (A 235–6).

Politically, Gandhi's principal target was the Asiatic Department. Hearing that bribes were being demanded from Indians and Chinese seeking entry into the Transvaal, Gandhi began to collect evidence. This was risky not only for him (his movements were watched) but also for the Indians and Chinese willing to help him. In the end he gathered what he thought was incontrovertible evidence against two officers. Confronted with the evidence and with witnesses brought by Gandhi, Johannesburg's police commissioner said he would detain and prosecute the two officers. He added, however, that a white jury was unlikely to convict whites accused by non-whites. When one of the accused absconded, the police chief obtained an extradition warrant and had the man brought to Johannesburg.

As expected, the all-white jury disregarded the compelling evidence and acquitted the two. But both the accused were cashiered by the Asiatic Department, which became 'comparatively clean', enabling the Asian community to save large sums in unpaid bribes. Gandhi's prestige rose, and it went up further when, on receiving a request, he agreed not to oppose the dismissed officers' applications for jobs with the Johannesburg municipality.

A description of Gandhi in 1903 has been left by a British writer, Arthur Hawks, who was in South Africa from April to June that year and met Gandhi in Johannesburg. Hawks thought the 33-year-old Gandhi to be 'about forty' and described him as wearing 'a small black moustache on a face not especially dark in colour, but very bright in understanding'. Hawks noticed Gandhi's 'soft voice, mellifluous diction, charm of manner' and 'exquisite English' and that he was 'without semblance of rancour'. Hawks also recorded that Gandhi's speech contained a 'faint' and 'intermittent' sibilance that at times turned an 's' sound into 'sh'.[3]

Ghetto and plague. A 'coolie location' or ghetto in Johannesburg called Brickfields claimed Gandhi's attention almost from the moment he arrived in the city. A number of ex-indentured Indians lived there on small plots leased for 99 years. The municipality's neglect combined with the ignorance of the overcrowded residents made the location totally insanitary, and the municipality was able to get a law passed for demolishing it. The residents were allowed the right to appeal against the amount of compensation offered by the municipality.

They engaged Gandhi for their appeals. Out of about 70 cases, he lost only one. While the residents were happy with their success, and grateful to Gandhibhai, as they called him, their location, where they had to live until new quarters could be found, was getting more squalid by the day – having decided on destroying Brickfields, the municipality had no desire to look after it.

Madanjit Vyavaharik, a Gujarati-speaking friend of Gandhi who had been a school-teacher in Bombay, was at the location on 18 March 1904 when he learnt that 23 Indians there were down with pneumonic or 'Black' plague, contracted at a gold mine where the plague had broken out.

'A remarkably fearless man', as Gandhi calls him, Madanjit broke open the lock of a vacant house and put all the patients in there. He also sent Gandhi a note in pencil: 'There is an outbreak of the plague. You must come immediately.'

Gandhi cycled to Brickfields, where he was joined by Dr William Godfrey, an Indian doctor, and also, at Gandhi's request, by four young Indians working in his office, all bachelors. An offer to assist from Ritch, who had a large family to support, was turned down. Godfrey, Madanjit, Gandhi and the four youths spent 'a terrible night of vigil and nursing', giving the patients such medicine as Dr Godfrey prescribed, keeping them and their beds clean, and trying to cheer them up. All the patients got through that night.

The town clerk, to whom Gandhi had written a note saying they had taken possession of the vacant dwelling, now placed an disused warehouse at Gandhi's disposal. Gandhi and a team mobilized by him cleaned the warehouse, collected some beds from charitable Indians and improvised a hospital. The municipality sent a European nurse, quantities of brandy for patients and helpers, and some equipment.

Despite urgings from the nurse, Gandhi and the other helpers did not consume the brandy, Gandhi for one being unsure of its usefulness even for the patients. With Dr Godfrey's permission, Gandhi put three patients under his earth treatment, applying wet earth bandages to their heads and chests. In the end, two of these three were the only ones to survive. Even 'the good nurse', as Gandhi calls her, who 'would fain have attended to the patients' but was 'rarely allowed … to touch them', succumbed.

'It is impossible to say,' Gandhi would write in the Autobiography, 'how the two patients were saved and how we remained immune' (A 257–61).

The Natal Mercury acknowledged Gandhi's 'yeoman service' (22 Mar. 1904). In a letter to the press about the plague, Gandhi held the municipality responsible for neglecting the location after taking it over, but he cooperated fully in efforts to prevent the plague from spreading. Advised by him, the location's residents abided by an order preventing passage into or out of it. They also agreed to move out with all their belongings and to have the location gutted.

Many residents had buried hoards of coins there. These had to be unearthed. Gandhi, who spent much of his time with the residents, became their temporary banker and persuaded the manager of *his* bank to accept, in coins of copper and silver, a total of about £60,000 from the location, after the coins were disinfected. After a tent city was raised by the authorities at Klipspruit Farm, about 13 miles from the city, the ghetto's residents were removed there by special train. The next day the location was put to the torch.

Addressing fellow-Indians, Gandhi asked for 'sanitation and hygiene' to be made 'part of our being'. Overcrowding had to be 'stamped out' and 'we should freely let in sunshine and air'.[4]

Indian Opinion

That South Africa should have an Indian-owned printing press and journal had long been the community's wish. In 1899, Gandhi had loaned money to help Madanjit Vyavaharik start the International Printing Press in Durban.

Early in 1903 Madanjit approached Gandhi with the idea of using the press for a weekly journal called *Indian Opinion* to be published in four languages, English, Gujarati, Tamil and Hindi. (South Africa's first non-European journal, started in 1884 in the eastern province by an African teacher, John Tengo Jabavu, was called *Native Opinion.*) Gandhi signalled his readiness to support *Indian Opinion* with his pen and if need be his money. Mansukhlal Nazar, associated with Gandhi in Durban from the 1890s, agreed to serve as unpaid editor, and Gandhi promised to send at least one article each week. The first issue came out on 4 June 1903.

Translating every item into three other languages and composing type in four languages was a challenge for the modest staff and the small press, but the journal soon satisfied a need, informing Indians of events across South Africa and in India, and enabling interested Europeans to know the Indian mind.

In the opening issue Gandhi said that the journal would highlight the 'undeserved and unjust' disabilities under which South Africa's Indians laboured and would also 'unhesitatingly point out' Indian faults.[5] Commenting on the first issue, *The Times of Natal* wrote that the Indian case had been 'very temperately and fairly' presented. Gandhi would later claim that he realized 'in the very first month' of *Indian Opinion* that while control on a newspaper from without was 'more poisonous than want of control', an 'uncontrolled pen' could also destroy. He would say that the journal trained him in self-restraint, compelled the critic too 'to put a curb on his own pen', and enabled the Indian community to 'think audibly' through letters and comments (A 253).

At the end of its first year, after Gandhi had spent around 30,000 rupees on the journal, he asserted that *Indian Opinion* had endeavoured 'never to depart from the strictest facts in dealing with the difficult questions that have arisen' and to write nothing 'with a view to hurt'. But its writers 'believed in the righteousness of the cause' they espoused and would 'always place before readers' facts 'in their nakedness'.[6]

Madanjit had been in Brickfields collecting subscriptions for *Indian Opinion* when the plague broke out. In March or April 1904 (around the time of the plague) Madanjit told Gandhi that he planned to return to India. He was not in a position to repay Gandhi's loans, Madanjit added, but Gandhi could take over the press and the journal if he wished, and enjoy its income. Gandhi 'accepted the offer and finalized the deal then and there'.[7]

Chhaganlal and Maganlal. Encouraged by Gandhi, his 24-year-old 'nephew' Chhaganlal Gandhi, had by this time arrived in Durban from Bombay and found employment at the International Printing Press. Chhaganlal's younger brother Maganlal, who had travelled with Gandhi to South Africa at the end of 1902 but could not get to the Transvaal, had done well at business in the countryside near the Natal towns of Tongaat and Stanger, in partnership with another clansman who had gone to South Africa in 1897, Abhaychand, grandson of Gandhi's uncle Tulsidas. Frightened at first by strongly built Zulus who invaded his village store, Maganlal, who was 22 in 1904, soon learnt the Zulu language and befriended his African customers.

Gandhi viewed these brothers (whose father Khushalchand had always been close to him) as a special charge and sought to train them from Johannesburg. On their part the young men, whose wives would soon join them in South Africa, responded warmly to him. After Maganlal and Abhaychand met Gandhi in Durban, an impressed Maganlal wrote to his older brother, who was in India at the time:

> *31 Oct. 1903.* Looking at his radiant face, we were overjoyed … Uncle is ranked here as an extraordinarily powerful figure and is held in high esteem even by veteran statesmen … He has to employ seven Indian and two European clerks in his office, besides a lady typist.[8]

Phoenix

Gandhi's response to the plague in Brickfields affected the *Indian Opinion* project in ways that surprised Madanjit, Nazar and everyone else involved with it, Gandhi included.

West & Polak. Two white men played a role in this. One was Albert West, a partner in a small printing firm in Johannesburg, described by Gandhi as a 'pure, sober, God-

fearing and humane Englishman'. Most evenings West was Gandhi's dinner companion at a vegetarian restaurant run by a German called Adolf Ziegler (at this time Gandhi seemed to eat both lunch and dinner out). Often, after dinner, the two took a walk together.

Having missed Gandhi at the restaurant during the outbreak of plague and read his letter to the press, an anxious West knocked on the door of Gandhi's apartment. Relieved when Gandhi appeared, West offered to assist the plague victims as a nurse. 'You are not needed here,' replied Gandhi, 'but will you consider going to Durban to look after the *Indian Opinion* press?' West agreed and left the next day to take care of the press in Durban for £10 a month plus a 50 per cent share in any profits, Gandhi having conveyed to West Madanjit's view that profits were likely.

Not long after this, Henry Polak, 'a young man sitting a little way off' Gandhi's table at The Alexandra, the restaurant run by Ada Bissicks, sent his card to Gandhi, who invited Polak, sub-editor of *The Critic,* to his table. Polak said he had been impressed by Gandhi's letter to the press. The conversation that followed revealed a similarity of views and started a friendship.

When West wrote from Durban that the finances of the press and journal were in a sorry state, and that there seemed no possibility of any profits, adding however that he would 'remain on', Gandhi had no choice but to go to Durban to get at the facts. Polak saw him off at Johannesburg station (Sep. 1904) and lent him a book for the 24-hour journey to Durban, saying that Gandhi was sure to like it.

The book was John Ruskin's *Unto This Last*. Gandhi could not put it down; it more than captured him. Before his train had reached Durban he was resolved to put the book's principles into practice. As he saw them, these were, firstly, the good of the individual was contained in the good of all; secondly, a lawyer's work had the same value as a barber's; and thirdly, a life of labour, of the tiller of the soil or the handicraftsman, was the life worth living. In embracing the social equality and simple life presented by *Unto This Last,* Gandhi may also have been influenced by his recent interactions with the residents of the now-demolished location. Acting instantly, Gandhi proposed to West that *Indian Opinion* should be removed to a farm on which everyone should labour, drawing the same living wage (£3 a month) and also help with the printing. Living outside the city, they would live the right life and also reduce *Indian Opinion*'s losses.

The remarkably flexible West, clearly also a believer in Gandhi, agreed. So did Chhaganlal and Maganlal, though making money had been their goal in coming to South Africa. The brothers agreed to move to any farm that could be found, as did a few others, but Madanjit (who would leave for India on 16 October 1904) thought the proposal foolish in the extreme, and Nazar made it clear that his editing would be conducted from Durban.

An advertisement for 'a piece of land near a railway station in the vicinity of Durban' receiving a response, Gandhi and West inspected a 20-acre estate 14 miles from Durban and two-and-a-half miles from Phoenix station. The land was wild and infested with snakes, but it also had a spring and some orange and mango trees. The estate was bought, along with an adjoining 80-acre tract, for £1,000 in all. It was not far from a centre started by a Zulu leader, John L Dube, later a founder of the African National Congress.

Parsi Rustomji gave Gandhi corrugated iron sheets and other building materials. Indian carpenters and masons who had joined Gandhi during the Boer War helped erect a 75-foot by 50-foot shed, and the press was moved there within a month of Gandhi's arrival in Durban. On 24 December 1904, the first Phoenix-printed editions were dispatched.

Apart from writing his pieces, Gandhi did not hesitate to advise Nazar on the rest of the journal. 'The Indians and the Europeans both knew that though I was not avowedly the editor of *Indian Opinion,* I was virtually responsible for its conduct' (A 252). Recalling, in the Autobiography, his role with the journal, he would claim that not a word he wrote over a ten-year period was consciously exaggerated, or written without thought or merely to please. At times history, biography and world events joined Indian and South African subjects in its columns. Abraham Lincoln, Booker T Washington, Elizabeth Fry and Florence Nightingale were featured. In 1905, a piece by Gandhi hailed Japan's victory over Russia in a naval battle, underlined the Asian nation's successful spying and scouting, and held that the secret of its 'epic heroism' was 'unity, patriotism and the resolve to do or die' (*Indian Opinion,* 10 Jun. 1905; 4: 313).

The Indian community 'made the paper their own' and about 10 per cent subscribed to it. The force behind *Indian Opinion* and the creator of the rural settlement in Natal could not, however, ignore his work in Johannesburg. He had to be there. Gandhi was delighted, therefore, when Polak offered to reside in Phoenix, for which he, after all, bore some responsibility. Giving *The Critic* a month's notice, Polak moved to Phoenix, where each participating family lived in a house of corrugated iron on a three-acre plot. Considerations of time and expense killed Gandhi's hopes of small brick houses, or mud-huts thatched with straw.

'By his sociability' Polak 'won the hearts of all' in Phoenix. Indeed he took to the settlement like a duck to water, but Gandhi soon needed him in his Johannesburg law offices, for Ritch, who was carrying a major burden there, wanted to go to England for further studies. Responding swiftly to a request from Gandhi, Polak left Phoenix and returned to Johannesburg, where he signed articles with Gandhi.

When the dedicated Mansukhlal Nazar died suddenly in January 1906, he was briefly followed as editor of *Indian Opinion* by Herbert Kitchin, an electrical engineer (and theosophist) who had joined the settlement. Later in 1906 Polak became the editor, functioning from Johannesburg. But the journal never became profitable, not even after its costly Tamil and Hindi editions were closed in 1906, and survived only on Gandhi's savings.

Family in Johannesburg, 1904–6. When pressed for time, Gandhi dictated, in English, his letters to Kastur, who had been left in India. Typed by Miss Dick and posted to Bombay, the letters were translated there into Gujarati and given to Kastur. In the middle of 1903, realizing that he was not likely to return anytime soon to India, Gandhi sent for his wife and boys, but difficulty in finding an escort and other hitches delayed their arrival until the last quarter of 1904.

The eldest son, Harilal, now 16, remained in India, at school in Bombay under Laxmidas's distant eye and interested in marrying Chanchal Gulab, an educated daughter of Haridas Vora of Rajkot, whom Gandhi knew and liked. Though he had reluctantly approved of Harilal's betrothal to Gulab, Gandhi was against an early marriage and unhappy with Harilal's decision not to accompany his mother and brothers to South Africa, and probably unhappy, too, with Laxmidas's supervision of Harilal.

When Kastur and Harilal's brothers emerged from their ship in South Africa, Gandhi's third son, six-year-old Ramdas, was wearing a sling, having broken an arm while playing with the captain. 'In fear and trembling' Gandhi 'undid the bandage, washed the wound, applied a clean earth poultice and tied the arm up again'. Daily, 'Doctor' Gandhi dressed the injury in this manner; in a month the arm was healed (A 272).

For his family Gandhi rented (again with the help of Ritch) a two-storey house with a garden in Johannesburg's upscale Troyeville area. Though this home into which Kastur, Manilal, Ramdas, Devadas and Gandhi moved was fair-sized, modern and in an enviable location, life inside it was being drastically simplified 'in the light of Ruskin's teaching' (A 275). There was a servant in the house, living 'as a member of the family', and 'the children used to help him in his work'. A municipal sweeper removed the night-soil from the house but Gandhi and his family, rather than the servant, cleaned the toilet. Bread was not bought at a baker's. Unleavened wholemeal bread was baked at home according to Kuhne's recipe, made from flour ground at home by two men working a hand-mill that Gandhi had purchased for £7.

At about this time, influenced by the notion of aparigraha, Gandhi decided to cancel his insurance policy. He was there himself, Gandhi reasoned, to support his family. If he were to die God would look after them, or they themselves would; he should not rob them of their self-reliance. 'What happened to the families of the numberless poor in the world? Why should I not count myself as one of them?' (A 231)

More difficult was a letter he wrote in May 1905 to Laxmidas, the head of the Gandhi family and the recipient thus far of a good chunk of Gandhi's savings. By 1902, Gandhi had sent him 60,000 rupees (some of the amount settling debts incurred by brother Karsandas), apart from repaying the 13,000 rupees spent on Gandhi's studies in England. Henceforth, Gandhi wrote, Laxmidas should not expect any money from him. Any savings now and in the future would go to *Indian Opinion* and to the Indian community in South Africa (A 233–4). Gandhi added that his ambitions now were 'very high,' he did 'not even recognize fear now,' and he was willing if need be to 'embrace death'.[9] A shaken and indignant Laxmidas accused Mohandas of wanting to be 'wiser than our father' and of neglecting the family (A 233–4). Gandhi's answer was that he now had a new and larger family.

Father and sons. Gandhi's companion at the hand-mill in the Troyeville house was Henry Polak, who had accepted his invitation to move in. Polak was a bachelor but not for long. As soon as Gandhi suggested that Polak should marry his fiancée, Millie, who was in England waiting for a propitious time for marriage, Polak announced to her that the time had come. Millie quickly arrived in Johannesburg, and Gandhi was best man at the civil marriage of Henry, a Jew, with the Christian Millie, who joined her husband in the home of the Gandhis.

We can only imagine the feelings of Kastur at having to share her home and husband, soon after rejoining him, with a white couple, and her reactions to the hard routine that Gandhi had introduced into their home. We do not have *her* recollections. Gandhi acknowledges 'some unpleasant experiences' between 'Mrs Polak and my wife', adding that such experiences 'happen in the best-regulated homogeneous families' and were only to be expected in his 'essentially heterogeneous family' (A 274).

As before in Durban, the boys were educated at home. Gandhi's earlier objection to a European school for his children had now been reinforced by his encounters with the Asiatic Department, with the 'coolie location' and with Ruskin. There is no evidence that in Johannesburg he even tried to have a private tutor. He seemed to think that he himself would make an adequate teacher. 'Had I been able to devote a least an hour to their literary education with strict regularity,' he writes in the Autobiography, referring to this Johannesburg phase, 'I should have given them, in my opinion, an ideal education' (A 276).

But *Indian Opinion*, the community's needs, his legal practice, Phoenix and the running of his home took up all his time, and he did not find the hour-a-day to teach his sons. He tried to instruct them (he says) on walks to his office and back from it, getting the boys to join him on these walks. Gandhi admits that even these 'street' instructions were liable to be interrupted or abandoned if someone else was 'claiming [his] attention'.

Gandhi would claim that in Johannesburg his boys learnt to grind wheat, 'got a good grounding in general sanitation', developed no 'aversion for scavenger's work', kept fit, did not fall ill, learnt nursing and enjoyed 'what I imparted to them by word of mouth' in Gujarati, which was the result of 'all that I had digested from my reading of various books' (A 275 & 301). For the boys, however, the deprivation of literary education in their childhood and early youth would remain a lifelong grievance. In the Autobiography Gandhi would offer a limited apology:

> My sons have therefore some reason for a grievance against me ... and I must plead guilty to a certain extent ... It has been their, as also my, regret that I failed to ensure them enough literary training (A 276).

Polak, from whom the boys learnt much, had 'very heated arguments' with Gandhi – not, apparently, about their not being sent to a school but about their father speaking to them in Gujarati rather than in English. 'With all the vigour and love at his command', Polak contended that the children would have a competitive advantage if they learnt English from childhood. Gandhi felt, on the other hand, that while daily contact with Europeans would in any case teach good English to his boys (it did), without a knowledge of Gujarati they would seem foreign to Indians – in Johannesburg in 1904–6 India was very much on Gandhi's mind.

What was best for his wife and children was not Gandhi's primary quest. He led his children and wife into a lifestyle he thought best for his goals: 'I sacrificed their literary training to what I genuinely, though maybe wrongly, believed to be service to the community' (A 276). His children doing scavengers' work, grinding wheat and speaking fluent Gujarati may have been an admirable example to a hierarchical, colonized community that saw indignity in manual labour and in a native tongue. Yet the family paid a price for his noble ambition, and if the Gandhi boys displayed gifts in the future, it was in spite of the inadequacy of their education.

East & West. The East-West merger we find around Gandhi is noteworthy for its time. The Polaks living in the Gandhi home, Gandhi's role in their marriage, Albert West's responsiveness and faithfulness to Gandhi, who soon got West also married, the stay thereafter of West, his wife ('a beautiful young lady' from a family of shoemakers in Leicester), and mother-in-law in Phoenix (which grew into a little village of several families, including those of Chhaganlal and Maganlal Gandhi), the partnership of brown and white against the plague, the almost simultaneous impact on Gandhi of the *Gita* and of *Unto This Last* – in the opening years of the 20th century these were unusual occurrences. However, we should note the absence from these events of South Africa's largest group, the Africans.

Another European whom Gandhi met 'accidentally' in Johannesburg in 1906 and who would interact significantly with him was a German Jew, Hermann Kallenbach, a flourishing architect who at his first meeting asked Gandhi about the Buddha's renunciation (A 293). We may note that Gandhi's reference in the Autobiography to his 'essentially heterogeneous family' in Johannesburg was at once followed by a correction: 'When we come to think of it, the distinction between heterogeneous and homogeneous is ... merely imaginary. We are all one family' (A 274).

Re-registration of the Transvaal's Indians, 1905–6. Signs that they were not wanted in the Transvaal were meanwhile adding to the insecurity of Indians. While every law that directly or indirectly discriminated against the British was repealed following the Boer defeat, anti-Indian laws were not only retained; they were compiled into a single manual for the convenience of officials, and all loopholes were diligently closed. Boer laxity became a thing of the past.

That some Indians had managed to buy land in auctions was bitterly resented by the whites, and Indian traders were marked out for dislike. The intention to bar, and if possible banish, enterprising Indians was masked by what Gandhi called a 'pseudo-philosophical' argument that the West and the Indians represented rival cultures that could not co-exist. One culture was supposed to be 'fond of good cheer, anxious to save physical labour, and prodigal in habits', the other frugal and otherworldly.

'If thousands of Orientals settled in South Africa, the Westerners must go to the wall.' Since self-preservation was a supreme right, Indians had to be kept out (S 83–4). However, the real reasons, as Gandhi saw it, were trade and colour. Indian trade clearly hit British merchants, and coloured skin was disliked.

In any case, officials in the Transvaal asked the territory's Indians to re-register themselves. The step was needed, they were told, to prevent illegal immigration. Despite the animus against them, in 1905 the Transvaal's Indians agreed, in negotiation with the authorities, to do this, even though no new law obliged them to do so. They agreed in the hope of avoiding new anti-Indian legislation, and to demonstrate their disapproval of illegal immigration. By early 1906, all the Indians in the Transvaal had exchanged their old permits for new ones.

Harilal. In May 1906 Harilal, who had stayed behind in India and was now 18, married Gulab. Believing that the two were still too young, Gandhi had asked Harilal to wait for marriage and join him meanwhile in South Africa. But Harilal was keen and so was Laxmidas, who arranged an expensive wedding and later asked Gandhi to reimburse him. The younger brother said he could not.

Gandhi and Kastur felt disappointment on another score: Harilal was not writing to them or answering their letters. Asking his son to realize that his parents were 'affected by separation' from their son, Gandhi recalled the long letters he wrote from London, when he was 19, to Laxmidas, who was 'like a father to me'. Added Gandhi (28 Dec. 1905):

Obviously, your mother would be more anxious [for] your letters. Still, you have not written even a small note ... You have not fulfilled my natural curiosity to know every aspect of your life, your thoughts, your desires, etc.[10]

But the dissatisfaction was mutual and the son had *his* grievances. He had received insufficient attention, he felt, from his father; and he did not approve of the changes in his parents' lifestyle.

Responding to the Zulu Rebellion, 1906. Just when Gandhi thought he had settled down in the Transvaal, albeit to a stricter life-pattern, a crisis occurred in Natal that broke up the Johannesburg establishment. After a Zulu chief rejected a new tax, a white man sent to collect the tax was assegaied; another white man was also killed. In punishment 12 Zulus were blown from the muzzle of a cannon before an audience that included several chiefs. The Zulu revolt persisted, and military action to crush it was announced.

Gandhi was quick to assess the significance of what had happened. He wrote in *Indian Opinion* of 'important events, the effects of which will not be forgotten for many years' and of 'great changes likely to take place in South Africa'. 'The Indians and other Blacks,'[11] he added, 'have much to ponder and act with circumspection' (*Indian Opinion* [Guj.], 7 Apr. 1906; 5: 162).

Though he doubted the wisdom of the revolt, Gandhi's sympathy was with the Zulus, 'who had harmed no Indian' (A 278). But in South Africa the Indians existed on British sufferance, and he again concluded, as he had over the Boer War, that they had to support the authorities. In *Indian Opinion* he wrote:

What is our duty in these calamitous times in the colony? It is not for us to say whether the revolt ... is justified or not. We are in Natal by virtue of the British power. Our very existence depends upon it. It is therefore our duty to render whatever help we can (*Indian Opinion* [Guj.], 14 Apr. 1906; 5: 179).

We should note here that even John Dube, the Zulu leader who ran the Ohlange Institute in Phoenix and would help found the ANC, expressed the view that while the Zulus had serious grievances, 'at a time like this we should all refrain from discussing them, and assist the government to suppress the rebellion'.[12]

Gandhi offered the governor of Natal, 'with the community's permission' (S 90), an Indian Ambulance Corps, and to Kastur and the Polaks he pointed out that if the offer was accepted the Johannesburg establishment would have to be broken up: Kastur and the boys would go to Phoenix, and the Polaks to a smaller home in Johannesburg. In the Autobiography Gandhi claims that he had Kastur's 'full consent to this decision' (A

278). Though often reacting against her husband's ways, Kastur did not try to block the unknown path when, from time to time, destiny opened it for him.

The governor accepted his offer, Kastur and the boys went to Phoenix, and Gandhi again found himself leading a 'battlefield' corps, this time comprising 12 south Indians, five Gujaratis, two from the Punjab and one from Calcutta. Fourteen out of the 20 were Hindus, and six Muslims. They served in undulating terrain in the Zulu country, in areas north of Phoenix and west of Stanger, including Mapumulo, Umvoti valley and Imati valley.

Clarity, chastity, certainty

Three chapters in the Autobiography – 'The Zulu "Rebellion"', 'Heart Searchings' and 'The Birth of Satyagraha' – describe this critical phase in Gandhi's life when he found a certainty about his mission and clarity about his road.

Gandhi and his colleagues were on active service in the Zulu terrain for four weeks in June–July 1906, carrying on stretchers Zulu friendlies mistakenly shot by British soldiers and nursing them as well as Zulu suspects whose wounds received from British lashes had festered for days. In addition Gandhi had to 'compound and dispense prescriptions for the white soldiers'. This was easy enough for Gandhi, who had learnt to do this in Dr Booth's little hospital. Noticing Gandhi's service, two whites who had led the bitter opposition to his return to Durban in 1896–7, a prominent butcher named Sparks and another man named Wylie, called on Gandhi to thank him (A 279).

But Gandhi quickly saw that the military campaign supported by him was only a man-hunt. Whatever his head may have advised, his heart was with the unfortunate Zulus, and 'every morning' he was assailed by bitter qualms as he heard 'rifles exploding like crackers in innocent hamlets' (A 281). His conscience was somewhat eased by the fact that he and his corps nursed innocent Zulus who would otherwise not have been cared for. Dr Savage, the 'very humane' doctor in charge of the ambulance, had told him that white nurses were not willing to attend to the wounds of the Zulus. In fact, white soldiers tried to dissuade the Indians from doing so. When the Indians did not heed them, the soldiers 'poured unspeakable abuse on the Zulus' (S 90; A 279). Though the Indians could not understand what the Zulus said, they could make out 'from their gestures and the expressions of their eyes' that they seemed to feel 'as if God had sent us to their succour' (S 91).

The Indians were serving in a sparsely populated, beautiful part of the country. 'Few and far between in hills and dales were the scattered kraals of the simple and so-called "uncivilized" Zulus.' With or without the wounded, Gandhi and his colleagues marched long distances, at times 40 miles a day. In his treks 'through these solemn solitudes',

Gandhi 'often fell into deep thought' (A 281). The horrors of war were 'brought home' to him with 'vividness', and Gandhi's conscience pricked him for being on the side of those who had practised great brutality. He was reminded of India's 1857 Rebellion, which too witnessed great brutality, including floggings and men blown from guns. That rising had only consolidated British power in India, even as the Zulu revolt seemed to be doing in South Africa.

As the psychoanalyst Erik Erikson puts it, the exercises of cleansing the gunshot wounds and binding rents made by the lash – the experience of 'witnessing the outrages perpetrated on black bodies by white he-men' – aroused in Gandhi 'both a deeper identification with the maltreated and a stronger aversion against all forms of male sadism'.[13]

But if in the Zululand solitudes Gandhi reflected on the pangs of the weak and the cruelties of the armed, he also realized the folly of being excited into violence against the strong-in-arms. And he saw that these latter were not really strong: the truly strong person was the pure in heart – the brahmachari, the celibate – especially if he was free also of the burden of possessions and thus capable of 'undertaking … the largest risks'. In his treks in the Zulu country, Gandhi seemed to sense there that he would have 'more and more occasions' for struggle, and that he would have to embrace what he had admired for years, brahmacharya, and also – 'as a constant companion in life' – poverty (S 91; A 282).

The less he had, the more he would become. He had to be lean and clean, and his battles and weapons too had to be unsoiled. In the Autobiography he recalls his choice: 'In a word, I could not live both after the flesh and the spirit' (A 281). But this purely spiritual wording is misleading, for it leaves out the political, strategic and pragmatic dimensions of Gandhi's Zululand decisions.

Caritas had indeed triumphed over Eros,[14] but a readiness to struggle had also triumphed over the survival instinct,[15] and a strategy of wisdom over that dictated by anger. The chastity vow was connected, too, to Gandhi's unwillingness to be tied down by more children (A 180), and also perhaps – although this is speculation – to a wish to prove to Harilal that sexual desire could be overcome.

In the Zulu country Gandhi sensed that he himself would fight well and on a large canvas. 'A mission … came to me in 1906, namely, to spread truth and non-violence among mankind in the place of violence and falsehood in all walks of life,' he would say in 1942.[16] He may not have used these exact words in 1906, but the sense of a calling was present. He would recall that the solemn decisions produced 'a certain kind of exultation'. 'Imagination,' he added in the Autobiography, 'also found free play and opened out limitless vistas of service' (A 281). By service he here chiefly seems to mean struggle.

That a struggle was ahead was suggested by letters and telegrams to him in Zululand asking him to return to the Transvaal, where new anti-Indian steps were being designed.

'My people were excited,' Gandhi would later recall, 'and there was talk of wreaking vengeance. I had then to choose between allying myself to violence or finding out some other method of meeting the crisis ... and it came to me that we should refuse to obey legislation that was degrading and let them put us in jail if they liked'. [17] Once again a crisis (which this time included an uneasy conscience) had become a springboard for Gandhi. This time the results were greater than before.

Within months of the Zulu rebellion, the Transvaal Indians launched their first non-violent defiance or, as it would eventually be called, satyagraha ('truth-force'), with Gandhi saying on 11 September 1906, 'I can boldly declare, and with certainty, that so long as there are even a handful of men true to their pledge, there can be only one end to the struggle, and that is victory' (5: 335).

In the Autobiography Gandhi says (A 284) that his Zululand decisions were a necessary 'preliminary ... to satyagraha'. Zululand had led to 'the gift of the fight'[18] that he would share with South Africa, India and the world. Every individual anywhere had the power to resist oppression, and non-violent resistance was legitimate.

Concluding justly that 'the turning point in Gandhi's personal life came in 1906' in Zululand, Jonathan Schell notes equally correctly that whereas in both East and West, holy vows have usually been accompanied by a withdrawal from the world and from politics, 'Gandhi proceeded in exactly the opposite direction'. His vows had freed him not from, but for, action.[19]

The Zululand decisions for chastity and poverty were similar to and yet different from 'giving God your life'. Cost at one level, freedom at another, and finality were written into his decisions, yet Gandhi was not abdicating personal responsibility for his life or control over it. While the God he spoke of (and prayed to) often seemed a personal God, in his Zululand reflections Gandhi focused on what he should do, not on what God might do. He would cry for God's help, but the burden was primarily his.

The Asiatic Law. As soon as the Corps was disbanded, Gandhi went to Johannesburg via Phoenix, where, as he recalls in the Autobiography, he 'eagerly broached the subject of brahmacharya with Chhaganlal, Maganlal, West and others'. He claims too to have 'consulted' his wife, who 'made no objection', but we do not know the details of this conversation.[20] Some in Phoenix, the Autobiography adds, 'set themselves bravely to observe the vow' and some 'succeeded also' (A 282).

We will look again and often at Gandhi's brahmacharya, but here let us note what he says in *Satyagraha in South Africa,* written before the Autobiography and revealing the growth of the political Gandhi even as the Autobiography recounts his spiritual/ethical/ dietetic experiments: 'On return from the war, I just met the friends at Phoenix and at once reached Johannesburg' (S 91).

'Eager' (as he tells us in the Autobiography) about the vow, he was just as eager, or even more, for action, and wanted '*at once*' (as *Satyagraha* informs us) to be where 'letters and telegrams' had asked him to return.

In the Transvaal a young man in the Asiatic Department called Lionel Curtis had argued that Indians exchanging their old permits for new ones was not enough. Re-registration by mutual consent, said Curtis, lacked the force of law. Worse, the process of mutual consent had raised the prestige of the Transvaal's Indians. To put them in their place, new legislation was needed, which could also serve as a model for the rest of South Africa and for parts of the Empire like Canada, Australia and New Zealand. Curtis's arguments found responsive ears, and on 22 August 1906 a *gazette extraordinary* of the Transvaal government published a draft, written by him, for amending the territory's Asiatic Law.

Arriving in Johannesburg, where he stayed with Hermann Kallenbach in the latter's house in Orchards, three miles outside the city, Gandhi took a copy of the *gazette extraordinary* 'to a hill near the house' to study the draft law and translate it into Gujarati. It required every Indian who was eight or older, male or female, to obtain a new certificate of registration from the Registrar of Asiatics and provide finger and thumb prints and other marks of identification. Failure to comply would invite a fine, imprisonment and/or deportation. Once obtained, a certificate was to be produced each time a police or government officer asked to see it; and police officers could enter private houses to inspect them. Gandhi saw 'hatred of Indians' in the offensive law, which he explained the next day to 'a small meeting of leading Indians', who were all as shocked as Gandhi had been.

One of them said in a fit of passion: 'If any man comes forward to demand a certificate from my wife, I will shoot him on the spot and take the consequences.' Gandhi 'quieted him' and told those gathered that the proposed law was 'the first step with a view to hound us out of the country'. If they acquiesced in it, the law would be replicated across South Africa; many more than the 10,000 to 15,000 Indians in the Transvaal would be affected.

But haste, anger and impatience would be a poor response. They had to 'calmly think out', Gandhi said, 'measures of resistance' and 'in time carry them out'. And they had to present 'a united front' (S 93–4). In an *Indian Opinion* editorial on 8 September he asked the community to learn from the self-sacrifice that Russian workers had recently shown in brave strikes against oppression, but to reject their violence.

'*We won't submit.*' On 11 September (the date is striking, in retrospect) the Jewish-owned Empire Theatre was 'packed from floor to ceiling' with Indians. Always a student of his audiences, Gandhi thought he saw 'in every face the expectation of something strange to be done or to happen'. Abdul Ghani, one of the oldest Indian residents of the Transvaal and chairman of the Transvaal British Indian Association, presided, and the meeting considered a resolution expressing solemn determination not to submit to the 'galling, tyrannous and un-British requirements' laid down in the proposed law and to suffer all penalties their resistance might invite.[21]

The audience heard Gandhi patiently as he explained the resolution. *Indian Opinion* would summarize his remarks:

> He had thought the matter over seriously and earnestly before he had given his opinion upon the step they should take, and he felt that it was their bounden duty to adopt the course laid down ... He admitted that the responsibility for the serious step ... was upon his shoulders, and he took the responsibility in its entirety.
>
> But he knew them; he knew that he could trust them, and he knew also that, when occasion required an heroic step to be taken – he knew that every man among them would take it (*Indian Opinion,* 22 Sep. 1906; 5: 333).

Speaker after speaker supported the resolution, and one of them, Haji Habib, another seasoned resident, said, 'We must pass this resolution with God as witness.' Habib 'went on solemnly to declare in the name of God that he would never submit to that law'.

Recalling the occasion in *Satyagraha,* Gandhi says that he was at first 'startled' and 'put on [his] guard' by Habib's reference to 'God as witness' and by his declaration 'in the name of God'. Then, 'in a moment', he 'thought out the possible consequences' and his 'perplexity gave place to enthusiasm'. He saw that the daunting responsibility 'a solemn oath' would place on his shoulders, and on the shoulders of the community, was also an opportunity to be grasped.

His eyes and instincts had told him that the assembly in the Empire Theatre was willing. The 'solemn oath' that Habib was asking for merged with his solemn decisions in Zululand, and with his vision there of great battles ahead. Here was the threshold of the first of these. He should summon his soldiers.

'A new principle'

Obtaining the chair's permission to explain the implications of Habib's remarks, Gandhi said that Habib had introduced a novel yet serious element. The God of Hindus and Muslims was one and the same. A pledge in the name of that God was not something to be trifled with. All present had to search their hearts and should take the pledge only if they were ready to carry it out.

If a majority of the Transvaal's Indians took the pledge and remained true to it, it was possible that the proposed law would be withdrawn. But it was also possible that only a minority would pledge themselves, and as a result invite ridicule, imprisonment, hunger, floggings, deportation and even death. But if 'even a handful of men' remained 'true to their pledge, there can be only one end to the struggle, and that is victory'.

Gandhi spoke in a Gujarati that Hindi-speakers too could follow, and his remarks were also translated into Tamil and Telugu. He ended by saying that while it was unlikely that he would be 'left alone to face the music', he was ready to stand on his own, and he asked those unsure of their 'will or ability to stand firm even when [they] are perfectly isolated' to declare their opposition to the pledge.

After the chair endorsed the proposal, 'all present, standing with upraised hands, took an oath with God as witness not to submit' to the proposed law (S 97–100). The next day an accidental fire destroyed the Empire Theatre, yet Gandhi felt that 'some new principle had come into being' there the previous day (S 102).

An upheaval in his family life had coincided with the birth of a new principle. The Zululand experience that led to 'the new principle' had separated him from his family and forced them to leave their upmarket Johannesburg house for a rough settlement in Natal. Earlier, his return to South Africa (in response to a cable) had led to a separation of two years, with the family left behind in Santa Cruz in Bombay. Before that, his prompt acceptance of the first invitation to South Africa had caused a three-year separation, as his London visit had done earlier. Embracing his destiny was Gandhi's priority, not the stability of his family, who stay put or move out as the situation might require. We should absorb this even as we note Gandhi's ability, time after time, to respond swiftly to a need or opportunity.

He is nailed not to a place, home or family but to an inner voice, or – perhaps we should say – to a people larger than his family. For their sake he will pull up old roots or send down new ones. He is free to fight for them; his family is compelled to adjust. He expands a tiny window into a large door for his oppressed people; his family is obliged to move into a more austere space.

For some time Gandhi and others would describe the Indians' response to the new law as passive resistance, but he was not satisfied with the English phrase. In 1907 *Indian Opinion* announced a small prize for an alternative, which Maganlal won with his suggestion of 'sadagraha' or 'firmness for the good'. Gandhi altered the prize-winning entry to 'satyagraha' or 'firmness for the truth'.

In September and October 1907 – a year after the Empire Theatre meeting – Gandhi extensively quoted the American, Henry David Thoreau (1817–62), in *Indian Opinion,* including Thoreau's statements about that government being best which governs the least, the duty of civil disobedience, and prison as the true place for a just man. Thoreau, Gandhi wrote, 'was a great writer, philosopher, poet, and withal a most practical man, that is, he taught nothing he was not prepared to practise in himself. He was one of the greatest and most moral men America has produced' (*Indian Opinion,* 26 Oct. 1907; 7: 279).

Gandhi would also acknowledge later that Thoreau 'invented' the idea of civil diso-bedience,[22] and that he had read Thoreau, whom he found 'so convincing and truthful', with 'great pleasure and equal profit'.[23] The evidence suggests that Gandhi's close and warm reading of Thoreau took place well after, rather than before, the Empire Theatre meeting, and that he found powerful confirmation and encouragement in Thoreau for what Zululand and the Asiatic Act had already engendered in him.

Using truth as a synonym for love, justice and the soul, and equating firmness with force, Gandhi would allow 'satyagraha' to be translated into English as truth-force, or love-force or soul-force. The American philosopher William James had called for 'the moral equivalent of war'. Gandhi felt he had found it.[24]

In Johannesburg – 1906

5

Hind Swaraj

South Africa and England, 1906–10

Still a Crown Colony in 1906, though assured by London of self-government in the very near future, the Transvaal required imperial consent for any new law. To urge Britain to reject the anti-Asian legislation, Gandhi and Haji Ojer Ali, an influential Muslim merchant, sailed for England early in October 1906, on the *Armadale Castle*.

Arguing that Gandhi represented not the Hindus but 'the Indian community as a whole', some Hindus in the Transvaal had wanted the deputation to include an additional Hindu 'to balance Ali'. The proposal, which was rejected, revealed Gandhi's non-communal standing as well as a 'Hindu/Muslim' element in the politics of South Africa's Indians (S 109).

In an *Indian Opinion* piece (17 Nov. 1906) Gandhi reported that the *Armadale Castle* was 'as big as a small town. There must be about a thousand persons on board, but there is no noise, no disorder.' He noted, too, that the English lawyer or businessman who had 'trekked long distances in the Zulu war and felt happy with dry bread' now did no work on the ship. 'He presses a button and an attendant stands before him. Why indeed should such a people not rule?' Gandhi asked. (He would say this sort of thing to Indians in South Africa, not to the British.)

But the people ruling the Empire from London knew who in South Africa they wished to placate. Though Lord Elgin, Secretary of State for the Colonies, said to Gandhi and Ali that the Empire could not support discrimination against Indians, and later indeed advised the King to withhold assent to the Transvaal law, he simultaneously assured Sir Richard Solomon, the Transvaal's representative in London, that the Empire would not intervene once the same law was passed by a self-governing Transvaal.

No inkling was given to Gandhi of this assurance to Solomon, who on his first visit to England after leaving its shores 15 years earlier lobbied with exemplary zeal. Along, when possible, with an often-ill Ali, Gandhi briefed public figures, including Campbell-Bannerman, the Prime Minister, Morley, the Secretary of State for India, and Curzon Wyllie, Morley's political secretary. He addressed about a hundred Liberal MPs and also approached MPs of other factions – imperialist, progressive and Irish. Two eminent London-based Parsis, Dadabhai Naoroji of the Indian National Congress and Sir Muncherjee Bhownugree, helped with some of the appointments.

Gandhi and Churchill. It was on this visit that Gandhi and Winston Churchill, Undersecretary for the Colonies and at this juncture a member of the Liberal Party, had their first (and last) meeting. This end-1906 interview with a 32-year-old Churchill was cordial enough; Gandhi, who was five years older, would say in 1935 that he retained 'a good recollection of Mr Churchill in the colonial office'.[1]

But from *My African Journey,* published two years later, we know what Churchill, who had been a correspondent in South Africa during the Boer War and had been taken prisoner, thought of Indian rights in Africa. He feared that 'Asiatics' might 'teach the African natives evil ways', saw the interests of whites and Indians as 'irreconcilable', and seemed to think that 'the brutal question' would be resolved only 'in a brutal fashion'. Added Churchill: 'The white artisan is invited to acquiesce in his own extinction ... by a competitor whom, he believes, he could strike down with his hands.' The phrase is evocative of the beating Gandhi had received in Durban in 1897 (of which Churchill may have heard). In London Gandhi invoked before Churchill what he believed to be an imperial norm: equal rights for Indians. Churchill would concede in *My African Journey* that 'the British Indian' had some rights 'as a human being' and 'as a British subject'.[2]

The climax of Gandhi's six weeks of lobbying in London was a large luncheon – 'about a hundred covers were laid' – where the South Africa British Indian Committee (SABIC), a standing committee for the protection of Indian interests in South Africa, was formed, with Lord Ampthill, a former governor and Viceroy in India, as its president and Louis Ritch as secretary.

Often working through the night, and writing an incredible 5,000 or so letters during the six weeks, Gandhi was helped by Indian students in London and by two young whites he had known in South Africa, Louis Ritch, now studying for the bar in London, and Symonds, a gifted 30-year-old who in Johannesburg had 'often humorously assured [Gandhi] that he would withdraw his support' if Gandhi was 'ever found ... in a majority' (S 112–13). In London, Symonds, who would die not long afterwards, took down Gandhi's dictation, typed letters, wrote addresses, affixed stamps and posted envelopes. Symonds 'toiled for us day and night without payment', Gandhi would write, and he would remember the 'sad parting' on the quayside on 1 December (S 113).

While in London Gandhi met British suffragettes fighting for women's rights and also Shyamji Krishnavarma (1857–1930), a Gujarati barrister and linguist who had studied in Oxford. Condoning violent means for Indian independence, in 1905 Krishnavarma had set up India House in Highgate for putting up and training young Indians in London, and also started a monthly, the *Indian Sociologist,* which attacked Gandhi's stand during the Zulu rebellion. Spending two nights in India House – an indication of his concern about its thinking – Gandhi proposed peaceful disobedience as an alternative to violence. Present at these discussions were young admirers of Krishnavarma, including a recent arrival from India, 23-year-old Vinayak Damodar Savarkar, a future ideologue of Hindu militancy.

On the way back along the west coast of Africa, Gandhi received (in the Portuguese island of Madeira) a joyous cable from Ritch: Elgin had advised the King to withhold assent. Two days after Gandhi left England, Churchill had indicated as much in Parliament. During the leg from Madeira to Cape Town, Gandhi, Ali and other Indian travellers therefore 'had quite a good time of it and built many castles in the air' (S 112).

They were undeceived on reaching Cape Town, where they learnt that Elgin had also assured the Transvaal of assent after the colony became responsible. On 1 January 1907 'responsibility' or self-government was granted. The first measure passed by the new Transvaal was the budget; the second, rushed through on 22 March, was the Transvaal Asiatic Registration Act (TARA), or the Black Act, as the Indians called it, which soon received London's consent. The appeal to Empire had totally failed. On 4 April Gandhi called on General Jan Christian Smuts, the Transvaal Interior Minister, and told him that the Indians could not accept TARA.

Harilal. In April Harilal, now 19 (and only 18 years younger than his father), arrived in South Africa with his wife Gulab (or Chanchal or Chanchi). Living, along with his father, in Kallenbach's place in Johannesburg, Harilal spent some time daily in Gandhi's law office, where Polak too worked. The father taught the son for an hour a day and urged him to 'maintain the habit of reading newspapers' even if for a few minutes every day. If he came across a word he did not understand, he should turn 'immediately' to the dictionary or his father 'or Mr Polak'.[3]

Soon, Harilal moved to Phoenix, where his wife was, and helped there with the printing of *Indian Opinion* and tried to involve himself in the settlement's other activities: carpentry, shoemaking, tailoring, cooking, grinding grain and farming. He also attended a school improvised by the inmates.

'We will fight.' Jolted by Britain's 'crooked policy', and disappointed that London had not tied the Transvaal's independence to its treatment of Indians, Gandhi probed the willingness of the Act's victims to fight. Contemplating risks to property and to their right of residence, quite a few had developed cold feet.

Yet on the night of 31 July about 2,000 Transvaal Indians gathered in the grounds of a Pretoria mosque. A friend of Gandhi's, William Hosken, came to address them. A business magnate, Hosken had been sent by the duo that ruled the Transvaal, General Louis Botha, the Premier, and Smuts, both heroes on the Boer side that had lost the war. In his remarks (translated 'word by word' by Gandhi), Hosken conveyed the duo's message: the Indians, who 'knew very well how powerful' the Transvaal government was, should not 'dash [their] heads against a wall'.

Having heard Hosken in absolute silence, the gathering clapped as he left, but the applause was meant for the fight that now seemed unavoidable. Gandhi said he took complete responsibility for advising Indians not to comply with TARA. Ahmad Muhammad Cachalia, a Meman trader with links to Surat, declared that he would face confiscation, deportation and even hanging rather than submit to the law. While mentioning hanging, Cachalia ran his fingers across his throat. Gandhi smiled in scepticism, a reaction he would be 'ashamed of', for Cachalia would soon prove his mettle, and Gandhi would later write that he knew of none to 'surpass Mr. Cachalia in courage and steadfastness' (S 123–4).

A new body, the Passive Resistance Association (soon to be renamed the Satyagraha Association) was formed – Gandhi did not want the Transvaal British Indian Association or its funds to attract the government's hostility. Hundreds of passive resisters peacefully picketed the offices where permits were to be issued and gave every Indian approaching the offices a pamphlet that explained the new Act and its consequences. An additional tactic was devised: hawkers and small traders would ply their trade without displaying their vendors' licences. Gandhi was also able to draw into the struggle the Transvaal's small Chinese community, also affected by TARA.

Indian Opinion sustained the resisters' spirits but also gave the authorities advance notice of their plans. Providing a rousing image, Gandhi wrote that each lamb-like Indian contained a lion inside, but he also offered a new definition of virility. Those reneging from a vow lost their manhood and hurt India's honour, he said, while those keeping a vow achieved manhood and burnished honour (*Indian Opinion,* 6 Jul. 1907; 7: 35). And he swiftly denounced resisters who threatened violence against Indians who sought permits; when the ones threatened obtained permits with police protection, the folly of violent talk became apparent to all resisters.

Some prominent Indians procured permits late at night, in secret, and far from any permit office, yet by 30 November 1907, the last date for registration, the Transvaal government was able to register only 511 out of the 13,000 Indians living in its territory. The rest had refused to comply.

Arrests. General Smuts responded with a policy of selective and, on the whole, courteous arrests. A group including Gandhi, Leuing Quinn, who led the Chinese community, and Thambi Naidoo, a Tamil trader who could, as needed, lead meetings or

do porter's work, were asked to appear before a Johannesburg magistrate to explain why they should not be deported. When they presented themselves on 28 December 1907, the judge asked them to leave the Transvaal by 10 January or return to the court to be sentenced.

By now Gandhi was calling the struggle satyagraha. British suffragettes active at this time and British Nonconformists opposing the Education Act in 1902 had spoken of their 'passive resistance'. Claiming that his struggle was different on two counts – it eschewed hatred and violence, and was a weapon for the strong, not the weak – Gandhi wanted a new name to distinguish it (S 103–7).

He had seen the itch for violence in some Indians in South Africa, in the group he had met in 1906 in India House in London, and in the news from India. On 6 December 1907 there had been a terrorist attack on the British Lieutenant-Governor's train near Midnapore in Bengal, and in April 1908 several people were killed by a bomb in Muzaffarpur in Bihar. In these methods Gandhi saw more travail for the oppressed, and he hoped that satyagraha would make them obsolete.

Some South African whites were unable to withhold their admiration. First meeting him in December 1907, Joseph Doke, a Baptist minister in Johannesburg, eight years older than Gandhi, recorded his impressions of the unusual Indian: 'a small, lithe, spare figure', 'a refined earnest face', 'a direct fearless glance', and 'the smile that lighted up the face ... and simply took the heart by storm.'[4]

In prison. On 10 January Gandhi, Quinn and Naidoo returned to the court. To be 'standing as an accused in the very court where [he] had often appeared as counsel' felt strange but Gandhi experienced not 'the slightest hesitation in entering the prisoner's box'.

He was awarded two months in prison. After being sentenced he was led to a side-room and shown a bench to sit on. Then the door was shut on him. Anxious thoughts raced through Gandhi's mind. His home and courts had vanished. He was a prisoner. Would he serve the full term? Two months would seem an age if other resisters did not join him. And so on, for some seconds, until Gandhi remembered that he had asked fellow Indians to recognize jails as His Majesty's hotels and imprisonment as bliss.

> How vain I was! Where had all this knowledge vanished? This second train of thought acted upon me as a bracing tonic, and I began to laugh at my own folly (S 137–8).

A policeman interrupted the smile and ushered Gandhi into a van which took him to the city jail, where he found it difficult to don the 'very dirty' clothes he was asked to change into. He was taken to a large cell where other Indians soon joined him. They told him his arrest had triggered a procession with black flags, and that some marchers had been flogged.

Finding that he had a free run of the prison library, he relaxed and read. Among the texts he dipped into were Carlyle's *Lives* of Robert Burns, Samuel Johnson, and Walter Scott, Bacon's *Essays,* Plato's Socratic dialogues, the Bible, the *Gita*, and an English translation of the Koran. He thought he should translate Carlyle and Ruskin into Gujarati.

In a few days many more Indians were in the jail, most of them vendors sentenced for refusing to show their licences. No matter where arrested or tried, all were given hard labour – the government had conveyed guidelines to magistrates. Soon the jail had about 150 Indian prisoners. Gandhi instructed them to observe jail rules.

On 28 January a friend of his, Albert Cartwright, editor of *The Transvaal Leader* and a supporter of the Indian position, turned up at the jail with the text of a proposed compromise that he claimed Smuts had approved. Detaining a multiplying number of Indians useful to the economy was not a comfortable option for the government; the Indians too could not indefinitely defy. Cartwright added what newly arriving prisoners had also told Gandhi, that the Indian leaders not in jail would accept any solution approved by him.

The essence of the 'settlement' he brought was an understanding, not put in writing, that if Indians underwent voluntary registration over a three-month period, the government would repeal the Black Act. There was, in addition, a written draft, which was vague. Amending the language, Gandhi signed the draft, as did Quinn and Naidoo. Cartwright was doubtful that Smuts would approve of the change but said he would take the signed document to Smuts.

In the afternoon of 30 January, the police superintendent of Johannesburg took Gandhi to Pretoria to meet Smuts, who said he accepted Gandhi's alteration. Reminding Gandhi, in a long talk, that he too was a barrister from one of the London Inns of Court, and claiming that English-speaking whites wanted TARA more than the Boers, Smuts praised the commitment of the Indian resisters. According to *Satyagraha,* Smuts added:

> I have consulted General Botha also, and I assure you that I will repeal the Asiatic Act as soon as most of you have undergone voluntary registration. When the bill legalizing such registration is drafted, I will send you a copy for your criticism (S 144).

When Smuts rose, Gandhi asked, 'Where am I to go? And what about the other prisoners?' Smuts laughed and answered that Gandhi was 'free this very moment' and that he was phoning to instruct the release of the others. As Gandhi 'had not a single farthing in [his] pocket', Smuts's secretary gave him the train fare to Johannesburg, where, immediately on arrival, Gandhi explained the settlement to the chairman of the Passive Resistance Association, Yusuf Mian, and other community leaders (S 144–5).

Around midnight Gandhi addressed about 1,000 Indians in Johannesburg who had quickly gathered in the grounds of a mosque. Deeming the settlement a victory, he asked the Indians to be as wholehearted in registering voluntarily as they had been in opposing compulsion.

Mir Alam. As soon as Gandhi sat down, Mir Alam, 'fully six feet in height and of a large and powerful build', stood up. A friend and client of Gandhi, Alam was one of the Transvaal's 50 or so Pathans, many of whom worked for him, making coir or straw mattresses. Alam asked Gandhi if they had to give ten fingerprints. Those with difficulties of conscience would not need to, replied Gandhi, but all the others should give ten fingerprints.

'What will you do yourself?'

'I have decided to give ten fingerprints.'

'It was you who told us that ten fingerprints were only required from criminals.'

'Yes I did, and rightly. But ... an indignity yesterday is today the hallmark of a gentleman. If you require me to salute you by force and I submit to you, I will have demeaned myself ... But if of my own accord I salute you as a brother or fellow man, that will be counted in my favour before the Great White Throne.'

'We hear you have sold the community to General Smuts for £15,000. I swear with Allah as my witness that I will kill the man who takes the lead in applying for registration.'

'One may not swear to kill another in the name of the Most High. However that may be, it is my clear duty to take the lead in giving fingerprints ... To die by the hand of a brother, rather than by disease ... cannot be for me a matter for sorrow.'[5]

When Yusuf Mian asked the audience what they thought, all, 'with the exception of a couple of Pathans present', endorsed the settlement. After two hours' sleep, Gandhi returned to the Johannesburg prison to meet his colleagues. An hour after he reached the jail, all the satyagrahis were released.

Assault. Authorities in Johannesburg worked with the satyagrahis to produce a new registration form. Gandhi, Yusuf Mian and some others decided they would fill it on 10 February.

That morning, when Gandhi went to his law office on Rissik Street, which was also the office of the Satyagraha Association, he found Mir Alam and his companions standing outside the premises. Noticing Mir Alam's 'angry eyes', Gandhi thought 'that something was going to happen'. After Yusuf Mian, Thambi Naidoo, and some others had joined

Gandhi in his office, the party set out on foot for the registration office, a mile away on Von Brandis Square. Mir Alam and friends followed. When Gandhi and party reached the premises of Messrs Arnot and Gibson on Von Brandis Street, Mir Alam accosted Gandhi and asked, 'Where are you going?'

While replying, Gandhi was hit from behind by a club. Sighing '*He Ram* (O God)', he passed out. Later he learnt that Mir Alam and his companions had given him more blows and kicks, some of which were warded off by Yusuf Mian and Thambi Naidoo, who were also hit. Some Europeans on the street caught the assailants as they were running away and handed them over to the police. An unconscious Gandhi was taken to the private office of J C Gibson.

Coming to, he saw Joseph Doke bending over him. Doke had found Gandhi 'lying on the floor, looking half-dead ... his face cut right open through the lip [and] an ugly swelling over the eye'.[6] When Doke asked him how he felt, Gandhi replied that apart from some pain in the jaw and the ribs he felt all right. He added, 'Where is Mir Alam?'

'He has been arrested along with the rest.'
'They should be released.'

The police were ready to take Gandhi to hospital but he accepted an invitation to Doke's home on Smit Street, to which he was moved in a carriage. Learning that Gandhi had been injured and taken to Doke's place, Montfort Chamney, the registrar of Asiatics, turned up there. Gandhi asked Chamney to bring the papers for his fingerprints. 'I had said I would be the first to register and have a pledge to keep.'

Next Gandhi sent a wire to the Attorney-General urging the assailants' release. (They were let off, but Mir Alam and his companions were later rearrested on a new charge: committing a crime on a public street. Though Gandhi refused to give evidence, Mir Alam and one other were given short sentences.)

A Dr Thwaites arrived at the Dokes' home and found that Gandhi's injuries were not serious. Stitching up wounds on the cheek and upper lip, the doctor enjoined liquid food and complete silence until the stitches were removed. As Gandhi would later write, though 'speech was forbidden me, I was still master of my hands'. For the community he wrote out a message:

They should not prosecute Mir Alam and company, who had acted in the only way they knew against what they thought to be wrong. Hindus should not retain anger against Muslims. Except for those with scruples of conscience, Asians should give fingerprints. And satyagrahis should 'fear none and nothing but God'.

Chamney returned with the papers. After Gandhi pressed his fingers first against an ink pad and then against the papers, he 'saw that tears stood in Mr Chamney's eyes'. Before closing his own eyes for a rest, Gandhi wrote out a note asking Doke whether his little daughter Olive would mind singing for him a hymn he liked, Cardinal Newman's 'Lead Kindly Light'. Doke 'called Olive by signs and asked her to stand at the door and sing the hymn in a low tone'. She did so:

Lead, kindly Light, amid the encircling gloom,
    lead thou me on!
The night is dark, and I am far from home;
    lead thou me on!
Keep thou my feet; I do not ask to see
    the distant scene;
One step enough for me.

All his life Gandhi would remember 'the whole scene' and 'the melodious voice of little Olive' (S 153–7); and 'one step enough for me' would endure as a guiding principle for him.

During the ten days that Gandhi stayed with the Dokes, hundreds of Indians of different classes visited Gandhi, including 'the humble hawker, basket in hand with dirty clothes and dusty boots' and prominent merchants. Though denounced among whites as black-lovers, the Dokes did not withdraw from Gandhi. Parting from them was for Gandhi 'a great wrench' (S 159).

Early in March, Gandhi travelled to Natal and explained the settlement at a meeting of the Durban Indians. The lights suddenly went off and a Pathan with a big stick rushed at Gandhi, but friends had formed a cordon around him. The next day Gandhi went to Phoenix, where Kasturba (as she was increasingly called, meaning 'Kastur-mother') and the boys were, including Harilal.

Discussing with his father the attack by Mir Alam, Harilal asked what he should have done had he been present: should he have watched his father being assaulted, or run, or hit the attacker? Gandhi's answer was that unless Harilal saw a non-violent way of defending his father, he should have used force.[7]

Sarvodaya. In May 1908 the Gujarati *Indian Opinion* began publishing Gandhi's translation of Ruskin's *Unto This Last*. To his Gujarati version Gandhi gave the title *'Sarvodaya'*, or 'the welfare of all'. Dissatisfied with the goal of 'the greatest good of the greatest number', Gandhi said that like Ruskin he wanted 'the advancement of all ... not merely of the greatest number', and of minorities as well (*Indian Opinion*, 16 May 1908). Like satyagraha, the term 'sarvodaya' was destined to find wide usage, and not merely in South Africa or India.

Betrayal. By 9 May 1908, 8,700 Indians had applied for registration. A new law validated the voluntary registrations but there was no mention of TARA being repealed. Smuts, who was turning into South Africa's most powerful politician, pleaded helplessness in the face of white opinion. The crunch came with an official declaration that residents of Indian origin returning to the Transvaal after 9 May would have to register under TARA and not be allowed the voluntary route, and with the enforcement of another anti-Indian law, the Transvaal Immigrants Restriction Act (TIRA), which in effect made it illegal for any Indian newcomer, no matter how well educated, to enter the territory. *The Transvaal Leader*, edited by Cartwright, asked for TARA's repeal, as did Doke in a letter to the paper, and William Hosken also intervened, but Smuts refused to budge, even though both Cartwright and Hosken confirmed that Smuts had promised repeal.

Feeling personally betrayed, but in order also to remain in tune with his angry base, Gandhi for the first time permitted himself the use of racial language (*Indian Opinion*, Guj., 27 Jun. 1908):

> When Japan's brave heroes forced the Russians to bite the dust of the battlefield, the sun rose in the east. And now it shines on all the nations of Asia. The people of the East will never, never again submit to insult from insolent whites (8: 405).

Convinced that a mild response would only confirm Indian inferiority in the white mind, the Satyagraha Association declared that certificates of registration would be burnt if TARA's repeal was not assured by the government. Certificates from Indians willing to burn them were collected, and a meeting was convened at 4 p.m. on 16 August in the grounds of the Hamidia mosque in Johannesburg. A large iron cauldron resting on four legs was installed in a corner of the arena. In solidarity, the Natal Indian Congress sent a delegation. As Gandhi pointed out to Smuts, each person in this group belonged to 'a different faith or clan of India'[8] – representing all of India was always Gandhi's concern.

A volunteer on a bicycle brought a telegram from the government expressing inability to repeal TARA. When this was read out, the assembled thousands, now free to burn their certificates, broke out in applause. Gandhi said that any who wanted their certificates back could have them before the pile was burnt; there was no shame, and even a kind of courage, he added, in claiming them back. No one wanted them, however, and none stood up when Gandhi asked those opposed to the burning to rise.

A number of certificates were added to the more than 2,000 previously handed in. Mir Alam came forward and said he had done wrong in assaulting Gandhi, at which Gandhi took hold of Alam's hand and assured him that he harboured no resentment against him. Saturated with paraffin, the pile was set ablaze by Yusuf Mian, the chairman. Many reporters covered the bonfire scene, London's *Daily Mail* likening it to the Boston Tea Party. Gandhi said he did not find the comparison inapt.

Tactics. Non-violent defiance of law was now practised in three ways: English-speaking Natal-based Indians entered the Transvaal. Transvaal residents went to Natal and returned without their certificates of residency. And hawkers traded without displaying their licences.

A Parsi accountant in his twenties, Sorabji Shapurji Adajania, who was fluent in English, stepped into the Transvaal and asked for his English to be examined. This was not done but Adajania was ordered to leave. When he refused, he was sentenced, in a packed courtroom where Gandhi was his defence lawyer, to a month in prison with hard labour. Also breaking the law, Daud Mohamed, president of the Natal Indian Congress, and Parsi Rustomji, both prosperous traders in Durban, and a number of English-speaking Indians in Natal, including Harilal, entered the Transvaal and, in consequence, the colony's prisons.

In 'the last months of 1908 the campaign reached a peak of intensity'.[9] The number of prisoners steadily grew, their ranks including traders, workers, hawkers and young-sters. But bigger traders stayed away, deterred by fines, prison terms and the risk to their businesses. Gallant roles were played by the Hamidia Islamic Society and the Tamil Benefit Society, and by a number of humble hawkers.

Gandhi took offence when he heard that an Indian in prison had objected to sleeping next to someone belonging to the scavenger caste. 'This was humiliating,' Gandhi wrote, adding:

> Thanks to these hypocritical distinctions of high and low and to the fear of subse-quent caste tyranny, we have ... turned our back on truth and embraced falsehood ... I wish that Indians who join this movement also resort to satyagraha against their caste and their family and against evil wherever they find it (*Indian Opinion,* 30 Jan. 1909; 9: 290–1).

Twice more in prison. Increasingly curtailed from 1906, Gandhi's legal practice had virtually ceased with his arrest at the end of December 1907, though he continued to use his legal knowledge to assist the struggle. In October 1908 he re-entered the Transvaal after visiting Natal and found himself in jail in the border town of Volksrust with 75 other Indian satyagrahis, for whom he briefly became the cook 'as only I could adjudicate on the conflicting claims to the ration supplied' (S 201).

During his nine weeks in the Volksrust prison, Gandhi and the other Indian prisoners broke stones, dug holes for trees and stitched caps on a sewing machine. The prison cap worn by black convicts and stitched by Gandhi would become the model in India for

the white cap, pointed at the front and the back, that hundreds of thousands of freedom
activists would wear after 1920, except that this Indian cap, known also as the Gandhi
cap, would be made from cotton spun and woven by hand.

Because he was needed as a witness in a case in Johannesburg, a warder took Gandhi
from Volksrust jail to spend a week at the Fort prison in Johannesburg. For this exercise
Gandhi, carrying his luggage, walked to Volksrust station in convict clothes, 'marked all
over with the broad arrow'. He did likewise from the station in Johannesburg to the jail.
Doke and his children walked alongside Gandhi to the prison. Others, too, recognized
the man walking in convict clothes and carrying a load as the attorney they knew and
admired.

In the Fort prison, a night in a cell with hardened criminals – 'wild, murderous-
looking, vicious Bantu and Chinese prisoners', as Gandhi would describe them – proved
difficult for him. Two of the prisoners appeared to threaten Gandhi with sexual assault.
They 'exchanged obscene jokes, uncovering each other's genitals', and 'jeered and laughed'
at Gandhi.[10] To fight his fears Gandhi recalled verses from the *Gita*, and he remained
awake all night, alert to the possibility of assault. In this prison Gandhi was grabbed,
lifted and tossed out of an open lavatory he had just occupied by 'a strong, heavily-built,
fearful-looking Native' who wanted to use it. Gandhi saved himself from a nasty fall by
catching hold of a door frame.[11]

Kasturba. A wire arrived in Volksrust from Albert West in Phoenix: Kasturba was
seriously ill. West suggested that Gandhi should seek parole or release, if need be by
paying a fine, and join Kasturba. Soldiers did not leave the battlefront, Gandhi answered.
Fighting in the Boer War, Lord Roberts had not gone to his son's funeral. He too would
remain on his battlefield.

To West, Harilal, and others in Phoenix, he sent suggestions for Kasturba's treatment,
and in a tender yet hard letter to 'Beloved Kastur', he said that though his heart had
been 'cut', the satyagraha prevented him from joining her. If she kept her courage and
took the necessary nutrition, she would recover. But if to his bad luck the worst were to
happen, she should not think that dying in separation was different from dying in his
presence. 'I love you so dearly that even if you are dead you will be alive to me.' Gandhi
added what he had told her before, that he would not marry again if she died before him
(9 Nov. 1908, 9: 210).

Kasturba survived. Later (10 Jan.) she underwent surgery in Durban without chloroform. Gandhi, who was present, marvelled at her 'wonderful bravery' but after a few days
her condition worsened, and her doctor, a friend of the Gandhis, declared that without
beef tea she would not recover. Asked by Gandhi whether she would take beef tea (he on
his part had disliked the idea), Kasturba said she would prefer to die in his arms. The
doctor's response was to withdraw his responsibility for her. Gandhi took her by rickshaw

to Durban station and carried her in his arms to the train, which took them to Phoenix station, where, instructed by Gandhi, West had brought a hammock, a party of six, a bottle of hot milk and another of hot water. In Phoenix Kasturba slowly gained strength under 'Doctor' Gandhi's hydropathic treatment.

But from 25 February to 24 May 1909 Gandhi was again in jail. Arrested along with Polak, he was kept in Volksrust for a week and then transferred in handcuffs to Pretoria, where he was placed in a dark narrow cell next to cells holding men convicted for attempted murder, sodomy and bestiality. The government's idea was to break Gandhi's spirit, for he was also handcuffed and marched on foot to a court where his evidence was demanded. But his spirit seemed to emerge stronger from these tests.

Scrubbing floors or sewing together worn-out blankets week after week, sitting on the floor and bending over his work, Gandhi developed severe neuralgia and his lungs were affected. But he 'read voraciously, whenever he could, even standing below the dim bulb, snatching whatever light he could. In three months he read thirty books.'[12]

Equation with Harilal. Among the 3,000 or 4,000 Indians who were jailed in 1908 and 1909 was Harilal. After a week's imprisonment in July 1908, Harilal continued his satyagraha. He was jailed for a month in mid-August and again, in February 1909, for six months. This spell was followed almost immediately by another half-year term starting in November 1909. Harilal's cheerful personality and his readiness to endure prison terms earned him the sobriquet '*Chhote* (Little)' Gandhi and his father's admiration, but the lad was unhappy about gaps in his education and dissatisfied with Phoenix.

When Harilal complained, Gandhi replied: 'If you feel that Phoenix smells badly, it is your duty to act in such a way that it gives fragrance. If your fragrance mixes [with it], the bad smell will decrease.'[13] The clever answer did not, however, address Harilal's desire for personal growth and normal schooling.

The father on his part wanted the son to be more open. Shortly after the Mir Alam attack, hoping to obtain an account of Harilal's life, Gandhi supplied details of his own day. He was living, Gandhi wrote, with Kallenbach, riding on a bicycle to work and back, working in the office from 9 a.m. to 5.30 p.m., waking in the morning between 6.30 and 7, taking the Kuhne bath, taking milk in the morning, fruits at noon, and milk and cherries etc. in the evening. Kallenbach was his companion at every meal, the fruit lunch being eaten in the architect's office. And so on.

But the gambit failed: Harilal did not provide the information sought by the father. Later Gandhi wrote to him about the Pathans still angry with him: Harilal was not to worry and should keep any disturbing news from his unwell mother. Added Gandhi: 'What if they kill me?... Most of the teachers had such a fate.'[14]

When the son was in jail, Gandhi sent detailed notes to Gulab, Harilal's wife, who had given birth to a girl, Rami. Gulab was to act as the mistress of the Gandhi home in the Phoenix settlement, look after Harilal's young brothers Ramdas and Devadas (keeping their nails clean), continue to breast-feed Rami for some more time (and take a good diet after supplying the feed), get good books and good poetry to read from Kasturba, and get plenty of fresh air.

Her moral character was Gulab's finest ornament. Piercing the ears and the nose and thrusting something into them was not civilized, though a ring on the hand would stop gossip. However, she should follow his suggestions only if convinced.[15]

Softer side. On another occasion, writing in appreciation of Harilal's going to prison, Gandhi said to his son: 'If I only talk about your shortcomings or always give you advice, do not think that I am unaware of your virtues. But these do not need to be sung.' Then he expressed a father's longing: 'Write to me at least sometimes …'[16]

Once when Gandhi was courting imprisonment while Harilal, free at the time, faced a difficult decision – perhaps on whether or not to defy the law again – the father wrote: 'On leaving you alone, the heart of a father is on fire. But I will have to go for the struggle. I leave all [to] your discretion.'[17]

His widowed sister Raliat's only son Gokuldas, who had spent several years under Gandhi's roof, died in 1908 in India, shortly after marrying. He was only 20 and had been close to Harilal. Gandhi wrote to relatives in India that he wanted to cry.[18]

Manilal. He softened similarly when writing from Pretoria prison in 1909 to his son Manilal, who was 17: 'As I write I want to draw you to my chest, and my eyes are wet because I cannot.' But in the same letter he had also written quite sternly about Manilal's career, about which the son had asked anxious questions: 'This much is clear that you are not to work as a barrister or a doctor. We are poor and wish to remain poor … Have faith that since you are serving others, you will not suffer privation.'[19]

Another letter from jail to Manilal, written in English, tried to assure the son that character-building was not going to be his sole exercise. 'Instruction in letters' was also taking place: The letter ended with 'love to all and kisses to Ramdas, Devadas and Rami'.[20]

In this letter (already quoted in Chapter 1) Gandhi added: 'Amusement only continues during the age of innocence, i.e., up to twelve years … Let me tell you that when I was younger than you are, my keenest enjoyment was to nurse my father. Of amusement after I was twelve, I had little or none.'[21]

In the autumn of 1909, when he was in England, Gandhi was delighted to learn from Manilal in Phoenix of the assistance he was giving to Albert West, who was unwell: 'I was extremely glad,' the father wrote. 'I read the letter twice. I felt proud of you and thanked God that I had such a son.'[22]

Devadas. When he was 'eight or ten', the youngest son found himself without Harilal and Manilal (who apparently were both in prison) and required to cheer up other Phoenix children, all younger than him, whose elders too were in jail. 'All felt very lonely and depressed.' Devadas's father, who was in Phoenix at the time, seated the children on a table and sang to them poet Nazir's lines about birds who chirped at dawn and dusk.

Minutes later, we too were singing the verses with him and romping and hopping on the table, our arms akimbo in imitation of the birds in the song, all our depression and loneliness gone.[23]

But this sort of fun was rare.

Kallenbach. Gandhi's acquaintance with Hermann Kallenbach, an architect 'of strong feelings, wide sympathies and childlike simplicity,' as Gandhi would describe him (S 163), 'ripened into very close friendship' (A 293). Two years younger than Gandhi, Kallenbach had studied architecture in Germany and designed hotels and department stores in South Africa. But (as Martin Green says) he seemed keener on simpler, airier, sunnier structures, using local materials and consistent with the landscape.

These were Gandhi's preferences too. As we have seen, in Johannesburg Gandhi now stayed with Kallenbach (for a while in a tent, while the architect built a new home in the Mount View suburb). The German Jew played provider, protector and follower. Kallenbach would insist that whatever he spent for Gandhi's subsistence in his home was a tiny fraction of what he was saving thanks to changes in his lifestyle inspired by Gandhi.

For some weeks after the attack by Mir Alam, Kallenbach walked behind Gandhi with a revolver concealed from onlookers and also from Gandhi, which was put away after Gandhi discovered a bulge in Kallenbach's jacket and the reason for it, and said to his friend ironically, 'You have taken over from God the burden of protecting me. I can now relax.'[24]

Gandhi was in Pretoria jail in April 1909 when he heard that Kallenbach's mother had died. Sending his condolences to his friend, Gandhi added: 'Need I say that among those of whom I think daily you are one? I am not with you in body but I am always with you in spirit … ' (96: 6).

Gandhi & Smuts. While in jail in Pretoria Gandhi received a couple of books sent by Smuts, an indication of the unusual relationship between the jailed and the jailer. Each was skilled in law and politics, each had had problems with 'the English', each needed to carry his constituencies in any settlement with the other, and each seemed, by turns, to respect and suspect the other.

If Gandhi felt betrayed by Smuts, the latter charged Gandhi with springing new demands on him (S 188–92). Yet even while attacking each other at meetings and in the media, the two negotiated a number of times during the struggle, face-to-face or through intermediaries, and kept channels open.

When in May 1908 Yusuf Mian, the BIA chairman, and Thambi Naidoo were again assaulted by some Pathans, Gandhi wrote to Smuts regarding 'the most violent member of the Pathan community, who has remained behind the scenes but who has been an active agent in having the assaults committed'. The letter (21 May 1908) did not name the man, whose identity the government knew only too well, but Gandhi called him a 'fanatic', speculated that 'he possesses no documents', and added, 'I certainly think that this man should be deported' (8: 332). But the South African establishment was not anxious to expel enemies of Gandhi, and the man – we do not know his name – was not deported.[25]

Life in Phoenix. The settlement struggled for money but its flowers and vegetables made an impression. The tall, strong, and, to begin with, hot-tempered Maganlal proved as good at gardening (and in composing type for *Indian Opinion*) as he had been at running a shop in the Natal hinterland.

His young nephew Prabhudas (Chhaganlal's son) noticed that Maganlal also changed from a nephew-beating disciplinarian into a gentler person. 'I was truly a human demon,' Maganlal would say, 'and do not know how many wrongs I would have committed in my angry blindness had [Gandhi] not changed my wild nature'.[26]

Busy organizing the Transvaal satyagraha, Gandhi made only short visits to Phoenix. On these visits the settlement's families were in their best clothes and spirits. Gandhi would call on each family, find out about everyone, and offer suitable words. Laughter rang out as much as advice, and there were rare and all-too-brief occasions when Gandhi's boys and other children and youngsters ran and played with him.

When, on one such occasion in a Phoenix grove, six-year-old Prabhudas, calling for Gandhi's third son, nine-year-old Ramdas, pronounced his name 'Laamdaash', Gandhi's response was to ask Prabhudas and all the boys present to shout 'hip, hip, hooray' as often and as loudly as they could. Including Prabhudas, all articulated the sounds, raising their voices until the ground shook. Next asked by Gandhi to say 'Hooray Ramdas,' Prabhudas managed to repeat the sounds correctly. Recalling the story in his *Jeevan Prabhat*, published after Gandhi's death, Prabhudas would remember that at the time of the incident he was fascinated by the gold gleaming from two of Gandhi's teeth and by Gandhi's airy shirt.

After the Indians started courting imprisonment, Phoenix was used for housing the dependents of the ones arrested, each Phoenix family taking in as many as they could. Gandhi personally persuaded the women in each family to accept the newcomers. Taking Muslim or Christian children into their homes was a difficult decision for the families of Phoenix's orthodox Hindus. Though they accepted Ibrahim, a Muslim boy, Chhaganlal and his wife Kashi would purify over a fire the utensils in which food for Muslims had been cooked, their son would later write.

For newcomers of different faiths and ages, classes were started in Phoenix, taught by those producing *Indian Opinion*. The presence of the newcomers underscored the need for multi-faith prayers and prayer songs, which became a permanent feature from 1908–09.

Hearing the bhajan or prayer song, 'Dear to me is Rama's name,' Parsi Rustomji 'exclaimed joyously, "Say Hormazd instead Rama."' 'The 'suggestion was readily taken up'. Husain Daud, who often stayed at Phoenix and 'enthusiastically joined' the prayers, taught others to sing a Muslim devotional, *Hai Bahare-e-bagh* ('Fleeting is the bloom of this world's garden'); and Joseph Royappen's suggestion that 'Christiana' should at times substitute 'Vaishnava' in Narsinh Mehta's oft-sung *Vaishnava Jana* was 'accepted with alacrity'.[27]

Gandhi probably first heard *Vaishnava Jana* in his boyhood. Perhaps it was sung to his ailing father. In any case, the opening line of this song by the Kathiawar-born 15th-century poet had become, and would remain, his favourite religious and social truth:

He alone can be called a Vaishnava [devotee of God] who knows the Other's pain.

Changes in Gandhi's lifestyle were reflected in Phoenix. Spicy and tasty snacks and meals, which everyone including Gandhi enjoyed, gave way to simpler non-spiced food which was increasingly eaten in Indian style by the Indian settlers, with fingers rather than with cutlery, and on Sundays in the open air in one of the choice spots that Phoenix offered.

To live like the poor and yet be efficient and scientific in the kitchen, on the farm and in the press was accepted as the goal. 'Through Phoenix we can find our soul and serve India,' Gandhi wrote to Manilal in 1909.[28]

Africans and Indians. Though located in the heart of the Zulu country, the settlement did not interact much with the surrounding population. And though Gandhi would in all spend about 18 years in South Africa, and write of that period in two books, he would relate few conversations with Africans and offer only brief descriptions (S 7–12) of their appearance, homes, languages, food and lifestyle. On occasion a few Zulus joined the multi-faith prayer sessions at Phoenix, and, as Albert West would recall, Zulu passers-by 'frequently call[ed] for a drink from our water-tank'.[29]

Nonetheless, as Prabhudas would remember, Kasturba and the wives of Chhaganlal and Maganlal at times spoke in low tones about possible Zulu attacks on Phoenix.[30] They were influenced by stories passed on by indentured Indians working in white-owned plantations about their assegai-wielding Zulu warders. The fears were baseless. The Zulus seemed to respect Phoenix and Gandhi. One of their leaders, John Dube, running his Ohlange Institute only a couple of miles from the Phoenix settlement, was friendly to Gandhi. The two had met in 1905, and in *Indian Opinion* Gandhi had written (2 Sep.

1905) of Dube, who would become the first president of the African National Congress, as an African 'of whom one should know'.

A few months later Gandhi praised the efforts of Tengo Jabavu (the founder of *Native Opinion*) to establish a college for Africans, writing of 'an awakening people' and of 'the great Native races of South Africa' and adding that 'British Indians in South Africa have much to learn from [Jabavu's] example'.[31]

Yet Gandhi himself was often biased and ignorant in respect of Africans. In 1894, shortly after arriving in South Africa, he had objected to attempts to drag Indians down to the level of 'a raw Kaffir', employing the pejorative expression for an African that many, including Africans, used at the time (1: 410). In a petition in 1899 he said (2: 270) that Indians 'were infinitely superior to Africans', and in 1902 he wrote of Zulus as a 'fine' but 'lazy' body of people (2: 464).

True, he had also written – on 25 October 1894, in a letter to *The Times of Natal* – that 'the Indians do not regret that capable Natives can exercise the franchise. They would regret if it were otherwise' (1: 410). But his political goal was dignity for South Africa's Indians, not justice for the country's Africans, though he acknowledged that 'children of the soil' could eventually claim full political rights, something he did not demand for the Indians, who were 'settlers' (*Indian Opinion* [Guj.], 24 Mar. 1906, 5: 135).[32]

Gandhi was at his most derogatory when he wrote in *Indian Opinion* (7 Mar. 1908) of African prison-mates convicted for crime who had appeared to threaten him: 'Many of the Native prisoners are only one degree removed from the animal and often created rows and fought among themselves in their cells' (8: 183).

Two months later, however, in a rare articulation, Gandhi offered a vision for all the races of South Africa. In a speech on 18 May 1908 at the YMCA in Johannesburg, he said:

[I]n studying the Indian question, I have endeavoured to study the question as it affects the Africans and the Chinese. It seems to me that both the Africans and the Asiatics have advanced the Empire as a whole; we can hardly think of South Africa without the African races ... They (the African races) are still in the history of the world's learners. Able-bodied and intelligent men as they are, they cannot but be an asset to the Empire ...

If we look into the future, is it not a heritage we have to leave to posterity, that all the different races commingle and produce a civilisation that perhaps the world has not yet seen? (8: 323)

Gandhi's understanding of Africans was growing, and after leaving South Africa for good he would recall times when, evidently, he held private talks with African leaders.[33] But these talks did not feature at the time in *Indian Opinion* or in his public utterances, and we do not know what was discussed. Any revelation of Indian-African meetings while he was in South Africa would have triggered white hysteria and demands for the expulsion of Indians.

At forty. We should understand what Gandhi had taken on as he neared his 40th birthday. He was commanding, on behalf of a small and not always united minority, a non-violent battle, making sure that it remained non-violent, defending satyagrahis in law courts and taking care of their dependents. He was conducting *Indian Opinion* week by week, supervising life in the Phoenix settlement, cultivating his links with friendly whites in South Africa, keeping sympathizers in India and England informed, and observing the Indian scene, which he hoped before long to influence.

He was writing numerous thoughtful letters every day and conducting experiments in diet and health. Finally, this now celibate 'father' of an expanding family was striving to retain the loyalty of his biological sons and others in his large family. Many in this family desired a less demanding, less risky and more normal life, even while admitting that their 'father', whom they loved despite the sudden changes he introduced from time to time, had involved them in a great enterprise for the soul and for India.

He seemed remarkable to more than his Phoenix followers. In 1908–9 Doke worked on a short biography, published first in November 1909, for which Gandhi described his Kathiawar background, his youth, including the London phase, and some of his South African experiences. And though the idea did not take off, the Bengal Provincial Congress Committee proposed in July 1909 that Gandhi be considered for the presidency of the Indian National Congress.

Deportations. The struggle in South Africa became harder once the government started deporting satyagrahis to India. Earlier deportations across the Transvaal border into Natal, the Orange Free State or Portuguese East Africa had not caused the same upheaval – deportees could return across the border, even if it meant going back to prison. Being sent to India was another matter for men who had families and property in the Transvaal.

Most deportees were ex-indentured men bound for south India with few relatives there. Gandhi had scant resources to assist them at the Madras end, but obtained the help of G A Natesan, whom he had met on his visits there. At Gandhi's instance, a young associate in the satyagraha, P K Naidoo, escorted the first batch of deportees. 'See first to their comforts and then to your own,' Gandhi instructed Naidoo (S 204). As a result of the deportations, 'many more fell away, and only the real fighters remained' (S 205). At one point Gandhi wondered whether he would be deported himself. 'Where they will deport me to, I cannot say,' he wrote to Harilal.[34] But deporting him to India was not really on the cards. The prestige around Gandhi ruled it out.

Yet now the struggle was no longer being 'joined by any highly educated men', except for the indefatigable Adajania, who was willing to be arrested any number of times (S 206). Dissuaded by the stakes, most big traders too kept themselves at a distance. Yusuf Mian in fact resigned as head of the TBIA and of the Satyagraha committee. He was replaced by Ahmad Cachalia who liquidated his business in order to free himself for the struggle. Another trader, Ebrahim Aswat, did likewise, but most merchants were not ready for such a bold step. The ex-indentured comprised the satyagraha's backbone. Since they were either Hindu or Christian, and the traders mostly Muslim, a Hindu-Muslim rift was a strong possibility at this juncture, but Gandhi, supported ably by Cachalia, took energetic steps to prevent it.

In July 1909, an 18-year-old prisoner from an ex-indentured family, Swami Nagappan, who had been made to work and sleep in a road-building camp at the height of winter, died of double pneumonia. Nagappan thought of the struggle till his last breath, his companions said (S 205).

Mission to England

Though martyrdom was hardly a widespread wish, Indians ready to give in to the government failed completely when they made a bid to oust Gandhi and his colleagues from the TBIA leadership. They also failed in their attempt to exclude Gandhi from a TBIA delegation sent to England at the end of June 1909.

Making an effort in England at this point was unavoidable: leaders of South Africa's whites were visiting England to secure a merger of all four colonies – the Cape, Natal, the Transvaal and Orange Free State – into a Union of South Africa. London's intervention in defence of Indian rights had to be sought before the merger; a united dominion would be stronger vis-à-vis London.

In June 1909, accordingly, the TBIA decided to send Gandhi, Ahmad Cachalia, Haji Habib and V A Chettiar to England, and another delegation of four, including Henry Polak, to India to mobilize opinion there. Cachalia and some others chosen were, however, arrested before they could leave. In the end Gandhi (who was travelling out of a sense of duty, not hope) and Habib went to England; and Polak, alone, to India. The Natal Indian Congress (NIC) too sent a delegation to England.

The *Kenilworth Castle* carrying Gandhi and Habib landed in Southampton on 10 July. The two stayed in England for over four months. Though he again worked extremely hard ('there was hardly a journalist or member of either House whom it was possible to meet whom we did not meet'), the mission failed (S 209).

There were several reasons. Firstly, British politicians were preoccupied with a budget crisis and summer holidays. Until Gandhi told him, Morley, the Secretary of State for

India, had not even known that Botha and Smuts were in London to finalize the South African union and dominion.

Secondly, while Dadabhai Naoroji was no longer in London to help (he was back in India), the two who were assisting Gandhi, Lord Ampthill, the president of SABIC, and Sir Muncherjee Bhownugree, did not see eye to eye.

Thirdly, the image of India and Indians had taken a beating following the murder, eight days before Gandhi landed in England, of Curzon Wyllie, political aide to Morley and a man Gandhi had met three years earlier. Wyllie was shot by a young Indian, Madanlal Dhingra, at a reception hosted by the National Indian Association in a South Kensington hall. Some Englishmen even imagined a link between extremist violence and satyagraha.

The main reason, however, was that the whites controlling the rich resources of South Africa were more important to London than the Indians of South Africa. Though Gandhi tried all he could, and though Ampthill secured the goodwill of other influential Englishmen for Gandhi, including Lord Curzon (Viceroy of India from 1899 to 1905), British ministers were reluctant to press Smuts and Botha.

For much of his time in England, heeding advice Ampthill had given, Gandhi lobbied privately. To be able to receive callers, he took a suite with a sitting room in the Westminster Palace Hotel. In the end, however, Ampthill informed Gandhi and Habib that Botha – influenced by the views of his white supporters – was opposed to repealing TARA, amending TIRA or letting even six educated Indians a year migrate to the Transvaal. Smuts was of the same view. But they were prepared to offer minor practical concessions.

To remove the colour bar from South Africa's laws, Gandhi was willing to restrict new Indian immigration to a mere six a year and to accept stringent educational tests for them, but Botha and Smuts, who were urging whites in Britain and Europe to move to South Africa, refused to modify the total ban on new Indians. The colour bar would stay. Translated by Gandhi, Habib told Ampthill that he would accept the terms and the tiny concessions. The Indians had suffered enough. He spoke, Habib added, for a majority of the Transvaal's Indians and for those holding the major portion of Indian wealth. Agreeing that he now represented a minority of the Transvaal Indians, Gandhi asked Ampthill to inform Botha that the satyagrahis would nonetheless continue to struggle; they wanted to honour their pledges and hoped that their self-inflicted suffering would soften General Botha's heart (S 208–10).

In October and November, after it was clear that he was getting nowhere with the British or the South African leadership, Gandhi reached out to the British public and press. This was done with the consent of Ampthill, who wrote a foreword for Doke's biography of Gandhi, which was published in England.

Many individual Britons responded to Gandhi and his accounts of the Transvaal satyagraha. At a meeting before the Emerson Club (8 October), he said that South Africa's 'grim prisons' were the gateways to the 'garden of God' where the 'flowers of self-restraint and gentleness' grew 'beneath the feet of those who accept but refuse to impose suffering' (10: 159). But he announced his direct opposition to the route of violence for national or racial rights. He had political assassinations too in mind when he said to the Emerson Club that war

> demoralizes those who are trained for it. It brutalizes men of naturally gentle character. It outrages every beautiful canon of morality. Its path of glory is foul with the passions of lust, and red with the blood of murder. This is not the pathway to our goal.

Meeting Britain's suffragette leaders again, Gandhi warmly described their struggle in *Indian Opinion* but added that the women's cause suffered when its supporters turned to violence.

Indian school of violence

The killing of Wyllie, which had been accompanied by the death of Cowasji Lalkaka, a Parsi doctor who tried to interpose himself between the victim and the assassin, Madanlal Dhingra, had highlighted the question of violence.

Many Indians studying in England seemed to support Dhingra's act. After writing in the *Indian Sociologist* that patriotic homicide was not murder, Krishnavarma, the editor, had slipped away to France. However, a cook at India House and other eyewitnesses gave evidence, and Dhingra was hanged on 17 August. Shocked by the killing and by its defence, Gandhi commented in the 14 August issue of *Indian Opinion:*

> It is being said in defence of Sir Curzon Wyllie's assassination that ... just as the British would kill every German if Germany invaded Britain, so too it is the right of any Indian to kill any Englishman ... The analogy ... is fallacious. If the Germans were to invade Britain, the British would kill only the invaders. They would not kill every German whom they met ... They would not kill an unsuspecting German, or Germans who are guests.

As Gandhi saw it, those who incited him were guiltier than Dhingra, who may have been courageous in inviting death, but the courage was the 'result of intoxication'. He added:

Even should the British leave in consequence of such murderous acts, who will rule in their place? Is the Englishman bad because he is an Englishman? Is it that everyone with an Indian skin is good? If that is so, there should be [no] angry protest against oppression by Indian princes. India can gain nothing from the rule of murderers – no matter whether they are black or white. Under such a rule, India will be utterly ruined and laid waste.

Much later it would be revealed that Savarkar, whom Gandhi had met three years earlier in London, had encouraged Dhingra's act and written the defence found on Dhingra's person. In 1909, however, Savarkar was concealing his involvement. On 24 October, he, Gandhi and Habib spoke together at a subscription dinner arranged by militant Indian students.

Keen to win the students to satyagraha and non-violence, Gandhi 'accepted unhesitatingly' their invitation to preside at the dinner.[35] In fact he arrived hours before the dinner, helped cook it, and laid the tables 'with gusto' before his identity was discovered. At least three of those at the dinner, V V S Aiyar, Asaf Ali and T S S Rajan, would later support Gandhi's movements in India. Recalling the occasion in the late 1940s, Asaf Ali would say that the October 1909 gathering was more interested in Savarkar than in Gandhi, and that Gandhi's words were 'calm, unemotional and devoid of rhetoric', while Rajan would claim that he 'found greatness in the Mahatma before the world knew him'.[36]

Before long, Savarkar would be captured by the British and sent to the Andaman Islands for a long imprisonment. The hatred he would later reveal for Gandhi was probably engendered in 1909, when Gandhi called those inciting Wyllie's murder guiltier than Dhingra.

The Gandhi of 1909 knew the reality of armed conflict better than London's young Indians. He had seen the Boer and Zulu wars at close quarters, studied the 1857 Rebellion with care, and taken at least three violent attacks on his own person (from whites in Durban, Indians in Johannesburg, and African prison-mates). But after his encounter with the young men fascinated by the Wyllie murder, who reminded him of Mir Alam's argumentations, he felt he had to forge a strategy for answering, as he put it, 'the Indian school of violence and its prototype in South Africa'.[37]

'Hind Swaraj'

He found clues for such a strategy in three texts he read while in England: a *Letter to a Hindoo* that Tolstoy had recently written, a comment in the *Illustrated London News* of September 1909 by G K Chesterton, and the socialist activist and poet Edward Carpenter's *Civilization: Its Cause and Cure*, which Gandhi read on 7 September.

Tolstoy's long *Letter* of 413 manuscript pages was written in response to a request for an article by Taraknath Das, then editing in Vancouver, Canada, an 'insurrectionary monthly'[38] called *Free Hindustan*. The monthly's masthead quoted the philosopher Herbert Spencer, as did Krishnavarma's *Indian Sociologist*. Though written in 1908, Tolstoy's *Letter* had for some reason not yet been published. Gandhi's old friend Pranjivan Mehta (who characteristically came to England while Gandhi was there) had found a typed copy being passed around in Indian circles in Europe and given it to Gandhi.

While intrigued by what Tolstoy had written, Mehta too was tempted, at this point, by the idea of bombs for independence, and discussed the question at some length with Gandhi, who found Tolstoy's epistle irresistible. Arguing that Indians should resist England non-violently and reject her civilization, the Russian's *Letter* added:

A commercial company enslaved a nation comprising 200 million people! ... What does it mean that 30,000 people, not athletes but rather weak and ill-looking, have enslaved 200 millions of vigorous, clever, strong, freedom-loving people? Do not the figures make it clear that not the English but the Indians have enslaved themselves?

Sending Tolstoy the copy that had reached him, Gandhi asked the Russian for permission to publish it, which came by return of post. Twenty thousand copies of the *Letter* were then printed in England by Gandhi, with Mehta providing the money. Later recalling his talks with Mehta at this time, Gandhi would say: 'Although he loved me, he thought I was foolish and sentimental. But I did place my point of view before him. It appealed to his heart. His attitude changed.'[39]

From Carpenter, Gandhi received the notion of civilization as a disease, though a curable one; Gandhi would set out to be its doctor, at any rate for Indians and India. He had found Carpenter's book 'very illuminating', Gandhi wrote to Polak (8 Sep.; 10: 75). Also welcome to Gandhi were these lines by Chesterton:

When I see ... the views of Indian nationalists, I get bored and feel dubious about them. What they want is not very Indian and not very national ... Suppose an Indian said: 'I wish India had always been free from white men and all their works. Everything has its own faults and we prefer our own ... I prefer dying in battle to dying in [a Western] hospital ... If you (the British) do not like our way of living, we never asked you to. Go, and leave us with it.'

Supposing an Indian said that, I should call him an Indian nationalist. He would be an authentic Indian ... But the Indian nationalists whose works I have read go on saying: 'Give me a ballot box. Give me the judge's wig. I have a natural right to be Prime Minister. My soul is starved if I am excluded from the editorship of the *Daily*

Mail.' Even the most sympathetic person may say in reply: 'What you say is very fine, my good Indian, but it is we who invented these things.'

Chesterton added: 'The right of a people to express itself in action is a genuine right. Indians have a right to be and to live as Indians. But Herbert Spencer is not Indian; his philosophy is not Indian philosophy.'[40]

These (varied) thoughts from Tolstoy, Carpenter and Chesterton were right up Gandhi's street. In fact he had felt and expressed them himself. Within a year of his arrival in South Africa he had written pejoratively (in the *Natal Mercury*) of 'the dazzling and bright surface of modern civilization' (3 Dec. 1894; 1: 185). The following year he had referred (in the *Natal Advertiser*) to 'the utter inadequacy of materialism' and of 'a civilization [whose] greatest achievements are the invention of the most terrible weapons of destruction' (1 Feb. 1895; 1: 206). On 20 August 1903 he had written in *Indian Opinion* of 'the tinsel splendour of modern civilization' (3: 209). Five years later, in 1908, he referred to Western civilization as a recent phenomenon ('only a hundred years old, or, to be more precise, fifty' (8: 459); and he knew that modern civilization and its weaponry had made colonialism possible. Gunpowder and Western civilization had merged in history and also, unashamedly, in the discourse of empire-builders.[41]

Bolstered by Tolstoy, Carpenter and Chesterton, these old insights of his were assembled in 1909 into a sharply defined theory and strategy. The theory was that violence and a diseased Western (or modern) civilization went together, as did satyagraha and Indian civilization, which though corrupted was sound at its core. The theory would strengthen Indians in their fight against Western domination, and the satyagrahis vis-à-vis the 'Westernized' agendas of the men who had inspired Mir Alam in South Africa and Madanlal Dhingra in England.

The strategy was that he, as an authentic Indian, would ask India, in the name of her soul and her past, to reject the imported mix of violence and Western civilization. In its place India should pit soul force against brute force, for satyagraha was not only the right way; it was also the Indian way. When Gandhi found that the reasoning worked with Mehta, he said to himself, 'Let me write down the argument' (77: 357).

This was the genesis of *Hind Swaraj* ('Indian Self-Rule'), written in Gujarati by Gandhi between 13 and 22 November 1909 on the 'good, strong, stamped stationery' of the *Kildonan Castle* on which he was returning to South Africa.[42] Very little in the 30,000-word manuscript, divided into 20 short chapters, was scratched out or written over. When the right hand needed a rest, Gandhi wrote with his left hand (a recourse he would employ for the rest of his life).

The swift and seemingly irresistible flow of the text on to the ship's notepaper, and the confidence its words exhale, suggest a sense in the author of a thrilling and promising discovery. To Kallenbach he wrote that he had produced 'an original work', and in the foreword he said, 'I have written because I could not restrain myself.'[43] After finishing *Hind Swaraj*, Gandhi translated, while still aboard the *Kildonan Castle*, Tolstoy's *Letter to a Hindoo* into Gujarati.

The argument of *Hind Swaraj*, addressed, interestingly enough, to India rather than to the Indians of South Africa, may be summarized as follows: At one level, swaraj or self-rule must mean an individual's rule over himself or herself. At the political level, it means home rule or self-government. But if it is to satisfy, self-government must be grounded on the control that leaders and citizens exercise over themselves. Also, Hindus, Muslims and others all belong to the composite Indian nation, which is perfectly entitled to self-government. Rejecting Western/modern civilization and its inseparable component, brute force, Indians must embrace the simple life, swadeshi (what one's own country makes), and satyagraha. Only non-violence suits the genius of India; violence is futile, Western and destructive of India's future.

Anthony Parel points out that in *Hind Swaraj* Gandhi gives India a modern concept of dharma or religion – a strong force, he knows, in India. Clarifying that by dharma he means 'that religion which underlies all religions', he separates religion from its divisive role, e.g. in setting Hindus and Muslims against each other, and also from its conventional Indian roles (in rituals or for demonstrating social status). Instead he employs dharma (which he equates with ethics and also with true civilization) for citizenship, liberty and mutual assistance.[44] This, of course, was how Gandhi had invoked religion for the Transvaal satyagraha. *Hind Swaraj* formulated the practice into a theory.

While attacking modern or Western civilization, *Hind Swaraj* values contact with it and praises individual Westerners; it steers clear of isolationism and rejects hatred. In his preface to the English version, Gandhi writes that he has 'endeavoured humbly to follow Tolstoy, Ruskin, Thoreau, Emerson and other writers, besides the masters of Indian philosophy'. He names the Westerners, not the Indians, he refers to.[45]

Also, in extolling the simple life and asking satyagrahis to embrace poverty, Gandhi's goal is the end of Indian misery. It is for removing want in India that he wants satyagrahis to limit their wants. *Hind Swaraj* asks India's Westernized elite – lawyers, doctors and the wealthy – to acknowledge their distance from the people and simplify their lives. In 15 words, all of a single syllable, Gandhi writes:

Those in whose name we speak we do not know, and they do not know us.

The tract concludes by saying: 'I bear no enmity towards the English, but I do towards their civilisation ... I have endeavoured to explain [swaraj] as I understand it, and my conscience testifies that my life henceforth is dedicated to its attainment.' Here Gandhi announces his life's mission, which is to attain India's Swaraj through satyagraha and thereby present satyagraha to the world.

The book's ideas are presented via a dialogue between an 'Editor' and an unnamed 'Reader', the latter arguing along lines that Savarkar and London's militant students (and also Mehta) had employed. Thus it is through the mouth of a modern newspaper editor that Gandhi excoriates Western civilization and elevates the Indian.[46]

Published in December 1909 in two successive issues of *Indian Opinion*'s Gujarati edition, *Hind Swaraj* came out in book form in January 1910. After the Bombay government confiscated copies of the book in March 1910, *Indian Home Rule*, an English translation that Gandhi himself had already dictated (to Kallenbach, at the latter's request), was quickly produced. It appeared on 20 March 1910.

Tolstoy's *Letter*, with a preface by Gandhi, was also soon published in *Indian Opinion*, in both English and Gujarati. In the preface Gandhi calls Tolstoy 'one of the clearest thinkers in the Western world, one of the greatest writers, [and] one who, as a soldier, has known what violence is', and adds that India would 'cease to be nationalist India' if it yields to 'reproduction on that sacred soil of gun factories and hateful industrialism'.[47] Again, Gandhi amalgamates guns, industrialism and the West, and suggests the superiority of the alternative triad of satyagraha, the simple life and India.

Tolstoy, to whom Gandhi sent a copy of *Indian Home Rule*, wrote back (10 May 1910) that the question of passive resistance raised in the book was 'of the greatest importance not only for India but for the whole of humanity' (10: 511). On 7 September 1910, when Tolstoy was 'vividly feeling the nearness of death', he wrote again to Gandhi. In what would be the Russian's 'last long letter', Tolstoy, who 'had noted in his diary how close Gandhi's work was to his own', said that the satyagraha in the Transvaal supplied 'most weighty practical proof' of what the two believed. Added Tolstoy:

> [Y]our work in Transvaal, which seems to be far away from the centre of our world, is yet the most fundamental and the most important to us (11: 474).[48]

But Krishnavarma, in a sharp attack on *Hind Swaraj*, called Gandhi 'an admirer of Jesus Christ' who was trying to put into practice 'the extreme Christian theory of suffering'.[49] Gandhi's identification of satyagraha with India, and of violence with the West, had clearly gone home, and Krishnavarma counter-attacked by linking Gandhi with a supposedly 'Western' religion.

We can move forward in time and acknowledge that Gandhi's strategy did succeed, in South Africa and India. Satyagraha baffled and frequently outwitted the British, and enabled Indians fighting under Gandhi to feel that they held the moral high ground. During Gandhi's lifetime satyagraha also marginalized 'the Indian school of violence'.

Indians accepted Gandhi as the authentic Indian and satyagraha as the Indian method, with many also agreeing that pro-violence Indians were the West's imitators.

Yet *Hind Swaraj* was a warrior's manifesto, not a scholar's survey. Gandhi's weapon for influencing India, it was less than pure truth. Alloyed with strategy, it did not hold the scales evenly between the East and the West, and Gandhi's thesis reinforced an old self-righteous sense that India was wiser and more spiritual than the West. This was not Gandhi's belief – we have seen and will see again that he was only too aware of Indian greed and cruelties, and there were aspects of the modern West that he admired. But *Hind Swaraj*'s reader is left with unquestioned Indian superiority.

The reader also takes away a rejection of technology, for *Hind Swaraj* attacks materialism (or greed) and technology (called 'machinery' in the text) in the same breath, and with the same intensity. We know that Gandhi was not blind to the relief that technology gave to people. He did not hate new things, and he could hate old things if they were useless.

But in *Hind Swaraj* Gandhi eschewed nuance and subtlety and sought stark contrasts. Its sweeping style was dictated by corroborated conviction and a compelling political instinct. The unqualified denunciation of Western civilization was also connected to Gandhi's experience as an ignored leader from the East in the England of 1909. We may see *Hind Swaraj* as an assertion of Eastern identity in a world and an age dominated by the West, and Gandhi's assertion of himself before an India that could only petition or throw a bomb here and there.

When, at the end of 1909, Henry Polak also returned to South Africa (from India), Gandhi, along with associates, was at Port Durban to welcome him. As his ship neared the pier, Polak waved from the deck. Standing on the pier along with his son Prabhudas, Chhaganlal was waving back when a port employee brusquely asked him to move aside.

Chhaganlal moved back a step and continued to address Polak. 'Get out!' the white employee shouted. 'Didn't you hear me? Get out!' He was about to shove Chhaganlal away when Gandhi's voice, twice as loud, was heard. 'HE SHAN'T MOVE AN INCH,' said the voice, whereupon the employee was escorted outside by his colleagues.[50]

In India Polak had spoken to several audiences about events in the Transvaal, but a tribute that Gokhale paid to Gandhi at the end-December session of the Congress in Lahore was based not only on accounts that Polak might have supplied but also on Gokhale's direct experience in 1902–3:

It is one of the privileges of my life that I know Mr Gandhi personally, and I can tell you that a purer, nobler, a braver and a more exalted spirit has never moved on this earth … [He] is a man among men, a hero among heroes, a patriot among patriots, and we may well say that in him Indian humanity at the present time has really reached its high-water mark.[51]

It was probably at this time (late 1909) that an incident mentioned by Gandhi in *Satyagraha* occurred. At a meeting in Lahore in support of the satyagrahis of South Africa, Gokhale saw (and obviously reported at some point to Gandhi) that Charles Freer Andrews (1871–1940), an Anglican priest sympathetic to Indian hopes, 'gave in their interest all the money in his possession' (S 291).

Shortly after the Great March, with Hermann Kallenbach (left) *and Sonja Schlesin – 1913*

6

A Great March

South Africa, 1909–14

The trip to London had dashed the last hopes of imperial intervention, and South Africa's Indians seemed to have lost their ardour for satyagraha. But Gandhi expected its revival and would wait for it.

Meanwhile he faced a huge task: taking care of the families of jailed or deported satyagrahis, and of satyagrahis who had lost their jobs. Early in 1910, Gandhi's burdens were lightened somewhat by a gift of 25,000 rupees from the industrialist Ratan Tata in Bombay and other contributions from India, including what C F Andrews had given. But what really rescued him was Kallenbach's offer of 1,100 acres of land he had acquired in Lawley, a mile from Lawley station and 21 miles from Johannesburg. Here Indian satyagrahis of all religious and social backgrounds, and their families, could live together and support one another.

He and Gandhi named the site Tolstoy Farm shortly before the Russian died in November 1910. Gandhi's obituary in *Indian Opinion,* bearing the heading, 'The Late Lamented Tolstoy the Great', said (26 Nov. 1910):

> Tolstoy is known to the entire world; but not as a soldier, though once he was reputed to be an expert soldier; not as a great writer, though indeed he enjoys a great reputation as a writer; nor as a nobleman, though he owned immense wealth. It was as a good man that the world knew him ... It is no small encouragement to us that we have the blessings of a great man like Tolstoy in our task (11: 176–7).

However, a year earlier Gandhi had also said, 'No one should assume that I accept all the ideas of Tolstoy' (*Indian Opinion,* 25 Dec. 1909; 10: 242). Seeking a better world from an

Indian platform, he did not agree with Tolstoy's sweeping denunciation of nationalism; and he agreed with only some of the Russian's criticisms of Hinduism. Yet the two were completely at one in their understanding of how India was lost to the British and in asking for a non-violent rejection of British rule.

Kallenbach. To name the new farm after Tolstoy was natural for him and for Kallenbach too, who had informed Tolstoy (via Gandhi) that he recognized himself in one of Tolstoy's novels, *A Confession,* a comment that 'greatly interested' the Russian.

Another novel, *David Copperfield,* featured in conversations between Gandhi and Kallenbach. Reading Dickens's story 'with avidity' after Kallenbach had recommended it to him, Gandhi asked Kallenbach to reflect on the character of the boy David's hero, Steerforth, who seduces and ruins the village beauty, Emily. Martin Green connects this to Gandhi's recollection of his boyhood admiration of Mehtab, in some ways a Steerforth-like figure, and points out that while David failed to improve Steerforth, and Mohan seemed to fail likewise with Mehtab, Gandhi succeeded with another dazzling figure, Kallenbach. In his friendship with Kallenbach, preserved in a remarkable correspondence, Gandhi set aside his caution against intimate or exclusive relationships. Offering Kallenbach a relationship that was warm, intimate, frank and mentoring, he received an exceptional friendship in return.

In June 1909 Gandhi wrote to Kallenbach that he did not understand the latter's 'extraordinary love' for him. On 30 August 1909, referring to Kallenbach's unfinished studies, Gandhi wrote: 'You remind me of friendships of bygone years of which one reads in histories and novels ... But is that almost superhuman love to exhaust itself in delicate attentions to me and mine, or will it not compel you to the study you know you need so badly to complete?'

Writing again in September 1909, Gandhi informs Kallenbach that his is the only photograph on the mantlepiece in the hotel room that Gandhi has taken in London, and that he is unable to dismiss Kallenbach from his thoughts. Two years later, when Kallenbach went to England, he drew up 'Articles of Agreement' with Gandhi in which he promised that he would neither marry nor look lustfully upon a woman. The return, the two agreed, would be 'more love and yet more love' between them – 'such love as, they hope, the world has not yet seen'.

Gandhi would write that he found partings from Kallenbach difficult yet inevitable, that Kallenbach should 'remember the meditation of the Yom Kippur' and 'constantly check [him]self'. Also, Kallenbach should watch Gandhi 'not with a friendly eye but with a highly critical and fault-finding eye'. It was foolish, Gandhi urged, to turn him into an idol. Gandhi would often not satisfy such expectations, and the result would be a hurt 'as if a dagger had gone through you'. 'Let the idol be broken. The residue will be a purer thing.'

Why a Kathiawari Bania and a German Jew should find each other in Johannesburg, and receive from the other what each needed, is one of the marvels of our story.

Tolstoy Farm. Trees on Tolstoy Farm provided an abundance of oranges, apricots and plums. There was a small house where five or six could live, and a spring about 500 yards from the house. Gandhi envisioned 'a sort of cooperative commonwealth' rising on the property, families of satyagrahis 'belonging to various (Indian) provinces and professing divers faiths' and training 'to live a new and simple life in harmony with one another' (S 214).

Kallenbach decided to live and teach on the farm he had made available. He who (in Gandhi's words) 'had been brought up in the lap of luxury and had never known what privation was', who 'had had his fill of all the pleasures of life' and 'secure[d] for his comfort everything that money could buy', was now happy 'to live, move and have his being on Tolstoy Farm' (S 223).

With 'mastery and exactitude' (Gandhi's words again), Kallenbach oversaw the construction of a residence for men, another for women, a house for himself, a school-house, and a workshop for carpentry and shoemaking. Aided by a European mason and Gujarati carpenters, the satyagrahis and their families managed the construction. For about two months, until the buildings were raised, everybody lived in tents. Joseph Royappen, 'a barrister free from barrister's pride', and Pragji Khandubhai Desai, who had not known discomfort hitherto, brought loads from the station and moved water from the spring. Gandhi felt that 'the weak became strong on Tolstoy Farm and labour proved to be a tonic for all' (S 217).

'Having founded a sort of village we needed all manner of things large and small from benches to boxes, and we made them all ourselves,' Gandhi would recall (S 219–20). Including children, the community was 75-strong. Its Muslims and Christians readily agreed, when Gandhi approached them, to an entirely vegetarian kitchen, even though Gandhi had been prepared to allow meat (including beef) on the Farm. But meat would have called for two separate kitchens and disrupted the Farm's budget.

To Maganlal, who was looking after Phoenix, where Kasturba and her sons continued to live, Gandhi wrote in August 1911:

My way of life has completely changed here. The whole day is spent in digging the land and other manual labour instead of in writing and explaining things to people. I prefer this work ... I regard the Kaffirs, with whom I constantly work these days, as superior to us. What they do in their ignorance we have to do knowingly. In outward appearance we should look just like the Kaffirs (11: 107).

This perhaps was the last time that he employed this pejorative word. While his using it and his assumption of African 'ignorance' reveal limitations in the South African Gandhi, this picture of Gandhi digging the Transvaal earth alongside Africans and believing in a superiority conferred by bread-labour is worth noting.

Kallenbach learnt to make sandals at the Trappist monastery at Marian Hill and taught it to Gandhi, who then passed it on to several others. The men on the Farm all wore 'labourers' dress but in the European style': workingmen's trousers and shirts imitated from prisoners' uniforms and tailored by the Farm ladies (S 224). The aim was to make the Farm 'a busy hive of industry' and 'the families self-supporting' and thus be ready to do 'battle with the Transvaal government' (S 219).

Farm-baked bread and 'coffee' made from wheat was the breakfast at six in the morning; rice, dal and vegetables constituted lunch at eleven; the evening meal at 5.30 p.m. was either wheat-pap and milk or bread and 'coffee'. The food was eaten from prison-style bowls with Farm-made wooden spoons. Multi-faith prayers, including prayer songs in Tamil, Telugu, Gujarati and Hindi, were held after the evening meal.

Enforcing the principle that 'the man who does not cover his waste deserves a heavy penalty even if he lives in a forest', Gandhi would claim that 'one could not find refuse or dirt anywhere on the Farm'. All waste water was used around trees, vegetable refuse and leavings of food employed as manure, and night-soil buried in pits. There were no flies (S 218–20).

Visits by train to Johannesburg on behalf of 'our little commonwealth' could only be done in third class, and non-business trips only on foot. Nothing could be spent on food or drink in the big city, but walkers could carry 'home-baked bread from which the bran was not removed' as well as groundnut butter and marmalade made on the Farm. On occasion people on the Farm, including Gandhi and Kallenbach, walked the 21 miles to Johannesburg and 21 miles back in the same day, starting the journey at 2.30 a.m. and reaching the city in six or seven hours. (Four hours and eighteen minutes was the best time recorded.) Gandhi would later claim that 'the youngsters thoroughly enjoyed the work on the Farm and the errands to the city' (S 218), and also that 'one day I walked fifty-five miles' (S 235).

However, schooling for the Farm's youngsters was again deficient. By the time (in the afternoon) that 'school' began, the teachers – Kallenbach, Gandhi and a couple of others – as well as their pupils were apt to be 'thoroughly exhausted by our morning labour' and compelled to doze (S 220). Moreover, on some days one of the teachers had to be in Johannesburg. The need to instruct in three languages (Gujarati, Tamil and Telugu) and to teach four religions (Hinduism, Islam, Zoroastrianism and Christianity) constituted additional challenges (S 220).

Yet there were gains. During Ramadan Hindu youngsters fasted alongside their Muslim farm-mates. Saved 'from the infection of intolerance', the children 'learnt to

With C F Andrews (left) *and W W Pearson in South Africa – 1914*

view one another's religions and customs with a large-hearted charity' and 'imbibed the lessons of mutual service, courtesy and industry' (S 221).

Boys and girls mixed freely. Gandhi 'fully explained the duty of self-restraint' but permitted children of both sexes to bathe at the spring at the same time, in his presence. In another bold experiment, all the youngsters slept together around Gandhi in an open verandah, with little more than three feet separating any two beds. The parents allowed this, and Gandhi felt that 'God safeguarded the honour of these boys and girls' (S 223).

One day, however, a young man 'made fun of two girls'. Gandhi 'trembled' at the news and admonished the culprit and his mates but also sought 'some sign' on the girls 'as a warning to every young man' and 'as a lesson to every girl that no one dare assail their purity'. After cogitating through a sleepless night, Gandhi concluded that the girls should have their 'fine long hair' cut off. In the morning he persuaded the two girls as well as the Farm's older women to agree. He would write 12 years later that the girls' hair was cut off by 'the very hand that is narrating this incident' (S 224). Both girls, Gandhi would write, were 'noble'. Yet though Gandhi claimed he was warning the boys and shielding the girls, it certainly looked as if the *girls* were being punished – we do not know if any punishment beyond chastisement was given to the boys. The incident stayed, and (going by the future remark about this 'very hand') perhaps preyed, on Gandhi's mind.

Confidence. Snakes were a continuing problem on the Farm, but before long the versatile Kallenbach read up on them, taught the community that only a few snakes were poisonous, and tamed a cobra. However, when a snake was found in Kallenbach's bedroom, Gandhi ordered it to be killed.

Gandhi's faith in satyagraha and the simple life, and its corollary of nature cures, had reached a new height, and 'Doctor' Gandhi's reputation grew after he cured an ex-indentured north Indian of asthma (by getting him to diet, quit tobacco and take sun baths) and the two-year-old son of the Lawley stationmaster of suspected typhoid (by regulating the child's diet and applying a cold mud poultice to the abdomen). Later, he would claim: 'I made many such experiments on the Farm and do not remember to have failed in even a single case' (S 234). The Lawley stationmaster became an ally and once even held up a train in order to allow two of the satyagrahis to catch it. At least in Lawley, the satyagrahis had become part of South Africa's life and landscape.

As Green puts it, at Tolstoy Farm Gandhi enjoyed the Robinson Crusoe pleasures, and simplicity exalted his spirit. 'My faith and courage were at their highest on Tolstoy Farm,' Gandhi would recall in the mid-1920s (S 222). Also, he seemed completely free from any regret regarding his 1906 chastity vow.

Harilal leaves

Gandhi's eldest son was a star at courting imprisonment. During the two-and-a-half years between 28 July 1908, when (at the age of 20) he was jailed as a satyagrahi for the first time, and 9 January 1911, when he emerged from his sixth and last imprisonment, Harilal was free in all for only ten months. In 1910, 18-year-old Manilal also won a series of brief prison terms plus a three-month sentence for hawking without a licence.

Gandhi praised Harilal for his satyagraha and referred to it with pride in a letter to Tolstoy. Yet the father-son relationship was rupturing. In the middle of 1910 Harilal sent his wife and two-year-old daughter Rami to India; a year later, shortly after the birth in India of Kanti, Rami's brother, Harilal departed, without telling his father.

He and Gandhi were in Johannesburg at the time, and Kasturba in Phoenix. A letter he left behind reproached Gandhi for being a deficient father and announced that Harilal was breaking all family ties; yet the 23-year-old son had taken a photo of his father with him. Gandhi searched all of Johannesburg for his boy and learnt (from Joseph Royappen[1]) that he had slipped away to Delagoa Bay in the Portuguese colony of Mozambique, *en route* to India.

Kallenbach rushed to Delagoa Bay, found Harilal, and brought him back to Johannesburg. Father and son talked from sundown to sunrise. During the long night Harilal charged that the father never praised his sons, favoured Maganlal and Chhaganlal, was hard-hearted towards his boys and their mother, and unconcerned about his sons' future. Harilal said he would go to India and make his own life. The tension had been brought to a head by Harilal's harsh jail terms. 'Six months was a barbarous punishment'[2] in South Africa at this time, and Harilal received it twice. But the father-son clash would have occurred even without the prison sentences.

Gandhi was absorbed in fashioning a new India, Harilal in finding a career. To Gandhi Harilal was one ward among many, and a difficult one at that. Harilal saw himself as his father's eldest son, entitled to a special relationship. Gandhi wanted his family to lose themselves in a new community of all races and classes; Harilal longed to find himself, and he disliked the community's rules.

To ten-year-old Devadas the eldest brother was a 'handsome' prison-going hero who 'parted his hair in the middle with beautiful curls on the forehead' and carried 'on his shoulder a huge leather bag' while 'engaged in deep conversation with Bapu as they walked together'.[3]

But the deep conversations were about differences. A major element in the son's resentment was Gandhi's decision in 1910 to send Chhaganlal rather than Harilal to study law in England with a scholarship provided by Pranjivan Mehta. It was for one of Gandhi's sons (for Manilal, it seems) that Mehta had first offered help,[4] but on Gandhi's request Mehta agreed that the scholarship could go to the most deserving person. (Gandhi was conceding that Indians in South Africa needed London-trained lawyers, no matter what he had said about lawyers in *Hind Swaraj*.)

After the overnight discussion, Gandhi announced (on the morning of 17 May 1911) that Harilal was leaving. Several saw him off at Johannesburg station, including Gandhi, who, as Pragji Desai would report, kissed his son, gave him a gentle slap on the cheek, and said in a tremulous voice, 'If you feel that your father has done any wrong to you, forgive him.'[5] And when Gandhi heard that on his way back to India Harilal had spoken in Zanzibar of the necessity of satyagraha, he sent his son a note of appreciation. He hoped that a shared political struggle might restore the broken bond.

Though unable to switch to a 'normal' family life, Gandhi had offered Harilal the sort of warmth that many Indian fathers of his generation extended to their sons. He would thus say (1910), 'I have great hopes from you.'[6] At other times, again like a typical father, he felt frustrated and angered by the son. 'I feel angry and feel like crying,' he wrote to his son when he learnt that Harilal was drifting after returning to India.[7] More than once the father simply said, 'Let's just be friends.' In a letter to Gulab in February 1912 Gandhi wrote, 'Live, both of you, as you wish and do what you like. I can have but one wish; that you should be happy and remain so' (12: 163).

Yet the father could not refrain from advising. (Here, too, he was typical of more than one generation of Indian fathers.) The son was 'independent', Gandhi told Harilal, and 'could do what he wanted', but what the father wanted was always spelt out. When Harilal wrote from Ahmedabad that he intended to take French as a subject for matriculation, Gandhi proposed Sanskrit instead. The son resisted what he saw as pressure. However, despite three attempts in Ahmedabad over a three-year period, Harilal failed to matriculate. Cards and gambling elbowed out studies.

The sharpness with which Harilal reacted to not being sent to England produced second thoughts in the father, who wrote in 1910, 'If you desire to go, I will send you,' and again, in 1912, 'I am ready to send you to England.'[8] But a condition was attached: after studying in London, Harilal should return to South Africa and serve the satyagrahis. (A similar promise had been extracted from Chhaganlal.) Disliking the condition and the delay in the offer, Harilal declined it. Unable to endure the English winter, Chhaganlal returned to India before completing his law course, and Mehta offered another scholarship for England, which Gandhi awarded to the faithful Adajania, thereby rekindling the grievance of Harilal (and Manilal).

However, Harilal's break with his father was not yet final. When, in 1912, Gokhale returned to India after a triumphal visit to South Africa that his father had organized, Harilal spoke at a reception for Gokhale in Bombay; and in 1913 there was talk of Harilal wishing to rejoin the satyagraha in South Africa. But it was not to be.

Charisma. Harilal's resentment of Maganlal and Chhaganlal was to some extent shared by Manilal and Kasturba, but Gandhi asked his nephews not to be swayed by it. The grudge, he explained, was in fact against him, and would not disappear if Maganlal and Chhaganlal were to leave, as they had offered to. Later (in 1918) Gandhi would speak of having found three colleagues in South Africa who were the sort of persons he was 'searching for': Maganlal, Henry Polak and Sonja Schlesin.[9]

Seventeen years old when she joined as Gandhi's secretary, replacing Miss Dick, Sonja Schlesin, 'a short stocky figure' who wore 'severely cut costumes',[10] had been introduced to Gandhi by Kallenbach, who said: 'This girl has been entrusted to me by her mother. She is clever and honest but she is very mischievous and impetuous. Perhaps she is even insolent. You keep her if you can manage her' (S 164–6).

Despite her age and temperament, Sonja Schlesin grew to become a colleague trusted by Gandhi with funds and major tasks. She had executive skills, excellent English, frankness and a readiness to serve at a low salary that she did not allow Gandhi to increase. If she took more than she needed, she said, she would betray 'the principle which has attracted me to you'. Indians of all kinds turned to Schlesin for help or advice, and Gandhi acknowledged her as 'the watchman and warder' of his office and movement (S 165–6). In her dealings with Gandhi, Sonja practised a freedom that Gandhi evidently liked. Wanting her to be articled (like Polak) to him and become a lawyer, he applied to the Law Society on her behalf. On the grounds that she was a woman, the application was rejected.

There was competition for Gandhi's attention between Kallenbach and Henry Polak but the two played different roles, with Polak, who was 11 years younger than Kallenbach, serving as Gandhi's political representative and interpreter, and Kallenbach as financier and helper. A loyal and talented aide, Polak was also a frank critic disconcerted by the sudden changes (in strategy, tactics, location) that Gandhi was apt to make. 'You have a most delightful habit,' Polak wrote in August 1911, 'of directing at my devoted head bolts from the blue, and then imagining that things will proceed just as before'.[11]

Recognizing in Polak 'a will to change the world'[12] and considerable journalistic skills, Gandhi also formed a direct relationship with Millie Polak, who saw that at times Gandhi showed feminine reactions. Noticing, to her surprise, that a Gandhi who idealized celibacy was warm towards a new-born child in Phoenix and its mother, Millie Polak thought that Gandhi differentiated, 'even as a woman does', between 'abstract principles and human needs and affections'.[13]

Millie felt the power of Gandhi's personality for many years, as did her sisters, and also Henry's sisters, whom Gandhi met in England in 1906 and 1909. Writing to Henry of the enthusiasm for his projects revealed by Maud, one of Henry's sisters, Gandhi wondered whether the enthusiasm resulted from the glamour of his personality. 'If so,' Gandhi added, 'I should be shot on sight, as a power more for harm than good.'[14]

If suspicious of his charisma, Gandhi was increasingly aware of it and of his growing fame. Doke's 1909 book on him had been followed in 1911 by three essays on Gandhi in the British journal *Open Road*, written by a Tolstoyan, Isabella Mayo, and in 1912 by a short book that Pranjivan Mehta wrote. Published in Madras, it was called *M.K. Gandhi and the South African Indian Problem.*

We should note, also, that for all the depth of his South African involvement, India was in Gandhi's sights. In a letter to Pranjivan Mehta in September 1911, he said:

> I shall be [in India] when the time comes. What more shall I say? All my preparations are meant to equip myself for work there (12: 61).

Truce. Though 'stray satyagrahis now and then went to jail' – most of them Tamil-speaking Indians from Johannesburg but also the valiant Sorabji Adajania, who courted another arrest in June 1910 – a visitor observing the even tenor of life on the fruit-blessed Tolstoy Farm was unlikely to suspect that its residents were fighters (S 236–7). Gandhi hoped that patience and peacefulness would prove of help when 'war' came.

The creation (in June 1910) of the Union of South Africa, with Botha as its Prime Minister, saw Smuts becoming the interior minister for the country as a whole. The Indians of all four territories, the Transvaal, the Cape, Natal and the Orange Free State, were in his charge, and he accepted Gandhi as their spokesman.

In 1911 the government of India prohibited the export of indentured labour to South Africa, a ban supported by Gandhi and sought also by Gokhale, who was a member of the Viceroy's advisory council. Apart from the indignity the indentured suffered, Gandhi wanted India to save face by stopping the export of the indentured before the new Union Parliament banned their import.[15]

Smuts knew that for the Transvaal Indians Gandhi had three demands: repeal of the Black Act; restoration of 'legal' equality by permitting the entry into the Transvaal of six or so educated Indians (which would remove the colour bar); and protection of the rights of all bona fide former residents, including arrested or deported satyagrahis. Though Smuts also knew that committed satyagrahis were now small in number, he was willing to concede Gandhi's demands if he could obtain the Indian community's acceptance of a new countrywide immigration law to replace the immigration laws of the four former colonies.

In May 1911 he and Gandhi signed a 'provisional settlement', which was published, in which Smuts said he would fulfil the satyagrahis' demands at the next session of the Union Parliament, and Gandhi pledged a suspension of satyagraha. A packed meeting of Johannesburg's Indians had endorsed the settlement on 27 April, after four hours of discussion.[16]

But Smuts ran into white opposition, especially from representatives of the Orange Free State, which had the most restrictive anti-Asian legislation in South Africa and from where, 20 years earlier, all but a handful of Indians had been expelled. Its representatives refused to accept even a notional right of Indians to immigrate; Gandhi on his part could not assent to an Orange Free State colour bar written into a South African immigration law. Smuts asked for more time, saying, among other things, that he wanted peace in South Africa during the coronation of George V, and Gandhi agreed.

In fact he welcomed the postponement. While a solution of the Transvaal grievances would finally enable Gandhi to return to India, he still needed to address another major issue. Primarily affecting Indians in Natal, this was the annual tax of £3 that every ex-indentured Indian had to pay. Gandhi knew that he could not return to India with dignity without tackling this harsh tax.

On 28 October 1911 *Indian Opinion* said that the £3 tax ranked with the Transvaal question as 'the most pressing' of the Indians' problems in South Africa as a whole; and a month later (25 Nov. 1911) the journal urged the Natal Indian Congress to work for the repeal of the tax 'at any cost'.

Gokhale's visit

The truce with Smuts was still in place in the summer of 1912 when Gokhale informed Gandhi that he was ready to visit South Africa.

For some time Gokhale and Gandhi had each been bidding to attract the other. The ailing Gokhale saw Gandhi as his political successor, wanted him in India, and had sought Gandhi's selection as president for the end-1910 session of the Indian National Congress. He was willing to accept the chair, Gandhi said, provided he could return to South Africa immediately after the session. Whether because of this condition or for other reasons, nothing came of the plan.

Gandhi's counter-proposal was that Gokhale should free Gandhi to return to India by visiting South Africa himself and helping its Indians. At the end of 1911, Gokhale said he would visit South Africa the following year, and in July 1912 he confirmed this from London, where he was, adding that the Secretary of State for India supported the proposed visit.

As he would later recall, Gandhi was 'simply overjoyed' (S 237). Gokhale would speak to South Africa's ministers on behalf of the Indian government and indirectly on behalf of the Empire; it would not be easy for the ministers to reject his pleas. And through Gokhale the Indian community could raise points not yet brought to the fore, such as the £3 tax.

Gokhale's charm, and Gandhi's management. Although Tolstoy Farm practised rigorous simplicity, Gandhi organized (in October and November 1912) a reception for Gokhale 'which even princes might envy' (S 237). Railway stations were decorated: at Johannesburg station Kallenbach designed what Gandhi approvingly called 'an ornamental arch of welcome', and 'rich carpets' (to use Gandhi's phrase again) were spread on the railway platform. A advocate of the simple life who saw the chase for the yellow metal as a sickness, Gandhi nonetheless ensured that the welcome address presented at the station to Gokhale was, in Gandhi's own words, 'engraved on a solid heart-shaped plate of gold from the Rand mounted on Rhodesian teak'. On the plate was a map of India flanked by two *gold* tablets, 'one bearing an illustration of the Taj Mahal and the other a characteristic Indian scene' (S 240). Gandhi also saw to it that Ellis, the mayor of Johannesburg, was present at the station. He sought grandeur and white participation in the welcome for Gokhale because India's prestige was involved, and also because he knew that the scale of the reception and white involvement in it would strengthen Gokhale's hand in talks with the ministers.

In Cape Town (the port of Gokhale's arrival), Gandhi persuaded Senator W P Schreiner, head of the illustrious Schreiner family, to chair 'a great meeting' attended by 'a large number of Indians and Europeans'. Planned by Gandhi, Gokhale's itinerary took him from Cape Town to the Transvaal towns of Klerksdrop, Potchefstsroom and Krugersdorp, with mayors presiding at town hall receptions in each place and the Indian community arranging separate meetings.

Then it was Johannesburg, where Gokhale addressed about 150 Europeans and 250 Indians at a banquet. The Indians paid a guinea each for the vegetarian dinner of 15 courses, the Europeans nothing. No wines were served. In Johannesburg, Gokhale (who was not in good health) stayed in Kallenbach's suburban home-on-a-hill, enjoying the view outside and the art inside, received visitors in a three-room office hired in the heart of the city, and held a private meeting with leading Europeans.

In Natal there were trips to Durban, Pietermaritzburg and Kimberley's diamond mines. Indians in these places spoke of the burden of the £3 tax, and Gokhale and Gandhi promised to work for its repeal. 'The clearness, firmness and urbanity of Gokhale's utterances' satisfied Gandhi, who thought that every idea expressed, and adjective used, had been just right (S 242-3).

The climax of the visit – 'a most important affair', as Gandhi would term it – was a two-hour interview in South Africa's capital, Pretoria, with Premier Botha, General Smuts and Fischer, an OFS politician who would succeed Smuts as interior minister (S 242-3).[17] Having so often fought the ministers, it was best, the two agreed, if Gandhi did not join this meeting. Gokhale would go alone.

Gokhale and Gandhi spent a whole night preparing for this meeting, even as they had collaborated on all the talks that Gokhale had given. After studying a long memo that Gandhi had prepared on the Indians' grievances, including the £3 tax, and 'post[ing] himself fully on every point', Gokhale 'went over the whole ground again in order to make sure that he had rightly understood everything'. If anything cropped up during the interview that was outside the brief provided by Gandhi, Gokhale was to say that he did not know and could not comment.

Returning from the interview, Gokhale said to Gandhi: 'You must return to India in a year. Everything has been settled. The Black Act will be repealed. The racial bar will be removed from the immigration law. The three-pound tax will be abolished.' Not convinced, Gandhi said he expected a lengthy fight and imprisonment rather than an early return to India. Yet Gokhale was not imagining things. Two days after his talks with the ministers, the Governor-General, Herbert John Gladstone, informed the Colonial Office in London that 'as regards the three pounds tax, the PM told me that he thought it would be possible to meet Mr Gokhale's views, though there might be strong opposition in Natal.'[18]

Gandhi and Kallenbach accompanied the India-bound Gokhale to Delagoa Bay in the Portuguese colony on the east coast, and thence on a steamer as far as Zanzibar. At Gandhi's instance, Gokhale 'minutely analyz[ed] for [him] the characters of the principal persons' he had met in South Africa. Discussing Gandhi's associates, Gokhale gave 'pride of place' to Sonja Schlesin for her energy, ability and service without expectation of reward (S 164).

Interestingly enough, Gokhale also 'analyzed [for Gandhi] the characters of all the leaders in India'. Twelve years later, after he had interacted with many of the leaders they discussed in 1912, Gandhi would write that Gokhale's 'analysis was so accurate' (S 245). Gandhi's account of these 1912 conversations makes it quite clear that Gokhale's visit was only secondarily for supporting the Indians' battle in South Africa. Its primary, if also connected, goal was to get Gandhi back to India.

It did not take long for Smuts to declare from his seat in Parliament that as the Europeans in Natal objected to the repeal of the £3 tax, the Union government could not arrange it. A 'deeply pained' Gokhale was assured by Gandhi that 'we would wring a repeal out of unwilling hands' (S 250). The way was now clear for Gandhi to include 'the despicable impost' as a cause of 'war' (S 249). In backing out, the government had let India's eminent leader Gokhale down, an offence that Gandhi would not fail to underline. In March 1913 he was handed another gift.

This was a verdict by Justice Malcolm Searle of the Cape Supreme Court that only marriages performed under Christian rites or registered by the Registrar of Marriages could be recognized in South Africa. By a stroke of the pen, the judgment nullified Hindu, Muslim and Zoroastrian marriages, outraging large numbers of women and men.

As Gandhi would later put it, 'God was preparing the ingredients for the Indians' victory' (S 251). While he and the other satyagrahis had been patiently waiting, 'there happened, or God brought to pass, events which no one had expected' (S 237).

When there was no positive response to a letter from Gandhi asking for legislation to validate Indian marriages, 'stubborn' satyagraha, in Gandhi's phrase, was decided upon by the Satyagraha Association of the Transvaal, irrespective of the number of willing fighters, and endorsed by the BIA, headed by Ahmad Cachalia (S 252).[19]

On 3 May Gandhi felt confident enough to claim in *Indian Opinion* that the likely satyagraha to come would be 'the purest, the last and the most brilliant of all'. The passage in July of a Union-wide Immigration Bill made confrontation inescapable. Though the Bill rendered the Transvaal's Black Act dead, it did not reverse the Searle judgment or deal with the £3 tax, or give even a theoretical right of entry to educated Indians.

Women to the fore

Informed by Gandhi of the implications of Searle's judgment, several Tamil women of the Transvaal said they were willing to go to prison, and publicly announced their intention to seek arrest unless the judgment was overturned.[20] So did Gujarati women in Phoenix, including Kasturba. Gandhi had been cautious about inviting his wife to resist, but she overheard his conversations with other women in Phoenix and demanded to join the battle.

Gandhi frankly asked Kasturba whether she would remain firm. If she trembled in the courtroom or, terrified by the hardships of jail, apologized to the government, Gandhi would not find fault with her, yet 'how would it stand with me? How could I then harbour you or look the world in the face?' (S 255)

It is cruel, this question mark against 'harbouring' his wife if she submits to the government. Kasturba replied:

> You may have nothing to do with me if being unable to stand jail I secure release by an apology. If you can endure hardships and so can my boys, why can't I? I am bound to join the struggle (S 255).

Kasturba and the others in Phoenix were told several times by Gandhi to join the satyagraha only if they felt they would hold on 'whether the struggle was short or long, whether the Phoenix settlement flourished or faded, and whether he or she kept good

health or fell ill in jail'. There was no shame, he explained, in staying out. All said they were ready (S 256).

The imminence of battle called for major changes. Tolstoy Farm was closed – its inmates were at last needed for the task for which they had been marking time. Not that Gandhi had an army at his disposal. In a message to Gokhale, who had inquired as to numbers, Gandhi wrote that satyagrahis he was sure of added up to a minimum of 18 and a maximum of 65 or 66 (S 250). But he was not going to limit the coming battle to his satyagrahis. The man who had seemingly disappeared into Tolstoy Farm was in fact monitoring a larger territory.

Strategy & tactics. He had realized, for one thing, that Phoenix, located in Natal, would be a more natural centre for a struggle against the £3 tax. Yet Natal's Indian elite was not eager for jail-going. In April 1913 two joint secretaries of the Natal Indian Congress (NIC) publicly voiced their dissent from satyagraha, and a public meeting of Indians seemed to support them.

Even before this signal from a section of the Indian elite, Gandhi was eyeing the indentured and the ex-indentured. He was alert, too, to the situation in the coalmines of northern Natal, not far from the Transvaal border, where many of the indentured worked. Confronted with a depressed economy,[21] these Indian workers, he suspected, would be more than open to a call in respect of the £3 tax.

In June he said in a letter to Kallenbach: 'I am resolving in my own mind the idea of doing something for the indentured men.'[22] What he came up with is revealed in Gandhi's account of 'the strategy [he had] thought out and unfolded before the Transvaal sisters', to quote his words (S 254). Gandhi told the Tamil-speaking women satyagrahis of the Transvaal that they should break the law by entering Natal. If they were arrested, it would make news – with luck, outside as well as inside South Africa. If not arrested (which was more likely, for governments did not want to publicize a satyagraha and arrested a satyagrahi 'only when they cannot help it'), the women 'should proceed to and post themselves in Newcastle, the great coal-mining centre in Natal [*36 miles south of the border*], and advise the indentured Indian labourers there to go on strike'. Gandhi figured that 'if the labourers struck in response to the sisters' appeal, government was bound to arrest them along with the labourers, who would thereby probably be fired with still greater enthusiasm' (S 253–4).

Simultaneously, 16 people from Phoenix, including four women (Kasturba, Chhaganlal's wife Kashi, Maganlal's wife Santok, and Pranjivan Mehta's daughter Jayakunvar Doctor) and Gandhi's third son, 15-year-old Ramdas, would move in the opposite direction; they would 'invade' the Transvaal by entering it without permits from Natal, and thus court arrest.

If the border police asked for their names and addresses, they should, Gandhi advised, refuse to reveal these. This would ensure their arrest, whereas disclosure of names and addresses would reveal their connection to Gandhi and probably result in their satyagraha being ignored.

The battle. Gandhi's anticipations proved remarkably accurate. The Phoenix party told the border police that they would reveal their names only in an open court. So they were arrested, sentenced on 23 September to three months' imprisonment with hard labour, and sent to the jail in Pietermaritzburg. The Transvaal women, however, were not arrested when they crossed into Natal, and again left alone when they hawked goods without permits. Walking the 36 miles to Newcastle, they 'set about their work according to the plans previously settled'. Accompanying them was Thambi Naidoo, a veteran satyagrahi and president of Johannesburg's Tamil Benefit Society. 'Their influence spread like wildfire,' and 'the pathetic story of the wrongs heaped up by the three-pound tax touched the labourers to the quick' (S 257).

On 15 October, 78 Indian workers at the Farleigh Colliery went on strike after hearing the Transvaal sisters. Gandhi, who had not quite been 'prepared for this marvellous awakening', left at once for Newcastle: he knew that he would have to look after the men striking at his call (S 257). Within a week *2,000* were out and in the following week *another 3,000* were also on strike. As Maureen Swan, a critical scholar of Gandhi's South African battles, notes, 'The swift success of the strike call derived from the fact that Gandhi had expressed a deeply-felt economic grievance by demanding the repeal of the tax.'[23]

On 21 October the Transvaal women were arrested, sentenced to three months' hard labour, and sent to Pietermaritzburg jail, where they joined the party from Phoenix. The picture of Kasturba and other innocent, respectable Indian women kept alongside ordinary criminals in a South African jail stirred the Indian heart, including in India, 'to its very depths'. In a speech in the Bombay Town Hall, even Pherozeshah Mehta, who had discouraged Gandhi's South African involvement, said that 'his blood boiled' at the picture; India, he added, 'could not sleep over the matter any longer' (S 258).

Unable to eat jail food, when they asked for a different diet the women were told that jail was not a hotel. Some emerged from prison as skeletons, and one young woman, 16-year-old Valliamma Munuswami Mudaliar, died on 22 February 1914, within days of her release and shortly after Gandhi had seen her tall, emaciated figure, 'a terrible thing to behold'. Asked by Gandhi whether she repented of having gone to jail, Valliamma replied that she would go again if needed and did not mind if she died as a result. 'The name of Valliamma will live,' Gandhi would later write, ' ... as long as India lives' (S 258–9).

Fatima Mehtab. Gandhi must have derived special satisfaction from the decision of Bai Fatima of Durban to offer satyagraha. Fatima was the wife of Sheikh Mehtab, who had stayed on in South Africa, working for Muslim merchants, after his 1895 ouster from Gandhi's house in Durban.

Though we do not have accounts of any conversations between Gandhi and Mehtab thereafter, Mehtab seems to have supported Gandhi's satyagrahas. Writing and singing patriotic songs (in Gujarati, Urdu and English) was one way in which he did this; he also often appeared at Parsi Rustomji's house in Durban to show support, which took some little courage, for by this time many of the Muslim merchants of Natal had become hostile towards satyagraha.

Inspired by the fight of the Transvaal women, Fatima, along with her seven-year-old son and her mother, Hanifabai, attempted to enter Volksrust by crossing the border. Asked to give fingerprints, she refused, whereupon, on 13 October, she and her mother were sent to prison for three months.

The scholar Martin Green has tried to discover some of Mehtab's doings in Durban. He thinks that Mehtab may have put on street-corner plays and taught at a mosque and possibly provided a 'convivial masculine presence, hearing and retailing gossip [and] reciting poems and songs'. According to Green, Mehtab finally acknowledged that Rajkot's 'timid little Mohan Gandhi' had won the 'struggle between the two of them over Gandhi's claim to be a moral hero and lawgiver'.[24]

The miners' march

Since the Natal Indian Congress, which he had founded, seemed hesitant about satyagraha, on 19 October Gandhi backed the formation of a new body, the Natal Indian Association (NIA), which started a strike fund.[25]

When light and water were cut off from some of the miners' quarters, which belonged to the mine-owners, and a few strikers were flogged, the choice was between going back to work or leaving the quarters with their families. Gandhi's host in Newcastle, a Christian Tamil called D Lazarus, fed and housed scores in his small house, but the stream of homeless miners was daily getting bigger.

Gandhi asked them to march out as pilgrims. If the marchers were willing to walk to the Transvaal border (35 miles) and then on to Johannesburg (125 miles) and beyond to Tolstoy Farm in Lawley (another 22 miles), he and Kallenbach would house them there. He would walk, eat and sleep with them. The disabled would be sent by rail.

In villages and towns along the way he would hope for provisions from Indian traders, or feed them with bread and sugar. If the government arrested them for crossing into the Transvaal and put them all in prison, that would speak to the world – and relieve Gandhi of the burden of feeding and housing them. Learning of the planned march, the mine-owners held talks with Gandhi in Durban. He told them that the strikers would go back to work the moment the tax was repealed, asked them to contact Smuts (which they did), and returned to Newcastle.

On the way to Durban and back (in a third-class compartment) Gandhi noticed that guards and other train staff 'would surround me, make diligent inquiries and wish me success'. The firmness of illiterate Indian mine-workers had astonished and impressed at least a section of South Africa's whites.

Early in the morning of 28 October, having rejected the option of returning to work, 'a continuous stream of pilgrims who [had] retired from the household life to the houseless one' set forth from Newcastle with their wives and children with bundles on their heads (S 263). Every bit of Gandhi's experience of the Boer War and Zulu Rebellion marches, and of organizing the Phoenix and Tolstoy Farm communities, was utilized on this trek, yet 'it was no joke to control a multitude' that he thought amounted to '5,000 or 6,000'.

The pilgrims' chief, or the army's general, had read out the rules to them. They were not to carry more clothes than necessary or touch another's property. Each marcher would daily get a one-and-a-half pounds bread and an ounce of sugar. If abused or even flogged, they were to remain patient and peaceful. If arrested they should submit; if Gandhi was arrested they should continue with the march.

Food collected by some of the Indian elites was distributed along the line of the march from the coal district to the village (33 miles from Newcastle) of Charlestown, on the Natal side of the border, with a population of about 1,000. However, two babies carried by their mothers died *en route* to Charlestown, one from exposure and the other falling while the mother crossed a stream.

For several days Charlestown served as the marchers' camp. Indian traders livi ig there made rice and dal available, and provided pots in which food was cooked on a ground next to the village mosque. Women and children were packed in the traders' houses, the men slept in the open. 'Luckily the weather was favourable, there being neither rain nor cold' (S 269).

Though alarmed by the influx, the district health officer, Dr Briscoe, cooperated with the marchers, if only to prevent the spread of disease. Gandhi ensured sanitation in the space occupied by the marchers; the workers joined him in the sweeping and scavenging. Recalling the experience later, Gandhi would write:

> Much can be done if the servant actually serves and does not dictate to the people ...
> Where the leader himself becomes a servant, there are no rival claimants for leader-
> ship (S 268).

In these sentences Gandhi hints that he was aware in 1913 that the route of service, including menial labour, could take him to unrivalled leadership, both in South Africa and in India.

Several experienced co-workers joined Gandhi in looking after the pilgrims in Charlestown, including Kallenbach, Sonja Schlesin, P K Naidoo and Albert Christopher. (Joseph Doke, who too would have offered support, had died in August in Rhodesia.)

A couple of miles across the border was the Transvaal town of Volksrust, where white residents were said to be excited and talking of disrupting the march. Visiting Volksrust ahead of the marchers, Kallenbach told a residents' meeting there that the Indians were entering the Transvaal not to settle there but to demonstrate opposition to an unjust tax. They would not retreat, Kallenbach added. The people of Volksrust should 'beware and save [themselves] from perpetrating a wrong'.

Also, Gandhi tried to reach Smuts over the phone from Charlestown and told the minister's secretary of the possibility of trouble in Volksrust, adding that the march would be stopped if Smuts promised repeal. Smuts refused to take the call. His secretary said to Gandhi: 'General Smuts will have nothing to do with you. You may do just as you please' (S 273). This brusqueness hurt Gandhi, who had enjoyed civil relations with Smuts for six years, but 'as I would not be elated by his courtesy, I did not weaken in the face of his incivility' (S 273–4).

At 6.30 a.m. the next morning (6 November) the march recommenced 'in the name of God'. From Charlestown hundreds had indeed turned back; however, the pilgrim band that continued consisted of 2,037 men, 127 women and 57 children. The idea was to march if possible 20 to 24 miles a day in a north-westerly direction and reach Tolstoy Farm in about eight days.

Volksrust. Smuts had said that he was aware that Gandhi 'would be glad to be relieved of further responsibility' for the marchers' needs.[26] He therefore did not arrest the marchers. Fortunately for them, the trouble predicted in Volksrust did not occur.

Despite his curtness when Gandhi phoned, Smuts may have alerted the town's authorities. In any event, no European in the streets of Volksrust attempted even a jest when the Indians marched through. 'All were out to witness [a] novel sight, while there was even a friendly twinkle in the eyes of some' (S 275). And a white baker in Volksrust agreed to send bread for the marchers at every halt.

> The baker did not take advantage of our awkward plight to charge us higher than the market rates, and supplied bread made of excellent flour. He sent it in time by rail, and the railway officials, also Europeans, not only honestly delivered it to us, but they took good care of it in transit and gave us some special facilities (S 273).

We must assume a role in eliciting this 'white' cooperation by persons like Kallenbach and Schlesin – and by Gandhi's personality, seen as being animus-free by numerous whites. As for the Indian workers, they were now calling him Gandhi Raja or King Gandhi; earlier he had been Gandhi Bhai or Brother Gandhi to them.

At 5 p.m. on 6 November, the caravan reached the scheduled halt, Palmford, about eight miles beyond Volksrust. The women who were carrying children in their arms were in no condition to continue further, and Gandhi handed them over to 'a good Indian shopkeeper' who lodged them and undertook to send them to Tolstoy Farm or, if the marchers were arrested, to their homes.

That night, when most were asleep in the open, Gandhi heard footsteps, saw a lantern and realized that he was being arrested. Rousing P K Naidoo, who was sleeping next to him, Gandhi told him that the march should proceed in the morning as planned. Also, the marchers should not be told of Gandhi's arrest until they halted for a meal, though anyone directly asking about Gandhi could be quietly told. If arrested, the marchers should submit. 'Naidoo had no fears at all.'

Lodged at the Palmford railway station for the rest of the night, Gandhi was taken by train in the morning to Volksrust, where he obtained bail, citing the more than 2,000 people that he was escorting (S 276). Kallenbach took him in a car to rejoin the marchers, along with the special reporter of *The Transvaal Leader*, who wrote 'a vivid description' of how the marchers welcomed Gandhi back.

Gandhi was rearrested at Standerton the next morning (8 November). (For some of this journey, the marchers took the route along which, in 1893, Gandhi had been roughed up.) The magistrate who had come to arrest him waited until Gandhi had completed distributing bread (and marmalade, presented by Indian traders) to the marchers.

'You are my prisoner,' he finally said, and took Gandhi to the courtroom, where five other marchers, including P K Naidoo and Rahim Khan, were also in the dock. Again Gandhi succeeded in obtaining bail; the others were jailed.

Occurring the next day, Gandhi's third arrest on the march was less courteous. Walking at the head of the marchers 'in a practically uninhabited tract of country' towards Greylingstad (about 50 miles south-east of Johannesburg), Gandhi was talking with Polak when a Cape cart drove up. From it alighted Gandhi's old friend Chamney, the principal immigration officer of the Transvaal, and a police officer, who asked Gandhi to move to one side and then said, 'I arrest you.'

Having instructed Polak to take charge of the marchers, Gandhi was urging them to keep the peace when the police officer sharply interrupted him and said he could not make a speech. Gandhi was bundled into the police vehicle, and the officer told the driver to 'drive away at full speed'. 'In a moment the pilgrims passed out of [Gandhi's] sight' (S 280).[27]

Gandhi would long remember the police officer's 'exercise of his brief authority'. 'The officer knew,' Gandhi would write, 'that for the time being I was master of the situation, for trusting to our non-violence he was alone in this desolate veldt confronted by 2,000 Indians' (S 280). 'It was easy enough,' he would say, 'for [the marchers] to cut to pieces those who arrested me,' but they were pledged to non-violence. Gandhi saw himself as a general battling General Smuts, and did not forget the insolence of a junior officer towards an opposing general in the latter's non-violent camp.

But he would remember, too, his pride that, counting on the Indians' non-violence, the rulers of South Africa could afford to send only a couple of officers to arrest the leader of a 2,000-strong army. 'It was the greatest testimony of merit the government of South Africa gave to the movement,' he would claim (24: 46).

Smuts's toughness and retreat. By now Smuts had resolved on toughness. Sentenced to nine months' imprisonment, Gandhi was sent all the way to Bloemfontein, deep in the interior of the Orange Free State, where there were hardly any Indians, so that no Indian could see Gandhi or carry messages from him. Also arrested were Kallenbach, who was sent to Pretoria jail, and Polak, sent to the prison in Germiston.

For 'a few happy days' Gandhi, Polak and Kallenbach were together in Volksrust jail, where new prisoners came every day and brought news. Among these was one Harbat Singh, aged about 75. Though not a miner, he had crossed from Natal into the Transvaal and was arrested on that count. Old men like him had not been asked to go to prison, Gandhi said to Harbat Singh, who answered that he could not help it when 'you, your wife and even your boys went to jail'. Saying that at his age Harbat Singh might not survive jail, Gandhi offered to arrange a release, but Singh's 'no' was unshakeable. On 5 January 1914, Harbat Singh died in Durban prison (S 283).

Whipping & shooting. For the marchers, many of whom had by now walked for about 110 miles, the government's retort was to pack them into trains, send them back to Natal, and force them to work in the coalmines as prisoners. Barbed wire converted collieries into 'outstations' of jails in the Natal cities of Dundee and Newcastle, and the Indians were ordered to go down into the pits and dig the coal out. Gandhi would call this 'slavery pure and simple' (S 286). But since the workers disobeyed, they were whipped, kicked and abused. This loss of temper and control proved counter-productive, for the outrage caused in India and Britain, and also in South Africa, compelled the government to retreat.

The coalminers were not the only workers to strike. There were stoppages across Natal in sugar plantations, the railways, hotels and restaurants. An arc of territory in coastal Natal was affected – from Tongaat down through Durban to Umzinto – and the interior cities of Pietermaritzburg and Ladysmith as well. At one point or another in November 1913, the great majority of Natal's 60,000 Indian workers were out.

The government's reply was to ask mounted military policemen to force workers back to work and to support employers and managers who flogged strikers. A striker in Durban was killed when the police opened fire on 16 November; two strikers were gunned down in an estate in Esperenza on 25 November. Two days later, five workers, Pachiappen, Ragavan, Selvan, Guruvadu and Soubrayen Gounden, were killed in the barracks of an estate in Mount Edgecombe. A worker with a paralyzed arm, Soorzai, also known as Amhalaram, was brutally flogged the same day in a plantation near the Phoenix settlement; he died two weeks later. Another worker, Narjia, died in prison. Scores were seriously injured.[28] Word of the repression was cabled by Reuters to India and Britain, where reactions were strong.

Settlement. From his sickbed in Poona, Gokhale asked for every detail and publicized it, and the Viceroy, Lord Hardinge, was obliged to call an emergency session of his council. On 27 November, from Madras, Hardinge publicly criticized the government of South Africa, asked for a commission of inquiry on which Indian interests would be represented and appeared to defend the satyagraha.[29]

Conferring privately across the seas, the Empire's high-tier officials in India, London and Pretoria concluded that the substance of Gandhi's demands would have to be conceded through the means of a commission that would save Pretoria's face. In early December Smuts announced that a three-man commission headed by Sir Richard Solomon, and including Ewald Esselen and Wylie, would inquire into the Indian strike. On 18 December, following a request by the commission, Gandhi, Polak and Kallenbach were released; the release of West and of the Transvaal and Phoenix groups, including Kasturba and Ramdas, followed.

Gandhi had welcomed his confinement in Bloemfontein, with its 'bearable discomforts', as 'a blessing' and 'a joy' (S 284). For the first time in years, he had the time and solitude to read. The need to keep alert from one second to the next had gone. The fact that he, an educated Indian, was now in the heart of the most jealously guarded white preserve, the Orange Free State, even if only as a prisoner, added to the satisfaction. The jail doctor became Gandhi's friend, as did the warden himself, since Gandhi supported his opposition to the doctor's pleas for favours to Gandhi. But the Bloemfontein 'rest' ended in about six weeks.

He had grasped that victory had come closer but was disturbed by the presence on the commission of Esselen and Wylie, 'well-known and able citizens' who had 'often expressed their dislike for the Indians' (S 292–3). On 21 December he wrote to Smuts asking for an additional member who had the Indians' confidence.

The same day, Gandhi appeared dressed as an indentured Indian labourer at a mass meeting in Durban, announced that to mourn the killed workers he would, for some time, eat only once a day, and asked others to do likewise. The meeting resolved not to give evidence before the commission unless a member acceptable to the Indians was added to it and kept alive the possibility of another strike. Smuts rejected the idea of an additional member. However, two intermediaries were by now on their way to South Africa.

One was Charles Freer Andrews, whose good friend, Rabindranath Tagore, was the 1913 winner of the Nobel Prize for Literature. When Gokhale learnt that Albert West, *Indian Opinion*'s acting editor, had been arrested (on 25 November) – even though West had followed Gandhi's instruction that he, along with Ahmad Cachalia, Maganlal Gandhi and Sonja Schlesin, should do nothing that could invite arrest – he wired Andrews to ask if he would go at once to South Africa. Andrews agreed. The other intermediary, also travelling from India, was Sir Benjamin Robertson, sent on a special steamer by Hardinge, the Viceroy. On 2 January 1914, Andrews, accompanied by his friend W W Pearson, arrived in Durban, two weeks before Robertson.

At his first meeting with Gandhi, Andrews, who was two years younger, bent down and, in traditional Indian fashion, touched Gandhi's feet. 'Pray do not do that,' Gandhi said, 'it is a humiliation to me'. Andrews said that Gandhi would have to accept such gestures when he returned to India.[30]

A strike at this juncture by European employees of the South African railways provided an ideal opportunity for a recommencement of the Indian struggle, but Gandhi declared that the Indians did not wish to embarrass the government. Any resumption would await the end of the railway strike. This announcement elicited a comment from a secretary to Smuts that the Indians' help in 'days of need' and their refusal to take to violence reduced the government to 'helplessness', preventing it from 'laying hands upon' the Indians (S 295).

Gokhale, through telegrams, and Andrews, in conversation, urged Gandhi not to boycott the commission, but Gandhi and his colleagues felt they would let the workers down if the boycott was withdrawn. What broke the deadlock was an understanding that the formal boycott would not exclude private talks between Gandhi, Smuts, Robertson and Andrews.

In Gandhi's opinion, Robertson was 'not entirely free from the usual weakness of the English official' (S 300). However, if Robertson was inclined to side with Smuts's point of view, Andrews sympathized with Gandhi's. Thus the parties were balanced, and a provisional settlement was arrived at.

On 21 January, Gandhi and Smuts exchanged letters spelling it out. All prisoners would be released and the Indians would stop the satyagraha pending the outcome of the commission and the introduction of legislation to provide relief. In his conversations with Gandhi, Smuts said that the commission was likely to endorse the main Indian demands. Mass meetings of Indians in several cities supported the settlement. On 21 February Andrews sailed for England; on 7 March the Solomon Commission submitted its report; and in May and June the two houses of the South African Parliament passed the Indians' Relief Act, or Act 22 of 1914.

The £3 tax was abolished, Indian marriages were restored to the pre-Searle position, and the rights of all bona fide former residents were assured. Though not included in the Act, the right of 'specially exempted' educated Indians to enter South Africa was conceded in correspondence between Smuts and Gandhi, in which Smuts also agreed that all existing laws would be 'administered in a just manner and with due regard to vested rights' (S 304). This last point was of special concern to Indian merchants, who continued to be denied opportunities to do business or own land or reside in many parts of South Africa, and feared the erosion of such rights as they had. Also not conceded by the Act was the right of South Africa's Indians to settle in a province of their choice. This was a demand that Gandhi had raised but not pressed during the march.

In his last letter to Smuts, Gandhi stated that 'some day or other these matters will require further and sympathetic consideration by the Government' and that 'complete satisfaction cannot be expected until full civic rights have been conceded to the resident Indian population' (S 304). Though much remained unachieved, Gandhi could say in the letter that

> The passing of the Indians' Relief Bill and this correspondence finally closed the Satyagraha struggle which commenced in September 1906 and which to the Indian community cost much physical suffering and pecuniary loss ... (S 304)

'General' Gandhi. We must acknowledge the acumen of satyagraha's general. He knew his often-hostile terrain and worked out his logistics; he understood his forces and his adversary's; and he cultivated people who could influence his adversary. Through Gokhale, and through reporters he had befriended, he worked successfully on Hardinge, who played a critical role in the endgame; and Gandhi's strategy, developed over the years, of enlisting allies from among the whites of South Africa delivered results. Smuts said on 11 March to the South African Parliament that Gandhi was able to function as he did in South Africa 'because he never advocated methods of violence to overthrow the state'.[31]

For his own army, Gandhi had built a talented and trustworthy staff and an effective chain of command. Planning his moves with deliberation, he also knew when to accelerate, stop or negotiate. His ability to anticipate the course of the battle was remarkable, as was his grasp of how the indentured would respond. Some Indian merchants, we saw, were critical of the Act and of Gandhi's failure to obtain redress for them. Considering that Gandhi had come to South Africa under their auspices and received their support for several years, the merchants' disappointment with him was natural. It was paralleled by the adoration of the indentured.

The irony was symbolized by the change between 1893 and 1914 in how Gandhi travelled and what he wore. When he first arrived in South Africa, he fought hard to travel first class and wore the smart European shirts and suits befitting a barrister. In 1914 he was travelling third class and wearing the clothes of the indentured.

His army did not win a complete victory, but it was a victory nonetheless, and even in 2006 it is hard to disagree with Gandhi's own assessment offered in the mid-1920s:

> Had it not been for this great struggle and for the untold suffering which many Indians invited upon their devoted heads, the Indians today would have been hounded out of South Africa. Nay, the victory achieved by Indians in South Africa more or less served as a shield for Indian emigrants in other parts of the British Empire ... (S 307)

A lapse in Phoenix and a fast. In July 1913, when Gandhi was in Johannesburg, he heard that two individuals in Phoenix were guilty of 'a moral fall'. Manilal, now 21, was one of them; a married Indian woman was the other. Confronted by letters from his father, Manilal at first denied any wrongdoing, which may have been encouraged by the woman. But when Manilal received a letter signed, 'Blessings from a father in agony', he broke down. In a letter that he asked Kallenbach to pass on to Gandhi, the son made a confession and asked for forgiveness.

Sending a telegram, 'I forgive you; ask God to forgive', Gandhi went to Phoenix where he announced that he would fast in atonement for a week and thereafter, for 20 weeks, eat only one meal a day. If the transgression was repeated, he would fast for three additional weeks. Though Gandhi found it hard to go entirely without food, the decision to fast transformed his appearance. One who had looked 'so sad and troubled ... as though the light had been quenched within him', as Millie Polak would recall, was suddenly completely at peace.[32] Manilal joined his father in this private fast of reparation, which was a precursor to Gandhi's 'public' fast in mourning for the killed workers.

Deaths of Laxmidas and Karsandas, & Kasturba's illness. Gandhi's rejection of family responsibilities as his first priority had not gone down well with Laxmidas, who 'year after year' sent 'curses by registered post' to the younger brother, as Gandhi would later recall.[33] But evidently the older brother thawed, acknowledged that what Gandhi was doing was necessary, and wrote that his dearest wish was to join him in South Africa.

This was not to be, for Laxmidas died in Porbandar on 9 March 1914. Karsandas, the middle brother, had died the previous June in Rajkot. On 11 March, a shaken Gandhi wrote to Chhaganlal about handling family matters if he, Gandhi, were also to die.[34]

The news of Laxmidas's death came when, her health damaged in jail, Kasturba lay critically ill. On 2 March Gandhi wrote to Harilal in India that she was 'hanging between life and death' (14: 97), and on 13 March he wrote to Andrews, with whom he had established a close relationship, 'Mrs Gandhi was near death's door last week. I have therefore done hardly anything else during the last ten days' (14: 118). The condition seemed not to improve, and on 1 April, writing to Gokhale, Gandhi expressed doubts about Kasturba's survival.[35]

He was proved wrong, and Kasturba would accompany Gandhi on his departure from Cape Town for England in July 1914 *en route* to India. Their sons and the rest of the Phoenix party would be shepherded directly to India by Maganlal in August. Following Andrews's suggestion, Gandhi had directed the Phoenix group to go first to a centre in the Himalayan foothills started by Mahatma Munshi Ram, later known as Swami Shraddhanand, and then east, near Calcutta, to Santiniketan, the educational centre created by Tagore. Close to both Munshi Ram and Tagore, Andrews had undertaken to arrange hospitality.

In different South African towns (Pretoria, Cape Town, Bloemfontein, Johannesburg, and the Natal cities of Durban and Verulam), the struggle's martyrs were honoured and the Gandhis bade farewell. Addresses in Durban and Verulam referred to Gandhi as a 'Mahatma', 'great soul'. He was seen as a great soul because he had taken up the poor's cause. The whites too said good things about Gandhi, who predicted a future for the Empire if it respected justice.

Before leaving, Gandhi presented Smuts with a pair of sandals out of a dozen or so pairs he had made on Tolstoy Farm. Later Smuts would say that he did not feel qualified to wear Gandhi's shoes, but in 1914 he was glad that Gandhi had left. To a friend he wrote, 'The saint has left our shores, I sincerely hope for ever.'[36]

If thus perceived as saintly (and difficult), we have seen that Gandhi was also a politician with brilliant instincts. Prayer was no doubt a daily part of his life, and we saw that in the latest campaign he once more acknowledged providential interventions, yet he relied primarily on his own untiring efforts, which were as sound and shrewd as he could make them. The Gandhi who inspired and led the great march was not exactly a shirt hanging on the line content to be blown about by the winds of God – he strove to create favourable currents. But he also astutely employed breezes that owed nothing to him.

It seemed beyond his capacity to also take on the cause of the Africans amidst whom he and the Indians of South Africa lived. Yet Gandhi's platforms in the opening decades of the 20th century, including his nationalism, were stepping-stones to a common humanity, and also to a future politics of an African-Indian alliance in South Africa. Even at the time, many Africans offered a silent blessing and a silent applause to the Indian satyagrahis. This came across in 1914 when Andrews's friend, the Reverend W W Pearson, interviewed the Zulu leader, John Dube, who was running the Ohlange Institute near the Phoenix settlement.

Recalling to Pearson a scene near Phoenix station that he had personally witnessed during the Indians' strike the previous November, Dube said he was 'amazed' by the non-violence and forbearance with which the Indians faced police brutality, and by their love for Gandhi Raja. Dube went on to say that Gandhi had tapped a vein in the Indian character that he was not sure existed in the Africans. In a comparable situation, Dube added, the Africans would hit back recklessly. 'If any brother of mine kills a white man after being excited, it would precipitate a great disaster upon us.' It was best not to risk it.[37]

Interviewed in 1976, Selby Msimang, an ANC founder-member, thought that the African leadership of Gandhi's time 'would have found Indian politics too radical to countenance an alliance'.[38] Though neither Gandhi nor any other Indian or African leader in South Africa in his time attempted a political alliance between Indians and Africans, the Indian struggle was paving the way for an African struggle. Recognizing this, Smuts himself had declared in 1908 that Indian defiance in the Transvaal could lead one day to 'Kaffir' or African defiance.[39]

To India via England. It was under Gokhale's guidance that Gandhi would start his public life in India. Eager to present satyagraha to India, Gandhi had accepted Gokhale's advice to say nothing, while observing everything, for a year. Since, for health reasons, Gokhale was in Europe and not in India, it was for England that Gandhi and Kasturba sailed on the *Kilfauns Castle* on 18 July from Cape Town.

Kallenbach, whom Gandhi proposed to take to India, was with them, carrying two pairs of binoculars. When he said that the items were an infatuation, Gandhi offered to throw them into the sea. Kallenbach agreed, Gandhi did so, and the Atlantic was enriched.

The ship was in the English Channel when the World War was declared. Gandhi's response was entirely in line with what he had done during the Boer and Zulu Wars: he offered to assist the Empire with an ambulance corps. This time it would consist of Indians studying or living in the UK. Some Indians complained that Gandhi was asking slaves to cooperate with their masters, but Gandhi was certain that an offer to assist would help the Indian cause.

Hearing of Gandhi's offer, Henry Polak cabled his protest from South Africa: how could the non-violent Gandhi even indirectly support a war? Gandhi's answer was that in a world where life lived upon life, and all humans were inextricably caught in the conflagration of violence, some compromise with it was inescapable. This was a moral justification for Gandhi's political decision as an Indian leader.

Officials in London accepted Gandhi's offer, and a number of Indians signed up. Among them was Sorabji Adajania, now studying law in England with the help of the second Pranjivan Mehta scholarship. About 80 received training for six weeks. But Adajania was indignant because the commanding officer did not consult any Indian, even

Gandhi, in his decisions, and because Oxford University undergraduates were ordering the Indians about. A mini-satyagraha was initiated, and a compromise reached.

In London Gandhi noticed that the city's 'the little [Muslim] world' was 'deeply moved' when 'Turkey decided to throw in her lot with Germany', presenting the Muslims with an almost impossible choice between the Empire, whose protection the Muslims claimed, and Turkey, the world's leading Muslim state whose Sultan was seen as the Khalifa or chief of the world's Sunni Muslims.[40]

At least two of the Indians Gandhi met in London (Sarojini Naidu, the poetess, and Jivaraj Mehta, a medical doctor) would become future colleagues. There were talks with Gokhale, who, interested in the course of the war, probed Kallenbach's detailed knowledge of German maps. And in a speech in August in which Gandhi evaluated the steadfastness of South Africa's Indian workers, he also revealed a noteworthy vision:

> These men and women are the salt of India; on them will be built the Indian nation that is to be.[41]

That is, he would seek to build an Indian nation (it remains to be built, he thinks) not around a religion or a race but on men and women (he takes care to refer specifically to women) ready to struggle, irrespective of their background.

However, pleurisy and a damaged leg handicapped Gandhi in London. The troubles flowed from his exertions and fasts before leaving South Africa, and from a diet restricted to fruit and nuts. Roberts, Undersecretary of State, and his wife Lady Cecilia called on Gandhi and tried to look after him, but in the end Roberts pronounced that in the English weather Gandhi was unlikely to improve or be able to do any ambulance work. Unable to cope with the fogs, Gokhale had left for India, and Gandhi decided that he and Kasturba should do likewise.

He tried hard to secure an Indian visa for Kallenbach, who held a German passport, but Viceroy Hardinge sent word that all German nationals were barred from India and an exception could not be made. 'It was a great wrench for me to part from Mr Kallenbach, and I could see that his pang was greater' (A 322). On 19 December 1914 the Gandhis sailed for Bombay aboard the *Arabia*.

Shortly after arrival in Bombay – 1915

With Kasturba – 1915

7

Engaging India

Ahmedabad-Bihar, Madras-Amritsar, 1915–20

Gandhi was 45 and had not seen the land of his birth for 12 years. His brothers were dead, but that was not the only reason for knowing that he was not returning to Rajkot. All of the Indian land towards which his steamer was making its way would be his battle-field and so his home – his karmabhoomi, as Indian tradition would call it – and all those living there his people. However, the people he was returning to felt that rather than being Indian, they were this or that, Punjabi or Bengali or Bohra or Meman or Patidar or Brahmin or Dalit or whatever.

Four years earlier, Rudyard Kipling, poet of Empire, had published, along with C L R Fletcher, a history book aimed at British 'boys and girls interested in the story of Great Britain and her Empire'. In that book Kipling underlined India's divisions:

> The extension of our rule over the whole Indian peninsula was made possible, first by the exclusion of any other European power, and secondly by the fact that the weaker states and princes continually called in our help against the stronger. From our three starting-points of Calcutta, Madras, and Bombay, we have gradually swallowed the whole country.[1]

Stating that the 1857 rebels were suppressed with the help of 'the gallant Sikhs and the Ghoorkas [*sic*]', Kipling added that three factors blocked Indian 'nationalism' after 1857: Muslim fear of Hindu rule; opposition by 'the native Princes'; and the 'complete indifference of the vast majority of the agricultural populations'.[2]

An Indian returning to India as a whole – to Indians in their entirety – Gandhi would answer Kipling by attempting to make all in India Indians. He would do this through personal example and, as he had indicated in that London utterance, through satyagraha. Swaraj through satyagraha, independence through non-violent resistance, would be his objective. And he would aim to enlist support for satyagraha from a variety of oft-quarrelling communities. He would need a base, of course, an Indian equivalent of Phoenix or Tolstoy Farm. And a staff – he would have to work assiduously to recruit it. As in South Africa, he would need money, and perhaps a journal like *Indian Opinion*.

Furthermore, he would need to spot the issues that move a people, and on which satyagraha could be offered. If possible, he would need also to create a link between himself and the common Indian people, even as he had managed to do with South Africa's Indian workers. For advice on all this, there was, fortunately, Gokhale, but Gandhi also had his own ideas.

He had expressed one of these in *Hind Swaraj*. Not the Indian elites (the 'lawyers and doctors' whom he linked in that manifesto to British hegemony) but peasants and ordinary Indians would be his chief partners. He had seen the symbiosis between himself and the poor in South Africa, and would aim for its replication in India. The Indian politicians he knew or knew about were focused either on British officials, or on *their* castes or communities in *their* regions, for whose political leadership they strove, not on the ordinary Indian. When they said that Indians must rule India, they meant that they rather than their elite rivals should replace the British. He would focus not on the 'enemy' (the British) nor on 'natural allies' (Gujaratis of his caste), but on the common people of all of India, and tap their power.

'While the other Indian politicians in their bid to inherit power from the British were directing their "correct grammatical whine" towards their foreign rulers [and] their rhetoric towards their own small class within their sub-regions',[3] Gandhi hoped to strengthen, somehow, the common Indian everywhere.

It is hardly surprising, then, that during the voyage Gandhi tried to learn Bengali, the language spoken in and around Santiniketan, where the Phoenix party had arrived in November. He and Kasturba were enjoying the voyage, even though neither was fit and the weather *en route* was either cold or stormy. For almost the first time since their marriage Kasturba had her husband wholly to herself – their children had left earlier with the Phoenix party, and there were no co-workers on board. The two, however, missed Kallenbach, to whom Gandhi wrote (23 Dec. 1914): 'The only thing to complete our happiness would be your presence. We always talk about you ... ' (14: 326)

He informed Kallenbach that he had switched back that day – 'somewhat to Mrs Gandhi's disgust' – from European-style clothes to the dress of the indentured of South

Africa; but he had also decided, as he wrote to Chhaganlal, that in India he would 'wear only our customary dress', i.e. the clothes of a Gujarati of their background (3 Jan. 1915; 14: 333).

The concern over clothes was part of the reflection on strategies in India. He did not feel he could revert to the European clothes he had given up, or appear in Bombay in the dress of an indentured coolie. His happiness on the voyage was in fact mixed with anxiety, the anxiety of one who sensed being on the threshold of a great undertaking. To West, who was editing *Indian Opinion* in Phoenix, he wrote:

> *23 Dec. 1914:* I have been so often prevented from reaching India that it seems hardly real that I am sitting in a ship bound for India. And having reached [India] what shall I do with myself? However, 'Lead Kindly Light, amid the encircling gloom, lead Thou me on.' That thought is my solace ... (14: 325).

'Before retiring I invariably read the *Bhagavad Gita* [and the] *Ramayana* and sing one hymn,' he wrote to Kallenbach (14: 326). Clearly he was seeking all the strength he could get. And he was being honest:

> *To Kallenbach, 30 Dec. 1914:* My mind wavers and longs for things which I had thought it had laid aside. How we are deceived! We fancy that we have got rid of particular desires but suddenly we discover that they were only asleep in us and not dead (14: 329–30).

It is interesting nonetheless to imagine the Gandhis aboard the *Arabia*, she having him all to herself, and he, always a good sailor, finding pleasure in the voyage and singing each night a prayer song as the ship ploughed its way across the waters.

The *Arabia* arrived in Bombay on 9 January 1915. Many went to the dock to welcome the couple, for the South African struggle had made news in India, and some insisted on pulling the vehicle in which the Gandhis rode after arrival. (One of the pullers, Valji Govindji Desai, who had been gripped by *Hind Swaraj,* became a lifelong co-worker.) Asked by reporters about his plans, Gandhi said he would follow Gokhale's advice and pass some time as an 'observer and a student' (14: 335).

Though unwell, Gokhale travelled from Poona to greet Gandhi, and there were several receptions in the big city, including one at which Pherozeshah Mehta presided, another attended by the greatly popular Bal Gangadhar Tilak, released only the previous year after a six-year incarceration, and a third given by Gujaratis. This last reception was chaired by the barrister Muhammad Ali Jinnah.

A Kathiawari like Gandhi, Jinnah, a thin Anglicized Muslim and a brilliant advocate, belonged to the Ismaili or Khoja branch of Shia Muslims. Seven years younger than the man he was welcoming, Jinnah was an influential figure in both the Congress and the Muslim League, like Gandhi a friend of Gokhale, and like Gokhale a member of the Imperial Legislative Council.

Off the ship and at these receptions Gandhi wore the plain if cumbersome clothes of a middle-class, conservative Hindu male from Kathiawar: a long cloak, a shirt under the cloak, a dhoti down to his ankles, and a heavy turban. The political and social leaders welcoming Gandhi turned out either in European dress or in ornate Indian costumes. Gandhi's appearance was odd in comparison, and so was his use of Gujarati in responding to the speeches of welcome. Through language and dress Gandhi was inviting a direct, personal link with non-elite Indians. On their part the embarrassed, shocked or amused elite leaders thought that the strange man they were welcoming would soon disappear into the Indian wilderness.

Calling, at Gokhale's urging, on Willingdon, the governor of Bombay, Gandhi gave a promise that Willingdon asked for: he would see the governor before taking any step against the government – the Raj at any rate was taking Gandhi seriously. A lot of travelling (and observing), much of it by train in third-class carriages, marked the months that followed. Gandhi went to Poona to talk with Gokhale (who assured funds for any base that Gandhi might set up); to Kathiawar to meet friends and relatives, including the widow of Laxmidas, and Kathiawaris who wished to honour him (some addressed him as 'Mahatma' Gandhi); to Bolpur near Calcutta to join his sons and the rest of the Phoenix party in Santiniketan (where Tagore too used the 'Mahatma' prefix); to Rangoon to meet Pranjivan Mehta, who had set up a jewellery business there; to Kangri in the Himalayan foothills to meet and thank Mahatma Munshi Ram; to Delhi, India's new (and ancient) capital, where Andrews's friend Sushil Rudra, principal of St Stephen's College, introduced Gandhi to the city's leaders, including Hakim Ajmal Khan and Dr Mukhtar Ahmed Ansari; and to South India to thank the Tamil and Telugu regions that had supplied the bulk of South Africa's marchers.

His long cloak and the turban proved a handicap for third-class train travel and were soon discarded. Footwear too was given up – in mourning, he said, for his deceased brothers. With a cheap Kashmiri cap replacing the turban, he brought himself a notch closer to the Indian poor. Travelling third class in overcrowded and dirty compartments was hard but also instructive for Gandhi and Kasturba, and led to lifelong attempts by Gandhi to educate travellers as well as rail authorities. It also separated him from other politicians. Fellow-passengers who had been impolite towards Gandhi, or for whom

Gandhi had made space, would find out who he was and express embarrassment, aston-
ishment and admiration.

On one of his journeys he met Motilal, a tailor in Wadhwan in Kathiawar, who
pleaded for a satyagraha against a customs cordon at Viramgam railway station where
passengers were harassed and delayed. After Motilal affirmed that he was ready to go
to prison, Gandhi spoke publicly of the Viramgam cordon and of the possibility of a
satyagraha against it.

When he complained to Governor Willingdon about the cordon, Gandhi was told
that only Delhi, not Bombay, could provide relief. Two years later, approached by Gandhi,
the Viceroy, Lord Chelmsford, ordered the cordon's removal. Viramgam thus marked 'the
advent of satyagraha in India' (A 339).

An ashram & its vows. Motilal, who earned his keep from an hour a day of stitching
clothes and gave the rest of his time to public work, became one of Gandhi's first
recruits in India, spending several days each month in the ashram that Gandhi started in
Ahmedabad in May 1915, a little more than four months after arriving in India.

To most Indians an ashram was a selfless and usually religious retreat. By calling his
base an ashram Gandhi revealed twin goals, making politics selfless and religion just.
And he did not mind the 'Hindu' connotation of 'ashram', for he intended to enter,
capture and change the Hindu platform, not to avoid it.

Discovering that Gandhi was more an Indian than a Gujarati, Mahatma Munshi
Ram had asked him to open an ashram in Hardwar. Others wanted him to work out
of Bengal. However, Gandhi chose Ahmedabad, the capital of British Gujarat, because
of its accessibility, its wealth (he hoped for donations), its past as a centre of handloom
weaving (he hoped for a revival of hand-spinning and hand-weaving), and because many
in his party were Gujarati-speaking. All-Indian that he was, to be rooted in his Gujarat
made sense.

The claims of Rajkot, strongly urged by some (perhaps including Maganlal), were
however rejected. Apart from being parochial and harder to get to, Rajkot was 'yellow'
or princely. Expecting to confront the British, Gandhi desired a 'red' base, a 'red' city,
moreover, that Indians themselves had created over the centuries, unlike Bombay,
Calcutta and Madras, which had all been made by the British.

An Ahmedabad-based barrister, Jivanji Desai, offered to rent his large house
in Kochrab, and Gandhi accepted. It would be called an ashram, but of what sort?
The names 'Sevashram' ('Abode of Service') and 'Tapovan' ('Abode of Austerity') were
proposed, but Gandhi was in no doubt about what he wished to convey. His would be
the Satyagraha ashram.

Those joining it would pledge themselves to eleven vows: non-violence, truth, non-
stealing, chastity, non-possession, bread-labour, control of the palate, fearlessness, respect

for all religions, swadeshi (India-made things), and the abolition of untouchability. The first five of these vows continued a well-established Hindu (and also Buddhist and Jain) tradition, but Gandhi intended to give each of the five a new meaning. The other vows were novel, radical even, and, to Gandhi, crucial. To Andrews, Gandhi wrote of the 'miserable, wretched, enslaving spirit of untouchability'. In respect of the vow of fearlessness, Gandhi said: 'My country is seized with a paralyzing fear. We may not open our lips in public, we may only talk about our opinions secretly.'[4] Those who ate without toiling were thieves to him; and there was no hope for India without swadeshi or religious tolerance. Armed with its unusual vows, this 'religious' ashram clearly harboured social and political goals as well.

Considered positions. He had been back in India only for six weeks when a telegram informed him that Gokhale had died. Gandhi 'had approached India,' he writes in the Autobiography, 'in the ardent hope of merging myself in [Gokhale], and thereby feeling free' (A 323). Suddenly, this influential figure who believed in him and had offered a political and financial umbrella was no more.

The meeting with Tagore, eight years Gandhi's senior, was warm and encouraging, and at Santiniketan (where the Phoenix party created a stir by doing its own cleaning, scavenging and cooking), Gandhi intrigued several talented individuals who would soon join him. One was Jivatram Kripalani of Sindh (1888–1982), who introduced himself as an instructor of history. Gandhi invited Kripalani to join him and make history. Another was the scholarly Maharashtrian, Dattatreya ('Kakasaheb') Kalelkar (1885–1981), who enrolled in the Kochrab ashram. Kalelkar had been a teacher in a Baroda school, Ganganath Vidyalaya, started by one who had studied in London at the same time as Mohandas, Keshavrao Deshpande. In the next two or three years, a migration from Ganganath Vidyalaya to Satyagraha ashram gave Gandhi gifted associates.

Gokhale's death freed Gandhi from the promise to merely listen and watch. Addressing (on 31 March, in Calcutta) a 'stupendously large gathering' of militant students, he described assassinations as 'absolutely a foreign growth' and said that those wanting to terrorize India should know that he, Gandhi, would 'rise against them'. On the other hand, if ever he chose sedition, he would openly advocate it; if the students were prepared to die, he would die with them (14: 396).

This speech created quite a stir. Among those affected were the colourful Ali brothers, the Oxford-educated Muhammad, who wrote powerfully in English and Urdu, and his older brother Shaukat. Like many Muslims in India and elsewhere, the brothers were troubled about Britain's attitude to Turkey, which had sided with Germany in the War but remained the world's leading Muslim state. The two met Gandhi and formed a bond with him.[5] Soon afterwards they were interned by the British.

At Mahatma Munshi Ram's ashram near the Himalayas, Gandhi was pressed by a staunch Hindu to display Hindu symbols on his person. Refusing to don the 'sacred thread' because, Gandhi pointed out, it was denied to lower castes, he agreed, however, to tie again, in orthodox Hindu fashion, the shikha or hair-knot at the back of his head. It was false shame, Gandhi now concluded, that had led him to discard the knot 27 years earlier, on the eve of his first journey to London. If the absence of the thread signified his rejection of Hindu hierarchies, the shikha conveyed his Hinduness. Once more Gandhi was taking a well-thought-out position. This had also been the case when he spoke in Gujarati in Bombay, or spoke out in Calcutta, or met the Ali brothers, or chose a site for his ashram, or chose its vows, or selected what he would or would not wear.

At the end of June Gandhi went again to Poona, the city of the late Gokhale, and of Tilak. In this city, where British officers of the Bombay presidency (of which Ahmedabad was a part) spent the rainy season, Willingdon, the Bombay governor, invested Gandhi with an imperial award, the Kaiser-i-Hind, for his services in South Africa.

Neither slow nor fast

But Gandhi's own ashramites, and his wife, were restive, for he had admitted a young untouchable couple into his ashram, Dudabhai Dafda and his wife, who belonged to the Gujarati-speaking community of Dheds or Dhedhs that worked with hides. Evidently, Gandhi told Kasturba that if she was unable to live with the Dhed couple 'she could leave me and we should part good friends'.[6] Kasturba yielded and stayed, but not Santok, Maganlal's wife, though she had been a satyagrahi in South Africa. Breaking conventions among kin in Ahmedabad was harder.

'There was a flutter in the ashram.' Santok fasted in opposition to the admission of Dudabhai and his wife; Gandhi fasted back; Santok and Maganlal packed their bags, said goodbye, and left (15: 46). Later, however, they returned, having, as Gandhi would say, 'washed their hearts clean of untouchability' (56: 178). But there was a flutter in the city as well, and in the ashram's vicinity. Dudabhai and others in the ashram were roundly abused when they tried to take water from a neighbourhood well, and money ceased to flow to the ashram.

Gandhi was thinking of moving the ashram into a Dhed settlement when a young industrialist in his twenties, Ambalal Sarabhai, quietly drove up with a wad of currency, handed 13,000 rupees to Gandhi, and went away (A 356–7). He and Gandhi had met only once before, in the Sarabhai home, to discuss prospects of an ashram in Ahmedabad, but Sarabhai had been impressed by Gandhi's readiness to address caste inequalities, which young Sarabhai had always found offensive.[7]

The tide soon turned, and Dudabhai and his wife, both showing forbearance, found increasing acceptance from neighbours, visitors and other ashramites. To Gandhi the incident showed 'the efficacy of passive resistance in social questions', as he wrote on 23 September to Gokhale's friend and colleague, V S Srinivasa Sastri. In this letter Gandhi also said that he expected his satyagraha enterprise to embrace Swaraj and social questions together (15: 46). He expected, also, to embrace the Hindu-Muslim question. His interest in the Ali brothers, and their interest in him, proved that, as did a relation-ship he was cultivating with Pandit Madan Mohan Malaviya (1861–1946), an orthodox Brahmin from Allahabad espousing Hindu interests in the Indian National Congress.

Unlike other politicians, Gandhi had seen (from the start of his South African days) the interconnectedness, practical and moral, of the three questions. Hindus would not *deserve* freedom from alien rule if they continued to treat a portion among them as untouchables; and caste Hindus were *unlikely to obtain* Swaraj if untouchables opposed it. And if they fought each other, Hindus and Muslims would neither *merit* nor *attain* independence.

Gandhi understood, too, the necessity of discovering the right pace on the three battlefronts. Patient work would be needed to attract Muslims and the untouchables on to the road to Swaraj. Yet he could not afford to be outflanked by Hindu militants tempting the Hindu high castes with an early Swaraj won via the bomb, a Swaraj, moreover, that the high castes would dominate; or, on the other wing, by Muslim extremists offering a revival of Muslim supremacy; or by radical foes of caste presenting dreams of instant equality among Indians, if necessary under British auspices. His thrusts should not be premature, nor his caution excessive.

As early as 20 February 1915, the day that Gokhale died, Andrews had asked Gandhi if he thought that satyagraha would soon come to India. 'It is difficult to say,' Gandhi had replied (A 342). Later in the year, a young man, Indulal Yagnik (1892–1972), asked Gandhi in Bombay whether he expected a following for civil disobedience in India. Gandhi replied:

> I am not very much worried about securing a large following. That will come in due course. But I do anticipate that a time may come when my large following may throw me overboard on account of my strict adhesion to my principles – and it may be that I shall almost be turned out on the streets and have to beg for a piece of bread from door to door.[8]

Confident about the short term and questioning about the long term, the 1915 Gandhi thus seemed aware that the palatable and the unpalatable would both issue from his lips. He also thought that Swaraj could co-exist with India's imperial connection. In April 1915 he said in Madras:

I discovered that the British Empire had certain ideals with which I have fallen in love and one of those ideals is that every subject of the British Empire has the freest scope possible for his energy and honour and whatever he thinks is due to his conscience ... Hence my loyalty to the British Empire (14: 417–18).

Yet from the moment of his return to India he looked for opportunities to try out satyagraha.

Harilal and Manilal. Gandhi's eldest son, now 27, was in Bombay when his parents landed, and accompanied them on some of their travels, and there were long father-son talks. But the gulf was not bridged. After Gandhi reimbursed Laxmidas's family in Rajkot for expenses incurred on Harilal, a formal separation occurred. On 14 March 1915 Gandhi wrote about it to Naraindas, brother of Chhaganlal and Maganlal and like them a close associate:

[Harilal] has parted from me completely. He will receive no monetary help from me. Gave him Rs 45 and he parted at Calcutta. There was no bitterness. Let him take any books or clothes of mine that he may want (14: 382).

At the end of March Gulab gave birth to her fourth child, Shanti. She and Harilal (who had given up the attempt to pass examinations) now had three boys and a girl. Shortly after Shanti's birth, Harilal wrote a disparaging 'Half-Open Letter' to his father and had it printed and circulated 'among a fairly wide circle', including Gandhi. At the last minute he dropped a plan to send the letter to the press. It contained bitter charges:

Our views about education are the main reason for the difference of opinion of the last ten years ... You have suppressed us [sons] in a sophisticated manner ... You have never encouraged us in any way ... You always spoke to us with anger, not with love ... You have made us remain ignorant ... I asked to be sent to England. For a year I cried. I was bewildered. You did not lend me your ears ... I am married ... with four children. I cannot ... become a recluse. Therefore I have separated from you with your permission.[9]

Devadas, younger than Harilal by 12 years and the youngest of Gandhi's sons, would say later that the letter was 'a landmark in [Harilal's] life and in his connection with the family'.[10] Yet in September 1915 Harilal accompanied his father on a journey to Bombay, where Gandhi needed to be. From Bombay Harilal went to Calcutta, where a Gujarati businessman had given him an office job. In Calcutta Harilal's fifth and last child, a

Kasturba (centre) circa *1918 with her sons Devadas (standing left), Manilal (seated right) and Ramdas (seated left)*

daughter, Manu, was born, with Kasturba helping during the delivery. After enjoying a whole year of hitherto-unknown contentment, Harilal lost his job over allegations that he had misappropriated his firm's funds and not repaid a loan.[11]

Twenty-four-year-old Manilal paid a high price in June 1916 for lending Harilal money from ashram funds and initially denying the fact to his father. He was expelled from the ashram, given a one-way ticket to Madras and a little money, and told to return only after earning the sum he had given Harilal plus the cost of the journey back. To Kallenbach, Gandhi wrote, 'Manilal has deceived me again ... [H]e is a very weak boy.'[12]

Before leaving, Manilal begged his father not to fast again. Though Manilal did not know at the time, Gandhi did fast for three days. On his journey south Manilal cried at his punishment and also at the grief he had once more caused his father. After his son had spent several hard weeks in Madras, Gandhi put Manilal in touch with friends there who partially helped him out. In his seven-month stay in Madras Manilal learnt Tamil and also weaving, from which he earned a quarter-rupee a day.

Confronting & recruiting

When, at the end of December 1915, the Indian National Congress met in Bombay for its annual session, Gandhi joined the proceedings and moved a resolution on Indians in the colonies.

In the year that followed, India heard a puzzling if also promising new voice. A country with numerous divides – rich/poor, high castes/untouchables, Hindu/Muslim, extremist/moderate, modernist/traditional, pro-British/anti-British, and so forth – could not at first make out where Gandhi stood. He seemed to tease each side while also offering his support to it.

In at least three ways he was different from other politicians. Firstly, he identified with the poor who seemed to accept him as their champion. Secondly, familiar with the British from his London and South African days, he approached them as an equal. Thirdly, he appeared to regard every place in India as his home.

If many saw him as a saint, others thought of him, to quote Sarojini Naidu's words in 1917, as a

fanciful dreamer of inconvenient and impossible dreams. For surely, the sudden appearance of Saint Francis of Assisi in his tattered robes in the fastidious purlieus of London or Milan, Paris or Petrograd today will be scarcely more disconcerting than the presence of this strange man with his bare feet and coarse garments, his tranquil eyes, and calm, gentle smile that disclaims, even while it acknowledges, the homage that emperors cannot buy.[13]

He was at his provocative best (or worst) on 6 February 1916, when he spoke in Benares at the founding of the Hindu University for which Annie Besant had laboured hard. Invited to the occasion along with several aristocrats and dignitaries, Gandhi spoke of the filth he had seen in the city and also compared the 'richly bedecked noblemen' seated on the dais with 'the millions of the poor'. There would be no salvation for India, he declared, unless the aristocrats stripped themselves of their jewellery.

In any case, added Gandhi, India would be rescued not by 'the lawyers, nor the doctors, nor the rich landlords', but by 'the farmer'. Referring, next, to the large numbers of police posted in the streets to protect the Viceroy who had opened the university, Gandhi said that life under such security would be a 'living death', to which assassination might be preferable (15: 148–55).

Mrs Besant and the noblemen were all shocked, Gandhi was asked to stop and the meeting abruptly closed. Erikson comments that on this occasion Gandhi's teasing may have turned into taunting, that he 'over-identified' himself with the potentially radical students who sat before him and whom he was aiming to attract, and that the students might have taken away anarchy rather than non-violence from Gandhi's words.[14]

Others, however, picked up a different message. A young Marwari industrialist, Ghanshyam Das Birla (1894–1983), who had welcomed Gandhi the previous year in Calcutta and joined in pulling his carriage, was captured by the speech, which produced a similar reaction in a 21-year-old scholar from Maharashtra, Vinoba Bhave (1895–1982). Bhave called on Gandhi at the Kochrab ashram in June 1916 and thought he saw in him both 'shanti' and 'kranti', the peace of the Himalayas and the fire of revolution. Two years later, Vinoba offered to serve Gandhi as a son. Impressed by the young man's mind and spirit, Gandhi wrote to him (Feb. 1918):

> Your love and your character fascinate me and so also your self-examination. I am not
> fit to measure your worth ... In my view a father is, in fact, a father only when he has
> a son who surpasses him in virtue ... I accept the role you offer to me as a gift of love.
> I shall strive to be worthy of it; and, if ever I become another Hiranyakashipu, oppose
> me respectfully as Prahlad, who loved God, disobeyed him (16: 251).

We should note Gandhi's apprehension, stemming from awareness of his radical goals, strong will and popularity, that he could end up as a tyrant like Hiranyakashipu.*

Before Benares, Gandhi had spoken to community meetings of Gujarat's Patels, Jains and Muslims in Surat and Navsari. After Benares he went again to Madras, and then, north-west of Gujarat, to towns in Sindh, part of Bombay presidency at the time.

---

* A legendary Hindu tyrant who wanted his son, Prahlad, to worship him, not God.

Everywhere large numbers turned out to see and hear him, and he was often introduced in awed terms. He said in Karachi (29 Feb. 1916) that if 'throughout India the hearts of the people [were] in a special degree drawn to [him]', it was because of the struggles of 'all those noble brothers and sisters of ours in South Africa' (15: 193).

But this was modesty. The truth was that many Indians drew hope from Gandhi's presence amidst them. In him they sensed both empathy and force. They felt that this strange man 'cared about them, understood their wretched plight and somehow had the power, even in the face of the rule of the great white sahibs in Delhi and the provincial capitals, to do something about it'.[15]

Gandhi's commitment was also drawing attention. When Lala Lajpat Rai of the Punjab expressed doubts about non-violence, Gandhi asked him not to fear 'the ahimsa of his father's faith'. Asserting that non-violence was the essence of Hinduism, Gandhi added (Oct. 1916) that his own loyalty to non-violence would remain unaffected even 'if I suddenly discovered that the religious books ... bore a different interpretation' (15: 253–4).

As for untouchability, he said in Madras on 16 February 1916: 'Every affliction that we labour under in this sacred land is a fit and proper punishment for this great and indelible crime that we are committing' (15: 173). And at the end of April he declared in Belgaum that he 'for one would oppose any part or class that wanted to set itself above the others'. If 'one particular class would dominate ... it would not be Home Rule' (15: 219).

His name and image were 'resonat[ing] among the Indian masses in a manner that was unprecedented',[16] and many among the poor, the 'untouchables' and the tribals started thinking of him as a deliverer.

Fought between competing European nationalisms, the First World War was stoking Indian nationalism as well, and the Empire's need for India's men and resources presented an opportunity for political advances. In 1916 'Home Rule' became a popular cry. Tilak, admiringly called Lokamanya ('Honoured by the people'), started a Home Rule League in Poona; in September Mrs Besant launched her Home Rule League in Madras.

Unity was another widespread desire, unity between the Congress and an extremist group lead by Tilak that had been forced out of the body in 1907, and also between the Congress and the Muslim League. Tilak, Mrs Besant and Jinnah were the lead players in these Home Rule and unity efforts. Gandhi's contribution was wholehearted but relatively small.

However, he played a major role in the Bombay Provincial Conference held in Ahmedabad in October, attended by, among others, Tilak and Jinnah. Convened by the

Gujarat Sabha (established in 1884 'to place the grievances and difficulties of the public before the government'), the conference brought extremists and moderates together. Gandhi proposed that Jinnah should preside, which he did, and Gandhi also moved political resolutions demanding the removal of the Viramgam customs cordon and of a bar on Mrs Besant's entry into the Bombay presidency.

At this conference Gandhi intrigued a man who would soon become a key ally, Vallabhbhai Patel (1875–1950), like Gandhi and Jinnah a London-trained barrister. The rugged, blunt and balding Patel, whose father was an impoverished peasant proprietor in Kheda district, had risen to become a brilliant criminal lawyer in Ahmedabad and the Gujarat Club's bridge champion. Vallabhbhai's older brother Vithalbhai, also a barrister, was a Gujarat representative on the Bombay Legislative Council. Hitherto Vallabhbhai had always laughed whenever friends at the Club talked about Gandhi – the crank, Patel would say, who thought that grinding grain and cleaning lavatories would fetch Swaraj. At the conference, however, Patel liked the seriousness in Gandhi's voice and the economy in his words.

Patel saw Gandhi again when the Congress met in December in Lucknow in the United Provinces. The Muslim League also convened there, and the two bodies agreed to work jointly for 'early self-government' on the basis of direct elections, separate electorates for Muslims and Sikhs, and quotas for religious minorities in provincial and central legislatures. Tilak, Jinnah and Annie Besant were the architects of this notable Lucknow Pact, and Gandhi a supporter who looked for ways to involve the Indian peasant in the call for self-government. Accordingly, he tried to address audiences in Lucknow and Allahabad in Hindi.

Jawaharlal Nehru (1889–1964), whom Gandhi would eventually call his heir and successor, saw him for the first time in Lucknow. The son of Motilal Nehru, a Kashmiri Brahmin who was a prominent Congress moderate and a leading lawyer in Allahabad, Jawaharlal had studied law in London, like Gandhi, Jinnah and Patel. Unlike these three, Jawaharlal had also gone to Harrow and Cambridge. To this thoughtful, sophisticated and good-looking 27-year-old, the Gandhi of December 1916 seemed 'very distant and different and unpolitical'.[17]

Champaran

Not everyone in Lucknow thought that, not, at any rate, Raj Kumar Shukla, who grew indigo in north Bihar as a tenant of British planters and sought help against their oppression. Introduced to Gandhi by Brajkishore Prasad, a lawyer from Bihar, Shukla pressed Gandhi to see for himself the plight of peasants working in Champaran in the foothills north of the Ganges, close to the Nepal border, and not far from Mount Everest.

Encouraged by his instincts, Gandhi indicated his willingness to do so. In April 1917, after Shukla had journeyed to Ahmedabad to renew his plea to Gandhi, he was ready to accompany Shukla to north Bihar. *En route*, in Patna, Bihar's capital, Shukla took Gandhi to the house of Rajendra Prasad, a lawyer he and other indigo-growers had engaged. However, the lawyer was out of town, and his servants, judging Gandhi to be of low caste, did not allow him to draw water from the well or use the lavatory in the house.

Prasad (1884–1963), 32 at the time, a Bihari Kayasth who had performed brilliantly at Calcutta University, would soon become a valuable colleague and in time assume the presidency of the Congress and later (from 1950 to 1962) of the Indian republic. Not finding Prasad, Gandhi contacted the Patna-based Muslim League leader, Mazharul Haq, who had been a fellow student in London.

Haq put Gandhi and Shukla on a train to Muzaffarpur in the north of the province, where they were met in the middle of the night by Kripalani, the history professor who had talked with Gandhi in Santiniketan, and a crowd of students. Though the welcoming party carried lanterns, Kripalani had trouble finding Gandhi because he was travelling third class.

The nub of the peasants' problem was the so-called 'tinkathia' regulation that forced them to grow indigo on part of their land even though its price was falling. Local lawyers, joined shortly after Gandhi's arrival by Rajendra Prasad and Brajkishore Prasad from Patna, confirmed Shukla's stories of oppression and coercion.

As had happened before – including in 1894 in Durban, in 1903 in Johannesburg, in 1913 in Newcastle – Gandhi saw an opportunity and instantly went for it. He told the clutch of lawyers from Patna and north Bihar that if they played their part he was willing to stay in the indigo area (about 1,000 miles from where he was born, and culturally a different world), make it his home, and fight. He was not asking Bihar's lawyers, Gandhi explained, to court imprisonment. But they should be willing to serve without fees as the peasants' stenographers, taking down their stories and complaints, and also translate for him documents he could not read (in Champaran these were sometimes written in Kaithi or Urdu) or speeches in the local dialect he could not understand. They agreed, and in so doing became, without realizing it, trainees for leadership in a national movement. Turning down a judicial post he had been offered, Rajendra Prasad said he would be content as a clerk and stenographer. Brajkishore Prasad said the same.

Accepting changes, the lawyers gave up caste rules and ate from a common kitchen: since all were 'engaged in rendering service', eating separately made no sense, Gandhi told them (94: 148). Over the following weeks, thousands of statements from the humble were diligently recorded by the elite, under Gandhi's supervision, in the Champaran district (west of Muzaffarpur town), where much of the indigo was extracted.

Energized by Gandhi's presence, the peasants acclaimed him as their guide. The planters objected and declared (in line with South African precedents) that Gandhi was 'An Unwelcome Visitor'. But Gandhi claimed the right to study the peasants' grievances, and the duty, thereafter, to advise the government. When he saw that the police were tailing him, Gandhi wrote to the district magistrate:

> *17 Apr. 1917:* I observed yesterday that a police officer followed the party all the way … We shall welcome the presence, if we may not have the assistance, of the police in the course of our mission (15: 344).

Assuming a right to defend the peasants, the 'outsider' Gandhi thus also wanted the authorities to assist him to collect facts that could go against them.

On 16 April Gandhi was served with a notice to leave Champaran by the first available train. In a letter to the district magistrate, Gandhi said he intended to disobey the order; and in a letter to the private secretary to the Viceroy, he said he felt obliged to return the Kaiser-i-Hind medal. And on 18 April, in Motihari, headquarters of the district of Champaran, he said in the courtroom:

> I have disregarded the order served upon me, not for want of respect for lawful authority, but in obedience to the higher law of our being – the voice of conscience (15: 345–6).

Gandhi had taken care, through letters, to keep a range of friends in the world outside Bihar posted on what was happening in Champaran – Andrews, Srinivasa Sastri, Malaviya, Polak, Kallenbach, Maganlal in Ahmedabad, and others. Some of these friends were in touch with the press, and at times Gandhi himself was.

The courtroom statement was big news across India. Reading it in Ahmedabad, Rao Saheb Harilalbhai 'shot up from his chair' at the Gujarat Club and said to those around him, 'Here is a man, a hero, a brave man! We must have him as [the Gujarat Sabha's] president.' Vallabhbhai Patel and others 'immediately concurred'.[18] There were similar reactions elsewhere. In Bihar, Kripalani asked Gandhi if he could join the ashram, and Rajendra Prasad, Brajkishore Prasad and several others were captured for life.

The Raj did not jail Gandhi. Not only was the expulsion order withdrawn; Gandhi was allowed to make his own inquiry and later made a member of an official committee of inquiry looking into the peasants' complaints. In October this committee unanimously asked for an abolition of the tinkathia system.

Why did Gandhi succeed? From South Africa Gandhi had brought equipment rare among India's elite politicians: familiarity with, and understanding of, the poor masses, and similar assets in respect of the white ruling class. On the one hand, he was able to befriend some British planters and officials, even if others remained hostile, and there was sympathy for him in New Delhi. On the other, he had support from Champaran's peasants as well as nationwide publicity, which meant that imprisoning or expelling Gandhi seemed riskier to the Raj than yielding to him. Moreover, indigo was losing commercial value worldwide, and the government had less of an incentive to stand up to Gandhi.

Meanwhile, Gandhi had brought Kasturba and other associates to Champaran, taught himself to write letters in Hindi, started schools, and tried to teach improved agriculture and sanitation to Champaran's villagers. On the last question, a British official called Merriman wrote to Morshead, commissioner of the Tirhut division that included Champaran: 'Personally, I think that if they are genuinely interested in the matter they profess, they will soon get sick of trying to teach hygiene to the Bihari cultivator.'[19]

Attacking Gandhi's mission in a letter in *The Statesman* of Calcutta, a prominent white planter called Irwin objected to Kasturba's presence in Champaran. Said Irwin: 'During the absences of her lord and master at Home Rule and such-like functions, Mrs Gandhi ... under the shallow pretence of opening a school, started a bazaar in [a] dehat' (16: 511–12). In his reply Gandhi said that Irwin had 'unchivalrously attacked one of the most innocent women walking on the face of the earth (and this I say although she happens to be my wife)'. Irwin's letter had also warned of Hindu-Muslim discord if Gandhi continued to speak, as he had done, of his attachment as a Hindu to the cow. Gandhi's answer revealed one who hoped to win and reform Hindus as well as Muslims. The 'Christians and Muslims living in India, including the British,' he wrote, 'have one day to give up beef'. But for that to happen Hindus would have to improve their treatment of the cow. Concerned that – 'contrary to the genius of Hinduism' – some Hindus 'would not mind forcing even at the point of the sword' the Muslim or the Christian to abandon cow slaughter, Gandhi added that he was committed to show 'the folly, the stupidity and the inhumanity of the crime of killing a fellow human being for the sake of saving a fellow animal'.[20]

Reshaping politics. There were two other victories in 1917. One, already mentioned, was the removal of the Viramgam customs cordon. In the other, Gandhi demanded, and obtained, a date from the government for the abolition of indentured emigration. But Congress leaders turned down Gandhi's proposal on another front: he had suggested that a hundred volunteers should march from Bombay to the Nilgiris to meet Mrs Besant, who had been interned there, and invite arrest if prevented from seeing her.

In September she was released, and in October Edwin Montagu, newly appointed Secretary of State for India, travelled from London to see if Indians could be granted more political opportunities. Tilak, Mrs Besant, Gandhi and Jinnah were among the politicians he met at the end of November. In his diary Montagu wrote that Mrs Besant had 'the most beautiful voice' he had ever heard, and that Jinnah was 'perfectly mannered' and 'very clever' but obstinate. Recognizing an ominous undercurrent of anti-British anger in India, Montagu also wrote in his diary that it was 'an outrage' that a man like Jinnah 'should have no chance of running the affairs of his own country'. Jinnah would have agreed. Walker, correspondent of the *Manchester Guardian,* told Montagu: '[Jinnah] believes that when Mrs Besant and Tilak have disappeared, he will be the leader.'[21]

As for 'the renowned' Gandhi, as Montagu called him, the diary recorded that he 'dresses like a coolie' and 'lives practically on the air'. Apparently Montagu said to Gandhi, 'I am surprised to find you taking part in the political life of the country.' Gandhi's reply, given (as he would later say in a letter to Andrews) 'without a moment's thought', was that he was in politics 'because without it I cannot do my religious and social work'. Gandhi added to Andrews that he thought 'the reply will stand good to the end of my life' (6 Jul. 1918; 17: 124).

In his diary Montagu summed up Gandhi as 'a social reformer', yet in some ways at least Gandhi was more practical than his fellow politicians, and keener than them to involve the people. He had, for instance, asked the Congress to collect signatures nationwide for a memorandum to Montagu demanding 'the early self-government' that the Congress and the League had asked for in Lucknow. The Congress accepted this proposal, and also Gandhi's suggestion that the memorandum should be drawn up in local languages. Thanks to him, there was 'an outburst of energy' in the Gujarat countryside, where more than 8,000 signatures were collected by the end of September 1917, a large figure for the time.[22]

In the first week of November 1917, Gandhi had given politics in Gujarat a new character while chairing, as the head of the Gujarat Sabha, a conference in Godhra in north Gujarat. First, he tore up the draft of the resolution of loyalty to the King with which every political conference in India began. Pointing out that gatherings in England did not pass 'loyalty' resolutions, Gandhi declared that 'loyalty could be presumed until they declared themselves rebels'. Next, affirming that Swaraj was dependent on 'widespread peasant backing', he urged every speaker, including Tilak, who had come from Poona, and Jinnah, who had come from Bombay, to speak in an Indian language. Tilak spoke in Marathi, and the anglicized Jinnah unwillingly 'stammered out a speech in Gujarati'.[23] The 'pressure' that Gandhi applied in Godhra would remain an unpleasant memory for Jinnah.[24]

At Godhra, Gandhi went with caste Hindu and Muslim leaders to a meeting where the 'untouchable' Dheds were also present. According to a police agent who took notes, Gandhi said: 'We Hindus and Muslims have become one; here we are in association with this Dhed community.' The higher castes would become 'fit for Swaraj', he said, when they stopped thinking of the Dheds as low (16: 135). Gandhi may not have known that untouchable leaders in Bombay had told Montagu that they would 'fight to the last drop of [their] blood any attempt to transfer the seat of authority in this country from British hands to the so-called high-caste Hindus'.[25] But, as we have seen, he knew instinctively that Swaraj, caste and the Hindu-Muslim question went together.

Finally, in Godhra Gandhi turned the Gujarat Sabha from a once-a-year gathering into a year-round body. Creating an executive committee of the Sabha, Gandhi persuaded Vallabhbhai Patel, the Ahmedabad-based barrister who was now also an influential member of the city's municipality, to serve as the committee's secretary. Patel's first task, Gandhi told him, was to seek the help of senior officials for ending 'veth' – the custom of forced, and usually unpaid, labour in the villages whereby a visiting officer often required a local carpenter to make pegs for the officer's tent, a potter to provide vessels and fetch water in them, a grocer to supply foodstuffs, a sweeper to clean, and so forth. Patel made some headway. Though Frederick Pratt, commissioner of the northern division of Bombay presidency and thus the Raj's principal officer in Gujarat, resented Patel's 'interference', he could not deny the impropriety of veth or prevent the entry into the countryside of Gujarat Sabha volunteers decrying the custom.

By this time Gandhi had enlisted another key aide. A lawyer and writer gifted in both English and Gujarati, Mahadev Desai (1892–1942) was 25 and had translated Morley's *On Compromise* into Gujarati. Two years after first meeting Gandhi, Desai placed himself at Gandhi's side. On 31 August 1917 Gandhi told Desai: 'I have got in you the man I wanted.' To Polak he wrote (8 Mar. 1918): 'Mr Desai … has thrown in his lot with me. He is a capable helper and his ambition is to replace you. It is a mighty feat' (16: 316). Until his death in detention at the age of 50, Desai would serve Gandhi as stenographer, typist, confidant, informant, interpreter, editor, helper and friend.

The peasants of Kheda. As 1917 turned to 1918, restive peasants in the district of Kheda gave Gandhi what looked like an opportunity to present satyagraha to rural Gujarat. Following torrential rains in October 1917 that destroyed an excellent crop of grain raised after a couple of bad years, two men from the district who had attended the Godhra conference, Mohanlal Pandya and Shankarlal Parikh, sought Gandhi's help for obtaining a suspension of the land tax.

In India's vast countryside, the land tax that peasant proprietors paid year by year was the bedrock (and practical proof) of British rule, even as earlier the impost had sustained (and symbolized) Mughal rule. Sometimes, in bad years, the British remitted the tax, but it was theirs to collect or let go. Kheda's collector of the land tax was, as everywhere else in India, the Raj's chief officer in the district and also the district magistrate, reporting to the commissioner of his division of the province (Frederick Pratt in Ahmedabad in this case) or, at times, directly to the provincial government in Bombay. Under the Kheda collector was a mamlatdar in each tehsil of the district, and under every mamlatdar several talatis or village revenue collectors.

It was this network of rulers, from the village talati up to the governor of Bombay presidency, that the Kheda peasants faced. Pandya and Parikh collected signatures from thousands of affected peasants, and the Gujarat Sabha urged the Bombay government to cancel the tax in some Kheda areas and postpone collection elsewhere in the district, but mamlatdars and talatis insisted on immediate payment of the tax. From Champaran, where he was trying to involve peasants in schools, sanitation, clinics and the breeding and care of cattle, Gandhi was summoned to Ahmedabad.

In the first week of January 1918, after he had cross-examined Pandya and Parikh and satisfied himself that the peasants' hardship was real, Gandhi asked the Gujarat Sabha to consider advising the peasants to suspend payment of the tax until a reply was received from Bombay. But he also laid down two conditions. One was that the Sabha's executive committee had to agree unanimously to the proposed line of action, and the other was that one of the committee should give 'all his time to the campaign until it was completed'.[26]

Though he did not name anyone, Gandhi had in mind the committee's secretary, Vallabhbhai Patel. He had been wooing Patel, pressing him to dine daily with him in the ashram, congratulating him from Champaran on work Patel had done for the municipality, and expressing appreciation for Patel's refusal to remarry though his wife had died in 1909. Patel, who nursed a deep bond with the peasants, said his heart 'danced' at the idea of a satyagraha in his Kheda, but giving up his practice for an indefinite period was a huge risk for his future and that of his two children. Nonetheless he offered his services, not, he would later insist, 'on the spur of the moment' but 'after mature consideration'.[27] Gandhi's other condition too was met when the lone committee member hesitant about satyagraha chose not to vote against the proposal.

Six years older than Patel and the same age as Gandhi, whom he had met and liked, Frederick Pratt* had served earlier as Kheda's collector and was fluent in Gujarati. Tough and experienced, he was convinced of the Raj's benevolence towards Gujarat's peasants. He told Gandhi:

In India, to defy the law of revenue is to take a step which would destroy all administration. To break this law, therefore, is different from breaking all other laws.[28]

In the five months of struggle that followed, Pratt was harder on Patel than on Gandhi, whom he called Mahatma Gandhi in some public utterances, and he and the mamlatdars

---

* His younger brother, William Pratt, would gain fame as the actor Boris Karloff.

were pretty hard on the peasants. Over 3,000 peasants had signed a pledge not to pay the tax and, despite seizures of property, most had kept it.

Thrilled by aspects of the peasants' attitude, Gandhi nonetheless questioned whether they had really understood his 'peaceful war'[29] – among other things he had heard that women and children had beaten up a mamlatdar who had seized buffaloes. But even as Gandhi wondered about the quality of this satyagraha, the Raj partially yielded and agreed that the impoverished would not have to pay the tax for a year.

As had happened over Champaran and indigo, Gandhi's relationship with the Viceroy in Delhi, Lord Chelmsford, had again proved helpful. Behind this friendship lay Gandhi's willingness to support the war effort unconditionally. As he said to Chelmsford, he wanted India to give 'ungrudging and unequivocal support to the Empire ... in the hour of its danger', which would enable Indians to reach 'all the more speedily' the status of Canada and Australia (A 403–5). Word that Gandhi should not be pushed too hard went from Delhi to Bombay and from there to Pratt in Ahmedabad. On 6 June 1918 Gandhi and Patel were able to announce victory and an end to the fight.

Though the Kheda exercise was over, Vallabhbhai Patel did not return to his practice. He would remain available to Gandhi, to whom Patel's decision was 'by itself' sufficient recompense for the efforts in Kheda (A 397). The Kheda experience and Gandhi's company had changed Vallabhbhai. The change in him in 1918 was recorded by Kripalani who, along with Rajendra Prasad, had travelled from Bihar to be with Gandhi in Ahmedabad and Kheda:

When I first met [Patel] he had just come under the spell of the personality of Gandhiji. He was living in a style then considered appropriate for a fashionable and young barrister. He soon left Ahmedabad to participate in the peasant satyagraha in Kheda. After some time I followed [Patel] there.

What I saw of his life then was a revelation to me! He had cast off his foreign dress and along with it the comfortable life he had led before. He lived with the workers, sharing the plain food, sleeping on the ground, doing everything for himself, including the daily washing of his clothes, and walking long distances in the villages ... [But he] was his usual self, full of fun and laughter.

The same phenomenon I witnessed again and again in the life of many of our leaders. As soon as they had the joined the fight for freedom, they seemed to have left their old life behind, never to be resumed. They were, as it were, born again as Indians.[30]

By the summer of 1918, that change had occurred in Kripalani himself, and in Rajendra Prasad, Mahadev Desai, and several others. These allies and recruits were captured as much by Gandhi's weapon, satyagraha, as by his personality. The weapon seemed an appealing alternative to the hazardous course of planting bombs and the humiliating course of petitioning; and the man himself seemed 'capable of turning the cowardly into the bravest of persons', as Patel remarked in Nadiad on 30 March 1918.[31]

As they moved and worked at Gandhi's side, these new colleagues also observed that he seemed to know when to start or end a battle, treated peasants and commissioners with the same courtesy, patiently wrote (or, now, dictated to Mahadev) numerous letters a day, and involved himself in virtually every aspect of a village's life: its sanitation, the condition of its women and untouchables, its educational needs, and how villagers 'used their spare time'.[32]

Textile workers, a fast & a mythical dimension. Alongside the Kheda effort, Gandhi was engaged in a shorter if more dramatic satyagraha on behalf of Ahmedabad's textile workers. He was in Champaran when he heard of their problems from the England-educated Anasuyaben Sarabhai, sister of Ambalal Sarabhai, the young industrialist who had quietly left money for Gandhi's ashram and was the city's leading mill-owner. Ambalal's unusual sister, however, was assisting the workers, who for long had been asking for an overdue increase in wages.

On returning to Ahmedabad Gandhi found that the workers' case was indeed strong. They had asked for a 35 per cent increase; the mill-owners had declared that 20 per cent was the maximum they would accept. Gandhi asked the mill-owners to refer the dispute to arbitration. When they refused, Gandhi advised the workers to go on strike if they were willing to abide by his conditions: no violence, no molestation of blacklegs, no begging for alms and no yielding.

'The leaders of the strike understood and accepted the conditions' and at a general meeting the workers pledged themselves to strike work and not resume it until arbitration or their wage demand was accepted. It was the first strike in Ahmedabad's history. The owners announced a lockout.

By this time the Satyagraha ashram had moved from its location in plague-stricken Kochrab to a larger, airier site on the banks of the Sabarmati. Daily, the strikers met under the shade of a babul tree near the ashram to be advised by Gandhi and Anasuyaben, who on occasion gave Gandhi a ride in her car. From time to time Gandhi met Ambalal and other mill-owners and asked for justice for the workers, only to be told that the workers were 'like our children' and that in family matters arbitrators had no place. Though on occasion Ambalal would come to the ashram for a meal (with a chuckle, Gandhi would have Anasuyaben serve her brother), the young industrialist did not budge.

For two weeks the workers were steadfast. Through daily leaflets Gandhi coached them in unity, or pointed out that they had the opportunity now to clean or repair their homes, or learn to read, or acquire new skills. But there were signs of flagging after the owners lifted the lockout and declared that workers accepting a 20 per cent rise were welcome. Several workers returned to work; some strikers seemed to threaten those returning; and Chhaganlal passed on to Gandhi a remark by a striking worker that Gandhi and Anasuyaben, who 'come and go in their car' and 'eat elegant food', could not understand the agonies of the starving.

On 15 March, when Gandhi sat again under the babul tree, he looked at 'a thousand disappointed faces' rather than 'the five thousand or more, beaming with self-determination' he had earlier seen. Realizing that he had to save a rapidly deteriorating situation, Gandhi quietly said, 'I cannot tolerate for a minute that you break your pledge. I shall not take any food nor use a car till you get a 35 per cent increase' (16: 364).

'Unbidden and all by themselves the words came to my lips,' he would write seven years later in the Autobiography (A 388). Unbidden perhaps, but surely not unconsidered. Five years earlier, in South Africa, he had twice deprived himself of food: first in response to his son's transgression, when he fasted for a whole week, and then in mourning for strikers killed by repressive officers, when for several weeks he lived on one meal a day. As Millie Polak had observed, the fast triggered by Manilal's indiscretion had transformed Gandhi's spirits. Now, in the context of another strike and a fall in morale, the thought of another fast was not unnatural.

Shaken, the workers swore that they would keep their pledge and do menial work instead to survive, but Ambalal went to Gandhi and burst out, 'This is between the owners and the workers. Where does *your* life come in?' Yet the owners could not ignore the fasting Gandhi if they wanted to face their relatives. 'For *your* sake and for *this* time' Gandhi was offered anything he wanted, but he insisted on a 'just' settlement.

An ingenious four-step formula was found after four days of negotiations. First the owners would accept arbitration by Principal Anandshankar Dhruva. Then the workers would resume work and get a 35 per cent increase for that day. On the following day, to help the owners keep *their* pledge, the workers would accept a 20 per cent increase. Thereafter they would get a 27.5 per cent increase to be adjusted against Dhruva's award. Some days after the four steps were taken, Principal Dhruva awarded 35 per cent.

On 19 March 1918 Gandhi broke his fast – his first political fast – before a hushed crowd. Commissioner Pratt asked to speak and said that as long as the workers 'followed Gandhi Saheb's advice, they would fare well and secure justice'.[33] Later Gandhi admitted that the fast had coerced the owners, including Ambalal (whose 'resolute will and transparent sincerity' he acknowledged), and also that he 'could not bear to see' the anguish, 'on account of my action', on the face of Ambalal's wife Sarladevi, who was 'attached to me with the affection of a blood-sister' (A 389). Yet the gains were solid: there was little ill will or bitterness during the struggle, the owners agreed to a standing mechanism for arbitration, and the workers formed the Ahmedabad Textile Labour Association, Gujarat's first union.

Gandhi also understood that the fast had raised his relationship with the Indian people to a mythical level. Across the seas, Gilbert Murray wrote in the *Hibbert Journal* (in July 1918, after Champaran, Ahmedabad and Kheda had happened) of 'a battle between a soul and a government'. Murray predicted that Gandhi would be 'a dangerous and uncomfortable enemy, because his body, which you can always conquer, gives you so little purchase upon his soul'.[34]

Audacious bids. Keen to forge a Hindu-Muslim alliance, Gandhi pressed 'his friend' the Viceroy to release the Ali brothers, who had been interned since 1915. The internment had enhanced the brothers' prestige in an India made increasingly resentful by the forced loans, coercive recruitment and rising prices caused by the World War. In December 1917 the younger brother, Muhammad Ali, India's most popular Muslim of the time, was named president *in absentia* of the Muslim League; his portrait occupied the chair in a League session in Calcutta that Gandhi took care to attend.

Called by the Viceroy to a War Conference in Delhi in April 1918, Gandhi repeated his plea for the brothers' release. At the conference Gandhi said in a one-sentence speech that he supported recruitment for the war. His words were spoken in Hindustani, which was unprecedented in the Viceroy's House. Gandhi had converted a gesture towards the Empire into a stroke for national pride.

Intensely aware of great Hindu-Muslim, India-Empire and Muslim-British gulfs, Gandhi dreamt of bridging all three. A month before the conference he confessed candidly (and privately) to Mahadev Desai: 'My mind refuses to be loyal to the British Empire and I have to make a strenuous effort to stem the tide of rebellion.' 'But,' added Gandhi, 'a feeling deep down in me persists that India's good lies in [the] British connection, and so I force myself to love them.' He also told Desai that while he saw that Hindus and Muslims did not 'today' see one another as brothers, there was 'no other course open to them', for they lived next to one another. Four months later, in another remark to Desai, he described the Muslims' anti-British anger, adding, 'I wonder how I am going to be able to win [the Muslims] over to love and non-violence.'[35]

At the Delhi conference Gandhi thought he could be accepted as the Empire's ally even while he championed the release of the Ali brothers and despite his Champaran and Kheda satyagrahas. The Kheda agitation was then at its peak, but Gandhi went out of his way to tell Chelmsford that he could not suspend it. The Viceroy seemed ready to consider Gandhi's unusual definition of an ally, but Sir William Vincent, the home member, told Gandhi, 'So far as I know, you have given a lot of trouble to the local authorities,' and added: 'Well, what have you done for the war? Have you brought a single recruit?'[36] Vincent's question propelled Gandhi into a recruitment drive in Kheda – he thought the district's hardy peasantry might provide soldiers. Also, he urged Tilak, Annie Besant and Jinnah to 'help the government with sepoys', arguing that unconditional support would fetch political advance.[37]

In July the political reforms on which Montagu and Viceroy Chelmsford had worked were announced. Gandhi said that the 'Montford' scheme, as it came to be called, was 'a strenuous effort to satisfy India' and 'should be accepted'. Amendments for improving it could be secured, he told Jinnah, if Indians helped with recruitment – or, as he said in a letter to Tilak, through satyagraha.[38] If Indians recruited and the British responded, satyagraha could stay sheathed. Otherwise, he knew, he might rise against the Empire. In June, when he was recruiting with ardour, he told Desai: 'We stand on the threshold of a twilight – whether morning or evening we do not know. One is followed by the night, the other heralds the dawn.'[39]

Failure and breakdown. Some of Gandhi's ashram colleagues told him (as Polak had done earlier) that recruiting soldiers did not seem like ahimsa to them. Gandhi's reply was that an Indian's ahimsa was often a mask for cowardice. Roundly declaring that Banias could not practise non-violence, he asked Kheda to display the Kshatriya spirit. Discipline – even military discipline – would be a step towards true non-violence and yield the strength with which 'we may even fight the Empire should it play foul with us'. If Kheda provided soldiers, it could help India move to the status of 'the Dominions overseas' and an Indian peasant could 'aspire to the viceregal office'.[40]

National interest was clashing with non-violence in his mind, yet the ethical dilemma too was real. The dilemma was similar, Gandhi argued, to the 'contradiction' over brahmacharya or celibacy, a quality that shone, he wrote to Maganlal on 28 July, only when displayed by those 'possessed of the highest virility', not when displayed by the impotent (17: 150). A letter to a British friend, Florence Winterbottom, bared Gandhi's conflict:

I am going through perhaps the severest trials of my life ... I want to raise men to fight, to deal death to men who, for all they know, are as innocent as they. And I fancy that through this sea of blood I shall find my haven ... I find men who are incapable through cowardice of killing. How shall I preach to them the virtue of non-killing? And so I want them to learn the art of killing! This is all awful ... Sometimes my heart sinks within me.[41]

Vallabhbhai joined Gandhi in a village-to-village recruiting effort in his district. Others in the party in Kheda included Mahadev Desai, Indulal Yagnik (who had invited Gandhi to Bombay in 1915 and helped with the Kheda tax campaign) and Mohanlal Pandya. They looked like soldiers on the march, or like Gandhi's ambulance units in South Africa.

But the attempt flopped. The struggle of Kheda's peasants against the land tax had reduced their warmth for the Raj, which had never been great. Risking their lives for the Empire was the last thing on their minds. Often the peasants hid themselves in homes

or fields when Gandhi and Patel arrived to discuss the war, and hesitated to offer accommodation or food. After ten weeks in the baking countryside, Gandhi was able to give
a hundred names to Commissioner Pratt, who was asked to find a location for training
the hundred. His own name was at the top of the list; he was willing, Gandhi said, to
stride up to German guns in France or wherever, but he would not carry a weapon. Patel
figured next. Many of the others listed were from the ashram.

However, on 11 August, when he was in Nadiad, Gandhi collapsed. The heat, his
failure with the peasants and, above all, the clash between the recruiting activity and
the non-violence that he and close associates felt to be the message of his life, contributed to a breakdown. Rajendra Prasad, visiting from Bihar and introduced by Gandhi
to Gujarat as a 'brother' who helped him forget the death of Laxmidas and Karsandas,
noticed that at this time Gandhi 'often wept' and said, 'I do not know what God's will
is' (16: 387).[42]

Exhausted in body, mind and soul, he had reached extremity. Ambalal and his wife
Sarladevi came to Nadiad from Ahmedabad and took Gandhi to their comfortable home.
A month with the Sarabhais and another in the ashram at Sabarmati led to a slow recovery,
but there were moments in between when Gandhi thought he was dying, and when he
did not wish even to talk or read. Germany's defeat ended his ordeal. The Empire did
not want any more soldiers, and Gandhi could forget recruiting.

Associates, friends, family. Among his friends, Andrews ('Charlie' to Gandhi) was
the only one to call Gandhi 'Mohan'. Kallenbach, who was not only prevented from
joining Gandhi in India but also detained in England for a spell, was never 'Hermann',
but Gandhi had written a letter to him every two weeks since returning to India. These
were addressed to 'My dear Friend' and signed, 'Old Friend'. Gandhi would ask the
German Jew if he was keeping up with his carpentry and diary-writing and the readings,
as evidently promised, of the New Testament, *Imitation of Christ*, and Edwin Arnold's
rendering of the *Gita*, and also seek Kallenbach's advice on a strong new interest – simple
devices that a poor Indian could use for weaving cloth and spinning yarn.

Gandhi would give Kallenbach an account of how Kasturba and the boys were faring.
Kasturba's temper or cooperation or illness or recovery would find mention, as also her
opposition to the 'untouchable' family's entry into the ashram. In some of these letters
to Kallenbach, Gandhi was at his tenderest.

22 Jul. 1915: I have unpacked our goods and as a perpetual reminder I am using your
favourite wooden pillow … In trying to reduce things to order, I ever think of you,
I ever miss you … But for better or worse we must live for some time in physical
separation (15: 32).

21 Dec. 1917: We may wither, but the eternal in us lives on. Thus musing ... my thoughts went to you and I sighed, but I regained self-possession and said to myself, 'I know my friend not for his form but for that which informs him.'[43]

On 15 November, the date that marked the Hindu New Year in 1917, Gandhi, writing from Champaran, said to Maganlal in the ashram that the gift he wished to send 'on this bright and happy day' was the gift of love or charity, which was lacking 'in you, in me, in many others'. After quoting the passage on love from Paul's First Letter to the Corinthians, Gandhi added:

Read this, chew the end, digest it. Read the original in English; translate it into Hindi. Do all you can, strain your neck and eye, but get a glimpse of this love or charity. Mira was stabbed with the dagger of love and she really felt the wound. If we too can get at this dagger ... we can shake the world to its foundations.[44]

In July 1918, in a blow to the Indian struggle in South Africa, Sorabji Adajania died at the early age of 35. In India, however, Gandhi had gathered several new helpers, including Jamnalal Bajaj, a Marwari businessman in Wardha in the Marathi-speaking country, and Kishorelal Mashruwala, a Gujarati intellectual also from Maharashtra.

After his spell in Madras, Manilal went back to South Africa, as did Ramdas. Gandhi hoped that Manilal would take on *Indian Opinion,* which was struggling in Phoenix. Ramdas sold cloth and worked for a tailor in Johannesburg – there was art and beauty in tailoring, Gandhi said. To Manilal, not content with life in Phoenix or with what his father had done for him, Gandhi wrote a long letter in July 1918:

I think I have given you many reasons to be angry with me. Please forgive me for this. I have pushed you about a good deal and that has interrupted your regular education. You can, however, forgive me only if you realize that this was inevitable ...

Just as I have had to pay for my experiments, so have you and Ba ... If you can somehow manage to be contented, you will also have peace. I have not harmed you intentionally. All I have done I did in the belief that it was for your good. Is not this enough to bring down your anger against me? (17: 165–8).

To 20-year-old Ramdas he wrote a similar, and warmer, letter:

27 Feb. 1918. If only you were with me, I would take you on my lap and comfort you. In the measure in which I fail to make you happy, I think I must be wanting in something ... Please think of any wrongs I may have done as unintended and forgive

me. I want you to come over to me after your experiments there are over. I shall do
my part to see you married. If you want to study, I shall help you ...

At the moment we are scattered wide apart. You there, Manilal in Phoenix, Deva
in Badharwa (Champaran), Ba in Bhitiharwa (Champaran), Harilal in Calcutta and
myself ever on the move from place to place (16: 291–2).

After his stint in Champaran, Devadas, 18 in 1918, was also sent to Madras to teach
Hindi there and seek thereby to bridge the gulf between south and north India. We may
note here that Gandhi did not ask his sons to recruit in the Great War, even though
Devadas for one seemed willing to enlist.

Truth, India and his family exerted different and at times conflicting pulls on Gandhi,
whose responses to the pulls were not always predictable, though Kasturba and the boys
felt that the family always came last. Gandhi could not always separate one tug from
another, or understand just what it was that was tugging at him.

Poor Harilal was leading a sad and isolated life when – in the summer of 1918 – his
wife Gulab went down with influenza in the home of her family in Rajkot. Learning that
Harilal was on his way to see her in Rajkot, Gandhi met up with his son at a station *en
route*, and when Harilal passed through Nadiad on his way back from Rajkot, the father
again located him in a rail compartment after searching for him in more than one train.
But there was not much by way of conversation between the father and the son, whose
pallor shook Gandhi. Yet it was Gulab who was now critically ill, and her three-year-old
son Shanti also. In October, first Shanti and then, a week later, Gulab died. Harilal and
Kasturba reached Rajkot after the deaths, and in Sabarmati Gandhi broke down. Gulab
had been his unhappy son's sole bulwark. For a period after this, the ill Gandhi sent a
letter a day to Harilal. On 26 November he wrote to his son that he was 'often ashamed
of the meanness of my mind' and offered to give Harilal 'the fullest benefit of my experiences' if he joined the father.[45] But the son could not bring himself to do that.

The following February Gandhi wrote a rare breezy and descriptive letter about
Harilal's four surviving children, who were now in the ashram in the care of their grand-
parents. The letter was addressed to 'The Satyagrahis' Firm', a title that Harilal and some
of his companions had acquired in South Africa.

To Harilal, 23 Feb. 1919: Just as I was beginning this letter, I had to make my room
a court of justice. The accused was Rasik, the complainant an innocent dog. Through
its howls it had loudly complained that somebody had soundly thrashed it.

My inquiry revealed that Rasik seemed to be the culprit. The accused confessed
his crime and, on further questioning, his previous offences. The judge (myself)
pardoned all his crimes, but he was warned ...

> As I am writing this, Kanti is holding the inkpot. He and Rami are reading the letter as it is being written and trying to improve upon it. The accused also is crouching behind one of the legs of the four-poster. Little Manu was giving out her shrieks of laughter at regular intervals, but now she is crying to be lifted to her bed.

The scene reminded him, Gandhi added, of Harilal's childhood, and a short playful verse ended the letter.[46] His condition had given Gandhi the time to write such a letter, but its mood was perhaps linked to an incident that found Gandhi going back on a vow, taken in South Africa and observed since then, not to drink milk.

Kasturba to the rescue. After surgery in Bombay on boils afflicting him, the doctors told Gandhi in January 1919 that he had no chance of recovery unless he took milk. Gandhi, who remembered that his father had died following boils, wanted to live. Some months earlier, on 2 October, his 49th birthday, he had no doubt dictated letters to Harilal and Devadas, the eldest and youngest sons, that they should be ready for his death. But that was when he still felt knocked out by the recruiting exercise. Now, in January 1919, there was so much he wanted to do.

It was Kasturba who brilliantly found a way out, reminding Gandhi that when he took the vow he had cows, not goats, in mind. Wasn't he troubled by how cows were being treated, and wasn't that behind the vow? Surely the vow left him free to drink the milk of a goat? Thus spoke Kasturba. After hesitating for 24 hours, Gandhi accepted his wife's ingenious if problematic solution, and began sipping goat's milk.

In so doing he came down, in his own mind and in the minds of some associates (including Polak), to soiled earth, but the fall also made him more forgiving of human weakness, and more admiring of his wife. According to Millie Polak, who visited India shortly after Kasturba's intervention, Gandhi said to her: 'You women are very persistent and clever,' with 'a twinkle in his eye and an intonation in the voice as though he almost admired Mrs Gandhi for the subtle distinction' that restored his health.[47] It helped recovery, though the months of breakdown and weakness left a lasting disability: henceforth he would find it difficult to speak while standing.

'A wonderful spectacle'

Gandhi did not know it, but his extremity in August 1918 had concealed an opportunity, and the inner conflict that produced the August crisis in Nadiad was but a prelude and a preparation, for February 1919 would see a remarkable *nationwide* intervention by him.

That was the month when the two anti-sedition 'Rowlatt' Bills, named after the judge heading the committee that recommended them, were introduced in the Imperial Legislative Council. The Bills authorized arrests without trial and trials without appeal for suspected seditionists and a two-year sentence for an Indian with a seditious leaflet in his pocket.

As had happened after the Ollivant incident in 1892 and over similar incidents in South Africa, Gandhi 'shook with rage'.[48] The Bills revealed a disrespect, contempt even, of Indians that was more real than the courtesies he had personally received from the Viceroy and from officials in Bihar and Gujarat. Indians were suspected 'subjects' when their dignity demanded that the Raj 'remain in India only as India's trustee and servant'.[49] Thus far Gandhi had pondered a *future* satyagraha to obtain what Montford lacked. Now he was certain that the 'deadly' Rowlatt Bills demanded an *immediate* response.[50]

He asked Vallabhbhai Patel for help. 'For what?' Patel asked. For satyagraha, Gandhi replied. When Patel said he was willing, Gandhi convened a gathering at the ashram of about 20 persons including Patel, B G Horniman, the British editor of the *Bombay Chronicle,* Sarojini Naidu, the poetess, Umar Sobhani, a Muslim mill-owner from Bombay, Anasuyaben Sarabhai, Indulal Yagnik and Shankarlal Banker, a home-rule activist from Bombay who had helped Gandhi and Anasuyaben during the textile strike. All signed a pledge that Gandhi had drafted:

> We solemnly affirm that in the event of these Bills becoming law and until they are withdrawn we shall refuse civilly to obey these laws and such other laws as a Committee to be hereafter appointed may think fit, and we further affirm that we will be faithful to truth and refrain from violence to life, person and property.[51]

Gandhi called the signatories 'the Indian covenanters' and their step 'most momentous'. For the first time since 1857, prominent Indians had publicly proclaimed their defiance of British laws. Kheda's peasants had also done so the previous year, but the British had dismissed them as a quarrelsome or insignificant lot. Now eminent Indians were openly pledging defiance. Gandhi correctly perceived a watershed in the Raj's history.

Knowing that neither the Gujarat Sabha nor the Congress was ready to organize any disobedience, Gandhi formed a new body, the Satyagraha Sabha, with himself as its president and Patel as secretary. Then he went to Delhi, plainly informed the Viceroy of his intentions, and heard Jinnah and Srinivasa Sastri powerfully attack the Bills in the Imperial Legislative Council. But 'strength' against 'sedition' seemed the Raj's priority, and the words of Gandhi, Sastri and Jinnah, who resigned in protest from the Council, were ignored.

Madras, at the other end of the country, was the ill Gandhi's next stop. He had been invited there by a 40-year-old lawyer, Chakravarti Rajagopalachari (1878–1972), who had sent Gandhi money for the South African struggle. In a 1916 paper, 'C R', as Rajagopalachari was also known, had argued that satyagraha could work in India as well. Shortly before Gandhi's arrival, this bespectacled and brainy Brahmin had moved to Madras from the town of Salem. He became Gandhi's latest recruit and secretary of the Madras Satyagraha Sabha.

Gandhi asked C R (a widower like Patel) if he had met Vallabhbhai, and added, 'I have found in him a most trustworthy man, staunch and brave.'[52] Inviting Rajendra Prasad and Kripalani to Gujarat and asking C R to link up with Patel were Gandhi's ways of building an all-India network. And he befriended Rajagopalachari's children even as he had befriended Patel's.

It was while staying in C R's home in Madras that Gandhi learnt that the Viceroy had signed one of the Bills into the Rowlatt Act. In 'the small hours' of the following morning, 23 March, when Gandhi was 'still in that twilight condition between sleep and consciousness', it occurred to him that as a protest against Rowlatt *all of India* should be invited to suspend work, fast, and pray on the approaching Sunday (A 414). He shared the idea with C R, adding that he was sure of a positive response at least in Bombay, Madras, Bihar and Sindh. Rajagopalachari fell in at once, and Gandhi drafted an appeal for an all-India hartal to be observed on 30 March. For wider participation the date was later changed to Sunday 6 April, but supporters in Delhi felt they should stick to the earlier date.

No part of the Congress endorsed Gandhi's call. By now many moderates had left the Congress to form a new Liberal party that seemed to have more leaders than followers, and most of the Congress's 'extremists' or nationalists had been put off by Gandhi's recruiting effort. Yet India responded magnificently. In Delhi on 30 March and a week later elsewhere, Hindus and Muslims joined hands as they observed a Black Sunday against the Black Act. It was the first nationwide political demonstration in India's long history. In a typical report, an intelligence officer called Moore informed the Madras government that the rally that day on the beach was 'unanimously considered to have been the largest gathering ... on such an occasion in Madras'. Moore noted that the humblest obeyed the call: 'Vendors of curd were not seen and even the women who sell rice cakes in the morning did not do so today.'[53] In Calcutta, 200,000 gathered. In the North-West Frontier Province, 28-year-old Abdul Ghaffar Khan organized a rally in Utmanzai, about 25 miles east of the Khyber Pass. As Gandhi would later write, 'The whole of India, from one end to the other, towns as well as villages, observed a complete hartal that day. It was a most wonderful spectacle' (A 415).

Answering Gandhi's appeal, a number of men and women fasted in Ahmedabad, Bombay, Madras, Karachi and elsewhere. Banned books (including *Hind Swaraj,* Thoreau's *Civil Disobedience,* and, interestingly enough, a biography of Mustafa Kamal of Turkey) were illegally sold; and an unregistered 'newspaper' called *Satyagrahi* was produced and illicitly sold in a number of places, Patel litho-copying it in his home in Ahmedabad and C R doing likewise in his Madras home.

Gandhi, who instructed that no one should be compelled to fast or suspend work, himself spent the day in Bombay, where he was invited to speak to over 5,000 in a mosque. Nothing would have encouraged him more.

At first the Raj chose to ignore the satyagrahis. Arresting them would enlarge their profile, and Gandhi's. But his pull was strong, and many across India were drawn into Gandhi's orbit. One of them was 29-year-old Jawaharlal, Motilal Nehru's son, who two years earlier had thought Gandhi unpractical. He now joined the Satyagraha Sabha in Allahabad.

The success of 6 April, including the joint participation of Hindus and Muslims, the rich and the poor, was aided by the national mood. Eighteen months after Montagu recognized it, Indian anger had grown along with the shortages and inflation left by the war. Soldiers returning from fronts where they were lauded returned to racial inequality at home. Resenting the British attitude to Turkey, India's Muslims welcomed Gandhi's call against Rowlatt and the opposition of most Congress leaders to Montford.

In an unprecedented gesture, Gandhi's friend Mahatma Munshi Ram, now called Swami Shraddhanand, was invited to speak in Delhi's Jama Masjid, the mosque that Shahjahan* had built in the 17th century. But a procession led by the Swami was fired upon, and a few were killed. There was an angry reaction, and the Swami and Hakim Ajmal Khan jointly summoned Gandhi to Delhi to restore peace.

No province was more restive than the Punjab, which had supplied the bulk of India's wartime soldiery. In March and early April the province was tense, and several of its leaders, including Satyapal and Saifuddin Kitchlew in Amritsar and Rambhuj Dutt Chaudhuri in Lahore, pressed Gandhi to visit the province and cool things down. Since Delhi, too, wanted him, Gandhi, accompanied by Mahadev Desai, boarded a train for Delhi and the Punjab on the night of 8 April.

The next day, shortly before the train reached Palwal station, which lay in the Punjab, Gandhi was served with a written notice to detrain and not enter the Punjab. He was told that his arrival would disturb the Punjab's peace. Asserting that he was proceeding to Delhi and the Punjab to allay unrest, not foment it, and believing that calming the Punjab was as much his task as the Raj's, Gandhi did not detrain. At Palwal he was forcibly removed, taken to Mathura for a night, and sent back to Bombay (by a goods train for part of the journey), but not before he had instructed Desai to convey to all concerned that they should not resent his arrest or commit violence. In the Punjab, meanwhile, the men who had invited Gandhi – Kitchlew, Satyapal and Chaudhuri – were arrested.

Violence. On 11 April Gandhi was released upon arrival in Bombay, where he ran into the Raj's mounted police who were charging a seething, stone-throwing crowd with

---

* Moghul emperor (1592–1666) in whose reign the Taj Mahal was built.

lances. There, right before Gandhi's eyes, were two results of his satyagraha: rioting by angry Indians, and unrestrained use of force by the Raj. Going straight to Griffith, Bombay's police commissioner, he complained about the conduct of the police.

'Do you know what has happened in Ahmedabad and Amritsar?' Griffith countered. Gandhi did not, and even Griffith did not know for certain, for telegraph wires had been cut. But serious violence had occurred, for which Griffith held Gandhi responsible. Gandhi answered that if he had been allowed to proceed to the Punjab there would have been peace there and also in Gujarat, but he also indicated that he was willing to consider suspending his campaign.

Gandhi was told that two or three Europeans had been killed in Ahmedabad, where the telegraph office, the collector's office, and parts of the railway station had been burnt down, and several Indians had died when the police started shooting. The news of his arrest, and a false story that Anasuyaben had also been arrested, had inflamed the city, which was placed under martial law. In the Punjab, five or six Europeans had been killed in Amritsar by a mob angered by the arrests of Satyapal and Kitchlew, an Englishwoman, Miss Sherwood, had been assaulted, and General Sir Reginald Dyer had assumed military command over the city.

That night Gandhi declared, in Bombay, that violence would spell the end of mass satyagraha. On 13 April, when he reached Ahmedabad, he went first to Pratt and found the commissioner 'in a state of rage'. Expressing regret for the violence, Gandhi added that martial law was not necessary and that he would cooperate with Pratt to restore peace. Pratt calmed down, agreed that Gandhi could address, the next day, a public meeting at the ashram, and agreed also to suspend martial law (A 422–3).

His recent illness and subsequent events had left Gandhi very weak, but that by itself was not why he asked Vallabhbhai to read out his speech at the ashram meeting. Gandhi wanted British officials as well as the people of Gujarat to know that Patel shared his remorse over the violence. Said Gandhi, via Patel's deep yet unemotional voice, on 14 April, to an audience of more than 10,000:

> Brothers, I am ashamed of the events of the last few days. Those responsible have disgraced me. In the name of satyagraha, we burnt down buildings, forcibly captured weapons, extorted money, stopped trains, cut off telegraph wires, killed innocent people, and plundered shops and homes.
>
> A most brutal rumour was set afloat that Anasuyaben was arrested ... Under the cloak of her arrest, heinous deeds have been done.
>
> We should repent and do penance. I would also advise you, if it is possible for you, to fast for twenty-four hours in slight expiation of these sins ... My responsibility is a million times greater than yours ... I will therefore fast for seventy-two hours.

If a redress of grievances is only possible by means of ill-will for, and slaughter of Englishmen, I for one would do without Swaraj and without redress.[54]

On 15 April, in a letter to Chatfield, the Ahmedabad collector, Gandhi sought particulars for sending help to the families of the British victims, and on 18 April he announced a temporary suspension of satyagraha.

Jallianwalla

The worst single incident in the annals of British rule in India, the Amritsar massacre, had occurred the day before Gandhi's Sabarmati speech, but he did not learn of it right away. Martial law, censorship and the cutting (or switching off) of telegraph and phone lines kept most of India in the dark for days.

After taking over in Amritsar, General Dyer prohibited public meetings, but not everyone knew of the ban. On the afternoon of 13 April, which was a Sunday and also the day of Baisakhi – significant to Sikhs and Hindus – over 10,000 people, Hindus, Muslims and Sikhs, most of them unaware of Dyer's ban and all of them unarmed, gathered at Jallianwalla Bagh, an open ground enclosed on three sides by five-foot-high walls.

The meeting had barely started when Dyer and 50 soldiers with rifles appeared and took possession of the entrance to the ground, which was also the sole exit. Without a single call for the crowd to disperse, Dyer ordered his men to open fire. For ten horrific minutes, the Raj's Indian soldiers from the Gurkha and Balochi regiments carried out the order. Almost every bullet found a victim. Official estimates said that 379 were killed and over 1,000 injured. Unofficial figures were higher.

Subsequent events were equally unbelievable. Sir Michael O'Dwyer, the governor of the Punjab, imposed martial law throughout the province. In Amritsar, Dyer ordered every Indian to crawl on the street where Miss Sherwood had been attacked, and every Indian seeing a British officer to offer a salute. Violators of Dyer's regulations were flogged at a public whipping post. The police opened fire in Lahore; elsewhere in the province two groups of peasants were bombed from the air. A revolutionary plot that did not exist was crushed.

Influential figures in the Empire shared Gandhi's view (and that of many Indians) that he could have calmed the Punjab. In a private cable sent in September from London, Montagu said to the Viceroy:

I have never heard of a case in which the appearance of Gandhi has not had a tranquillizing effect. It certainly had in Ahmedabad and Bombay during the recent riots ... So far as I can hear, Gandhi is a man who has always kept his word.[55]

Others thought differently. Lord Willingdon, now the governor of Madras, called Gandhi a 'Bolshevik'.[56] Men like Willingdon asked for the stick. Colleagues who had doubts 'stiffened into amoral solidarity' and 'Englishmen backed each other right or wrong'.[57]

Gandhi believed that it was the Raj's short temper that caused the Jallianwalla killings, and he also felt that to order 'innocent men and women' to 'crawl like worms on their bellies' was worse than the massacre (A 426). On 21 April he cabled the Viceroy sharply protesting the flogging orders. But he did not absolve his countrymen. Like the British, they too, he said, had gone 'mad'.[58] And he did not absolve himself. Launching a satyagraha before training a cadre that could keep it non-violent was, he said in July in Nadiad, a 'Himalayan miscalculation' on his part.[59] Yet he was not going to abandon satyagraha, even though, in a letter written on 12 April, Tagore had cautioned him about it (17: 464–5).

'Young India' & 'Navajivan'. Three of the Sabarmati 'covenanters', Umar Sobhani, Shankerlal Banker and Indulal Yagnik, were between them bringing out two journals, Young India, a weekly in English from Bombay, and Navajivan, a monthly in Gujarati from Ahmedabad, and were also associated with the nationalist daily, the Bombay Chronicle. At the end of April, in one of the Raj's drastic measures, Horniman, the British editor of the Chronicle, was deported, and publication had to be suspended.

In response, Sobhani, Banker and Yagnik requested Gandhi to take over the editorship of Young India and Navajivan and with their help bring out Young India twice a week and Navajivan every week. Gandhi agreed, and on 7 May 1919 the first number of Young India, New Series, came out. When, soon, the Chronicle resumed publication, Young India reverted to being a weekly but now published, for Gandhi's convenience, in Ahmedabad, along with Navajivan, which first appeared as a weekly on 7 September. Gandhi now possessed what he had hoped for from the moment of his return to India: vehicles to communicate his message.

The spinning wheel. Linking India's poverty to the destruction of Indian weaving and to British rule, Gandhi in Hind Swaraj had asked India's intellectuals to 'take up the handloom'. When he wrote this in 1909, he had seen neither a loom for weaving nor a wheel for spinning, yet he imagined energy – economic, political and psychological – flowing from 'looms' plying in a number of homes.

Much later, in 1938, after the charkha (spinning wheel) and khadi (hand-spun and hand-woven cloth) had become popular across India, Gandhi would say (in Bannu, in the North-West Frontier Province):

The charkha is not my invention. It was there before ... God whispered into my ear: 'If you want to work through non-violence, you have to proceed with small things, not big' (74: 160–1).

Practical necessity forced Gandhi to find the charkha soon after the ashram was founded in 1915. Gandhi and his associates had resolved firstly to wear only hand-woven cloth made from Indian yarn and secondly to make the cloth they needed. A few handlooms were accordingly set up in the ashram, and Maganlal and some others learnt weaving.

But Indian spinning mills wanted to turn all their yarn into mill-made cloth, not sell it to hand-weavers. Gandhi therefore asked associates to search for spinning wheels that could make yarn. At the Godhra conference of November 1917, a woman called Gangaben Majmudar, who had 'already got rid of the curse of untouchability and fearlessly moved among and served the suppressed classes' (A 442), promised him that she would locate a wheel. She found not one but hundreds in Vijapur in the princely state of Baroda, all lying in attics as 'useless lumber' (A 443). Women who in the past plied the charkhas told Gangaben that they would spin again if someone supplied slivers of cotton and bought their yarn. Gandhi said he would meet the conditions, his friend Umar Sobhani supplied slivers from his Bombay mill, and the ashram received more hand-spun yarn than it could cope with. Maganlal now organized the production in the ashram of improved spinning wheels.

An increasing number in and around the ashram and elsewhere in Gujarat learnt the art of spinning, including Gandhi. Gangaben found carders who made slivers by hand, eliminating dependence on mills. And before long, khadi or khaddar, cloth made from start to finish by hand, was seen again in shops, homes and streets in one Indian town after another.

Khadi was rougher, thicker, heavier and more expensive than mill-made cloth, and tore more easily. But it brought precious coppers to all willing to spin or weave, including poor landless labourers, the unemployed, the underemployed and the malnourished. For others the ancient and yet very new cloth offered proof of honest, patriotic labour. Quickly it became a symbol of dignity and of a bond between lowly and well-off Indians. It was a symbol, moreover, that could be touched, felt, seen and displayed. Every man or woman who wore khadi, or carded, span, or wove for it, felt tied by its threads to Mahatma Gandhi, to the poor, to Swaraj, to satyagraha. Gandhi himself became deeply attached to the hum of the charkha, which, he would say, 'had no small share in restoring [him] to health' in Bombay in the latter part of 1918 (A 444).

He was staying at the time in Mani Bhuvan, the home of Pranjivan Mehta and his relatives. Women who had become his allies plied the charkha in his room. By the summer of 1919 Gandhi was entitled to feel that his *Hind Swaraj* instincts regarding what he had erroneously called the 'loom' were being confirmed. The charkha and khadi connect Gandhi to Kabir, the 15th-century weaver and north Indian poet who, like Gandhi, sought to bridge the Hindu-Muslim divide, and to Thiruvalluvar, the earlier weaver-poet, possibly from the 6th century, who preached compassion and equality in south India.

The Punjab and Saraladevi Chaudhurani. Still barred from entering the Punjab, Gandhi demanded a full investigation into the Amritsar massacre and the punishments that had followed. In September the Raj announced that the Hunter Commission would conduct an inquiry, and in October he was told that he could enter the Punjab.

On 24 October 1919, three weeks after he had turned 50, Gandhi arrived in Lahore for the first time in his life. 'The railway station was from end to end one seething mass of humanity,' he would later recall. 'The entire populace had turned out of doors in eager expectation, as if to meet a dear relation after a long separation, and was delirious with joy.' (A 430) Many of the Punjab's political leaders were still in detention, including Rambhuj Dutt Chaudhuri, in whose house Gandhi was put up. Pandit Malaviya, the Congress president, Swami Shraddhanand from Delhi, and Motilal Nehru from Allahabad were also in Lahore. So was Charlie Andrews.

Dissatisfied with the Hunter Commission's terms of inquiry, Malaviya, Gandhi, and the others decided to organize a parallel investigation, to be conducted by a Congress committee comprising Gandhi, Motilal Nehru, Calcutta's brilliant lawyer Chitta Ranjan Das (1870–1925), the barrister M R Jayakar from Bombay, and the jurist Abbas Tyabji of Gujarat. It was Gandhi, primarily, who shouldered the burden of the committee, spending about three months in different parts of the Punjab and interviewing numerous witnesses on the inhumanities perpetrated. And in the end it was he who wrote the committee's report, claiming that all statements about which 'there was the slightest doubt' were excluded from it (A 431).

On his Punjab tour Gandhi promoted khadi and the charkha and found the Punjab's women responsive. He also sought funds for a Jallianwalla memorial, not, Gandhi under-lined, to engender 'ill-will or hostility to anyone', but as 'a symbol of the people's grief' and a reminder of 'the sacrifices, through death, of the innocent' (19: 307). Donations seemed slow in coming until Gandhi declared that he would, if necessary, sell his ashram in Ahmedabad to finance the memorial. This declaration was a factor in the decision of a young man, Pyarelal Nayar (1900–82), to join Gandhi. Encountering him during his Punjab tour, Pyarelal thought that Gandhi conveyed 'a calm assurance of strength' and 'an access to some hidden reservoir of power which could find a way even through an impenetrable granite wall'.[60]

But something now happened to Gandhi that he had not bargained for. He felt power-fully drawn to Saraladevi, the 47-year-old Bengali wife of Rambhuj Dutt Chaudhuri, his Lahore host who was in jail at this time. A niece of Tagore (her mother, Swarnakumari was one of the poet's two sisters), Saraladevi was the editor in her husband's absence of his journal, *Hindustan*.

Gandhi would have first seen her first 18 years earlier, in December 1901, when Saraladevi conducted the orchestra for the opening song at the Calcutta Congress session that Gandhi attended. She had composed the song, and 58 singers joined in performing it. We have no record of any comment about her at that time by Gandhi, but a book that Saraladevi wrote in the 1940s suggests that they may have met during the 1901 session. She thought of Gandhi at the time, she would say, 'as a possible South African contributor' to a journal she was editing, *Bharati*.[61] She was 29 then. While there is no evidence of anything passing between them at that time, we know from Gandhi's Auto-biography (written between 1925 and 1929) that in 1901 he spent some hours with her father, Janakinath Ghosal, one of the Congress secretaries. Evidently Gandhi answered correspondence for which Ghosal had no time, and the secretary 'insisted on [Gandhi] having lunch with him'. Gandhi found Ghosal 'talkative' and also (after discovering Gandhi's history) embarrassed that he had given Gandhi 'clerical work' (A 199).

Gandhi's 1901 meeting with Saraladevi may have been cursory, but it is likely that he remembered her. A photograph of her at graduation (published in Green's book) suggests an impressive appearance. An unusually talented singer and writer, Saraladevi went on to train Bengali youth in militant patriotism, thereby attracting the attention of the police. Earlier she was a Vivekananda disciple, and the Swami is said to have wanted her to accompany him to the West.

In 1905, a year of tension in Bengal over its partition, she married Rambhuj Dutt Chaudhuri of the Punjab, already twice a widower, and an Arya Samajist. This she did at the instance of her parents, who may have felt that in Lahore their daughter would be safe from the arm of Calcutta's police. At 33 Saraladevi was older than most brides of her time, and her husband apparently called her 'the greatest shakti in India'.[62]

How much of her career between 1901 and 1919 was known to Gandhi is unclear. When visiting Lahore in 1909 Polak stayed in the home of Saraladevi and her husband (where many a visitor to Lahore was put up), but we do not know if Gandhi suggested this arrangement.

On 27 October 1919, within days of his arrival in Lahore, Gandhi would write to Anasuyaben in Ahmedabad: 'Saraladevi's company is very endearing. She looks after me very well' (19: 84). The following months saw a special relationship that Gandhi called 'indefinable' after its character changed in June 1920.[63] In between he had not only overcome his caution regarding exclusive relationships but even thought of a 'spiritual marriage', whatever that may have meant, with Saraladevi.

Though at 47 her frame held no allure, to Gandhi she conveyed an aesthetic and political appeal around which Eros too might have lurked. Cultured in both Indian and Western terms, she wrote and spoke well and had, in Gandhi's view, a 'melodious' singing voice (95: 271). Politically, she could be imagined as embodying not only the prestige of a Tagore connection but also the spirit of the presidency of Bengal, and, in addition, the strand of violence in India's freedom effort. A merger with her might bring him closer to winning all of India to satyagraha.

Whether or not he consciously toyed with such considerations, they probably influenced him. In 1933 he would also say (to Father William Lash and E Stanley Jones) that he had been prevented from 'rushing into hellfire' by the thought of Kasturba and because of interventions by his son Devadas, Mahadev Desai and another young relative, Mathuradas Trikamji, grandson of his half-sister, Muliben (59: 196 & 227).

In 1935 he would say to Margaret Sanger, after referring to Kasturba's illiteracy, that he had 'nearly slipped' after meeting 'a woman with a broad, cultural education' but had fortunately been freed from a 'trance'. He was speaking of the 1919–20 attraction.[64] The remark in the last page of the Autobiography about his experiences (after 'returning to India') of 'the dormant passions lying hidden within me' seems also to recall the 1919–20 period (A 454).

Another element may also have been at work: perhaps this 'endearing' woman and aesthete who 'looked after' him 'very well' gave Gandhi the emotional support that he, a man who in his world was always giving, seldom received but always needed, whether or not he or others in his circle of followers and associates recognized the need. The supremely self-assured founder and general of satyagraha bore more aches in his bosom than he or those around him realized, and if India and truth spoke to him, so did his very human, if also greatly subjugated, self.

Martin Green, who more than others has researched this relationship and the career of Saraladevi, speaks of Gandhi 'closing the door that had opened before him' and adds: 'He and she together would certainly have made an extraordinary political combination.' Yet Green also notes the unstable nature of the relationship, and of Saraladevi's personality, which apparently included a 'sense of being unappreciated' and contradictory elements of strength and indecisiveness, drive and inertia, feminism and male appeasement. While in some ways a 'headstrong feminist', she also supported polygamy if the first wife was infertile. Gandhi seems to have opposed her; he 'argued' with Saraladevi on this question, he would tell Sanger.[65]

Between the end of October 1919 and the middle of February 1920, Gandhi spent some weeks in Delhi but the bulk of the time in the Punjab, travelling to conduct his inquiry (and promote khadi) or working on his report in the home of the Chaudhuris in Lahore. Saraladevi often accompanied Gandhi on his travels in the Punjab, spoke or sang at his meetings, wore and championed khadi, and asked the Punjab to absorb the meaning of satyagraha. Both she and Gandhi spoke of their disappointment that many in the province had taken repression lying down.

By the end of December Rambhuj Dutt Chaudhuri was released. Gandhi would say, in a report for *Navajivan* written on 23 January: 'Where earlier I had seen a woman, separated from her husband and living all alone, the image of a lioness, I saw today a happy couple ... I saw a new glow on Smt. Saraladevi's face. The face which had been lined with care was today bright with joy' (19: 358). By this time the couple's teenage son Dipak had been sent to Sabarmati, where ashramites questioned the relaxations that Gandhi seemed to propose for the boy. And when, in March 1920, Saraladevi was herself at the ashram, there was criticism of the time Gandhi spent talking with her.

For four to five months – between January and May 1920 – Gandhi was clearly dazzled by her personality and seemed to fantasize that Providence desired them together to shape India to a new design. He wrote to her that he often dreamt of her, and that she was a great shakti. In February 1920 *Young India* carried a song by Saraladevi on the front page, and *Navajivan* another poem by her, along with Gandhi's comment that it was 'perfect'.[66]

But his son Devadas and others (Desai, Mathuradas and C R were among them) questioned Gandhi and asked him to think of the consequences for Kasturba, people like them and Gandhi himself if he continued the special relationship with Saraladevi. 'It was their love which chained me so tightly and strongly' and saved him, Gandhi would say to Father Lash (59: 196).

An autobiography that Saraladevi later wrote makes no reference to the relationship. Nor does Gandhi's, though a few letters and recorded conversations reveal his thoughts on it. 'It was so personal I did not put it into my autobiography,' he said to Sanger. Rambhuj Dutt Chaudhuri had died in 1923, but Saraladevi and her son Dipak were very much alive when the Autobiography was written and Gandhi could not have referred to the episode without hurting her again.

Saraladevi was heartbroken when Gandhi informed her that their relationship could not continue as once thought. The change seems to have occurred in the middle of June 1920, for on 12 June, after receiving a telegram from Gandhi, Rajagopalachari wrote to him: 'Had your telegram. Words fail me altogether. I hope you have pardoned me.'[67] We can infer that Gandhi's telegram (its text is not known) signified a change in the relationship to one who had voiced his concern.

Determined to secure the change, Rajagopalachari wrote Gandhi a strong letter on 16 June. Addressed to 'My dearest Master,' the letter said that between Saraladevi and Kasturba the contrast was similar to that between 'a kerosene oil Ditmar lamp' and 'the morning sun'. Asserting that Gandhi had nursed a 'most dreadful delusion', C R added: 'The encasement of the divinest soul is yet flesh ... It is not the Christ but the shell that I presume to warn and criticize. Come back and give us life ... Pray disengage yourself at once completely.'[68]

The break was made. Devadas has written that when he was leaving for a course of study in Benares (probably in the summer of 1920), his father 'suddenly stepped forward and with great love kissed me on the forehead'.[69] Gandhi was showing gratitude, and not just love, to his 20-year-old son. He would say in August in a letter to Kallenbach, 'Devadas is with me, ever growing in every way and every direction' (21: 131). And to Saraladevi he wrote on 23 August that Mathuradas and other allies were right to be 'jealous of his character, which was their ideal'. To deserve their love, which was 'so pure and unselfish', he would, he told her, 'surrender all the world' (21: 196).

A shattered Saraladevi complained that she had 'put in one pan all the joys and pleasures of the world, and in the other Bapu and his laws, and committed the folly of choosing the latter'.[70] She demanded an explanation, which Gandhi finally tried to offer in a letter he sent in December 1920:

> I have been analyzing my love for you. I have reached a definition of spiritual [marriage]. It is a partnership between two persons of the opposite sex where the physical is wholly absent. It is therefore possible between brother and sister, father and daughter. It is possible only between two brahmacharis in thought, word and deed …
>
> Have we that exquisite purity, that perfect coincidence, that perfect merging, that identity of ideals, the self-forgetfulness, that fixity of purpose, that trustfulness? For me I can answer plainly that it is only an aspiration. I am unworthy of that companionship with you … This is the big letter I promised. With dearest love I still subscribe myself, Your L.G. (22: 119)

The initials stood for 'Law Giver', the title with which she had rebuked Gandhi. A brave effort, the letter could not assuage Saraladevi's feelings. In the years that followed she would criticize Gandhi, at times accusing him of allowing non-violence to break out in hatred, and at other times saying that he possessed a Christo-Buddhist rather than a Hindu frame of mind (24: 400).

Communication did not cease, however. In the 1940s, at her suggestion, Gandhi suggested Dipak's name to Jawaharlal as a possible match for his daughter Indira. That idea did not work out but after Saraladevi and Gandhi were both no more, Dipak married Radha, the daughter of Maganlal Gandhi. Saraladevi and Gandhi had known of this romance. After giving some of her time to the education of girls, Saraladevi turned to spirituality and in 1935 adopted a guru. She died in 1945.

What, if anything, Gandhi told Kasturba about the episode is not known, but we must assume that she noticed both the attachment and its severance. Others too would have told her, including Devadas, who was devoted to his mother. We must assume also that the relationship shocked and wounded Kasturba while it lasted, and that its ending enhanced her prestige in circles around him. Writing about her in the letter he wrote to Kallenbach after a two-year gap, Gandhi said in August 1920: 'Mrs Gandhi is at [the]Ashram. She has aged considerably but she is as brave as ever.' (21: 132)

Twelve years later Gandhi would write to Ramdas that he did not want any of his sons

> to behave towards his wife as I did towards Ba ... [S]he could not be angry with me, whereas I could with her. I did not give her the same freedom of action which I enjoyed ... My behaviour towards Ba at Sabarmati progressively [changed] ... and the result was that ... [h]er old fear of me has disappeared mostly, if not completely (11 Aug. 1932; 56: 316–17).

Though Gandhi did not mention it in the letter, the Saraladevi episode, which occurred a year after Kasturba's life-saving intervention over milk, may have contributed to the improvement in his attitude.

Khilafat & 'Non-cooperation'. Agitated by signs that the victorious Allies intended to end the Turkish Sultan's custodianship of Islam's holy places in Arabia, Palestine and Iraq, many of India's Muslim leaders met in Delhi in November 1919.

After recalling a promise by the Prime Minister, Lloyd George, on 5 January 1918 that the Allies were not 'fighting to deprive Turkey of the rich and renowned lands of Asia Minor', a promise that had enabled Indian Muslims to enlist as soldiers for the British, the gathering searched for a suitable response to what seemed both a betrayal and a sacrilege, for the Turkish Sultan, the head or Khalifa of the Sunni faithful around the world, had protected Islam's holy places for centuries (19: 447).

Invited to the deliberations, where indignation with the British was marked and he was viewed with some suspicion, Gandhi asked the Muslims to be firm but also wise. Boycotting all foreign cloth was more sensible, he said, than singling out British products, and in any case it would be laughable for an assembly where everyone had 'some article of British manufacture on his person' to declare a boycott of British imports (A 434).

At this, Maulana Hasrat Mohani, who had demanded the boycott of British goods, countered that boycotting all foreign cloth was not very practical either. However, Mohani added, 'Let that stand, but give us something quicker.' Gandhi's response, conveyed in his still rough Hindustani, contained a single English phrase for which he could not readily find a Hindustani word. Once more he was ready for the moment of opportunity.

'We can respond with *non-cooperation*,' Gandhi said. If the Allies and the British played foul with Turkey, 'which may God forbid', Indians could refuse to cooperate with British rule. They could return the Raj's titles and honours and withhold cooperation even from the tempting councils the Montford scheme was offering (A 435).

The Delhi gathering decided to wait for the decision of the Allies, but 'non-cooperation' intrigued many Muslim minds, and Gandhi had moved a step closer to his goal of a Hindu-Muslim front.

The Amritsar Congress and the Reforms Act. Its principal leaders were all present when, in December, the Congress met for its annual session in Amritsar, on a site chosen for its proximity to Jallianwalla Bagh. Released on the session's eve, the Ali brothers were a large draw. Tilak, Annie Besant and Jinnah were present, as also Malaviya, the retiring president, and Motilal Nehru, who succeeded him. The Bengalis were led by Chitta Ranjan Das and Bipin Chandra Pal, both famed for their oratory.

However, thanks to the Rowlatt satyagraha and his response to the Punjab repression, Gandhi, still not fully fit, was the people's star. Motilal Nehru acknowledged as much when from the chair he referred to 'Mahatmaji',[71] and Jinnah, too, spoke of 'Mahatma Gandhi'.[72] Supporting Gandhi in Amritsar was a second line of leadership attracted by him, including Vallabhbhai Patel from Gujarat, Jawaharlal Nehru from Allahabad, Rajagopalachari from Madras and Rajendra Prasad from Bihar.

The Montford scheme, now passed by the House of Commons as the Reforms Act, was the main item before the plenary, but after what had happened in the Punjab it appeared impossible to accept what the British offered. Tilak, Das and Pal led the attack on the Act, but Malaviya, Motilal Nehru and Annie Besant seemed willing to try it out.

In the end, a resolution moved by Gandhi and seconded by Jinnah was accepted. Through it the Congress declared that it would work the Reforms Act even though it was 'inadequate' and 'disappointing'. Gandhi said that the release of the Ali brothers had encouraged him to hope that the British would respect Indian sentiments, including over the Punjab wrongs and the Khilafat question.

Redefining honour

Concerning the Punjab, Gandhi drafted for the subjects committee a resolution that condemned the massacre and also the violence of Indian mobs. A record of the discussion on this resolution has been left by a delegate, K M Munshi, a lawyer and author from Bombay who would hold senior positions in independent India:

> The hearts of most of us revolted at the latter part of the resolution ... This must have been Mrs Besant's work, many thought; she was after all British. One Punjab leader gave expression to the feeling rather crudely: no one born of an Indian mother, said he, could have drafted this resolution. Lokamanya too was indignant and so were Pal and C.R. Das; and the latter part of the resolution was lost by an overwhelming majority.

The next day the President wanted the committee to reconsider the resolution as Gandhiji, he said, was very keen on it. There were vehement protests. Ultimately Gandhiji was helped to the table to move that the resolution be reconsidered. He spoke sitting. Out of respect the house sat quiet but with ill-concealed impatience.

Referring to the remark that no son born of an Indian mother could have drafted the resolution, Gandhiji stated that he had considered deeply and long whether as an Indian he could have drafted the resolution, for indeed he had drafted it. But after long searching of the heart, he had come to the conclusion that only a person born of an Indian mother could have drafted it.

And then he spoke as if his whole life depended upon the question ... When he stopped, we were at his feet ... The resolution was reconsidered and accepted in its original form.[73]

Other remarks by Gandhi in Amritsar were recorded by Pyarelal Nayar. Gandhi's voice, Pyarelal would say, was 'full-chested and so distinct that it could be heard clearly to the farthest end of the vast gathering in that pre-mike era.' Said Gandhi:

The Government went mad, but our people also went mad. I say, do not return madness with madness but return madness with sanity, and the situation will be yours.[74]

From England, where he was on vacation, Frederick Pratt, the commissioner in Ahmedabad, sent a 'private' letter to Gandhi:

A week or two ago when I read the account of your speech in the Amritsar Congress... I felt that I would like to write and congratulate you on the stand you took ...

Our relations in the past have not been harmonious. Speaking for myself only, I feel sure that there have been hard thoughts and hard words against you, which were not justified. But the future matters more than the past, and I wish to grasp the hand of fellowship and cooperation in the same spirit in which you extended it in your admirable speech.[75]

Pratt's gallant letter indirectly acknowledged that in Amritsar Gandhi had given a new meaning to Indian honour, enabled the Congress to capture the moral high ground, and put the Empire on the defensive. According to Munshi, 'the old guard were routed' at Amritsar and 'Gandhiji was left in possession of the field'.[76]

Restructuring the Congress. Gandhi was also left holding a baby, for the Congress asked him to write a new constitution for the party. Two years earlier he had restructured the

Gujarat Sabha. Now he offered a new design for the Indian National Congress (22: 170–78). In the constitution he proposed, any adult accepting the Congress's goal ('Swaraj within the Empire') and paying four annas (one-quarter of a rupee) a year could become a Congress member. Where referring to a member's rights and roles, Gandhi's draft, approved in December 1920, spoke of 'he' or 'she', and 'him' or 'her'.

Democratically-elected committees would function at all levels – village or town, taluka, district, province and all-India. Unlike the Raj's provinces, Congress provinces would be linguistic and include adjacent princely territories, but the Congress would not interfere in the internal affairs of princely states. Elected annually by votes from each provincial unit, the Congress president would nominate a Working Committee of 15 which would function round the year and where the president would only be *primus inter pares*.

Popular membership, admitting persons from princely states, specifying that women were welcome, and the proposed committees, including the Working Committee at the apex, were all new ideas. Emboldened by Amritsar, Gandhi was looking to forge a people's Congress as well as an efficient, and if necessary fighting, machine.

8

The Empire Challenged

India, 1920–2

For some months after the Amritsar session, Gandhi encouraged his younger allies' interest in the provincial legislatures created by the Reforms Act. Elections for these legislatures were set for November 1920. Though vital issues were reserved for the British governor and his nominated council, the new legislatures, chosen by a partial franchise, would possess tempting powers. So Vallabhbhai announced his candidature for the Bombay legislature from Kheda, and in Madras Rajagopalachari drafted a manifesto for the Congress nationalists.

But influential events intervened in March and May, and Gandhi's suppressed sense that he would rise against the Empire came true. The first event concerned Turkey and its Khilafat. Muhammad Ali, who led a deputation to England in March urging Prime Minister Lloyd George not to remove Islam's holy places from Turkish control, was told by the Premier that there was no reason for Turkey to escape the 'justice, the pretty terrible justice', that Germany and Austria had received.[1]

Gandhi responded by calling Khilafat 'the question of questions' and saying that 'the terrible, stern justice for Turkey must be tempered with the pledged word … of the British Empire' (*Young India,* 31 Mar. 1920).

Yet on 14 May India learnt of the Treaty of Sèvres, which not only deprived Turkey of all her colonies and of Greek-majority areas, but placed Mecca and Medina under a pro-British chieftain, and gave Britain a mandate over Iraq, which contained Karbala and Najaf, and also over Palestine, which included Jerusalem. All of Islam's holiest sites were thus placed under the direct or indirect influence of Britain, while France, another non-Muslim country, was asked to 'advise and assist Syria'.

If Muslim India's indignation had solidified by mid-May, all of India was offended

Chakravarti Rajagopalachari – 1930

before the end of the month by the report of the Hunter Commission on the excesses in the Punjab. While confirming the facts summarized in Gandhi's account, the Hunter Report drew weak conclusions and absolved the Punjab governor, O'Dwyer, of all responsibility. General Dyer was held guilty of 'a grave error of judgement' and deprived of his command, but that could not soothe the wounds caused by O'Dwyer's harsh decrees. There was worse to come. The House of Lords passed a motion in support of Dyer and British admirers presented him with a sword of honour and £20,000.

The simultaneous resentment of Hindu and Muslim India was a rare phenomenon. For over six decades, the Raj had worked painstakingly and successfully to prevent a Hindu-Muslim front. The last time something similar had happened was in 1857, when Hindus and Muslims of the Empire's Bengal army had mutinied. Involving only a part of India, that rebellion was ruthlessly and effectively crushed. This time, however, Gandhi had non-violent weapons for baffling the British, and he hoped to involve all of India. As he would say in Madras on 12 August, and repeat the thought in Calicut on 18 August, India had been given 'an opportunity which is not going to recur for another hundred years' (21: 145 & 183).

Suddenly, three deep longings of his seemed realizable: Hindu-Muslim unity, if Hindus made common cause with Muslims; weaning Muslims from violence, if they were offered the option of non-violent non-cooperation; and the end of British rule, if Hindus and Muslims jointly withheld their cooperation from the Raj.

We have seen that this last was his heart's desire but so far the head had ruled it out. Now, with the Empire rejecting its principles, he felt he had no choice. Moreover, India was so bitterly estranged from the Empire that if he did not lead an all-Indian as well as a non-violent fight, others were likely to incite Muslims, Hindus and Sikhs to separate, violent, regional and (as 1857 had proved) futile rebellions.

The chance of a lifetime seemed the only possible option, and it found Gandhi ready. After all, he had begun cultivating the Ali brothers (and other Muslim leaders) within weeks of his return from South Africa, and from April 1919 he was preparing the ground for challenging the Empire over the Punjab.

Sharply disagreeing with Gandhi's stand on Khilafat, Henry Polak, now living in England, accused him of 'narrowness', which he linked to Gandhi 'being cooped up in India and not knowing anything of the new life in Europe'.

Yet new events had occurred or were looming in the Middle East as well. In November 1917, well before the post-war reallocation of the Ottoman Empire's lands, the British Foreign Secretary, Balfour, had announced a British commitment for 'a national home for the Jewish people' in Palestine. Their close comradeship in South Africa notwithstanding, a British Jew and an Indian aiming for Swaraj and Hindu-Muslim partnership could not take the same view of the Middle East.

To Polak, 27 Mar. 1920: Now for the Khilafat. I do not mind your differing from me so violently as you do ... I can only say that the new life in Europe appears to me to be abhorrent for its total disregard of sanctity of promises and of its idolatrous worship of brute force and money. Being in the thick of it, you are unable to feel the foul stench that modern Europe is filling the world with. I who stand outside it know what it means ... [I]f I could but see you face to face, I would certainly endeavour to convert you to my view (20: 186).

For a while criticism of Gandhi's Khilafat position came also from Andrews, who underlined the right of Arab and Armenian territories to be free of Turkish domination. Gandhi's reply touched on the European powers' commercial motives.

To Andrews, 25 May 1920: I have said always that absolute guarantees may be taken from the [Turkish] Sultan about non-interference with the internal administration of Armenia; similarly for Arabia.

The position created by the peace treaty is simply intolerable. The Arabians have lost what independence they had under the Sultan because they were more than a match for him. And now if the king of Hejaz and Amir Feisal can help it, Arabia and Mesopotamia will be drained dry for both these men will be puppets in the hands of British officers whose one aim would be to make as much money as possible for the European capitalists (20: 359).

Writing a month later in *Young India*, Gandhi referred pointedly to Britain's interest in 'the oil of Mosul' (30 Jun. 1920; 20: 432). The Hunter Report had come on top of the Treaty of Sèvres, and Gandhi asked Andrews 'to realize with me the enormity of the double crime of the present British administration or make me see my folly and correct myself!' (20: 411)

His call. Now asking Indians *not* to take part in the elections due in November, Gandhi also spelt out, in a *Young India* article in early May, the gains he expected from non-cooperation: Hindu-Muslim friendship – Muslims were likely to respond positively to Hindu support over Khilafat – and an honourable relationship between India and Britain.

In this article of 5 May Gandhi also outlined a four-stage strategy for non-cooperation. In the first stage Indians should return titles and honorary posts. Later, when leaders gave the word, Indians should think of quitting civilian jobs with the government. The more distant third and fourth stages would involve withdrawal from the police and the military, and non-payment of taxes (20: 285–8).

Quick to accept non-cooperation, some Muslim leaders requested his leadership. To them he addressed direct words about the practical consequences of non-cooperation:

If there is no spirit of sacrifice at least they should get rid of a man like myself. I can secure no diplomatic triumph. I can only guide along the difficult, narrow and thorny path of self-sacrifice ... [2]

And also about non-violence:

Navajivan, 16 May 1920: I told them that non-cooperation would be possible only if they gave up the idea of violence. Even if there was a single murder by any of us or at our instance, I would leave. They agreed, and understood that non-cooperation was, in many respects, a more potent weapon than violence (20: 318).

Admitting that many Muslims responding to non-cooperation did 'not believe in my doctrine of non-violence to the full extent', that 'if some of them could offer successful violence, they would do [so] today', and that they were not 'free from hatred', he yet hoped that by 'joining my love with their hatred' he could 'diminish the intensity of that hatred' (*Navajivan*, 18 Apr. 1920; 20: 214).

Violence was very much in the air, and in Muslim rhetoric, as was the notion of hijrat – migration from defiled to purer lands. A land ruled by a race destroying Khilafat was deemed defiled, and India's Muslims were exhorted to migrate to a Muslim country. Gandhi advised against hijrat, but in the spring of 1920 several thousand Indian Muslims (mostly Pathans from the North-West Frontier Province, including Abdul Ghaffar Khan) moved into Afghanistan. After a few months' privation and several deaths they returned.

Some enraged Muslims hinted at the possibility – 'for the purpose of forcing better peace terms' for Turkey – of an invasion of British India from Afghanistan. Gandhi not only attacked the idea in *Young India* (23 Jun. 1920); he said that in the event of such an invasion it would be 'the duty of every Hindu to resist any inroad on India', even as it was the duty of Hindus to join Muslims in non-violent non-cooperation (20: 419).

Jinnah, Ajmal Khan, Ansari & Azad. At the end of April, on the urgings of activists like Sobhani, Banker and Yagnik, Gandhi had accepted the presidency of the All-India Home Rule League. This did not go down well with Annie Besant, who had founded the League, or with Jinnah, one of its leading members, both of whom were wary of non-cooperation. Still, Gandhi now had a platform of his own in case the Congress found non-cooperation too hot, and he sought the help of Jinnah's wife Ruttie, whose trust he had evoked, for winning her husband over.

To Mrs Jinnah, 30 Apr. 1920: Please remember me to Mr Jinnah and do coax him to learn Hindustani or Gujarati. If I were you, I should begin to talk to him in Gujarati or Hindustani. There is not much danger of you forgetting your English or your misunderstanding each other, is there? ... Yes, I would ask this even for the love you bear me (20: 258).

Whether or not Ruttie did as he urged, Jinnah remained cool to Gandhi's plans. Though resenting the treatment of Turkey, Jinnah was troubled by Gandhi's interest in direct popular action, for he was a constitutionalist preferring hard negotiations in dignified chambers and in the English language.

However, a Central Khilafat Committee of India's Muslims embraced non-violent non-cooperation, and several leading Muslim figures allied themselves to Gandhi, including the Ali brothers and two prominent medical practitioners from Delhi whom Gandhi had first met in 1915, Hakim Ajmal Khan (1863–1927) and Mukhtar Ahmed Ansari (1880–1936). Ajmal Khan had in fact returned his British medal in March.

Another key Gandhi ally from 1920 was Calcutta's Abul Kalam Azad (1888–1958), a brilliant writer, orator and Islamic scholar who had captivated Muslim India with his Urdu journals *Al Hilal* and *Al Balagh,* and whom the Raj had interned in Ranchi in Bihar from 1916 to 1920. A devout Muslim with Arab links on his mother's side, Azad had always held that cooperating with Hindus violated no Islamic injunction. In 1920 Azad, who had briefly endorsed hijrat, announced his support for non-violent non-cooperation, while clarifying that he was accepting non-violence as a policy, not a creed. The Ali brothers had said the same thing.

Audacious letter. Taking longer to make up its mind, the Congress said that its decision on non-cooperation would be made at a special session in Calcutta in September. Not waiting for its decision, Gandhi announced at the end of June that non-cooperation would begin on 1 August, unless the terms for Turkey were revised and redress obtained over the Punjab.

To Lord Chelmsford, the Viceroy, who had admitted that the Treaty with respect to Turkey contained 'terms which must be painful to all Moslems',[3] he penned, on 22 June in Delhi (in the home of his host, Principal Rudra of St Stephen's College), a bold, sombre letter that merits an even longer quotation than here provided:

Your Excellency, As one who has enjoyed a certain measure of Your Excellency's confidence and as one who claims to be a devoted well-wisher of the British Empire, I owe it to Your Excellency and, through Your Excellency, to His Majesty's Ministers, to explain my connection with and my conduct in the Khilafat question.

At the very earliest stage of the War, even whilst I was in London organizing the Indian Volunteer Ambulance Corps, I began to interest myself in the Khilafat question. I perceived how deeply moved the little Mussulman world in London was when Turkey decided to throw in her lot with Germany.

On my arrival in India in the January of 1915 I found the same anxiousness and earnestness among the Mussulmans with whom I came in contact. Their anxiety became intense when the information about the secret treaties leaked out ... The peace terms and Your Excellency's defence of them have given the Mussulmans of India a shock from which it will be difficult for them to recover ...

I consider that as a staunch Hindu wishing to live on terms of the closest friendship with my Mussulman countrymen, I should be an unworthy son of India if I did not stand by them in their hour of trial ...

So far as I am aware Mussulmans and Hindus have as a whole lost faith in British justice and honour. The Report of the Majority of the Hunter Committee, Your Excellency's Despatch thereon, and Mr Montagu's reply have only aggravated the distrust ...

Your Excellency must be aware that there was a time when the boldest though also the most thoughtless among the Mussulmans favoured violence and that hijrat has not yet ceased to be the battle-cry.

The school of hijrat has received a check if it has not stopped its activities entirely. I hold that no repression could have prevented a violent eruption, if the people had not had presented to them a form of direct action ...

I venture to claim that I have succeeded by patient reasoning in weaning the party of violence from its ways. I confess that I did not – I did not attempt to – succeed in weaning them from violence on moral grounds, but purely on utilitarian grounds. The result for the time being at any rate has however been to stop violence ...

At the same time I admit that non-cooperation practised by the mass of people is attended with grave risks. But ... not to run some risks now will be to court much greater risks, if not virtual destruction of law and order.

But there is yet an escape from non-cooperation. The Mussulman representation has requested Your Excellency to lead the agitation yourself as did your distinguished predecessor at the time of the South African trouble. But if you cannot see your way to do so, and non-cooperation becomes a dire necessity, I hope that Your Excellency will give those who have accepted my advice and myself the credit for being actuated by nothing less than a stern sense of duty. *I have etc.,* M. K. GANDHI (20: 413–16)

The letter was in effect a claim that he, brown-skinned, unarmed and without office, was guiding the country more effectively and justly than all the Raj; and a demand that the present Viceroy should support Gandhi even as the previous incumbent, Hardinge, had done.

Maganlal's misgivings. In his own ashram, however, Maganlal, its head when Gandhi was absent, complained that Gandhi was not giving enough time to the ashram or to the spiritual life. The involvement with politics in general and Muslims in particular troubled Maganlal and others in the ashram (most of them Hindus from conservative backgrounds), just as his stand over admitting the Dheds had done five years earlier. Saraladevi, too, was a major issue, if one about to die down, between Gandhi and his closest ashram colleagues.

In addition, Maganlal was surprised that Gandhi seemed open to the idea of a car for the ashram. Finally, Maganlal felt that Gandhi was losing both physical strength and spiritual lustre. Gandhi's 'power, in virtue of which everyone was obliged to listen to what you said,' had disappeared. The reply sent to Maganlal (4 May 1920) was every bit as self-assured as Gandhi's letter to the Viceroy.

While conceding that he had lost his 'former fire', Gandhi termed the loss purely physical. 'My illness has disabled me,' he wrote. 'The steel-like strength of my body' had gone. 'Did anyone ever see me going for a change of air? Well, that is what I do now.' But he added:

> My staunchness has not disappeared. My ideas have grown stronger and more piercing. My indifference to worldly pleasures has increased. What I used to see but dimly has now become clearer to me. I have grown more tolerant, so that I am less particular about others [doing what I want them to do].

As for the car, Gandhi said:

> Economically, I saw that a car would be an advantage. We certainly use cars a good deal. The question was whether we could accept a car as a gift. I did not think it quite proper to give an immediate reply on my own. For two days I struggled hard against the idea but, thinking of Lyall,* I softened and thought that I would accept the gift if you also desired that I should.

On Khilafat, Gandhi wrote:

> If I had not joined the Khilafat movement, I think, I would have lost everything. In joining it I have followed what I especially regard as my dharma ... I am uniting Hindus and Muslims ... [I]f non-cooperation goes well, a great power based on brute force will have to submit to a simple-looking thing.

---

* We do not know about Lyall or his needs.

The Khilafat movement is a great churning of the sea of India. Why should we be concerned with what it will produce? All that we should consider is whether the movement itself is a pure and worthy cause.

In the end Gandhi reminded Maganlal that Doke had called him 'a pathfinder' and had wanted to call his book 'Pathfinder' or 'Junglebreaker' rather than 'An Indian Patriot', the title for which Polak had successfully pressed (20: 281–4).

The regret about his 'abandoning spirituality for politics', expressed by not just Maganlal, was memorably answered in *Young India* (12 May 1920). Repudiating any notion that he was a saint, Gandhi added:

But though by disclaiming sainthood I disappoint the critic's expectations, I would have him to give up his regrets by answering him that the politician in me has never dominated a single decision of mine, and if I seem to take part in politics, it is only because politics encircle us today like the coil of a snake from which one cannot get out, no matter how much one tries.

I wish therefore to wrestle with the snake, as I have been doing, with more or less success, consciously since 1894, unconsciously, as I have now discovered, ever since reaching the years of discretion.

Gandhi was acknowledging an attraction to politics ever since his boyhood. But he insisted that he was introducing the religious spirit into it.

Quite selfishly, as I wish to live in peace in the midst of a bellowing storm howling round me, I have been experimenting with myself and my friends by introducing religion into politics.

Let me explain what I mean by religion. It is not the Hindu religion, which I certainly prize above all other religions, but the religion which transcends Hinduism, which changes one's very nature, which binds one indissolubly to the truth within and which ever purifies (20: 304).

He was saying two things. One, he preserved his balance in the tempest of politics by holding tight to a firmly-fastened religious bar or rail. Two, that that religious bar or rail was something moral and universal, transcending Hinduism.

Despite such explicit clarifications, Gandhi was seen, and knew he was seen, as a (or, by many, *the*) symbol of Hinduism. Not, to be sure, as the founder of a new Hindu sect or order, but as a man of action, a karmayogi, who represented the Hindu world to Hindus, Muslims, the Empire and others. Useful politically, this image was a challenge also to the Hindu world, to which gradually yet surely Gandhi was introducing the touchstones of rationality, fairness and compassion. Becoming India's best-known and most-loved Hindu, he had acquired the stature to instruct the Hindu world in resisting domination from without, and intolerance from within.

Nobly conscientious, Maganlal had sacrificed his dreams and life for Gandhi. But he wanted his hero to settle down, not cut new paths. On the other hand, Harilal, refusing stubbornly to be rooted to anything and forever in debt, responded enthusiastically to non-cooperation and for a while wore the simple white khadi cap, copied from a prison uniform in South Africa, that became a symbol of the non-cooperation struggle.[4]

It was not easy for the righteously loyal Maganlal to recognize either the significance of his uncle's newest undertaking or the depth of the personal struggle within one aiming at historic changes even while caught in a doomed human relationship that had appeared to promise so much. Maganlal was too close to Gandhi, and too focused on his duties at the ashram, to appreciate the vigour, innovative enterprise, boldness and self-denial of the 50-year-old Gandhi who in 1920 took on the Empire and took up his people's burdens while shutting the door to a possibly satisfying relationship with a talented woman.

Defying fatigue and weakness, only sleeping a few hours a night, Gandhi travelled, wrote letters and articles, spoke at meetings, persuaded face-to-face, and debated in the press. There were meetings in Allahabad (early June), in Bombay (early July), in cities in the Punjab (Lahore, Amritsar, Rawalpindi, and Jullundur in the middle of July), Sindh (late July), in south India (August) and in Gujarat (late August). In his talks Gandhi explained non-cooperation, asked for non-violence, and claimed, as in his letter to the Viceroy, that it was the non-cooperation alternative that had prevented violence. Pyarelal would afterwards recall:

> One day I counted fifty-six letters which he had written in his own hand. Each of them he carefully read from the date line to the final detail of the address before handing them for dispatch. At the end of it he was so exhausted that, pressing his throbbing temples between his two hands, he flung himself down on the hard floor just where he was sitting, without even spreading the bedding he was leaning against. He simply pushed it aside.[5]

Tilak is no more. Hindu caution regarding non-cooperation had been ended by the Hunter Report, and in fact Hindus were not indifferent. Even Tilak, jealous of the Hindu interest, had said at the end of May 1920 that 'Hindus would support' Muslim decisions on Khilafat.[6] The comment recalled Tilak's lead for the 1916 pact where, in exchange for Muslim support, the Congress had accepted a separate Muslim electorate.

However, worn out by diabetes and years in prison, Tilak, the man who had taught Indians to say 'Swaraj is my birthright', died on 1 August, the day non-cooperation was to start. Gandhi shouldered the bier, stood beside the flames that took away the Loka-manya's 64-year-old body, and composed a tribute calling Tilak 'a giant among men', 'the idol of his people' and 'the lion' whose voice was 'hushed' (21: 111).

Later that day Gandhi sent a letter to the Viceroy returning the medals he had received for services in South Africa and saying that after the double let-down over Khilafat and the Punjab, he retained neither respect nor affection for the Raj. Across India, many returned their medals. In his reply Chelmsford called non-cooperation 'the most foolish of all foolish schemes'.

The Calcutta session. While many Indians disagreed with the Viceroy, several Congress leaders did not. They mounted a bid to thwart non-cooperation at the Calcutta session in September. Motilal Nehru met Jinnah off his train and talked tactics. Also cool towards non-cooperation were Annie Besant, Bengal's Chitta Ranjan Das and Bipin Chandra Pal, Pandit Malaviya of Benares, and the man who would preside, Lala Lajpat Rai of the Punjab, who had been away in America when the Jallianwalla killings occurred.

This was a formidable line-up of older leaders, but the rank and file were with Gandhi, as was the younger leadership, including Patel, C R, Prasad, Jawaharlal and Azad. Before the Calcutta meeting, Patel, who had given up all thought of entering the Bombay legislature, had organized a Gujarat conference that endorsed non-cooperation and asked Hindus to support Muslims 'heart-broken' by the treatment of Turkey.[7]

Sensing the mood in Calcutta, including that of his son, Motilal switched and voted for Gandhi's resolution asking for non-cooperation. In his speech Gandhi cited the sentiment he had found throughout India – once more his travelling had helped him. Malaviya, Das, Pal, Jinnah, and Mrs Besant spoke in opposition, but Gandhi's resolution was carried by a large majority, 1,855 votes to 873.

The resolution asked for return of the Raj's honours and titles, a boycott of the Raj's councils and of the November elections, a boycott of foreign goods and a gradual with-drawal by students and lawyers from the Raj's schools, colleges and courts. The word 'gradual' was a concession to reality: even enthusiasts were not ready right away to leave the Raj's institutions, or to ask their children to do so.

We may note that on this visit to Calcutta, Gandhi stayed with his son Harilal, on Pollock Street. Also meeting in Calcutta, the Muslim League passed without opposition a similar resolution championed by Shaukat Ali. Presiding over the League's session, Jinnah spoke of Rowlatt, 'the Punjab atrocities' and 'Khilafat, a matter of life and death', and conceded that some kind of non-cooperation was unavoidable.

But he fell out with Gandhi the following month when, at Gandhi's instance, the Home Rule League changed its constitution and name. By 42 votes to 19, the body decided that henceforth it would seek, simply, 'Swaraj', rather than 'Self-govern-ment within the Empire', and be called Swarajya Sabha. One of the outvoted 19, Jinnah had asked for retention of the reference to the Empire. Charging that the meeting was not competent to change the body's constitution, Jinnah resigned, as did 18 others.

Disagreeing on the constitutional point, Gandhi had recommended 'Swaraj' because it left open the question of India's link with the Empire, which could be retained or broken as needed. He requested Jinnah to return and invited him to 'take your share in the new life that has opened up before the country'. The suggestion that he had to be offered a role did not go down well with Jinnah, who responded with sarcasm and expressed his fears regarding Gandhi's agenda:

> I thank you for your kind suggestion offering me 'to take my share in the new life that has opened up before the country'. If by 'new life' you mean your methods and your programme, I am afraid I cannot accept them, for I am fully convinced that it [sic] must lead to disaster.[8]

Though unclear whether he was dealing with a singular or a plural noun, Jinnah was clearly predicting violence.

Nagpur session. Despite the Raj's hope that 'the sanity of the classes and masses alike would reject non-cooperation', November provided evidence that at least the masses were embracing it. Two-thirds of India's electors boycotted the voting for the new legislatures. Jinnah was among the boycotters, but he was one of only three leaders, Annie Besant and Malaviya being the other two, who signalled their opposition to Gandhi's agenda when, in December, the Congress met in Nagpur for its annual plenary session.

As chairman of the reception committee, the Wardha-based Jamnalal Bajaj, Gandhi's ally from 1915, organized the session, which was chaired by C Vijiaraghavachariar from the south, but the Gandhian programme needed no props. The country's preference was plain to everyone, and those who had opposed non-cooperation in Calcutta advocated it in Nagpur. Das moved the resolution endorsing it, and Lajpat Rai and Pal backed Das. Annie Besant did not attend. In town but unwell, Malaviya sent a message opposing non-cooperation. It was heard with respect but not heeded. Only two persons, one from UP and the other from Sindh, voiced dissent when Das's resolution was put before the house. Their names are not known.[9]

At Nagpur the Congress also accepted the new bottom-up structure for its organiza-tion that Gandhi had proposed. Three general secretaries were appointed for the coming year: Motilal Nehru, Ansari and Rajagopalachari. For the first time in its history, a campaign against untouchability was made part of the Congress programme. Finally, as the Home Rule League had done, the Congress changed its aim from 'Swaraj within the Empire' to just 'Swaraj'.

Jinnah was emphatic in his opposition to this change, and at first Das and Pal agreed with him. Later Jinnah was left alone in dissent, and when he referred in his remarks to 'Mr Gandhi' and 'Mr Muhammad Ali', there were shouts that he should say 'Mahatma' and 'Maulana'. Gandhi urged the audience to respect Jinnah and his choice of words, but the Bombay barrister felt he had had enough. After Nagpur he left the Congress.

Jinnah's keenness on the link with the Empire was in line with an important strand in Muslim thinking that went back to Sir Sayyid Ahmad Khan (1817–98), who had founded the Aligarh Muslim University (AMU). Pointing out that Hindus would dominate any democratic self-government in India, Sir Sayyid had asked the qaum, his Muslim community, to invoke the Empire's protection.

On the other hand, as Gandhi recognized, many Hindus, too, 'believe[d] that British rule serve[d] ... to protect Hinduism' from possible Muslim attacks. But he felt that nothing could be 'more humiliating' to Hindus than the idea that despite being three times more numerous than Muslims they needed British protection. If Hindus took the unexpected opportunity that lay before them – 'the like of it will not come again for a hundred years,' he repeated – and supported the Muslims, the latter were likely to respond positively. If they did not, the Hindus were strong enough to take care of themselves (*Navajivan*, 29 Aug. 1920; 21: 209–10).

Two poles & a new spirit

From 1920 onwards, Indians seemed conscious of two political poles, one represented by the Empire and the other by Gandhi. Those gravitating openly to the second pole, non-cooperators and their supporters, identified themselves by wearing khadi and often by spinning on a charkha. Muhammad Ali donned khadi, as did his old mother. By the end of 1921, hundreds of thousands were doing so.

Two million charkhas spinning across India was part of the Congress's (and Gandhi's) positive agenda, which also included a fund, in the name of Tilak, of one million rupees and a Congress membership of one million. If, said Gandhi, the positive and negative targets were all reached, India would find Swaraj in a year. Whether or not the Empire was dismantled, Indians would experience self-government.

Heeding the call for non-cooperation, top lawyers ended their practice, among them Chitta Ranjan Das in Calcutta, Motilal and Jawaharlal Nehru in the UP, Patel in Ahmedabad, Rajagopalachari in Madras, and Prasad in Patna. Though not knowing what the future held, hundreds of successful lawyers joined them in walking away from the courts.

Subhas Bose as president of the Haripura Congress, followed by Maulana Azad and Jawaharlal
Nehru – 1938

The boycott of elections to the Raj's councils (for which regional parties, independents and a new Liberal party formed by some of the former Congress moderates provided candidates) was impressive. Two-thirds of those qualified to vote stayed away, and Sir Valentine Chirol, writing for the London *Times,* recorded that 'at a freshly swept polling station' near Allahabad, not a single voter showed up from eight in the morning to twelve noon.[10]

Objecting to the Raj's control over their colleges, thousands of bright young men and women walked out. Many streamed into squalid villages and city slums to propagate khadi or Hindustani or Hindu-Muslim unity or the removal of untouchability or to recruit members for the Congress. Others entered newly-started national colleges, including the Jamia Millia Islamia in Aligarh, the Gujarat Vidyapith in Ahmedabad and other colleges in Calcutta, Patna, Maharashtra and Madras. Muhammad Ali, the prime mover over the Jamia, to which many AMU students and professors migrated, became its first rector after the poet Iqbal declined the position despite an appeal from Gandhi, who had said to Iqbal, 'The Muslim National University calls you.'[11]

Across the land potential leaders surfaced. Recently returned from England, 25-year-old Subhas Chandra Bose (1897–1945) gave up a plan of entering the Raj's civil service, joined the stir and, following a suggestion from Gandhi, became Das's lieutenant and the head of a new national college in Calcutta. After Gandhi visited Patna and Abul Kalam Azad made a stirring speech there, 19-year-old Jayaprakash Narayan (1902–79) 'flung his textbooks into a dam', quit the Raj's educational system – though only a few weeks remained for him to write his university examination in Patna – and joined the newly-started Bihar Vidyapith.[12] Men like Bose and Narayan would acquire national, and wider, fame, but hundreds of others joining the movement in province after province would also provide leadership in the future to either small or large constituencies.

In some regions (including large parts of Gujarat), non-cooperators fanned out to every single village, literally. People wore a new cloth, walked with new companions, talked on new subjects, did things they had not done, went to places they had not seen. After a year the Congress had six million new members, the Tilak fund target was fully reached, and hundreds of thousands of charkhas were humming.

A Congress worker in Andhra said to Gandhi that the spinning wheel should feature in the flag of free India. Agreeing enthusiastically, Gandhi proposed that the flag should be in three colours – orange for India's Hindus, green to represent Muslims, and white to represent all the others—and made from khadi cloth. Thus was born the Congress flag, the basis, on independence, of India's national standard.

In 1921, when many Indians actually expected 'Swaraj in one year', a fresh spirit blew away the cloud of fear. It seemed to blow away also the veils standing between Indians, especially between Hindus and Muslims, who began to fraternize in unprecedented ways.

Muslims were invited to meals in the homes of orthodox Hindus; Hindu leaders were invited to speak in mosques. As a gesture toward Hindus, Muhammad Ali stopped eating beef; departing from age-old practice, numerous Muslim homes celebrated Eid without beef.

Towards the end of 1921, Muhammad Ali declared: 'After the Prophet, on whom be peace, I consider it my duty to carry out the commands of Gandhiji.'[13] Observing what was happening, Lord Reading (the former Rufus Isaacs), who replaced Chelmsford as Viceroy in April 1921, wrote to his son of the 'bridge over the gulf between Hindu and Muslim' that was being erected.[14]

The new spirit touched another important community: the Sikhs. Groups of Sikhs struggled non-violently to free their religious shrines, the gurdwaras, from the control of often-corrupt priests, and the Akali movement was born.

The untouchables. The caste front saw progress but also challenges. Criticisms in the press and a whispering campaign followed an announcement (in October 1920) that the new national university in Ahmedabad, the Gujarat Vidyapith, would not admit students from schools that excluded 'untouchables'. The journal *Gujarati* alleged that Christians like Andrews had influenced Gandhi's stand against untouchability, and orthodox Hindus told Gandhi that 'the movement for Swaraj will end in smoke' if Antyajas (as the 'untouchables' were referred to in Gujarat at the time) were admitted to the national schools.[15]

Gandhi answered that he would rather reject Swaraj than abandon the 'untouchables' (*Navajivan,* 5 Dec.; 22: 57), but the threat of returning to the Imperial pole did not come only from caste Hindus. Some leaders of the 'untouchables' also thought that salvation for their people was 'only possible through the British Government'.[16] In April 1921 Gandhi asked a meeting of the 'untouchables' in Ahmedabad to assert their self-respect:

I prayed ... today: 'If I have to be reborn, I should be born an untouchable, so that I may share their sorrows, sufferings and the affronts levelled at them, in order that I may endeavour to free myself and them from that miserable condition.'

You should not ask the Hindus to emancipate you as a matter of favour. Hindus must do so, if they want, in their own interests ... You should now cease to accept leavings from plates ... Receive grain only – good sound grain, not rotten grain – and that too only if it is courteously offered ... (23: 45–7)

The 'I should be born an untouchable' sentence had emotion but also realism. Gandhi sensed that in the end the untouchables would accept the lead only of one of their own. But he would try to win them (and shame the orthodox) by acknowledging the offence

of untouchability. In *Navajivan* he had written that cruelties to the untouchables constituted 'an outrage grosser than that in the Punjab against which we have been protesting'
(22: 316). At the Ahmedabad meeting he was again brutally frank:

> What crimes for which we condemn the Government as Satanic have we not been
> guilty of towards our untouchable brethren? ... We make them crawl on their bellies;
> we have made them rub their noses on the ground; with eyes red with rage, we push
> them out of railway compartments – what more than this has British rule done? (23:
> 44)

Still, he would ask the 'untouchables' not to see caste Hindus as irredeemable enemies.
'The Hindus are not sinful by nature,' he told the 'untouchables'. 'They are sunk in
ignorance ... ' (23: 47)

The Gandhi pole was immersed in conflict and complexity over caste, yet it contributed to 'untouchable' dignity and high-caste shame, and instilled in many caste Hindus
a long-term commitment to justice for the 'untouchables'.

Tribals. In the new climate, 'adivasis' (original inhabitants) listed by the Raj as 'scheduled
tribes' and in some cases as 'criminal tribes', also fought for dignity. In 1921–2 there was
tribal unrest in parts of western, southern and eastern India, led by local figures inspired by
Gandhi. These protests were not always non-violent or supported by Gandhi himself, but
associates of Gandhi (including Indulal Yagnik, Amritlal Thakkar and Jugatram Dave)
had by this time started work on ashrams for tribals in southern Gujarat.[17]

The spirit also touched opium-taking and prostitution. Andrews would later write
of 'old abuses ... being swept away' and of a 'treasured memory' of two hours that he and
Gandhi spent in Barisal in Bengal with 'sisters' who used their bodies for subsistence.[18]

Learning of what was happening in India and why, a Unitarian minister in New York,
John Haynes Holmes, declared in a sermon in April 1921 that Gandhi was 'unquestionably the greatest man living in the world today'.[19]

Hurdles

But the non-cooperation train ran into hurdles. The biggest was sent by the Turks.
Emerging as Turkey's man of destiny, fighting the Greeks and the British and forming a
government of his own in Ankara, Mustafa Kamal derided the person for whom India's
Muslims seemed ready to die, the Sultan of Turkey. In February 1921 a Khilafat conference that Gandhi attended urged the Sultan to enlist the rising leader's partnership,
but the two Turkish governments were at war, and there was no sign that Kamal was
interested in Khilafat.

Increasingly desperate, the Ali brothers made intemperate speeches. Muhammad Ali remarked that he would assist an Afghan army that invaded and freed India and returned home. Hindus were troubled, and Reading, the Viceroy, confronted Gandhi with the brothers' speeches, whereupon Gandhi said he would either obtain apologies or dissociate himself from them.

At Gandhi's instance the Ali brothers apologized. To a friend Muhammad Ali wrote that he had expressed regrets because 'we had made up our mind to bring about a complete entente between Hindus and Muslims' and also 'to prove to Gandhi that we have enough respect for our colleague and leader's advice'.[20]

Praising their move in *Young India* (1 Jun. 1921), Gandhi wrote of the 'big burden' the brothers carried and of their responsibility for 'the prestige of Islam' (23: 216–17). Montagu and Reading conceded that the recantation prevented a breach between the brothers and Gandhi, but Montagu also thought that Gandhi's insistence on the apology 'must have left very unpleasant thoughts in their minds which are all to the good'.[21]

Although Gandhi's alliance with the Ali brothers survived the apology, suspicion was injuring partnership at the grassroots. In both communities, voices whispered that the other side talked about non-cooperation but retained government jobs. This undercurrent of suspicion and rivalry can be seen in a comment by the Pakistani writer, Sheikh Muhammad Ikram, on a 1921 fatwa in the Punjab asking Muslims to leave the Raj's police and army.

> The fatwa was widely hailed by Hindu newspapers of the Punjab, who had complained of Muslim preponderance in the police and the army, but it had no serious results as very few soldiers and policemen obeyed it.[22]

But the most damaging episode occurred in Malabar in the Malayali country in August 1921. Many of the Malabar Moplahs, Muslims with a trace of Arab blood and a background of fanaticism, were tenants of Hindu landlords. Alleged insults to their religious leaders brought them into violent rebellion, first against the government and then against their landlords. 'Independence' was declared, arson and murder occurred, and some Hindus were forcibly converted.

The Raj moved thousands of soldiers into the area. In the full-scale military operation that ensued, over 2,000 were killed (mostly Moplahs) and over 24,000 convicted of rebellion or lesser crimes. These figures, withheld for many months, were not known in 1921, but stories of rebellion and forcible conversion spread across the land, injuring Hindu-Muslim trust. The rebellion was local both in origin and aims. No propaganda for Khilafat had been permitted in the Moplah country, which had neither seen nor heard the Ali brothers. Yet in March 1922 the Raj's home member would speak of 'the many

Hindus killed and dishonoured in Malabar and of the thousands of Moplahs misled and driven to death and ruin by the incitements of Mohamed Ali, Shaukat Ali, and those who think like them.'[23]

In October Gandhi gave his reactions to the Moplah events. It was short-sighted but typical of the Raj, he said, that he and other non-cooperators were barred from entering Malabar. Not wishing 'to give non-cooperators the credit for peacefully ending the trouble', the authorities were 'desirous of showing once more that it is only the British soldier who can maintain peace in India'.

Muslims, added Gandhi, should go beyond 'verbal disapproval' and 'feel the shame and humiliation of the Moplah conduct about forcible conversions and looting'. Whether Hindus or Muslims, the vulnerable 'must be taught the art of self-defence'. Fighting was better than fleeing. Finally, Gandhi drew a wider, prophetic lesson:

> *Young India,* 20 Oct. 1921: We … have neglected our ignorant countrymen all these long centuries. We have not felt the call of love to see that no one was left ignorant of the necessity of humaneness or remained in want of food or clothing for no fault of his own. If we do not wake up betimes, we shall find a similar tragedy enacted by all the submerged classes. The present awakening is affecting all classes. The 'untouchables' and all the so-called semi-savage tribes will presently bear witness to our wrongs against them if we do not do penance and render tardy justice to them (24: 447–9).

The Moplah tragedy not only gave the Raj a powerful means to discrediting the Khilafat movement and breaking the Hindu-Muslim alliance; it sparked off mutually hostile movements for protecting the two communities from each other. But in August 1921 its impact seemed confined to Malabar, and the non-cooperation train continued to roll.

Debate with Tagore

It rolled on despite serious questioning by Tagore. Indians were treated to an absorbing debate between him and Gandhi, with Tagore using the columns of Calcutta's *Modern Review,* Gandhi replying in *Young India,* and other journals discussing the debate. In an article in May 1921 Tagore urged Gandhi to strive to unite East with West, not merely Indians with one another, and expressed disapproval of 'the intense consciousness of the separateness of one's own people from others'.

Gandhi replied that the aim of non-cooperation was not 'to create a Chinese wall between India and the West' but to 'pave the way to real, honorable and voluntary

cooperation'. Tagore said he was disappointed with 'non' as the first syllable of a great movement. Answering that weeding was as important as sowing, Gandhi pointed out that the *Upanishads* described God first of all as '*Neti*' – 'Not this'. Added Gandhi:

> *Young India, 1 Jun. 1921*: I hope I am as great a believer in free air as the great Poet. I do not want my house to be walled in on all sides and my windows to be stuffed. I want the cultures of all the lands to be blown about my house as freely as possible. But I refuse to be blown off my feet by any (23: 215).

In October Tagore rejoined the debate with 'The Call of Truth' in *Modern Review*. The coercion that some non-cooperators were employing troubled him, as also Gandhi's focus on spinning and weaving, but the poet seemed most concerned at a new item in the non-cooperation programme, introduced from 1 August 1921: the burning of foreign cloth.

Saying that in Gandhi 'divine providence has given us a burning thunderbolt of truth' and that 'the Mahatma has won the heart of India with his love', and asking Gandhi to go beyond merely asking India to 'spin and weave, spin and weave', Tagore added:

> Consider the burning of cloth, heaped before the very eyes of our motherland shivering and ashamed in her nakedness ... How can we expiate the sin of the forcible destruction of clothes which might have gone to women whose nakedness is actually keeping them prisoners, unable to stir out of the privacy of their homes?

Tagore's challenge evoked an eloquent response, 'The Great Sentinel', that also spelt out Gandhi's understanding of the Indian scene. After welcoming the poet's warning against bigotry and intolerance, Gandhi added lines that reveal a writer's enjoyment of his writing, a rare occurrence for one who had chosen fighting over writing as a career.

> *Young India, 13 Oct. 1921*: When there is war the poet lays down the lyre, the lawyer his law reports, the schoolboy his books.
>
> To a people famishing and idle, the only acceptable form in which God can dare appear is work and promise of food as wages. God created man to work for his food and said that those who ate without work were thieves. Eighty per cent of India are compulsory thieves half the year. Is it any wonder if India has become one vast prison?
>
> Why should I who have no need to work for food spin? Because I am eating what does not belong to me. I am living ... on my countrymen. In burning my foreign clothes I burn my shame. I must refuse to insult the naked by giving them clothes they do not need instead of giving them work which they sorely need. I would give them neither crumbs nor cast-off clothing but work.

True to his poetical instinct the Poet lives for the morrow and would have us do likewise. He presents to our admiring gaze the beautiful picture of the birds early in the morning singing hymns of praise as they soar into the sky. These birds had their day's food and soared with rested wings in whose veins new blood had flowed the previous night. But I have had the pain of watching birds who for want of strength could not be coaxed even into a flutter of their wings.

The human being under the Indian sky gets up weaker than when he pretended to retire. The hungry millions ask for one poem – invigorating food. They cannot be given it. They must earn it. And they can earn it only by the sweat of their brow (24: 412–17).

Andrews shared Tagore's distaste for cloth-burning and thought it smacked of violence and racialism. Gandhi's defence was that all foreign objects were not being boycotted or destroyed. That would have been 'racial, parochial, and wicked'. Non-cooperation was 'not anti-British', he insisted. Had he not unveiled portraits (in February 1921) of Lord Hardinge and Lady Hardinge while opening a national medical college started in Delhi by Hakim Ajmal Khan?[24]

The targeting of foreign cloth, Gandhi argued, was a response to the reality of racialism. Indians were undoubtedly 'filled with ill-will' to the British, but he sought to transfer 'the ill-will from men to things'. Where Tagore and Andrews feared that Gandhi was abetting ill will, he claimed he was deflecting it.

Empire shrinks. The Empire's authority shrank as villagers settled cases out of court. Its revenues shrank as liquor sales went down. And its prestige shrank when in city after city influential persons threw foreign hats, caps, suits and shawls into a blaze. The Congress's strength rose as gold, silver and cash were contributed to the Tilak Swaraj fund. Thousands of women, including many Muslim women emerging from burqas, flocked to give jewels, or yarn spun by them, to Gandhi and the Ali brothers.

The two poles were clashing in dignified style. In May Gandhi had six meetings with Reading and they talked for 13 hours in all. Reading recorded his reactions:

He is convinced to a point almost bordering on fanaticism that non-violence and love will give India its independence and enable it to withstand the British government … Our conversations were of the frankest; he was supremely courteous with manners of distinction.[25]

But a visit to India that the Prince of Wales was to make in November set limits to seditious talk. In July these limits were crossed when, at a meeting in Karachi, the Ali brothers (who continued to cling to the illusion that Mustafa Kamal and the Sultan would come together) said that Muslims could not serve or enlist with British armies in the event of hostilities between Britain and the forces of Kamal.

On 14 September, when Gandhi and Muhammad Ali were together on a south-bound train, vainly hoping to visit Malabar, Muhammad Ali was arrested in Waltair in the Telugu country. Elsewhere, the older brother too was apprehended. Offered immediately in his speeches and later in *Young India,* Gandhi's response was strong:

> *Young India, 29 Oct. 1921*: The Ali brothers were charged with having tampered with the loyalty of the sepoy and with having uttered sedition ... But sedition has become the creed of the Congress ... Every non-cooperator is pledged to preach disaffection towards the Government ... But this is no new discovery. Lord Chelmsford knew it. Lord Reading knows it. We ask for no quarter; we expect none from Government (24: 347).

Meeting in Bombay in early October, Gandhi and several close colleagues (including Das, the Nehrus, Lajpat Rai, Patel, C R and Sarojini Naidu) issued a manifesto that declared that it was 'the duty of every Indian solder and civilian to sever his connection with the Government'. The Prince of Wales's tour would be peacefully and courteously boycotted, and the climax would be mass civil disobedience – a refusal to pay taxes – in an area to be named later.

Vallabhbhai and his brother Vithalbhai were asked to select a region in Gujarat that possessed firm and non-violent satyagrahis. In early November, the Ali brothers were sentenced to two years, and Gandhi announced that a reply would be given in the Bardoli taluka of Surat district, recommended by the Patel brothers. Scores of national schools functioned in this taluka, which also had a large number of spinners and khadi-wearers. Moreover, several in Bardoli had returned from South Africa, where they had taken part in satyagrahas. But about half of the population were tribals, and only a few in the Congress or among Gandhi's associates had worked with them. Gandhi asked 'that this be rectified'.[26]

Since Surat was one of Britain's first outposts on the subcontinent, it was fitting to challenge the Empire in a Surat taluka. Confident that Bardoli would mount a successful battle, Gandhi wrote in *Young India* of talukas 'throughout the length and breadth of India' seeking 'to plant the flag of swaraj' after 'it floats victoriously at Bardoli'.[27] He was imagining the sort of dramatic expansion that had occurred in South Africa in 1913.

The general's rules and strange uniform. This general kept himself in communication with his officers and soldiers and also travelled on a prodigious scale. In October he claimed:

Hardly anyone could have toured India as I have done in the last thirteen months ...
I covered the country from Karachi in the west to Dibrugarh in the east and from
Rawalpindi in the north to Tuticorin in the south (*Navajivan,* 9 Oct. 1921; 24:
393).

Indians thronged railway stations at all hours of the day and night to see Gandhi as he
passed through. At times his usually admirable patience snapped. While travelling one
night between Gorakhpur and Benares, he first pleaded with and then shouted at a crowd
that would not allow him or Kasturba or Mahadev to sleep. Finally, Gandhi slapped
himself hard three times. After the second slap, a passenger said to him, 'What will be
our plight if you yield to anger?' A humbled Gandhi related the incident in *Navajivan,*
which is how we know of it (20 Feb. 1921; 22: 358).

The mounting pressures of each day drew from him the device of a weekly day of
silence. 'Perfect truth is in silence alone,' he had written in December 1920 (22:11). By
April 1921 he had decided that he would not speak on Mondays, unless there was an
emergency. The silent Monday would last for the rest of his life.

Altering his uniform, the general announced on 22 September that he was reducing
the size of his lower garment. Instead of a dhoti going down to his ankles, he would
now wear only a waist-to-knee dhoti, or loin-cloth, as it would be called, keeping it as
neat and clean as he could. He said his encounter with the misery of the famine-stricken
of East Bengal had led to the decision, as also the arrest of Muhammad Ali, plus the
criticism of many that khadi was too expensive for them. A shorter khadi dhoti would
compete in price with an imported standard-length dhoti. In any case, 'the dress of the
millions of agriculturists in India is really only the loin-cloth, and nothing more'. He
was aware, he wrote, that he might be called 'a lunatic'. But he said he felt helpless. It
was the only response he could make to an India 'where millions have to go naked' (*The
Hindu,* 15 Oct. 1921; 24: 349–50).

Rajagopalachari, who was with him when Gandhi first appeared in the shortened
dress, expressed his disapproval, as did a few other colleagues, while the governor of
Madras, Lord Willingdon, expressed a private hope that Gandhi 'would not die of
pneumonia as a result!'[28] Yet Gandhi was firm about his latest sartorial change, once
more made, he would say, with 'deep deliberation' (24: 349–50).

The man. Glimpses of Gandhi amidst the heat and lulls of the non-cooperation
struggle were jotted down by Krishnadas from Bengal, who had joined Gandhi because
Mahadev Desai had been deputed to assist Motilal Nehru with the Allahabad newspaper,
the *Independent.*

Krishnadas saw in Ahmedabad (Oct. 1921) that at the end of the ashram's evening
prayers, Gandhi 'made friendly enquiries of each inmate ... present' and 'in course of

conversation he made such humorous hits that he set the whole audience roar with laughter'.[29] When Lajpat Rai arrived for talks with Gandhi and sat down for lunch, the host used to receiving 'almost royal honours' from Indian crowds was 'engaged in the task of driving away' noisy dogs who disturbed the guest (K 93).

When reverting to generalship, Gandhi was 'firm with the meddlesome' and gave instructions 'so fast' that it was only 'with difficulty' that he could be followed (K 109). Who should defy a ban and who should not, and when, where, and how defiance should occur were questions that Gandhi tackled through letters and telegrams and in his journals. And he focused on details, including the care of the families of those entering prison.

Krishnadas also thought that Gandhi's appearance changed from one moment to another. 'Sometimes he has appeared to me like a young man of twenty-five, pursuing his work with infinite and indomitable energy. At other times, again, his look has been that of an octogenarian, a shrivelled figure bent with the weight of years' (K 92).

Reading aloud Gandhi's mail to him, Krishnadas noticed that while eulogies left Gandhi 'cold and indifferent', he listened to 'criticism or condemnation' with 'rapt attention'. He heard Gandhi speak of Pyarelal, the secretary who had joined from 1919, as a 'scholar' and an 'encyclopaedia' (K 83–4), and felt that Gandhi protected the 'independence, self-respect and individuality' of aides like Swami Anand, who helped edit *Navajivan,* and Valji Desai, who played a similar role with *Young India* (K 93). However, while Gandhi's 'best wishes were unremittingly showered upon his devoted followers, as between opponents and friends, his love and tenderness were reserved more for the former than for the latter' (K 74–5).

According to Krishnadas, Kasturba loyally and uncomplainingly cooked for Gandhi's guests and had an instinctive understanding of Gandhi's needs. But her health suffered if she had to cook for guests for a long time. Gandhi said to Krishnadas, 'When she feels thoroughly worn out by hard work, she, poor thing, neither grumbles nor protests, but simply weeps' (K 81).

Discovering, at the post-prayer conversation one day, that Kasturba was unaware of the illness of an ashramite, Gandhi said to her, in front of the gathering: 'If Devadas had fallen ill, you would have known of it long ago; but how is it that you do not keep yourself informed when others fall ill?' (K 81) He had upheld equality but she, humiliated in public, must have wept later in private.

Devadas's 'courtesy, readiness to oblige others and ... cheerful and calm exterior' impressed Krishnadas, who thought that Gandhi was developing his 21-year-old son 'by slow, imperceptible degrees'. Gandhi apparently said to Krishnadas: 'There is not an iota of fear in Devadas's composition. Where other people would think thrice before venturing ... Devadas without the least hesitation would ... enter.' (K 82)

According to Krishnadas, Gandhi's 'tenderest' feelings were directed towards his five-year-old granddaughter, Manu, the youngest of Harilal's motherless children, and Lakshmi, the seven-year-old daughter of Dudabhai, the 'untouchable'. Like a 'rock' much of the time, conveying 'imperturbable gravity', Gandhi would however unbend and relax whenever Lakshmi or Manu engaged him (K 84).

Setback. The Bardoli plan was upset when riots occurred in Bombay during the visit of the Prince of Wales (the future Edward VIII), who landed there on 17 November. Those joining the ceremonies of welcome – mostly Parsis, Anglo-Indians and Jews – became targets of Hindu-Muslim mobs. The saris of a few Parsi women were pulled at. Foreign caps donned by some men were forcibly removed and burnt. Some Parsi-owned liquor shops were wrecked. Five constables were murdered, and in five days of riots and police shooting, 53 Hindus and Muslims were killed.

Gandhi was in Bombay at the time. Confronting the rioters in the streets, he declared that the Swaraj he had witnessed 'stank in his nostrils' and that 'Hindu-Muslim unity has been a menace to the handful of Parsis, Christians and Jews' (25: 129). A fast by him ended the rioting, but a shaken Gandhi postponed the Bardoli rebellion, saying that the Congress would decide on it at the end of December. In a 'special word' to his Muslim 'brothers', he asked them to recognize that Muslims had played the leading part in the rioting (25: 139).

He also summoned Devadas, earlier deputed to help prepare Bardoli, and announced that should fresh violence break out in or near Bombay, he would send Devadas into its centre. He was ready, he said, to sacrifice a loved son. In another move, he asked the Congress Working Committee to form an All-India Volunteer Corps, the Hindustani Seva Dal, for controlling demonstrations.

Bombay had come in the way of Bardoli, and 'how to maintain peace in India' became the 'primary object of his activities' (K 164). But he could not call off India's great uprising, could he? The momentum of India's energy was clashing with the momentum of Gandhi's truth. On 8 December he spelt out his thinking in *Young India*:

I believe in loving my enemies. I believe in non-violence as the only remedy open to the Hindus, Mussalmans, Sikhs, Parsis, Christians and Jews of India … We must by our conduct demonstrate to every Englishman that he is as safe in the remotest corner of India as he professes to feel behind the machine gun … In our strength must we humble ourselves before our Maker (25: 218–19).

Yet when, following the riots, the Raj curbed the press and banned meetings, Gandhi's response was to encourage non-cooperators across the land to court imprisonment by defying the bans. One by one at first, then by the tens and soon, by the hundreds and the thousands, Indians embraced imprisonment. They included Das, the Nehrus, Lajpat Rai, C R and Azad.

The leaders' arrests sent Gandhi into 'high spirits', and when he learnt that Das's wife Basanti Devi and other women in Bengal had also courted arrest, Gandhi looked 'like a child brimming over with sheer joy', Krishnadas thought. 'His whole frame seemed to be tingling with joy' and he appeared to sway with delight as he walked (K 169–70). Distinguished women had conquered the fear of jail. Risking their jobs, thousands of men had non-violently defied the Empire. In spirit at least, Swaraj had arrived.

His son Manilal was in South Africa, and Ramdas about to return from there, but Harilal, the eldest, joined the non-cooperation movement in Calcutta and was arrested on 10 December. A 'very pleased' Gandhi 'at once sent a wire to Harilal expressing his satisfaction', and Kasturba too seemed happy. 'I also have done three months' hard labour in South Africa,' she said (K 171).

Gandhi himself was not arrested because he had not yet disobeyed the law, and because the Raj did not wish to risk uncontrollable unrest. But he knew he could be taken any day. To Kallenbach he wrote, 'I am expecting to be deported. Even execution has been suggested ... But I know that not a blade of grass moves without His will' (8 Feb. 1922; 26: 112).

Climax at hand

Hoping to ensure the Prince of Wales a grand, undisturbed welcome in the Christmas season, Viceroy Reading explored a deal. If the Raj released most prisoners, lifted its bans, and promised a committee to look into India's grievances, would the Congress call off its boycott and its Bardoli plan? Through Malaviya, the Viceroy sent the offer to the incarcerated Chitta Ranjan Das, who was the Congress's president-elect. From jail Das recommended the deal to Gandhi, who said he would go along if the Ali brothers too would be released, and if there was agreement beforehand on the timing and composition of the grievances committee. Reading turned down the conditions, and the gambit collapsed.

The atmosphere was tense by the end of December. Scores of leaders and about 30,000 others were behind bars. Some newspapers, including the *Independent* in Allahabad, had been banned; Mahadev Desai too had been jailed; and Gandhi had sent Devadas to Allahabad to fill Desai's place and organize if possible a hand-written version of the *Independent*.

The Congress held its year-end session in Ahmedabad, its deliberations chaired in Das's absence by Hakim Ajmal Khan, and resolved that the Bardoli defiance would start in January. At Gandhi's instance all Congress volunteers were required to sign a pledge of non-violence and desist from any defiance not cleared by the Working Committee.[30]

The climax was at hand. Another truce was, however, proposed by Jinnah, who was in Ahmedabad for a parallel Muslim League session. At his urging Gandhi attended, on 15 January, an All Parties Conference in Bombay that asked him to postpone Bardoli and asked the Raj to release prisoners, withdraw bans and convene a Round Table Conference. Gandhi agreed to put off Bardoli until February, but Reading rejected the Bombay proposals.

On 29 January, 4,000 khadi-clad Bardoli residents pledged their willingness to stop paying taxes and 'to face imprisonment and even death without resentment'.[31] Gandhi said to them the next day that Swaraj would come not through a show of hands but from a readiness to lose property and, if need be, life; they declared that they would not pay revenue to the Raj unless and until he asked them to.

On 1 February Gandhi sent Reading an ultimatum. Political prisoners should be released, bans lifted and Congress workers given full freedom. If this did not happen, the Bardoli rebellion would start. The Viceroy replied that the Raj would not surrender. Gandhi, now issuing a leaflet a day to his soldiers, sent Reading a rejoinder and declared that the non-violent rebellion would start on 12 February.

Before that date, however, Gandhi was, in his words, 'stabbed in the back' by a mob in eastern UP, and he called the whole thing off.

Anti-climax

On 5 February 1922, in a place called Chauri Chaura near the town of Gorakhpur, an angry crowd of about 4,000 Hindus and Muslims surrounded a police unit that had taken shelter in its post after exhausting its ammunition. Minutes earlier, two had been killed by police bullet; a few days earlier, a sub-inspector had evidently roughed up a non-cooperator who was an ex-soldier. The police post was set alight and fleeing constables were hacked to pieces or forced back into the flames. Twenty-two policemen lost their lives at the hands of a crowd that was shouting 'Mahatma Gandhi *ki jai* ("Victory to Mahatma Gandhi")'.[32]

Not all these details were immediately available to Gandhi, but the newspapers of 8 February carried a story on the incident, and that day or the next, Gandhi also received a wire about it from Devadas who, remembering his father's wish to send him to the scene of any violence, had gone to Chauri Chaura from Allahabad.

But the news struck Gandhi dumb, and he knew he had to withdraw his Bardoli challenge, due on 12 February. To every Working Committee member not in prison, and a few others, he at once sent a letter inviting them to a discussion in Bardoli on

11 February. He was 'violently agitated', Gandhi added. To Devadas he sent a general's telegram that could not conceal a father's concern:

> *9 Feb. 1922:* Your wire. Send full accurate reports. Keep people non-violent. Get all information. Tell workers am deeply grieved. Keep calm. God will bless you ...
> Bapu (26: 136)

The previous day, before learning of Chauri Chaura, Gandhi had written to Kallenbach: 'Devadas has shaped wonderfully' (26: 112). For *Navajivan* Gandhi wrote:

> I am certainly the one most responsible for the crime of the people of Gorakhpur district, but every genuine non-cooperator is also responsible for it. All of us should be in mourning for it. But the matter can be further discussed only when we have more details. May God save the honour of India and of non-cooperators (26: 148).

On 10 February he spoke to his Bardoli associates about putting off the defiance. 'Almost everyone declared with one united voice that it was unthinkable to suspend the fight at this stage; that if Mahatmaji retreated ... the whole country would be disgraced before the world' (K 225). Vithalbhai Patel, who had taken charge of the Bardoli exercise, objected strongly. Three dissenters, however, thought that not to suspend would be worse.

Though the Working Committee was yet to meet, Gandhi announced to the gathering on 10 February that he was calling off the Bardoli disobedience. Malaviya, who was present, said that Gandhi was showing an out-of-the-ordinary greatness, but almost everybody else seemed stunned and demoralized. The next day the Working Committee grudgingly accepted Gandhi's decision.

On 13 February he drafted, for *Young India,* 'The Crime of Chauri Chaura'. Claiming that God had spoken to him through the incident, Gandhi added:

> 'But what about your manifesto to the Viceroy and your rejoinder to his reply?' spoke the voice of Satan. It was the bitterest cup of humiliation to drink. 'Surely it is cowardly to withdraw the next day after pompous threats to the government and promises to the people of Bardoli.' Thus Satan's invitation was to deny Truth ...
>
> I put my doubts and troubles before the Working Committee and other associates whom I found near me. They did not all agree with me at first. Some of them probably do not even now agree with me. But never has a man been blessed, perhaps, with colleagues and associates so considerate and forgiving as I have ...
>
> The drastic reversal of practically the whole of the aggressive programme may be

politically unsound and unwise, but there is no doubt that it is religiously sound, and
I venture to assure the doubters that the country will have gained by my humiliation
and confession of error ...

The people of Bardoli are in my opinion the most peaceful in India. But Bardoli
is but a speck on the map of India. Its effort cannot succeed unless there is perfect
cooperation from the other parts ...

The tragedy of Chauri Chaura is really the index finger ... If we are not to evolve
violence out of non-violence, it is quite clear that we must hastily retrace our steps
and re-establish an atmosphere of peace ...

Let the opponent glory in our humiliation or so-called defeat ... Chauri Chaura
must stiffen the Government, must still further corrupt the police, and the reprisals
that will follow must further demoralize the people. [But] if we learn the full lesson
of the tragedy, we can turn the curse into a blessing (*Young India*, 16 Feb. 1922; 26:
177–83).

His error – of 'having been the instrument, however involuntary, of the brutal violence
by the people at Chauri Chaura' – required penance and punishment. So he went on a
five-day fast.

Gandhi spoke of an inner compulsion, but the outer context also influenced him. In
January and early February he had received reports of indiscipline in Calcutta, Allahabad,
the Punjab and elsewhere, and among different communities – Hindu, Muslim, and
Sikh.[33] Coming on top of the Bombay riots, the reports had deeply troubled Gandhi. As
he would say in a letter to a dismayed (and imprisoned) Jawaharlal, Chauri Chaura 'was
the last straw'.[34]

Moreover, Gandhi had suspected that suspension was going to be inevitable before
long, for Mustafa Kamal (who would soon expel the Sultan, for whom he had no use,
from Turkey) had knocked the bottom out of the Khilafat issue. To suspend out of moral
necessity made political sense.

Gandhi was bombarded with protests from behind prison walls by Das, the Congress
president, the Ali brothers, Motilal Nehru, Lajpat Rai, Jawaharlal, C R, Azad, and scores
of others. Even Mahadev Desai was put out. They wanted to know why, as Rajagopalachari put it, 'there should be a call for stopping our struggle for birthrights [because
of] every distant and unconnected outburst'.[35] Later, C.R. changed his mind, as did
many others including Jawaharlal, who would write: 'All organization and discipline was
disappearing ... Gandhiji's decision was right. He had to stop the rot and build anew.'[36]
But some did not, and wondered about the Mahatma's political acumen.

The constructive programme. On 11 February 1922, when the Working Committee
agreed to the suspension of all aggressive activities, Shankarlal Banker asked Gandhi not

to leave non-cooperators 'suspended in mid-air'. They needed an alternative programme of action (K 229). Gandhi's response, which the Working Committee endorsed, was that workers should

- recruit for the Congress, ensuring that those joining understand 'the creed of truth and non-violence';
- spin daily for a fixed time;
- introduce the charkha, 'the wheel of prosperity and freedom', in every home;
- visit 'untouchable' homes and find out their wants;
- induce national schools to receive 'untouchable' children;
- visit homes damaged by the drink curse;
- help establish real panchayats (village councils); and
- help to place national schools on a proper footing (*Young India,* 16 Feb. 1922; 26: 181–2).

Gandhi assembled a team for promoting the constructive programme, did some travelling, and wrote his notes and articles, but his arrest was imminent. With India's public demoralized, it would not invite uncontrollable unrest.

Yet strong words remained to be exchanged. In a speech in Parliament, Lord Birkenhead warned India of Britain's 'hard fibre' and Montagu, the Secretary of State for India, declared that if the existence of the Empire was in question, India could not successfully challenge with success 'the most determined people in the world'.

In *Young India* Gandhi answered (23 Feb.) that India's demand indeed 'involved the existence of the Empire' and that India's spirit, which would 'neither bend nor break' before 'the most determined people in the world', was ready for 'all the "hard fibre' that can be transported across the seas' (26: 217–19).

Arrest and trial

On the afternoon of 10 March, when Gandhi returned to Ahmedabad station after a quick visit to Ajmer, a British soldier who had been watching the passing Gandhi from his train window 'with wide and curious eyes, stretched out his hand' and said, 'Mr Gandhi, I must shake hands with you.' Gandhi wholeheartedly offered his hand, 'which was immediately grasped', and the soldier 'stammered out some words' from 'the fullness of his heart' that our witness, Krishnadas, could not hear (K 258).

Gandhi was 'in an exceptionally happy mood', though that day he also wrote to Devadas, 'You are making separation from you more and more unbearable every day. I feel it, however much I wish that I did not' (26: 345). Shortly after ten that night, Dan

Healey, the superintendent of police, arrived outside the ashram with a posse, informed Anasuyaben that Gandhi was to be arrested, and added that he could take his time.

Her news did not surprise Gandhi. After his ashram family had sung for him a favourite prayer-song, *Vaishnava Jana*, he walked towards the police party, saying to himself, 'O the happy day! The best thing has happened.' Along the path he embraced Maulana Hasrat Mohani, the politician (and poet) who had often disagreed with Gandhi. Three days later, in a letter to his friend Revashankar Jhaveri, he would say:

> I was arrested only after I had eradicated my anger, had undergone atonement and purified myself. What better lot can there be for India or for me? (26: 362)

Kasturba and a few others, including Krishnadas, were permitted to accompany Gandhi to the jail not far from the ashram. Shortly before midnight they left Gandhi on his bed in a verandah outside his cell (Krishnadas had been allowed to make Gandhi's bed), and returned to the ashram (K 260–1). Much of India grieved but there were no demonstrations. As Reading remarked, 'Not a dog barked.' There was no barking because some Indians heeded Gandhi's instruction to respond to his arrest with constructive work while others had been stunned by his Chauri Chaura decision.

On 18 March Gandhi was tried in the Shahi Baug Circuit House in Ahmedabad for inciting disaffection towards His Majesty's Government. Three *Young India* articles of his, published in September and December the previous year and in February 1922, were presented as evidence. The printer and publisher of *Young India*, Shankarlal Banker, was also arraigned under the same section (124A) of the law.

History has recorded the short public trial of the Empire's unusual foe. We know that Justice Robert S Broomfield had two entries in his calendar for that day: 'Golf' and 'Try Gandhi.' At the trial Broomfield was courteous and also moved. The accused pleading guilty to the charges, the judge asked Gandhi if he wished to say anything more. Gandhi, who in preceding days had faced his conscience, now wanted the Empire to face its own. After outlining the transformation of a believer in the Empire into its foe, he said:

> I came reluctantly to the conclusion that the British connection had made India more helpless than she ever was before, politically and economically. A disarmed India has no power of resistance against any aggressor if she wanted to engage in an armed conflict with him ...
>
> She has become so poor that she has little power of resisting famines. Before the British advent, India spun and wove in her millions of cottages just the supplement she needed for adding to her meagre agricultural resources ...

Little do town-dwellers know how the semi-starved masses of India are slowly sinking to lifelessness ... Little do they realize that the Government established by law in British India is carried on for this exploitation of the masses.

No sophistry, no jugglery in figures can explain away the evidence that the skeletons in many villages present to the naked eye ...

I have no personal ill will against any single administrator, much less can I have any disaffection towards the King's person. But I hold it to be a virtue to be disaffected towards a Government which in its totality has done more harm to India than any previous system.

Accepting his responsibility for the madness in Chauri Chaura in February and in Bombay in November, he said: 'I know that my people have sometimes gone mad; I am deeply sorry for it.' But he did not regret that he had summoned his people:

I knew that I was playing with fire. I ran the risk and, if I was set free, I would still do the same ... I wanted to avoid violence. I want to avoid violence. Non-violence is the first article of my faith. It is also the last article of my creed. But I had to make my choice. I had either to submit to a system which I considered had done an irreparable harm to my country, or incur the risk of the mad fury of my people bursting forth when they understood the truth from my lips.

Non-violence was the alpha and omega of his *means:* of *his* means – not all Indians subscribed to them. His *ends* included India's equality with Britain; he had to protect the self-respect of his people.

I do not ask for mercy. I do not ask for ... clemency. I am here to invite and cheerfully submit to the highest penalty that can be inflicted upon me for what in law is a deliberate crime and what appears to me to be the highest duty of a citizen.

Justice Broomfield sentenced Gandhi to six years and Banker for a year plus another six months if he did not pay a fine of 1,000 rupees. He also made remarks showing that the Empire, like its foe, had an unexpected face:

Mr Gandhi, you have made my task easy in one way by pleading guilty to the charge. Nevertheless, what remains, namely, the determination of a just sentence, is perhaps as difficult a proposition as a judge in this country could have to face.

You are in a different category from any person I have ever tried or am likely to have to try ... In the eyes of millions of your countrymen, you are a great patriot and a great leader. Even those who differ from you in politics look upon you as a man of high ideals and of noble and of even saintly life …

[But] it is my duty to judge you as a man subject to the law, who has by his own admission broken the law and committed what to an ordinary man must appear to be grave offences against the State.

I do not forget that you have constantly preached against violence and that you have on many occasions, as I am willing to believe, done much to prevent violence, but having regard to the nature of your political teaching and the nature of many of those to whom it is addressed, how you could have continued to believe that violence would not be the inevitable consequence, it passes my capacity to understand …

If the course of events in India should make it possible for the Government to reduce the period and release you, no one will be better pleased than I.

Remarking that the sentence was 'as light as any judge would inflict on me', Gandhi added, 'I must say that I could not have expected greater courtesy.'

'Then,' reported *Young India*, 'the friends of Mr Gandhi crowded round him as the Judge left the court, and fell at his feet. There was much sobbing on the part of both men and women. But all the while Mr Gandhi was smiling and cool and giving encouragement to everybody who came to him' (23 Mar. 1922; 26: 377–86).

Maniben Patel, the daughter of Vallabhbhai, present along with her father, observed Gandhi's 'peaceful, sombre and sweet face' as he heard the sentence, the complete silence prevailing in and around the packed courtroom – 'it was as if the birds and animals too were still, and people had stopped breathing' – and the sadness that followed. 'When asked why they were looking sad, people broke down and wept' (*Navajivan,* 18 Mar. 1923).

Summing up. In 1920, the fates appeared to bring Indian liberty and Hindu-Muslim partnership within reach, and all that seemed needed was the application of Indian will. Surfacing all across India, Gandhi looked capable of mobilizing that will. In February 1922, Lajpat Rai, by no means an unquestioning ally, said:

> Never before in the experience of living men did a leader so successfully and unfailingly appreciate the genius of his people and feel their pulse as Mahatma Gandhi has done over the last three years. I wonder if ever in the history of India a single person has had so much influence over the masses of India … [37]

However, as Chauri Chaura revealed, that influence was not deep enough. Moreover, Gandhi's charisma was joined to what seemed, at first sight at any rate, a great contradiction. For many Indians, Gandhi's position – 'I cannot and will not hate Englishmen;

nor will I bear their yoke'[38] – was hard to comprehend. For them fighting and hating went together.

And yet Gandhi had come pretty close. As Lord Lloyd, who was the governor of Bombay when, in his province, Bardoli was planned and abandoned, would say to a British journalist in November 1923:

> He gave us a scare. His programme filled our gaols. You can't go on arresting people for ever, you know, not when there are 320 million of them, and if they had taken the next step and refused to pay our taxes, God knows where we should have been. Gandhi's was the most colossal experiment in the world's history, and it came within an inch of succeeding. But he couldn't control men's passions. They became violent, and he called off the programme.[39]

From his prison and later as a free man, Chitta Ranjan Das criticized Gandhi's 'bungling'. In Das's view, Gandhi blundered in rejecting the deal offered in November 1921 and again, three months later, in calling off Bardoli. Young Subhas Bose, gifted with a solemn, driven personality, joined in these criticisms, as did others, but it was beyond Gandhi, given his life-goals, to abandon the Ali brothers in November or non-violence in February.

If Indians unable to refrain from violence let Gandhi down within India, and Mustafa Kamal destroyed Khilafat outside, the struggle was also weakened by the unwillingness of the bulk of India's educated classes to risk their Empire-linked careers. Thousands showed great courage, but tens of thousands of others did not. Their reluctance to defy the Empire was as human as the demonstrators' difficulty in remaining non-violent.

But many middle-class Indians, and those at the upper rungs of India's hierarchies, were also afraid of the wider consequences of Gandhi's non-cooperation call – of likely challenges to their domination over land, the lower castes and the poorer classes. 'The present awakening is affecting all classes,' Gandhi had observed while reacting to the Moplah rebellion. Many Indians feared the awakening and doubted Gandhi's capacity to control it.[40]

Though Gandhi's call did not strike deep roots everywhere, it stirred (as we saw) the aggrieved or suppressed in far corners of India. These included 'untouchables', tribals, tea-garden workers, low and peasant castes, Sikhs, and subjects of India's princes.[41] It also affected many of the Raj's employees, Indian as well as British, one result of which was that Indians entering prison were at times treated with courtesy and even respect.

Many on Gandhi's team realized that though the battle was lost, the war was not over. As Rajagopalachari reflected in prison, 'The nation is too weak; too far gone in economic misery to be able to fight and win in one campaign. We have to carry on many campaigns before we can reach our goal.'[42]

Tagore, for his part, regretted that Gandhi fought for India rather than for humanity as a whole, but Gandhi thought he had to stand on a rock of national self-respect to wage any wider battle. Making an opposite complaint, others said that Gandhi was too broad and too Indian, and not focused enough on what *their* India needed, on what was most wanted by Hindus, or Muslims, or Sikhs, or Dalits, or some other *section* of Indians.

Hindu-Muslim trust would drop markedly in the period following Gandhi's arrest, yet the deterioration occurred not because of his Khilafat-linked non-cooperation call but in spite of it. While his summons for abandoning the Raj's offices clashed with material interests, his plea for Hindu-Muslim partnership often ran counter to deeply held (and constantly fuelled) prejudices in both communities.

The Ali brothers would slowly drift away from Gandhi, and so would Hindu leaders like his host in 1915, Swami Shraddhanand. Yet for people to switch from a common struggle to separate Hindu or Muslim campaigns was not a new event in Indian history. It had happened earlier, immediately after the 1857 Rebellion. What was new was the continuing commitment of many Hindus and Muslims to a united struggle for Indian independence.

Even those who did not remain connected, or joined the Muslim League or an exclusively Hindu body, acknowledged the import of what had happened in 1920–2. As Afzal Iqbal, the future biographer of Muhammad Ali, would write:

These events formed a psychological watershed in the development of modern India … For the first time India witnessed a mass movement which shook the country and nearly paralysed the British rule. For the first time India realized a new pride and discovered a sense of unity … For the first time, in a rare manifestation of amity and accord, Hindus and Muslims drank from the same cup … [43]

For all the shock and demoralization caused by the suspension, other emotions too were engendered, including pride in Indian hearts and respect in British ones. As Geoffrey Ashe would mark, India's leader had refused to 'lead his people along the old paths of bloodshed and terror and cheated hope'.[44]

Elsewhere in the world (the Mexican poet, Octavio Paz, would point out) violent wars for independence had often become 'breeding grounds for warlords' and for 'militarism, coups, uprisings, and civil wars'.[45] Gandhi, who had waged another sort of war for another sort of outcome, was now in prison and in fact happy to be there. But he was not finished.

9

Building Anew

India, 1922–30

At midnight on 20/21 March 1922, Gandhi and Banker were removed from Sabarmati prison and put on a special train to Poona, where they were lodged in Yeravda jail. Gandhi had taken with him his charkha and a few books: the *Gita*, the ashram's book of prayer-songs, the *Ramayana*, a dictionary, a translation of the Koran, and a Bible sent by American students. The Yeravda jailer confiscated the spinning wheel, whereupon Gandhi said he would not eat if he could not spin. The charkha was restored.

On 1 April Devadas and Rajagopalachari (who was released on 20 March) were allowed to meet Gandhi in the jail superintendent's office on the first floor of the prison tower, with the superintendent and the jailor supervising the interview. Following instructions left by Gandhi, C R had taken over as *Young India*'s editor. He wrote in the journal that his 'heart leapt' when he sighted 'the old and familiar source of inspiration and joy' (6 Apr. 1922). But Devadas burst out crying when his father was made to stand on a slab of stone while the superintendent and the jailor sat in comfortable chairs.

Also standing at the interview, of course, Rajagopalachari and Devadas learnt that Gandhi was sleeping on a flimsy blanket in a solitary cell, locked in at night, using some of his books as a pillow, and was denied newspapers and periodicals. After the interview Rajagopalachari wrote in *Young India* (6 Apr. 1922) that India's rulers were unaware of their 'privilege of being custodians of a man greater than the Kaiser, greater than Napoleon ... greater than the biggest prisoners of war'.

Two years later Gandhi himself would say: 'Man is nothing. Napoleon planned much and found himself a prisoner in St Helena. The mighty Kaiser aimed at the crown of Europe and is reduced to the status of a private gentleman. God had so willed it. Let us contemplate such examples and be humble' (*Young India*, 9 Oct. 1924; 29: 236).

Life in prison

Gandhi thus compared his experience with history's great confrontations. After advancing to topple the Raj, he was now, like Napoleon, in prison. Like the Kaiser, he too had aimed at the crown, if only to remove it. Humility was indeed called for, as was acceptance of bitter results.

But he was not accepting defeat. One day, God willing, he would resume his fight. Meanwhile he would read, reflect – and spin. Newman's truth, 'One step enough for me', had become Gandhi's own. For now the clear next step – for him and, in his view, for the country outside – was constructive work, and his favourite form of it was spinning.

He and Banker practised it in Yeravda, and he also kept periods of silence, sometimes for a week at a time. A few restrictions were removed after newspapers printed Rajagopalachari's findings. Gandhi was given a pillow and allowed some exercise in a yard and read books sent by friends or available in the jail library.

The last time he had read uninterruptedly was more than eight years previously, in a South African prison. In Yeravda, giving six hours a day to books, he went through scores: Gibbon's volumes on the decline and fall of Rome, Kipling's songs of Empire, the *Mahabharata*, Plato, Jules Verne, Macaulay, Shaw, Walter Scott, *Faust*, Tagore, Wells, Woodroffe, *Dr Jekyll & Mr Hyde*; histories of Scotland, of the Sikhs, of India, of birds, of cities; biographies of Pitt, Columbus, Wilberforce, Paul of Tarsus, Kabir; several Christian, Muslim and Buddhist books and a series of Hindu texts; the writings of Vivekananda, Dayananda Saraswati, Aurobindo and Tilak, and of his own younger colleagues including Kalelkar and Mashruwala; and much more.

The menu is rich, large and varied. The Empire's challenger is thus also, in his mid-fifties, a scholar with an appetite. At times he copies lines into a notebook, including these from Goethe's *Faust*:

My poor sick brain is crazed with pain/ And my poor sick heart is torn in twain.

For all his cheerfulness in Yeravda, Gandhi's brain surely asked difficult questions and his heart too felt wounded.

Writer. In Yeravda, Gandhi hoped also to write, and there are hints that from the time he expected his arrest – following Chauri Chaura, that is – Gandhi's mind turned to the possibility of working on at least three projects: a history of his South African battles, his autobiography, and an interpretation, in support of non-violence, of the *Mahabharata* and the *Gita*.

For the next five years or more, writing in fact would vie with spinning for first place in Gandhi's personal agenda of constructive work. Two years after his arrest, when a critical turn in his health forced the government to release Gandhi, he would publicly announce that he had made considerable progress with the South African story and that he hoped in addition to write his autobiography and interpret the *Mahabharata* (27: 6).

Much earlier, in March 1922 – before he was brought to Yeravda – Gandhi had asked his son Manilal, now editing *Indian Opinion* in South Africa, to send to India the manuscript papers, correspondence files, collections of press cuttings, and books he had left behind in South Africa. Gandhi did not receive this material in Yeravda, but we can infer that he was thinking of the history of satyagraha in South Africa (Letter of 17 Mar. 1922; 26: 368–9). He had 'long entertained a desire to write a history of that struggle,' for as its general he knew things no one else did.[1] Moreover, the story of that struggle might help in understanding what the non-cooperation struggle lacked and what a future struggle would need.

While broad, his reading in Yeravda was controlled. Since there were no lamps in his cell, it had to be done by day, and he would not give it more than six hours. Four clear hours were daily given to spinning and carding, and at dawn and sunset he performed his prayers, reciting texts and singing bhajans, most of the time to himself.

He saw the spinning as a spiritual exercise also. In a letter he wrote in April to Ajmal Khan, the acting Congress president, Gandhi said that while his mind at times wandered when he read the *Gita*, the Koran and the *Ramayana*, 'not an impure thought enters my mind during the four hours [of spinning]' (23: 134). A diary into which he regularly entered a few lines, though not every day, mentions the books he read and the visitors permitted to see him or Banker. One entry states that he wrote an apology to Banker – we do not know for what.

While cherishing his seclusion, Gandhi longed at times for company. He enjoyed that of the diffident Banker for some of most days but wished for more. Asked to name relatives who might qualify to visit him, Gandhi provided a list of nine, most of whom were not his kin by blood. Kasturba's name was mentioned last, as 'Mrs Gandhi'. Their son Ramdas and Lakshmi Dudabhai, the 'untouchable' girl, were named, as also Ameena Bawazir, a Muslim girl in the ashram, and another girl, 15-year-old Moti Lakshmidas, who had been ailing – Gandhi would not pass up any chance to make a statement about inclusiveness. (26 Apr. 1923; 26: 429)

Told that he could send a letter every three months, he chose to write the first one, in mid-April 1922, to Hakim Ajmal Khan, the acting Congress president but also (Gandhi explained to the jail chiefs) a personal friend. The letter contained no politics but several messages to family and friends, including Das and Motilal Nehru, that Gandhi hoped would be forwarded. Through the letter Kasturba was requested not to worry or attempt to visit him in jail – Gandhi feared that, like Devadas, she too would cry. The letter was stopped by the Raj. He could write, Gandhi was told, to a family member, not to others. In that case he would prefer not to write the quarterly letters,

he replied. But, obtaining permission, he did write a couple of times, including, once, to Jamnalal Bajaj.

This was soon after a visit by Kasturba and Ramdas, their third son. Now 24 years old and recently back from South Africa, Ramdas had spoken of his wish to marry. Through Bajaj Gandhi advised Ramdas that if he had to marry he should find a virtuous girl from a poor family, not look for a rich girl (5 Oct. 1922; 23: 139–44).

Before Gandhi's arrest, Manilal, now over 30, had also communicated his keenness to marry. Gandhi had discouraged him. 'The day you marry you will lose your lustre,' the father wrote, adding, 'My relation with Ba today is that of brother and sister, and the fame I have is due to it.' 'However,' said Gandhi at the end of the letter, 'do what you wish, but not what I wish. If you simply cannot do without marrying, do think of marriage by all means' (17 Mar. 1922; 23: 101–2).

Bajaj had sought the imprisoned Gandhi's advice on keeping the mind free of lustful thoughts. Recommending bland food, prayer and a passion against the wandering eye, Gandhi also asked Bajaj to recognize the difference between a thought straying into the mind and the will's response to it. 'If I were to allow all my thoughts to rule my actions, I should be undone. At the same time, we must not fret about these evil thoughts' (5 Oct. 1922; 23: 139–41).

At Yeravda he composed, in Gujarati, a short 'primer' for children. Two of its 12 chapters reproduced bhajans – *Vaishnava Jana* and another song praising God as the universe's loving creator. In other chapters a rural mother and her daughter and son converse about playing, exercising, studying, brushing teeth, cleaning the body, tending flowers and trees, and doing house work, which the son too is expected to join in. Admitting that the conversations were somewhat 'artificial', and not drawn from the typical village home, Gandhi thought they might be found useful nonetheless. In prison he also prepared a short concordance of the *Gita*, with an index, giving 15 minutes daily – no more and no less – to this exercise.

He was daily frisked for weapons or other banned material, at times roughly. During one such exercise a European warder touched Gandhi in the groin. At first Gandhi thought of speaking about the misconduct to the superintendent, whose respect he had quickly won, but he chose instead to talk directly to the warder, whose ways evidently improved. When other warders were harsh to him or to other prisoners, Gandhi again sought to correct them without involving the jail chiefs. Indulal Yagnik, a fellow-prisoner permitted to see Gandhi from time to time, recorded an incident involving Adan, a Somali convict who had become a warder:

One evening our Negro warder from Somaliland was bitten by a scorpion on his hand. He gave a shout. Mr Gandhi was quickly on the spot ... He first asked for a knife to cut the wound ... But he found the knife dirty. So missing no moment he quickly washed the area round the wound and applying his lips to the wound began to suck out the poison. He went on spitting after sucking and eventually stopped when Adan felt relief.[2]

But Gandhi protested strongly when some satyagrahi fellow-prisoners were flogged for refusing to work as ordered. When Gandhi's request to meet them was denied, he threatened to fast. Yielding, the jail officials restricted flogging to those who assaulted prison staff.

In April 1923 Banker completed his sentence and was released. Going to Yeravda's gates to greet him, Rajagopalachari thought that Banker's soul had been 'polished by a master hand' during his obligatory retreat for 13 months in Gandhi's company (*Young India*, 19 Apr. 1923).

Missing his faithful prison-mate, Gandhi was glad when, on 16 April, Devadas, now 23, made his second visit to Yeravda. In between, the son had spent several months in prison in Allahabad, after saying at his trial there: 'We Indians do not joke when we say that jail is the only abode which a self-respecting man can choose for himself at this time.'[3] Walking to the prison gate to see his son off, Gandhi found Vallabhbhai, who was waiting outside. Breaking into a broad smile, Gandhi exclaimed, 'What a gift I have had today!'[4]

If thoughts of defeat did not assail Gandhi, thoughts of death did. We know, from what he would write after his release, that he reflected on the mystic Hallaj, who had died for his beliefs. Mortality was also underlined by sharp abdominal pains from April 1923. On 5 May and again ten days later, Colonel Maddock, the Poona-based surgeon-general of Bombay presidency, examined Gandhi, and on 18 May Kasturba was allowed to meet her husband, who had been moved to the jail's European wing, which was less harsh.

The problem seemed to subside but may have been a factor in Gandhi recounting, from November 1923, the story of the South African battles led by him. Without the aid of documents or notes, he started dictating it to Yagnik, in Gujarati. He wanted the story told before he died.

Congress disunity

Outside, the thousands emerging from prisons and other politically conscious Indians were confused and divided. The Congress had preferred challenging the Empire to entering the Raj's councils, but constructive work was less exciting than either. But not for everyone. Vallabhbhai, for instance, had raised a million rupees for Gujarat Vidyapith, and men like him and Rajagopalachari had advanced the fight against untouchability in their areas. These two, and Bajaj, Rajendra Prasad, Devadas and Vinoba Bhave, were also involved in a morale-boosting if localized satyagraha in Nagpur that restored the right to fly the Congress flag. In another part of the country, Akalis who in accordance with custom were collecting firewood (for their temple's common kitchen) in Guru-ka-Bagh, ten miles from Amritsar, refused to be cowed by police lathis. Group after group went to fell wood and non-violently took beatings until their right to the fuel was acknowledged.

But flags and firewood could not match the attraction of councils, for which elections were due again in November 1923. Motilal Nehru, released in June 1922, and Chitta Ranjan Das, freed two months later, proposed a reversal of the policy of boycotting the councils. They were backed by many, including Vithalbhai Patel, who spoke of 'smuggling into the enemy fort with a view to conquering it' and argued that Congress members would 'wreck' the councils from the inside if it proved impossible to influence them.

His brother Vallabhbhai pointed out that the fortress of the enemy was located not in the largely decorative legislatures but in the impenetrable estates of the Viceroy and the governors, who would rule by ordinances no matter what the councils said.[5] Claiming that debates and votes could nonetheless embarrass the Raj, many in the Congress – the Pro Changers as they were called – called for a new policy. The No Changers were led by C R, Patel, Rajendra Prasad and Jamnalal Bajaj. At the end of 1922, when the Congress met for its annual plenary session in Gaya in Bihar under the presidency of Das, Rajagopalachari proved to be the star performer. The No Changers won the debates and the votes.

But Das, Motilal Nehru and Vithalbhai responded by forming a Swaraj party that claimed to be the Congress's pro-council wing. Much acrimony resulted, and a third group led by Azad and Jawaharlal tried in vain to restore unity, but the Swarajists contested the November elections and won several seats. Motilal Nehru entered the Central Legislative Assembly from Allahabad. Defeating independents and a Liberal Party candidate, Vithalbhai was elected from one of Bombay city's two seats, Jinnah winning the other seat, which was reserved for Muslims. In Bengal the Swarajists led by Das emerged as the largest single group, and in the Central Provinces they were the majority. Elsewhere, they were outperformed by local parties and independents.

Pro Changers and No Changers signed a truce of sorts in December 1923 when the Congress met in Bezwada (Vijaywada), with a recently released Muhammad Ali in the chair. Non-cooperation was reaffirmed as Congress policy but endorsement was also offered to the Swarajists' entry into the councils, with the clarification that they represented themselves, not the Congress.

Surgery and release

On 12 January 1924, after his abdominal pains had returned in extreme form and an emaciated Gandhi had been removed to Sassoon Hospital, Colonel Maddock diagnosed appendicitis. (Later, when there was criticism at the delay in identifying the problem, Gandhi defended the doctors by saying that appendicitis was not easy to diagnose, which at the time was indeed the case.)

On Maddock offering to approach doctors he wanted, Gandhi named Dr Jivraj Mehta and Dr Dalal, but neither could be quickly traced, whereupon Gandhi wrote a letter authorizing Maddock to perform the surgery. On 12 January, a power outage forced Maddock to operate under torchlight, but the operation was successful. The Raj publicly announced the news. Though saved by Maddock from a predicament, the Raj could not continue to detain Gandhi, for it knew that India loved him, everybody knew that he was ill and weak (those allowed to visit him thought he was half his usual size), and everybody remembered that two years earlier he had called off a national struggle because of Chauri Chaura.

On 5 February, when he was still at Sassoon Hospital, he was informed that because of his condition he was being unconditionally released. Though Gandhi expressed regret that the release was tied to his health, India felt a wave of delight. But he was too ill to leave the hospital. When, on 10 March, he finally emerged into the open air, his 'very efficient English nurse' (to quote from what Gandhi wrote two months later), speaking with 'a smile curling round her lips' and an 'insidious twinkle in her eyes', asked Gandhi to remember that he, 'a fierce boycotter of everything British', as she called him, had been operated upon by a British surgeon with British surgical instruments, and received British drugs and the ministrations of a British nurse.

The nurse's 'last triumphant sentence' was that the umbrella shading him on his way out of the hospital was British too. But when Gandhi answered that the boycott he had asked for was not of British or imperial goods but of cloth made outside India – whether in Britain, Europe, America or anywhere else – and that he had asked for it for the sake of the charkha and the women and men of India's villages, the spirited nurse evidently remarked that she might wear khadi herself (*Young India*, 15 May 1924).

Goals in 1924. A Bombay businessman, Narottam Morarjee, offered his seaside home in Juhu for Gandhi to convalesce. There Gandhi came to some conclusions. For one thing, he would rule out leading another attack on the Raj before March 1928, when his six-year sentence would expire. Since India in any case was too divided to fight, he would aim for reconciliation – in India as a whole and in the Congress – promote constructive work and safeguard his vision for the Hindus in an increasingly intolerant climate. Finally, he had to start thinking of an Indian leadership after him.

He revealed himself and some of his thoughts at a meeting on 31 August in Bombay's

Excelsior Theatre, after ardent non-cooperators had booed speakers who had been non-cooperation's critics. Gandhi asked the disturbers to stand up and apologize, which they did. Then Gandhi said that his own nature had two sides, 'the severe and the mild'. The former, he admitted, had alienated 'my wife, son and departed brother'. When he wore that face, added Gandhi, his concealed love had to be 'looked for'. Now (he seemed to claim) India would see his gentler side (29: 65).

Opposition, ingenuity, unity. The No Changers in the Congress wanted Gandhi to crush the Pro Changer rebellion; the Pro Changers hoped he would bless it. At first Gandhi suggested a clear division of responsibilities to resolve the quarrel, the Swarajists engaging with the councils and the No Changers keeping charge of the Congress. Wanting, however, a say in the party as well, Motilal Nehru (who had been elected leader of a 45-strong Swarajist group in the Central Assembly) and Das rejected the proposal.

At an AICC meeting held in Ahmedabad in June 1924, Gandhi saw the strength of the sentiment against positions dear to him. Not only was council-entry defended, but Das and others attacked and almost defeated a resolution of Gandhi's that condemned the murder of an Englishman in Calcutta. 'Your way has been tried from 1920. Now give our way a chance.' This seemed to be the message to him from Das, Motilal Nehru, Vithalbhai and several others.

Gandhi was challenged in the Congress on another front: there was a demand for a boycott of all products of the Empire. As the Sassoon Hospital nurse had found out, Gandhi opposed this policy. He felt it smacked of hatred, could touch off violence and was impractical. By contrast, he claimed, his alternative of a boycott of foreign cloth was a practical proposition, for the charkha, together with India's textile mills, could make all the cloth India needed. If an anti-British boycott signalled a step towards violence, its alternative, the charkha, became – to him and his critics – a symbol of non-violence.

India had the undoubted right, Gandhi argued, to adopt 'the time-worn method' of violence, but superiority of arms would enable the British to crush Indian violence and extend their rule indefinitely. Gandhi also warned that Hindus and Muslims were bound to use violence against each other, and not merely against the British, so that if independence was somehow won by assassination, it would descend on a Hindu or a Muslim state, not on an India for all (*Young India*, 22 May 1924; 24: 99–102).

Though he prevailed in the votes at Ahmedabad, the attacks on his policies hurt Gandhi so much that he openly wept at the session and said that he felt 'defeated and humbled'. But he bounced back and offered, in an ingenious move, to give in to the Swarajists over the councils if they supported him on khadi. They agreed, and a Gandhi-Das-Nehru pact was signed to end the Congress infighting. Gandhi accepted that the Swarajists were in the councils on the Congress's behalf, and the Swarajists agreed that only those who plied the charkha could become members of the Congress. Instead of paying four annas a year, Congress members would henceforth turn in hanks of yarn. If not spinning themselves, they could hand in yarn made by others. Gandhi had lost on the councils but won on khadi, which he (and others) interpreted as non-violence.

In 1924 the Raj arrested several Swarajists in Bengal, including Subhas Bose. Gandhi's response was to ask the Congress to support the arrested men by owning them. The No Changers felt aggrieved at Gandhi's generosity towards the Swarajists but remained loyal, and hoped for a realization of Gandhi's belief that the Swarajists would 'retrace their steps when experience has disillusioned them'.[6]

Yet non-cooperation was in effect given up in 1924. Hoping that three planks – khadi, Hindu-Muslim harmony and a struggle against untouchability – would add up to a new platform of national reconciliation, Gandhi invited everyone, including the Liberal Party, to converge onto it.

Cracks in the bridge

The Hindu-Muslim issue presented a huge challenge. Gandhi called it 'the question of questions', employing the phrase he had used five years earlier about Khilafat. The bridge that Reading had acknowledged was cracking, thanks in part to the Raj's diplomacy.

In February 1924, the month of Gandhi's release, a Muslim member of the Viceroy's executive council, Sir Muhammad Shafi, spent three hours with the Ali brothers and obtained, as he wrote in his diary, a promise from the brothers not to oppose the 'organizing of the Muslim community for … defending and promoting Muslim interests'. Shafi had 'emphasized' to them 'the danger to Islam' from the 'shuddhi and sangathan movements' started among Hindus following the Moplah tragedy of August 1921.[7]

Those calling for shuddhi (purification or reconversion) and sangathan (consolidation) included Gandhi's old friend, Swami Shraddhanand. The man who in 1919 had been invited to speak in Delhi's Jama Masjid was now a Hindu first. In 1922, when his demand for Congress funds for shuddhi was turned down, he left the Congress and forged new links with the Hindu Mahasabha, founded in 1915, hoping to make that body more resolute in championing 'Hindu interests'.

In 1923, Gandhi's adversary from 1909, Vinayak Damoder Savarkar, who two years earlier had been moved from the Andaman Islands to Ratnagiri jail, had a tract published entitled *Who is a Hindu?* Promoting 'Hindutva' or 'Hinduness', the tract argued that only those who saw India as both a homeland and a holy land could be patriotic, a reasoning that rendered Muslims and Christians unpatriotic by definition. When, in 1911, Savarkar first entered his cell in the Andamans (to serve a life sentence for a role in the 1909 assassination of the collector of Nasik, a Sanskrit-literate British officer called

A M T Jackson), the British were his enemy number one, but before long Muslims took that position.

He sent an apology to the Raj. Conditionally released in 1924 but confined to Ratnagiri district until 1937, when he was freed, Savarkar continued, it seemed, to believe in the manliness of certain acts of violence, and in 'the national duty' of patriots to kill 'the nation's enemies'. This came across from his writings in the 1920s, 1930s and later. Much earlier, in a history of the 1857 Rebellion that he wrote in 1909 (the year when he and Gandhi had met, and when Gandhi had condemned the Wyllie murder, which he had encouraged), Savarkar had refused to condemn the brutal killings of British women and children.[8] On a range of current and historical questions, Savarkar thus stood sharply opposed to Gandhi.

In August 1923 the Hindu Mahasabha endorsed Savarkar's line and called for shuddhi and for the formation of Hindu self-defence squads. There were parallel Muslim movements for tabligh (spreading the word) and tanzim (organization). Both sides, Hindu and Muslim, claimed to be acting in defence, but Hindu-Muslim riots occurred nonetheless, including eleven significant ones in 1923 alone.[9]

While Muslims, including Muhammad Ali, complained to the released Gandhi about shuddhi and sangathan, and about statements by Hindu leaders like Pandit Malaviya, Lala Lajpat Rai and Swami Shraddhanand, Gandhi also received 'unprintably' abusive letters from Hindus who attacked him for having roused Muslim passion, which they claimed now targeted Hindus, not the British. Did he not know, Gandhi was asked, of Muhammad Ali's response when accused by Muslims of being 'a follower of Mahatma Gandhi in his religious principles'? Ali had replied that while 'in actual character' he could not think of anyone 'entitled to a higher place than Mahatma Gandhi', he nevertheless regarded 'the creed of even a fallen and degraded Mussulman [as] entitled to a higher place' than that of the then imprisoned Gandhi.[10]

Even the heightened polarization did not require comparison in such terms. In the uproar that inevitably followed, some demanded Ali's resignation as the Congress chief. Gandhi's comment was that a molehill – Ali's effort to underscore his loyalty to Islam – had been made into a mountain.

Essay & an indiscretion. As long as Hindus and Muslims were jointly fighting the British, some crucial and divisive questions could be set aside. Now Gandhi was obliged to address them directly. He did so at the end of May in a wide-ranging *Young India* essay that merits close attention.

Entitled 'Hindu-Muslim tension: Its cause and cure', the essay began with the 'indictments' that Gandhi was receiving. If Hindus alleged that Gandhi's position on Khilafat had enhanced the prestige of the Maulvis, who had now 'proclaimed a kind of jehad against us Hindus', Muslim complainants charged that Hindus had tricked

Muslims by quietly returning to the Raj's courts, colleges and councils, whereas Muslims had stayed out.

One Muslim critic said that the Aligarh College had been 'utterly spoilt' by non-cooperation and lamented that a man like Muhammad Ali, who in the past had done 'solid work for the Muslim community', was 'won over to your side and he is now a loss to the community', even though, fortunately, only 'a few' Muslims continued to remain 'in your camp'.

Rejecting the charges, Gandhi wrote in the essay that he was 'totally unrepentant'. If he had been 'a prophet and foreseen all that has happened', he would have still done what he did. 'The awakening among the masses' was 'a tremendous gain' and he would do nothing 'to put the people to sleep' again.

Pointing out that recent riots had claimed Muslim as well as Hindu victims, and declaring that the Punjab, where newssheets from both sides vied with one another 'in using abusive language and reviling the religion of the opponent', was 'the seat of the trouble', he said that attempts to justify violence constituted the biggest challenge confronting India. Quoting a Muslim friend who had said to him, 'Violence is the law of life' and 'I must hate my enemy', Gandhi added that some Hindu critics, too, found non-violence 'repugnant'.

'Some of my Hindu friends tell me that killing is a duty enjoined by the *Gita* under certain circumstances.' His own firm view was that the *Gita* 'inculcated the duty of eradicating the evil within us without hesitation, without tenderness'. But there were Hindus who 'scornfully rejected my interpretation'. 'I feel the wave of violence coming,' Gandhi warned.

He was not asking Indians, Gandhi pointed out, to respond with absolute non-violence to villainy, or against 'thieves, robbers, or ... nations that may invade India'. However, 'the means for the attainment of Swaraj must be non-violent'. Secondly, Hindus, Muslims, Christians, Sikhs and Parsis 'must not settle their differences by resort to violence'. Hindu-Muslim disputes should be settled through arbitration or in courts of law:

> It must be common cause between the two communities that neither party shall take the law into its own hands, but that all points in dispute, wherever and whenever they arise, shall be decided by reference either to private arbitration or to the law courts if they wish. This is the whole meaning of non-violence [in] ... communal matters ...

If attacked, Hindus should of course fight to protect their loved ones. A rabbit fleeing a terrier and a muscular Zulu cowering before English lads were examples of cowardice, not of non-violence. He had heard, Gandhi wrote, that Hindu homes had been looted in

Saharanpur in western UP, and a housewife assaulted, but the locality's Hindus had not put up a fight. 'As a Hindu I am more ashamed of Hindu cowardice than I am angry at the Mussulman bullying,' he said. Added Gandhi:

> There is no doubt in my mind that in the majority of quarrels the Hindus come out second best. My own experience but confirms the opinion that the Mussulman as a rule is a bully, and the Hindu as a rule is a coward. I have noticed this in railway trains, on public roads and in the quarrels which I had the privilege of settling ... Where there are cowards, there will always be bullies.

The essay made other points. Reviling the other religion in the name of shuddhi and tabligh should be publicly condemned. The facts of each reported riot should be dug out. Goondas* alone could not be blamed; respectable Hindus and Muslims too were accountable, for they created the climate where goondas flourished.

Middle-class Hindus eager to play religious music near a mosque should not enlist 'untouchables' who 'feared not death' as a shield. Such exploitation of 'our "untouchable" brothers can serve neither Hinduism in general nor the suppressed classes in particular'. As for the cow, over which riots had occurred, its protection should start with better treatment of cattle by the Hindus, not with attacks on Muslims over the cow. 'The half-starved condition of the majority of our cattle is a disgrace to us.'

The essay asked Muslims not to think of Hindu leaders like Malaviya, Lajpat Rai and Shraddhanand as enemies. While not perfect, these leaders were certainly 'not past praying for'. Hindus were given identical advice. True, Maulana Abdul Bari, the Lucknow-based preceptor of the Ali brothers, had made hurtful remarks. But he had been quick to apologize. The Ali brothers were 'not faultless'. Yet, 'being full of faults myself, I have not hesitated to seek and cherish their friendship'. Their 'pan-Islamism [was] not anti-Hindu'.

He was not going to forsake his friends, whether Hindu or Muslim, Gandhi declared. 'We have to discover points of contact and with faith in God work away for the common good.' Quoting a recent remark by Jinnah, 'Hindu-Muslim unity means Swaraj', Gandhi said he agreed with it. His conclusion was that 'a lasting heart unity' – 'so necessary for both' communities – was natural and possible (*Young India*, 29 May 1924; 28: 43–62).

Except for the sweeping generalization about Muslims being bullies and Hindus cowards, the essay was notable for its balance, clarity, frankness and common sense. What it said about 'the coming wave of violence', the centrality of the Punjab, and the exploitation of Dalits for violent clashes was prophetic as well.

---

* Goondas = criminals/hooligans.

But the generalization, easily removable from its context, was felt to be unfair and damaging by Muslims and welcomed by the Hindu section that wished to stereotype Muslims. Unusually for him, Gandhi had been carried away. He did not check himself because he sensed a contest for the Hindu heart between two visions of the future, his own and that of a growing anti-Muslim school of Hinduism, and wished his strength of feeling for fellow-Hindus to come across.

We do not know whether (or how much) Gandhi knew in May 1924 of the ideas and plans of Savarkar, or of preparations for the 1925 birth of the Rashtriya Swayamsevak Sangh (RSS) in Nagpur. That Gandhi was aware of communal riots in Nagpur in 1924 is known – he tried to send Motilal and Jawaharlal Nehru and Abul Kalam Azad to Nagpur to investigate. In any case, the remarks in the essay about 'the scornful' rejection of his interpretation of the *Gita* and the current of violence he could feel coming disclose Gandhi's live consciousness of the hostility that threatened his bond with the Hindus.

All the same, Gandhi's bullies-and-cowards remark did not meet the standard of caution included in a set of norms for writers and journalists that he would spell out a year later:

> I may not write in anger or malice. I may not write idly. I may not write merely to excite passion … Often my vanity dictates a smart expression or my anger a harsh adjective. It is … a fine exercise to remove these weeds. The reader sees the pages of *Young India* fairly well dressed-up and is inclined to say, 'What a fine old man this must be!' Well, let the world understand that the fineness is *carefully* and prayerfully cultivated (Emphasis added; *Young India*, 2 Jul. 1925).

Let us also note that Gandhi, now nearing his 55th birthday, calls himself, for the first time, an old man.

In November 1924, in a challenging remark that again revealed his alertness to a possible 'wave of violence', Gandhi equated violent nationalism with imperialism. 'Violent nationalism, otherwise known as imperialism, is the curse. Non-violent nationalism is a necessary condition of corporate or civilized life' (*Young India*, 27 Nov. 1924; 29: 385).

A riot & a fast

Though Gandhi had said that Hindu-Muslim unity was natural and possible, the climate was against it. Yet he made a notable bid for it, occasioned by violence in September 1924 in Kohat in the North-West Frontier. Inflamed by a poem derogatory of the Prophet, a crowd of Kohat's Muslims had surrounded a building where many Hindu families lived. Shots fired from the building caused Muslim casualties and further enraged the Muslims, who were also angered by a local Sikh's alleged liaison with the wife of his Muslim gardener.

A number of Hindus were killed in the violent reaction that ensued, and there was an allegation that three Hindu housewives were abducted, forcibly converted and remarried. Professing conversion to save their lives, some Hindu males shaved off their tufts and recited the kalima, declaring their supposed Islamic belief. The offending poem was withdrawn but Muslim anger did not subside. With the Raj's support, Kohat's Hindus and Sikhs fled to Rawalpindi.

In unconfirmed bits and pieces, the news of Kohat reached a Gandhi already stricken by a sense of helplessness. What he had said or written had not brought the two communities together. His national pride too had been hurt. 'The world is watching,' he wrote, ' – some with glee and some with sorrow – the dogfight that is proceeding in our midst' (*Young India*, 25 Sep. 1924; 29: 211). There was a sense, also, of guilt. If Hindus seemed to think that non-violence was cowardice, perhaps he was partially responsible. As he would say to Mahadev Desai on 18 September, the Hindus 'could charge him with breach of faith', for he had asked them to believe in the Ali brothers who, most Hindus thought, had let Gandhi down. On 19 September he told Shaukat Ali: 'I cannot bear to hear people accusing you and your brother of having broken your promises to me' (29: 193).

As Gandhi admitted (*Young India*, 25 Sep. 1924), '[H]andling large masses of men, dealing with them, speaking and acting for them [was] no joke for a man whose capacity God has so circumscribed' (29: 198). Yet people like the Ali brothers had not done more to ease his burden; they had not made Hindus feel that Gandhi's trust in them was vindicated. In *Young India* he would write (4 Dec. 1924):

> I am in the world feeling my way to light 'amid the encircling gloom'. I often err and miscalculate. My trust is solely in God. And I trust men only because I trust God. If I had no God to rely upon, I should be like Timon, a hater of my species (29: 408).

Helplessness above all, but also hurt, guilt and blame had turned Gandhi into a 'smouldering mass', to use his phrase. The news of Kohat 'lit [the mass] aflame' (29: 211). His response was to announce a 21-day fast as 'a penance and a prayer'. At first thinking of a 40-day fast, he later settled on a shorter period of trial and told a few friends that he would end the fast even earlier if he found that death was the only alternative (29: 228).

When he decided on the fast, Gandhi was a house guest of Muhammad Ali in Delhi, *en route* to Kohat – along with, he hoped, the Ali brothers. He consulted no one about the fast, not his family, nor close co-workers like Desai, nor his host. Ali criticized the decision, protesting that as Gandhi's host *and* as the Congress president he should have been consulted, and that if Gandhi did not survive the fast, Hindus would attack Muslims. From her sickbed Ali's old mother, Bi Amman, who wore khadi, implored Gandhi not to fast. Journeying from Bombay, Shaukat Ali tried to dissuade Gandhi, as did many others.

Gandhi, unmoved, replied to Bi Amman that he would have carried out her command as coming from his own long-deceased mother, but he had to obey a call from God. The many Hindus who pressed him to reconsider (Saraladevi was one of them) were reminded that Rama had gone to the forest despite his mother's entreaties.

Also journeying to Delhi, and fearing that a Gandhi yet to recover fully would not survive 21 days of starvation, Rajagopalachari speculated that the fast was born of Gandhi's grief at the failure of Muslim leaders to appreciate Hindu suffering or return his gestures.

Gandhi's own explanation was broader. 'To revile one another's religion, to make reckless statements, to utter untruths, to break the heads of innocent men and to desecrate temples or mosques' had become the order of the day. As the author of an energy that had become self-destructive, he *had* to respond, he said (29: 211). Yet a more personal impulse, too, was indicated when Gandhi said: 'I cried out to God even like Draupadi* when she seemed abandoned by her five brave protectors. And her cry [was not] in vain. "Rock of Ages, cleft for me; Let me hide myself in Thee"' (29: 198).

Muhammad Ali's home, where the fast began on 17 September, stood on the Ridge, on the outskirts of Delhi, from where in 1857 the British had begun their recapture of Delhi. Nearby rose a memorial marking the mutiny. The scene inside Muhammad Ali's home was also powerfully symbolic: Gandhi fasting, surrounded by prominent Hindu and Muslim leaders (Swami Shraddhanand, Motilal Nehru, Das, Rajagopalachari, the Ali brothers, Ajmal Khan, Ansari, Abul Kalam Azad and others) and also by two Britons, Andrews, who came at once, and Foss Westcott, the Bishop of Calcutta.

Across the country people were stirred and also anxious. A practised faster who well understood his body, Gandhi however fully expected to survive and said as much to all enquirers. Among other things he was making amends to the Hindus and strengthening his bond with them. This was indicated by the references to Rama and Draupadi, and confirmed by a 'personal' letter to readers of *Navajivan*, signed, 'Your servant, Mohandas Gandhi', that he wrote in Gujarati soon after the fast began (28 Sep. 1924).

In this letter he said that while he himself would always practise complete non-violence, that could not be everyone's response. 'The sword indeed has a place in the world, but not cowardice.' His readers had the duty to 'protect [their] wards by using the

---

* Draupadi = a central character in the *Mahabharata*, wife to five Pandava brothers.

sword if necessary'. Saying that he had always 'put his soul' into *Navajivan* and written not 'even one word there without God as witness', Gandhi added that he had nonetheless been 'tortured' by the thought that he may perhaps have harmed his readers by unwittingly suggesting that cowardice was non-violence. After starting to fast in penance, he felt better (29: 218–19).

If the fast's 'penance' was a signal to the Hindus, its 'prayer' seemed meant, firstly, for Congress leaders. He wanted them to burn for Hindu-Muslim unity. 'Divided, we must ever remain slaves,' he had said to Ajmal Khan in a letter written as far back as March 1922, just after he was arrested, adding that if 'a sufficient number' of Hindu and Muslim leaders preserved an unbreakable faith in unity, it would 'permeate the masses' (26: 356).

The prayer was also addressed to the Muslim community. On 19 September he told Shaukat Ali: 'I would ask Muslims to befriend the Hindus if they think it is not contrary to their religion. [If they feel it is contrary,] then I am sure I should have no cause to live any more. I should die.' (29: 194) During the first week of the fast he spoke in a similar vein:

I have not a shadow of doubt that Islam has sufficient in itself to become purged of illiberalism and intolerance (*Young India*, 25 Sep. 1924; 29: 189).

The Ali brothers responded with gracious gestures. Both plied the charkha and showed Gandhi their yarn. Again and again Shaukat Ali called Gandhi 'my chief' and spoke sadly of Gandhi's 'bed of sorrow' in his younger brother's house, where the entire household had turned vegetarian during Gandhi's stay. Gandhi said he had not received 'warmer or better treatment than under Muhammad Ali's roof', and added: 'I am experiencing here the richest love. It is more than bread for me' (29: 212).

Towards the end of the fast, in *his* symbolic gesture, Muhammad Ali purchased a cow from a butcher and asked Gandhi to gift it to a Hindu cow-shelter. But we must assume that the brothers felt targeted by the fast, and we know that they did not see eye-to-eye with Gandhi over the violence in Kohat.

The fast exposed Gandhi's vulnerable if also creative face. The self-possessed general of 1921, one whom Hindus and Muslims had fervently and unquestioningly followed, was revealed in 1924 as somebody who could also feel weak, guilty and abandoned. And when Gandhi starved himself, he was also – despite all the confidence he expressed about his body's capacity – struggling, and entirely dependent on the water he had allowed himself, on Kasturba and others joining him to assist, on doctors, on his God.

The dependence increased his humility and warmth, and he wrote or dictated affectionate, caring letters to Jawaharlal, Rajagopalachari, Vallabhbhai and his daughter Maniben, Bajaj, Birla, Lakshmi Dudabhai and several others.

Referring, just before the fast, to 'my own dearest relations', Gandhi had said (*Young India*, 4 Sep. 1924): 'Sometimes love's anguish left deep scars on the loved ones, but it let much deeper ones on the lover's bosom.' (29: 75) Aware that he had often hurt those dearest to him, he agonized, most of the time secretly.

He wrote warmly to Devadas, who while translating for *Navajivan* a typed English text of Gandhi's explanation of his fast, where it was stated that the fast arose from 'hopelessness', had rectified the word to 'helplessness'. '[Y]ou have, as it were,' the father wrote, 'proved your title to be my heir. May God give you long life and may He advance your beautiful character and proficiency' (21 Sep. 1924; 29: 207).

On the 20th day of the fast, Gandhi made the remark (quoted at the start of this chapter) about the humility taught by the fates of Napoleon and the Kaiser. Added Gandhi: 'During these days of grace, privilege and peace, I have hummed to myself a hymn we often sing at the Satyagraha Ashram, *"Raghuvar tum ko meri laaj"*' (29: 236).

The hymn was by Tulsidas, the 16th-century poet who had popularized the *name* of Rama, the prince-hero of the classical epic *Ramayana*, as a path to the divine and a force greater than the prince; and the lines that Gandhi was humming were entreaties from 'a sinner of old' to One who 'protects the weak' and 'removes the sin and misery of mankind'. A similar sentiment was contained in the plea to the Rock of Ages that, as we saw, Gandhi had spontaneously recited (and perhaps sung inwardly as well).

At the end of the 21st day, Gandhi asked for full, unhindered freedom of worship in temples and mosques, and put it to his friends present to be willing to lay down their lives for Hindu-Muslim friendship. Ajmal Khan and Abul Kalam Azad promised their total commitment. At Gandhi's request, Vinoba Bhave recited from the *Upanishads*; Imam Bawazir, who like Bhave had travelled from the Sabarmati ashram, recited the *Fateha*; and Andrews sang, 'When I survey the wondrous Cross'. To his host, Gandhi said, 'You are more than a brother to me.' Adding, 'God is great and merciful', he broke his fast, sipping orange juice handed to him by Dr Ansari.

Andrews stayed at Gandhi's side throughout the fast and was deeply affected. He thought his friend had taken upon himself the sins of his Hindu and Muslim compatriots. Long after the fast Andrews would say: 'No more impressive event has happened in India's recent history.'[11]

For a while at least, many others in India also seemed touched, but perhaps the fast's most significant impact was on the leaders gathered around the starving Gandhi, who saw that Hindu-Muslim unity would not come without a price.

Gandhi recognized that one man willing to pay that price was Motilal's son, Jawaharlal, whose active cultivation and grooming by Gandhi dates from this time. When the fast started, Gandhi wrote to a 'stunned' Jawaharlal asking him not to be anxious, but Jawaharal ran to Gandhi's bedside, taking his seven-year-old daughter Indira with him.*

A month after the fast ended, Gandhi proposed to Jawaharlal the formation of a 'flying Hindu-Muslim column' that would quickly reach any riot area and investigate (29: 323). This message was soon followed, in the middle of November, by a greeting to Jawaharlal for his 35th birthday, and days later, by a telegram sent when Jawaharlal and his wife Kamala lost a new-born child. While a host of others also received similar messages at this time from Gandhi, his interest in Jawaharlal, growing in the crucible of the fast, was exceptional.

Polarization

Yet polarization was proceeding apace. In 1925, a group of Maharashtrian Brahmins, led by Keshav Baliram Hedgewar (a doctor who had taken part in the non-cooperation movement but concluded that 'yavan-snakes† reared on the milk of non-cooperation were provoking riots in the nation with their poisonous hissing'[12]) and backed by Savarkar, formed the Rashtriya Swayamsevak Sangh (RSS) in Nagpur. Declaring that the strengthening of Hindu Dharma, Hindu Culture, and the Hindu Nation was its aim, the RSS equated Hindu interests with Indian interests. Towards its goal the RSS would organize, across India, shakhas (branches) of Hindu young men of all castes. The youths would be asked to wear khaki shorts and taught to sing Hindu nationalist verses, to drill, to practise the use of sticks and, at times, daggers, and to salute the 'bhagwa' or the saffron banner reportedly used by Brahmin Peshwas during their assaults on Muslim chieftains in the 18th and 19th centuries. On crucial questions of Indian nationhood – Hindu-Muslim relations, militarization, the use of violence, and an Indian flag – the RSS ideology was thus fundamentally opposed to Gandhi's. The ideology was incorporated in the RSS programme, which indicated, among other impulses, a concern among Brahmin elites at Gandhi's popularity with peasant-caste and other 'low-caste' masses and their increased assertiveness. Whereas Gandhi saw 'the awakening among the masses' as 'a tremendous gain', Hedgewar lamented that following non-cooperation the 'Brahmin/non-Brahmin conflict was nakedly on view'.[13] As a counter-strategy, the RSS would strive to unite all Hindu castes against the presumed threat from Muslims.

Gandhi was aware of differences among Hindu nationalists. Unlike the RSS, men like Shraddhanand and Lajpat Rai seemed as keen on independence as on Hindu interests,

---

* Indira Nehru (1917–84), later married to Feroz Gandhi (no relation to Mahatma Gandhi), was India's prime minister from 1966–77 and 1980–4.
† Yavan = a pejorative term for foreigner or Muslim.

while Malaviya (like Lajpat Rai a member of the Central Assembly) was opposed to violence in any Hindu-Muslim confrontation. And though Lajpat Rai thought that Muslim history and Muslim law constituted 'an effective bar' to Hindu-Muslim unity, he did not prescribe a second-class status for Muslims or Christians.

With Shraddhanand, Lajpat Rai and Malaviya, Gandhi had built excellent personal relations and a partial ideological rapport. Unlike Savarkar or the RSS, these three would probably have shared a sentiment that Gandhi expressed in May 1925:

> I have had in my life many an opportunity of shooting my opponents and earning the crown of martyrdom, but I had not the heart to shoot any of them. For I did not want them to shoot me ... I wanted them to convince me of my error. I was trying to convince them of theirs (*Young India*, 7 May 1925).

Yet, in December 1926, Swami Shraddhanand was assassinated by a Muslim in Delhi, and a Hindu-Muslim alliance became even more difficult. Lajpat Rai would die in 1928, after being hit by police lathis in a pro-independence demonstration.

A year earlier (in August 1927), in a letter to Ghanshyam Das Birla, Lajpat Rai had this comment to make about Gandhi:

> The best man to learn manners from is Mahatma Gandhi. His manners come very near perfection, though there is nothing perfect in this world. Great as he is, the greatest of us all, he is very particular in his behaviour towards his friends and co-workers.[14]

But Gandhi's manners and reasoning proved insufficient to restore trust. Frustrated but unrepentant, he would say in 1925:

> I cannot accept that Malaviyaji and others are enemies of Muslims. Nor can I agree to calling [Muhammad] Ali an enemy of the Hindus. I can never agree to the rule of blood for blood and temple for a mosque. But who listens to me? (35: 317)

The Raj did not allow Gandhi and the Ali brothers to visit Kohat. In December 1924, Gandhi visited Rawalpindi without the Ali brothers and met refugees from Kohat. The following February, he and Shaukat Ali together visited Rawalpindi, where some Muslims came from Kohat to present their version, but the two investigators reached different conclusions. Shaukat Ali underlined the Hindu poet's inflammatory verses, while Gandhi emphasized the condoning by Kohat's Muslim leaders of killing, abduction and forced conversions.

Though Shaukat Ali expressed his opposition to forced conversion, he was not willing to put his signature to Gandhi's findings. Going against Ajmal Khan's advice, Gandhi published the two separate reports in *Young India* on 29 March 1925. A public that had closely followed the joint visit to Rawalpindi was in his view entitled to know the result, even if it was split.

The Ali brothers slowly drifted away from Gandhi. 'We still love one another,' Gandhi wrote after publishing the differing reports. Yet their partnership was coming apart, and many Muslim minds entertained the thought that Gandhi had become, or perhaps always had been, a leader of and for Hindus.

Later in 1925, when word came from Kabul that an Ahmadi* would be stoned to death – in accordance, it was claimed, with Islamic law – and Gandhi expressed in *Young India* his unhappiness with that form of punishment, another Khilafatist leader, Maulana Zafar Ali Khan, said that if Gandhi wished to retain his prestige among Muslims, he should not comment on their internal matters. Gandhi answered that he sought not prestige but love, which he would strive to win through service.

But he was no longer winning Muslims. Although men like Ajmal Khan, Ansari, Azad and Ghaffar Khan remained with Gandhi and dismissed the notion that he was merely a Hindu leader, the days when Muslims were exhorted to 'fill the jails at the bidding of Gandhi' and to 'follow Mahatma Gandhi unflinchingly' had ended.

Withdrawal. Reviving Hindu-Muslim partnership or launching another strike against British rule looking unlikely in the near future, Gandhi was free to focus on khadi and untouchability and on his writing. The political arena was more or less abandoned by him, though he had agreed, when asked by both wings of the Congress, to preside at the body's end-1924 session, held in Belgaum. However, president Gandhi dropped C R, Patel and Bajaj from the Working Committee he formed. These leaders would be honed through constructive work for future battles that Gandhi fully expected; and the Swarajists would not confront an adversarial Working Committee.

Rajagopalachari started an ashram in Tiruchengode in the Tamil country. Prasad was associated with Patna's Sadaqat ashram, started in the early 1920s by Gandhi's friend from his student days in London, Mazharul Huq, and Bajaj undertook to keep these and other ashrams viable. The ranks of spinners and weavers grew, as did campaigns against untouchability and liquor, and 'untouchables' were enlisted into the ashrams.

With Gandhi's blessing and approval, Vallabhbhai joined and chaired the Ahmedabad municipality, and Jawaharlal the Allahabad one – unlike the glamorous provincial councils, city municipalities ran schools and employed numbers of people, including 'untouchables', and offered tangible opportunities for assisting the public. These men

---

* Ahmadi = a member of the heterodox Islamic Ahmadi or Ahmadiyya sect.

had not renounced the fight for independence. As C R explained in March 1926 in Patna, where Prasad had invited him to address students of Patna National College, soldiers like him had not retired. In their ashrams they were making ammunition for future battles. The nation's ability to suffer was this ammunition but it had been used up. Some days later, in Ahmedabad, Rajagopalachari again used a militant metaphor; the spindle that made cotton thread was, he said, the Indian masses' pistol.

Satyagraha against untouchability. After 1924 Gandhi reached out again, in Gujarat and elsewhere, to push his campaigns for khadi and against untouchability, dowry and liquor. At most meetings caste Hindus and 'untouchables' sat in different enclosures; on occasion the former would remove the dividing cordon and make history; at other times hosts would purify their vessels after Gandhi and his companions had polluted them – having consorted with the 'untouchables', the Gandhi party too was deemed tainted. At the port town of Mandvi in Kutch, for example, the chairman of the reception committee threw the welcome address at Gandhi from several feet away, as he could be honoured but not touched.

Gandhi backed a satyagraha begun in 1924 in the town of Vykom (Vaikkam) in the princely state of Travancore against a longstanding denial to untouchables of the use of public roads adjacent to a temple and to Brahmin homes. Though forced at times to stand in waist-deep floodwater, the satyagrahis kept up their opposition for months, peacefully entering the forbidden streets and picketing barriers. Visiting Vykom, Gandhi proposed a referendum of caste Hindus on the question – he was certain that only an orthodox minority would defend the prohibitions.

The demand was rejected but in June 1925 prohibited roads on three sides of the temple were thrown open to the 'untouchables'. The victory was incomplete, for the road to the temple's east was still closed to 'untouchables', but all of India had seen the obduracy of the orthodox and followed the Vykom satyagraha, a milestone in the battle against untouchability.

Autobiography

Gandhi's *Satyagraha in South Africa* was serialized in *Navajivan* and *Young India* during 1924 and 1925; and from the end of 1925 the Autobiography began to appear in the two journals. The lull in politics made the writing possible; associates had always urged him to recall his life story; his illnesses may have supplied arguments for recalling it; and writing it would be an exercise in reflection and introspection.

But we may surmise that Gandhi also saw political value in relating a story that confirmed the image of a servant of truth and a loyal Hindu. For a little over three years – from the end of 1925 to February 1929 – the two journals carried a weekly autobiographical instalment. Titled 'My Experiments with Truth', the account ended with the Nagpur Congress of December 1920.

Either Mahadev or Pyarelal translated Gandhi's weekly instalments into English; at times the translation was revised by Gandhi. Many of the lapses, petty thoughts and struggles in Gandhi's life from childhood to 1920 were frankly related in an autobiography which in its personal honesty seemed to have very few precedents. 'It is not without a wrench that I have to take leave of the reader,' he wrote in the final piece, adding, 'I have spared no pains to give a faithful narrative'.

Yet some things were left out. In the first instalment he referred to things 'known only to oneself and one's Maker' that were 'clearly incommunicable' and would not find a place. We can only speculate on what these were. Bitter complaints to the Almighty, unbecoming in an iconic believer? Aches about unfulfilled hopes? Immodest apprehensions of a special calling? We do not know.

Some things known to a few others were also left out – for instance the episode involving Saraladevi, who was very much alive and would have been wounded afresh by any account of it. The events involving Sheikh Mehtab were recounted but, as noted earlier, he was not named.

The Gita. For nine months in 1926–7 he gave discourses in Gujarati on the *Gita*, which were published in *Navajivan*. This exercise too was part of his battle to clarify, and win, the Hindu mind, and not merely his tribute to a text that meant much to him.

Gandhi's core arguments in the *Gita* commentaries, which he presented at the end of morning prayers at the ashram, were as follows: The battlefield setting of the *Gita* is allegorical, not historical. The chariot in which Krishna and Arjuna ride is not real either. The human body is the true chariot, Arjuna the human mind, and Krishna the Indwelling Guide. God as Krishna wants humans to fight in their hearts the daily battle of courage against meanness, not a bloody battle against enemies. After exhorting repeatedly against anger and hatred in the *Gita*, why would Krishna ask for killing, a deed inseparable from anger or hatred?

True, the *Gita*'s first chapter and the start of the second describe a battle, but the rest of the 18-chapter text is a treatise on self-control and on union with the divine; no one could call the *Gita* a textbook on warfare. Finally, since the message of the *Mahabharata* was the folly of war, which killed most characters in the epic and left the world a virtual void, how could the *Gita*, if it was part of the epic, plead for its opposite?

Aware of the *Gita*'s influence in India, Gandhi wanted to enlist that influence on behalf of satyagraha and against violence.

Caged lion

In November 1925 Gandhi wrote to Dr Ansari that he felt 'like a caged lion', that there were things 'buried deep down in my bosom' that were far weightier than what he wrote of in his journals, and added that he did 'not fail to advertise them daily before the Unseen Power' (33: 208).

He was alluding to, among other things, the Hindu-Muslim polarization and the self-imposed embargo ('not before March 1928') on himself. But he seemed to feel that before long he would lead a big battle again, and was sustained by faith in his bond with the masses. In January 1926 he wrote:

Between the masses and myself there is a bond which defies description, but is never-theless felt alike by them and me. I see in the fellowship with them the God I adore … Whether I live in the Ashram or in their midst, I work for them, think of them, and pray for them. I want to live only for them – and so for myself (*Young India*, 7 Jan. 1926).

Always reminding himself of his humanness, he said in February 1927, 'Whenever I see an erring man, I say to myself: "I have also erred"; when I see a lustful man, I say to myself, "So was I once"; and in this way I feel kinship with everyone in the world' (*Young India*, 10 Feb. 1927). A month later he wrote:

The Mahatma I must leave to his fate. Though a non-cooperator, I would gladly subscribe to a bill to make it criminal for anybody to call me Mahatma and to touch my feet. Where I can impose the law myself, i.e. at the Ashram, the practice is criminal (*Young India*, 17 Mar. 1927).

Yet he refused, in his mind, to abandon a destined role:

When I think of my littleness and my limitations on the one hand and of the expec-tations raised about me on the other, I become dazed for the moment; but I come to myself as soon as I realize that these expectations are a tribute not to me, a curious mixture of Jekyll and Hyde, but to the incarnation, however imperfect but compara-tively great in me, of the two priceless qualities of Truth and Non-violence (*Young India*, 8 Oct. 1925).

And in March 1927 he seemed to sense that something might again stir the masses:

Whether [my message] will produce an impression in my lifetime or not, I do not

care, and as the days roll on and as the agony of the masses become prolonged, it will
burn itself into the heart of every Indian who has a heart to respond to the message
(*Young India*, 24 Mar. 1927).

The man conscious of a destiny, of a bond with the masses and of their agony, was also,
however, a friend to individuals. Ghanshyam Das Birla has recorded a conversation at
four one morning 'in the bitter winter of 1926' at a railway station in Delhi, where Birla,
whose wife Mahadevi was critically ill, had gone to see Gandhi, who was arriving from
the Punjab and booked on a connecting train to Ahmedabad.

At the station Birla asked Gandhi ('in a warm, easy way'), 'Will you be stopping
over?' *Gandhi:* 'No, I have to be on my way.' Silence from Birla. *Gandhi:* 'Why did you
ask?' *Birla:* 'Oh, nothing.' *Gandhi:* 'No, you had a reason.' *Birla:* 'I mean, there's a lady,
she's on her deathbed. She desires your darshan, but you are not stopping over, how can I
ask you to come.' *Gandhi:* 'I won't stop over but I will come with you.' *Birla:* 'It's bitterly
cold, and the place is nearly twelve miles from here.' Gandhi: 'Nothing to worry about.
I'll come and catch my train at the next station.' Arguments from Birla. *Gandhi:* 'Not
one word more. Get inside the car.'

Continues Birla's story:

> In those days we didn't have the closed cars we do now. It was really wintry, and
> imagine the icy wind along with it [for] ten miles through the jungle. Arriving, he
> asked the ailing lady, 'How are you?' Her eyes opened in surprise ... She said, 'You
> are here. I am so happy ... I can die in peace.' He replied. 'Take God's name and be at
> peace.' He stayed there ten minutes and boarded his train at the next station ... Such
> was the man who captivated me.[15]

Marking time, and the Swarajists' problems. In June 1925 Das unexpectedly died in
Darjeeling, within days of Gandhi's visit to him, when a bond had been formed. 'I
realized not only how great [Das] was, but also how good he was,' Gandhi wrote in *Young
India* (18 Jun. 1925; 32: 5).

Gandhi's response to his death was to announce a posthumous concession to Das, who,
despite the Das-Motilal pact with Gandhi, had never liked the link between spinning
and Congress membership. Gandhi said he was now willing for people to pay cash if
they could not spin. Rajagopalachari and other No Changers felt terribly let down, but
Gandhi wanted to honour Das and win over his supporters.

On Gandhi's advice, the Swarajists chose Sarojini Naidu as the Congress president
for the end-1925 session in Kanpur; Srinivasa Iyengar, who had resigned his post as
advocate-general in Madras, for the end-1926 session in Gauhati; and Dr Ansari for the

Madras session of December 1927. To show his support, Gandhi attended the sessions but they lacked fervour, largely because in the legislatures the Swarajists were obstructing one another, not the Raj.

After Motilal Nehru accepted a nomination to a committee of the Raj on cadet training, and Vithalbhai Patel became president of the Central Assembly, Tambe, a Swarajist leader in the Central Provinces, went further and in 1925 joined the provincial executive council. When Motilal condemned Tambe's action, he was criticized in turn by other Swarajists.

Allies & intimates

In October 1924 Manilal, who was slowly winning difficult battles in South Africa to keep *Indian Opinion* and Phoenix going, made a brief visit to his father in India. That year Romain Rolland, eminent novelist, pacifist and admirer of Tolstoy, published a study of Gandhi that commanded wide and sympathetic attention in Europe; and in the following year Gandhi was joined at Sabarmati by Madeleine Slade, the 33-year-old daughter of a British admiral, who having read Rolland's book was encouraged by him to go to Gandhi.

Gandhi admitted Miss Slade into the ashram. Tall, authoritative and plain, but also enthusiastic and musical, Miss Slade Indianized herself, wore a khadi salwar and kameez, learnt to spin, speak Hindustani and clean lavatories, and accepted the name that Gandhi gave her, Mira, after the medieval Rajput princess who renounced everything for God. Gandhi greatly liked her. To Rolland he wrote:

> *13 Nov. 1925:* What a treasure you have sent me! ... I shall leave no stone unturned to assist her to become a bridge between East and West. I am too imperfect to have disciples. She shall be fellow-seeker with me and as I am older in years and therefore presumably in spiritual experience, I propose to share the honour of fatherhood with you. Miss Slade is showing wonderful adaptability and has already put us at ease about herself (33: 218).

Living in a one-room hut close to the cottage of the Gandhis, Mira became a helper, ally – and disciple, despite what Gandhi wrote to Rolland.

Not all his allies were disciples or followers. Some (like Motilal Nehru, Das, Ajmal Khan, Ansari, Lajpat Rai, Rajagopalachari, Vallabhbhai Patel, Abul Kalam Azad, Rajendra Prasad and Jawaharlal) were political associates, though Patel, Rajagopalachari and Prasad were also followers in that they always held to Gandhi's line. Jawaharlal was in a category of his own, remaining a loyal follower despite often expressing disagreement.

Some allies (Bajaj, Birla, Sarabhai, Pranjivan Mehta) were financial supporters; of these Bajaj saw himself as a follower as well, in fact, as Gandhi's fifth son.

Other non-political colleagues who enjoyed proximity with Gandhi were thinkers, or persons of the spirit, or of literature or journalism, or social activists: people like Vinoba Bhave, Kaka Kalelkar, Kishorelal Mashruwala, Swami Anand, Ravishankar Vyas, Mohanlal Pandya, Narhari Parikh, Jugatram Dave, Amritlal Thakkar, Valji Desai, Narayan Khare, Shankarlal Banker, Anasuya Sarabhai and others.

Some in this category were Gandhi's associates on *Young India* and *Navajivan* or in the ashram or in work with 'untouchables', tribals, peasants or industrial workers. Many in this group called themselves disciples but to Gandhi they were colleagues. Most (like Gandhi's political colleagues) had circles of influence of their own. Their work and links brought Gandhi strength, and he also enjoyed the stimulating and often frank companionship that many in this group, and his political associates, offered.

We can think of another small category of – simply or above everything else – friends: Andrews, Pranjivan Mehta, and a few others like Mathuradas Trikamji, who was a relative as well.

Another small group (Mahadev Desai, Maganlal, Pyarelal, Krishnadas, Devadas, Kasturba, Mira) were allies/followers/aides who spent much of their time with him, and who sought to serve his person as well as his causes. Persons in this category had a more intimate relationship with Gandhi. This was not of course a constant or unchanging group (the other categories too were changing ones).

The ones named include his wife as well as one of his sons: we have seen that neither Kasturba nor Devadas could claim an exclusive relationship with Gandhi, who thought of and addressed Mahadev, Maganlal, or Pyarelal as a son, and Mira as a daughter. They in turn called him Bapu, which is how most in every category addressed him. Not everyone; we have seen that Andrews called him 'Mohan'.

Visiting Sabarmati in 1925, Andrews thought he saw a 'combination of discipline and love' there. Children 'came flocking around [Gandhi]', there was 'no feeling of fear or awe within his environment' and 'any aloofness or assumption of superiority' in Gandhi was 'unthinkable'.[16]

When she visited the Sabarmati ashram in the 1920s, Pyarelal's young sister Sushila found Kasturba doing 'more than her full quota of work' in the kitchen and 'extraordinarily active'. Noticing 'amazing agility' and 'neatness' in Kasturba, Sushila 'hardly ever saw her sitting near Bapu'. Yet Kasturba's 'watchful eyes followed him all the time' and she 'saw to it that all his needs were supplied'.[17]

A picture of Kasturba would also be provided by another resident of the ashram at this time, Prabhavati Narayan:

At Ba and Bapu's lodgings ... there was a kitchen which served the guests of the Ashram as well. It had gradually become a common mess serving fifteen to twenty persons. A few Ashramites helped Ba in her culinary chores. But most of the work was done by Ba herself, and she took great delight in serving her guests.[18]

Sons and marriage. In 1926 Manilal, sending a message via Ramdas, sprang a surprise: he wished, he said, to marry Fatima ('Timmie') Gool, daughter of Yusuf Gool, a Cape Town merchant who had migrated from near Surat, and of Gool's Cape Malay wife, Wahieda. Timmie was willing. Manilal had known the large Gool family since 1914 when, on the eve of their return to India, all the Gandhis had stayed with the Gools in Cape Town. The father's response was clear. Marriage between a Hindu and a Muslim was fraught with difficulty. Would one of the two convert? To what religion would offspring belong? Moreover,

> your marriage will have a powerful impact on the Hindu-Muslim question ... You cannot forget nor will society forget that you are my son. If you enter into this relationship ... I fear you may no more be the right person to run *Indian Opinion.* It will be impossible for you, I think, after this to come and settle in India (3 Apr. 1926; 35: 12).

'You are a free man', Gandhi added, 'so I cannot force you to do anything.' But we have seen that stark warnings, explicit or implicit, accompanied this reminder of freedom: an end to an editorship that meant everything to Manilal, and the probability that father-son relations would break. A father who had himself shut a hazardous door in 1920 was six years later asking his 34-year-old son to close a similar opening.

Manilal had entertained hopes that his father would approve: after all Gandhi was committed to Hindu-Muslim friendship and had consciously nurtured a multi-faith life in Phoenix, Tolstoy Farm and Sabarmati. But the son was mistaken. The father was not willing to jeopardize his work in South Africa and India by blessing Manilal's marriage to a Muslim girl. As Manilal's granddaughter and biographer, Uma Dhupelia Mesthrie puts it, 'Ever the obedient son, Manilal once again bowed to his father's wishes.'[19] Intervening at this point, Kasturba asked Gandhi to find another bride for Manilal.

If differences of opinion meant hostility, Gandhi would write in *Young India* (17 Mar. 1927), 'my wife and I should be sworn enemies of one another'. Yet on this occasion he agreed with his wife. After associates, including Jamnalal Bajaj, were consulted, Manilal's parents settled on a 19-year-old Gujarati girl living in Akola in Maharashtra: Sushila, a Bania like the Gandhis though not a Kathiawari, and a niece of Kishorelal Mashruwala, Gandhi's *Young India* and *Navajivan* colleague.

The marriage took place in Akola in March 1927. Gandhi having urged his son to start 'the marriage with honesty', Manilal informed Sushila of his 'abandoned plans to marry Timmie' and of the earlier Phoenix episode as well. (Timmie, who remained single, eventually forgave Manilal, it appears.[20]) In a letter to Manilal, who would return to South Africa with his bride, the father wrote:

> 8 Feb. 1927: I want a solemn assurance from you that ... you shall honour Sushila's freedom; that you shall treat her as your companion, never as your slave ... that you shall take your pleasure only with her consent (38: 96–7).

Sushila's father was well off but at Gandhi's instance the wedding was kept utterly simple. All gifts for the bridal pair were transferred to nationalist funds. From Manilal's parents the couple received a copy of the *Gita*, another of ashram prayer-songs, a 'takli' or spindle for spinning, and two rosaries made of yarn spun by Gandhi.

Some months before this marriage, a Gandhi continuing to think of possible death had written a will declaring he owned no property and bequeathing anything found to be his to the Satyagraha ashram. For much of the first half of 1927 Gandhi was again quite weak and ill. Doctors having asked him to avoid the heat, he spent several months in Bangalore (where a giant khadi exhibition was mounted) and in the Nandi Hills nearby, with Rajagopalachari serving as host, companion and door-guard, keeping out unwanted callers.

A surprise was in store for guest and host both: 27-year-old Devadas, who had been close to Rajagopalachari for about nine years, proposed marriage to his youngest daughter, Lakshmi, who was only 15. She accepted, but the two also agreed not to marry without parental consent. Though not common, a marriage between a Bania and a Brahmin was different from a Hindu-Muslim wedding, and neither Gandhi nor Rajagopalachari cited the caste issue while asking Devadas and Lakshmi to wait. The girl's ability, at her age, to know what she wanted was the question.

The two were told that parental permission was possible if after a few years spent without seeing or writing to each other they still wanted to marry. Devadas returned to north India, while Lakshmi went with her father and a recovering Gandhi to Ceylon, where, as in the Karnataka country, khadi was vigorously sold and advocated, and untouchability attacked.

In January 1928 Ramdas, older than Devadas by two years, married Nirmala Vora at the ashram. Like Manilal's, this too was a marriage arranged by parents, and the couple received the same gifts that were given to Manilal and Sushila. Also Kathiawari Banias, the Voras had made several marriage connections with the Gandhis – Harilal's wife had been a Vora too, as also the wife of Samaldas, son of Laxmidas.

After a short religious ceremony Gandhi addressed Ramdas and Nirmala, the families and ashramites. He was 'nearly moved to tears' while speaking of the poverty he had imposed on his sons. Ramdas was asked to be the bride's 'true friend' and 'not her master'. 'You will both earn your bread by the sweat of your brow as poor people do ... Let the *Gita* be to you a mine of diamonds.'[21]

As for Harilal, he continued a life of wandering and indebtedness, with his parents or the sisters of his late wife looking after his four surviving children. In 1927 he published criticisms of his father. Gandhi wrote to his friend from South Africa, Ritch, that Harilal was 'a brave boy in one sense'. His was 'an open rebellion'.[22]

Expressions

In 1925 Gandhi travelled widely in eastern and northern India and in Gujarat, and in 1927 in southern India and in Ceylon, but, unusually for him, the year in between, 1926, was almost wholly spent in the ashram, though he briefly toyed with, but declined, invitations to visit Finland and the USA.

To the Americans inviting him he wrote, 'If I can say so without arrogance and with due humility, my message and methods are indeed in their essentials for the whole world.' However, results in India would speak more to America than any talks by him:

> [I]f the movement that I seek to represent has vitality in it and has divine blessing upon it, it will permeate the whole world without my physical presence in its different parts ... (*Young India*, 17 Sep. 1925)

Writing and speaking remained part of his life, and there were revealing or robust expressions of what he stood for. One was a review in 1927 of Katherine Mayo's controversial book, *Mother India*, in which the American author exposed India's insanitation and other defects, with the aid, at times, of Gandhi's comments, while praising the efforts of British rulers and Indian princes.

Conceding that the book was 'cleverly and powerfully written', Gandhi called it the report of an 'inspector of open drains and their stench' and added, 'She says in effect with a certain amount of triumph, "The drains are India."' Yet he also said:

> Whilst I consider the book to be unfit to be placed before Americans and Englishmen (for it can do no good to them), it is a book that every Indian can read with some degree of profit. We may ... not repudiate the substance underlying the many allegations she has made. It is a good thing to see ourselves as others see us. We need not even examine the motive with which the book is written (*Young India* 15 Sep. 1927; 40: 105–14).

Rejecting the option of whipping up hatred against the British, he wrote, 'I cannot love Muslims or Hindus and hate Englishmen,' and added, 'By a long course of prayerful discipline I have ceased for over forty years to hate anybody' (*Young India*, 6 Aug. 1925). A year later he repeated the idea:

> *15 Jul. 1926:* We cannot love one another if we hate Englishmen. We cannot love the Japanese and hate Englishmen. We must either let the law of love rule us through and through or not at all. Love among ourselves based on hatred of others breaks down under the slightest pressure ... (36: 46)

At Kanadukathan in the Tamil country, where he was welcomed by Chettiars, a trading community whose members had prospered in Malaya and Burma, Gandhi spoke with refreshing if brutal frankness on the clutter of objects in his hosts' homes:

> When I saw your houses choked ... I felt oppressed with this inordinate furniture. There is ... hardly any room to sit or to breathe ... Some of your pictures are hideous and not worth looking at ... [T]his lavish display ... obstructs the free flow of pure air and it harbours dust and so many million germs that float in the air.
>
> If you give me a contract for furnishing all these palaces of Chettinad I would furnish them with one tenth of the money but give you a much better accommodation and comfort than you enjoy today and procure for myself a certificate from the artists of India that I had furnished your houses in a much more artistic fashion than you have done (22 Sep. 1927; 40: 141–5).

The Gandhi speaking thus was after all a colleague of the architect and decorator, Kallenbach. He was responsive, too, to nature's patterns. Travelling with him in eastern India and to Ceylon, Kalelkar found that Gandhi 'at times drew my attention to nature's beautiful scenes, especially to the glories of dawn and the dipping sun'. Kalelkar was struck too by the 'tidiness with which he conversed with others, did his work, washed his face, chopped vegetables, folded clothes ...'[23]

Untouchables and Hinduism. In Chettinad and elsewhere, Gandhi denounced untouchability, dowry and Hindu-Muslim suspicion, and presented the charkha as a weapon against multiple wrongs. Though not 'political', his travelling replenished his bond with the masses. An incident in December 1927 illustrates both the interest that Gandhi aroused among 'untouchables' in remote areas and his approach to reform.

He and Andrews were in Bolgarh in Orissa, 31 miles from the nearest railway station, when, as Gandhi would report in *Young India*, a pariah with a half-bent back, wearing only a dirty loincloth, came crouching in front of us. He picked up a straw and put it in his mouth and then lay flat on his face with his arms outstretched. He then raised himself, folded his hands, bowed, took up the straw, arranged it in his hair ...

The man was about to leave when Gandhi asked him to wait. Answering Gandhi's questions, he said he was an 'an "untouchable" living in a village six miles away, and being in Bolgarh for the sale of his load of faggots and having heard of me, he had come to see me. Asked why he had taken the straw in his mouth, he said that this was to honour me.' Placing a straw in the mouth and chewing it was a gesture that 'superiors' had long required from 'inferiors' in different places, including, across the subcontinent, on the North-West Frontier. At times the 'inferior' was also expected to utter, 'I am your ox.'[24]

Gandhi, who wrote that he was 'writhing in agony' while witnessing the scene of self-humiliation, obtained from the man a pledge 'never again to take that straw in your mouth for any person on earth; it reduces a man's dignity', and two other promises: he would not consume liquor or what 'untouchables' across India were often required to eat, carrion (*Young India*, 22 Dec. 1927; 41: 51–2).

Three months earlier, Gandhi had silenced Brahmin priests in Kumbakonam who wanted to read out Hindu texts in defence of untouchability and child marriage:

The proper way of upholding Hinduism [is] not by quoting isolated texts but by acting through the inner voice of conscience. Nothing that was opposed to truth and love could be dharma according to Hindu shastras (*Bombay Chronicle*, 16 Sep. 1927; 40: 105).

Himalayan peaks, an inner cave. In the summer of 1929, after spending several days in Kausani in the Himalayas, when he wrote an introduction to the Gujarati original of his *Gita* translation and commentary, Gandhi shared with his readers – in Gujarati – 'the thoughts that overpowered me again and again' as he looked 'at the row of snow-capped Himalayan heights glittering in the sunlight', but for which 'there would be no Ganga, Jamuna, Brahmaputra and Indus; if the Himalayas were not there ... there would be no rainfall ... and ... India would become a desert like the Sahara'.

The quiet days in the Himalayas constituted an exceptional break for one who lived and moved with multitudes and could almost never merely commune with nature. Added the reflecting Gandhi (tr. from Gujarati):

If children were to see that sight, they would say to themselves that that was a mountain made of [their favourite milk-sweet], that they would like to run up to it and, sitting on top of it, go on eating that sweet. Anyone who is as crazy about the spinning wheel as I am would say that someone has ... made a mountain of cotton like an inexhaustible stock of silk ...

If a devout Parsi happened to come across this sight, he would bow down to the Sun-God and say: 'Look at these mountains which resemble our [priests] clad in milk-white puggrees just taken out of boxes and in gowns which are equally clean and freshly laundered and ironed, who look handsome as they stand motionless and still with folded hands, engrossed in having the darshan of the sun.'

A devout Hindu, looking at these glittering peaks which collect upon themselves water from distant dense clouds would say: 'This is God Siva Himself, the Ocean of Compassion ... who by holding the waters of the Ganga within His own white matted hair saves India from a deluge.'

Yet there was something even more life-sustaining:

> Oh, reader! The true Himalayas exist within our hearts. True pilgrimage ... consists in taking shelter in that cave and having darshan of Siva there (*Navajivan*, 14 Jul. 1929; 46: 267–9).

His *Gita* commentary and the introduction he wrote for it in Kausani were weapons in Gandhi's battle to identify a Hinduism that was moral rather than racial or national, related more to the soul than to India's soil.

The man & his ashram

Maganlal dies. In April 1928 Maganlal unexpectedly died in Patna, after contracting an illness, and Gandhi was heartbroken. He wrote to Maganlal's father Khushalchand and wife Santok that his loss was greater than theirs, and his grief equal. In *Young India* he referred to Maganlal's numerous skills – in carpentry, gardening, weaving, printing, engineering, management and more – and added:

> He whom I had singled out as heir to my all is no more ... Let not the reader imagine that he knew nothing of politics. He did, but he chose the path of silent, selfless constructive service. He was my hands, my feet and my eyes. The world knows so little of how much my so-called greatness depends upon the incessant toil and drudgery of silent, devoted, able and pure workers, men as well as women. And among them all Maganlal was to me the greatest, the best and the purest.

As I am penning these lines, I hear the sobs of the widow bewailing the death of her dear husband. Little does she realize that I am more widowed than she. And but for a living faith in God, I should become a raving maniac for the loss of one who was dearer to me than my own sons ... (*Young India*, 26 Apr. 1928; 41: 450–2)

As he neared and passed his 60th birthday, a Gandhi continuing to travel (north India and Sindh in the early months of 1929, Burma in March, Andhra in April, UP in October) seemed conscious both of an imminent struggle and of the passage of time.

In February 1929, time claimed Gandhi's 17-year-old grandson Rasik, Harilal's second son, whom Gandhi had helped raise. A cheerful, outgoing lad, Rasik was in Delhi with his uncle Devadas, who was teaching Hindi and spinning to students of Jamia (which had moved from Aligarh to Delhi's Karol Bagh). Rasik joined Devadas in teaching spinning but caught typhoid. Dr Ansari, who was also the Jamia chancellor, 'wore himself down for Rasik', as did Devadas, but the boy could not be saved. Harilal and Kasturba arrived just before the end. Gandhi underlined Rasik's 'noble sentiments' of devotion and duty, and called his death 'enviable', but he admitted his deep grief in an article in *Navajivan*. He gave it the heading, 'Sunset in the Morning' (45: 108–10).

'I see old age approaching me,' he wrote shortly after he reached 60 (*Navajivan*, 15 Dec. 1929; 48: 92).

Controversies. Readers were kept informed of his latest dietetic experiments (he was again trying to subsist on uncooked food) and of what he thought of social customs, generally in response to questions. When a young woman wrote to him that she wanted to leave a cruel, already-married and much older man to whom her father had married her when she was a child, and to marry a younger man of her choice, Gandhi published his reply in the newly launched Hindi edition of *Navajivan*:

> The marriage that was forced on Lakshmi Devi cannot be considered a religious marriage. In a religious marriage, the girl should be told to whom she is getting married, her consent should be obtained for the marriage and if possible, she should be given an opportunity to see the prospective bridegroom. Nothing of the kind was done in Lakshmi Devi's case. Secondly, she was too young for wedlock. Therefore she has a perfect right to refuse ... to recognize it as marriage.
>
> The only heartening feature of this tragedy is that her mother is with her ... I would request Lakshmi Devi's father not to regard adharma as dharma and stand in her way. I hope Lakshmi Devi will remain steadfast in her resolution in the same brave and modest spirit that she has shown in writing this letter for publication, and will marry the young man who wishes to be bound to her in holy wedlock.[25]

The ashram's espousal of celibacy also raised issues. For instance, Prabhavati, daughter of the Bihar Congress leader, Brajkishore Prasad, and married in 1920 (at the age of 14) to Jayaprakash Narayan, had lived in the ashram from 1922, when her husband left to study in the USA.

Close to both Kasturba and Gandhi and looked after by them, Prabhavati had become a wholehearted ashramite and taken the vow of celibacy, as had some other ashram women. She had done so in her teens and in her husband's absence, though Gandhi asked her not to confirm the vow until Jayaprakash approved. Yet a question-mark remained on the soundness of vows like hers.

Freedom within families, and in the ashram. A man whose son and daughter-in-law had stayed for a while in the ashram, after which the daughter-in-law had given up the veil, complained that Gandhi's advice to youth to differ from seniors if their conscience so demanded was damaging relations within the family. The man also took objection to women in the ashram sometimes touching Gandhi, and his touching girls in the ashram.

In his reply, published in *Navajivan*, Gandhi said that he believed in teaching self-control to those joining him but also in giving them complete freedom. All his sons, and grandsons 'who have come of age', enjoyed 'complete independence', he said, adding:

> My eldest son openly goes against me. I am not unhappy over this ... I keep up my relationship with him as a father ... He signs his letters to me as 'your obedient son'. I do not feel that he is insulting me by doing so ... Obedience has its limits.

Claiming that he did not 'know of any other place in India' where women enjoyed the degree of freedom they had in his ashram, he added that their relationship with him was of mothers, sisters or daughters. If they touched him, it was 'in a motherly spirit'. His touching them was like 'a father innocently touching his daughter in public'.

> I never enjoy privacy. When young girls come out for a walk with me daily I put my hands on their shoulders and walk. The girls are aware of the fact and everyone else also knows that that touch is an innocent one without any exception.

He did not claim, Gandhi added, a 'yogic' exemption from human nature. 'Like all others, I too am a creature made of earth, subject to the same sexual instinct.' Still, just as other fathers safely touched their daughters, he touched the ashram girls. Moreover, not only was he 'bound by the pledge of having only one wife', even Kasturba 'stays with me merely as a friend'.

In short, Gandhi was asserting his right to practise and offer freedom on the basis of his and others' vows, his of celibacy and theirs of celibacy or restraint. Indicating that he gave himself a latitude not available to others, Gandhi added: 'Except me no other man touches young girls as no such occasion arises at all. A fatherly relationship cannot be established at will.'[26]

Physically touching those he felt close to was one of Gandhi's traits. Putting his hands on the shoulders of the ashram's boys as he walked, at times lifting his feet off the ground and letting the youngsters carry him for a while,[27] or resting his arms on the shoulders of the ashram's girls and women while walking, or slapping young and old on the backs, or stroking a blessing on their heads, or embracing the grieving 'as if he was absorbing their agony into his own heart',[28] he gave affection through contact and also, we must assume, received it back.

This need for physical contact with an inner circle was part of his make-up. We saw earlier that at the age of 22, after returning to Rajkot from London, he walked with his hands on the shoulders of nephews and nieces; and we will see that the practice would continue to attract questions. This tactile familiarity with some co-existed with a degree of reserve with others, and also, as we have seen, with a striving for perfect purity or chastity.

With Mira, for instance, Gandhi seemed careful, perhaps because he was conscious of his love for her, which was nourished by her assistance, abilities (which included a sharp political sense) and a fine singing voice. It was also a response to her love for him, which seemed boundless. Gandhi's feeling for her easily overcame his awareness of Mira's possessive and imperious aspects, which put others off. However, to cure her dependence on him Gandhi often sent her away for spells, which she found hard.

For her part Mira thought Gandhi's singing attractive. In the evening of her life she would recall a pre-dawn moment in Sabarmati: 'He was the first to arrive for the morning prayer and as it was time he started chanting it. His voice was beautiful.'[29]

Earlier, in September 1928, Gandhi's decision to put a calf at the ashram to sleep had invited sharp protests. Informed that the calf was beyond recovery, Gandhi consulted others at the ashram and then, in his words, 'in all humility but with the clearest of convictions I got in my presence a doctor kindly to administer the calf a quietus by means of a poison injection' (*Young India*, 30 Sep. 1928; 43: 58). Mira, who was present at the scene, noted that Gandhi 'stooped down and took the heifer's front leg' while the injection was being given.[30]

Among several angry letters he received afterwards was one from a Jain who apparently wrote, 'Gandhi, you killed that cow, and if I do not kill you in return, I am no Jain.'[31]

Political succession

Though Gandhi had welcomed the awakening of the non-Brahmins and of the 'untouchables', he would not exclude Brahmins from leadership roles. When young anti-Brahmin activists in Karaikudi in the Tamil country gave Gandhi a pamphlet where Rajagopalachari was disparaged, Gandhi not only defended C R; he said, in September 1927, that Rajagopalachari would be his successor:

> You do not know the man. If Rajagopalachari is capable of telling lies, you must say that I am also capable of telling lies. I do say he is the only possible successor, and I repeat it today ... The pamphlet shows how you are fed on lies ... You may offer stubborn battle if you like, but build your foundation on truth (on or before 25 Sep. 1927; 40: 155).

Gandhi's poor health in 1927 had imparted urgency to the question of succession. Rajagopalachari was not the only candidate. There were at least four others: Vallabhbhai, three years older than Rajagopalachari, Jawaharlal, 14 years younger than Vallabhbhai, Bihar's Rajendra Prasad, five years older than Jawaharlal, and Bengal's Abul Kalam Azad, four years younger than Prasad.

Apart from Azad, all were lawyers who had abandoned their practices (Vallabhbhai and Nehru were, in addition, London-trained barristers, like Gandhi) and all had refused to join the Swarajists. Of the five C R had been the first to understand satyagraha, and he had a flair for articulating it that surpassed that of the others. In 1922, after Gandhi was jailed, it was C R who successfully led the charge to defeat the Pro Changers, and on three issues critical to Gandhi – Hindu-Muslim unity, opposition to untouchability and khadi – he stood solidly with Gandhi. But his prospects were not improved by Devadas's proposal to his daughter: Gandhi would think several times before recommending a potential relative. The fifth candidate, Bengal's Abul Kalam Azad, was a year older than Jawaharlal. An ideologue of political Islam and also of Hindu-Muslim unity, Azad, who had been close to Das, had tried to unite Swarajists and No Changers.

We saw that from the 1924 fast Gandhi had turned his attention towards Jawaharlal, whom he identified as a passionate foe of intolerance. In April 1926 he wrote to Romain Rolland introducing Jawaharlal, who was in Europe with his ailing wife Kamala, as 'one of my dearest friends and co-workers',[32] yet young Nehru's fascination with aspects of Marxism and the Soviet experiment made Gandhi cautious for a while, and towards the end of 1927 there was a sharp difference between the two.

At issue was a demand for the Congress to declare Complete Independence as its goal for India, ruling out Dominion Status. Led by Jawaharlal and Subhas Bose (recently released from incarceration in Mandalay in Burma), a radical wing succeeded in getting a resolution to this effect passed at the end-1927 Congress session, held in Madras.

Gandhi, who was absent from discussions, was unimpressed. The Congress had not fought for some time and did not have the training or weapons to fight. In the circumstances, the resolution reminded Gandhi of 'prisoners in chains spitting frothy oaths only to provide mirth for their gaolers'. Also, the resolution needlessly ruled out a possibly useful option.

> Dominion Status can easily become more than Independence, if we have the sanction to back it. Independence can easily become a farce, if it lacks sanction. What is in a name if we have the reality? A rose smells just as sweet ... (*Young India*, 12 Jan. and 6 Sep. 1928)

Jawaharlal defended his position in letters to Gandhi but backed away when Gandhi asked him to announce a parting of the ways. 'Am I not your child in politics?' he wrote to Gandhi.[33]

The lull breaks

In October 1927 the new Viceroy, Lord Irwin, who had taken over from Reading in April 1926, summoned Gandhi to Delhi. Gandhi, who was in the south, took a boat from Mangalore on the west coast to Bombay and thence a train to Delhi, where Irwin told him, and some other Indian politicians, that a statutory commission led by Sir John Simon would tour India early in 1928 and make constitutional proposals. Saying to the Viceroy that the information could have been sent in a one-anna envelope, Gandhi returned to his ashram.

When it quickly transpired that the Simon Commission would be all-white, with no Indian associated, new life was breathed into what for four years had been a quiescent front against the Raj. The implication that Indians were incapable of contributing to an Indian constitution offended almost all politicians – No Changers, Swarajists, Liberals and others, including Lajpat Rai, Jinnah and Muhammad Ali.

Meeting in Madras at the end of 1927, the Congress asked Indians to boycott the Commission; with Gandhi's full approval, it also asked a panel chaired by Motilal Nehru to draft, in consultation with all parties, an Indian constitutional scheme.

The slogan 'Simon Go Back' was raised across India when the Commission toured India from February 1928. Crowds gathered in numerous places and were beaten back. In Lucknow a lifelong disability was inflicted on the Congress leader, Govind Ballabh Pant, who hurled himself against police lathis to shield Jawaharlal Nehru. Later in the year, in Lahore, Lajpat Rai, 63 years old and unwell, was seriously hurt when the police hit him during a demonstration. Eighteen days later he died.

The passing of Lajpat Rai and Ajmal Khan (who had died in December 1927) removed two of Gandhi's important allies, but as 1928 rolled on, and Gandhi's personal deadline of March 1928 was crossed, not only did India seem ready to fight again; in a remarkable satyagraha in Gujarat, Vallabhbhai Patel led the peasants of Bardoli to victory.

Bardoli. This taluka was where, but for Chauri Chaura, the 1922 attack on the Raj would have been launched. In 1925, when Gandhi and Vallabhbhai were touring Gujarat for khadi and against untouchability, Gandhi had said in Bardoli:

> I for one am never going to give up my hope for Bardoli ... I have come here to say to Vallabhbhai also that if he wills it he can, by his power and influence, retrieve Bardoli's glory ... I am not asking people today to go to jail. We shall go to jail in future.[34]

That year, 1925, Patel became president of a federation of four ashrams located in the taluka. Working from these ashrams, associates of Gandhi had taught spinning and weaving to all castes, and reading to many 'untouchables' and tribals, and weaned many villagers from liquor. In the process they had forged strong links with the populace, even though their work with the Dublas and other tribals and the 'untouchables' had led to occasional friction with the land-owning Patidar (Patel) and Anavil castes.

The chance for a battle came in 1928, when land revenue in Bardoli taluka was increased by 22 per cent. Simultaneously, 23 Bardoli villages were placed in a higher tax category. The peasants wanted to defy what for many was a double blow and approached the ashramites, who in turn approached Gandhi and Patel. Gandhi gave the green light; and Patel agreed to lead the fight.

This general was served by a gifted staff, including several who had enlisted with Gandhi soon after his return from South Africa (Mohanlal Pandya, Ravishanker Vyas, Jugatram Dave, Swami Anand, Darbar Gopaldas), a few (like Khushalbhai Patel) who had served in the South African battles, and leaders from the soil (like Kunverji and Kalyanji Mehta). He also had a seasoned adviser, Gandhi. But the battle was won because of Vallabhbhai's leadership, which was confident, earthy, blunt and forceful, the solidarity of the peasants and the work over the years of the taluka's ashrams.

In August 1928, after four months of struggle during which lands and cattle were confiscated because the peasants did not pay the tax, the increase was virtually scrapped and much of the seized property returned. The peasants had neither yielded nor hit back nor lost (or taken) a single life – it was a victory for non-violence. It was also a joint Hindu-Muslim fight, supported by the old judge from the region, Abbas Tyabji, and Imam Bawazir from Sabarmati.

Unlike the cancelled satyagraha of 1922, which aimed explicitly at Swaraj, the goal of the 1928 struggle was only economic. Even though Patel was the GPCC president, the Congress was kept out of it, as were its national leaders. But all of India followed the satyagraha's ups and downs. The morale-boosting victory brought Patel nationwide fame and also a title the peasants of Bardoli had given him, Sardar ('Chief').

Calcutta Congress, Dec. 1928. The aspiration of 'Bardolizing' all of India was expressed by many, and Motilal Nehru suggested to Gandhi that Patel should preside at the next Congress session. Otherwise, added Nehru, 'Jawahar would be the best choice.'[35] Gandhi's response was to ask Motilal himself to chair the session – Motilal and his panel had consulted widely and worked painstakingly to produce a constitutional scheme, the Nehru Report as it came to be called, which was ready by August 1928.

White horses pulled Motilal Nehru's chariot in Calcutta, but a radical wind blew across the session, thanks to Jawaharlal and, even more, to Subhas Bose, who was six years younger than Jawaharlal and had emerged as Das's heir and Bengal's most popular figure. Designated 'Commander' of the Congress's volunteer force, Bose wore a military uniform during the session. Opposing the Dominion Status spelt out by the Nehru Report, Subhas and Jawaharlal demanded a call for Complete Independence. Gandhi proposed a compromise: if within two years the British did not concede Dominion Status and the rest of the Nehru Report's recommendations, the Congress would fight – and ask for Complete Independence.

Two years? Jawaharlal replied that he could not wait for two minutes. Yet when Gandhi said that the waiting period could be reduced to one year, Jawaharlal and Bose agreed, in committee, to the modified compromise. However, when Gandhi's resolution, mentioning a deadline of 31 December 1929 for Dominion Status, was presented at the open session, Bose moved an amendment asking for a complete break with the British, and Jawaharlal supported Bose. Gandhi's reaction was blunt:

> You may take the name of independence on your lips but all your muttering will be an empty formula if there is no honour behind it. If you are not prepared to stand by your words, where will independence be?[36]

Bose had many supporters at the Calcutta session. Though his amendment was lost, it received 973 votes, compared with 1,350 cast against. As for Gandhi, he was now ready to intensify sentiment against British rule but wary of inciting racial hatred. In October 1928 he wrote:

> I have nothing to be ashamed of if my views on Ahimsa are the result of my Western education. I have never tabooed all Western ideas, nor am I prepared to

anathematize everything that comes from the West as inherently evil (*Young India*, 11 Oct. 1928).

Agreed constitution?

Jinnah and Muhammad Ali arrived in Calcutta with their 'Delhi Proposals' for an Indian constitution and stressed three key demands: statutory Muslim majorities in the Bengal and Punjab legislatures; the separation, from Bombay presidency, of Sindh, which would create a new Muslim-majority province; and a one-third share for Muslims in the Central Assembly.

If, said Jinnah and Ali, the Congress backed these proposals, Muslims might give up the separate Muslim electorate to which the Congress had agreed under the 1916 Lucknow Pact, and which the British had accepted.

Jinnah was hoping to revive an earlier equation with Motilal Nehru. Through the Nehru Report the Congress on its part had accepted the separation of Sindh, asked for joint electorates, and proposed the end, in every province, of weightage, a provision from the Lucknow Pact that gave minorities a higher-than-proportionate share in every provincial legislature. In India's largest Muslim-majority provinces, Bengal and the Punjab, the provision had become a sore point with Muslims, for it seemed to give non-Muslims a chance to rule.

Doing away with weightage, the Nehru Report laid the ground for Muslim majorities in Bengal and the Punjab without mandating them. (Before his death Lajpat Rai had criticized statutory Muslim rule, and the Punjab's Sikhs were also opposed.) As for the Central Assembly, the Nehru Report gave the Muslims a quarter of the seats, matching the population percentage.

The differences between the Nehru Report and the Delhi Proposals did not appear large. The prospect of joint electorates was attractive to many in the Congress who thought separate electorates undermined the sense of a common nationality. Addressing a conference of all parties, Jinnah and Muhammad Ali presented their case with passion. However, no agreement resulted.

Though describing Jinnah as 'a spoilt child', the lawyer and Liberal leader Tej Bahadur Sapru had urged the Congress to concede his demands and 'be finished with it'. But his colleague M R Jayakar said that Hindu groups had accepted the Nehru Report with 'great difficulty' and would urge 'violent and arrogant' claims if the issue was reopened.[37]

Telling Jinnah that he was personally prepared to concede the Muslim demands, Gandhi pointed out that the Sikhs had declared that they would back out if changes were made to the Nehru Report.[38]

The only concession the Congress offered was to raise the Muslim share in the Central Assembly from 25 to 27 per cent. Mindful of the strength of Hindu and Sikh feeling, the Congress leaders were in addition unsure that Jinnah and Muhammad Ali spoke for Muslims as a whole. Denouncing joint electorates, Sir Muhammad Shafi had split from Jinnah, and the poet Iqbal, an increasingly influential figure in Muslim politics, had supported Shafi.

After Calcutta a bitterly disappointed Jinnah spoke of 'a parting of the ways'[39] and an angry Muhammad Ali formally left the Congress, asking Muslims to stay away from it. As for Gandhi, his mind was on a possible fight with the Raj. He had sensed its likelihood, saying in October that he hoped to hit upon a path of struggle 'which I may confidently commend to the people' (*Young India*, 11 Oct. 1928).

The lure of violence. Also on Gandhi's mind was a fascination for violence in young Indians. Lajpat Rai's injury and death had been followed (in December 1928) by the revenge killing in Lahore of a police officer, J P Saunders, and by an incident in April 1929 in the Central Assembly in Delhi, when two young men, Bhagat Singh and Batuke-shwar Dutt, threw a couple of crude bombs and bundles of leaflets onto the Assembly floor. The two were arrested and tried for this incident and also for their involvement, which was soon established, in the Lahore killing. The sensational character of the Lahore and Delhi incidents, the defiant demeanour, during their trial, of Singh and Dutt, and the revelation that the Lahore killing was part of a revolutionary conspiracy in which other youths were also involved, thrilled many in India.

Gandhi responded with a *Young India* article, 'The Cult of the Bomb'. Insisting that the votaries of 'revolutionary terrorism', as they described their ideology, did not represent the Indian masses, he underlined its hazards.

Firstly, 'every time violence has occurred we have lost heavily'. Military expenditure rose, and there were harsh reprisals. 'The masses in whose name, and for whose sake, we want freedom, have had to bear greater burdens.' Secondly, it was 'an easy natural step' from 'violence done to the foreign ruler' to 'violence to our own people', to anyone seen as an obstruction.

Once killing was made respectable, India's weak and crippled would be at risk. Violence against Indian oppressors was also unwise, for, 'maddened with rage over their coercion', they would 'seek the assistance of the foreigner in order to retaliate'. By contrast, said Gandhi, India had seen in 1919–22 the results of non-violence:

Mass awakening came no one knows how. Even remote villages were stirred. Many abuses seemed to have been swept away ... The system of [forced labour] vanished like mist in ... several other parts of India, wherever the people had become awakened to a sense of the power that lay within themselves ... It was true swaraj of the masses attained by the masses (*Young India*, 2 Jan. 1930; 48: 184–6).

The incidents of violence intensified Gandhi's search for a non-violent satyagraha that would attract young Indians hungry for defiance and sacrifice. In February 1929, when *Young India* and *Navajivan* published the last instalment of the Autobiography, Gandhi asked Jawaharlal, a general secretary of the Congress, to prepare the party for a non-violent campaign in the following year.

Ghaffar Khan. In the summer of 1929, Gandhi and Abdul Ghaffar Khan of the Frontier province met in Lucknow. The 39-year-old Ghaffar Khan had followed Gandhi closely ever since the 1919 stir against Rowlatt, which the Pathan leader had joined, and seen Gandhi at different Congress sessions, but this was their first meeting. Jawaharlal, who had known Ghaffar Khan's older brother, Dr Khan Sahib, from their days as students in Britain, brought Ghaffar Khan to Gandhi.

Their talk – about the Pathans living in the Frontier province, in Afghanistan, and in the tribal territories in between – was heartening to both. Well aware of the history of British reprisals and anxious to overcome the revenge code of the Pathans, Ghaffar Khan was convinced about non-violence. In September 1929, within weeks of the Lucknow meeting, he launched (in his village Utmanzai), the Khudai Khidmatgars, a body of 'servants of God' pledged to serve the Pakhtuns, and if necessary struggle for them – non-violently.

By this time Gandhi had been given the Congress chair, which he renounced. Ten provincial committees of the Congress having proposed his name, Gandhi's election was announced, but he successfully pressed the Congress to place Jawaharlal in the chair.

Jawaharlal vs. Patel

Gandhi had been desired as president because a fight would need a general, negotiations with the British would need a seasoned interlocutor, and there was 'yet the Hindu-Muslim knot to undo'.

Declining the office, Gandhi cited his lack of energy and added (*Young India*, 1 Aug. 1929): 'The battle of the future has to be fought by younger men and women. And it is but meet that they are led by one of themselves.' His own gifts were independent of any office and would not be kept back. Continued Gandhi:

In my opinion the crown must be worn by Pandit Jawaharlal Nehru ... Older men have had their innings ... Responsibility will mellow and sober the youth, and prepare them for the burden they must discharge.

Jawaharlal had proved an able secretary. Also,

by his bravery, determination, application, integrity and grit he has captivated the imagination of the youth of the land. He has come in touch with labour and the peasantry. His close acquaintance with European politics is a great asset in enabling him to assess ours.

Admitting his 'intellectual differences' with Jawaharlal, Gandhi added:

[T]hose who know the relations that subsist between Jawaharlal and me know that his being in the chair is as good as my being in it ... [O]ur hearts are one. And with all his youthful impetuosities, his sense of stern discipline and loyalty make him an inestimable comrade in whom one can put the most implicit faith.

Moreover,

a President of the Congress is not an autocrat. He is a representative working under a well-defined constitution and well-known traditions. He can no more impose his views on the people than the English King ... And it is the Congress as a whole with which, when the time is ripe, British statesmen will have to deal (46: 329–31).

So Jawaharlal was empowered, and also informed of his limits, while others were told that they were not powerless. Gandhi was presenting Jawaharlal as first among equals. If need arose, the others together could overrule the chair. Gandhi's influence on Jawaharlal would be an additional check.

Vallabhbhai, in particular, was on Gandhi's mind. As Subhas Bose would later recall, 'The general feeling in Congress circles was that the honour should go to Sardar Valla-bhbhai Patel.'[40] Five provincial committees had proposed the hero of Bardoli, but on Gandhi's prompting Patel instantly withdrew in favour of Jawaharlal, who had been suggested by three committees.

In preferring Jawaharlal over Patel at this stage, Gandhi was strongly influenced by the age factor. Vallabhbhai, only six years younger than him, was more like a younger brother to Gandhi, whereas Jawaharlal, 20 years younger, was like a son. Patel was an indispensable part of Gandhi's team, Jawaharlal the potential leader of the new generation. And Gandhi clearly hoped that the move would help 'to wean Nehru himself from the drift to the far left', apart from encouraging young radicals increasingly tempted by militant or Communist ideas to remain with the Congress.[41]

British proposal, Lahore Congress. At the end of October, Irwin, the Viceroy, announced that the British government wished to meet Indian leaders in London during the coming year. To pave the way, four Indian leaders – Gandhi, Motilal Nehru, who was in the final weeks of the Congress presidency, Vithalbhai, president of the Central Assembly, and Jinnah, president of the Muslim League – were invited to meet Irwin in Delhi on 23 December, eight days before the Congress deadline was to expire.

Hours before the meeting, a bomb exploded under a special train carrying the Viceroy, who, however, escaped without injury. After describing the incident to the leaders, Irwin broached the political question, asking, 'How shall we start?' Gandhi's response was direct: 'Will the London conference proceed on the basis of Dominion Status?' When Irwin said he could offer no such assurance, the gathering dispersed.[42]

Now the ball was in Congress's court, which held its December-end plenary session outside Lahore, on the banks of the Ravi. The cold was bitter, yet, as the Congress historian, Pattabhi Sitaramayya, would write: 'The heat of passion and excitement, the resentment at the failure of negotiation, the flushing of faces on hearing the war drums – oh, it was all in marked contrast with the weather.'[43]

Led by Ghaffar Khan, the Khudai Khidmatgars were conspicuous at the session. At midnight on New Year's Eve, Jawaharlal hoisted the Congress tricolour. Britain having failed to promise Dominion Status, the Congress was now pledged to struggle for Complete Independence. In his presidential address, the 40-year-old Jawaharlal spelt out his socialist and republican hopes for the long run, but the immediate question was how the Congress would do battle.

For an answer, all eyes turned to Gandhi, who asked, firstly, for a nationwide test of readiness. Let Indians across the land, he said, meet on 26 January, raise the tricolour, and take a pledge of independence and of willingness, if instructed, to break laws. Secondly, he asked for the resignation of Congress's representatives in the legislatures. Finally, he said that in due course he would announce when, where and how the struggle should commence, and over what question.

Meanwhile, for goodwill but also to underline the non-violent character of the impending struggle, Gandhi asked the Congress to congratulate Irwin on his escape. Subhas Bose at once opposed the idea, and many in Lahore backed him. Votes were taken, and Bose lost only narrowly. He walked out, as did Srinivasa Iyengar, the two forming the Democratic Party as a bloc within the Congress.

In a little over three weeks, on 26 January 1930, Gandhi would know whether Indians were ready for another round of struggle. He would be disappointed if they were not. But it would be harder if they were ready, for then he would have to present a strategy of non-violent war.

10

Assault – with Salt

India, England, India, 1930–2

How did one coax an aggrieved yet disarmed, heterogeneous and divided populace to launch an assault on a powerful Empire? On 18 January 1930 Tagore called at the ashram and asked Gandhi about his strategy. 'I am furiously thinking night and day,' replied Gandhi, 'and I do not see any light'.[1] But he had reached some conclusions. One, during the first stage only trained ashramites, committed to non-violence, would be deployed; the model they presented could thereafter be followed by the untrained. Two, he would order a halt if violence entered his movement but not if extraneous violence occurred.

On 26 January, tens of thousands gathering in different parts of India soberly assented to a statement-cum-pledge, drafted by Gandhi, that called British rule a 'four-fold disaster' – economic, political, cultural and spiritual. Calling submission to that rule 'a crime against man and God', the statement asserted the right of Indians to freedom and to the fruits of their toil, and 'the further right to alter or abolish a government withholding such rights'. Also affirmed was the right, under Congress instructions, to disobey laws 'without doing violence, even under provocation' (48: 215).

As for the content of the disobedience, Subhas wanted the creation of a parallel government, while Bajaj suggested a march to the Viceroy's House in New Delhi, Vallabhbhai a fight over land revenue (an understandable choice in the light of Bardoli) and Rajagopalachari attacks on the sale of liquor.

Not everyone thought Indians were ready for a fight. One of Gandhi's closest colleagues and a key Muslim ally, Dr Ansari, cautioned him that the climate for giving battle was worse than in 1919–22, when rising prices, the Rowlatt legislation, martial law and Khilafat had united Indians against the British. Now, in contrast, Indians entertained hopes from a new Labour government in Britain and from the seemingly warm attitude of the Viceroy, Lord Irwin, a conservative politician from a landed family in Yorkshire. Some Indians meeting him thought that the Viceroy was interested in a 'Christian' approach to Indian nationalists. In a letter to Gandhi, Ansari added that Hindu-Muslim unity was at a low point, the Sikhs (again unlike in 1920) had turned against the Congress, the Congress was divided, and the youth seemed drawn to violence (48: 524–8).

At 3.30 a.m. on 16 February, Gandhi wrote a reply to Ansari. Agreeing that 'the Hindu-Muslim [question] is the problem of problems', Gandhi suggested that Muslims should nonetheless have no fear as long as the Congress 'act[ed] on the square under all circumstances' (48: 324–5). Two weeks later, in another letter to Ansari, Gandhi said: 'We cannot achieve [Hindu-Muslim] unity through any conference. But we can through fighting for common causes' (3 Mar. 1930; 48: 369).

Devadas, for one, agreed with some of Ansari's reservations and said so to his father. However, the Working Committee authorized Gandhi to plan and direct the promised battle. His colleagues had no agreed plan of their own, and in any case they had learnt over the years to respect Gandhi's judgement.

In the middle of February his 'furious' search ended: the intuition came to him 'like a flash'[2] that the assault should be over salt.

Salt? By taxing the manufacture and sale of salt, the government was injuring 'even the starving millions, the sick, the maimed and the utterly helpless'. Nature had gifted salt to India, but Indians could not collect or use it without paying a tax much higher than the cost of gathering it. All were hurt by the salt law, and all could defy it. Satyagrahis near the coast could defy the law simply by walking to where the salt lay and scooping it up. Indians in the interior could perform satyagraha by buying or selling 'illegal' salt.

Gandhi pictured a march to the sea by his ashramite army, with himself at its head, if the British did not arrest him earlier. The defiance would provide striking scenes, exert maximum pressure with the minimum risk of violence, and would be hard for the British to crush: could they police the entire coastline? Gandhi thought that satyagraha could spread quickly from the ashramites to the general public, as had happened 16 years earlier in South Africa.

In the climate of 1930, the salt tax held another virtue for Gandhi: all could jointly oppose it, Hindus and Muslims, peasants and the landless. The poor needed salt more than the rich, who got it from all their foods. As Gandhi put it:

Next to air and water, salt is perhaps the greatest necessity of life. It is the only condiment of the poor. Cattle cannot live without salt. Salt is a necessary article in many manufactures. It is also a rich manure.[3]

Moreover, unlike defiance over land revenue, defiance of the salt tax would not cost peasants their land or cattle. The British had indeed yielded over land revenue in Bardoli, but that was because the Bardoli satyagraha had been carefully disconnected from any campaigns for Swaraj. Now Swaraj was the central goal, and the British would not be merciful. Looking for a fight that would not ruin the participants, Gandhi picked on salt.

It had long been germinating in his mind. Almost 40 years earlier, as a student in London in 1891, he had spoken of 'salt, a heavily taxed article'. In 1909 his *Hind Swaraj* had referred to it; and he had mentioned it on numerous other occasions. It was a question, moreover, that Naoroji and, later, Gokhale had raised. Thanks to the salt tax – the simplest and most regressive form of taxing every Indian, including the poorest – British salt was easy to sell in India, and the government of India obtained 2 per cent of its revenue from the tax on it.

Also, salt was a powerful emblem, featuring in proverb, scripture and everyday speech, and the only inorganic thing that all humans ate. It preserved, disinfected, embalmed. Salt could cause harm too, of course – we have found Gandhi himself experimenting with salt-free diets, if always to return to its moderate use. But that did not detract from salt's symbolism, or the tax's iniquity.

Clarity about salt changed Gandhi. Thereafter, an observer thought, Gandhi spoke at ashram prayer-meetings with 'a peculiar glow in his look and voice, as of one pregnant with inspired inner thought and prayer'.[4] For several days he kept the idea to himself and some close colleagues. Confidentiality was essential for preparation and also for preventing premature arrests. But several associates were informed in February, including Mahadev, Vallabhbhai, Mohanlal Pandya and Ravishankar Vyas, and the last three were asked to select a route for the march and its destination on the coast, where salt would be illegally collected.

Letter to the Viceroy. In the last week of February Gandhi spelt out guidelines for a satyagraha without mentioning that it would be over salt. And in a letter to the Viceroy written on 2 March (but not made public for a week or so) he listed the removal of the salt tax as one of 11 demands the British would have to concede if they did not want to face satyagraha. After repeating the indictment of a 'four-fold' ruination, he demanded

1) Total prohibition, 2) A better rupee/shilling ratio, 3) Halving of land revenue, 4) Abolition of salt tax, 5) Halving of military expenditure, 6) Reduction in official salaries, 7) Tariffs on foreign cloth, 8) Reservation of coastal shipping for Indian ships, 9) Release of political prisoners save those convicted for murder or attempted murder, 10) Abolition of the Criminal Intelligence Department or control over it by elected representatives, and 11) The right of Indians to licensed firearms.

The writer is revealed as a formidable nationalist far removed from the image of an ascetic plying his spinning wheel. This ahimsa advocate is not willing to give up any Indian right, not even the right to a gun. Equally, the list reminded Indians that their fight was for more than a couple of words ('complete independence') – it was for a better life for the common Indian. Addressed to 'Dear Friend', Gandhi's demands were couched in non-violent language, yet the letter was even stronger than the one sent ten years earlier to Chelmsford. Irwin was reminded, among other things, of the huge salary he was drawing from Indian revenues.

Gandhi sent the letter not by post but by the hand of a young British sympathizer who was in the ashram at the time, Reginald Reynolds. Gandhi claimed that by choosing Reynolds as his messenger he had 'forge[d] a further check upon myself against any intentional act that would hurt a single Englishman'.[5]

'My ambition,' Gandhi told the Viceroy in the letter, 'is no less than to convert the British people through non-violence and thus make them see the wrong they have done to India' (48: 366). There was no reply from Lord Irwin, but on 12 March Gandhi received a four-line letter from Cunningham, the Viceroy's secretary, stating that Lord Irwin 'regrets to learn that you contemplate a course of action which is clearly bound to involve violation of the law and danger to the public peace' (48: 367).

On 5 March, from the ashram prayer ground, Gandhi made the first public announcement about the choice of salt. His political colleagues were shocked. Neither Jawaharlal nor his father was impressed, and a displeased Vallabhbhai stayed away from early planning meetings called by Gandhi. The truth was that in February 1930 no part of India was agitating over the salt tax, which seemed a minor irritant to educated Indians, including many of Gandhi's associates. Indulal Yagnik, for example, spoke dismissively of striking 'the fly of the salt act' with the 'sledge hammer of satyagraha'.[6]

There was chuckling in British and pro-British circles. 'Let Gandhi soon eat his own salt,' was one remark. After Gandhi announced his plan, *The Statesman,* Calcutta's British-owned journal, wrote:

> It is difficult not to laugh, and we imagine that will be the mood of most thinking Indians. There is something almost childishly theatrical in challenging in this way the salt monopoly of the Government.[7]

Destination, route, and marchers. After reconnoitring southern Gujarat, Mohanlal Pandya and Ravishankar Vyas selected a coastal village in Surat district, Dandi, where waves from the Arabian Sea usually left layers of salt, as the destination for the marchers. Dandi was more than 200 miles south of the ashram and close to Bardoli. Pandya and Vyas also proposed villages and towns in Kheda, Bharuch and Surat districts that the satyagrahis should walk through on their way to Dandi.

Gandhi vetted the list, picking villages where he thought he could (a) draw officials away from the Raj, (b) promote khadi and sanitation, (c) attack untouchability, and (d) advance Hindu-Muslim friendship. But the route and destination were not announced until 9 March. He was equally particular that only the disciplined and the committed would march. Since they would be defying laws in pursuance of Gandhi's tough letter to the Viceroy, they were bound to invite arrest, perhaps for long terms. Beatings were likely and death could not be ruled out. Fifteen years after its founding, the Satyagraha ashram would show whether it lived up to its name.

Its members were bound to vows, to one another, and to Gandhi, who had seldom failed to spend time with the ashram's sick or laugh with the young ones. Differences existed among ashramites, and bickering too, but they had become a family. Narayan, son of Mahadev Desai, would later recall that if some in the ashram lost a dear one, 'more soothing than Bapu's words would be the way he came to them and embraced them. It was as if he was absorbing their agony into his own heart. If away, Bapu would write to them daily.'[8]

However, for his march Gandhi would not accept the very young, the old, those with heavy family responsibilities, or women – the last because it would not be chivalrous to use women as a shield.

Guidelines. He laid down detailed rules for the marchers. They should be willing to suffer unto death, cause no violence, injury or insult to British rulers or their Indian servants, and refrain from swearing or cursing. They should neither salute nor insult the Union Jack. If a communal fight appeared likely to start, the satyagrahis should intervene and prevent it. When arrested, they should obey prison rules and not demand special facilities from the authorities or maintenance for dependents from the Congress. But they should refuse to shout slogans like 'victory to the government' or eat food that was unclean or rudely served.

At this time the roughly 200-strong ashram community had 'reached its zenith of physical energy and moral strength', Mira would write. 'Every morning and evening Bapu spoke in the prayers, and an atmosphere of uplifting inspiration filled the air.'[9]

Sensing a strong response from beyond the ashram as well, Gandhi expected early arrest and left clear instructions for 'When I am Arrested'. Vallabhbhai, whose doubts were short-lived, would lead the marchers in Gandhi's absence.

Once the idea of a salt attack was announced (5 March), the British debated whether to put Gandhi away immediately or when he actually violated the Salt Act. Arresting now would add to his prestige and provoke an instant reaction. It would be cleverer to let his weird plan flop before arresting him. The British assumed, too, that a coastal corner of Kheda district, where Vallabhbhai's fellow Patidars were firm foes of their rule, would be the chosen site.

Vallabhbhai arrested. On 7 March 1930, Vallabhbhai, who was passing through the Kheda village of Ras, was arrested there, to his and Gandhi's surprise. After he had agreed, following pressure from Ras's residents, to address them, officials tailing Patel handed him an order not to speak. By this time thousands had gathered to hear him. When Patel said he would speak to them, he was arrested. Alfred Master, collector of Kheda and the district magistrate, sentenced Patel to three months.

On 8 March Gandhi addressed 50,000 incensed Indians on the banks of the Sabarmati, said that his 'right hand' had been removed, and asked the audience to pledge themselves to 'follow Sardar Vallabhbhai to jail, or win complete independence', but 'only if you have the strength to act upon' the pledge. Thousands raised their hands in affirmation.[10]

The next day Gandhi announced that in three days he and more than 70 others would begin a march to the Surat coast and hope to reach there early in April, in time for observing the National Week, as the 6–13 April period had been called from the time of the struggled that culminated in the Amritsar massacre on 13 April 1919.

By now hopes were high. On 10 March, when over 2,000 attended the ashram's evening prayers, Gandhi explained the strength and subtlety of satyagraha:

Everyone is on the tip-toe of expectation, and before anything has happened the thing has attracted world-wide attention ... Though the battle is to begin in a couple of days, how is it that you can come here quite fearlessly? I do not think anyone of you would be here if you had to face rifle-shots or bombs ...

Supposing I had announced that I was going to launch a violent campaign, not necessarily with men armed with rifles, but even with sticks or stones, do you think the Government would have left me free until now? Can you show me an example in history, be it England, America or Russia, where the State has tolerated violent defiance of authority for a single day? But here you know that the Government is puzzled and perplexed.

And you have come here because you have been familiarized by now with the idea of seeking voluntary imprisonment ... Supposing ten men in each of the 700,000 villages in India come forward to manufacture salt and to disobey the Salt Act, what ... can this Government do? Even the worst autocrat you can imagine would not dare to blow regiments of peaceful civil resisters out of a cannon's mouth (48: 395–6).

Yet he knew he would soon be jailed, and death too was possible. He and the other marchers were stepping out of the ashram for good, to return, if alive, only after India was free. On the evening of 11 March he said:

Even if the Government allows me to march tomorrow morning, this will be my last speech on the sacred banks of the Sabarmati. Possibly these may be the last words of my life here ... But let there be not a semblance of breach of peace even after all of us have been arrested ... Let no one commit a wrong in anger. This is my hope and prayer. I wish these words of mine reached every nook and corner of the land ... I shall eagerly await the news that ten batches are ready as soon as my batch is arrested.

After his arrest, he said, Jawaharlal, the Congress president, would advise, but regional commanders were already in place, including Rajagopalachari in the south, Rajendra Prasad in Bihar, J M Sen Gupta in Bengal, Ghaffar Khan in the Frontier, Mahadev Desai for Gujarat off the route of the march. If the commanders were arrested, the battle would throw up new leaders, Gandhi said.

The march

In the early morning of 12 March 1930, joy and sadness, pride and fear, and prayer songs marked the departure of Gandhi and 78 (or, by another count, 80) others.[11] Pyarelal, 30, and 35-year-old Chhaganlal Joshi (the ashram's manager after Maganlal's death) walked just behind Gandhi. The rest represented 15 Indian provinces, with Gujarat offering the largest number and Maharashtra the next highest. There were two Muslims, a Christian, and four 'untouchables' in the mainly Hindu band.

Arriving from South Africa, Manilal, now 38, joined the party, as did Kanti, Harilal's 20-year-old son. Pandit Narayan Khare, 44, the ashram's music teacher, was also a marcher, carrying his tanpura,* even though his son Vasant had died of smallpox a few days earlier. At 35, Valji Desai, translator into English of some of Gandhi's writings, was a senior member. A Gujarati studying in America, Haridas Muzumdar, 25, and Kalelkar's sons, Satish, 20, and Bal, 18, were among the many youngsters in the group, the youngest being 16-year-old Vithalal Thakkar.

All the marchers received garlands and tilak from young girls. Those bidding farewell recalled settings-forth from history and the epics, and many among the tens of thousands who crammed Ahmedabad's streets cried, thinking they were seeing the marchers for the last time. Kasturba pressed a tilak on Gandhi's forehead and garlanded him with handspun yarn. Kalelkar gave him a bamboo staff. Precisely at 6.30 a.m. the march commenced. Jawaharlal, who was present, wrote:

Today the pilgrim marches onward on his long trek. Staff in hand, he goes along the

---

* Tanpura = Indian drone instrument similar in appearance to a sitar.

dusty roads of Gujarat, clear-eyed and firm of step, with his faithful band trudging along behind him. Many a journey he has undertaken in the past, many a weary road traversed. But longer than any that have gone before is this last journey of his, and many are the obstacles in his way. But the fire of a great resolve is in him, and surpassing love of his miserable countrymen. And love of truth that scorches and love of freedom that inspires.[12]

All the marchers wore khadi and most donned a simple white khadi cap. Everyone including Gandhi (who did not wear the cap) carried a shoulder-bag containing a bedroll, a change of clothes, a takli for spinning, a diary and a drinking mug. His pocket-watch hanging conspicuously from his waist, Gandhi, now 61, was the oldest walker of the lot but also the most experienced and indeed among the quickest, though suffering from blisters and fatigue. Throughout the long march of around 220 miles,[13] most of the others struggled to keep up with him.

This marching army was also a moving ashram: its general (or father) required of each marcher that he would daily pray, spin and keep a diary, which Bapu could ask to read. With Gandhi continuing to write numerous letters a day and several articles a week, it was a mobile office as well.

Gandhi also spelt out, ahead of the march, what he expected from a village *en route*: the simplest food (which the marchers were ready to cook); clean space for sleeping; and 'an enclosed space for the satyagrahis to answer calls of nature'. Inside the leader who hoped (by picking up salt) to liberate India and convert England was a researcher as well. Gandhi asked that at each halt the following information should be kept ready for him:

> The village population (how many 'women, men, Hindus, Muslims, Christians, Parsis, etc.'); the 'number of untouchables' and the education, if any, they were getting; the number of boys and girls in the village school, if one existed; the number of cattle, of spinning wheels, and of khadi-wearers; the amount and rate of land revenue; the size of any common grazing ground; the consumption of salt (*Navajivan,* 9 Mar. 1930; 48: 392–3).

Arrangements were not left wholly to chance. Eighteen students of Ahmedabad's Gujarat Vidyapith went ahead of the marchers to help hosts organize spaces for cooking, sleeping and praying, and to help dig latrine trenches. Selected by Kalelkar, the Vidyapith vice-chancellor, these oft-unnoticed members of the Arun Tukdi (Sunrise Unit) were not only crucial to the march's efficiency; they were also reserve marchers, ready to replace arrested ones.

Many places *en route* gave a hugely enthusiastic response. In some towns (including

Nadiad, Borsad, Bharuch and Surat) populations poured out into 'festooned streets sprinkled against dust'[14] when the marchers passed through, and often there were immense meetings. In several villages along the way, but also elsewhere in Gujarat, functionaries resigned their jobs with the Raj and aligned themselves with 'the movement'. Buoyed by these indications, the AICC swiftly and briefly met in Ahmedabad (21 March), asked provincial units across India to prepare defiance, and authorized presidents of all Congress committees, national, provincial, and local, to nominate successors. 'Chains of command [were] forged and battle plans mapped out.'[15]

But a few villages on Gandhi's route were cautious, in part because of his stand over the 'untouchables'. At the village of Dabhan (on 15 March), Gandhi 'walked straight through the village past the temple and the village square' to the quarters of the 'untouchables', where 'he drew water from the well and bathed', embarrassing but also challenging his high-caste reception committee, who had not expected Gandhi to draw water even from their 'pure' well: a servant should perform that sort of task.[16] In Gajera (21 March) Gandhi asked the caste Hindus welcoming him to let the 'untouchables' of the village join the gathering. Most did not mind, and the 'untouchables' sat down along with the rest, but some high-caste women left.[17]

Asked, in the village of Ankhi (21 March), about non-violent ways of treating an oppressive officer, Gandhi answered that both compassion and sternness had a place. Any official found in distress, white or brown, even someone like General Dyer, had to be quickly helped, but an arrogant officer abusing his power should 'get neither food nor drink, neither a bed, nor matches, nor even fodder for his horse'.[18]

Two things troubled Gandhi on the evening of 29 March. One, he heard that Muzumdar, the 'American' student in the party, had accepted an offer of ice cream at an earlier halt. Two, he had seen some marchers goad a servant who carried on his head a heavy petromax lantern to walk faster. After arrival that night in Bhatgam, Gandhi expressed his 'scorching truth':

> We are very weak, easily tempted. There are many lapses to our debit ... Even today some were discovered ... In the light of these discoveries, what right had I to write to the Viceroy the letter in which I have severely criticized his salary which is more than 5,000 times over average income? ...
>
> We are marching in the name of God. We profess to act on behalf of the hungry, the naked, and the unemployed ... No labourer would carry such a load on his head. We rightly object to begar [forced labour]. But what was this if not begar? Remember that in Swaraj we would expect one drawn from the so-called lower class to preside over India's destiny.

Even the intelligence officer taking down the remarks noted that the atmosphere became 'electric'.[19]

An 'unlawful deed' is multiplied. By now Sykes, the Bombay governor, wanted to arrest Gandhi, as did Alfred Master and Master's superior in Ahmedabad, Joseph Garrett, but Irwin and his advisers hesitated. They had been informed that Gandhi's blood pressure was 'dangerous' and his heart 'none too good' and that with the physical and mental load he was carrying he could die before reaching Dandi.[20] Also, some of his Indian friends, including, it seems, Vithalbhai Patel, the central assembly president, had told Irwin that the salt march, more humorous than dangerous, was bound to invite ridicule. Arresting Gandhi, on the other hand, would not only glorify him; it could trigger widespread unrest.

So on 5 April, 24 days after leaving the ashram, Gandhi and his army reached Dandi without being arrested. Admitting that he had been 'wholly unprepared for this exemplary non-interference' from the government, Gandhi credited it to 'world opinion which will not tolerate repression' even of 'extreme political agitation' when that agitation remained non-violent. But he did not think that 'actual breach of the salt laws' would be tolerated by the British.[21] Journalists from India and beyond had gathered in Dandi. For them Gandhi wrote out a crisp sentence: 'I want world sympathy in this battle of Right against Might.'

Early next morning, on the first day of National Week, Gandhi bathed in the ocean, stepped up to where the salt lay, scooped some of it up with his fingers, straightened himself, and showed what he had collected to the multitude around him. It was neither a large quantity nor very pure – the Raj's police had done its best to clear the spot of clean salt. Yet the 'unlawful deed' had been done. Sarojini Naidu, who was present, addressed him as 'Law Breaker'. A satyagraha had been executed, and in the days and weeks that followed, in one form or another, hundreds of thousands emulated it across India. The response was even larger than what Gandhi had hoped for. As Jawaharlal would later put it, 'It seemed as though a spring had been suddenly released.'[22]

The restraint that Gandhi had imposed on himself and his associates for six years – the retreat into ashrams, the focus on constructive work and on the evil of untouchability – had contributed to the power of the release. After the long self-suppression, satyagraha spread like 'prairie fire' (to use the second metaphor that Jawaharlal employed[23]) from Gandhi and his marchers to India as a whole.

In hundreds of places across India, salt was illegally made, or carried, or sold, or bought. Often the action was en masse. In south Kheda's coastal village of Badalpur, around 20,000 people illegally gathered salt on 13 April, under a full moon. By mid-June there were resignations in over half of Kheda's villages: the district had de-recognized the Raj. Bengal witnessed a 'spectacular' march,[24] and in the south Rajagopalachari led an army of 100 carefully selected satyagrahis on a 145-mile trek to Vedaranyam on the Bay of Bengal. Those providing food or accommodation to the marchers were harassed and in several cases imprisoned, but the populace supported C R. On 30 April his marchers were able to defy the law, make salt and invite arrest. The officer who had tried to suppress the Vedaranyam march, J A Thorne, reported: 'If there ever existed a fervid sense of devotion to the Government, it is now defunct.'[25]

A bigger eruption occurred at India's opposite end, in the far North-West. Offended by the arrest on 23 April of their beloved leader, Ghaffar Khan, hundreds of Khudai Khidmatgars protested in Peshawar, standing up to machine guns, horses and lathis. Ordered to open fire on a crowd of unarmed Pathans in Peshawar's Kissa Khwani Bazar, Indian soldiers of the Raj's Garhwal Rifles disobeyed the order, staging *their* non-violent revolt. For five days Peshawar belonged to the Khidmatgars, not to the British.

The Raj's response. Admitting 'surprise' at 'the dimensions' of the movement,[26] Irwin and his officers curbed the press, banned *Young India* and *Navajivan,* banned the Working Committee and other Congress-affiliated bodies, and decided to rule through ordinances, bypassing the Central Assembly where Indian members, whether Swarajist or liberal, were increasingly sympathetic to the disobedience.

Still leaving Gandhi and his band alone, the British imprisoned many elsewhere while also using physical force to recover illegal salt. Beatings were judged cheaper and more effective than jail terms. 'Salt in the hands of satyagrahis represents the honour of the nation,' Gandhi replied. 'It cannot be yielded up except to force that will break the hand to pieces' (*Young India,* 10 Apr. 1930).

Another British tactic was to remove salt from expected sites of attack. Left free in Dandi but denied salt to collect, the original marchers felt frustrated. Some were permitted to go elsewhere to join or ignite defiance, but the majority remained around Gandhi, whose answer to the lull in Dandi was two-fold.

Women come forward. Firstly, he permitted women to join the struggle. As Sykes, the Bombay governor bearing the brunt of the Salt March, acknowledged to the Viceroy, Gandhi's meetings were drawing more and more women:

There is no doubt that Gandhi has a great emotional hold as evidenced by the numerical support of his demonstrations and the popular enthusiasm, largely among the younger generation and increasingly amongst women and girls, which has been more than was expected.[27]

In an article that appeared in *Navajivan* on 6 April, and in *Young India* four days later, Gandhi called 'the impatience of some sisters to join the good fight' a 'healthy sign' and added oft-to-be-quoted sentences about women and non-violent action:

To call woman the weaker sex is a libel; it is man's injustice to woman ... If by strength is meant moral power, then woman is immeasurably man's superior. Has she not greater intuition, is she not more self-sacrificing, has she not greater powers of endurance, has she not greater courage? ... If non-violence is the law of our being, the future is with woman (*Young India*, 10 Apr. 1930; 49: 57–9).

Women, Gandhi said, could picket sales of liquor and foreign cloth. The idea was enthusiastically accepted at two meetings of women, one held at Dandi on 13 April and the other in Vijalpur on 16 April. Because of barriers set up by the government, many women had to walk 12 miles to attend the Dandi gathering. Kasturba was present at these meetings, as also Karnataka's Kamaladevi Chattopadhyaya (her husband was Sarojini Naidu's brother) and Gujarat's Hansa Mehta (a Hindu), Mithu Petit (a Zoroastrian) and Amina Tyabji (a Muslim).

On 27 April a letter went to the Viceroy, signed by 28 women (Hindus, Muslims and Parsis), expressing opposition to the sale of liquor and foreign cloth. However, it was Gandhi who had drafted the letter. Among the signatories were the wife and sister of Ambalal Sarabhai, Maganlal's widow, and Mahadev Desai's wife.

Raiding a salt depot. Conscious of the lull felt by the marchers, Gandhi scouted the area around Dandi (not hesitating to use a car for the purpose) and came up with his second riposte: a raid on three great salt heaps in a government depot in Dharasana, about 25 miles south of Dandi. Towards the end of April he announced at meetings with journalists that he would lead the raid on the depot.

By this time thousands had been arrested across the country, including Jawaharlal, Jamnalal Bajaj, Ravishankar Vyas, Darbar Gopaldas and Mahadev Desai, and two of Gandhi's sons, Ramdas, arrested not far from Dandi, and Devadas, who was taken in Delhi for selling contraband salt. In addition, hundreds had been beaten because they did not let go of the salt in their hands. Peshawar had erupted, and C R and his 100 were closing in on Vedaranyam.

The declaration of a raid by Gandhi was reported in Indian, British and American newspapers, and Irwin was bound to arrest the rebel-in-chief. Still, Gandhi wanted to inform the Viceroy directly of his intention. In an improvised hut in Karadi, where he was camping, five miles east of Dandi, Gandhi worked on a letter to Irwin until late on the night of 4 May. Unless the salt tax was removed and private salt-making allowed, he and his companions, Gandhi wrote, would 'set out for Dharasana' and 'demand possession of the Salt Works' (49: 260–3).

But Irwin was not waiting for a letter. About 40 minutes after midnight, three officers (two British and an Indian), accompanied by between 20 and 30 rifle-armed Indian policemen, entered the camp, walked quietly past marchers sleeping under the stars and mango trees, and stepped inside Gandhi's hut. By now sound asleep, with a marcher and a woman visitor sleeping on the floor on either side of his bedstead, Gandhi was woken up by lights flashed into his face.

'Do you want me?' Gandhi asked, even though he knew the answer. In response to another question, he was informed that his arrest was under Regulation 25 of 1827, which authorized detention without trial. A new speech by him from the dock was not what the Raj wanted.

By this time everybody in Karadi was up but prevented by the police from reaching close to Gandhi, who instructed his grandson Kanti to prepare a bedroll he could take, and Valji Desai to send to *Young India* the nearly completed letter for Irwin.

'May I wash and brush my teeth?' Gandhi asked the Raj's officers. He could but should be quick, was the answer. In a few minutes Gandhi was ready, having also picked up a couple of taklis and a bundle of cotton slivers. As Tom Weber, the Salt March's Australian researcher, puts it, it was 'a cool and organized performance for an old man who had had less than two hours' sleep'.[28]

Obtaining the officers' permission, Gandhi asked Pandit Khare to sing *Vaishnava Jana*, the bhajan with which the march had commenced. With head bowed and eyes closed the prisoner heard the song. Then he was taken away. Fifty-eight years later, one of the Karadi men present at the arrest would break down while describing the scene.[29]

The marchers had treasured their time with Gandhi, feeling that 'they were something special' to him. 'I felt like a son to him' or 'He was like a father to me' would be general memories, but there was also a feeling of being individually needed by Gandhi, e.g. to take care of his correspondence if Pyarelal was not around, or to assist if Gandhi had a problem with spinning.[30]

Driven in a lorry to a level-crossing a few miles away, Gandhi was transferred there, in darkness, to the Frontier Mail, which made an unscheduled stop on its long journey from the North-West Frontier to Bombay. Some hours later, at 6.40 in the morning of 5 May, the Frontier Mail made another unscheduled halt north of Bombay, just short of Borivli. Swiftly and quietly, Gandhi was removed to a Buick and driven all the way to Yeravda jail in Poona, a journey of 125 miles, but not before being greeted by two American journalists who had correctly guessed that the Buick and the British soldiers they had noticed around the rail track north of Borivli were meant for Gandhi. He recognized the journalists and gave them, on being asked, a short message for Americans: they should 'study the issues closely and judge them on their merits'.[31]

A doctor accompanied the police party that took Gandhi to Yeravda, where goat's milk was made available for him, and he was allowed to spin and use a sewing machine as well. He expressed appreciation, but others could not help thinking that Gandhi had been arrested under cover of darkness by rulers who feared the multitude, because they took him for a prophet.

Marchers arrested. As had been arranged, the Muslim jurist, Abbas Tyabji, who was 75 and had a flowing snow-white beard, took over the leadership of the marchers, who were joined also by Jugatram Dave. On the morning of 12 May, after being blessed by Kasturba and Mrs Tyabji, the marchers set off for the Dharasana salt depot. After they had walked a few minutes, several hundred policemen surrounded the marchers and ordered them to turn back. Though some thought that refusal might result in the police opening fire, all shouted that they were not turning back.

They were arrested and sentenced: Tyabji for six months' simple, Dave for six months' rigorous, and the rest for three months, except for four adjudged to be minor, who were cautioned and let off, and who promptly joined another party planning to raid Dharasana. Here the salt heaps were successfully defended by a cordon of ditches and barbed wire and by 25 rifle-armed soldiers and about 400 policemen, commanded by six British officers. On 21 May Sarojini Naidu, Manilal Gandhi, Imam Bawazeer and Pyarelal led around 2,500 satyagrahis in an attack that fetched headlines across the world even if no salt was collected.

Successive columns wading through ditches and trying to reach the barbed wire were attacked with iron-tipped lathis. Scores were brutally hit in the head and shoulders but not one raised a hand against the police. The ground where they fell was soon blood-soaked. So were the blankets in which satyagrahi first-aid teams removed the injured to a 'hospital' tent nearby.

World learns of Dharasana. Present at the scene and watching, an American corre-spondent, Webb Miller of the United Press, sent a graphic report that created a worldwide sensation:

Slowly and in silence the throng commenced the half-mile march to the salt deposits. A few carried ropes for lassoing the barbed-wire stockade ... As the throng drew near the salt pans they commenced chanting the revolutionary slogan, Inquilab Zindabad (Long Live the Revolution) ...

Suddenly, at a word of command, scores of native police rushed upon the advancing marchers and rained blows on their heads with their steel-shod lathis. Not one of the marchers raised an arm to fend off the blows. They went down like nine-pins. From where I stood I heard the sickening whacks of the clubs on unprotected skulls ...

Then another column formed ... They marched steadily with heads up ... The police rushed out and methodically and mechanically beat down the second column ... The blankets used as stretchers were sodden with blood ...

The Gandhi men altered their tactics, marched up in groups of twenty-five and sat on the ground near the salt pans, making no effort to draw nearer ... Finally the police became enraged by the non-resistance ... They commenced savagely kicking the seated men in the abdomen and testicles ...[32]

Beating was still preferred to jailing, but several were arrested, including Naidu, Manilal, Imam Bawazeer and Pyarelal. Turning up at Dharasana, Vithalbhai Patel, who had seen the logic of events and resigned his presidency of the Central Assembly, declared:

All hope of reconciling India with the British Empire is lost for ever ... I cannot understand how any government that calls itself civilized could deal as savagely and brutally with non-violent, unresisting men as the British have this morning.

Vithalbhai's comment, too, was sent out to the world by Miller. Little salt was captured in Dharasana, but, as J C Kumarappa claimed in *Young India* (29 May), 'Our primary object was to show the world at large the fangs and claws of the Government in all its ugliness and ferocity. In this we have succeeded beyond measure.'[33] A Christian from the Tamil country, Kumarappa was a Columbia-trained economist who had recently joined the Gujarat Vidyapith as a professor.

Smaller raids and beatings continued for a few more days, and a Gujarat Congress report would claim that in all 2,699 volunteers were sent into the field, 1,333 wounded, and four died of their injuries.

Sense of independence. A bigger raid took place in Bombay city on 1 June 1930, targeting salt pans in Wadala. Around 15,000 assembled in support, and a number, including women and children, 'splashed through slime and mud to reach the salt pans'.[34] This time a large quantity of salt was collected. There were lathi charges on the crowd, the infantry too was called, and numerous arrests made, but Bombay was experiencing a sense of independence.

Visiting the city, the British journalist and Labour Party leader, H N Brailsford, wrote of the Congress's boycotts, marches and rallies:

More sober and orderly meetings I never saw ... The speeches were certainly what lawyers call 'seditious', but they were never incitements to disorder. Invariably they preached non-violence ... When the speakers talked, the more devoted members of the audience, men as well as women, would take out the little hand-spindle, the takli, and twist it placidly and indefatigably as they listened.[35]

In Delhi, Harry Haig, Home Secretary to the Government of India, privately conceded that the Congress seemed to run the streets of Bombay, noting that the numbers and discipline involved in Congress marches and 'the brushing aside' of police control of traffic 'have combined to produce a vivid impression of the power and success of the Congress movement'.[36]

Elsewhere, too, the Raj's prestige slipped, if not as dramatically. It slipped despite bans on several units of the Congress, despite large-scale arrests, and despite ten ordinances that Irwin promulgated between mid-April and mid-December, exercising an 'arbitrary rule ... wielded by no previous Viceroy'.[37]

When Jawaharlal was arrested, his father became acting president of the Congress. When, in June, he too was arrested, Motilal Nehru named Vallabhbhai Patel, whose release came at the end of June, to the chair. By this time even Malaviya, always wary of confrontation, had resigned from the Central Assembly. On his request, Vallabhbhai nominated Malaviya to the Congress's illegal Working Committee. Patel also asked 'every house in the country to be the office of the Congress committee, and every individual to be the Congress in himself'.[38] At the end of July, Vallabhbhai, Malaviya, and several others were arrested in Bombay for disobeying an order to disperse. Released but rearrested in December 1930, Patel named Rajendra Prasad to succeed him as acting Congress president.

About 90,000 Indians were arrested for defying laws during the 1930 movement. Except in the Frontier Province, the proportion of Muslims courting arrest was, however, small, and Sikhs too seemed to stay away from the fight. Nonetheless 'unlawful' salt was collected, moved, sold or bought all across India, foreign cloth was boycotted, and previously bought foreign cloth set aflame. Import of cotton piece-goods came down by 75 per cent, khadi sales rose by 60 per cent and liquor sales were curbed by an expanding corps of picketing women.

Despite Gandhi's injunctions, some violence from the Indian side occurred in Karachi (where two Congress volunteers died of injuries sustained while restraining a mob), in Calcutta, in Peshawar and in Chittagong in eastern Bengal, where an armed band raided the police armoury, killed the guards and made off with guns and ammunition.

But these incidents were eclipsed by the sheer scale of India's non-violent assault in 1930. Referring to it the following year, Churchill charged that the Indians had 'inflicted such humiliation and defiance as has not been known since the British first trod the soil of India'.[39] Another old Harrovian, Jawaharlal, would write in his autobiography that he 'felt a little abashed and ashamed for having questioned the efficacy of this method when it was first proposed by Gandhiji'.[40] Writing, one prisoner to another, to Gandhi, Nehru said (28 Jul. 1930):

May I congratulate you on the new India you have created by your magic touch!

What the future will bring I know not but the past has made life worth living and our prosaic existence has developed something of epic greatness in it.[41]

Land revenue withheld. When, on 19 March, the marchers had passed through the village of Ras, where Vallabhbhai was arrested, Patidar farmers told Gandhi that they would not pay land tax. Having precipitated Patel's arrest, they would atone by undertaking a defiance their hero had desired.

Times had changed, Gandhi warned. The 1928 Bardoli action in Surat district was for removing an economic grievance. Now, in a struggle as different 'as the earth is from the sky', they were talking of 'removing a government'. The Raj would be at its harshest. But the men of Ras, confident of sanctuary and support from kinsfolk in Sisva and Jharola, adjacent villages in the princely state of Baroda outside the Raj's direct control, and confident too that fellow-farmers would not buy forfeited lands, would not be budged. Though he wrote in *Navajivan* that Ras's farmers were 'attempting the impossible', Gandhi did not obstruct them.[42]

Ras lay in Keda district's Borsad taluka. Thirteen other villages of the taluka joined Ras in the defiance over land revenue. After Gandhi's arrest, Bardoli also decided to withhold the land tax, and at the end of May Kheda's Patidar peasants (many with relatives in Baroda villages) said they would extend the defiance to the whole district.

Determined to punish the rebels, Alfred Master brought forward the date for collecting revenue, frustrating the farmers' plan to sell standing crops and remove proceeds to Baroda. He also gave free rein to the mamlatdar of Borsad taluka, Mohanlal Shah, who offered to crush the resistance by thrashing and jailing Congressmen, and by encouraging the area's Baraiyas and Patanvadiyas, poorer peasants whose forebears had lost lands through indebtedness to Patels, to buy the lands the Patels were forfeiting.

Patanvadiyas loyal to Ravishankar Vyas, who had worked in the area, refused to take Patidar lands even if offered free, but others were willing, and the Master-Shah tactics, backed at times by the looting and burning of Patidar homes, were effective. Hundreds of families lost land, and thousands of Patidars left Kheda for villages in Baroda, as did many peasants from Surat and Bharuch districts: in February 1931 Baroda officials would count some 28,000 hijratis or migrants. They were paying a high price, but the men of Ras, and others like them in southern Gujarat, seemed unrepentant.

The prisoner

Gandhi did not know for how long he would be incarcerated, for Regulation 25 of 1827, last used a quarter of a century earlier, allowed the government to detain a person indefinitely. Kalelkar was his cellmate in Yervada Central Jail but Gandhi was not allowed to meet any of the political prisoners kept there, who included Vallabhbhai, Sarojini Naidu and Jairamdas Daulatram of Sindh.

Kalelkar would later write that a prison cook overcame a limp thanks to Gandhi's prescriptions, and that Gandhi made friends with – and gave Gujarati lessons to – the Irish jailer, Patrick Quinn. Evidently, Quinn carried in his shirt pocket a two-line note written by Gandhi: 'Be kind to prisoners. If provoked, swallow your anger.'[43]

Enjoying Kalelkar's company and the time to spin, Gandhi improved the quality and quantity of his yarn. And a sewing machine sent by a friend in Poona, Lady Premlila Thackersey, enabled him to improve the tailoring he had learnt in South Africa.

Letters. Allowed to write as many non-political letters as he wished, Gandhi wrote 60 to 80 every week: to children in the ashram, Dandi marchers, family members, associates, friends. After inspection and delays, the letters were sent in a bunch to the ashram and forwarded from there by the new manager, Narandas Gandhi (Maganlal's brother). Many were replies to letters that Gandhi was allowed to receive. He liked getting them, and complained good-humouredly if some did not write.

In his earliest letters he gave 'Yeravda' as his address. This was soon changed to 'Yeravda Palace' and then, a few letters later, to 'Yeravda Mandir' (Yeravda Temple). Often he dealt with questions raised in the ashram, or of diet or health. An unfertilized egg, he wrote, was more 'vegetarian' than milk.[44] Advice was frequently spelt out, but the letters also contained love, appreciation, imagination, gratefulness, faith, reflection, humour, or concern.

To Mira (Miss Slade), who had packed and sent Gandhi's spinning wheel, who loved Gandhi and was loved by him, 12 May: Yours is the first letter I take up to write from the jail and that on the silence day. I have been quite happy and have been making up for arrears of rest. The nights here are cool and as I am permitted to sleep right under the sky, I have refreshing sleep ... It was a great treat to receive the wheel so thoughtfully sent and with things so carefully packed in it (49: 274).

To 'Birds', the ashram children, 12 May, from 'Yeravda Palace': Birds are real birds when they can fly without wings. With wings any creature can fly. If you, who have no wings, can fly, you will feel no fear at all ... See, I have no wings and still I fly every day and come to you ... There is Vimla, and here are Hari, Manu and Dharmakumar. You also can fly with your minds and feel that you are with me (49: 279).

To Kasturba, 12 May: How good it was that I met you all on Sunday evening [4 May] and accompanied you back as far as your camp! I was very happy that I did so. God is showering His kindness on me. Let all the women write to me (49: 280).

To Devadas, arrested in Delhi, from 'Yeravda Mandir', 13 May: Since I do not know where you are, I write to you at the Ashram address. There is God to worry for us all and we need not, therefore, worry on account of one another. You know about me, that ultimately I never come to harm. God always clears my path. (49: 283)

To Bali and Kumi, sisters of Harilal's deceased wife Gulab (or Chanchal), who were looking after Harilal's children, 26 Jul.: I got Bali's letter. Kumi also should write. I don't mind your having taken away Manu [*Harilal's youngest daughter*]. Anything which pleases you two sisters pleases me. Your love for these children sometimes brings tears of joy to my eyes. (49: 388)

To Pandit Narayan Khare, the ashram music teacher, 21 Aug.: Your voice as you used to sing at the time of prayers haunts me every day. (49: 455)

To Sushila, wife of Manilal, who had visited her husband in jail, 24 Aug.: I hope you always find Manilal with a smile on his face and joking. Does he read anything in jail? (50: 3)

To Narandas Gandhi, 24/26 Aug.: How is Devadas's health? Tell him that I often think of him. Has Ramdas's health recovered? (50: 5)

To Narandas, 5/9 Sep.: If Dudabhai [*the 'untouchable' whose daughter Lakshmi was in the ashram*] is eager to have Lakshmi with him and if the latter wishes to go, do not stop her (50: 41).

To Mira, 28 Sep.: Narandas tells me you are not hitting it off with Kumarappa. Charity is our talisman. I should let him do as he pleases. (50: 90)

To Prema Kantak, a woman from Maharashtra who taught the ashram's children, loved and revered Gandhi and wanted to keep his wooden sandals, 2 Oct. (Gandhi's birthday): If you wish, you may certainly keep the wooden sandals. But what will you do with those bits of wood? Keep them if you think that they will add an inch or two to your stature ...

I used to keep with me a photograph of my father. I had hung his photographs in the drawing-room and the bedroom when I was in South Africa. When I used to wear a chain, it had a locket which contained small photographs of my father and elder brother. I have now put them away. That does not mean that I feel less reverence for them now.

If I tried to keep with me photographs of all [I revere], I would have no room to put them in. And if I tried to keep their wooden sandals, I should have to acquire a piece of land for the purpose. As a man of experience, I advise you, therefore, to follow me when I am walking on the right path. That will be a thousand times better than keeping my wooden sandals ... (50: 104)

To Henry Polak, who had disagreed with the 1930 defiance but sent a birthday greeting, 20 Oct.: My dear Henry, I had your and Millie's loving message. You are never absent from my mind. How is Leon? (50: 156)

To Andrews, 12 Nov.: My dear Charlie ... I think of you every day and that often. Love. Mohan (50: 224)

To J C Kumarappa, who had written of his misgivings regarding vows, 16 Nov.: The strongest men have been known at times to have become weak ... Hence the necessity of vows, i.e., invoking God's assistance to give us strength at the crucial moment. But I must not strive with you. It seems to me that we mean the same thing but express it differently – you in Spanish and I in Italian, shall we say? (50: 240)

For Mira's sake he *daily* translated into English a verse or bhajan from the ashram *Bhajanavali*, at times asking Kalelkar for his understanding of a Sanskrit, Gujarati, Hindi or Marathi original. Begun on 5 May, the exercise was completed on 15 December. It involved 224 careful if short translations. From Yeravda, Gandhi also sent detailed Gujarati commentaries on each of the ashram's 11 vows.

In November, his sentence served, Kalelkar was released. This was a loss for Gandhi, but he was soon allowed the company of Pyarelal, also a prisoner in Yeravda.

Negotiations. Obtaining permission from Irwin, Sir Tej Bahadur Sapru and M R Jayakar called on Gandhi in the middle of August to explore a truce. They brought with them, from Naini Jail in the UP, the two Nehrus and Bihar's Syed Mahmud, again courtesy of Irwin. The two intermediaries, the three north Indian prisoners, and four Yeravda detainees, Gandhi, Vallabhbhai, Sarojini Naidu and Jairamdas Daulatram, conferred together on 14 and 15 August, and Sapru and Jayakar took the Congress's terms for a truce to Irwin.

There could be a withdrawal of disobedience, the Congress leaders said, if the British were prepared to concede India's right to leave the Empire, if Gandhi's 11 points were satisfactorily addressed, and if free collection of salt was allowed. The Viceroy rejected these terms.

In November and December Sapru and Jayakar attended a Round Table Conference

(RTC) that Ramsay MacDonald convened in London. The Congress boycotting the conference, MacDonald admitted its unrepresentative character and adjourned it. From London, Sapru and Jayakar cabled word that Congress leaders should await their return before reacting publicly to the RTC's outcome. Their plea coincided with an unexpected statement from Irwin, who declared in Calcutta that it would be 'a profound mistake' to 'underestimate the meaning of nationalism'. 'Strong action by the Government', the Viceroy added, could never 'wholly cure' it.

Release. On the morning of 26 January 1931 – exactly one year after the Congress's independence pledge – Gandhi was told that he was being released. Jawaharlal, Patel, Rajagopalachari and all the Working Committee members were also set free that day, and the ban on the Committee was withdrawn. Irwin said the releases were ordered to make discussions possible.

> *Gandhi to Narandas, 26 Jan.*: We were informed this morning that Pyarelal and I are to be released ... My present feeling is that I shall be leaving peace and quiet and going into the midst of turmoil (51:71).

That evening the Associated Press of India sent out a story from a railway station just west of Poona:

> While waiting on the platform of the Chinchwad station to board the train for Bombay, Mr Gandhi gave the following message to the Indian people: 'I have come out of jail with an absolutely open mind, unfettered by enmity, unbiased in argument and prepared to study the whole situation from every point of view.'
>
> Q. 'What is your opinion regarding the immediate release of all political prisoners?'
>
> A. 'I most sincerely believe that every political prisoner now in jail for being connected with my civil disobedience movement should be liberated immediately, and none of us as leaders should be happy as long as any of our brethren or sisters are in Jail.'
>
> Asked if he was happy at being free once again, he replied: 'I really do not know.' Mr Gandhi expressed great appreciation of the treatment he received in jail, and when asked if he expected to go back again in the near future, Mr Gandhi replied: 'Possibly, you never know' (51: 71–2).

Pact with Irwin

Twelve years younger than Gandhi, Edward Frederick Lindley Wood, scion of a landed family in Yorkshire, was made Lord Irwin in 1925 and Viceroy of India in 1926. Publicly acknowledging, to the dismay of several Delhi officials, 'the spiritual force which impels Gandhi',[45] Irwin also made private remarks that encouraged liberals like Sapru, Jayakar and Srinivasa Sastri.

Prodded by these three, the now lawful Working Committee authorized Gandhi to talk on the Congress's behalf with Irwin, and accompanied him to Delhi to be available for consultation. In the meantime, however, Motilal Nehru, 69, ailing, and released some months earlier, had died in Lucknow on 6 February 1931.

Beginning in New Delhi on 17 February, Gandhi's talks with the Viceroy spanned a 16-day period and were held in the Viceroy's new palace, designed by Lutyens, of red and white sandstone and multi-hued marbles. Containing a mile-and-a-half of corridors and 340 rooms, and occupying five-and-a-half acres on a 16-acre ground, the building sought to proclaim that the Raj was both grand and permanent.

The Viceroy's visitor was lodged five miles away in Daryagunj, in the home of the Muslim doctor and Congress leader, Mukhtar Ahmed Ansari. From this home Gandhi walked to the Viceregal palace to talk with Irwin, and walked back to report to the Working Committee, on some days performing the routine twice.

In London Churchill uttered a famous alarm. It was 'nauseating', he said, that 'a seditious Middle Temple lawyer [*this was an error – Gandhi had joined the Inner Temple*] now posing as a fakir' was 'striding half-naked up the steps of the viceregal palace to parley on equal terms with the representative of the King-Emperor'.[46] Churchill added: 'The truth is that Gandhism and all it stands for will have to be grappled with and finally crushed.'[47]

To Indians the scene that so offended Churchill seemed merely appropriate. After a series of long talks, the rebel and the Viceroy signed an accord on the night of 4 March, the Irwin-Gandhi Pact, as the Raj called it, or the Gandhi-Irwin Pact, as Indians described it.

Against a Congress agreement to suspend disobedience and take part in the Second RTC in London in the autumn, the Raj agreed to release all those imprisoned in the 1930 disobedience, withdraw its ordinances and bans on Congress units, return unsold confiscated lands, allow residents of coastal areas to make their own salt and permit non-aggressive picketing of shops selling liquor or foreign cloth.

Independence was not offered. The salt tax was not lifted. Lands that had been sold were not to be returned. Yet most Indians rejoiced because tens of thousands were being released, and because the Pact implied equality between Britain and India, between the Viceroy and Gandhi, between the Raj and the Congress and, at the grassroots, between the Raj's policeman and the non-violent law-breaker. Now the men and women of the Congress could freely collect salt or, with impunity, picket cloth or liquor shops 'under the eye of the very policeman who was till yesterday jumping upon them like a wolf on a fold'.[48] Psychologically, it was a revolution.

But there was disappointment as well. Neither Bose nor Jawaharlal, the Congress president, liked the clause in the accord committing the Congress to 'consider further the constitutional scheme discussed in the Round Table Conference', which seemed several steps short of complete independence. Patel on his part felt aggrieved by the failure to win back all the lands forfeited by the Gujarat peasants.

Bhagat Singh's fate. Across India the young were unhappy that the amnesty did not apply to all political prisoners. Bengali youths imprisoned for militant activities were not freed, and – the bitterest disappointment – there was no commutation of the death sentences passed on Bhagat Singh, Sukhdev and Rajguru for the 1928 killing, in Lahore, of Saunders. Could the young rejoice when three heroes of theirs were to hang?

Before agreeing to sign the accord, Gandhi 'put it to member after member of the Working Committee, individually, and asked whether he should break on prisoners, on lands, on anything, on everything …'[49] Despite dissatisfactions, no one counselled a break. The members knew they were obtaining a settlement, not laying down a victor's terms. On every point Gandhi had bargained hard. When he told Irwin that he had to honour Patel's promise that peasants would get their lands back, Irwin replied, truthfully, that he too had given a commitment to Sykes, Garrett and Master that sold lands would not be returned.

But the Viceroy agreed to urge the Bombay government to reinstate village headmen who had resigned and help non-governmental efforts for the return of sold lands. In addition, Gandhi was told by Irwin that Ansari could attend the London RTC on behalf of the group of nationalist Muslims: this was important for Gandhi, who knew that anti-Congress Muslims would be vocal at the London conference.

Yet Irwin firmly rejected Gandhi's plea for the lives of Bhagat Singh, Sukhdev and Rajguru. Claiming surprise that 'the apostle of non-violence should so earnestly be pleading the cause of the devotees of a creed so fundamentally opposed to his own', Irwin also felt that it would be 'wholly wrong to allow my judgement to be influenced by purely political considerations'. In Irwin's view, the death sentence for killing a police officer was 'directly deserved'.[50]

After the three were hanged, Gandhi acknowledged that while he strove for commutation, neither he nor the Working Committee had made it a breaking point. Apart from Irwin's own position, London was resolute on the question. If Gandhi had called for a Congress boycott of the Second RTC, the sentences would still have been carried out, but the door of dialogue that seemed to be opening – 'the second door to Swaraj',[51] as Gandhi called it – would have closed.

Irwin told Gandhi that Churchill was bound to accuse him of betraying Britain.[52]

The Viceroy was correct. Churchill complained that 'the lawless act has now been made lawful' by Irwin's concessions, that 'Mr Gandhi and Congress have been raised to a towering pedestal,' and that appeasement had been offered to those who had 'inflicted such humiliation and defiance as has not been known since the British first trod the soil of India'.[53]

At a press conference in Delhi on 6 March, when Indian, British and American journalists talked with Gandhi, he sparkled.

> *Journalist*: Will you press for Purna Swaraj [Complete Independence] at the RTC?
>
> *Gandhi*: We will deny our very existence if we do not press for it.
>
> *Journalist*: What was it that turned the tide in the negotiations?
>
> *Gandhi (smiling)*: Goodness on the part of Lord Irwin and perhaps [*a bigger smile from Gandhi*] equal goodness on my part as well.
>
> *Journalist*: Do you expect Purna Swaraj in your life time?
>
> *Gandhi*: I do look for it most decidedly. I still consider myself a young man of sixty-two.
>
> *Journalist*: Do you prefer English people as a governing race to other races?
>
> *Gandhi*: I have no choice to make. I do not want to be governed except by myself.
>
> *Journalist*: Would you agree to become the Prime Minister of the future Government?
>
> *Gandhi*: No. It will be reserved for younger minds and stouter hearts.[54]

One of the correspondents interacting with Gandhi was William Shirer of the *Chicago Tribune,* the future author of *The Rise and Fall of the Third Reich* and of *Gandhi: A Memoir.* According to Shirer, Gandhi said to him at this time, 'You will see, my dear Mr Shirer! We shall gain our freedom – in my lifetime.'[55] Twenty-seven years old in 1931, Shirer was drawn to Gandhi. Recalling a moment during the Delhi talks when, on Gandhi's request, he typed out a statement dictated by Gandhi, the reporter would say:

> I was so moved by some of his words and the simple, sincere way in which he spoke them that at moments I had difficulty in putting them down on my typewriter.[56]

Karachi Congress. The Working Committee chose Vallabhbhai as the new Congress president. Only one person resented the appointment, older brother Vithalbhai, who felt that his sacrifice of the Central Assembly presidency had gone unrewarded.

En route to Karachi for the Congress plenary, Gandhi again urged Irwin to spare the lives of Bhagat Singh, Rajguru and Sukhdev, saying that peace would be endangered, and his own position rendered 'almost too difficult' if the hangings were carried out. In this 'final appeal', Gandhi's last sentence was, 'Charity never faileth' (51: 290–1). On 23 March, the day on which the letter was sent, the three were hanged.

When Gandhi arrived at Karachi station on 25 March, incensed young men greeted him with black flags and shouted 'Down with Gandhism'. He thought they would physically attack him. Instead they presented him with flowers made of black cloth and escorted Gandhi to the car brought for him. On the night of 26 March, addressing the plenary under the 'canopy of heaven', as Desai put it, Gandhi praised the young men's courtesy, and added:

> I think they had a right to [condemn] me, if they felt that I was betraying the country … I want to win them over by love. Having flung aside the sword, there is nothing except the cup of love which I can offer to those who oppose me.

'One's head bends before Bhagat Singh's bravery and sacrifice,' Gandhi had said at a press conference (51: 301). At the plenary he added:

> But I want you also to realize Bhagat Singh's error … I declare that we cannot win Swaraj for our famishing millions, for our deaf and dumb, for our lame and crippled, by the way of the sword. With the Most High as witness I want to proclaim this truth …
>
> Do you think that all the women and the children who covered themselves with glory during the last campaign would have done so if we had pursued the path of violence? Would our women, known as the meekest on earth, would women like Gangabehn, who withstood the lathi-blows until her white sari was drenched in blood, have done the unique service they did if we had violence in us?
>
> And our children – our vanarasena [monkey-army]. How could you have had these innocent ones, who renounced their toys, their kites and their crackers, and joined as soldiers of Swaraj – how could you have enlisted them in a violent struggle? We were able to enlist as soldiers millions of men, women and children because we were pledged to non-violence (51: 305–9).

In a *Navajivan* tribute to Bhagat Singh's courage (29 March 1931), Gandhi repeated his rejection of assassination:

> If the practice of seeking justice through murders is established amongst us, we shall start murdering one another for what we believe to be justice. In a land of crores [millions] of destitutes and crippled persons, this will be a terrifying situation (51: 316–17).

Sole representative. The success of the previous year's struggle ensured unity at the Karachi session, which endorsed the Gandhi–Irwin accord, with Jawaharlal moving, and Subhas Bose seconding, a resolution for ratification, and authorized Gandhi to attend the RTC as the Congress's sole representative, with plenipotentiary discretion over last-minute proposals.

Giving Gandhi colleagues in London would mean excluding others, a hard and divisive exercise. Should president Patel go but not Jawaharlal? Jawaharal but not Bose? Why not Rajagopalachari? In any case, India would require leaders during Gandhi's absence. Covering the Karachi session, Shirer thought Gandhi functioned there as 'the consummate politician'.[57]

Karachi also adopted a significant resolution on fundamental rights in a free India. Collaboration between Jawaharlal and Gandhi produced the text of this resolution, which Gandhi moved. 'By passing this resolution,' he said, 'we make it clear to the world and to our own people what we propose to do as soon as we come into power' (51: 329).

It committed the Congress to freedom of expression, religion, thought and assembly; equality regardless of caste, sex or creed; a minimum wage and limited working hours; a secular state ('Swaraj will favour Hinduism no more than Islam, nor Islam more than Hinduism,' Gandhi explained[58]); the abolition of untouchability and serfdom; removal of the salt tax; and state ownership or control of key industries.

Communal strife in Cawnpore (Kanpur) coincided with the Karachi session. Indians were stirred by the death there of 41-year-old Ganesh Shankar Vidyarthi, editor of a Hindi weekly and prominent UP Congressman, who was killed while attempting to prevent a Hindu-Muslim clash. In *Young India* Gandhi wrote (9 Apr. 1931) that Vidyarthi's 'heroism [was] bound in the end to melt the stoniest hearts, melt them into one' (51: 361).

Willingdon and disappointment. The relationship with Irwin offered hope but in the provinces British officials tried to block the Viceroy's concessions. In Gujarat, Garrett and Master resisted the reinstatement of pro-Congress village chiefs and refused to help rebels recover their lands, and there was obstruction in other provinces as well. At Gandhi's instance Irwin had Master transferred, but after 18 April there was no Irwin to go to. He had been succeeded as Viceroy by Lord Willingdon, former governor of Bombay and Madras, who had called Gandhi a 'Bolshevik' in 1919 and thought Irwin 'a simple man' whom Gandhi had 'deluded'.[59] Three years older than Gandhi, the new Viceroy, born George Freeman Thomas, had been a Liberal MP before being made a baron and Canada's governor-general (1926–31). A lord-in-waiting and tennis partner to George V, he seemed to prefer India's princes to its politicians.

Finding Willingdon indifferent to repeated complaints about violations of the Pact in Gujarat, the Frontier Province, and the UP, and to pleas for the release of the Bengal prisoners, Gandhi announced on 11 August, 18 days before he was to sail for London, that he would rather not go for the RTC.

A failure to re-enlist Muslim partners had also affected him. Shaukat Ali, with whom Gandhi talked for two days in Bombay, evidently first accepted and then rejected Gandhi's proposal of an alliance formula: a one-third share for Muslims in a central assembly plus joint electorates.[60]

But Sapru and Jayakar busied themselves once more, and in three days Gandhi, Patel, Jawaharlal and Ghaffar Khan found themselves in Simla, where Gandhi had a meeting with Willingdon that he felt was 'bereft of all grace'.[61] Willingdon rejected every demand save one. He would not intervene in the UP or the Frontier or Bengal, and, no, Ansari could not be a delegate at the RTC. But he was willing, the Viceroy said, to order an inquiry into lands in Bardoli.

The tiny concession tipped the scale for Gandhi; and Patel, Nehru, and Ghaffar Khan also urged him to go. But Gandhi's faith in 'the second door' to freedom had all but gone. He announced in Simla that 'notwithstanding the suspension of disobedience' the Congress would, if forced, seek relief in 'defensive direct action'.[62] Gandhi knew that this 'relief' would mean fresh suffering for his soldiers. Hoping against hope, he would go to England, not primarily to attend the RTC but to talk with the British people.

As aides to go with him, he picked Mahadev Desai, Devadas, Pyarelal and Miss Slade. Asked by a journalist about Mira, Gandhi laughed and answered, '[W]hy shouldn't I bring her? She is a most useful assistant and, besides, she is anxious to see her mother who lives in England' (51: 276). But he took no close political companions.

To Rajagopalachari, 28 Aug. 1931: There are two men whom I would like by my side in London, you and Jawaharlal ... You will both help me, like the others, by being [in India]. Only, your presence with me would have lightened my burden (53: 294).

England

On 29 August 1931 Gandhi and party boarded the *Rajputana* in Bombay. Forty-three years had passed since he last sailed, as a nervous if eager teenager, from India to England – his later visits to England (in 1906, 1909 and 1914) had been made from South Africa. This time he was going on India's behalf.

A country he knew and in some respects admired, England was also, however, India's master. Moreover, Gandhi was well aware that its rulers, the RTC hosts, were going to treat him not as the voice of India (which is how Irwin had seen him) but only as one of several Indian representatives. Since reaching the British people was his true goal, he accepted an invitation to live in a community centre in Bow in the East End called

Kingsley Hall, founded by two sisters, Doris and Muriel Lester. A pacifist, internationalist and feminist, Muriel had visited the Sabarmati ashram and invited Gandhi and his party to live in the Hall's 'cells', as she called them.

He enjoyed the sea voyage, with Mira, the admiral's daughter (who wore Indian clothes and shaved her head like an Indian nun), pronouncing that as a sailor Gandhi was 'out and away the best' among his party.[63] When an impish young fellow-passenger on the *Rajputana* presented him with a 'journal' called 'Scandal Times' and asked for comments, Gandhi removed the pin from the sheets, which he returned, kept the pin, and said, 'Thank you.'[64]

Egyptians resentful of European hegemony turned up at Suez and Port Said but were not allowed to meet the Empire's chief rebel. The poet Ahmad Shauqi had exhorted Egyptians that as Gandhi passed by they should,

Stop to welcome him, from close quarters sitting in boats and also from a distance in whatever way possible. He is a guide and pathfinder like Confucius ... He has inspired in Hindus and Muslims the spirit of mutual love and with his spiritual powers brought the two swords in one sheath. He is a great powerhouse which generates the power to tame predators.[65]

In Marseilles, where he took a train for Calais, hundreds, including scores of journalists, mobbed Gandhi, and on 12 September about 5,000, including many Indians, greeted him in Folkestone. Later in the day a large throng of east Londoners welcomed Gandhi when he arrived at Kingsley Hall.

He told a correspondent of the *Evening Standard* (12 Sep.) that he would 'wear his loin-cloth in London, but would protect himself from the weather with shawls and rugs'. Asked if he would see any plays, Gandhi remembered long-forgotten pleasures in his reply:

At one time I used to attend the Lyceum. I liked Shakespeare's plays – I adored the incomparable Ellen Terry – I worshipped her, but that was before the advent of melodrama. The only reason I will not attend theatres in London is because I shall not have time. I am not the dreadful old man I am represented to be. Actually I am a very jolly fellow. I could almost be described as Scotch. I am very careful of my sixpences (53: 347–8).

On the evening of 13 September he had a long talk, at the Dorchester, with the Prime Minister, Ramsay MacDonald. The son of a poor Scottish farmer, the Labour PM had been heading, from the end of August, a Tory-dominated 'national government' unpopular with most Labour MPs. Gandhi found MacDonald feeling helpless: it was the Depression, unemployment was high, the pound was falling and the Premier's base was weak.

In any case, India was not England's chief concern. Moreover, policy regarding India remained in the hands of officials who thought that Indians could not rule themselves. Worst of all, from Gandhi's angle, was the certainty that various delegates from India – Muslims, princes, Parsis, Anglo-Indians, Europeans and men like Bhimrao Ambedkar from Maharashtra, who led an important body of the 'untouchables' – would declare at the RTC that the Congress did not represent their India.

The RTC. Still, 'whilst there is yet a little sand left in the glass',[66] he would make an attempt. In his first speech to the RTC, he depicted the Congress's inclusive character, named some of the Muslim, Parsi and Christian presidents it had chosen, spelt out its commitment for the rights of minorities, 'untouchables' and women, acknowledged British qualities and claimed that India was relevant even to Britain's economic crisis:

Time was when I prided myself on being, and being called, a British subject. I have ceased for many years to call myself a British subject; I would far rather be called a rebel than a subject. But I have aspired, I still aspire, to be a citizen, not of the Empire, but in a Commonwealth; in a partnership – if possible, if God wills it, an indissoluble partnership – but not a partnership superimposed upon one nation by another ... [E]ither party should have the right to sever the connection ...

I wondered, even as I was sailing towards London, whether we ... at the present moment would not be a drag upon the British Ministers, whether we would not be interlopers. And yet I said to myself: It is possible that we might not be interlopers ...

India, yes, can be held by the sword! I do not for one moment doubt the ability of Britain to hold India under subjection through the sword. But what will conduce to the prosperity of Great Britain ... an enslaved but rebellious India, or an India an esteemed partner with Britain to share her sorrows ... ?

And so I said to myself whilst I was nearing the shores of your beautiful island, perchance it might be possible for me to convince the British Ministers that India as a valuable partner, not held by force but by the silken cord of love ... might conceivably be of real assistance to you in balancing your Budget, not for one occasion but for many years.

What cannot two nations do, one a handful, but brave, with a record for bravery perhaps unequalled, a nation noted for having fought slavery, a nation that has at least claimed times without number to protect the weak; and another a very ancient nation, counted in millions, with a glorious and ancient past, representing at the present moment two great cultures, the Islamic and Hindu cultures ...

And supposing that God fires both Hindus and Mussulmans represented here with a proper spirit, so that they close ranks and come to an honourable understanding ... (53: 364–5)

Covering the RTC in London after having followed, for seven months, Gandhi's doings and speaking in India, Shirer thought that this speech, delivered from the heart and without notes, was 'the greatest one of his long political life'.[67]

Reaching out. Gandhi walked morning and evening along the streets of Bow, plied the spinning wheel daily in his 'cell', which had no table, chair or bed (he slept on the floor), prayed morning and evening in Kingsley Hall (where a goat was installed to provide Gandhi's milk), and received callers in his cell.

Residents of Bow crowded their windows to stare at the strange figure walking past their homes. Hearing that they wanted to see him, Gandhi visited a woman in a hospital and a sick man in his home. Successfully badgering their parents, children joined Gandhi in his early morning walk. Muriel Lester observed that Gandhi 'was delighted and took his walk with them, their rosy faces like apples, and big scarves round their necks'. The children called him Uncle Gandhi and 'were sad to see he had no socks on and used to try to make him wear warmer clothes'.[68]

At a 'joy night' in Kingsley Hall, a woman called Martha Rollason patted Gandhi 'on the shoulder' and said, 'Come on, Mr Gandhi, let's have a dance.' Muriel Lester thought Gandhi 'looked awfully pleased to be asked'[69] but he did not try to dance. At the Dorchester Hotel, the *maître d'*, a man called Charles, greeted Gandhi, reminding him that they had taken dancing lessons together in 1889. Gandhi, who remembered, exclaimed, 'Charlie!'

Assigned by Scotland Yard to protect Gandhi, Sergeants Evans and Rogers walked behind Gandhi and would 'come back wiping their brow with sweat, trying to keep up with Mr Gandhi'.[70] The two went wherever Gandhi went, and kept the long hours he did. Throwing himself into the life of Bow but also conferring, in hotels or chambers in London's West End, with delegates and British leaders, Gandhi usually worked past midnight and slept, on an average, for about four hours a night. The pattern of 1906 and 1909 was thus repeated. Much earlier, right after his student years, he had written in *Guide to London* that England's climate was conducive to hard work.

To meet textile workers hurt by the Depression and by the Indian boycott of foreign cloth, he went to Lancashire for two days. Andrews (who brought himself to England for the Gandhi visit) had proposed this trip. Gandhi told the workers that he sympathized with them but asked them to think of Indian hardships as well. Following Gandhi to Lancashire, Shirer thought that 'the bluff ... cotton-mill hands' gave one who had called for the boycott 'a tumultuous welcome'.[71]

Gandhi also visited the Empire's nurseries (Eton, Cambridge, Oxford) and its engines (Birmingham, Nottingham, Manchester). Finding his clothes, food and routine irresistible, journalists wrote many stories about him, which also, inevitably, touched on the Indian struggle. Though most large papers buried Gandhi's remarks in small spaces on an inside page, the press stories and Gandhi's face-to-face encounters revealed a bluntness to which the British people, the Empire's shareholders, were not accustomed:

> The object of our non-violent movement is complete independence for India, not in any mystic sense but in the English sense of the term, without any mental reservation. I feel that every country is entitled to it without any question of its fitness or otherwise. As every country is fit to eat, to drink and to breathe, even so is every nation fit to manage its own affairs, no matter how badly ... The doctrine of fitness to govern is mere eyewash. Independence means nothing more or less than getting out of alien control.[72]

To a group in Oxford he said:

> The long and short of it is that you will not trust us. Well, give us the liberty to make mistakes ... I do not want you to determine the pace [of Indian self-government]. Consciously or unconsciously you adopt the role of divinity. I ask you for a moment to come down from that pedestal (54: 87–8).

'How far would you cut India off from the Empire?' he was asked. 'From the Empire entirely,' Gandhi answered, 'from the British nation not at all'. To Eton students he said: 'It can be no pride to you that your nation is ruling over ours. No one chained a slave without chaining himself' (54: 82). Courteously but clearly he indicated that if the RTC failed the Congress would have to resume disobedience.

Tea with the King. All delegates were invited to tea at Buckingham Palace but George V (Willingdon's friend) disliked the idea of receiving Gandhi. Churchill's line had influenced the King, who moreover had not forgotten the Indian boycott of his son's visit ten years earlier. 'What!' he exclaimed to Samuel Hoare, Secretary of State for India, 'Have this rebel fakir in the Palace after he has been behind all these attacks on my loyal officers!'

Political advisers persuaded the King that Gandhi could not be left out, and despite his own reluctance Gandhi went to the royal reception, wearing what he always wore. Asked afterwards whether he felt comfortable about his dress, Gandhi replied, 'The King had enough on for both of us.'

After Hoare introduced Gandhi to him, the King asked, 'Why did you boycott my son?' 'Not your son, Your Majesty, but the official representative of the British Crown,' Gandhi answered. Then the King, who according to Hoare, 'evidently thought it was his duty to caution Gandhi on the consequences of rebellion', uttered 'a grave warning': 'Mr Gandhi, I won't have any attacks on my Empire.' Replied Gandhi: 'I must not be drawn into a political argument in Your Majesty's Palace after receiving Your Majesty's hospitality.' Hoare would write that 'Gandhi's savoir-faire saved the situation'.[73]

Despite a request sent in by Gandhi, Churchill refused to meet him. But Gandhi agreed to sit for a sculpture that Churchill's left-leaning cousin, Clare Sheridan, wanted to do. Gandhi said to her, 'You must tell him [Churchill] … that now that you've met me, I am not as bad as reputed.'[74]

Friends arranged meetings with Bernard Shaw, Charlie Chaplin, Hewlett Johnson (later called the 'Red' Dean of Canterbury), Maria Montessori and former Prime Minister Lloyd George. In Shaw, socialistic, Irish, and a vegetarian to boot, Gandhi found similarities of outlook, but Chaplin he had not even heard of before. He also met old colleagues like the Polaks, a newer friend and former foe, Lord Irwin, an older foe-and-friend, General Jan Smuts, and spoke, as he had done over 40 years earlier, to the London Vegetarian Society. Lord Sankey, a member of the MacDonald cabinet and prominent at the RTC, complained that Gandhi surrounded himself in England with 'churchmen, cranks, and faddists',[75] and no doubt others were put off too, while some like the Labour MP J F Horrabin, who was a journalist and cartoonist as well, were struck by Gandhi's 'twinkling' appearance.

Horrabin noticed the twinkle a number of times: when he took a more famous cartoonist, Low, to meet Gandhi, when Gandhi talked with an unnamed Tory MP 'with a highly aggressive manner', and again, 'when, in my Gower Street flat, he sat surrounded by a small crowd of journalists'. At this last occasion Gandhi apparently 'twinkled for a couple of hours'.[76]

RTC & Ambedkar. 'I want to turn the [Delhi] truce … into a permanent settlement,' Gandhi said on 1 December. 'But for heaven's sake give me, a frail man, sixty-two years gone, a little bit of a chance' (54: 228). Despite his pleas, British Ministers refused to spell out a timetable for Indian independence.

Instead, they questioned the Congress's right to speak for India and pointed to RTC delegates opposed to the Congress. Perhaps the most articulate of these was 40-year-old Bhimrao Ambedkar (1891–1956), a brilliant scholar and lawyer born into a family of Mahars, one of Maharashtra's 'untouchable' groups. After humiliations in school and college, Ambedkar had gone on to earn doctorates in London and New York. In 1927, as a rising leader of the untouchables, Ambedkar had mobilized over 10,000 of his people in Mahad for a satyagraha for access to water from a public tank. After a rally where Gandhi's portrait was displayed, Ambedkar and the others marched to the tank and drank forbidden water. Later, the town's Brahmins arranged a ceremony to restore the tank's purity.

But Ambedkar's warmth towards Gandhi did not endure. When, shortly before the RTC, they first met in Bombay, Gandhi took Ambedkar to be a radical Brahmin fighting untouchability. (He did not, however, say this to Ambedkar, and quickly realized his mistake.) Recognizing Ambedkar's ability and commitment, and conceding in London (54: 18) that Ambedkar spoke 'for that particular part of the country where he comes from', Gandhi insisted, 'however, that for India's 'untouchables' as a whole he himself was the truer representative.

For years he had championed their cause. In December 1929 he had said that 'chamars,* weavers, cobblers and Dheds, etc., among us ... had attained the highest knowledge' and added, 'Should it then be surprising if one of them, by virtue of the strength of his services, becomes the President of the State?' (48: 128)

Often expressed by Gandhi, such sentiments appeared paternalistic to Ambedkar, who wanted 'untouchables' to be led by their own. Criticizing Gandhi for not frontally attacking the caste system, Ambedkar was, in addition, fearful that independence would strengthen caste Hindu domination, a fear that Gandhi shared. Shortly before leaving for London, Gandhi had said:

> If we came into power with the stain of untouchability unaffected, I am positive that the 'untouchables' would be far worse under that 'Swaraj' than they are now, for the simple reason that our weaknesses and our failings would then be buttressed by the accession of power (53: 168).

Nonetheless, the RTC saw a bitter clash between Gandhi and Ambedkar. Demanding a separate electorate and reserved seats for the 'untouchables', Ambedkar challenged Gandhi's right to speak for his people, even as Muslim delegates, disowning Gandhi's leadership, insisted on a separate Muslim electorate. Neither Gandhi nor the Congress could reject a Muslim electorate, which had been accepted in the 1916 Lucknow Pact signed by the Congress and the Muslim League. Though both sides complained about the Pact, they had not agreed on an alternative.

But a separate electorate for 'untouchables' was contrary to all that Gandhi had worked for. He (and other reformist caste Hindus) had broken the barrier of untouchability and built a slender bridge on which many caste Hindu and 'untouchables' were courageously walking. A separate electorate would restore the barrier, weaken the bridge and reverse the reform process among caste Hindus.

---

* Chamars = 'untouchable' group working with hides.

Worst of all, it would 'divide the Hindu community into armed camps' (54: 119) and expose 'untouchables' to greater hostility. During a discussion at Friends House, the Quaker centre in Euston, Gandhi claimed (31 Oct.) that he was one 'who feels with them and knows their life' and added:

> The untouchables are in the hands of superior classes. They can suppress them completely and wreak vengeance upon the untouchables who are at their mercy. I may be opening out my shame to you. But … how can I invite utter destruction for them? I would not be guilty of that crime (54: 119).

In a bid to woo Ambedkar in London, Gandhi sent Devadas to him and tried also to involve Sir Mirza Ismail, a Muslim delegate. In a speech to the Indian Majlis, a mainly Muslim association of Indians in Britain, Gandhi spelt out his sympathy:

> I have the highest regard for Dr Ambedkar. He has every right to be bitter. That he does not break our heads is an act of self-restraint on his part … The same thing happened to me in my early days in South Africa where I was hounded out by the Europeans wherever I went. It is quite natural for him to vent his wrath (54: 84).

Not only were the attempts unsuccessful; to the delight of British officials, Ambedkar and leaders of some other groups at the RTC formed a united front of anti-Congress minorities to prevent the RTC from endorsing Gandhi's demands.

Gandhi told Shirer that he had never felt more humiliated,[77] but a response began to stir inside of him, and he was ready with his reply when, on 13 November, the so-called Minorities Pact was announced. Signed, among others, by Ambedkar and the Aga Khan, the Pact demanded separate electorates in Indian legislatures for Muslims, 'untouchables', Christians, Anglo-Indians and India-based Europeans.

Arguing that a separate electorate for the 'untouchables' means 'the perpetual bar sinister', Gandhi added:

> I would not sell the vital interests of the untouchables even for the sake of winning the freedom of India. I claim in my own person to represent the vast mass of the untouchables … I claim that I would get, if there was a referendum of the untouchables, their vote, and that I would top the poll.
>
> Today there is a body of Hindu reformers who are pledged to remove the blot of untouchability. Sikhs may remain as such in perpetuity, so may Mohammedans, so may Europeans. Will untouchables remain untouchables in perpetuity?

Referring to 'the two divisions' in every village that separate electorates would entrench, Gandhi suggested that those demanding separation 'do not know their India, do not know how Indian society is today constructed'. He ended with a declaration:

> I want to say with all the emphasis that I can command that if I was the only person to resist this thing, I would resist it with my life (54: 158–9).

In other words, he would fast unto death.

Farewell to London. But Gandhi would not leave London with any sense of defeat. On 1 December he uttered words that must be unique in the story of empires. Addressing Britain's leaders, including the Prime Minister, Gandhi punctured the balloons of unreality in the RTC chambers, defended the Congress's claims, asserted India's right to rebel, said that negotiation – the 'second door to Swaraj'– had failed, and announced, in effect, a second wave of assault:

> I live under no illusion. I do not think that anything that I can say this evening can possibly influence the decision of the Cabinet ...
>
> All the other parties at this meeting represent sectional interests. Congress alone claims to represent the whole of India, all interests ... It may not always have lived up to the creed. I do not know a single human organization that lives up to its creed ... But the worst critic will have to recognize ... that ... its message penetrates the remotest village of India ...
>
> Congress ... has been accused of running or desiring to run a parallel Government; and in a way I have endorsed the charge ... [You should] welcome an organization which could run a parallel Government and show that it is possible for an organization, voluntarily, without any force at its command, to run the machinery of Government even under adverse circumstances ...
>
> I heard several speakers ... saying what a dire calamity it would be if India was fired with the spirit of lawlessness, rebellion, terrorism and so on ... As a schoolboy I had to pass a paper in history also, and I read that the page of history is soiled red with the blood of those who have fought for freedom ...
>
> The dagger of the assassin, the poison bowl, the bullet of the rifleman, the spear and all these weapons and methods of destruction have been up to now used by what I consider blind lovers of liberty and freedom, and the historian has not condemned [them].
>
> The Congress then comes upon the scene and devises a new method not known to history, namely, that of civil disobedience ... But ... I am told that that is a method that no Government in the world will tolerate ... No government may

tolerate civil disobedience, but governments have to succumb even to these forces
...

A nation of 350 million people does not need the dagger of the assassin, it does not need the poison bowl, it does not need the sword, the spear or the bullet. It needs simply a will of its own, an ability to say 'No', and that nation is today learning to say 'No'...

He ended by expressing thanks:

[M]y thanks to all – from Their Majesties down to the poorest men in the East End, where I have taken up my habitation ... They have accepted me ...

[A]lthough ... the Lancashire people had perhaps some reason for becoming irritated against me, I found no irritation, no resentment even in the operatives. The operatives, men and women, hugged me ... I shall never forget that.

I am carrying with me thousands upon thousands of English friendships. I do not know them, but I read that affection in their eyes as early in the morning I walk through your streets. All this hospitality, all this kindness will never be effaced from my memory no matter what befalls my unhappy land (54: 219–31).

'With an eye and mind as pointed as a needle, he penetrated in a moment any sham.'[78] This was how Hoare, the Secretary of State for India, assessed Gandhi's performance at the RTC.

But, Depression and all, the Empire too had worked out its response: it would crush any new rebellion. Shortly before he left England, Gandhi was given a hint by Hoare that he and other Congress leaders should be ready to be arrested again.

Indian events. Mahadev conveyed the message to Patel, who quickly drew up a list of leaders to lead the Congress, one after the other, if he was arrested: Rajendra Prasad, Rajagopalachari, Ansari, Saifuddin Kitchlew, and the Sikh leader, Sardul Singh Caveeshar.

The climate was worsening in India. In Bengal, a cycle of violence and repression was followed by an ordinance superseding all laws. The UP too saw an ordinance sidelining laws after some peasant groups talked of withholding land revenue. In the Frontier Province there were restrictions on Ghaffar Khan and his brother Dr Khan Sahib. And in Gujarat, Vallabhbhai broke off from the Bardoli inquiry that Willingdon had reluctantly ordered; Patel had found the inquiry one-sided and superficial.

'I came a seeker after peace, I return fearful of war.'[79] This is what Gandhi was quoted as saying when, after a three-month stay in England, he left Victoria Station by train for Folkestone and thence by steamer for France.

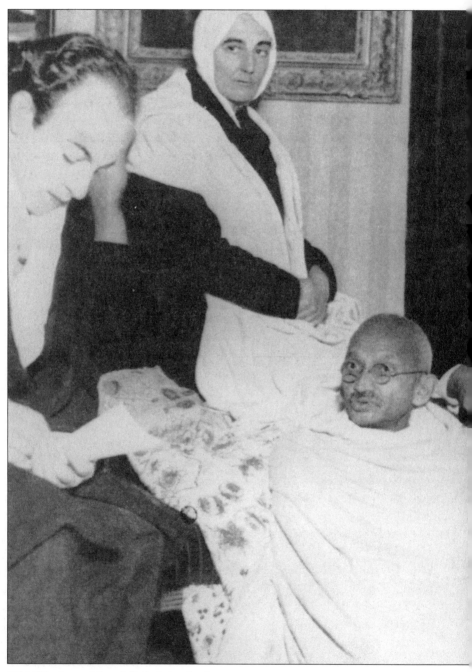

With Mira (second from left) *in Switzerland – 1931*

Children at Kingsley Hall had given Gandhi, for his birthday, 'a woolly lamb, a little doll's cradle, and some other things'. Muriel Lester observed that as Gandhi left England he placed the presents 'on the window sills of every carriage that we changed into' and kept them with him during the Channel steamer crossing.[80]

Europe en route. Gandhi and his party spent five days in Switzerland, mostly with Romain Rolland in Villeneuve, and four days in Italy, where he met Mussolini and visited the Sistine Chapel. He had not visited these countries before. At Gandhi's request, the British government gave Sergeants Evans and Rogers a paid holiday in Italy while he and his party were there.

For several years Gandhi's interpreter for Europe, Rolland (who had introduced Mira to Gandhi) was now inclining towards Marxism. Perhaps because Beethoven had first brought Mira into touch with him, Rolland played some Beethoven for the Indian party. Mira, Mahadev, Pyarelal and Devadas were much taken by the piece, but Gandhi seems merely to have said to Rolland: 'It must be beautiful, because you say so.'[81] Rolland spoke to Gandhi of the menace of fascism and counselled against his seeing Mussolini, who had expressed a wish to meet Gandhi. Assuring Rolland that he would be wary, Gandhi in turn advised carefulness about Soviet Russia. 'I follow the Russian experiment with a fundamental distrust,' he said (54: 261).

He took in Switzerland's loveliness, saying to an audience in Lausanne (8 Dec.): 'As the train was slowly gliding by your beautiful lake and as we passed the villages so beautifully clean, I could not but be entranced by the sublimity of the beauty.' He also said, in response to a question, that after repeating for years that God was love and truth, he now preferred to say that truth was God. 'What is truth?' he was asked. Gandhi replied: 'A difficult question, but I have solved it for myself by saying that it is what the voice within tells one.' But did not different inner voices speak differently? Apparently they did; hence, said Gandhi, the need for non-violence in pressing your version (54: 269–70).

In Rome he stayed with friends of Rolland, declining to be entertained by the state. Weapons displayed outside Mussolini's office repelled him and he noticed Mussolini's 'catlike' eyes,[82] but he enjoyed the paintings in the Vatican and wished he had the time to study them. He was glad too to meet Tolstoy's oldest daughter in Rome. Princess Maria, daughter of Italy's King, called on him.

As Desai and Mira both noticed, Gandhi was deeply moved, in the Sistine Chapel, by a crucifix on the altar. In *Young India* he wrote (31 Dec. 1931):

> It was not without a wrench that I could tear myself away … I saw there at once that nations like individuals could only be made through the agony of the Cross and in no other way (54: 304).

Crackdown

On 14 December 1931, at Brindisi, he boarded the *Pilsna,* which reached Bombay on 28 December. By this time Jawaharlal and the Khan brothers had been arrested. Kasturba, a grim-looking Patel and Rajagopalachari went up to the ship to meet Gandhi and gave him the news. He called it the Viceroy's Christmas present.

That evening he told a mammoth gathering at Azad Maidan that he was ready for either cooperation or struggle with the Raj. Then, authorized by the Working Committee, he asked for an interview with Willingdon. Simultaneously, Gandhi informed the Viceroy that while the Congress condemned 'assassination' and 'methods of terrorism' in 'unmeasured terms', it would also have to resist 'measures of legalized Government terrorism' (54: 349).

Willingdon took this as impudence. In the hours before dawn on 4 January, Gandhi and Patel were arrested. Other blows quickly followed. Not only all Working Committee members but leaders in every city and large village were put behind bars. Congress units were banned. Assemblies were prohibited. Meetings and processions were lathi-charged or fired upon or broken up by mounted policemen. Promising 'peace' in six weeks, Willingdon assured his admirers that the very name of the Congress would be finished. All offices and ashrams linked to the Congress were raided. Defying peasants lost more land. Press censorship was imposed, and all of India came under ordinance rule.

India hit back. Thousands defied the ordinance and the bans. In two months Willingdon had more political prisoners than Irwin at the height of the 1930 fight. The ordeal was as fiery as Gandhi had feared. Faced with overcrowded jails, officers of the Raj turned to the lash. Though the whip was not widely employed, the lathi was freely swung. According to the Congress historian, about 75,000 were arrested in January and February 1932, and about 300,000 to 400,000 beaten with lathis.[83]

Yeravda again. Between return and arrest Gandhi had managed to do a few necessary things in Bombay. He sent two English watches to Sergeants Evans and Rogers – the watches had to be English, he had said to his aides. Also, after consulting Rajagopalachari and Kasturba, he told Devadas that the son had proved himself and could now marry Lakshmi. But marriage remained distant, for soon Devadas too would be behind bars.

When the police came for Gandhi in the early hours of 4 January, it was Devadas who roused his father at Mani Bhuvan, where they were staying – the house belonged to relatives of Pranjivan Mehta. There was a farewell from Kasturba, who had been without her husband for the four months of his trip to England and was again losing him, seven days after his return. She told him, with tears in her eyes, 'Please pardon me if I have offended you in any way.' Recalling the remark later to Patel and Desai, his prison companions, Gandhi would say, 'She was afraid we might never meet again on this side of the grave.'[84] After the parting with Kasturba, Gandhi and his son walked arm in arm to the police vehicle.

Once more Regulation 25 of 1827 was invoked and there was no trial. Gandhi and Patel were driven to Yeravda where they were joined, two months later, by Desai, who was transferred from another prison. From newspapers made available to them, the three learnt that Kasturba too had been arrested, released after a few weeks, rearrested, and sentenced for six months.

Gandhi thought he would be in jail for five years this time. Even so, every hour was put to use. There were walks morning and evening, and prayers twice a day, and spinning. Patel started on a course of Sanskrit, cut twigs for brushing teeth (for Gandhi, Desai and himself), and made envelopes from waste paper.

The Raj permitting non-political correspondence, Gandhi daily wrote or dictated numerous letters, with Desai and at times Patel taking dictation. Letters he wrote to Kasturba, who was kept in Sabarmati jail, were not delivered to her, and some of her letters were not given to him. In his prison in Gorakhpur in eastern UP, Devadas fell dangerously ill with typhoid, but letters the worried father wrote to his son were held up for days by censors who did not know Gujarati.

Manilal, who was back in South Africa, was also unwell, and Harilal was quarrelling with the sisters of his late wife over the affairs of his children. Gandhi was thus living with deep, if mostly suppressed, anxieties. A hurtful letter from Harilal elicited this response:

27 Apr. 1932. [C]ontrary to my usual practice, I am preserving your letter so that, when you have awakened, you may see the insolence of your letter and weep over it and laugh at your folly ... not to throw it in your face then but only that I may laugh at it ...[85]

To Devadas, the father wrote (23 Jun. 1932):

Harilal's glass is always red. When he was conceived, I lived in ignorance. The years when he grew up were a time of self-indulgence. I certainly did not drink, but Harilal has made up for that. I sought my pleasure only with one woman. Harilal seeks his with many. It is only a difference of degree, not of kind.[86]

In another letter to Devadas (17 Jul. 1932), he said: 'All those who form or keep connections with me must pay a heavy price. It can be said that Ba has to pay the heaviest' (56: 205). A month later, writing to Ramdas, Gandhi again reflected on Kasturba's hardships:

I would not like any of you to behave towards his wife as I did towards Ba ... [S]he could not be angry with me, whereas I could with her. I did not give her the same freedom of action which I enjoyed ... (11 Aug. 1932; 56: 316–17)

Studying the stars. Gandhi practised his Urdu in Yeravda and studied the stars with the aid of a telescope loaned by Lady Thackersey. 'The stars address silent discourses to us,' he said (1 Jul. 1932). 'It is holy companionship.' In a letter to Kalelkar he imagined humans landing on planets and stars:

> It may perhaps be that on being able to reach the planets and the stars one will get the same experience of good and evil that one gets here on earth. But truly divine is the peaceful influence of their beauty and coolness at this great distance ... All these thoughts have made me a keen watcher of the infinite skies ... (56: 232)

In August he heard that Pranjivan Mehta had died in Rangoon. His inability to assist the Mehta family in its hour of need tormented him. To Mehta's nephew he wrote:

> *4 Aug. 1932:* A beautiful nest is in danger of being ruined ... I had no greater friend than Doctor in this whole world, and for me he is still alive. But I am unable to do anything from here to keep his nest whole, and that makes me unhappy (56: 286).

Desai's diary. Thanks to Desai's diary, we have a record of life and conversations in this Yeravda confinement. The three prison-mates befriended a jail cat and its kittens, with Patel at times also teasing them. Appreciating Patel's commitment to envelope-making and Sanskrit, Gandhi commented that Vallabhbhai went after useless paper (14 Jun. 1932) with 'the intentness in a cat's mind for a mouse' and learnt Sanskrit 'with the speed of an Arab horse' (28 Aug.).

Put away by the Raj, Gandhi had to find a way of regaining the initiative, but not knowing when he would be released made this hard. He and his companions tried to gauge British intentions from the talk of Raj's officers visiting them. After the commissioner of Poona called, Desai jotted down Gandhi's comment (27 Mar.) that his remarks were an 'echo of the table-talk of the ruling class'.

Gandhi was clear, however, about one move he would make: if His Majesty's Government separated the 'untouchables' in elections for the new legislatures that were being proposed, he would fast unto death. He had said as much in London. Two months after his arrest, he repeated the warning in a letter to Secretary of State Hoare.

The Yeravda three smarted on learning of Hoare's comment on the Indian disturbances: 'Dogs may bark but the caravan passes.' In October the trio heard the noise of a propeller above them – Willingdon was landing in Poona for a race. 'Thousands of rupees for one race meeting!' Gandhi said. Patel thought the Viceroy wanted 'to show that he is the ruler and Gandhi only a prisoner'.

Letters that outwitted censors sometimes gave news of the struggle outside. Winning his jailers' permission to meet some new prisoners, Gandhi learnt that places like Kheda seemed to be giving a good fight, but there were reports of fatigue as well.

On its part the Raj tried to read the minds of its Yeravda guests. On 26 May the jailer, a Major Mehta, probed the three about Mussolini. Was he not 'remarkable' and 'a beautiful personality'? 'As beautiful as a tiger,' said Mahadev. 'A cruel man,' said Gandhi. The next day Patel showed Gandhi a newspaper picture of Italian boys of eight to ten years receiving military training. 'When they grow up,' Patel remarked, 'they will help Mussolini to destroy the world.'

'You are right,' Gandhi replied. 'And Winston Churchill is a great admirer of Mussolini's ... What powerful opponents we have! But resist them we must, till the end of time.' In Yeravda in the summer of 1932, that last phrase held an ominous meaning.

The oft-sarcastic Patel would speak (11 Apr.) of Gandhi's time in England as 'the months you wasted in that country'. When the papers reported that Irwin had made a speech defending Willingdon's policy, Patel said (30 Apr.), 'See how your friend is behaving himself.'

Some of this was banter, and there were other ways too in which Vallabhbhai made his companions laugh. Usually reserved before Gandhi, Patel had become sparklingly spontaneous as a prison-mate. On 24 November, Desai recorded this conversation:

Today there was an open letter {to Gandhi} from a correspondent who signed himself as 'one who had the misfortune of living in your age'.
Bapu: 'Tell me, what sort of reply should I send him?'
Patel: 'Tell him to poison himself.'
Bapu: 'Would it not be better to say that he should poison me?'
Patel: 'I am afraid that will not help him. If he poisons you and you die, he would be sentenced to death. Then he would take his chance of rebirth along with you. It is much better that he poisons himself.'

'Sardar Vallabhbhai is with me. His jokes make me laugh until I can laugh no more, not once but several times a day.' Thus wrote Gandhi in reply to Srinivasa Sastri, who had asked if solitude did not lead to depression.[87]

If his companions eased his time, Gandhi did his bit for them, instructing Desai, for example, to 'place orders' with the jailer 'for a cooker, rice and dal' for the benefit of Patel and Desai. Finding (27 Mar.) that mosquitoes were harassing Vallabhbhai, Gandhi 'wrote a note to the jailer suggesting that he get a mosquito net at once'; it being a Sunday, he asked a warder to take the note forthwith to the jailer's house.

Ever the reformer, Gandhi tackled Patel on his manner of preparing a drink of 'lemon juice with a little soda bicarb'. He told Vallabhbhai (26 Apr.): 'You are holding the spoon wrongly. It should be held only with the handle. The other end is for stirring the drink. Again, you wiped the spoon with your handkerchief with which you wipe your mouth.' Yet Gandhi was deeply moved by Patel's care of him. He would later say, 'His affection and love overwhelmed me and reminded me of my Mother.'[88]

Thoughts of mortality were natural in Yeravda. On 11 June Gandhi spoke of death 'some day or the other', whereupon Patel chastised him: 'No, no. Don't leave us in the lurch. Bring the ship to the shore and then go where you like. And I will go with you.' You are not to go before independence. After that we would leave together. Such was the 'understanding' Patel reached with Gandhi in Yeravda.

Vallabhbhai was making envelopes on 25 May when Gandhi abruptly asked him: 'Which portfolio in the Swaraj cabinet would you like reserved for you?' 'I will take the beggar's bowl' was the alert Patel's instant response.

Gandhi replied: 'Das and Motilal used to discuss what posts they would occupy. Muhammad Ali thought he should become education minister and Shaukat Ali wanted to be the commander-in-chief.' 'Well,' added Gandhi, 'Swaraj is still to come.' Das, Nehru and Muhammad Ali being dead, and Shaukat Ali no longer a comrade, Patel would surely find a top portfolio in any Swaraj cabinet, but Gandhi's question to him indicated that he saw another as Prime Minister.

Talk of ministries, however, was not entirely wild, for by now Gandhi had made a significant decision. If 'real power' was transferred to provinces by the new constitution for India that London was working on, then, said Gandhi to Patel on 28 March (within three months of their arrest), 'we should capture the legislatures'.

A Congress government in Bombay, the UP or another province might be able to restore lands lost by rebelling peasants. Three months later, Gandhi repeated the thought to Patel, who agreed. Thus far the two had been wary of the Raj's councils. Now, in altered conditions, they were willing to see in the councils a possible response to Willingdon's repression.

Missile from prison

Aware that the final decision on separate electorates lay with the Prime Minister, the Yeravda trio wondered where MacDonald would come down.

6 July 1932:

Patel: MacDonald's award [*on electorates*] is sure to go against us.

Gandhi: I still have hope that MacDonald will stand up against the Tories.

Patel: You are wrong. They are all birds of the same feather.

Gandhi: Still I think he has his own convictions.

Patel: If he really had them would he have sold himself to the Tories? He does not wish to get off our backs.

Gandhi: [I agree] no Englishman would like to give up control over India …

Desai: Is [MacDonald] going to oppose separate electorates for Muslims?

Gandhi: No, but he cannot gulp down such electorates for the 'untouchables'.

Six weeks after this conversation, on 17 August, HMG's Award was announced: the 'untouchables', or the 'Depressed Classes' as they were formally described, would have a separate electorate. The next day Gandhi wrote to the Prime Minister that he would 'resist your decision with my life'. Unless the decision was revised, he said, he would cease taking 'food of any kind save water with or without salt and soda' from noon on 20 September.

He had thought out his tactics in detail. Asking the jail authorities to cable his letter to London, Gandhi also asked the Prime Minister to have the letter published, arguing that he wanted 'public opinion to be affected'. At the same time he bound Patel and Desai to secrecy. When they protested, Gandhi answered: 'It is far better that this should come upon everybody suddenly … Sudden shock is the treatment required.' Gandhi told Patel and Desai that it was necessary, in particular, 'to give a shock' to two men: Malaviya, the country's most respected orthodox Hindu, and Rajagopalachari, the acting Congress president who was also a champion of Hindu reform. Scholarly Brahmins both, and arrested for defying the 1932 bans, they were now out of prison. They could summon gestures of caste Hindu repentance that might persuade men like Ambedkar to forgo a separate electorate.

He wanted, said Gandhi, to 'sting the Hindu conscience'. If Hindus were not prepared to banish untouchability, they should sacrifice him 'without the slightest hesitation'. From behind thick walls a prisoner was forcing the Congress, Hindu society, the 'untouchables' and HMG to think again. To save Gandhi's life, would India's Hindus abandon practices of untouchability? If they did, would Ambedkar soften his position? If he did, would MacDonald revise his award? These were the questions of September 1932. To win Ambedkar's agreement, Gandhi said he would not only accept reserved legislature seats for the 'untouchables', he would give them twice as many seats as had been offered in HMG's award. (Gandhi's figures were closer to population ratios.) But 'untouchable' legislators should be elected by a general, not separate, electorate.

On 12 September, when Gandhi's correspondence with MacDonald and Hoare was released to the press, the impact was electric. Telegrams piled up at Yeravda, Downing Street and the Viceroy's House in New Delhi. Malaviya summoned Hindu leaders to an urgent conference in Bombay.

Mass meetings throughout India asked Gandhi not to fast and MacDonald to change his award. Replying to Rajagopalachari's telegraphed plea against the fast, Gandhi said:

I expect you to rejoice that a comrade has a God-given opportunity for a final act of satyagraha in the cause of the downtrodden (57: 33).

In other messages to caste Hindus, Gandhi said this was but the beginning. Henceforth 'an increasing army of reformers' would resist 'social, civic and political persecution of the Depressed Classes'. The issue was of 'transcendental value, far surpassing Swaraj'. He believed, Gandhi said, that his 'cry will rise to the throne of Almighty God' (57: 97).

A day before the fast was to start, a historic commitment was made. The Bombay meeting of caste Hindu leaders resolved that 'one of the earliest Acts of the Swaraj Parliament' would be to assure to 'untouchables' equal access to 'public wells, public schools, public roads and all other public institutions' (57: 118).

Once the fast started, relatives and negotiators were permitted to visit Gandhi. Allowed to join her fasting husband, Kasturba greeted him with the words, 'Again the same old story!' Gandhi had in fact longed to see her, and knew that she wanted to see him.[89] The fast had opened prison locks.

Recovering from typhoid, Devadas too was released and allowed to see his father. Gandhi advised him to say that 'as his father's son' he would rather 'forfeit his father's life' than see the suppressed classes injured. When the press published a letter from Devadas, the father, writing to Lakshmi, the girl the son hoped to marry, said: 'See what a beautiful letter Devadas has [written]' (57: 78).

In numerous letters written on the eve of the fast and in the hours before dawn on the 20th, Gandhi urged his nearest and dearest not to grieve if he died. To Khushalchand Gandhi, his older cousin (father of Chhaganlal, Maganlal and Narandas), who over the decades had remained close to him but also retained orthodox practices, Gandhi wrote on 19 September:

I am sure you will welcome the yajna* which begins tomorrow. If you approve of it as holy, I request you both to send me your sincere blessings. If I leave this world before

---

* Sacrificial offering or ritual.

you, please do not grieve, but rejoice that you had a younger brother whom God had granted the strength to complete such a yajna. You have ever been more than a brother to me. At this hour of dawn, your younger brother bows to you ... (57: 69)

In a letter to Mira written on the morning of the 20th, Gandhi admitted that when he wrote to MacDonald announcing the fast, he 'thought of you and of Ba' and hesitated, for he knew that they would be shaken. Continued Gandhi:

[F]or a time I became giddy. How would you two bear the thing? But ... the letter went. No anguish will be too terrible to wash out the sin of untouchability. You must therefore rejoice in this suffering and bear it bravely ... Just think and realize that there is no meaning in having the last look. The spirit which you love is always with you (57: 81).

Tagore rushed to see the fasting Gandhi, who lay on a cot under a mango tree, and for several minutes buried 'his face in the clothes on Gandhiji's breast'. Malaviya and C R called on the man stretched out under the tree. So did Ambedkar and other leaders of the Depressed Classes, including M C Rajah and P N Rajbhoj.

That mango tree in a prison yard became the national stage. Ambedkar's first words were, 'Mahatmaji, you have been very unfair to us.' 'It is always my lot to appear to be unfair,' Gandhi replied. According to Pyarelal (who also joined Gandhi, witnessed proceedings and later recorded them in a book), 'The redoubtable Doctor [Ambedkar], strongly supported by his colleagues, fought every inch of the ground.'[90]

The fast undoubtedly put pressure on Ambedkar, who felt the weight of Gandhi's all-India support, but orthodoxy felt an even greater weight. Defying hoary prohibitions, temples across India opened their doors overnight to 'untouchables'. In city after city, Brahmins and 'untouchables' dined together. Sarojini Naidu's daughter, Padmaja, thought she was witnessing 'a catharsis' cleansing Hinduism of 'the accumulated corruption' of centuries, and Tagore felt that a 'wonder' was 'happening before our very eyes'.[91]

After interviewing Gandhi, a reporter from the British-owned *Times of India* wrote (24 Sep.):

Under the shade of a small mango tree was Mr Gandhi lying on a cot covered with a prison blanket. At the end of [his answers,] Mr Gandhi leant back, weak from exhaustion, onto his bed. Immediately two of the jail doctors were at his side to render what help they could. But Mr Gandhi seemed to derive most comfort from Mrs Gandhi, who although obviously suffering, seemed delighted to have the opportunity of altering his pillow, rubbing his forehead with olive oil and quietly talking to him (57: 114–15).

On the evening of 24 September, leaders of 'untouchables' and of caste Hindus gathered round the tree signed the 'Poona Pact'. Malaviya signed first, followed by Ambedkar, who was followed by Rajagopalachari and Rajendra Prasad. 'Untouchable' leaders Rajah, Srinivasan and Gavai also signed.

As Gandhi's condition had entered the danger zone, word of the agreement was cabled to London, where MacDonald and his ministers accepted it, modifying the earlier award. At 5 p.m. on the 26th, after news of the alteration had reached Yeravda, Gandhi broke his fast, sipping orange juice handed to him by a relieved Kasturba. To Gandhi's joy, Tagore was present, and also Parchure Shastri, a fellow-prisoner from the ashram, who was afflicted with leprosy.

Gandhi's acceptance of reserved seats was matched by the acceptance of a common electorate by Ambedkar and other 'untouchable' leaders. Incorporated later in India's Constitution, the agreement has endured, surviving charges that Gandhi's fast had coerced Ambedkar – that fear of caste Hindu reprisals on 'untouchables' had forced Ambedkar's hand in Poona. The record of the 1932 fast and negotiations conveys no such suggestion. At that time Ambedkar said he had been 'surprised, immensely surprised' to find 'so much in common' between Gandhi and himself. 'If you devoted yourself entirely to the welfare of the Depressed Classes,' Ambedkar said to Gandhi, 'you would become our hero.'[92]

A statement Gandhi composed (26 Sep.) said that he saw 'the hand of God' in 'the glorious manifestation throughout the length and breadth of India during the past seven days'. Expressing his 'Hindu gratitude' to 'Dr Ambedkar, Rao Bahadur Srinivasan and … Rao Bahadur M. C. Rajah,' Gandhi added:

> They could have taken up an uncompromising and defiant attitude by way of punish-ment to the so-called caste Hindus for the sins of generations.
>
> If they had done so, I at least could not have resented their attitude and my death would have been but a trifling price exacted for the tortures that the outcastes of Hinduism have been going through for unknown generations. But they chose a nobler path and have thus shown that they have followed the precept of forgiveness enjoined by all religions. Let me hope that the caste Hindus will prove themselves worthy of this forgiveness … (57: 123–4)

To caste Hindus he conveyed a warning:

The political part of [the settlement] ... occupies but a small space in the vast field of reform that has to be tackled by caste Hindus during the coming days, namely, the complete removal of social and religious disabilities under which a large part of the Hindu population has been groaning.

I should be guilty of a breach of trust if I did not warn fellow reformers and caste Hindus in general that the breaking of the fast carried with it a sure promise of a resumption of it if this reform is not relentlessly pursued and achieved within a measurable period (57: 123–5).

Four days later, in a letter to Andrews, he said:

30 Sep. 1932: I did expect a mighty response from the orthodox, but I was unprepared for the sudden manifestation that took place. But I shall not be deceived. It remains to be seen whether the temples opened remain open and the various other things done persist (57: 134).

For the moment, however, a 63-year-old prisoner had made history on two counts. One, lying flat on his back under a jail-yard tree, he had imposed his will on a stern Empire. Two, he had awakened the long-dormant conscience of Hindu society.

In Wardha – 1939 (Original photo: Udit Gopal)

11

Negotiating Repression

In and out of prison, 1932–6

Willingdon, too, could count gains. Indian defiance had petered out, Gandhi's non-violent soldiers were exhausted and in many cases uprooted, and Gandhi himself was behind bars, cut off from family and most colleagues, his subversive ashram almost empty, his seditious journals banned.

His success on the 'untouchable' issue was no doubt a fly in the ointment, yet the Raj did not silence Gandhi on that question. After his fast ended, other jail restrictions were quickly re-imposed, but he was not barred from commenting on untouchability. The Raj's hope was that Gandhi would draw fire both from orthodox Hindus and from men like Ambedkar. Patel and Desai feared that the Raj's calculation might prove right, but Gandhi seized the opening his fast had created. His pen and heart were hungry to interact again with his people, even if solely over the evil of untouchability.

From September 1932 he started calling the 'untouchables' 'Harijans' ('People of God'), a phrase first proposed in 1931 by an 'untouchable' reader of *Navajivan,* who cited that usage by Gujarat's 15th-century saint-poet, Narsi Mehta (the author of *Vaishnava Jana*). Calling himself a 'self-chosen Harijan', Gandhi would explain (28 Apr. 1933) that

> The term has not been coined with a view to perpetuating the separate identity of Harijans ... The term 'untouchable' savours of contempt ... [I]n so far as untouchables have a distinct identity we must have a name by which to call them ... Let us pray that this separateness may be done away with so that all of us may become fit to be called 'Harijans'– men of God. A friend rightly said that today caste Hindus have become 'Arijans'– enemies of Hinduism.[1]

Week after week he wrote from prison on the question, and the press published his comments. On 5 November 1932 he reminded caste Hindus of 'the wrongs we have heaped' on the heads of the 'untouchables':

> Socially they are lepers. Economically they are worse than slaves. Religiously they are denied entrance to places we miscall 'houses of God'. They are denied the use, on the same terms as the caste men, of public roads, public hospitals, public wells, public taps, public parks and the like, and in some cases their approach within a measured distance is a social crime, [or] ... their very sight is an offence.
>
> They are relegated for their residence to the worst quarters of cities or villages where they practically get no social services. Caste Hindu lawyers and doctors will not serve them ... Brahmins will not officiate at their religious functions. The wonder is that they are at all able to eke out an existence or that they still remain within the Hindu fold. They are too downtrodden to rise in revolt against their suppressors (57: 332).

From February 1933 he was even permitted to edit, from his cell, a new journal, the English-language *Harijan,* which was soon joined by the Gujarati *Harijanbandhu* ('Brother to Harijans'), and the Hindi *Harijan Sevak* ('Servant of Harijans').

Also, he blessed two bills moved in the Central Assembly by an elected member, Ranga Iyer, one seeking to prohibit discrimination against Harijans, and the other making it unlawful for an orthodox minority to bar Harijans from entering a temple. The second Bill arose from the failure of a reformist majority of worshippers at the Guruvayur temple in Kerala to have the temple opened to Harijans.

Patel pointed out to Gandhi that while Malaviya opposed Ranga Iyer's bills, Ambedkar had said that the 'untouchables' did not really care about temple entry. Desai said he thought 'we would be crushed between the upper and the nether stones of the orthodox Hindus and the followers of Ambedkar'. Patel's advice was that Gandhi should 'let the two parties quarrel', not allow himself 'to come between' the two. Disagreeing, Gandhi told Patel and Desai (16 Feb. 1933) that 'millions of Harijans' could not be allowed to 'feel that they have been left to their fate'.

Through *Harijan* Gandhi encouraged Rajagopalachari to leave the Congress chair and lobby in New Delhi for the bills. The idea of C R lobbying in an Assembly the Congress had boycotted made many uneasy, and from his prison in the UP Nehru sent Gandhi a strong protest.

But Gandhi knew what he was doing: the author of non-cooperation was now starting to prepare his countrymen to accept the Raj's councils. As we know, for about a year now – from April in the previous year – Gandhi had been thinking, with Patel's full agreement, of 'capturing the legislatures', a switch in strategy dictated by Willingdon's repression.

Another debate with Ambedkar. Though he had signed the Poona Pact, Ambedkar continued to clash with Gandhi. Declining Gandhi's request for 'a message' for the opening issue of *Harijan,* he nonetheless sent a 'statement' where he said that nothing short of 'the destruction of the caste system' would finish untouchability: outcastes existed because there were castes. Ambedkar also indicated a readiness to leave the Hindu fold.

On his part Gandhi linked untouchability not to the existence of castes but to the notion of high-and-low, and saw 'an attack on untouchability' as also 'an attack on this 'high-and-low-ness'. On 14 February Gandhi said:

> If this doctrine of utmost superiority and utmost inferiority, descending from father to son for eternity, is an integral part of Hinduism ... then I no more want to belong to it than does Dr Ambedkar. But ... there is no superiority or inferiority in the Hinduism of my conception.
>
> I invite Dr Ambedkar to shed his bitterness and anger and try to learn the beauties of the faith of his forefathers. Let him not curse Hinduism without making an unbiased study of it, and if it fails to sustain him in his hour of need, by all means let him forsake it (59: 275).

Ambedkar was not persuaded. At the other end, bowing before orthodox pressure, Ranga Iyer would withdraw his bills, and there were ugly demonstrations by purist 'sanatanists' against Gandhi. An old friend, Ranchhoddas Patwari (whose temporary loan had assisted Gandhi's 1888 journey to London), demanded precise replies to 88 questions (all patiently answered by Gandhi), predicted that Gandhi's stand against orthodoxy would wreck the Congress, suggested that Gandhi had 'completely forsaken dharma', and spoke of a break between them (58: 436–46).

But Hindus who wanted reform felt Gandhi to be their champion, as did Hindus who cherished Hindu unity, and so did a great many 'untouchables'. Once again seeing more clearly than his critics, Gandhi realized that the bulk of the Hindu community would follow him and that the purists were isolating themselves. To Nehru he wrote:

> *15 Feb. 1933:* The fight against sanatanists is becoming more and more interesting if also increasingly difficult ... The abuses they are hurling at me are wonderfully refreshing. I am all that is bad and corrupt on this earth. But the storm will subside. For I apply the sovereign remedy of ahimsa – non-retaliation. The more I ignore the abuses, the fiercer they are becoming. But it is the death dance of the moth round a lamp (59: 278–9).

Another fast. He consolidated his position through a fresh fast, this time 'a self-purificatory' one for 21 days, undertaken in May 1933. The last one had put pressure on orthodoxy and also on Ambedkar. Now, making no demands of anyone, he would put pressure only on himself. Since fasting was a time-honoured Hindu practice, the self-imposed ordeal underlined his Hinduness. It also brought about his release.

We should not assume that he anticipated all his gains before starting the fast. According to his own account of its origin, for two or three nights he was agitated and could not sleep. Reports from the ashram of indiscipline and of friction between a Harijan and other members had troubled him, and the attacks by Ambedkar and the sanatanists were on his mind. When he retired on the night of 29 April he had no idea (he told Vallabhbhai the next morning),

> that something was coming up … But after eleven I woke up, I watched the stars, repeated Ramanama but the same thought would persistently come to my mind: 'If you have grown so restless, why don't you undertake [a] fast? Do it.' The inner dialogue went on for quite some time. At half past twelve came the clear, unmistakable voice: 'You must undertake the fast' (61: 40).

If they would give it, Gandhi sought (through scores of separate letters) the approval of Tagore, Malaviya, Srinivasa Sastri, Jawaharlal, Andrews, Anasuya Sarabhai and other friends. Feeling fit and fully expecting to survive the fast, Gandhi also thought that his power to influence events would be enhanced by it:

> The evil (of untouchability) is far greater than even I had thought it to be. It will not be eradicated by money, external organization and even political power for Harijans, though all these three are necessary. But to be effective, they must follow or at least accompany … inward power … This can only come by fasting and prayer (61: 38–9).

The news that the imprisoned Gandhi would fast for 21 days to purify himself produced an electric effect all over again. From afar Smuts cabled his anxiety, as did hundreds of others from across India, but Gandhi may have been most affected by a telegram from Harilal, who said, 'I undertake to do anything you would ask me to, but please do give up the fast.'

'If I could get Harilal back,' Gandhi remarked to Kalelkar, who was with him, 'I would fast for forty-two days.'[2] To his son Gandhi cabled back: 'Your letter touches me. If this fast means your return to pure life it would be doubly blessed. See me. I shall try to guide you. God bless you' (61: 94).

Devadas, 'my youngest son and valued comrade', as Gandhi called him, made (in his father's words) a 'fervent personal appeal, strengthened by a copious flow of tears' (61: 86). C R protested, as did Patel, and from Sabarmati prison, where Kasturba had returned and Mira too was lodged, the latter sent a cable on behalf of Kasturba and herself:

Got news of fast only today. Ba wishes me say she greatly shocked. Feels decision very wrong but you have not listened to any others so will not hear her. She sends her heartfelt prayers. I am stunned but know it is the voice of God and in that sense rejoice even in midst of anguish. Deepest prayers. Love.

In his cabled reply, Gandhi said:

2 May 1933: Tell Ba her father imposed on her a companion whose weight would have killed any other woman. I treasure her love. She must remain courageous to end. For you I have nothing but only thanks to God for giving you to me. You must prove your bravery by sustained joy over this newest of God's missions for me. Love (61: 49).

Kasturba was allowed to join him in Yeravda, and a grateful Gandhi wrote to Mira: 'Ba has responded magnificently. Her courage has been a source of the greatest strength to me' (61: 72). As for Mira herself, Gandhi acknowledged that her ordeal as a solitary prisoner in Sabarmati prison would be 'more searching' than his own (61: 137).

On the night of 8 May, some hours after the fast began, the Raj released Gandhi, not wishing to risk his death in custody. This could not have been a complete surprise to Gandhi. Mahadev was also set free. Declaring that he would not take advantage of his release, Gandhi asked M S Aney, the acting Congress president, to announce a six-week suspension of disobedience.

Leaving Vallabhbhai behind in Yeravda, Gandhi, Kasturba and Desai moved to 'Parnakuti', the Poona home of Lady Premlila Thackersey. Aided by Kasturba's 'nursing and massaging and preparing his feeds with all her devoted and loving care' (to quote Desai), the fast, begun on 8 May, was endured fairly easily by him (61: 146).

After Gandhi had fasted for 13 days, his friend-cum-grand-nephew Mathuradas Trikamji, who also had joined to help, said in a letter:

I am writing these lines from a corner from where I constantly … look at him. He lies in his cot like a sweet child, beaming with brightness (61: 142).

As during previous fasts, a confident, demanding general had turned into a dependent, child-like, serene and adorable person. On 29 May, Gandhi thanked 'the doctors and other friends who have poured their affection on me during these days of privilege and grace', and added:

> Within a minute or two I am going to break the fast. In His name and with faith in Him was it taken, in His name it terminates ... You will not expect me to make a speech on this occasion. It is an occasion for taking the name and singing the glory of God (61: 143).

Responding to repression

Breadwinners had gone to prison for long periods in 1930 and 1932, and many were still inside. Donations to the Congress were banned, and its funds had either been seized or dried up. As Gandhi recognized in a letter to Andrews, Willingdon's ordinance rule had 'struck the people dumb'. The masses were 'terror-struck' and 'the well-to-do' were 'trembling in their shoes' through fear of the Raj. 'And so there is a kind of dead calm which even in my bed, isolated though I am from contact with people through the orders of doctors, I can't help sensing.'

But Gandhi was not giving up, for, he wrote to Andrews, 'time ... counts in our favour', and there was 'a certainty of the final triumph' (61: 164).

Andrews had asked Gandhi to concentrate on untouchability removal 'for the whole remainder of your life, without turning to the right or the left'. Recalling that Gandhi had 'again and again' said that with untouchability Indians were 'not fit' for swaraj, Andrews asked his friend not to try 'to serve two masters'.[3] This was what Ambedkar too had urged, but Gandhi turned down the advice:

> *To Andrews, 15 Jun. 1933*: Now for your important argument about untouchability. But there is this initial flaw about it. My life is one indivisible whole. It is not built after the compartmental system – satyagraha, civil resistance, untouchability, Hindu-Muslim unity, [etc.,] ... are indivisible parts of a whole ...
>
> You will find at one time in my life an emphasis on one thing, at another time on other. But that is just like a pianist, now emphasizing one note and now other. But they are all related to one another.
>
> Therefore you see how it is utterly impossible for me to say: 'I have now nothing to do with civil disobedience or Swaraj!' Not only so ... Full and final removal of untouchability ... is utterly impossible without Swaraj ... Love. Mohan (61: 163–6).

As to how to work for Swaraj, Gandhi would try a modified strategy. During two conversations held in Poona on 1 and 2 June 1933, Gandhi and C R agreed that the mass struggle should come to an end.

Confirming the conclusion that Gandhi and Patel had reached in Yeravda, Gandhi and C R also agreed that it might be necessary at some point to 'think of taking power in our hands', even under 'the constitution they [the British] are framing'. Meanwhile a small number should keep up the struggle, and Gandhi should ask Willingdon for an interview, even though 'we will get the same reply from the Viceroy' (61: 480–4). Deliberating in Poona in Gandhi's presence, Aney and other free Congress leaders endorsed the new approach.

Devadas married. On 16 June 1933, after six years of waiting during which Devadas, his father and Rajagopalachari had all gone to prison more than once, and Devadas had been on the brink of death, he and Lakshmi were married, in 'Parnakuti' in Poona.

Because the bride and groom belonged to different castes, the ceremony was performed by a young reformist priest from Maharashtra, Laxman Shastri Joshi. Gandhi, Kasturba, Rajagopalachari and a handful of guests attended. Gandhi addressed the couple, but it took him 'over five minutes to gather sufficient strength to speak', for he was not only weak from the fast, he was deeply moved:

> Devadas, you know my expectations about you. May you fulfil them … Who knew that your wedding would take place under the roof of the pure-souled Lady Thackersey? Who knew that a man of great learning and spotless character like Laxman Shastri would be found to act as priest?
>
> You have today robbed Rajagopalachari of a cherished gem. May you be worthy of it!
>
> May God protect you! Only He protects, for He is the father, mother, and friend, everything rolled into one. Let your life be a dedication to the service of the motherland, and of humanity. May you both ever be humble, and may you both walk in fear of God always! (From *The Hindu* and *The Hindustan Times*, 17 Jun. 1933; 61: 167–8)

A concerned father was again revealed in a letter that Gandhi sent to Mira (21 Jun.): 'Nothing is certain as to where Devadas is to stay in future or what he is to do. It is enough that both he and Lakshmi are very happy …' (61: 180)

Rebuff, response & the break-up of the ashram. In the middle of July Gandhi sought an interview with Willingdon 'with a view to exploring possibilities of peace' and received the expected rebuff (61: 228). Gandhi's response was two-fold. One, he would personally offer disobedience in Gujarat. Two, he would disband the Sabarmati ashram before the

Raj seized it – movables from the ashram had already been confiscated to recover fines or taxes that the ashramites had refused to pay.

With the disbandment, every inmate was expected to 'constitute a walking ashram, carrying with him or her the responsibility for realizing the ashram ideal … in prison or outside' (61: 274). This was a tough and painful decision, arrived at after consulting ashramites not in prison. Like Gandhi, they were willing to offer individual disobedience: when thousands across India had lost property, Gandhi could not exempt his ashram, and its members could not play safe.

However, Gandhi freed the ashram's Harijans from the contemplated action: he did not want them to lose their dwellings or their school. He made sure, too, that the ashram's stock of khadi, looms and charkhas, its cattle, and its cash were transferred to trusts independent of law-breaking activities; and the 11,000 books in the ashram library were gifted to the Ahmedabad municipality. But he would vacate the Ashram's land, buildings and crops before the Raj took them by force.

In a letter asking the Home Secretary in Bombay to take over the property, Gandhi indicated what the ashram, his 'first constructive act on return to India in 1915', had meant to him:

> 26 Jul. 1933: Every head of cattle and every tree has its history and sacred associations. [The ashramites] are all members of a big family. What was once a barren plot of land has been turned by human endeavour into a fair-sized model garden colony. It will not be without a tear that we shall break up the family and its activities (61: 266–9).

At 64, Gandhi was breaking up what had been his home for 16 years, repeating previous (and always wrenching) exercises in Phoenix, Tolstoy Farm, Johannesburg, Durban, Bombay and Rajkot.

Arrests again. On 31 July he declared that he would march with Kasturba and several companions towards the Kheda village of Ras, where many peasants had lost their lands. That night he and his party were arrested and confined in Sabarmati jail. On 2 August he, Kasturba and Desai were transferred to Yeravda. On 4 August he was released but ordered to stay in Poona. When he tried to move out of Poona, he was arrested again and sentenced to a year.

Across India several hundred individuals, including C R and Prasad, again defied the Raj and once more found themselves in prison. Patel and the Khan brothers were in jail continuously from January 1932. Released in August 1933, Jawaharlal was rearrested in February 1934. Within a few weeks of his marriage, Devadas too was arrested near Delhi, where he had hoped to start a career in journalism, when he refused to sign a pledge forswearing disobedience.

Two prominent Congressmen not in prison, and not in India, were Vithalbhai Patel and Subhas Bose, who disapproved of Gandhi's focus on untouchability. In May 1933 the two declared from Austria that Gandhi's leadership had failed, but in October Vithalbhai died in a clinic near Geneva.

Fast, release and reflection. In India the new arrests did not greatly lift morale. Not that Gandhi or anybody else thought they would. The disobedience struggle seemed to be on its last legs, and Congress supporters dispirited and in disarray.

Bitterly disappointed at not finding Patel in Yeravda – the Raj had removed him to Nasik Jail – Gandhi demanded facilities in his cell for Harijan work. When these were denied, he began a fast on 16 August. Two days later he declined an offer of conditional release. On 20 August, his condition worsening, he was moved to Sassoon Hospital, where he had had his appendix removed in 1924. Three days later, when it appeared that he would not survive, he was unconditionally released. Kasturba, along with some other women, remained confined in Yeravda.

His release, Gandhi said on 25 August, 'is a matter of no joy for me. Possibly it is a matter of shame that I took my comrades to prison and came out of it by fasting' (61: 339). But instead of repeating a cycle of defiance, arrest, fasting, release and rearrest, he chose 'not to take the offensive' until August 1934, when his one-year sentence would expire.[4] Meanwhile, he would do Harijan work.

Had repression defeated satyagraha? Gandhi once more faulted himself and other satyagrahis, not satyagraha. Their satyagraha had been imperfect, he said. But the truth was that repression called for flexibility; mechanical defiance was merely ruinous. As we have seen, Gandhi was willing, if quietly at first, to examine the option that several in the Congress were now advocating: entering the Raj's councils and capturing office in the provinces.

HMG's scheme. This thinking was encouraged by a White Paper on political reform in India that HMG had issued in March 1933. The White Paper offered wide powers to elected provincial legislatures and proposed a new federal assembly where princes or their nominees would fill a third of the seats.

Neither Gandhi nor anyone close to him could countenance a major role by hereditary princes in a federal assembly, but provincial power merited a look. Though a provincial ministry would be circumscribed by reserve powers vested in the Viceroy and the governor, it might, among other things, restore the freedom fighters' lands and help with a future fight.

In September 1933, Jawaharlal, enjoying an interval between prison terms, talked privately and at length with Gandhi in Poona. More upset than Gandhi by the petering out of defiance, and less willing to recognize the value of provincial office, Nehru was also troubled by Gandhi's concentration on the Harijan question; he saw a 'danger' of 'other issues obscuring' the goal of independence.[5]

In a letter written after the talks, Gandhi sought to reassure his younger colleague: 'I have no sense of defeat in me and the hope in me that this country of ours is fast marching towards its goal is burning as bright as it did in 1920.'[6]

A new base, and touring India again. Later in September he moved to Wardha, near Nagpur. Situated at the eastern end of the Marathi country, Wardha was Jamnalal Bajaj's town, hotter than Ahmedabad but close to India's geographical centre. At the end of August, after Gandhi had vacated Sabarmati, Bajaj urged Gandhi to make Wardha his base. Vinoba Bhave was already in the region – Gandhi had sent him there in the early 1920s – running an ashram and enjoying Bajaj's support and loyalty.

Within days of arriving in Wardha, where he was put up in Bajaj's garden guest-house, Gandhi seemed to adopt it as a home and started giving 'Satyagraha Ashram, Wardha' as his address on letters he wrote.

In November, after he had gained strength, Gandhi, now 64, began another all-India tour, this time with an exclusive focus against untouchability. With his wife, Desai, Pyarelal and other companions in jail, he had new aides and travelling colleagues, but after her release in the new year Mira joined the party.

Between November and March he visited Nagpur and the Berar (Vidarbha) area of the Marathi country; Bilaspur and the large tribal tract of Chhattisgarh; the Hindi-speaking Mahakoshal region of central India; Bhopal and Delhi and places adjacent; Bezwada and over 70 towns and villages in the Telugu country; the Kannada and Malayalam regions; the Tamil country; the Coorg area; and Mangalore, Belgaum, Bijapur and other places in south-western India.

Everywhere he collected money for the Harijan cause, wrote for his new weeklies, visited quarters where Harijans lived, sought their entry into temples, and insisted that any welcome address presented to him in a town or village should describe the condition of its Harijans. After a huge earthquake on 15 January 1934 destroyed towns and villages in north Bihar, Gandhi sought money for Bihar as well but refused, despite urgings by some, to divert Harijan funds to earthquake relief.

New debate with Tagore. A newly released Rajendra Prasad raised funds and organized relief in Bihar, as did the government, and Gandhi sent his associate Kumarappa to serve as the custodian of Bihar's relief funds. In remarks in Tinnevelly and Tuticorin in the Tamil country, Gandhi observed that 'the government and the people have become one' in face of the calamity.

Also, however, he controversially suggested that the earthquake was 'a divine chastisement' for 'the great sin' committed for centuries by the so-called higher castes against Harijans, a 'calamity handed down … from century to century' (63: 38–40).

Criticizing Gandhi's 'superstitious' argument, Tagore said that the logic 'far better suits the psychology of [Gandhi's] opponents than his own', and that the orthodox were likely to 'hold [Gandhi] and his followers responsible for the visitation of Divine anger' (63: 516). But Gandhi could not resist using the earthquake to drive home the iniquity of untouchability.

[W]hilst we have yet breathing time [*he said on 24 Jan.*], let us get rid of the distinctions of high and low, purify our hearts, and be ready to face our Maker when an earthquake or some natural calamity or death in the ordinary course overtakes us (63: 40).

In March and April, he spent more than four weeks in Bihar's devastated areas, consoling victims and supporting Prasad's relief work, and again linked the calamity to untouchability. There were angry protests from sanatanists, who came with black flags to his meetings.

These drew immense crowds, as his meetings in southern and central India had done. He interpreted the vigorous response of caste Hindus to his attacks on the doctrine of high-and-low as a sign that 'untouchability has become weak and limp'.[7]

The 'non-political' tour was also reviving Congress confidence and demonstrating Gandhi's continuing appeal. On 2 April 1934 a bolstered Gandhi made – in Saharsa, Bihar – the statement of retreat that he had been waiting to make:

[A]fter much searching of the heart I have arrived at the conclusion that in the present circumstances only one, and that myself and no other, should for the time being bear the responsibility of civil resistance ...

I must advise all Congressmen to suspend civil resistance for Swaraj as distinguished from specific grievances. They should leave it to me alone ... I give this opinion as the author and initiator of satyagraha ... I am quite convinced that this is the best course in the interests of India's fight for freedom (63: 247–9).

In another significant move, he summoned colleagues from the disbanded Sabarmati ashram to Patna and told them that they should not hesitate to look for jobs, or imagine that he wanted them to court jail again. His sons Ramdas and Devadas, he said, had gone into jobs (Devadas was freed in February 1934); he did not like it but had not objected. Others too should feel free 'to start earning'. 'Only those who are willing to die and get buried in jail should go there.'

Hinting that a struggle phase had ended, Gandhi, however, added that those 'who are out today, earning money' would find a future 'opportunity' to 'plunge' again into a sacrificial battle 'of their own accord'.[8] Such a battle would have to be waged again; he knew better than to hope that the British would leave India through constitutional talks.

'This lull does not affect the march,' he wrote to Agatha Harrison, a Quaker friend. 'It is a precursor to the full awakening' (63: 73).

Opening doors. Yet, without suspending disobedience the Congress could not hope for a lifting of the bans on Congress bodies, or for a chance to contest the elections to the Central Assembly, due in November that year, or to contest provincial elections due later. With the suspension Gandhi opened doors for those in the Congress, but in an ingenious qualification that saved self-respect, his own and that of the Congress, he also reserved himself as a possible satyagrahi.

The last person elected as the Congress president, Vallabhbhai, was still in prison, and not expected to be out until mid-July. After six months of freedom, Jawaharlal, Patel's immediate predecessor, was again in jail for no one knew how long. The Frontier's Khan brothers too were behind bars. But Gandhi felt he had the duty to initiate an inescapable change. He knew that Patel agreed at least partially with him, and he was confident that Nehru too would come round.

In his prison Nehru was jolted, writing in a diary that Gandhi's announcement 'bowled him over', and fearing he would have to break with Gandhi.[9] Despite his readiness 'to capture' legislatures, Vallabhbhai too felt 'puzzled' and 'pained' that Gandhi had 'snatched away the weapon with which he had armed the people'.[10] But C R (released in February 1934), Prasad, Ansari and a great majority of the Congress acknowledged Gandhi's realism.

> *Gandhi to Patel, 18 Apr. 1934:* I hope you have fully understood my decision ... I feel that [it] was absolutely correct. It has been taken neither too late nor too early ...
>
> I think it is our duty to give full freedom to Congressmen who favour entering the legislatures. It is but right that those who daily attend legislatures in their thoughts should do so physically as well ... Is it not better that one who daily eats jalebi* in his imagination should eat the real thing and know the wisdom or folly of doing so? ...
>
> I see that [Rajagopalachari] fully approves of the move ... Rajendrababu has been in favour of it from the beginning (63: 408).

Catching Gandhi's signal, Haig, the home member in Delhi, announced that an AICC meeting called to ratify Gandhi's call would not be banned. In May the AICC met in Patna in Gandhi's presence, confirmed the suspension, and agreed that the Congress as such, rather than Swarajists acting on its behalf, would enter legislatures. In June, bans on most Congress bodies were lifted. Mindful of the elections due in November, Gandhi asked Ansari to chair a Congress Parliamentary Board (CPB).

---

* Jalebi = an Indian sweet.

Kasturba

Gandhi exchanged weekly letters with his wife in Yeravda jail. Not allowed to correspond with anyone else, Kasturba could, however, see copies of the Gujarati weeklies *Harijanbandhu* and *Jam-e-Jamshed*. She asked Gandhi to include a spiritual discourse in his weekly letter, which he usually did. He also described for her the places he was in, or events such as the Bihar earthquake, and week by week gave news of dozens of people she was interested in.

Harilal's habit of getting into trouble and into the newspapers, the courage of his son Kanti, who was in jail as a satyagrahi, the situation with Kasturba's brother Madhavdas, Manilal's struggles in South Africa, the eyes of Ramdas's daughter Sumitra, the playfulness of Manilal's daughter Sita, the pregnancies of Ramdas's wife Nirmala and Devadas's wife Lakshmi, how Mahadev and Pyarelal were faring in their jails, her health or his — such were the subjects they wrote about.

The couple's concern for each other came across. Though separated, they were together in anxiety while their great-granddaughter Kusum (born to Rami, Harilal's daughter) lay seriously ill. When Kusum died, Gandhi wrote to Rami and Rami's sister Manu:

1 Feb. 1934: Even I, though my heart is as hard as stone, felt grieved for a moment. Both you sisters will have calmed down [by the time] you get this letter ... Keep writing to me. I will expect a letter from Rami. Ba will be very much pained at the news (63: 76).

Occasionally there was humour. 'You should now stop worrying about Manilal,' Gandhi wrote to Kasturba on 8 March. 'I hope you do remember that he is past forty now' (63: 262). What he wrote on 6 April probably gave her, and Gandhi himself, some relief:

I have now decided to stop all others from going to jail. I alone should offer satyagraha. Hence, when all of you are released you will not have to offer satyagraha again for the present (63: 359).

Released at the end of May, Kasturba joined her husband in June.

Bomb. Between April and August, the month when he completed his all-India Harijan tour, Gandhi was in Assam, north and south Bihar, Orissa, Bombay, Poona, Gujarat, Ajmer in central India, Sindh, the Punjab, Bengal, UP and Bihar again. Once more, and for the fifth time, he had covered virtually all of India, mostly by third-class train, partly by car, and often on foot. Once more great numbers greeted him everywhere, drawing and giving strength.

Harijans and reformists thrilled to him. In places visited by him schools or hostels

Kasturba Gandhi – 1938 (Original photo: Kanu Gandhi)

for Harijans were set up; temples opened doors to Harijans; and Gandhi collected funds for the Harijan Sevak Sangh, or the Servants of Harijans Society.

His sanatanist opponents were violent at times. In Benares his portrait was burnt, and in Karachi a Hindu carrying an axe was apprehended before he could attack Gandhi. In Orissa, Gandhi was abused near Puri's famed Jagannath Temple, from which Harijans were barred. On 25 April he escaped an attack by lathi-wielding sanatanists when he alighted at Jasidih station in Bihar. Prevented by the welcoming party from hitting Gandhi, they repeatedly struck the car he entered, but he was not hurt.

Two months later, on 25 June in Poona, an unknown assailant threw a bomb at a car thought to be carrying Gandhi for a talk at the Municipal Building. Occupants were injured but Gandhi was not in the car. Informed of the attack on reaching the venue, he referred to it in his remarks:

> I have had so many narrow escapes in my life that this newest one does not surprise me. God be thanked that no one was fatally injured by the bomb …
>
> The sorrowful incident has undoubtedly advanced the Harijan cause … I am not aching for martyrdom, but if it comes in my way in the prosecution of what I consider to be [my] supreme duty … I shall have well earned it …
>
> Let those who grudge me what yet remains [of my life] know that it is the easiest thing to do away with my body. Why then put in jeopardy many innocent lives in order to take mine which they hold to be sinful? …
>
> I have nothing but deep pity for the unknown thrower of the bomb. If I had my way and if the bomb-thrower was known, I should certainly ask for his discharge (64: 94).

The bomb-thrower in Poona was not caught or identified, and we do not know whether he had any links to the group that would eventually kill Gandhi. The following month, in Ajmer, Pandit Lalnath, a sanatanist leader, was hit on the head. Gandhi visited him to apologize.

Congress politics

As July progressed, all eyes were on Gandhi, whose self-imposed abstention from politics was to end on 3 August. Would he exercise the right, now confined to him alone, to defy the Raj and court imprisonment? If he did, could the Congress think of contesting elections?

By now back in Wardha, Gandhi fasted for a week from 7 August, in reparation, he said, for the attack on Lalnath. Later, after Patel (freed in July) and Rajagopalachari had conferred with Gandhi, a relieved C R said in a letter to Devadas: 'It is fairly certain that he will NOT go to prison.'[11]

Released on an 11-day parole because of his wife's illness, Jawaharlal sent Gandhi (13 Aug. 1934) a long, bitter letter about the state of the Congress. Grudgingly reconciled to the suspension of disobedience, and ready to imagine, 'under certain circumstances, entering a legislature myself', Nehru, however, spoke of himself as 'a revolutionary' resenting opposition in the Congress to 'the advanced and fighting elements in the Congress ranks' (64: 455–62).

The last phrase referred chiefly to a Socialist Party born inside the Raj's prisons in March 1934. Envisaged as a party within the Congress, its leaders were Jayaprakash Narayan of Bihar (who had returned to India in 1930), Narendra Deva and Rammanohar Lohia from the UP, Minoo Masani, Yusuf Meherally, and Asoka Mehta of Bombay, and Achyut Patwardhan of Maharashtra.

A professed socialist but not a member of the new faction, Jawaharlal was in some ways their hero, yet they felt an allegiance also to Gandhi, who publicly welcomed the group's formation while expressing disapproval of violence and class war and claiming that his voluntary poverty made him a truer, real-life socialist.

However, a majority in the Congress, led by Patel, C R and Prasad, were wary of socialism, and to Jawaharlal's dismay the Working Committee, with Gandhi's approval, warned against 'loose talk'. Asking Jawaharlal not to be hard on the Working Committee, Gandhi added (17 Aug. 1934): 'I fancy that I have the knack for knowing the need of the time ... After the explosion I want construction' (64: 302–3).

Resignation. At the end of August, Gandhi gave Nehru (who was back in jail), Patel, C R, Prasad, Azad and other colleagues a shock, announcing that he was retiring from the Congress! In a letter (5 Sep.) addressed to Patel – the last elected president of the Congress – Gandhi explained that cogitation during the travelling, 'non-political' months had led to the decision. Finding that many who differed from him suppressed their views, he saw himself as a 'stifling' force, 'arresting [the] full play of reason' (64: 394–6).

Division in the Congress had influenced him, he said. Patel, C R and Prasad, all three holding conservative economic views but seen as Gandhi's loyal colleagues, nursed sharp misgivings about the socialists, but Gandhi felt a bond with the latter as well, and we know of his faith in Nehru.

Was he then with the rightists or the socialists? He felt he was for both sides and against neither. The best way of not lending his weight to either side was to leave the Congress. The two groups should fend for themselves, if necessary have it out with one another, and find their levels. If a need arose, he would try from outside to unite the groups.

Then there was his advancing age, plus the attacks on his person – the Congress should learn to think of a future without him. Finally, Gandhi sensed that his retirement could facilitate a settlement between the Congress and the Raj. If this did not come about, and another clash proved necessary, the Congress could always summon him to lead it.

Azad protested, and a disconcerted Rajagopalachari argued that Gandhi would 'surely be disappointed' if he thought that he could retire and still keep the Congress or himself 'politically important', but Gandhi was being astute. 'I do not retire to a cave,' he told Rajagopalachari. 'I hold myself at everybody's disposal.'[12]

His retirement would in fact enable the Congress to present a cooperative face while the chief rebel remained in the wings, available, when the time came, to resume fighting.

Released in August 1934, the Khan brothers spent several weeks with Gandhi, Bajaj and Desai in Wardha, and Ghaffar Khan had his teenage daughter Mehr Taj brought from England to study there. Gandhi seems to have probed Ghaffar Khan about presiding at the Congress session set for the last week of October in Bombay: retirement did not mean taking his hands off. Wary, however, of all-India burdens, the Frontier leader declined Gandhi's 'offer'.

Another possible candidate, Rajagopalachari, had felt disqualified 'on account of my ignorance of Hindi',[13] and the choice fell on Rajendra Prasad, whose work for earthquake relief had enhanced his reputation. While praising Prasad as one 'whose sacrifice for the nation, judged whether in quality or quantity, is not to be excelled', Gandhi made sure, through his letter to Patel (5 Sep.), that the Congress knew what he thought of the absent Nehru, who had 'many years of service in front of him':

I miss at this juncture the association and advice of Jawaharlal who is bound to be the rightful helmsman of the organization in the near future (64: 394–6).

It was a measure of Patel's fibre, and of his own candour, that Gandhi could write plainly to Vallabhbhai that Jawaharlal would be the future leader.

Gandhi was not breaking with the Congress, only redefining his relationship with it, yet sending the resignation letter gave him a pang. 'It is not with a light heart,' he wrote, 'that I leave this great organization' (64: 394–6). To the session in Bombay, chaired by Prasad, Gandhi said:

I am not going out as a protest against anything inside the Congress. I am going out so that Congressmen may think and act for themselves. My retirement does not in any way mean that I am not ready to come back whenever my help is needed.

I am leaving the Congress to lift the weight which has been suppressing it, in order that it may grow, and I may grow myself ... I am leaving in order to develop the power that non-violence has ...

If you have given me the position of a general commanding an army, you must allow that general to judge whether he serves the army by being at its head or whether he serves the army by retiring and giving place to lieutenants who have served well.

If you believe that I have been a fairly wise general, you must believe in my judgement even now ... [14]

Starting again

It was like starting all over again. He had broken up his home and ashram, resigned from the Congress, moved across from western India to a stopgap base in central India, and suspended disobedience for all save himself. His future seemed uncertain, and the Wardha address temporary.

When Dietrich Bonhöffer (the German pastor who would be executed in 1945 for an alleged role in a plot to kill Hitler) asked, in a letter posted in London, whether he and a friend could spend some time with him in India, Gandhi replied (1 Nov. 1934):

If you and your friend have enough money for return passage and can pay your expenses here, say, at the rate of Rs 100 per month each, you can come whenever you like. The sooner the better so as to get the benefit of such cold weather as we get here. The Rs 100 per month I have calculated as the outside limit for those who can live simply. It may cost you even half the amount ...

With reference to your desire to share my daily life, I may say that you will be staying with me if I am out of prison and settled in one place when you come ... [I]f I am travelling or if I am in prison, you will have to be satisfied with remaining in or near one of the institutions that are being conducted under my supervision (65: 274–5).

Brahmacharya. As he indicated at the Bombay session, Gandhi hoped that a personal strengthening would accrue from his latest renunciations. He also hoped to work on himself, for he linked the apparent success of repression to his imperfections. Part of his response related to brahmacharya. If he acquired that quality in perfection, he seemed to think, all opposition might evaporate, whether of the Raj, the intellectuals, the sanatanists, Ambedkar, or Muslims suspicious of the Congress.

Convinced that 'there must be some men who have something of the woman too in them', he revived earlier efforts to join their ranks. 'If men and women can never live together without getting disturbed by sex attractions, their brahmacharya is not brahmacharya,' he said in a letter (addressed to Pandit Khare) in September 1934:

Do not mother and son, father and daughter, brother and sister so live? Why, then, cannot men and women who are not so related live likewise? If we are sincere, we shall progress through our mistakes and realize one day that what seemed impossible has become possible.[15]

Five years earlier (as we saw in Chapter 9), some Sabarmati co-workers had objected to Gandhi's practice of placing his hands on the shoulders of women while walking, but he had defended himself, claiming, 'Never has an impure thought entered my being during or owing to the practice.' In Bajaj's guest-cottage in Wardha he resumed the practice, following a natural inclination.

In September 1935, however, Gandhi stopped the practice when he learnt that a young man visiting Wardha had molested a girl after professing sisterly feelings towards her. But he was not happy. Whether advance towards perfect chastity was hindered or helped by the freedom he assumed with women became a major subject of debate in Gandhi's mind and with co-workers; and from time to time he resumed or suspended the practice.

Though acknowledging (in the columns of *Harijan* and in letters) that he had not attained perfect purity in thought, and admitting, in 1936, that he experienced involuntary discharges more frequently in his sixties in India (at intervals of several months rather than several years) than in his thirties and forties in South Africa, Gandhi seemed to conclude that freedom with women – his sisters and daughters as he viewed them – helped his (and their) quest for perfection, though there also were moments when he thought he might be deceiving himself.

In the late 1930s, this freedom included his taking a bath in the presence of others, including women, and their sleeping near him. The women included Sushila Nayar, Pyarelal's sister, who had trained as a doctor and was 22 in 1936, Rajkumari Amrit Kaur, 47, an unmarried Christian from a family, formerly Sikh, that ruled the princely state of Kapurthala, Prabhavati, the 30-year-old Sabarmati 'graduate' married to the socialist leader, Jayaprakash Narayan, and Amtus Salaam, from a prominent Muslim family in the princely state of Patiala.

In September 1934, writing to Prema Kantak from Wardha, Gandhi wrote, 'There is a terrace here for sleeping,' and named those sleeping near him: 'Amtus Salaam, Vasumati, Amala [Margarete Spiegel, a German Jew], Ba when she is here, Om [Bajaj's daughter] and Prabhavati' (65: 31).

In his middle and late sixties, when the national scene offered little cheer, Gandhi found comfort and security in his apparently lust-free proximity to his female associates/aides.

Politics, economics & village India. If tensions marked Gandhi's chastity drive, his political or economic thinking was free of doubts. His retirement from the Congress was joined to a plan to strengthen the body's rural links. In his 1933–4 tour of much of India, Gandhi had seen that though khadi provided employment to around 220,000 women and 40,000 men in nearly 6,000 villages, other village industries were needed to combat rising rural unemployment.

He therefore created an All-India Village Industries Association as an autonomous and non-political affiliate of the Congress. J C Kumarappa was asked to lead the new association from Wardha, where Bajaj offered 20 acres of orange orchards for experiments in village industries: how to make things like paper, soap and jaggery* in a village, or make processes like hand-pounding rice more efficient, and so forth. In memory of one who had helped build Phoenix and Sabarmati, Gandhi named the site Maganwadi.

Repudiating a charge that he was against technology, Gandhi said: 'Is not this charkha in front of me a machine? We do want machines but do not wish to become their slaves. We should make the machine our slave' (65: 225). In another comment, he said:

> The problem with us is not how to find leisure for the teeming millions inhabiting our villages. The problem is how to utilize their idle hours, which are equal to the working days of six months in the year (*Harijan*, 16 Nov. 1934; 65: 354).

In an interview in November 1934 with a left-leaning anthropologist, Nirmal Kumar Bose, Gandhi spelt out his philosophical objection to state socialism:

> The State represents violence in a concentrated and organized form. The individual has a soul, but as the State is a soulless machine, it can never be weaned from violence to which it owes its very existence.
>
> I look upon an increase of the power of the State with the greatest fear, because although while apparently doing good by minimizing exploitation, it does the greatest harm to mankind by destroying individuality, which lies at the root of all progress (65: 316–19).

Central Assembly elections. 'So far as I can see the future,' Gandhi said in a letter at the end of October 1934 to his Quaker friend, Agatha Harrison, 'there is no likelihood of my initiating or precipitating mass civil disobedience for some years to come' (65: 276). And in November he openly asked voters to send Congress candidates to the largely symbolic Central Assembly. The results gave 61 seats to the Congress and its allies, including a dozen won by the Nationalist Party led by Malaviya.

---

* Jaggery = unrefined sugar.

This was close to a sweep of 'general' and 'untouchable' seats, and a delighted Gandhi referred (23 Nov.) to 'the wonders [the Congress] has worked with the least amount of expenses' (65: 395). In a house of 146, the so-called ENO group (Europeans plus Nominated members plus Officials) had 47 plus the support of around 16 loyalists, representing landholding or other privileged interests. Led by Jinnah, a bloc of 18 legislators elected from Muslim seats formed a third group.

Barred from the Frontier. Released in August 1934 after more than 30 months of detention but not allowed to return to their province, the Khan brothers provided Gandhi with enjoyable company in Wardha in the last quarter of 1934, strengthened his hopes of Hindu-Muslim partnership and produced in him a wish to 'bury [him]self' in a Frontier village. However, on 7 December, while Ghaffar Khan and all his four children were together for the first time in years, the Frontier leader was rearrested for alleged sedition.

Via a letter sent by his private secretary, Willingdon barred Gandhi from entering the NWFP. Some months later (June 1935), when a violent earthquake ravaged Quetta in Baluchistan and Gandhi asked for permission to visit that province, permission was again denied.

Harilal

In September and October 1934, Harilal, now 46, wrote unexpected letters to his father. Saying that he wished to start a new life, Harilal added that he was learning spinning and other khadi processes from his daughter Manu, and wanted to settle down and remarry. Several letters were exchanged.

Afraid and yet willing to believe his son (Kasturba was sceptical), the father said he would be glad if Harilal married a widow, and offered to ask friends to help Harilal if he was serious about a fresh start. On 17 October Gandhi wrote to his son:

> I can't stop thinking about you all the time ... You are constantly in my thoughts.
> If I had time, I would go on inflicting long letters on you. If the change that you
> have described endures ... I would be extremely happy in this the last stage of my
> life (65: 187–8).

In February 1935 Gandhi invited Harilal to stay with him in Wardha, and the son came, his body looking ravaged, the face thin and stained, his hair dishevelled. For a while it looked as if the son would recover, and he and his parents enjoyed one another's company. Apparently, Harilal told Gandhi that he wanted to stay in a village and serve. In that case, Gandhi responded, 'I would love to die in your lap.'[16]

When Harilal repeated that he wanted to marry again, Gandhi did not express any objection. Margarete Spiegel, a German schoolteacher who had lost her job in Berlin, being a Jew, and was in India because of an interest in Gandhi's lifestyle, thought she might marry Harilal, who seemed willing, but the idea came to nothing, and in May Harilal returned to Rajkot.

To Narandas Gandhi, who was now Rajkot-based, Gandhi wrote: 'God knows where Harilal's destiny will lead him. We must ask only this favour from God that our prodigal son should not be lost again.'[17] But Harilal found it hard to stay in a job or in one place, or without liquor or borrowed money.

In April 1936 he met his parents in Nagpur and told them 'how he was amused by the attentions that were being paid to him by the missionaries of rival faiths'. Some weeks later, on 30 May, while Gandhi and Kasturba were in Bangalore, the newspapers announced that Harilal, now 48, had secretly converted to Islam and had been accepted on Friday 29 May as a Muslim in one of Bombay's main mosques, and now bore the name Abdulla. A shattered Kasturba conveyed her reaction in a letter to Harilal's daughter Rami:

> I am very unhappy, but what to do? In fact I feel very ashamed ... We have lost a jewel. The jewel has gone into the hands of Musalmans.[18]

Gandhi thought the conversion stemmed from compulsive habits. 'He must have sensation and he must have money,' he wrote to Amrit Kaur (1 Jun. 1936: 69: 75). But the publicized conversion to Islam of Gandhi's son was more than a personal or family matter. It demanded a public response. On 2 June Gandhi issued a press statement:

> The newspapers report that about a fortnight ago my eldest son Harilal, now nearing fifty years, accepted Islam and that on Friday last ... he was permitted to announce his acceptance amid great acclamation and that, after his speech was finished, he was besieged by his admirers who vied with one another to shake hands with him.
>
> If his acceptance was from the heart and free from any worldly considerations, I should have no quarrel ... But I have the gravest doubt about this ... Everyone who knows my son Harilal, knows that he has been for years addicted to the drink evil and has been in the habit of visiting houses of ill-fame.
>
> God can work wonders. He has been known to have changed the stoniest hearts and turned sinners into saints, as it were, in a moment. Nothing will please me better than to find that ... he had ... suddenly become a changed man ... But the Press reports give no such evidence ...
>
> Harilal's apostasy is no loss to Hinduism and his admission to Islam is a source of weakness to it if, as I apprehend, he remains the same wreck that he was before.

My object in addressing these lines to my numerous Muslim friends is to ask them to examine Harilal in the light of his immediate past and, if they find that his conversion is a soulless matter, to tell him so plainly and disown him, and if they discover sincerity in him to see that he is protected against temptations so that his sincerity results in his becoming a God-fearing member of society.

I do not mind whether he is known as Abdulla or Harilal if, by adopting one name for the other, he becomes a true devotee of God, which both the names mean (*Harijan*, 6 Jun. 1936; 69: 76–8).

Harilal's son Kanti visited his father and wept at his condition. Soon there were stories of Abdulla Gandhi preaching Islam in different parts of the country but also of disorderly conduct by him and proceedings against him. A humiliated Kasturba 'gave vent to her feelings one morning in Delhi' before Devadas, who transcribed her pain into 'An Open Letter from a Mother to her Son' that newspapers published on 27 September. The letter also offered a glimpse into Gandhi's heart, piercing its steel casing, and into her own:

Dear son Harilal, Now it has become hard for me even to live. How much pain you are inflicting on your parents in the evening of their life, at least think of that a little.

Your father does not speak anything about this before anybody. But the shock that your behaviour causes breaks his heart to pieces. God has given him strong willpower ... But I am a weak, aged woman, and I am unable to endure the mental torture caused by you.

Your father daily receives letters from many persons complaining against your behaviour. He has to gulp down the bitter drink of all this infamy. But for me you have not spared a single place where I can go. Out of shame I cannot move with ease among friends or even strangers. Your father has always forgiven you; but God will never tolerate your behaviour.

Every morning when I wake up I have a fear in my heart; what if there are reports about your new evil doings in the newspapers. I long ardently to meet you; but I do not know your whereabouts. You are my eldest son, and you are now fifty years of age. Perhaps you may insult even me.

You have changed your ancestral religion. That is your personal affair. You like those who give you money but you spend the money on drinking and after that you deliver discourses from the pulpit ...

Addressing Muslims who celebrated the conversion, Kasturba added:

The powerless voice of a wounded mother will surely stir someone's heart ... What you have been doing would not be reasonable in the eyes of Khuda*.[19]

Harilal's first reaction (not wholly inaccurate, as we know) was that his mother 'didn't write this letter. Someone else wrote it and signed her name.'[20] He also claimed he would stop drinking if his parents embraced Islam.[21] But the conversion was not genuine, and before the end of the year he reconverted to Hinduism in an Arya Samaj ceremony and adopted a new name, Hiralal.

Mahadev Desai's son Narayan has left a first-hand account of an encounter at about this time, in the company of the Gandhis, with Harilal:

One day when our train stopped at a station on our way back to Wardha, we heard a cry from the crowd different from the usual: '*Mata Kasturba ki jai.*'

It was Harilalkaka. He was emaciated. His front teeth were gone. His hair had turned gray. From a pocket of his ragged clothes he took an orange and said, 'Ba, I have brought this for you.'

Breaking in, Bapu said, 'Didn't you bring anything for me?'

'No, nothing for you ... All the greatness you have achieved is only because of Ba. Don't forget that!'

'Oh, there is no doubt of it! But now, do you want to come with us?'

'Oh, no. I only came to see Ba. Take this orange, Ba. I begged for it and now I give it to you. It's only for you, all right? If you are not going to eat it yourself, give it back to me.'

Ba promised to eat the orange. Then she too pleaded with Harilalkaka to come with us.

Harilalkaka's eyes were full of tears. 'Leave off such talk, Ba. There is no way out of this for me.' Our compartment had pulled away from him when Ba realized, 'I didn't even ask the poor boy if he wanted anything to eat. We have a basket full of fruits. My dear child must be dying of hunger.'

But by then the train had left the platform. Amidst the cries of '*Gandhiji ki jai!*' we could still hear the faint cry, '*Mata Kasturba ki jai.*'[22]

Ambedkar & conversion

It was Ambedkar who had made conversion a hot topic. On 14 October 1935, shortly after reports of atrocities against Harijans in Kavitha village in Gujarat's Ahmedabad

---

* Khuda = God.

district, he announced at a Depressed Classes conference in Yeoli in Maharashtra that though born a Hindu he did not intend to die one.

He had been speaking in this vein from 1933. Hindu society, he said, was resisting reform; Gandhi had rejected his plea to become 'a dictator like Kemal Pasha or Mussolini in social and religious matters';[23] and there was no future for the 'untouchables' within Hinduism. The Yeoli conference resolved to look for a religion that gave them equality. Gandhi offered an immediate comment:

> I can understand the anger of a high-souled and highly educated person like Dr Ambedkar over the atrocities as were committed in Kavitha and other villages. But religion is not like a house or a cloak which can be changed at will …
>
> [C]hange of faith by him and those who passed the resolution will not serve the cause which they have at heart; for millions of unsophisticated, illiterate Harijans will not listen to him and them … especially when it is remembered that their lives, for good or for evil, are intertwined with those of caste Hindus (68: 65).

Yet Gandhi concluded that on his part he should now criticize the caste system directly. Thus far, in order to demonstrate his loyalty to Hindu tradition, Gandhi had defended an 'ideal' caste system (the so-called 'varnashrama' dharma) as a division of occupations based on equality and aptitude, while admitting that the ideal did not exist in practice.

On 16 November 1935, in a noteworthy shift, Gandhi said of the caste system, 'The sooner public opinion abolishes it, the better.' The *Harijan* article in which he wrote this was entitled, 'CASTE HAS TO GO'. As for Ambedkar, though Christian, Muslim and Sikh groups made eager approaches to him, he seemed in no hurry to choose a new religion.

A year later, in November 1936, Andrews again brought up the question of conversion. While (he said) he himself had 'discarded the position that there is no salvation except through Christ long ago', he nonetheless wanted to know what Gandhi would 'say to a man who after considerable thought and prayer said that he could not have his peace and salvation except by becoming a Christian'.

> *G*: I would say that if a non-Christian, say a Hindu, came to a Christian and made that statement, he should ask him to become a good Hindu rather than find goodness in change of faith.
>
> *A*: I cannot in this go the whole length with you, though you know my own position. But supposing the Oxford Group Movement people changed the life of your son, and he felt like being converted, what would you say?

G: I would say that the Oxford Group may change the lives of as many as they like, but not their religion … If a person wants to believe in the Bible let him say so, but why should he disregard his own religion? This proselytization will mean no peace in the world. Religion is a very personal matter.

We should, by living the life according to our light, share the best with one another, thus adding to the sum total of human effort to reach God … My position is that all the great religions are fundamentally equal. We must have the innate respect for other religions as we have for our own. Mind you, not mutual toleration, but equal respect (*Harijan*, 28 Nov. 1936; 70: 58–60).

Extremely reluctant to endorse changes in faith, and apprehensive of violence arising from competition for souls and numbers, Gandhi however acknowledged, as we have seen, that persons like his son Harilal and Ambedkar were entitled to choose their religious home.

That mass conversions might be flawed was admitted by some Christian missionaries, and John R Mott, the American founder of the YMCA, told Gandhi in November 1936 that he regretted 'unseemly competition' among missionaries to baptize 'untouchables'. Still, Mott asked whether it was wrong to 'preach the Gospel with reference to its acceptance'.

Gandhi's reply betrayed a preconception regarding the 'untouchables' similar to an earlier bias about Africans that he had grown beyond. He asked:

Would you, Dr Mott, preach the Gospel to a cow? Well, some of the 'untouchables' … can no more distinguish between the relative merits of Islam and Hinduism and Christianity than a cow … If you must share [the Gospel] with the Harijans, why don't you share it with Thakkar Bapa and Mahadev? Why should you go to the 'untouchables' and try to exploit this upheaval? (*Harijan*, 19 and 26 Dec. 1936; 70: 77–8)

Reported in *Harijan*, the comment drew protests, including one sent by a gifted young Congressman in Bihar, Jagjivan Ram, who came from an 'untouchable' caste.[24] Explaining, Gandhi said that no offence was meant ('the cow is a sacred animal'), and he added that it was the caste Hindus' fault that 'thousands of Harijans' had been left in a state where they could not 'understand the merits and demerits of different religions' (*Harijan*, 9 Jan. 1937; 70: 258–9).

It is unlikely that Jagjivan Ram's feelings were assuaged. Did Gandhi really think that Dalits were incapable of clear or independent thinking? Part of him certainly carried this prejudice, but we have also seen Gandhi's references to talented 'untouchables' worthy of occupying India's highest offices; and he was well aware of the abilities not only of Ambedkar but also of Jagjivan Ram and several other Dalit leaders. What Mott's remark brought out was not Gandhi's calm view but a reaction of fear-cum-resentment, typical of many Hindus, at the thought of 'losing' some of their numbers.

Act of 1935. In July 1935 the British Parliament passed a new statute for India, the Government of India Act. In line with the 1933 White Paper, the Act of 1935 gave substantial autonomy to soon-to-be-elected provincial legislatures, while retaining British control over the Central Assembly.

At the end of August 1935, Gandhi cabled the Viceroy asking for the unconditional release of Jawaharlal, whose wife Kamala lay critically ill in Europe. Nehru was freed, and a Gandhi who had 'retired' from the Congress asked Jawaharlal to succeed Prasad as president.

Convinced that it was Rajagopalachari's turn to take the chair, Vallabhbhai had pressed Gandhi to nominate the southerner, and Gandhi had sent C R a feeler. Claiming fatigue, and aware in any case of Gandhi's wish, Rajagopalachari demurred, and Gandhi informed Patel that he had 'asked Jawaharlal with [C R's] consent'.[25]

Held in Lucknow with Nehru in the chair, the Congress plenary of March–April 1936 witnessed 'an acrimonious verbal duel' between Jawaharlal (whose wife had died in February) and Patel.[26] Two issues sharply divided them: in his presidential address, Jawaharlal spoke of socialism as a vital creed in which he believed with all his head and heart; and he also made plain his dislike of office-acceptance. Patel was sceptical of socialism and open to provincial office, positions that C R and Prasad shared.

Unwilling to divide the Congress, Nehru went along with Lucknow's decision not to reject provincial office in advance, and he also refrained from joining the Congress Socialist Party. In fact Lucknow lived up to Gandhi's hope, which was that Nehru should have his head but the others should not lose their voices.

Present but silent in Lucknow, an unwell Gandhi in effect chose the Working Committee. Led by Patel, Prasad and C R, the old guard comprised a majority in the new team, and the three socialists included in it (Jayaprakash, Narendra Deva and Achyut Patwardhan) 'owed their appointment not to Jawaharlal but to Gandhi', as Patwardhan would put it.[27] Also included was Subhas Bose, who was in prison again, this time for returning to India against the Raj's wishes. Kripalani was retained as general secretary, a position to which (on Patel's urging) he had been appointed in 1934.

Within weeks, however, Nehru sparked off a crisis, remarking publicly that he had consented to the new Working Committee 'against his better judgement'. Patel's reaction was that the remark had left the majority in 'a humiliating position in which I for one would not agree to stay at any cost'. Seven members (Patel, Prasad, C R, Kripalani, Bajaj, Jairamdas Daulatram and Shankarrao Deo) sent in their resignations.[28]

Nehru's response was to offer to resign himself, but Gandhi intervened and all resignations and offers to resign were withdrawn. 'I look upon the whole affair as a tragicomedy,' Gandhi said to Jawaharlal, who had complained of intolerance from his colleagues, asking him not to compel the Congress to choose between him and them. Added Gandhi: 'If they are guilty of intolerance, you have more than your share of it. The country should not be made to suffer for your mutual intolerance.'[29]

Cooperation and even harmony soon arrived, helped by the elections, due early in 1937, where success was desired by supporters as well as opponents of office-acceptance. But in May came a blow: Dr Ansari died at the age of 56. In a tribute (16 May) in *Harijan*, 'A Great Friend Gone', Gandhi spoke of Ansari's unwavering commitment to Hindu-Muslim unity, his skill as a doctor and free treatment of the poor, and of his patients' faith in him: 'They had many proofs of the Doctor's friendship when they thought God had forsaken them.' (69: 1) On Ansari's death Patel became the chairman of the CPB and received full cooperation from Nehru.

> *Patel to Gandhi, 26 Aug. 1936*: We have been getting on beautifully this time … It has been more like a gathering of family members. The manifesto was prepared and passed almost unanimously … I cannot speak too highly of Jawaharlal. We found not the slightest difficulty in cooperating with him.[30]

Sevagram

Because the flow of visitors in Wardha left him with no peace, and also because he wanted to live with poor Harijan villagers, in the summer of 1936 Gandhi moved to the village of Segaon, five miles from Wardha. Bajaj owned three-quarters of Segaon's land, and Mira had lived there for a few weeks.

Segaon had a population of 639 (most of them 'untouchables'), no post office, telephone or clinic, and plenty of snakes, malaria and typhoid. The 'road' to it from Wardha was often unusable. Still, in March 1936 Gandhi asked Bajaj to build a mud hut in Segaon where he and Kasturba could live, and another hut for his aides Mahadev and Kanti (Harilal's son). Mira already had a small hut in Segaon for herself. Gandhi told Bajaj that to meet visitors he would travel to Wardha, in transport that Bajaj might provide. Otherwise he would live in and off the Segaon land, and thereby also focus everyone's attention on India's villages.

This was the origin of what soon grew into Sevagram ('Village of Service') ashram, Gandhi's new abode. More allies and aides joined Gandhi to live in Sevagram, as Segaon was renamed, and those wanting to meet him often went there. 'Doctor' Gandhi spent much time teaching the villagers the use of steam inhalations, mud packs, wet

sheets, and enemas, and treating them with iodine, quinine, castor oil and sodium bicarbonate.

But he also contracted malaria, and could not easily shake it off. Though most villagers were indifferent to his suggestions for sanitation, Gandhi was gradually able to introduce spinning, weaving and tanning, and to enlist local help in road-making. He also achieved partial success in breaking down untouchability. Before long the high-caste headman of the village was eating ashram food prepared by local Dalits.

Trains between Bombay and Calcutta on the east-west route, and between Delhi and Madras on the north-south route, stopped at Wardha station. Soon many Indians, and quite a few non-Indians, were travelling to the centre of the country – by train to Wardha and thence on foot or by bullock-cart to Sevagram – to meet a self-styled crank in his late sixties who was 'developing' a hot, arid, snake-infested village while also keeping a sharp and steady finger on India's political pulse.

In one significant detail, the New Delhi picture altered. Willingdon finally retired in 1936 and was succeeded as Viceroy by Victor Alexander John Hope, the Marquess of Linlithgow (1887–1952), a Conservative politician from Scotland. Earlier in the year King George V, whose tea party Gandhi had attended, had died. Gandhi sent a cable of condolence to Queen Mary.

Patel vs. Nehru

In November 1936 Jawaharlal indicated a desire to be the Congress president for 1937 as well, and Patel exploded. To Mahadev Desai he wrote: 'The decked-up groom-prince is ready to marry at one stroke as many girls as he can find.'[31] Once more Vallabhbhai urged Gandhi to invite C R to the chair.

> *Gandhi to Rajagopalachari, 21 Nov. 1936*: Sardar is desperately anxious for you to wear the thorny crown. I shall be pleased if you will, but I have no heart to press it on you. If you [can] be persuaded into shouldering the burden, you should unhesitatingly say yes and end the agony of the Sardar (70: 105).

But C R still felt tired, or unsure that Gandhi really wanted him, or perhaps he was thinking of the premiership of Madras. In any case he declined again. Patel hoped that Govind Ballabh Pant of the UP could be chosen. Suggesting Pant's name in a letter to Desai, in effect a letter to Gandhi, Patel said he would quit if Nehru was repeated, adding, 'Jivat [Kripalani] too is very cut up.'[32]

When Nehru declared that those considering him for another term should 'bear in mind' that he was a socialist,[33] Patel was asked by supporters to stand himself. He was

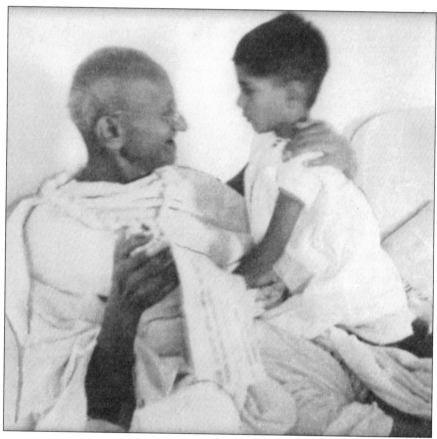

With the author, his grandson – 1936

willing, his name was announced, and Gandhi seemed happy with the idea. However, as Kripalani would recount,

> Jawaharlal approached Gandhiji and told him that he felt that one term of eight months was not sufficient for him to revitalize the Congress. He would like a second term of office ... Gandhiji remained thoughtful for some time. Then he said, 'I shall see what can be done.' I was present when the conversation between Gandhiji and Jawaharlal took place.[34]

Though disappointed by Nehru's keenness, Gandhi understood his value as a Congress president in the elections that were now in full swing; he also understood the damage a rebuffed Jawaharlal could inflict. And he saw a chance to clinch Nehru's adherence to group decisions. Asking Vallabhbhai to withdraw, Gandhi also drafted a statement for Patel to make.

> *To Patel, 24 Nov. 1936*: If you do not like the draft, write out another, and if you think it your duty to enter into competition, do so. You may change the draft where you think it necessary. Whatever you do must be done with confidence, because we shall have to cross many deserts.

Vallabhbhai withdrew. He also issued the statement that, as Nehru well realized, Gandhi had written out for him:

> After consultations with friends I have come to the conclusion that I must withdraw from the contest ... At this critical juncture, a unanimous election is most desirable. My withdrawal should not be taken to mean that I endorse all the views Jawaharlalji stands for. Indeed, Congressmen know that on some vital matters my views are in conflict with those held by Jawaharlalji. For instance, I do not believe in the inevitability of class war.
>
> [Also], I can visualize the occasion when the acceptance of office may be desirable to achieve the common purpose. There may then be a sharp division of opinion between Jawaharlalji and myself. We know Jawaharlalji to be too loyal to the Congress to disregard the decision of the majority.
>
> The Congress President has no dictatorial powers. He is the chairman of a well-knit organization ... The Congress does not part with its ample powers by electing any individual no matter who he is.[35]

Of Gandhi's relationship with Jawaharlal, Martin Green has aptly said, 'Without

falsifying himself, Gandhi found a dozen ways to charm and attach Nehru.'[36] He was
– as required – warm, breezy, thoughtful, admiring or tender. Moreover, he helped in
the marriages of Nehru's sisters. Yet he was also willing to be detached from or by the
younger man, and ready to speak frankly to him.

This mix of warmth, helpfulness and candour was, however, what Gandhi offered
(with variations of tone) to a large number: to Patel and Rajagopalachari, to Sarabhai,
Bajaj and Birla, to Desai and Pyarelal, to Vinoba, Kalelkar and Swami Anand, to Tagore
and Malaviya, to Andrews and Kallenbach, to Mira, Amtus Salaam and Amrit Kaur, and
a host of others of different types and in different relationships with him.

Accepting Gandhi's and Patel's terms, Nehru clarified that 'it would be absurd for
me to treat this presidential election as a vote for socialism or against office-acceptance'.[37]
While Patel and Nehru entertained hard thoughts about each other in 1936, they fell
in with a larger design, playing complementary roles. If Jawaharlal 'shot through the
country like an arrow'[38] and sought votes, Patel, as the CPB chairman, helped select
candidates and raised funds.

In December 1936 the Congress met for a plenary in a Maharashtra village, Faizpur.
This too was the 'retired' Gandhi's idea, part of the exercise to strengthen the Congress's
rural bonds. The artist Nandalal Bose came from Santiniketan to design the village
venue, Tilak Nagar as it was called, and Shankarrao Deo supervised the logistics and the
sanitation. It was an impressive show.

Finally released but barred from returning to the Frontier, Ghaffar Khan was present
at the Faizpur session. Gandhi went there and said (25 Dec.), 'I have cast all my cares on
the broad shoulders of Jawaharlal and the Sardar' (70: 211–12).

12

Dream under Fire

1937–9

The polls of February 1937 gave the Congress the opportunity to form ministries in eight provinces: on its own in the UP, Madras, Bihar, the Central Provinces and Orissa, and with allies in Bombay, Assam and the Muslim-majority province of the NWFP, where Dr Khan Sahib, the 'older brother', was elected to head the Congress-led alliance. Save in Bombay's Maharashtra region, where Ambedkar's party won several seats, India's 'untouchables' voted solidly for the Congress, as did caste Hindus, despite sharp attacks from sanatanists.

Except in the Frontier Province, however, the Congress received only a small share of the Muslim vote. Led by Jinnah, who had been elected as the League's 'permanent' president in 1934, the Muslim League scored well in Muslim seats in Hindu-majority provinces, where it was presented as the protector of threatened Muslim interests, but less so in the Punjab, Bengal, Sindh and the NWFP, where Hindus were in a minority. Leading the Congress campaign, Nehru had asked Indians to choose 'between the Congress and the British'. Jinnah replied (January 1937): 'I refuse to line up. There is a third party – the Muslims. We are not going to be dictated to by anybody.'[1]

In May 1937, before it was clear that the Congress would accept office but after his spat with Nehru, Jinnah sent Gandhi a private, verbal message via B G Kher, a fellow-lawyer who was also the leader of the Congress party in the Bombay legislature. In it he said that Gandhi should give a lead in forging Hindu-Muslim unity. More concretely, it seems, Jinnah wished to explore a Congress-League coalition in Bombay.

Gandhi was reluctant. Maybe he was put off by Jinnah's retort to Nehru. Maybe he felt he could not discuss office-sharing with Jinnah before the Congress had decided on accepting office. In any case he sent Jinnah a written answer in general but discouraging terms:

Mr Kher has given me your message. I wish I could do something, but I am utterly helpless. My faith in unity is as bright as ever; only I see no daylight ... (22 May 1937; 71: 277)

Nehru, who was the Congress president, was against taking office. While keeping its options open, the Congress had in fact resolved to 'wreck' the 1935 Act under which provincial ministries would be formed, for that Act also provided for a federal assembly where unelected princes (or their nominees) could vote. At Nehru's initiative, the UP Congress Committee passed a resolution opposing office-acceptance.

None in the Congress liked the federal part of the 1935 Act, but Patel was for acceptance of provincial office, as was Rajagopalachari, now the leader of the Congress party in the Madras legislature, to which he had been elected from a university seat. The question went to the 'retired' Gandhi, who said he would counsel acceptance of office provided the Viceroy, Lord Linlithgow, gave an assurance that governors would not overrule elected ministers.

Sapru, the constitutional lawyer, thought that Gandhi was asking for a 'fantastic' assurance, which, if offered, would contravene the 1935 Act.[2] To Sapru's and others' surprise, Linlithgow met Gandhi halfway. In a public statement the Viceroy said:

There is no foundation for any suggestion that the Governor is free or entitled or would have the power to interfere with the day-to-day administration of a province outside the limited range of responsibilities specially confided to him.

Treating the statement as 'a sign from Britain that it would cooperate', Gandhi advised the Congress to accept office. When the Working Committee met in Wardha in the first week of July, no one, not even Nehru, opposed the advice. Office-acceptance was authorized.

Gandhi was gambling that the duality in the Congress's relationship with the Raj – participation in government by its foes – would work in the Congress's favour, even as Linlithgow hoped it would work to the Empire's advantage. Though hoping that provincial power would help the Congress, Gandhi was also aware, as was the Viceroy, that power could soften the Congress, and that association with the Raj could compromise it in the eyes of the Indian people.

By the middle of July 1937 seven Congressmen were nonetheless installed as premiers: C R in Madras, Kher in Bombay, G B Pant in the UP, Shrikrishna Sinha in Bihar, N B Khare in the CP, Dr Khan Sahib in the NWFP, and Bishwanath Das in Orissa. A year later, in Assam, Gopinath Bardoloi became the Congress's eighth premier.

Gandhi described the installation of Congress ministries as 'an unwritten compact between the British Government and the Congress ... a gentleman's agreement, in which both sides are expected to play the game'.[3]

Bombay & UP, Punjab & Bengal. When it became clear that the Congress would take office, Jinnah sent word to Patel, the CPB chairman, suggesting the inclusion of two League legislators in the Bombay ministry. Patel said they could be taken if all the League MLAs merged with the Congress legislature party, a condition rejected by Jinnah, who wanted partnership in a coalition government and did not wish the Congress to control his MLAs.

A Congress-League coming together seemed more likely in the UP, where, apparently without Jinnah's consent, provincial League leaders (Khaliquzzaman and Nawab Ismail Khan) negotiated with the Congress. The Congress leaders in these talks included Nehru, Azad (who was asked by the CPB to supervise ministry-formation in the UP), Pant (leader of the Congress legislature party in the UP), Kripalani, the UP-based general secretary of the all-India Congress, and Narendra Deva, a socialist member of the Working Committee.

The Congress negotiators agreed to two League ministers in a cabinet of six, where Rafi Ahmed Kidwai, Nehru's loyal ally in the UP Congress, would be a third Muslim member. The decision overruled objections from Hindu nationalists who thought that three Muslim ministers were too many, as well as from leftist Muslims and Congress Muslims, who wanted ministerships for their nominees, not the League's. However, the deal collapsed because the Congress again sought to absorb the Muslim League MLAs in its legislature party, a demand rejected by the League legislators.[4]

The smugness of the Congress of 1937, which electoral success had boosted, comes across in letters regarding the UP negotiations exchanged between Nehru, Azad and Prasad.[5] On 21 July Nehru wrote to Prasad: 'We came to the conclusion that we should offer stringent conditions to the UP Muslim League group and if they accepted them in toto then we would agree to two ministers from their group.' One condition, said Nehru, was 'the winding up of the Muslim League group in the UP and its absorption in the Congress'.[6] And although prescient anxiety can be detected in letters from Wardha that Gandhi sent at the time to Nehru, he seemed in no position, for all his influence, to override the views of the UP Congress and of the Congress negotiators.[7]

In the Punjab, where the League won only two seats, Sir Sikandar Hyat Khan of the Unionist Party of landlords and farmers (Muslim, Sikh and Hindu) became the premier. A stable government proved elusive in the smaller Muslim-majority province of Sindh. In Bengal, where the Congress emerged as the largest single party (with 60 seats), the premiership went to Fazlul Huq of the Krishak Praja Party (KPP), which championed the cause of East Bengal's largely Muslim peasantry and won 35 Muslim seats. After Jinnah offered Huq the number one position, a coalition of the KPP, the League (which had 40 seats), and some smaller groups formed a government.

Pro-landlord elements in the Bengal Congress blocked a possible alliance between the Congress and Huq's party, which was seen as too radical. In the Punjab, on the other hand, radical sections of the Congress prevented the party's association with the Unionists, who were seen as pro-landlord and soft towards the British.

Though the Muslim League had not done as well across India as he had hoped, Jinnah had found a new mission. Uniting all Muslims against what he increasingly termed the 'Hindu' Congress now took precedence over working with other Indians against British rule. Jinnah profited, too, from the rhetoric of Savarkar, who, presiding at the 1937 session of the Hindu Mahasabha, said:

> I warn the Hindus that the Mohammedans are likely to prove dangerous to our Hindu nation ... India cannot be assumed today to be a unitarian and homogeneous nation, but on the contrary there are two nations in the main: the Hindus and the Moslems in India.[8]

Men like Savarkar, as well as sanatanists opposed to Gandhi over caste, attacked Gandhi as not being Hindu enough. Yet Jinnah insisted on seeing him and the Congress as exclusively Hindu. Not caring where the Unionists or Huq stood on land reform or vis-à-vis the British, Jinnah promised them the League's full backing as long as they resisted advances from the 'Hindu' Congress. Huq was given Bengal's premiership, and Sikandar assured, through a Jinnah-Sikandar pact, that the League's Punjab unit would not defy him. In October 1937 Huq publicly embraced Jinnah at a Muslim League session in Lucknow and signed the League pledge. Sikandar too attended the session and acknowledged Jinnah as his leader at national level.

Muslims in Hindu-majority provinces were asked by Jinnah to recognize 'Hindu domination'. Within months of the Congress assuming office, he declared:

> All along the countryside, many of the 10,000 Congress committees and even some of the Hindu officials are behaving as if Hindu Raj had already been established.[9]

When Gandhi protested, Jinnah complained that Gandhi had remained silent while Nehru and the others were belittling the League. Gandhi asked to be used as a bridge by Jinnah, who countered by asking Gandhi for a specific offer, and by continuing to press the allegation of Hindu Raj. Muslims in the UP and other Hindu-majority provinces increasingly believed him.

After years in the political wilderness, including some spent as a lawyer in England, Jinnah now held a strong set of cards. Had Gandhi missed a trick over that feeler from Jinnah? The League leader never sent another.

Congress ministries. To prevent Congress ministers becoming 'addicted' to office, Gandhi asked, and Nehru and Patel agreed, that their salaries be limited to 500 rupees a month, with a travel allowance of no more than 250 rupees a month. To make it harder for the Raj to soften them, ministers and MLAs were barred from attending functions sponsored by the governor or senior British officials. To reduce divide-and-rule opportunities, ministers were required to obtain their premier's consent before meeting the governor.

Each side, the Congress and the Raj, was testing the waters. An early tussle occurred when Congress ministries ordered the release of political prisoners, and governors in the UP and Bihar blocked it. The Raj was opposed not so much to the releases as to a precedent of being bypassed on a critical issue. Gandhi and Patel advised premiers Pant and Sinha to resign, which they did. There was a flurry of cables between the provincial capitals and New Delhi, and between New Delhi and London. Unwilling to see a break, the Raj did not immediately accept the resignations, whereupon Gandhi made a conciliatory statement. The crisis could be avoided, he said, 'if the governors were left free to give an assurance that their examination of cases was not intended to be usurpation of the powers of the ministries'.[10] The governors gave the desired assurance and then allowed the releases.

Gandhi's interventions were rare. He did not choose the premiers. This was done by Congress legislators, generally on Patel's advice, with Nehru, Azad and Prasad also playing a role. And it was the Patel-led CPB that had given Congress tickets to the legislators.

The ministries carried out the Congress agenda. Lands were returned to the rebels of 1930 and 1932. Water was taken to dry villages. Debts of impoverished peasants were cancelled. Temples were opened to Harijans. Land reform bills were brought before legislatures. Though hard to enforce, bans on liquor seemed to improve life in hundreds of thousands of poor homes. Prisoners' diet was improved. Khadi uniforms were prescribed for sections of government employees.

In much of India, the Congress appeared to grow in both power and popularity, and indeed closer to its dream of Swaraj. As a reminder of that dream, every session of the AICC and of a Congress-controlled legislature demanded 'representative government' at the centre and a popularly elected constituent assembly for devising a structure of democratic governance.

Jawaharlal complained, however, that Congress ministers were excessively concerned with law and order. When, in November 1937, C R authorized the arrest of S S Batlivala, a Bombay socialist, for a speech in Madras province that allegedly incited violence, Nehru protested to Gandhi. He also proposed that premiers be required in such cases to obtain direction from the Working Committee. Neither Gandhi nor the

With Azad and Vallabhbhai Patel in Bombay – 1940

Working Committee agreed with Nehru, though ministers were asked not to object to criticism.

Subhas Bose. Gandhi involved himself in the Congress presidency: his choice for Nehru's successor was Subhas Bose, who had been released in March 1937. We do not know what Nehru thought, but C R and Patel were opposed. Among other complaints, Patel alleged that before he died in Europe his brother Vithalbhai had been misled by Bose. He also questioned Bose's balance. 'I have seen that Subhas is unsteady,' Gandhi replied, 'but no one except him can be the president.'[11]

Next to or as much as Nehru, Subhas was the hero of the young, an important factor for Gandhi, who was thinking of the future. Also, Subhas was fully committed to Hindu-Muslim unity. In addition, Gandhi felt that Bose, to Jinnah a less familiar face than Gandhi, Nehru or Patel, should have a chance to negotiate a settlement with the League leader.

Subhas presided at the plenary held in February 1938 in the village of Haripura in Bardoli taluka, on the banks of the Tapti. For the session, as Nehru would concede, Patel 'built a magnificent town',[12] with a waterworks, a printing press, a hospital, a garden, a bank, a post office, a telephone exchange and a fire engine. Two thousand volunteers ran the kitchens and kept the sanitary areas clean. Once more Nandalal Bose came from Santiniketan and produced 200 paintings, and Gujarat's artists Ravishankar Raval and Kanu Desai created their pieces.

Haripura reaffirmed the Congress's dual policy towards the Raj, as also its policy towards the princes, which was dual too. The princes were advised to understand the times they were living in, while their subjects, keen on democratic rights, were told that individuals in the Congress would assist them. Gandhi (and, under his advice, the Congress) remained wary of pushing the princes deeper into the arms of the British. The alienation of so many Muslims was bad enough.

Preserving unity among Congress leaders was a constant challenge. 'Sardar and I are close to each other, we are as one, we work alike and we think alike,' Gandhi said in Haripura,[13] but in a letter to Patel he had to use another tone.

20 Feb. 1938: Devadas complained against your speech today. Then Jayaprakash came and spoke about it in great distress. I think your speech was unduly severe. You cannot win over the socialists like that.[14]

Mahadev Desai. At the end of March 1938 – while he, Kasturba, Mahadev and several others were in Orissa – Gandhi heard that Kasturba, Mahadev's wife Durga, and a female relative of Durga's had gone inside Puri's Jagannath Temple, which Harijans could not enter. (Four years earlier, Gandhi had been abused near this temple's entrance.) He was shocked, and troubled too, for he was told that 'the whole of Puri' was talking about Kasturba's visit inside the temple. 'Even the stationmaster asked us, "Did Kasturba really enter the temple?"'[15]

Chastised by Gandhi, the women wept. Kasturba said she was wrong to have gone inside. Gandhi's strongest rebuke, however, was reserved for Desai. He should have instructed the women not to go in, Gandhi told him. Mahadev's son Narayan, 15 at this time, was praised; though accompanying the women he had refused to go inside. At a public meeting in Delang, near Puri, Gandhi referred (30 Mar. 1938) to the transgression:

> It is my daily prayer, as it should be the prayer of you all, that if untouchability does not perish it were far better that Hinduism perished ...
>
> I felt humbled and humiliated when I knew that my wife and two ashram inmates whom I regard as my daughters had gone into the Puri temple. The agony was enough to precipitate a collapse. The machine recorded an alarmingly high blood-pressure ...
>
> The three ... went in ignorance. But I was to blame, and Mahadev was more to blame in that he did not tell them what their dharma was ... He ought to have thought also of its social repercussions ...
>
> How are we to carry to [the Harijans] the conviction that we are with them through thick and thin, that we are completely identifying ourselves with them, unless we can carry our families – our wives, our children, brothers, sisters, relatives – with us ... ?

If Indians developed true instead of false dharma, added Gandhi, its 'power [would be] such that the sword would drop from the Englishman's hand' (73: 69–70).

While Gandhi's blood pressure rose alarmingly, Mahadev felt he could take it no more. He thought Gandhi was making a mountain out of a molehill, and asked to be allowed to leave. As he put it, Gandhi, 'who has performed several spiritual operations using the chloroform of love, had performed this one without that chloroform'. In *Harijan* he cried out:

> To live with the saints in heaven is a bliss and a glory, But to live with a saint on earth is a different story (*Harijan*, 9 Apr. 1938; 73: 457).

But he was denied permission to leave.

> *To Desai, 31 Mar. 1938*: I will tolerate thousands of mistakes, but I can never part

with you ... If you decide to leave me, will Pyarelal stay on? And if Pyarelal leaves, will Sushila stay? ...

They will all run away. Lilavati will simply go mad ... And yet how can I prevent anybody from running away? (73: 73–4)

The letter reveals Gandhi's dependence on his close aides, and his fear of losing them. Later in the year Gandhi enthusiastically backed a plan, originating with Kallenbach, to give Desai, and perhaps Mira as well, a break in South Africa.

To Desai, 5 Nov. 1938: I certainly liked the idea about a sea voyage. I like Kallenbach's suggestion very much indeed. You may go and see the field of my battles. I should like you very much to see Phoenix, Tolstoy Farm, the house in which I used to stay in Durban, the Johannesburg office, etc. Manilal will dance with joy.

But it might be difficult to take Durga [*Desai's wife*] and Bablo [*their son Narayan*] as far as that. I should like Bablo to remain with me. And moreover, a visit to South Africa would mean at least four months. South Africa is not less big than India. Go and see the four Colonies. And you must not miss the Victoria Falls ...

It is worth going there even if only for the sake of meeting Miss Schlesin. Kallenbach will perhaps have a time that he will remember for ever. The climate there is beyond praise. Think over it. If you feel inclined, I am certainly ready to send you. If Mirabehn wishes to go, I am ready to let her go (74: 95–6).

Unhappily, the plan was never realized.

Protecting a dream. March and April 1938 were difficult months. Apart from the crisis in Puri, a major reason was his awareness that Muslim separatism was growing even as independence seemed nearer. Jinnah, now the chief spokesman of Muslim separatism (or, to use the phrase Jinnah preferred, of Muslim nationalism), was gaining noticeably in strength. Also, the Hindu Mahasabha was preaching Hindu-Muslim incompatibility. Would India find civil war along with, or instead of, Swaraj?

While they lasted, the anti-British struggles of the early 1920s and the early 1930s had concealed Indian divisions. The 1937 elections and the negotiations that ensued revealed that India was larger than the Congress, and that the Congress could not contain all of India's competing groups, let alone resolve all their mutual conflicts.

No one before Gandhi had tried to bond with every Indian group, or to persuade the Congress to do the same, but the task was beyond him, the Congress or any human agency. Not only that: seeking a bond with all Indians angered some of them. Thus both Jinnah and Savarkar attacked Gandhi's effort to win Muslims to the Congress, Jinnah accusing him of 'poaching', and Savarkar charging that Gandhi was indifferent to Hindu interests.

At the end of 1936, sensing a menacing divide and a yen for violence, Gandhi had said to students who wanted a message:

> What new message can I give you at the age of sixty-eight? ... Assassinating the body of course does not matter, for out of my ashes a thousand Gandhis will arise. But what if you assassinate or burn the principles I have lived for? (70: 225)

In March 1938 he initiated correspondence with Jinnah. The two agreed that they should talk face to face, but Jinnah brusquely declined Gandhi's invitation to meet in Sevagram, and Gandhi agreed to call on him in his Bombay home.

Pride had to be swallowed ('I wrote to Jinnah that I would even go and meet him,' Gandhi would say to ashram colleagues[16]) but there was a deeper unease, for Jinnah had written to him that the 'only basis' for productive talks was for both sides to accept that the League represented India's Muslims while Gandhi and the Congress spoke for India's Hindus.[17]

Jinnah was asking Gandhi to disown his life so far. Rejecting Gandhi's suggestion that he meet with Maulana Azad to begin with, Jinnah said he would prefer to talk with Gandhi and then, if necessary, with Subhas, the Congress president. Gandhi agreed to a meeting at the end of April in Bombay, but about three weeks before it, for, he would say, 'the first time in my public and private life', he seemed to lose self-confidence. Admitting this publicly on 22 April, Gandhi added, 'I find myself for the first time during the past fifty years in a Slough of Despond' (73: 117).

He was on the brink of knocking down the British thesis that there was no such thing as an Indian nation, or that Indians could not govern themselves, when Jinnah loomed up, ready to prove Gandhi wrong. But the Jinnah barrier was joined to something else, an incident that Gandhi took as a sign of personal infirmity.

This personal 'failure' – which we will look at later in this chapter – seemed for a while to unnerve him for the Jinnah interview. On the other hand, anxiety about the interview, and fear of losing Mahadev, may have contributed to the 'failure'. In any case, Gandhi would fight his loss of confidence. In the 22 April statement he said:

> I may not leave a single stone unturned to achieve Hindu-Muslim unity ... We are friends, not strangers. It does not matter to me that we see things from different angles of vision. I ask the public not to attach any exaggerated importance to the interview. But I ask all lovers of communal peace to pray that the God of truth and love may give us both the right spirit and the right word and use us for the good of the dumb millions of India (73: 118).

On 28 April he and Jinnah talked for three-and-a-half hours. Later, Gandhi's reaction was: 'He is a very tough customer. If the other members of the League are of the same type, a settlement is an impossibility.'[18] The 'way out', Gandhi thought, was 'a unilateral undertaking' by the Congress to allay Muslim anxieties.

Yet since 'every attempt must be made to arrive at a mutual understanding', he urged Subhas also to try with Jinnah.[19] Observing that Subhas was 'a good listener', Gandhi thought it possible that 'he may succeed where others might have failed'.[20] Held in May, the Bose-Jinnah talks were nonetheless also unsuccessful.

In the Frontier

Gandhi's ability to reconnect with Muslim India had been hurt by the deaths of Ajmal Khan and Ansari, but he still had three influential Muslim allies, the Bengal-based Abul Kalam Azad and the Frontier's Khan brothers.

In July 1937, after Gandhi's positive role in the Congress's office-acceptance became plain, the new Viceroy, Linlithgow, wrote to Gandhi proposing a meeting. Gandhi not only replied, gracefully, that he too was thinking of a meeting, he made two requests from his side: Ghaffar Khan should be allowed to return to the NWFP, and he, Gandhi, should be allowed to go there.

Ghaffar Khan returned to the Frontier, Nehru followed him there in October 1937, and Gandhi in May 1938, just after his meeting with Jinnah. Gandhi's visit was preceded by that of Mahadev, who in 1935 had produced a short book on the Khan brothers, *Two Servants of God,* based on interviews during the brothers' 1934 stay in Wardha. Struck by Ghaffar Khan's 'submission or surrender to God', Desai had found the older brother less strict in Islamic observance. 'My brother offers the namaaz[*] on my behalf also,' Dr Khan Sahib told Desai.[21]

After a week in the Frontier in May 1938, Gandhi returned there for five weeks in the autumn of 1938, and again in July 1939, when he was accompanied by Kasturba. On all three trips Ghaffar Khan was his host, guide and interpreter. At Peshawar's famed Islamia College, founded in 1908, Gandhi asked his Muslim audience to reflect on the boundaries of their community:

> Islam ... believes in the brotherhood of man. But you will permit me to point out that it is not the brotherhood of Muslims only but universal brotherhood ... The Allah of Islam is the same as the God of Christians and the Ishwar of Hindus.[22]

---

[*] Namaaz = formal Muslim prayer.

With Ghaffar Khan in the Frontier Province – 1938 (Original photo: Kanu Gandhi)

The province's Hindu and Sikh minorities, troubled by raids by tribes descending into the Frontier's settled areas, were told by him that self-defence was everybody's birthright. 'I do not want to see a single coward in India,' Gandhi said on 25 October 1938 in the walled city of Bannu. Yet Gandhi also asked the Hindus and Sikhs to realize that the tribesman was 'a human being, just like you and me, and capable of responding to the human touch'.

He had met several tribesmen following his arrival in the province, Gandhi added, and he 'did not find that their nature was essentially different from human nature elsewhere'. Then he challenged the Hindus:

> You are a community of traders. Do not leave out of your traffic that noblest and precious merchandise, love. Give to the tribesmen all the love you are capable of, and you will have theirs in return.[23]

Unwell when he arrived for his second visit, Gandhi quickly recovered in the peace and quiet of the Khan brothers' village, Utmanzai. After Gandhi had complained, Badshah Khan, as Ghaffar Khan was known among his Pathans, disarmed the men guarding the house where Gandhi stayed, but he refused to dismiss the guards.[24]

During Gandhi's travels across the NWFP, Ghaffar Khan's Khudai Khidmatgars (KKs) were posted along his route, villages were festooned with arches, and tribal Pathans stood on perches to watch him. Everywhere Gandhi spent long sessions with KK groups, asking them to learn punctuality and crafts, and, as he put it in the town of Tank in Dera Ismail Khan district, 'to become a living wall of protection to your [Hindu and Sikh] neighbours'.[25]

Remembering that a Pathan, Mir Alam, had attacked him in South Africa, Gandhi probed the KKs on their non-violence. When a Khidmatgar confessed that he would depart from non-violence in case of 'abuse of their revered leaders', Gandhi said, 'I know it is no joke for a Pathan to take an affront lying down.'[26] Speaking to KKs in Tank, Gandhi made a remark that would be quoted often in the future:

> A small body of determined spirits fired by an unquenchable faith in their mission can alter the course of history.[27]

Even more interesting were two other statements Gandhi made in the Frontier. One was on the gender question in the Pakhtun country. Gandhi tackled it indirectly, narrating (on 23 October, in Hungoo) his personal experiences with Kasturba:

> I used to be a tyrant at home ... I used to let loose my anger at Kasturba. But she

bore it all meekly and uncomplainingly. I had a notion that it was her duty to obey me, her lord and master, in everything.

But her unresisting meekness opened my eyes and slowly it began to dawn upon me that I had no such prescriptive right over her. If I wanted her obedience, I had first to persuade her by patient argument. She thus became my teacher in non-violence. And I dare say, I have not had a more loyal and faithful comrade in life.

I literally used to make life a hell for her. Every other day I would change my residence, prescribe what dress she was to wear. She had been brought up in an orthodox family, where untouchability was observed. Muslims and untouchables used to frequent our house. I made her serve them all, regardless of her innate reluctance.

But she never said 'no'. She was not educated in the usual sense of the term and was simple and unsophisticated. Her guileless simplicity conquered me. You all have wives, mothers and sisters at home. You can take the lesson of non-violence from them.[28]

In July 1939, on his third visit, Gandhi made another memorable statement. By now many of the subcontinent's Muslims were receptive to the line that Indian independence would mean Hindu rule. Speaking in Abbottabad in the Frontier's Hazara's district, he said:

If you dissect my heart, you will find that the prayer and spiritual striving for the attainment of Hindu-Muslim unity goes on there unceasingly all the twenty-four hours without even a moment's interruption whether I am awake or asleep ... That dream [of Hindu-Muslim unity] has filled my being since the earliest childhood.

The greatest of things in this world are accomplished not through unaided human effort. They come in their own good time. God has His own way of choosing His instruments. Who knows, in spite of my incessant heart prayers, I may not be found worthy for this great work.

We must all keep our loins girt and our lamps well trimmed. We don't know when or on whom His choice may fall. You may not shirk your responsibility by shoving it all on me. Pray for me that my dream may be fulfilled in my life ... God's ways are more than man's arithmetic.[29]

We have a record of some of the Frontier conversations between Gandhi and Ghaffar Khan. In October 1938, recalling their first meeting nine years earlier, Gandhi said to Badshah Khan:

For years, ever since we met each other, it has been a pet dream of mine to visit the tribal areas, go right up to Kabul, mix with the trans-border tribes and try to understand their psychology. Why should we not go forth together, present to them our viewpoint and establish with the tribesmen a bond of friendship and sympathy?[30]

Ghaffar Khan said to his guest:

> This land, so rich in fruit and grain, might well have been a smiling little Eden upon this earth, but it today has fallen under a blight. Violence has been the real bane ... The entire strength of the Pathan is today spent in thinking how to cut the throat of his brother ...
>
> The non-violent movement is the greatest boon that God has sent us ... We used to be so timid and indolent. The sight of an Englishman would frighten us. [Our] movement has instilled fresh life into us and made us more industrious. We have shed our fear and are no longer afraid of an Englishman or for that matter of any man. Englishmen are afraid of our non-violence. A non-violent Pathan, they say, is more dangerous than a violent Pathan.

'I have been accused,' Badshah Khan added, 'of having a lashkar of one lakh of Khudai Khidmatgars to help the Hindus to subdue the Muslim population!'[31] When, in November 1938, the two parted at Taxila, 'our eyes were wet,' Gandhi recorded in an article in *Harijan*.[32] Earlier he had spoken at a Peshawar public meeting of

> the wonderful and affectionate allegiance of the people to [Badshah Khan] as their general ... Not only the Khudai Khidmatgars, but I noticed wherever I went that every man, woman and child knew him and loved him. They greeted him most familiarly. His touch seemed to soothe them. [Badshah Khan] was most gentle to whoever approached him. The obedience of the Khudai Khidmatgars was unquestioned. All this has filled me with boundless joy.[33]

A major element in this joy was the knowledge that, thanks to the Khan brothers, a vital Muslim-majority province trusted him and the Congress.

Subhas Bose

At the end of 1938 Subhas said he wanted a second term, even as Jawaharlal had had. Bose made it plain, moreover, that in his second term he expected executive authority, so that, for example, he could pull out all the Congress ministries, if that seemed desirable.

Subhas's stance was in part a response to developments in Europe, where, on 29

September 1938, Premiers Neville Chamberlain (Britain) and Edouard Daladier (France) signed with Adolf Hitler (Germany) and Benito Mussolini (Italy) the Munich pact, permitting Hitler to do as he pleased with Czechoslovakia. To Bose, a vulnerable Britain and France, a bold Germany and a confident Italy added up to an opportunity for mass disobedience in India, ending what he saw as the Congress's humiliating association with the Raj.

Gandhi's reaction to Munich, on the other hand, was to say in a letter to Jawaharlal, 'What a peace at the cost of honour!' (Letter of 4 Oct. 1938; 74: 77) In *Harijan* he wrote (8 Oct.):

> I do not profess to know European politics. But it does appear to me that small nationalities cannot exist in Europe with their heads erect. They must be absorbed by their larger neighbours. They must become vassals.
>
> Europe has sold her soul for the sake of a seven days' earthly existence … England and France [have] quailed before the combined violence of Germany and Italy (74: 98).

Soon Gandhi wrote about Hitler and his drive against the Jews (*Harijan*, 26 Nov. 1938):

> If there ever could be a justifiable war in the name of and for humanity, a war against Germany, to prevent the wanton persecution of a whole race, would be completely justified. But I do not believe in any war.

The last sentence showed that the violence of war was an issue with Gandhi. Even as he condemned Hitler, he proposed, both to the Jews and the Czechs, 'the superior alternative' of non-violence resistance. He did not know that in November 1937 Indian non-violence and Britain's 'appeasement' of it had been ridiculed by Hitler. Speaking to Irwin, now Lord Halifax and a minister under Chamberlain, Hitler had said:

> All you have to do is to shoot Gandhi. If necessary, shoot more leaders of Congress. You will be surprised how quickly the trouble will die down.[34]

To return, however, to Bose. He was reported to have been 'in contact with the German consul in Calcutta … negotiating some arrangement'. K M Munshi, the minister for law in Bombay, received this information from the Raj's central director of intelligence and forwarded it to Gandhi.[35] It appears, too, that Bose's 'admiration for Mussolini was then known to many'.[36]

Reading the 'message' from Europe differently, Gandhi would have been troubled by Subhas's apparent comfort with authoritarian rulers. But he had another reason for not wanting Bose reappointed: disturbed by Jinnah's attitude, Gandhi had 'instinctively felt' that Azad should be picked.[37] If Jinnah could not be conciliated and had to be fought, it made sense to have a Muslim as the Congress president. So Gandhi advised Bose not to offer himself again, and Nehru did likewise, but, certain of his destiny, Subhas announced his candidacy.

In the middle of January 1939, after Gandhi and Patel had talked to him in Bardoli, Azad agreed to stand against Bose, whereupon Patel, who had been proposed himself by some PCCs, formally withdrew his name. Fighting the charismatic Bose was a tough proposition, however, especially for one like Azad who lived in Bengal, where Subhas enjoyed passionate support. Within days of agreeing to stand, Azad also withdrew.

There was one possible opponent to Bose left in the lists: Pattabhi Sitaramayya from the Telugu country, whose name had been proposed by the Andhra PCC. Though hardly a famous figure, Pattabhi was publicly endorsed (at Gandhi's instance) by Patel, Prasad and five other Working Committee members, who, however, did not quote Gandhi.

Bose sought Nehru's support. Both saw themselves as socialists, and association with the Raj was distasteful to both of them. But they saw the European scene differently. If Bose was impressed by Mussolini, Jawaharlal had supported the anti-Fascists of Spain. As for India, while Bose could now think of himself as an alternative to Gandhi, Nehru would not defy Gandhi. He stayed out of the Bose-Pattabhi contest.

While most in the Working Committee were with Pattabhi, many of the Congress rank and file shared Bose's view that European events, and the possibility of a war between Germany and Britain, justified a return to the policy of defiance. Popular opinion, too, was increasingly anti-British, accusing Britain of wanting democracy in Europe but restricting self-government in India. Scenting a possible victory, Bose fought back, accusing 'Sardar Patel and other leaders' of unfairness and 'moral coercion' in endorsing Pattabhi. He also suggested that 'a compromise on the Federal Scheme' was likely 'between the Right Wing of the Congress and the British Government during the coming year'.[38] Nehru, no lover of the Right Wing, said publicly that the aspersion was unjust.

Calling Bose's statement 'amazing', Patel said he knew of 'no member who wants the Federation', and added that he and his colleagues had 'a perfect right to guide the delegates'.[39] But a majority of the delegates rejected the guidance. On 29 January, Subhas was re-elected, obtaining 1,580 votes as against Pattabhi's 1,375.

Though his sympathies were widely known, Gandhi had remained silent during the campaign, but after the result was known he said publicly:

Since I was instrumental in inducing Dr Pattabhi not to withdraw his name as a candidate when Maulana Saheb withdrew, the defeat is more mine than his (Statement of 31 Jan. 1939; 74: 14).

Making it plain that the Congress had to choose between him and Bose, Gandhi allowed Patel and C R to lead a campaign that forced Subhas to resign. Efforts for a compromise by Subhas and his older brother Sarat were resisted by the old guard.

When, in March, the Congress met for its plenary on the banks of the river Narmada, in Tripuri village in the Central Provinces, Govind Ballabh Pant moved a resolution calling upon the president 'to appoint the Working Committee in accordance with the wishes of Mahatma Gandhi'. Seconding the resolution, C R mercilessly ruled out a compromise:

There are two boats on the river. One is an old boat but a big boat, piloted by Mahatma Gandhi. Another man has a new boat, attractively painted and beflagged. Mahatma Gandhi is a tried boatman who can safely transport you. If you get into the other boat, which I know is leaky, all will go down, and the river Narmada is indeed deep.

The new boatman says, 'If you don't get into my boat, at least tie my boat to yours.' This is also impossible. We cannot tie a leaky boat to a good boat, exposing ourselves to the peril of going down.[40]

Gandhi was not in Tripuri but in his former home, the princely state of Rajkot, engaged in a battle for democracy there that we will look at later in this chapter. Subhas was present but quite ill; it was his portrait that 52 elephants pulled in Tripuri for the Congress's 52nd annual session, and Sarat read out his brother's address.

But Pant's resolution was easily carried, even though, once more, Nehru (and most Congress socialists) remained neutral. Refusing to implement the Tripuri directive, Bose resigned as president, and Prasad was elected in his place. In July, after Bose announced a day of protest against the Working Committee's condemnation of propaganda against Congress ministers, he was, 'with great regret', declared barred from elective office for three years. His revolt had been put down.

But Gandhi hoped for a restoration of his tie with Subhas. In November 1939 he wrote to him: 'For the time being you are my lost sheep. Some day I shall find you returning to the fold, if I am right and my love is pure.'[41]

Sex, love and lust. In December 1935, in Wardha, Margaret Sanger, the birth-control pioneer from New York, and Gandhi had a frank discussion, spread over two days, on sex, love and lust. According to Desai, who was present at the talks, Gandhi 'poured his whole being into his conversation. He revealed himself inside out, giving Mrs Sanger an intimate glimpse of his own private life' (*Harijan*, 25 Jan. 1936; 68: 190–4).

The two agreed on small families but not on contraceptives, Gandhi saying contraceptives would encourage immorality and Sanger asking whether couples could really restrict sexual union to two or three occasions in their lives together. Gandhi accepted that hard cases might justify contraceptives but said that he himself would not prescribe them, though he could ask for union to be confined to a wife's 'safe' period. Pressed by Sanger, Gandhi conceded that sexual union for procreation also partook of lust.

When Sanger suggested that she saw nothing wrong in multiple marriage partners, Gandhi disagreed. Recalling his relationship with Saraladevi, without naming her, he said: 'Could we not develop a close contact, I said to myself? This was a plausible argument, and I nearly slipped. But I was saved. I awoke from my trance, I don't know how. I was saved by youngsters who warned me.'[42]

Love, non-violence and African-Americans. Why not 'love' instead of 'non-violence'? The question was asked in February 1936 when two African-American couples, Howard and Sue Bailey Thurman and Edward and Phenola Carroll, met Gandhi in Bardoli.

Visits that Mira and Muriel Lester had made to the USA in 1934, and an earlier visit by Andrews in 1929, had helped many black Americans know more about an Indian they had been excited about from at least 1917, when Hubert H Harrison referred in an essay to Gandhi's call for Indian self-reliance.[43] W E B Du Bois's journal, *The Crisis,* had featured Gandhi in July 1921 and frequently thereafter, and another renowned black leader, Marcus Garvey, had also often spoken of Gandhi. The Thurmans and Carrolls thus represented an expanding constituency of African-American interest in Gandhi.

Answering their question, he said that for one thing 'love in the English language has other connotations too'. Moreover, in a world of 'strife and bloodshed, [with] life living upon life', 'non-violence' could suggest love plus struggle, whereas 'love' on its own might not, said Gandhi, while admitting his warmth for 'love in the Pauline sense'.

Gandhi seemed to value this encounter for more than one reason. He had always likened untouchability to slavery and remembered the unnamed African-American who helped him out in Pretoria in 1893; and he saw similarities in India's fight against imperialism and black America's struggle against racism.

Desai, who was present at the interview, told Thurman, then dean of Rankin Chapel in Howard University, that in all his years with Gandhi he had never seen him 'greet a visitor so warmly'. At the interview (Thurman would later recall), Gandhi asked 'persistent, pragmatic questions about American Negroes, about the course of slavery, and how we had survived it'.[44] Was colour prejudice growing or dying? Did American law recognize marriages between blacks and whites? And so forth.

When Sue Bailey Thurman asked Gandhi how non-violence would be applied against lynching, he suggested black non-cooperation 'unto self-immolation' against the lynching community, while admitting that his own non-violence was imperfect. At his request the Americans sang a Negro spiritual, and when Howard Thurman remarked on the similarity between the spirituals and what they had heard from him, Gandhi said:

> Well, if it comes true it may be through the Negroes that the unadulterated message of non-violence will be delivered to the world (*Harijan*, 14 Mar. 1936; 68: 237–8).

A year later, two other African-American leaders, Benjamin E Mays and Channing H Tobias, met with Gandhi in Sevagram. Tobias asked, 'What word shall I give to my Negro brethren as to the outlook for the future?' Replied Gandhi: 'With right, which is on their side, and the choice of non-violence as their only weapon, if they will make it such, a bright future is assured.'[45]

Evangelists. Christian ministers and evangelists (John Mott, Frank Buchman, E Stanley Jones, Toyohiko Kagawa, Sherwood Eddy and others) never stopped visiting him and Gandhi developed close relationships with several without conceding a need to become a Christian, and without approving efforts to proselytize. His oft-expressed view was that lovers or servants of Christ should serve but not desire or ask for converts. 'You can only preach through your life. The rose does not say: "Come and smell me"' (to John Mott, Nov. 1936; 70: 77). But he enjoyed his friendships with committed Christians.

Stanley Jones noted a set of opposing qualities in Gandhi: he was of East and West, the city and the village, a Hindu influenced by Christianity, simple and shrewd, candid and courteous, serious and playful, humble and self-assertive. The blend produced 'a sweet savour,' Jones said, but, he added, 'the preponderating impression he leaves is not sweetness but strength'.[46]

When, in 1929, John Mott asked Gandhi what weighed most on his mind, Gandhi spoke not of alien rule but of 'our apathy and hardness of heart, if I may use the Biblical phrase ... towards the masses and their poverty'.

In December 1938 Mott and Gandhi met again in Sevagram. By this time Munich had occurred, and Gandhi conceded that since 'the best mind of the world has not imbibed the spirit of non-violence', the world 'would have to meet gangsterism in the orthodox way' (74: 274).

Probed by Mott on God's interventions in his life, Gandhi spoke of his being enabled to survive assaults in South Africa, the money he received at moments of greatest need for his struggles, the inspiration that he felt led to the nationwide hartal of 1919, and the 'voice' that directed the fast of May 1933. Mott next asked about the place of silence in his life. Replied Gandhi:

It has now become both a physical and spiritual necessity for me. Originally it was taken to relieve the sense of pressure. Then I wanted time for writing. After, however, I had practised it for some time I saw the spiritual value of it. It suddenly flashed across my mind that that was the time when I could best hold communion with God (74: 270–7).

Crying out to God? Yet, in his case, communion with God only rarely meant (or produced) a cry for relief, help or a miracle. He sought strength and wisdom but did not spare himself in his division of labour with God. As Gandhi saw it, his burden was chiefly for himself to carry.

Mott (in December 1936): What affords you the greatest hope and satisfaction?
G: Faith in myself born of faith in God.
M: In moments when your heart may sink within you, you hark back to this faith in God?
G: Yes. That is why I have always described myself as an irrepressible optimist.
M: So am I. Our difficulties are our salvation. They make us hark back to the living God.
G: Yes. My difficulties have strengthened my faith which rises superior to every difficulty, and remains undimmed. My darkest hour was when I was in Bombay a few months ago. It was the hour of my temptation. Whilst I was asleep I suddenly felt as though I wanted to see a woman.

Well, a man who had tried to rise superior to the sex instinct for nearly forty years was bound to be intensely pained when he had this frightful experience.

I ultimately conquered the feeling, but I was face to face with the blackest moment of my life ... Many Christian friends are jealous of the peace I possess. It comes from God who has blessed me with the strength to battle against temptation.
M: I agree. 'Blessed are the pure in heart, for they shall see God' (report of meetings on 13–14 December in *Harijan*, 26 Dec. 1936; 70: 79–80).

Thus his response to temptation is shock and a resolve for greater personal strength, while conceding that such strength 'comes from God'. Human striving is what he has practised over a lifetime, but he is more than familiar with the view that without God's grace nothing is possible. He accepts this truth, and indeed has experienced it.

But he has also, in one part of him, resisted this truth. While his Christian friends equated grace with Christianity, many Hindus had made grace an excuse for inaction. He answers faith in Jesus, and Hindu fatalism, with faith in his discipline. Christian friends marvel at his commitment to what they see as Christian morals, while Hindus think of him as one of their faith's most effective modern exemplars.

On his part he never forgets the warning of his Christian friends, which is also the teaching of the Bhakti poets he loves, including Tulsidas and Narsi Mehta, that freedom from sin is impossible without divine intercession. Time and again, in the Autobiography and elsewhere, he records the warning. Yet crying out to God is only rarely his style; if it occurs, it does so behind the scenes, unrecorded. Otherwise, each crisis is primarily a signal for greater self-effort, and he seems convinced of God's blessings if he but obeys his mind-cum-conscience.

Shivering & an unusual remedy

All the same, turmoil – physical and emotional – stalked Gandhi in the late 1930s in Sevagram. There the Gandhis' hut was largely Kasturba's, for he usually slept in the open, with two or three of his aides, generally women, sleeping near him. Not enjoying any exclusive relationship with her husband, Kasturba was remarkably friendly to the women assisting him. One of them, Prabhavati Narayan, would recall:

> During winter days in Sevagram, I used to go into Ba's room after the early morning four o'clock prayer. And Ba always insisted: 'Prabha, Go and sleep for some time.' Even in freezing weather Ba used to sweep the room; then she would heat water for the bath, and after the cleaning and dusting were over she would come to wake me up. Warm water was always ready for my bath.[47]

When, at some point in 1937, doctors ordered an ill Gandhi to sleep indoors, Kasturba at once announced, 'Bapu will sleep in my hut.' Sushila has recalled the occasion:

> Ba's room was small. There were one or two other persons who used to sleep near Gandhiji. Ba vacated the room for Bapu and his companions and she slept on the verandah with her little grandson Kanu [Ramdas's son]. She never for a moment grudged making room for others beside her own husband.[48]

Gandhi felt guilty the next morning and said:

> Poor Ba has never had a room to herself. This hut I had constructed specially for her use and I myself supervised all the details. I thought she should have some comfort and privacy in her old age and now I have taken possession of it.[49]

More than that, Gandhi had begun or would soon begin an unusual practice. Assailed by fits of trembling, he would find relief through one of his women aides lying down beside him.

'If Gandhi got the shivers on wintry nights, why not reach for an extra blanket instead of a girl?'[50] We have no direct answer from Gandhi to the obvious question that William Shirer would ask after Gandhi's death. Yet the curious remedy was not, in history, an unprecedented recourse. As Erikson notes, the Bible speaks of King David who was unable to feel any warmth though covered at night with many clothes, whereupon a young woman called Abishag 'was brought to the king'. She 'cherished the king and ministered to him, but the king knew her not' (Kings 1: 3,4).

We have seen that trembling and shaking marked Gandhi from his boyhood. In April 1939 Pyarelal would write in *Harijan* that the shaking was, 'an old symptom that seizes him whenever he receives an acute mental shock' and that it was usually set off 'by a sudden attack of sharp pain near the waist'.[51] We do not know what contributed to the shivering in 1937, or whether or not it was a medical condition, or related to the violence he had received over the years,[52] misery over Harilal, the scale of what he had taken on, or whatever. Nor do we know whether Gandhi was aware of the precedent of King David.

In retrospect we mark a natural progression: someone long dependent on the physical touch has his young aides first sleep near him and then right up against him. No matter what its immediate or longer-term cause, the shivering was answered by a woman aide lying down beside him – with Kasturba's full knowledge.[53]

'Whatever I used to do, Ba knew everything,' Gandhi would claim in 1947, in a letter to Harilal's son Kanti.[54] There is no record of her opposition to the 'remedy'.

Not only did the practice continue for several weeks during the winter of 1937–8, Gandhi began to defend it as an experiment in chastity and indeed as a means for enhancing it, in himself and in the companion. Perhaps he was rationalizing an embarrassing 'remedy' that had become a need. Yet there was no suggestion or allegation from anyone involved, then or later, that open or concealed lust was at work. As far as he knew himself, he said, the practice was lust-free.

He had a shock, however, on the night of 7 April 1938. (This was within days of Mahadev saying he wanted to leave, and while Gandhi was exploring a meeting with Jinnah.) While he and his aides, including Prabhavati, who was 32, and Sushila, 24, slept in the open in Sevagram, he experienced an involuntary emission. A week later, on 14 April, he experienced a discharge again. In a private note written for co-workers (2 Jun.), he would say:

> I felt ashamed. After the experience [of 7 April] I hardly slept that night. I was restless. I walked about on the terrace and calmed myself a little ... I felt that I

was not fit to accept service from Sushila and Prabhavati who slept close to my bed.

After the [pre-dawn] prayer, I first recounted to them what I had been through and then told them that I would not be taking service from them. But both took this decision very badly. Within twelve hours I reviewed my decision and continued to take service from them.

But my distress did not cease. On the 14th I had another type of experience which increased my shame and added to my anguish ... While I was caught in that whirlpool, I had to meet Mr Jinnah ... I had lost my self-confidence ...

But a doubt arose after my experience of the 7th April ... Why have my thoughts and my mind not become purer and purer? ... Could the contact with women have obstructed my path in some subtle way? Who can answer that question? The only solution is that unless God Himself answers it, I should try to shun all physical touch and understand my own mind and conquer it ...

I should not have undertaken the experiment if it was so terrible. If it was worth undertaking, I should have encouraged all my colleagues to pursue it on my condition. My experiment was a transgression of the limits prescribed by brahmacharya ...

Only he who can observe complete brahmacharya can give complete training in non-violence ...

After a great deal of thought I have [decided that] I should not take any service from women which involves physical contact, unless it is absolutely unavoidable ... I must not touch them in jest or in affection ...

Before I took the vow of brahmacharya and after, I touched numerous women in a light-hearted way or in affection. I have not experienced any adverse effect thereby and have not known any woman who may have been sensually aroused.

Who can say where the future will lead me? My strongest desire is to submit lovingly to God and let myself be driven whither He wills.

It was my clear duty to convey this much to my co-workers. I assume that any co-worker who wishes will let me know his reactions and point out any error he may find in my thinking (note of 2 Jun. 1938, marked 'Unrevised'; 73: 214–15).

The note is full of doubt and inconsistency. He links his 'fall' to the liberties he had taken, but 'who can answer' for certain? Curbing his freedom 'might' strengthen him; his decisions are final but also alterable, for instance if women like Sushila and Prabhavati are upset; he is not really sure what God wants or 'where the future will lead me'. The experiment is over for now but not necessarily for ever.

Learning of his 'fall', Mira suggested at the end of April that Gandhi should reduce or end physical contact with women. We may observe that she was never part of the 'experiment'. In respect of Mira, Gandhi always spoke of himself as a father, as a male, never claiming (as he did with other women aides) that he was their 'mother' or 'sister', and perhaps, too, he felt unsure about Mira's brahmacharya in any 'experiment' involving the two of them.

In his reply (3 May 1938) to Mira, Gandhi wrote disapprovingly of the traditional Hindu notion of 'nine fortifications' against the charms of women. Parts of the letter are quite moving:

> I like your letter for its transparent love ... The problem however is not so simple as you have put it ... What is the value of the species that requires the nine fortifications? You are quite right in describing my experiment as new. So is my experiment in ahimsa. The two hang together.
>
> Remember that my experiment has natural limitations. I may neither tempt God nor the Devil ... In your next letter you must tell me in concrete terms what definite changes I should make so as to fit in with your idea. Should I deny myself the service rendered by Sushila? Should I refuse to have malish [massage] by Lilavati or Amtul Salaam for instance? Or do you want to say that I should never lean on girls' shoulders?
>
> Needless to say you won't pain me at all by telling me frankly whatever you think I should do to get out of the terrible despondency. Just now I am most in need of support from those who surround me with service and affection, undeserved as it seems to me, for the time being.
>
> In guiding me remember that what I am doing I have done all my life you may say. And my brahmacharya has become firmer and more enlightened ... I felt I was progressing. That degrading, dirty, torturing experience of 14th April shook me to bits and made me feel as if I was hurled by God from an imaginary paradise where I had no right to be in my [uncleanness].
>
> Well, I shall feel pride in my being parent to so many children, if any of them will give a lifting hand and pull me out of the well of despair (73: 41–2).

Apparently disagreeing with Mira, Sushila (who was a doctor) protested at Gandhi's word that he would not touch her. The note of 2 June was a response to conflicting advice, and to the conflict in his own mind.

The uncertainties were repeated in several letters he wrote at this time to Pyarelal, Sushila, Mira, Mahadev and others. Relationships among his co-workers and theirs with him seem tense and fragile at this point. In some letters he implores Pyarelal and Sushila not to leave him, says his own imperfections lay behind a wrong accusation he seems to have made (in respect of Sushila's behaviour towards Mahadev), and at times uses a tone, extremely rare in him, of plaintiveness. He also thanks Sushila for 'your resolute stand'. 'Even though you came to me as a daughter, you have acted like a mother' (73: 211).

On 1 June he wrote to Sushila: 'Now I have *more or less* [*emphasis added*] decided that with the exception of Ba I will not accept from any other woman any service involving physical contact' (73: 210). Two days later, however, he wrote to Pyarelal: 'When she [Sushila] comes on her own I shall of course embrace her in spite of my having stopped taking service from women' (Letter of 3 Jun. 1938; 73: 219–20).The service he was speaking of included preparing and serving his meals, assisting with his bath and giving him an oil massage.

In a letter (11 Jun. 1938) to another co-worker, Balwantsinha, Gandhi said that his 1935 decision not to place his hands on the shoulders of women did not 'mean that I would never place my hand on the shoulder of any girl whatsoever'. Stating, further, that he was used to bathing in the nude in the presence of some women, Gandhi added:

> From the very beginning I have regarded Sushilabehn in the same way as Ba, as an exception ... I would like to give up physical contact even with these two if it were possible, but I have no desire to do so at the cost of the deep hurt which I would be causing them while my heart feels no sin in the contact of these two.
>
> I have caused Ba much pain. I still occasionally do, but I have no courage nor any desire to inflict any further pain on her ...
>
> Once I intended to give up all personal services from Sushila but within twelve hours my soft-heartedness had put an end to the intention. I could not bear the tears of Sushila and the fainting away of Prabhavati. I did not even want to ...
>
> Sushila has been present in the bathroom while I have bathed in the nude and in her absence Ba or Prabhavati or Lilavati have attended on me ... Pyarelal has been in attendance occasionally but I have never felt any embarrassment in being seen naked by a woman ... whose relations with me cannot come under any kind of suspicion (73: 235–6).

Co-workers were indeed troubled. A colleague from 1915, Amritlal Thakkar, who had given himself to work for Harijans and tribals and was called Thakkar Bapa, was 'pained', Gandhi was informed (73: 267). Mahadev too seemed perturbed.[55]

However, if some associates, and also part of his mind, asked Gandhi to give up closeness with women, that advice was resisted by an unwillingness to break what had become a dependence, which would also mean breaking hearts in a close circle of women. This was not a *closed* circle: some left while others joined. In the late 1930s, it included Lilavati Asar from Bombay (who was only 14 in 1938), Prabhavati Narayan, Amtus Salaam, a faithful Muslim from Patiala state in eastern Punjab, and Sushila Nayar.

Kasturba, special in the circle but not perhaps critical to it, had learnt to tolerate other women sharing the space and chores around Gandhi, and grew close herself to some of them. At least once, and possibly several times, she insisted that her husband should 'take service from the girls'.[56] Oddities and all, there was remarkable trust, respect and affection between the two. We should note here, too, that the honest account that Gandhi gave in the Frontier Province of his harshness to Kasturba was offered immediately after the turmoil of the 1938 summer.

Striving to be womanlike (as well as manlier than anyone else), Gandhi too felt part of this intimate, feminine circle, where he found the love that helped him fight his outer battles.

Yet perhaps we should at least register Gandhi's claim that also at work was his sense of how a non-violent general's power is acquired or lost, and of his personal calling. The thought that he was a pioneer in chastity as much as in satyagraha clashed with the advice against closeness with women, which was ended only to be resumed, suspended, revived, extended ...

What is beyond doubt is his dependence on physical closeness and contact. This closeness (as he claimed to Mira) has precise limits, yet it solaces, comforts, renews him. It recalls his mother, who loved him and believed in him as no one else ever did in his boyhood, and whom, as he thought, he loved as no one ever loved a parent. He seeks and offers at night a mother's warmth, and is ready before every dawn to fight every battle thrown at him, to fight it with greater virility than any other Indian.

Sense of duty. Trembling (or the remedy for it) did not affect Gandhi's sense of duty. Not harboured for long, 'loss of confidence' was never allowed to paralyze him. In 1938 he made two visits to the NWFP and one to eastern India; and in 1939 he went to Gujarat, UP, Calcutta, Bihar and the Frontier Province.

Every day, whether travelling or in Sevagram, and including when he felt trapped in a Slough of Despond, he wrote dozens of letters and gave of himself to several callers. The routine of waking at 3.30 a.m., praying twice a day, spinning for an hour or more, and spending time with the sick did not change. Every week he wrote for *Harijan*, now a political as well as a social reform journal, offering advice to Congress ministries and to his non-political followers. And whenever necessary he intervened in Congress affairs: his role over the Subhas Bose presidency was not an isolated case.

His looks depended on the beholder. To some he was small and ugly. He certainly was not tall at five-foot-six. He had large ears (like Mickey Mouse's, as a later generation would say) and 'his fat nose pointed downwards, and his lower lip pushed up to meet it'.[57]

But he also looked 'like a polished nut, all bright and shiny, with no spare flesh'.[58] An American journalist who would soon get to know him, Louis Fischer, thought the body did not suggest an old man. It had long arms and well-formed fingers and Gandhi's hand-clasp was firm. Fischer found Gandhi's skin soft and smooth, with a healthy glow. More than one observer called his look 'coppery'. Meeting him in 1939, the British journalist Francis Watson thought that Gandhi shone 'with coppery well-being'.[59]

A daily oil massage no doubt heightened the quality of his skin but Gandhi, a keen and pragmatic student of health, had also looked after himself over the years, eating carefully and walking several miles a day. 'Just as a pregnant woman takes care of her health for the sake of the baby in her womb, I take care of myself for the sake of the Swaraj that is supposed to be in my womb,' he had said in 1930 to Kalelkar. Watson noticed 'coiled energy in the angular body'[60] when Gandhi sat. When he walked, his straight back and brisk steps became apparent.

Most found his appearance striking rather than plain, and youthful rather than old, and remembered especially his laughter. He smiled, grinned, chuckled or laughed heartily, and usually those meeting him also found themselves laughing. As Nehru and others found, Gandhi usually brought a breeze to a room he entered.[61]

Yet Gandhi's gaiety was perhaps secondary to his sorrow. Nehru noticed 'deep pools of sadness' in Gandhi's twinkling eyes, and Hansa Mehta spoke for all who sat sensitively near him when she said: 'There must have been something terribly pathetic about him, for I always felt deeply moved in his presence.'[62] Some of the sadness undoubtedly came from self-suppression: he couldn't do what he had wanted to do. 'If I have given up anything for national service,' he had said to Kalelkar back in 1915, 'it is my interest in English literature'.[63] In that remark literature stood for a range of joys he had denied himself.

Then there was his eldest son. Every reminder of Harilal's distress was a knife-thrust. Moreover, since Gandhi's longings were huge, involving a large country and at times a larger humanity, life had acquainted him with disappointment going beyond his son or family.

A toll was taken, too, by his inner conflicts – over chastity, as we have seen, but also over who at any given time were more 'his people' or 'family' than others, and over how hard or soft he should be with those close to him. An important layer of his suppressed unhappiness was formed by the tension between the voices of truth and India, a tension that at times had obliged him to live with violence.

Yet the oft-concealed melancholy served as a spur. Any reminder of his sadness led him always to a reminder of a task that was his to complete. In him melancholy was the twin of destiny – and usually a prelude to a chuckle.

Like his sadness, Gandhi's gaiety, too, had inner and outer sources. He believed in the triumph, no matter how slow, of good, and found 'delight in life ... in the scheme of this universe';[64] he felt he had been given rich truths to share with the world, some of which he had seen wonderfully demonstrated; he seemed to find something of value in every person he encountered; and each day saw at least some of his wishes fulfilled, even if most others remained unmet.

And though he sought to influence the world, he did not seek followers. In March 1940 he would tell a gathering of associates:

> Let no one say that he is a follower of Gandhi. It is enough that I should be my own follower ... You are not followers but fellow students, fellow pilgrims, fellow seekers, fellow workers.[65]

One way of making sense of his sleeping alongside his 'sisters' or 'daughters' is to see it as a response to the weight on his shoulders: the load of personal pain and disappointment plus the burden of his large battles. He is in effect carrying India on his shoulders. He loses balance under that impossible load, and seeks comfort in unconventional ways, but the load is never dropped.

Though he would be called the father of India he was also India's son, carrying India the way the boy Shravana carried his parents in the scene that Mohan saw in his childhood and never forgot. Shravana died before their death and the parents wailed as Indians would wail when Gandhi would die; but carrying the load required strange twists and adjustments. Gandhi's practices were particular and peculiar, but the cargo was safely carried.

Stories. In 1939, a Marathi paper claiming to be devoted to 'the organization of Hindus' suggested that Gandhi's brahmacharya was 'a cloak' to hide his 'sensuality' and mentioned Sushila. And the *Bombay Chronicle* carried a story that Edward Thompson, a British historian interested in India, had said something similar to British MPs, on the basis, apparently, of distorted versions of Gandhi's confessions published in some Marathi papers. Asked to reply, Gandhi wrote a piece in *Harijan* that included his analysis of the calumniators:

> Poor Dr Sushila Nayyar has been dragged before the public gaze for the crime of giving me massage and medicated baths, the two things for which she is the best qualified among those who surround me. The curious may be informed that there is no privacy about these operations which take over one-and-a-half hours and during which I often go off to sleep but during which I also transact business with Mahadev, Pyarelal or other co-workers.
>
> The charges, to my knowledge, began with my active campaign against untouchability. This was when it was included in the Congress programme and I began to address crowds on the subject and insisted on having Harijans at meetings and in the

Ashram. It was then that some sanatanists, who used to help me and befriend me, broke with me and began a campaign of vilification ...

If I were sensually inclined, I would have the courage to make the confession ...

[T]he manner in which my brahmacharya came to me irresistibly drew me to woman as the mother of man. She became too sacred for sexual love. And so every woman at once became sister or daughter to me ...

I found myself enjoying the confidence of many sisters, European and Indian, in South Africa. And when I invited the Indian sisters in South Africa to join the civil resistance movement, I found myself one of them. I discovered that I was specially fitted to serve womankind.

To cut the (for me enthralling) story short, my return to India found me in no time one with India's women. The easy access I had to their hearts was an agreeable revelation to me. Muslim sisters never kept purdah before me here even as they did not in South Africa.

I sleep in the Ashram surrounded by women for they feel safe with me in every respect. It should be remembered that there is no privacy in the Segaon Ashram.

If I were sexually attracted towards women, I have courage enough, even at this time of life, to become a polygamist. I do not believe in free love – secret or open (*Harijan,* 4 Nov. 1939; 77: 60–2).

Chastity, power & calling. Earlier, in an article published in July 1938, he had put his beliefs, and also his doubts, into words for the public:

[T]here must be power in the word of a satyagraha general – not the power that the possession of limitless arms gives, but the power that purity of life, strict vigilance, and ceaseless application produce.

[A]n impure thought is a breach of brahmacharya; so is anger. All power comes from the preservation and sublimation of the vitality that is responsible for creation of life. If the vitality is husbanded instead of being dissipated, it is transmuted into creative energy of the highest order ...

My brahmacharya was not derived from books. I evolved my own rules for my guidance and that of those who, at my invitation, had joined me in the experiment. If I have not followed the prescribed restrictions, much less have I accepted the description found even in religious literature of woman as the source of all evil and temptation.

It is not woman whose touch defiles man but he is often himself too impure to touch her. But recently a doubt has seized me as to the nature of the limitation that a brahmachari or brahmacharini should put upon himself or herself regarding contacts with the opposite sex.

I have set limitations which do not satisfy me.

My faith in non-violence remains as strong as ever. I am quite sure that not only should it answer all our requirements in our country, but that it should, if properly applied, prevent the bloodshed that is going on outside India and is threatening to overwhelm the Western world …

[God] will perhaps take me away when I am no longer wanted for the work which I have been permitted to do for nearly half a century. But I do entertain the hope that there is yet work for me to do, that the darkness that seems to have enveloped me will disappear, and that, whether with another battle more brilliant than the Dandi March or without, India will come to her own demonstrably through non-violent means (23 Jul. 1938; 73: 316–20).

Writing two months before Munich, Gandhi refers, if only in passing, to the likelihood of war in Europe and, let us note, the possibility of another 'brilliant battle' in India.

Rajkot. If 'British' provinces now enjoyed self-government, should not princely states move towards popular rule? This natural question had come to the fore at the Haripura Congress of March 1938, and while Gandhi remained anxious not to solidify the alliance of India's princes with the Empire, he blessed the emergence of Praja Mandals or People's Associations in the states and permitted some Congress leaders to lend support.

Rajkot was in a sorry condition. Its ruler, Dharmendrasinh, feeble and irresponsible, had squandered funds and allowed Virawala, his diwan (a successor, that is, of Kaba Gandhi) to auction monopolies for selling rice, matches, sugar and cinema tickets. Imposing a 14-hour day on workers in the state-owned textile mill, Virawala sold a monopoly for gambling as well and proposed mortgaging Rajkot's powerhouse.

A young man called U N Dhebar, who led a people's campaign against the monopolies and asked for a closure of gambling shops on religious holidays, was arrested, and many were beaten. Vallabhbhai Patel intervened. In September 1938 he went to Rajkot and said, 'We are not desirous of dethroning the ruler. We wish to limit his authority.'[66]

The Raj seemed to act in defence of the people of Rajkot. A British diwan, Sir Patrick Cadell, took over from Virawala and released Dhebar. But Virawala retained power as the prince's private adviser and drafted a letter signed by Dharmendrasinh that requested E C Gibson, the resident for the Kathiawar states (a successor, that is, of Charles Ollivant), to recall Cadell. Gibson's response, however, was to ask for Virawala to leave Rajkot.

Cadell stayed on and Virawala left, but when Dhebar and his fellow activists revived their campaign they were jailed. In their support, Patel's daughter Maniben campaigned in villages in Rajkot state. She was arrested on 5 December.

Virawala now came up with a cunning strategy for returning to power. Telling Patel that Indians like him, Virawala and Dharmendrasinh should settle 'without the knowledge of Cadell', he also ensured that Gibson and Cadell were kept informed of Patel's supposed untrustworthiness.[67]

On 28 December a settlement between Patel and the ruler was announced. Dhebar, Maniben and the others were released, and Dharmendrasinh promised a committee to prepare a scheme of reforms and said it would consist of seven chosen by Patel and three by himself. However, even as Patel announced the end of the popular unrest and imagined that 'the speed and drama of the settlement had baffled the resident',[68] Gibson began complaining to Dharmendrasinh about Patel. Three weeks after signing the settlement, the prince revoked it. Not only that: Cadell was removed and Virawala reinstated as diwan! At Patel's instance a struggle was announced. It was ruthlessly repressed. Newspapers were kept out of Rajkot, meetings were banned, and those defying bans were beaten and deprived of their property.

'The movement for liberty within the [princely] States is entering a new stage,' Gandhi wrote in *Harijan* (28 Jan. 1939). Apart from Rajkot, he noted repression in states in the Orissa region and in Jaipur in Rajputana, and the danger from caste and religious divisions in Travancore. Told often that his involvement with untouchability and the Hindu-Muslim question weakened the focus on British rule, Gandhi was criticized for opening yet another front. In particular, he was warned against allowing himself to be dragged into the Rajkot tangle, which coincided with Subhas Bose's bid for re-election.

But Gandhi had always known that the journey to independence would have to take in the princely states. As for Rajkot, the betrayal of Patel, his stalwart right hand, had to be answered. Moreover, Rajkot was his own state, and it was in his presence that Dharmendrasinh's father Lakhajiraj had said in 1925: 'I myself wish to be Gandhiji's lieutenant. Why may I not surpass even Vallabhbhai?'[69]

Rajkot was also where Kasturba had spent her youth. When, in December, Maniben was arrested, she asked Gandhi to let her go there. But she had fainted in Devadas's house in Delhi only days before, and her husband thought her 'too weak' for the exercise. At the end of January she again asked to go. This time Gandhi let her. In *Harijan* he wrote (4 and 11 Feb. 1939):

> My wife feels so much ... that though she is as old as I am and much less able than myself to brave such hardships as may be attendant upon jail life, she feels she must go to Rajkot (75: 1).
>
> She felt a personal call. She could not sit still whilst the other daughters of Rajkot were suffering for the freedom of the men and women of the State. Rajkot is no doubt an insignificant place on the map of India. But it is not insignificant for me and my wife (75: 45).

Early in February Kasturba, accompanied by Maniben and Mridula Sarabhai (Ambalal's daughter), entered the state. All three were arrested, detained in a shabby place and told falsely that Gandhi had taken ill in Sevagram. Reminding his wife that she had 'now become a State guest',[70] Gandhi wrote to her every day, and she to him. She became ill, he too was unwell, and each worried about the other.

> *To Kasturba, 9 Feb.:* For the time being I have given up taking help from the girls. Do not feel uneasy. Do not worry. I shall see what to do. Sushila of course continues to look after me (75: 59).

Kasturba's travail stirred many across India and affected her husband. At the end of February he felt he had to go himself to Rajkot. There Virawala called on Gandhi, prostrated himself before him, and stayed for three-and-a-half hours, but questioned the authenticity of the 28 December settlement. Also, he insisted on being present when Gandhi met Dharmendrasinh. In a letter to Gibson, the resident, Gandhi said that to think of the prince as a 'responsible, thinking ruler' would be 'giving currency to a fraud', and that Virawala, 'the virtual ruler of Rajkot', was 'utterly unreliable' (4 Mar. 1939; 75: 148–9).

On 3 March Gandhi started a fast and said he hoped the Viceroy would 'induce fulfilment' of the ruler's promise to Patel. Recalling his mother (it was natural to do so in Rajkot), he said:

> Fast[ing] is in my blood and bones. I imbibed it with my mother's milk. My mother fasted if someone was ill ... if she was in pain ... in season and out of season. How can I, her son, do otherwise?[71]

Three days later an anxious Kasturba was released, as also Maniben and Mridula. More significantly, Gibson's ultimate boss, Lord Linlithgow, the Viceroy, suggested in a message to Gandhi that the dispute over the end-December settlement could be referred to the Chief Justice of India, Sir Maurice Gwyer.

Accepting the suggestion, Gandhi ended the fast four days after starting it. Given on 3 April after a presentation by Virawala, Gwyer's ruling completely vindicated Patel, and the Viceroy declared that the Raj wanted the settlement implemented. Gandhi thanked Linlithgow, but the impressive victory was short-lived. Refusing to admit defeat, Virawala stoked the fears of minorities in Rajkot. Many of the state's Muslims, Garasias (landowners), and Bhayats (the ruler's kinsmen) joined what was billed as a campaign to prevent minority interests being crushed by Patel's nominees.

Ring of violence. There was talk of a threat to Patel's life. Then, on 16 April, a 600-

strong mob of sword-swinging Bhayats and lathi-carrying Muslims broke up a prayer meeting that a barely fit Gandhi, some months shy of his 70th birthday, was conducting in Rajkot, and tried forcibly to disperse a cordon of unarmed volunteers around Gandhi.

Remaining at Gandhi's side, Kalelkar's 26-year-old son Bal, who had been a Dandi marcher in his teens, 'suddenly noticed that Bapuji's whole body began to shake violently'. Bal Kalelkar thought that the shaking

> was not out of fear; his face could tell how free from fear he was. The physical reaction was his revolt against the disgusting atmosphere of violence.[72]

Pyarelal, who was not far, wrote what we have already quoted. He would say that the shaking was set off by a sudden attack of sharp pain near the waist, 'an old symptom that seizes him whenever he receives an acute mental shock'. Added Pyarelal:

> For a time he stood in the midst of that jostling crowd motionless and silent, his eyes shut, supporting himself on his staff, and tried to seek relief through silent prayer ... As soon as he had sufficiently recovered, he reiterated his resolve to go through the demonstrators all alone. He addressed a Bhayat, who stood confronting him: 'I wish to go under your sole protection, not co-workers.'[73]

Bal Kalelkar's account suggests that this time the prayer was not silent, that Gandhi cried out to God:

> Suddenly he closed his eyes and started praying. I could hear him saying Ramnam with an intensity of devotion that could never be surpassed. I joined him in his prayer and to keep time to our chanting of God's name I started patting my hand on his back ...
>
> The prayer worked. When Bapuji reopened his eyes there was a new strength that appeared then like magic. In a firm tone he asked all the volunteers to quit that place at once and leave him absolutely alone at the mercy of the hired goondas ...
>
> Then he called the leader of the gang who was busy breaking up the congregation and told him that he was absolutely at his disposal if he cared to argue out his point; if not, would he tell what he proposed to do next? To everyone's amazement the thugs' violence melted like ice. The leader of the gang stood before Bapuji with folded hands ... That evening he walked all the way home with one hand on the shoulder of the leader of the gang.[74]

But we should take note of the younger man's role in this story of trembling yet victorious courage. The affectionate, trusting beat of Bal's palm had aided Gandhi's renewal.

Admitting defeat. Though they allowed Gandhi to walk away unmolested, the Bhayats were in no mood to let their dominance of Rajkot be ended by Patel's nominees and men like young Dhebar. They, the Garasias and the Muslims – the minorities that Virawala had mobilized – made up only about 15 per cent of the population but provided the bulk of the police and of the state's muscle-power. With their support Virawala was able to block the implementation of the settlement. On 24 April Gandhi left Rajkot 'empty-handed, with body shattered and hope cremated', as he put it (75: 298).

Reflection was called for. A campaign for the mere beginnings of representative government in Rajkot had evoked hostility from significant minorities. The fight against feudalism had stoked fires in caste and communal groups. Moreover, to defeat feudalism he had turned to the chief agent of imperialism.

It was the Viceroy who had given him and Patel, and the majority of the people of Rajkot, their 'victory'. By asking Linlithgow to intervene, Gandhi had enhanced the Raj's prestige. He knew perfectly well that if others – Jinnah, the princes, the landlords, Ambedkar, Savarkar and the like – were to ask the Raj to help out, the Viceroy would not necessarily reject their overtures, or go along with Gandhi's views.

The plea to Linlithgow was perhaps inopportune as well, for Subhas had lately accused Congress leaders close to Gandhi of planning a deal with the British. In May 1939 Gandhi formally renounced Gwyer's unenforceable award and said he had erred in asking for the Viceroy's aid. The fight for 'liberty within the States' would have to be waged again, at another time, perhaps in another way.

India was complex, as was the journey to independence. The Rajkot exercise confirmed this. Did it do more? It certainly forged new leadership. Dhebar (1905–77) would become chief minister of Saurashtra in 1948 and president of the Congress from 1955 to 1959. It also brought new prestige to Kasturba and new depth to an old if taxing relationship between the Gandhis.

When, in July, the two went to the North-West Frontier Province (his third visit), hosts thought that Kasturba was 'in wonderful form, even more so than Bapu'.[75] In any case Gandhi insisted that 'Rajkot has been to me a priceless laboratory' (*Harijan,* 29 Apr. 1939; 75: 298).

Hitler, Jews, Palestine

In November 1938 Gandhi spelt out, in response to pressing requests, his views on German militarism and how to resist it, the persecution of Jews and the bid for a Jewish home in Palestine:

My sympathies are all with the Jews. I have known them intimately in South Africa.

Some of them became life-long companions. Through these friends I came to learn much of their age-long persecution. They have been the untouchables of Christianity ...

But my sympathy does not blind me to the requirements of justice ... Palestine belongs to the Arabs in the same sense that England belongs to the English or France to the French. It is wrong and inhuman to impose the Jews on the Arabs ... The nobler course would be to insist on a just treatment of the Jews wherever they are born and bred ...

But the German persecution of the Jews seems to have no parallel in history. The tyrants of old never went so mad as Hitler seems to have gone. And he is doing it with religious zeal. For he is propounding a new religion of exclusive and militant nationalism ...

If I were a Jew and were born in Germany and earned my livelihood there, I would claim Germany as my home even as the tallest gentile German may, and challenge him to shoot me or cast me in the dungeon; I would refuse to be expelled or to submit to discriminating treatment.

The calculated violence of Hitler may even result in a general massacre of the Jews by way of his first answer to the declaration of such hostilities. But if the Jewish mind could be prepared for voluntary suffering, even the massacre I have imagined could be turned into a day of thanksgiving and joy that Jehovah had wrought deliverance of the race ...

And now a word to the Jews in Palestine ... The Palestine of the Biblical conception is not a geographical tract. It is in their hearts. But if they must look to the Palestine of geography as their national home, it is wrong to enter it under the shadow of the British gun. A religious act cannot be performed with the aid of the bayonet or the bomb. They can settle in Palestine only by the goodwill of the Arabs ...

I am not defending the Arab excesses. I wish they had chosen the way of non-violence in resisting what they rightly regarded as an unwarrantable encroachment upon their country ... (*Harijan,* 26 Nov. 1938; 74: 239–42)

There is no way of knowing how, if born a Jew in Germany, Gandhi would have organized non-violent resistance there. We have seen in him a calling to present non-violence joined by a strong pragmatism. He never asked Indians to invite a massacre from the British, or Hindus, Muslims or 'untouchables' to invite a massacre from their Indian foes. The real commander of a non-violent battle was very different from the professor of a remorseless non-violent ethic.

Martin Buber, the Jewish philosopher, protested at Gandhi's willingness to prescribe satyagraha without understanding German realities. The sufferings of Indians in South

Africa or in British-ruled India paled, he said, before the Jewish experience of Nazi horrors. He had 'long known and honoured' Gandhi's voice, Buber said, but could non-violence be asked of Jews in Germany by one who had often said, with reference to India, that violence was preferable to cowardice or bondage?[76]

The editor of a Jewish journal suggested that Gandhi's 'zeal for Hindu-Muslim unity' had made him 'partial to the Arab presentation of the case, especially as that side was naturally emphasized in India', but Gandhi answered that he would not 'sell truth' either 'for the sake of India's deliverance' or 'for winning Muslim friendship'. Gandhi added:

> I am painfully conscious of the fact that this writing of mine will give no satisfaction either to the Editor of *Jewish Frontier* or to my many Jewish friends. Nevertheless I wish with all my heart that somehow or other the persecution of the Jews in Germany will end and that the question in Palestine will be settled to the satisfaction of all the parties concerned (*Harijan*, 27 May 1939; 75: 416).

Kallenbach. Early in 1939 Hermann Kallenbach spent two months in Wardha. The old friends were extremely happy at being together again, though Kallenbach took ill for some of the time. He gave Gandhi more information on what was happening to Jews in Germany. Gandhi wrote in *Harijan*:

> I happen to have a Jewish friend living with me. He has an intellectual belief in non-violence. But he says he cannot pray for Hitler. He is so full of anger over the German atrocities that he cannot speak of them with restraint. I do not quarrel with him over his anger. He wants to be non-violent, but the sufferings of fellow Jews are too much for him to bear (*Harijan*, 18 Feb. 1939; 75: 39).

Letter to Hitler. Other Western friends asked Gandhi to write to Hitler, hoping that a plea from this strange yet prestigious figure who lived far from Europe might have some effect. In any case it could do no harm. In July, while Gandhi was in the Frontier, a letter from Gandhi ('As at Wardha, CP') was posted, addressed to 'Herr Hitler, Berlin, Germany':

> *23 Jul. 1939:* Dear Friend, Friends have been urging me to write to you for the sake of humanity. But I have resisted their request, because of the feeling that any letter from me would be an impertinence. Something tells me that I must not calculate and that I must make my appeal for whatever it may be worth.
>
> It is quite clear that you are today the one person in the world who can prevent a war which may reduce humanity to the savage state. Must you pay that price for an

object however worthy it may appear to you to be? Will you listen to the appeal of one who has deliberately shunned the method of war not without considerable success? … Your sincere friend, M.K. Gandhi (76: 156–7)

The Raj did not allow the letter to be delivered, a fact of which Gandhi was unaware when, after the outbreak of the Second World War, he published its contents in *Harijan* (9 Sep. 1939; 76: 312).

Congress & the coming war. Horror at Hitler's war machine did not take away India's right to make her own decisions. With Gandhi's support the All India Congress Committee declared in May 1939 that the Congress would oppose 'all attempts to impose a war without the consent of the Indian people'.[77]

On 10 August 1939 the Working Committee once more spelt out, again with Gandhi's full support, Congress policy on the approaching war in Europe:

In this world crisis the sympathies of the Working Committee are entirely with the people who stand for democracy and freedom, and the Congress has repeatedly condemned Fascist aggression in Europe, Africa and the Far East of Asia as well as the betrayal of democracy by British imperialism in Czechoslovakia and Spain.

The Congress has further clearly enunciated its policy in the event of war and declared its determination to oppose all attempts to impose a war on India (76: 430).

Thus German fascism and British imperialism were both to be opposed. To those who knew, the former was more hideous by far, but British rule was closer to home. Now out of the Congress, Subhas saw no difference between the two. Jawaharlal did, but after 22 August, when a Russo-German pact was signed, his sympathy for the Soviet Union made Nehru less inclined to separate British imperialism from German fascism. 'In the event of a war breaking out the Congress ministries may have to resign,' he said.[78] On the other hand, C R and the other Congress premiers met under Patel's chairmanship and agreed that 'cooperation with the British should be wholehearted if an understanding was arrived at between the Congress and the government'.[79]

On 1 September Hitler's armies moved into Poland. Two days later, Prime Minister Neville Chamberlain declared that Britain was at war with Germany. Within hours Lord Linlithgow announced that India too was at war. The Congress was not consulted. A partnership that Gandhi had carefully forged with the Raj had ended, as had the world he had known for two decades.

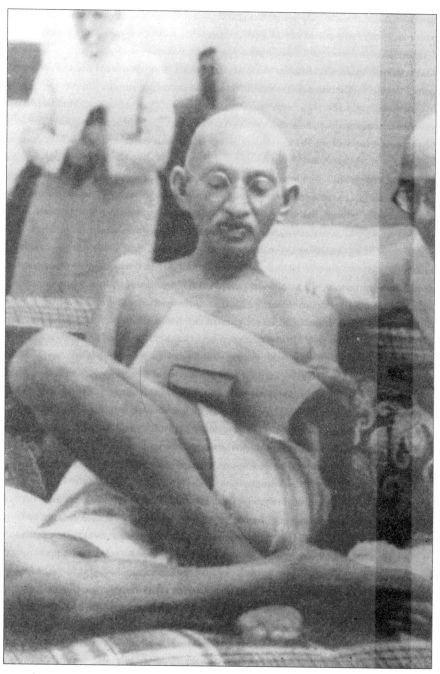

At the Quit India meeting of the AICC – 1942 (Original photo: Central Camera Company)

13

'Quit India!'

Wardha, Bombay and Prison, 1939–44

On 2 September 1939 the Viceroy sent a wire to Wardha informing Gandhi of Germany's attack on Poland and inviting him to Simla. Some other Indians were also invited. 'Sorry terrible news,' Gandhi replied. 'Taking earliest train. Arriving Simla fourth morning.'

He left the same day. Before he and his party boarded the train, telegrams went out asking the Working Committee to assemble in Wardha from 9 September. Starting from Bombay, Patel joined Gandhi's train at Itarsi. Later, from Jhansi station, telegrams were sent to Jinnah, Bose and Jayaprakash inviting them to join the Working Committee's deliberations. Gandhi was bidding for an Indian consensus. In *Harijan* he wrote (9 Sep.):

> [I]n the midst of this catastrophe without parallel … Congressmen and all other responsible Indians individually and collectively have to decide what part India is to play in this terrible drama (76: 312).

Gandhi's sympathy lay with England, but he knew that Indians would not support the war without an assurance of independence at the end of it, and without the immediate participation of national leaders in the government in New Delhi.

After a journey of two nights, he told Linlithgow in Simla (4 Sep.) that he viewed the war 'with an English heart'. Although, he added, only the Working Committee could commit the Congress, he himself was for the Congress giving unconditional support to Britain and France – unconditional but non-violent.

When he spoke to the Viceroy of the possibility of bombs falling on Westminster Abbey and the Houses of Parliament, tears came to his eyes. He did not suppress the tears because he wanted the Viceroy to know how he felt. Linlithgow was warm and courteous but unmoved. The war had hardened the imperial mind. In a statement to the press the next day, Gandhi referred to the tears – he wanted Indians and his British friends also to know how he felt. He added, however, that with his 'out-and-out non-violence' he did not 'represent the national mind'. The remark carried two implications. One, he might not stand in the way if the Working Committee offered India's armed support. In fact his statement also said:

> Yet it almost seems as if Herr Hitler knows no God but brute force and, as Mr Chamberlain says, he will listen to nothing else (*Harijan*, 9 Sep. 1939; 76: 312).

The second implication was that the 'national mind' did not necessarily share his sympathy for England, France and Poland. He on his part would say in a cable to Ignacy Jan Paderewski, Poland's celebrated pianist-politician: 'My whole heart is with the Poles in this unequal struggle ... Their cause is just and their victory certain, for God is always the upholder of justice' (76: 314). As Gandhi noted, others in India had reacted differently.

> At Delhi, as I was entraining for Kalka [*en route to Simla*], a big crowd sang in perfect good humour, to the worn-out refrain of '*Mahatma Gandhi-ki-jai*,' 'We do not want any understanding' ... [T]hey were admonishing me not to have any understanding with the Viceroy (76: 313).

It was the same on the way back to Wardha. At every station Subhas's supporters asked Gandhi why he was sentimental about England. Had he no tears for endangered German sites?[1] Accompanying Gandhi, Patel heard this reaction.

The India of September 1939 was not ready to offer unconditional support to a Britain that had put the country at war without consulting its leaders. Anger at Britain was a cloud over Hitler's terror. If Britain assured India's independence, the cloud could vanish. Instead, the cloud thickened, for as soon as war was declared the British Parliament empowered the Viceroy to override or take over India's provincial governments.

The war for freedom in Europe had cut back self-government in India. When the Working Committee met in Wardha, with Prasad in the chair, Subhas and Jayaprakash were present, but not Jinnah. Bose demanded that no 'Indian men, money and resources' should go into the 'imperialist war'.[2] Jawaharlal too was 'in a combative mood,' as Prasad would put it.[3]

Gandhi's proposal of unconditional non-violent support was shot down by the Working Committee. No one agreed with him. For the first time in 19 years his younger colleagues banded together to vote him down. Though anticipated and accepted by Gandhi, the outcome was a milestone that he and everyone else registered, and he regretted, for more than most he understood the cards the British held in India, and the risks in antagonizing a Britain at war.

Nehru's resolution declaring opposition to fascism but asking Britain to spell out her war aims and their application to India was easily passed. Jawaharlal was expressing the national opinion when he said that friendship between India and England was 'possible but only on equal terms', and that a lorded-over India could not fight for the freedom of Poland.[4] To respond from day to day to the Raj's war policies, the Working Committee asked Nehru to head a three-member 'war' committee, comprising himself, Patel and Azad.

Endorsing the Working Committee resolution, Gandhi praised its author as an 'artist' who had 'compelled India, through the Working Committee, to think not merely of her own freedom, but of the freedom of all the exploited nations of the world', one who could 'not be surpassed in his implacable opposition to imperialism' but was yet 'a friend of the English people' and indeed 'more English than Indian in his thoughts and make-up' (76: 327). These truthful comments were part of Gandhi's strategy. Despite Linlithgow's unresponsiveness, he was still hoping for a Congress-Raj partnership in New Delhi similar to what had been worked out in the provinces.

Some British voices asked HMG to be far-sighted. The *Manchester Guardian* wrote of 'a historic opportunity to secure Indian support' and Clement Attlee, the Labour Party leader, pleaded for 'imaginative insight'.[5] A group of British officers in the Punjab privately urged the Viceroy to proclaim 'in a few stirring words' his 'belief that a war for freedom could only end in the freedom of India'.[6] But the imperial mind, now also a mind focused on the war, seemed closed to such advice.

In September, October and November Gandhi had more meetings with Linlithgow when he spelt out what the Congress wanted, but the Viceroy, personally courteous and even warm to Gandhi, was unbending over policy. He and Zetland, the Secretary of State for India, described the Congress's demands as blackmail. Britain was doubtless in a life-and-death struggle, but this interpretation was unjust. The Congress's demands were neither sudden nor unexpected nor conceived after the declaration of war. Since accepting office in 1937, the Congress and its provincial legislators had passed resolutions every few months asking for constitutional advance at the centre. Zetland, for one, conceded that the Congress was only 'reasserting' its claims.[7]

But Zetland, Linlithgow and their superiors in London, backed by their juniors in the Raj in India, hated the idea of hastening Indian independence. Their counter to Gandhi's 'sympathy' offensive, to the Congress resolution and to liberal British voices, was the reliable device of divide-and-rule. Linlithgow was frank in a letter to the King:

As soon as I realized that I was to be subjected to heavy and sustained pressure designed to force from us major political concessions as the price of Congress's cooperation in the war effort, I summoned representatives of all the more important interests and communities in India, including the Chancellor of the Chamber of Princes and Mr. Jinnah ... and interviewed them one by one ... a heavy and trying task, but well worth the trouble.

The Viceroy added that it had been decided not to 'give to Congress what they are asking for, which is an understanding ... that India will be given political independence at the conclusion of the war'.[8]

Like Gandhi, Linlithgow had realized the importance of Jinnah, who after declining Gandhi's invitation accepted that of the Viceroy in early October. Jinnah informed Linlithgow that the Muslim League would support the war effort if, but only if, Muslims' interests were protected to its satisfaction in any future Indian constitution; and he did not ask for immediate steps towards independence. Unlike the Congress, he could wait for independence, for by now many Muslims in India felt that the Hindu and not the Briton was their chief foe.

In November Gandhi and Nehru had talks in New Delhi with Jinnah, giving the Viceroy (as he confessed to Zetland) 'one or two rather anxious moments'.[9] For one meeting with Linlithgow, Gandhi and Jinnah arrived together at the Viceroy's House in one car (Jinnah's). 'I urged that we at least make the appearance of unity by going to the Viceroy together,' Gandhi would later recall.[10] But Jinnah had no intention of helping the Congress. The same being true of most princes and of Ambedkar, Linlithgow was able to claim that the Congress did not speak for all of India.

In October, when Patel and Prasad also had talks with the Viceroy, the latter evidently told Patel that if the Congress did not offer support the British would 'have to take the Muslims' help', a remark that caused Patel to regret the rejection of Gandhi's advice of unconditional support.[11]

On 17 October the Raj gave its formal reply to the Congress's resolution and demands: 'HMG have not themselves defined with any ultimate precision their detailed objectives in the prosecution of the war.' However, after the war ended Indians could hold constitutional talks with the British. During the war the Congress could, if it wished, send representatives to a consultative committee.[12]

This reply spelt the end of what some months earlier Gandhi had described as the Congress's 'alliance with the British Government'.[13] The Working Committee asked all provincial ministries to resign, though it did so in 'studiedly moderate' words, as Gandhi would say. Costly as loss of office would be, loss of face with the Indian masses would be worse.

Rajagopalachari's ministry in Madras resigned on 27 October. While anxious to give 'wholehearted support to Britain in the fight against gangsterism personified',[14] C R thought Britain had 'simply thrown away a great opportunity' of enlisting Indian friendship.[15] By 27 November all Congress ministries were out of office, including Dr Khan Sahib's in the NWFP, and governors ruled with the help of nominated advisers.

Hitler's war had shattered the Congress-Raj alliance. Jinnah said Muslims had reason to celebrate. Ambedkar said the Dalits also felt that way. Leading a movement in the Tamil country that simultaneously targeted Brahmins, the Hindi language and north Indians, E V Ramaswami Naicker said he too was joyous. Their parties observed 22 December 1939 as Deliverance Day.

Nursing a leprosy patient. While he was in Simla to meet the Viceroy, one person on Gandhi's mind, as Narayan Desai would recall, was Parchure Shastri.[16] Once a member of the Sabarmati Ashram, and present in Yeravda jail in 1932 when Gandhi broke his fast, Shastri was a Sanskrit scholar and leprosy sufferer who, after being shunned everywhere else, had asked for permission to live and die in the Sevagram Ashram. Admitting Shastri, Gandhi added that permission to die would not be granted.

A hut was built for Shastri not far from the Gandhis', and Gandhi himself regularly nursed and massaged him. After improving for a while, Shastri would eventually succumb in 1945, but his stay under Gandhi's supervision in Sevagram inspired associates of Gandhi to start a therapeutic colony for leprosy sufferers near Wardha.[17]

Andrews dies. In February 1940 Gandhi visited his friend Andrews, the friend also of Tagore and many others and especially the downtrodden, who lay ill in Calcutta. 'Mohan, Swaraj is coming,' said Andrews from the sickbed from which he would not rise. Later, Gandhi sent Mahadev to be with the patient but early on 5 April Charles Freer Andrews died. In *Harijan* Gandhi wrote of the only person to call him 'Mohan' in his adult life:

> Nobody probably knew Charlie Andrews as well as I did ... When we met in South Africa, we simply met as brothers and remained as such to the end ... It was not a friendship between an Englishman and an Indian. It was an unbreakable bond between two seekers and servants ...
>
> If we really love Andrews' memory, we may not have hate in us for Englishmen, of whom Andrews was among the best and the noblest (*Harijan*, 13 Apr. 1940; 78: 128–9).

Jinnah & 'Pakistan!'

From the last quarter of 1939, the person most on Gandhi's mind was Jinnah, under whose leadership the Muslim League had attracted hundreds of thousands of new members in the late 1930s. At the end of October 1939, Gandhi acknowledged 'the tremendous fact' that the Muslim League looked upon 'the Congress as the enemy of the Muslims' (77: 66).

More disturbing was a call that Gandhi first heard in a letter that October. A school-teacher, probably from the Punjab and described by Gandhi as 'a Muslim friend', asked for 'the recognition of Muslims as a separate nation' (*Harijan*, 28 Oct. 1939: 77: 27). Others too were voicing such a demand (mostly Muslims but also some Hindus), Jinnah sounded close to embracing it, and Gandhi felt he had to answer it comprehensively:

Why is India not one nation? Was it not one during, say, the Moghul period? Is India composed of two nations? If it is, why only two? Are not Christians a third, Parsis a fourth, and so on? Are the Muslims of China a nation separate from the other Chinese? Are the Muslims of England a different nation from the other English?

How are the Muslims of the Punjab different from the Hindus and the Sikhs? Are they not all Punjabis, drinking the same water, breathing the same air and deriving sustenance from the same soil? What is there to prevent them from following their respective religious practices? Are Muslims all the world over a separate nation? Or are the Muslims of India only to be a separate nation distinct from the others?

Is India to be vivisected into two parts, one Muslim and the other non-Muslim? And what is to happen to the handful of Muslims living in the numerous villages where the population is predominantly Hindu, and conversely to the Hindus where, as in the Frontier Province or Sind, they are a handful?

The way suggested by the correspondent is the way of strife. Live and let live or mutual forbearance and toleration is the law of life. That is the lesson I have learnt from the Koran, the Bible, the Zend-Avesta and the Gita (*Harijan*, 28 Oct. 1939: 77: 27).

RSS. A different perspective, in some ways justifying Jinnah's new line, was offered from the Hindu side in 1939 by Madhav Sadashiv Golwalkar, who had succeeded Hedgewar as the head of the Rashtriya Swayamsevak Sangh (RSS). In *We, or Our Nationhood Defined*, Golwalkar wrote:

Germany has ... shown how well nigh impossible it is for races and cultures, having differences going to the root, to be assimilated into one united whole, a good lesson for us in Hindusthan to learn and profit by ...

The foreign races in Hindusthan must either adopt the Hindu culture and language, must learn to respect and hold in reverence Hindu religion, must entertain no idea but those of the glorification of the Hindu race and culture, i.e., of the Hindu nation and must lose their separate existence to merge in the Hindu race, or may stay in the country, wholly subordinated to the Hindu nation, claiming nothing, deserving no privileges, far less any preferential treatment – not even citizen's rights.[18]

This was, among other things, a repetition of Savarkar's 1937 claim, noted earlier, that Hindus and Muslims were different nations. The war was sharpening India's partisan swords.

Gandhi's moves. Acknowledging Jinnah's rising stature, from January 1940 Gandhi started calling him Quaid-e-Azam ('The People's Leader'), the honorific that many Muslims were by now using. Gandhi made three other moves.

Firstly, to refute Jinnah's charge that the Congress was a Hindu body, he asked Azad to succeed Prasad as its president. Secondly, he tried to get closer to the Muslim premier of the Punjab, the Unionist leader, Sir Sikandar Hyat Khan.[19]

Thirdly, noting that the League chief had aligned himself with Ambedkar and Ramaswami Naicker and was said also to be meeting Savarkar, Gandhi encouraged Jinnah, referring to him as 'my old comrade', to lead all the anti-Congress forces in India and if possible push the Congress to second place. Better an anti-Congress movement across India than separating Muslims from India.

> If the Quaid-e-Azam can bring about the combination, not only I but the whole of India will shout with one acclamation, 'Long Live Quaid-e-Azam Jinnah' (*Harijan*, 20 Jan. 1940; 77: 222–3).

But Jinnah did not take the bait. 'India is not a nation,' he commented. 'It is a subcontinent composed of nationalities.'[20] More than willing to fight the Congress, henceforth he would fight even more the notion of one India, and encourage men like Ambedkar and Naicker to fight it also.

At the end of 1939, Linlithgow remarked to Jinnah that a separate state was the logical implication of his stand, whereupon, according to Linlithgow, Jinnah 'blushed'.[21] But in January he said publicly that Hindus and Muslims were not only distinct, they were two nations. And in March 1940, when the League met in Lahore, the call for separation was formally and dramatically made.

'Pakistan'. In a resolution moved by the premier of Bengal, Fazlul Huq, the League declared that it would accept nothing short of 'separate and sovereign Muslim states, comprising geographically contiguous units ... in which the Muslims are numerically in a majority, as in the north-western and eastern zones of India.'[22] But the units or their boundaries were not specified, and there was also a suggestion of more than one Muslim state being demanded.

Pointing out that the resolution did not name the provinces that would constitute the new state, a delegate at Lahore expressed the fear that its imprecise wording would justify partitioning the Punjab and Bengal. In his answer, Liaqat Ali Khan, the League's general secretary, defended vagueness:

> If we say Punjab that would mean that the boundary of our state would be Gurgaon, whereas we want to include in our proposed dominion Delhi and Aligarh, which are centres of our culture ... Rest assured that we will [not] give away any part of the Punjab.[23]

Ten years earlier, at a meeting in Lucknow, the poet Iqbal had first asked for a consolidation of Muslim areas in the subcontinent's north-west. Muslims of the eastern zone were not part of Iqbal's scheme, which envisaged a 'Muslim India within India', or a separation that was not complete. Also, Iqbal said that the Punjab's eastern areas, where Hindus and Sikhs outnumbered Muslims, could be excluded from his Muslim zone.

Soon afterwards, a man called Khwaja Abdur Rahim thought of 'Pakistan' or 'Land of the Pure, an amalgamation of the Punjab, the Frontier Province, Kashmir, Sindh, and Balochistan. In 1933 a student in Cambridge, Chaudhry Rahmat Ali, used the expression in print and gave it currency.

The Lahore resolution of 1940 demanded something larger but more vague than what Iqbal had asked for in 1930, and did not use the word 'Pakistan'. But the press needed a name for the state or states that the resolution sought. 'Pakistan' was remembered, the Lahore resolution soon became known as the 'Pakistan' resolution, and the League adopted the term.

Azad's perspective. At Ramgarh in Bihar, where the Congress met ten days before the League's Lahore gathering, Abul Kalam Azad delivered a stirring presidential address:

> I am a Muslim and proud of the fact. I am indispensable to this noble edifice. Without me this splendid structure of India is incomplete.
>
> It was India's historic destiny that many human races and cultures and religions should flow to her, and that many a caravan should find rest here ... One of the last of these caravans was that of the followers of Islam. This came here and settled here for good.
>
> We brought our treasures with us, and India too was full of the riches of her own precious heritage. We gave her what she needed most, the message of human equality. Full eleven centuries have passed by since then. Islam has now as great a claim on the soil of India as Hinduism.
>
> Everything bears the stamp of our joint endeavour. Our languages were different,

but we grew to use a common language. Our manners and customs were different, but they produced a new synthesis ... No fantasy or artificial scheming to separate and divide can break this unity.[24]

Jinnah's answer to this, given in Lahore, was that Hindus and Muslims could 'never evolve a common nationality' and that 'to yoke together two such nations under a single state' would destroy any fabric of government. *The Times* of London reported that prolonged cheering almost drowned Jinnah's remark when he said he would 'give his life to achieve' a Muslim state.[25]

Even though Sikandar Hyat Khan opposed the Lahore resolution in the Punjab legislature, saying he did not want 'a Muslim raj here and a Hindu raj there',[26] and the Khan brothers remained firm in the Frontier, the bulk of the subcontinent's Muslims seemed to cheer Jinnah more than Azad. When Azad proposed a conversation with him, Jinnah sent back a rude telegram:

> I refuse to discuss with you, by correspondence or otherwise ... Can't you realize you are made a Muslim show-boy Congress President? ... The Congress is a Hindu body. If you have self-respect resign at once.[27]

Gandhi's response. The call for Pakistan presented Gandhi with a dilemma. Launching a struggle would now not only invite repression from a Britain at war; it could also ignite Hindu-Muslim violence. Yet doing nothing would demoralize the Congress base. Gandhi's answer was to recommend selective and disciplined disobedience by carefully chosen individuals, under his own direction.

More serious than the dilemma on strategy was the attack on Gandhi's vision that the Pakistan demand represented. He responded in several ways. For a start, he *questioned* the doctrine behind it:

> The 'two nations' theory is an untruth. The vast majority of Muslims of India are converts to Islam or are descendants of converts. They did not become a separate nation as soon as they became converts.
>
> A Bengali Muslim speaks the same tongue that a Bengali Hindu does, eats the same food, has the same amusements as his Hindu neighbour. They dress alike. I have often found it difficult to distinguish by outward sign between a Bengali Hindu and a Bengali Muslim ...
>
> When I first met [Jinnah], I did not know that he was a Muslim. I came to know his religion when I had his full name given to me. His nationality was written in his face and manner ...

Were the Ali Brothers and their associates wrong when they hugged Hindus as blood brothers and saw so much in common between the two? (*Harijan*, 6 Apr. 1940; 78: 109)

Religion binds man to God and man to man. Does Islam bind Muslim only to Muslim and antagonize the Hindu? Was the message of the Prophet peace only for and between Muslims and war against Hindus or non-Muslims? Are eight crores of Muslims to be fed with this which I can only describe as poison? ...

I have lived with and among Muslims not for one day but closely and almost uninterruptedly for twenty years. Not one Muslim taught me that Islam was an anti-Hindu religion (*Harijan*, 4 May 1940; 78: 178–9).

He *warned* Muslims against division, calling it 'suicidal' (*Harijan*, 4 May 1940; 78: 183).

I should be failing in my duty, if I did not warn the Muslims of India against the untruth that is being propagated amongst them ...

It is worse than anarchy to partition a poor country like India whose every corner is populated by Hindus and Muslims living side by side. It is like cutting up a living body into pieces (speech of 16 Sep. 1940, *Harijan Sevak*, 12 Oct. 1940; 79: 231).

He *hoped* that the Muslim masses would reject the call:

But I do not believe that Muslims, when it comes to a matter of actual decision, will ever want vivisection. Their good sense will prevent them. Their self-interest will deter them. Their religion will forbid the obvious suicide which the partition would mean (*Harijan*, 4 May 1940; 78: 183).

He *rejected* separation personally:

It makes no difference to me that some Muslims regard themselves as a separate nation. It is enough for me that I do not consider them as such (*Harijan*, 4 May 1940; 78: 183).

But he *conceded* that separation was possible:

If the vast majority of Indian Muslims feel that they are not one nation with their Hindu and other brethren, who will be able to resist them? (*Harijan*, 30 Mar. 1940; 78: 93)

I know no non-violent method of compelling the obedience of eight crores of Muslims to the will of the rest of India, however powerful a majority the rest may represent (*Harijan*, 6 Apr. 1940; 78: 109).

Pakistan cannot be worse than foreign domination. I have lived under the latter though not willingly. If God so desires it, I may have to become a helpless witness to the undoing of my dream. But I do not believe that the Muslims really want to dismember India (*Harijan*, 4 May 1940; 78: 178).

And he *offered* a *sort* of separation:

The Muslims must have the same right of self-determination that the rest of India has. We are at present a joint family. Any member may claim a division (*Harijan*, 6 Apr. 1940; 78: 109).

Five months later, however, he *declared he would resist* any bid to force partition. In apparent contradiction to what he had said in April and May, he asserted in September that partition would be prevented:

I do not say this as a Hindu. I say this as a representative of Hindus, Muslims, Parsis and all. I would say to Muslim brethren, 'Cut me to pieces first and then divide India. You are trying to do something which was not attempted even during the Muslim rule of 200 years. We shall not allow you to do it' (speech of 16 Sep. 1940; *Harijan Sevak*, 12 Oct. 1940; 79: 231).

C R's successful dissent. The months from March to August in 1940 saw a serious division in the Congress high command, with Rajagopalachari dissenting from Gandhi and marshalling impressive support. At issue was the impact on India of Allied reverses in Europe. In the spring and summer of 1940, Norway, Denmark, Holland, Belgium and even France fell before Hitler's *blitzkrieg*.

While C R thought the reverses would persuade the British to settle with the Congress, Gandhi did not think the British wanted an honourable deal. At Ramgarh (March 1940) he had told the Working Committee that he was now 'stiffer' towards the British and that selective disobedience was unavoidable. 'I do not find any honest response from the other side,' he said.[28] Rajagopalachari's reaction was that the British would crush wartime disobedience.

But divide-and-rule had put Gandhi off. His sympathy had drained away. Nine months after it had started, Gandhi looked at the war with an Indian rather than an English heart.

Churchill at the helm. In May 1940, some weeks before the fall of France, Churchill replaced Chamberlain as Britain's Prime Minister. More than his colleagues, Gandhi was aware of the intensity of Churchill's attachment to the Empire. Unlike them he had interacted with Churchill, meeting him in 1906 and being rebuffed by him in 1931.

Later, in 1935 in London, Churchill had told Gandhi's industrialist friend Birla that 'Mr Gandhi has gone very high in my esteem since he stood up for the untouchables.' Informed of the remark, Gandhi authorized Birla to write to Churchill that Gandhi retained 'a good recollection of Mr Churchill when he was in the Colonial Office'.[29] Meeting Birla again in 1937, Churchill asked him to 'give your leader my greetings'.[30]

But Gandhi was too seasoned to imagine that those earlier niceties would matter with the War Premier. Though Churchill's famous remark that he had 'not become the King's First Minister in order to preside over the liquidation of the British Empire' was two years away, Gandhi knew what not to expect from Premier Churchill. And he knew that Churchill would use the Pakistan cry, a proof of Indian disunity, to justify the *status quo.*

In the third week of June, a day after France appealed to Hitler for peace, the Working Committee met in Wardha. C R, however, imagined that Britain might want, as an ally, 'a free India when she has lost France'.[31] If the Congress offered to prosecute the war, it might gain its goals of independence and, immediately, a share in the government. He argued his case gently, clearly and persuasively. He argued it in the name of non-violence, saying that fighting a war was on occasion the best way of ending violence, and he recalled Gandhi's 1918 bid to recruit soldiers for the British.

'I don't want to be instrumental in militarizing the masses,' Gandhi told his colleagues.[32] Yet could non-violence work in a war between nations? Could it work in Europe?

Meeting to formulate its approach to the Raj in India, the Working Committee found itself debating the feasibility of non-violence in the war in Europe. Unwilling to acknowledge any weakening in his faith, Gandhi declared that European nations and, if it came to that, India, should defend liberty not 'with the force of arms' but 'with the force of non-violence' (*Harijan,* 22 Jun. 1940; 78: 343–5).

When a majority in the Working Committee, including President Azad and Patel, disagreed with him, Gandhi asked to be absolved from its decisions. His wish was granted. After four days of deliberations, the members said they had

> come to the conclusion that they are unable to go the full length with Gandhiji. But they recognize that he should be free to pursue his great ideal in his own way, and therefore absolve him from responsibility for the programme and activity which the Congress has to pursue ... in regard to external aggression and internal disorder (78: 350).

Influenced by Rajagopalachari, Congress leaders seemed willing, for a price, to switch from Gandhi to the Raj, from the charkha to the gun. Glimpses of power and the passage of time were factors with them: Patel was now 65, Rajagopalachari 62, Prasad 56, Azad 52, and Nehru 51.

When, at the end of June, Gandhi went to Simla for a prior appointment with Linlithgow, he told the Viceroy that 'this was [his] last interview'. Henceforth the Viceroy 'should send for the president of the Congress if he must have an offer on behalf of the Congress'(78: 393).[33]

To the Working Committee meeting in Delhi in early July, Gandhi recounted what Linlithgow told him in respect of the new Congress policy:

> You want to defend India, you want aeroplanes, battle-ships, tanks, etc. We will give you all these. This will serve our purpose and also yours. This is the golden opportunity. You should come and get equipped. Under pressure we will go forward double speed.[34]

Dismay. What pleased the Viceroy dismayed Gandhi. Was his non-violent struggle going to end in India's militarization, and that under the Empire's aegis? This strike against his vision, coming from his closest Congress colleagues, felt even worse than the blow Jinnah had delivered. Gandhi told the Working Committee: 'I cannot do this. This is not for me.'

He also asked his colleagues to see the pressure the Raj was applying to mobilize Indian resources:

> This process ... was gentle and not much felt till the French capitulation. I cannot conceive my remaining silent or sitting at ease with this coercion going on unhampered.[35]

He knew that tens of thousands of Indians were recruiting for the war, which offered much-needed employment in a poor country with a large population. Asked about 'Harijans who voluntarily want to enlist as recruits', he said that no attempt should be made to dissuade them.[36] But recruits were joining England's war, not India's. In Europe Britain's allies were collapsing – the sun was setting, he said, on the Empire.[37] Time was on their side. Was this the moment to appeal to the British?

As for Hitler's success, Gandhi wrote in *Harijan*: 'What will he do with his victory? Can he digest so much power? ... [The Germans] will not be able to hold all the conquered nations in perpetual subjection.'[38] To the Working Committee Gandhi also said that Indians would offer non-violent resistance if Japan, Germany's eastern ally, were to move across Asia into India.[39]

C R was not persuaded. Gandhi said: 'I had not in the past the slightest difficulty in carrying Rajaji with me, his intelligence as well as his heart, but since this office question cropped up, I saw that our thoughts were running in different directions.'[40] But he also failed to carry most of the others. Before long even Nehru agreed with C R's reasoning. Among the prominent leaders, only Ghaffar Khan and Kripalani remained with Gandhi.

A remark he made in the summer of 1940 reveals the disturbance that the war's trends, the Pakistan demand and his colleagues' interest in the Empire's armaments had caused in Gandhi:

I sometimes feel like taking shelter in flight, not to seek cloistered peace, but in the stillness of utter isolation to know myself, to see where I stand, to catch more effectively the faint whispering of the 'still small voice within'.[41]

Let AICC ratify. Though disappointed that his words 'lacked the power of convincing the Sardar and Rajaji',[42] Gandhi asked the AICC to endorse the Working Committee's offer to Britain. Its members, he said, were the Congress's leaders, as sincere as he was, and possibly wiser. C R had shown 'persistency, courage and skill' (*The Hindu*, 9 Jul. 1940), and Vallabhbhai had held 'fast to his convictions'.[43] Despite the knock he had taken, Gandhi was not going to disown his team, divide the Congress or risk its break-up. Simultaneously, he advised the British, in a *Harijan* piece, 'not [to] reject the hand of friendship offered by the Congress'.[44]

Unreal appeal. In another *Harijan* article, 'To Every Briton', he elaborated his faith in non-violence in the war in Europe. Claiming that the war was 'brutalizing man on a scale hitherto unknown', he proposed non-violent non-cooperation as an alternative and added:

All distinctions between combatants and noncombatants have been abolished. No one and nothing is to be spared. Lying has been reduced to an art. Britain was to defend small nationalities. One by one they have vanished, at least for the time being ...

I appeal for cessation of hostilities, not because you are too exhausted to fight, but because war is bad in essence ...

You will invite Herr Hitler and Signor Mussolini to take what they want of the countries you call your possessions. Let them take possession of your beautiful island, with your many beautiful buildings. You will give all these, but neither your souls, nor your minds ...

This process or method, which I have called non-violent non-cooperation, is not without considerable success in its use in India. Your representatives in India may

... tell you that our non-cooperation was not wholly non-violent, that it was born of hatred.

If they give that testimony, I won't deny it. Had it been wholly non-violent ... I make bold to say that you who are India's masters would have become her pupils and, with much greater skill than we have, perfected this matchless weapon and met the German and Italian friends' menace with it ... (*Harijan*, 6 Jul. 1940; 78: 386–8).

On Gandhi's request the Viceroy conveyed this 'appeal' to HMG in London. On 10 July Linlithgow wrote to Gandhi:

I have now heard from them that with every appreciation of your motives they do not feel that the policy which you advocate is one which it is possible for them to consider, since in common with the whole Empire they are firmly resolved to prosecute the war to a victorious conclusion (78: 389).

An offshoot of Gandhi's debate with the Working Committee, the appeal was not a serious initiative. Its writer made an academic case for non-violence, whereas the Gandhi who conducted India's non-violent campaigns had his feet on the ground. And when the British led by Churchill fought back not only with determination but also with weapons, Gandhi acknowledged their valour.

AICC endorses. Subhas Bose and Jayaprakash, both opposed to overtures to the British, were in jail by this time. Before his arrest Subhas had asked for mass defiance and for the formation of a provisional national government. In August a prominent leader of the Congress socialists, Rammanohar Lohia, was jailed. Always on the lookout for younger leaders he could buttress, Gandhi made several positive references to Jayaprakash and Lohia in *Harijan*.

From prison, Jayaprakash made an unsuccessful appeal to Nehru to oppose C R's line and work for mass disobedience. Gandhi was not willing to go that far, but he acknowledged that Subhas and Jayaprakash were more representative than C R of 'the smouldering discontent' (Gandhi's phrase) of the Indian people.[45]

On 27 July, in Gandhi's absence but as urged by him, the AICC, meeting in Poona, endorsed the Rajagopalachari proposal. In protest, Ghaffar Khan resigned from the Congress. He did not want to associate himself with any support for a violent war.

Britain's reply. On 8 August the response to 'the Poona offer' came through a Viceregal statement. Provided, it said, the Raj, the Congress, the Muslim League and the princes reached an agreement, some politicians would be included in an expanded Viceroy's Council in which the Viceroy would retain his veto. At the end of the war, a body to be set up 'with the least possible delay' would 'devise the framework of a new constitution'.

The statement assured Muslims and other minority 'elements in India's national life' that Britain would never allow 'their coercion into submission' to a majority government. Indeed, the British would not permit a government 'whose authority is directly denied by large and powerful elements in India's national life' (79: 466–8).

Rather than the Congress, Jinnah and the princes had been placated. A shocked C R said he was 'angry',[46] and Patel remarked that the British government 'has begun to show itself in its true colours'.[47] To Gandhi, Patel said, referring to his secession, 'It shall never happen again in our lifetime.'[48]

Limited satyagraha. Quickly pressed to resume guiding the Congress, Gandhi revived the idea of disciplined disobedience by selected individuals. Anything larger would 'embarrass ... the British people or the British government when their very existence hung in the balance',[49] could spark off Hindu-Muslim disturbances and perhaps bring the Raj and the Muslim League closer to each other. Anything smaller would 'kill the Congress'[50] by divorcing it from mainstream India, now increasingly restive against tightening British control.

What imperial order would chosen satyagrahis flout? That which curbed free speech, said Gandhi. A resolution that Gandhi drafted for the AICC declared that while the Congress could not 'withhold their admiration for the bravery and endurance shown by the British nation in the face of danger and peril', it would insist on 'the free expression of public opinion'.[51] With Nehru's help he devised a restrained yet unlawful two-sentence slogan:

> It is wrong to help the British war effort with men or money. The only worthy effort
> is to resist all war with non-violent resistance.[52]

Calling on the Viceroy, Gandhi asked that Indians be given the right to recite the slogan. Linlithgow rejected the plea, and the stage was set for the campaign of individual civil disobedience (ICD).

Between October 1940, when ICD commenced, and the summer of 1941, more than 15,000 Indians courted prison, receiving terms ranging between nine and 15 months. Recommended in the first instance by provincial Congress committees, ICD candidates were finally chosen or approved by Gandhi personally, mainly on the basis of their support of non-violence, spinning, caste equality and Hindu-Muslim friendship.

Each resister recited the slogan as he or she walked until arrested by a police officer, who was often informed in advance. Some recited the words because they opposed violence, more because they opposed the Empire. Generally, the first sentence was uttered with greater conviction. No violence occurred, and over Christmas no satyagraha was offered. The most disciplined of the several all-India campaigns that Gandhi had

initiated, and dramatic in its restraint, ICD preserved the Congress and the spirits of its members and supporters.

For inaugurating ICD, Gandhi picked Vinoba Bhave, thereby bringing to national and global attention the most gifted individual, perhaps, among his 'non-political' associates. From the 1920s, Vinoba had been conducting an ashram of his own near Wardha. Throughout his association with Vinoba, which began in 1916, Gandhi had thought the younger man his superior in self-control and learning.

A scholar of religious texts and of languages, Vinoba had quietly taken part in all previous satyagrahas, spending several hard terms in prison. This time Gandhi wanted him to lead. In *Harijan* he explained why:

> For perfect spinning probably he has no rival in all India. He has abolished every trace of untouchability from his heart. He believes in communal unity with the same passion that I have. In order to know the best mind of Islam he gave one year to the study of the Koran in the original. He therefore learnt Arabic ...
>
> He has an army of disciples and workers who would rise to any sacrifice at his bidding. He is responsible for producing a young man[53] who has dedicated himself to the service of lepers. Though an utter stranger to medicine this worker has by singular devotion mastered the method of treatment of lepers and is now running several clinics for their care ...
>
> This will perhaps be the last civil disobedience struggle which I shall have conducted. Naturally I would want it to be as flawless as it can be ... [54]

On this occasion Gandhi kept himself out, for his arrest could trigger what he was keen to avoid: mass participation and unrest. Also, he wanted to remain available in case the Viceroy wished to negotiate.[55] On 21 October Vinoba was arrested. Ordered not to report the arrest in his journals, Gandhi suspended their publication and said:

> Let everyone become his own walking newspaper and carry the good news from mouth to mouth ... The idea here is of my telling my neighbour what I have authentically heard. This no Government can overtake or suppress. It is the cheapest newspaper yet devised and it defies the wit of Government, however clever it may be.
>
> Let these walking newspapers be sure of the news they give. They should not indulge in any idle gossip. They should make sure of the source of information, and they will find that the public gets all the information that they need without opening their morning newspaper ... (*Harijan*, 3 Nov. 1940; 79: 330)

Jawaharlal was chosen to follow Vinoba but before he could utter the two sentences he was arrested on 31 October, charged with sedition in earlier speeches, and sentenced to four years. This was a severity that Gandhi wanted to protest with a fast but in the end did not. Before the year ended, Azad, Patel, C R, Prasad, all other nationally known Congress leaders and hundreds more were also in jail.

During their incarceration, Hitler invaded his supposed ally, the Soviet Union on 22 June 1941. In India this meant support hereafter for Britain's war from the small but not insignificant Communist party and some other leftist groups.

Bose and JP. Earlier, on 27 January 1941, Subhas Bose had dramatically escaped from the house in Calcutta where he was interned, secretly made his way to Afghanistan, and thence to Germany. In October 1941 Jayaprakash Narayan, jailed in Deoli, was caught trying to slip out, via his wife visiting him, a sheet that allegedly encouraged his followers outside to commit acts of sabotage. The Raj publicized the incident.

Bose's escape thrilled many in India. Despite conflicts with him, Gandhi also seems to have been impressed. This was Azad's assessment, apparently based on remarks that Gandhi later made to Azad.[56] Though Azad did not quote Gandhi, we know what Gandhi had said earlier, shortly after Subhas's arrest the previous summer. Giving an account of a conversation in June 1940 with Subhas, who espoused mass disobedience, Gandhi wrote in *Harijan* (13 Jul. 1940):

> He told me in the friendliest manner that he would do what the Working Committee had failed to do ... I told him that, if at the end of his plan there was Swaraj during my lifetime, mine would be the first telegram of congratulation he would receive ... But I warned him his way was wrong ...
>
> So long as Subhas Babu considers a particular course of action to be correct, he has the right, and it is his duty, to pursue it whether the Congress likes it or not ... [I]f success attends his effort and India gains her freedom, it will justify his rebellion, and the Congress will not only not condemn his rebellion but welcome him as a saviour.[57]

Gandhi's press statement issued after the Raj's exposure of Jayaprakash's failed attempt may also provide a clue to his reaction to Bose's escape:

> Assuming the correctness of the charge against Jayaprakash Narayan, the method advocated by him is against the policy of truth and non-violence adopted by the Congress, and he deserves the severest condemnation. But it ill becomes the Government to condemn or discredit it. Frankly, all nationalist forces, no matter by what name they are described, are at war with the Government.
>
> And, according to the accepted canons of war, the method adopted by Jayaprakash

Narayan is perfectly legitimate. He has had his training in America for seven long years and is a student of the methods adopted by Western nations in their fight for freedom. To practise deception, to resort to secret methods and even to plot murder, are all honourable and turn the perpetrators into national heroes.

Are not Clive and Warren Hastings British heroes? If Jayaprakash Narayan was in the British Diplomatic Service and by secret diplomacy achieved something of importance, he would be covered with distinction ...

While Jayaprakash Narayan remains the patriot we have known him, [Indians] must realize that his method is harmful in the extreme while a non-violent struggle is going on.[58]

While most of his political associates were in prison, Gandhi remained, in his words, 'buried in Sevagram'. Apart from visits in February 1941 to Bombay and Allahabad, he stayed put and felt fully confident:

> I have got strength and resourcefulness enough to lead this battle ... I shall do better and clearer thinking in Sevagram than anywhere else, simply because I have built up there an atmosphere for my growth. With the march of time my body must decay but, I hope, not my wisdom. I seem to see things more clearly with the advance of age. It may be self-deception, but there is no hypocrisy.[59]

In July 1941 he thought he would send satyagrahis to prison in a steady flow 'for no less than five years',[60] presumably his estimate at this time of how long the war might last.

On 7 August Tagore died. Braced over the years by the poet's criticisms, and comforted by his support, Gandhi had in recent months raised funds for Santiniketan. 'In the death of Rabindranath Tagore,' his tribute said, 'we have not only lost the greatest poet of the age, but an ardent nationalist who was also a humanitarian ...' (80: 436)

August 1941 was also the month in which Churchill and President Roosevelt signed the Atlantic Charter, declaring their 'respect' for 'the right of all peoples to choose the form of government under which they will live' and their 'wish to see sovereign rights and self-government restored to those who have been forcibly deprived of them'. But in the following month Churchill stated explicitly that the Atlantic Charter would not apply to India.

Patel was released (from Yeravda) in August 1941 and C R two months later. 'All eyes are on you including mine,' Gandhi wrote, with shrewd suspicion, to Rajagopalachari.[61] And on 31 October he wrote to Patel: 'I hear it is your birthday today ... Remember we are not to go until we have attained Swaraj.'[62]

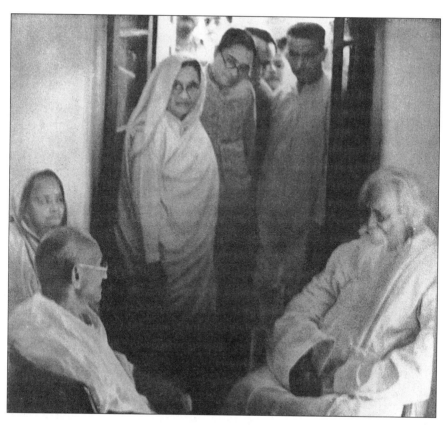

(Seated) *Kasturba, Gandhi and Rabindranath Tagore in Calcutta – 1941*
(Original photo: S Shaha)

Clearly he was curious about what his colleagues had been thinking while in prison. In his jail in Trichy in the Tamil country Rajagopalachari had received a message from Sikandar Hyat Khan, the Punjab premier, brought by a visitor, Kasturi Srinivasan, editor of *The Hindu.* Hyat Khan proposed a joint Congress-Muslim League move to the British and C R showed interest, but Linlithgow, sticking firmly to divide-and-rule, told the governor of Madras that Srinivasan should not have been allowed to meet Rajagopalachari, and Hyat Khan was pressured to abandon his initiative.[63]

Long months in jail had persuaded C R to seek a rapprochement with the Raj or Jinnah or both. On the other hand, Vallabhbhai, who suffered greatly from illness (with a suspicion of cancer) while in Yeravda, seemed content to await Gandhi's lead. In his UP prison, Jawaharlal felt conflicting tugs: revulsion at Nazism and fascism, distress over Russia's suffering, anger at British control of India, loyalty to Gandhi and bewilderment at some of Gandhi's actions.

On 4 December 1941, all ICD prisoners, including Azad, the Congress president and Nehru were released. Most had served out their sentences, and it was hard for the Raj to justify detaining Nehru longer than the rest. Not only that, Nehru was thought likely to advocate a softer line towards the Raj, an assessment based on his warmth for the Soviet Union, Britain's ally from June. A statement announcing the releases expressed the government's confidence 'in the determination of all responsible opinion in India to support the war effort until victory is secured'.[64]

Gandhi's response was to say that without a change in policy the releases would not 'evoke a single responsive or appreciative chord' in him. He felt the 'government will be soon disillusioned' if it thought that 'the prisoners will have changed their opinions in their self-invited solitude'.[65] ICD would continue, Gandhi added, though Working Committee and AICC members would not court re-arrest for the time being.

Pearl Harbor, & another Congress offer. Within three days of the releases, Japan attacked Pearl Harbor and drew America directly into the war. Rajagopalachari felt confirmed in his views. Now, surely, with a war in Asia as well as in Europe, the British would give much to obtain the Congress as an ally. Quickly he mobilized support, beginning with president Azad's.

Once more he won a majority of the Working Committee, which met in Bardoli at the end of December, even though this time both Patel and Nehru voted against him. C R's resolution recognizing the 'new world situation' and offering cooperation, including military support, to the Allies, if India's freedom was declared, was passed. Said Gandhi to his colleagues:

So far as I am concerned, even if I was given the utmost power conceivable, even if I was made the Viceroy of India today, would I ask the people of India to take up the

sword to keep the Empire alive? … Am I to abandon the very boat which has brought
me quite close to the shore?[66]

But the 1940 exercise was repeated. Despite Gandhi's pre-Pearl Harbor assertion, ICD
was suspended, and he was released from leading disobedience. Despite his disagreement Gandhi again asked the AICC, which met in Wardha in January, to endorse the
Working Committee's 'Bardoli' offer to Britain. Though Nehru, Patel and Prasad spoke
against it – Nehru saying that Rajagopalachari's was 'a primrose path' – C R's advocacy,
Japan's sweep across the Pacific, the draw of power and Gandhi's counsel won the AICC's
ratification.

At Wardha Gandhi explained why he was asking for endorsement. Firstly, he did not
wish to split the Congress. Secondly,

It is no longer open to the Government and the Congress critics to say that the
Congress has banged the door against negotiation on the doctrinaire ground of non-
violence. The resolution throws on the Government the entire burden of wooing the
Congress by meeting its legitimate demands and securing its participation in the
war effort.[67]

Thirdly, said Gandhi, 'We have a right to take a step back for jumping forward.'[68] He
was saying that if, as he expected, Britain failed to respond positively, a struggle could
again be launched.

The *Harijan* weeklies were revived. If the authorities tried to censor them, said
Gandhi, he would reply with satyagraha on his own behalf, not in the name of the
Congress. Short of sealing his lips, he was for giving the Bardoli offer every chance.

C R noted, in a letter to Devadas (1 Jan. 1942), that despite their differences Gandhi
was 'wonderfully good to me', adding, 'But what wonder really? He was ever that.'[69]
Gandhi was good and thoughtful also towards Patel. Keeping him in Sevagram for 40
days, Gandhi treated him with mud packs, hip-baths, walking and diet control.

Succession. Gandhi and his colleagues were friends as well, their relationships enriched
by more than two decades of common struggle. Their reunion after a year's separation
was not a small thing. But some tension was introduced into it on 15 January, when
Gandhi told the AICC that 'not Rajaji, nor Sardar Vallabhbhai, but Jawaharlal will be
my successor'.[70]

This was not a new thought. Indeed Gandhi prefaced the remark with the words, 'As
I have always said'. Yet being named and eliminated could not have been pleasant. No
record of how Patel or C R reacted seems to exist, but an activist from Rajasthan who was
present, Ramnarayan Chaudhary, saw that Nehru, hitherto cross-legged on the ground

with a bolster behind his back, 'sprang from his seat' when he heard the remark and sat down atop the bolster.[71]

Admitting differences between him and Nehru, including over non-violence, Gandhi yet added:

> You cannot divide water by repeatedly striking it with a stick. It is just as difficult to divide us ... He says whatever is uppermost in his mind, but he always does what I want. When I am gone he will do what I am doing now. Then he will speak my language too ...
>
> I would like to think that when the occasion arises India would defend herself through non-violence and thus be a messenger of peace to the whole world. Jawahar will also then work for it – not for war.[72]

Bajaj dies. February brought a blow: Jamnalal Bajaj's sudden death from a stroke. Granted his wish to be treated as Gandhi's 'fifth son', Bajaj had returned a title the British had given him and adopted Gandhi as a father, giving him funds, the Sevagram ashram and support for every item in the constructive programme. A devastated Gandhi tried to encourage Janakidevi, Bajaj's widow, and their children. He wrote:

> Death has taken a mighty man. Whenever I wrote of wealthy men becoming trustees of their wealth for the common good I always had this merchant prince principally in mind ...
>
> His simplicity was all his own. Every house he built for himself became a dharmashala. His contribution as a satyagrahi was of the highest order. In political discussions he held his own. His judgements were sound ...
>
> Where am I to get another son like him now? ... But ... a calamity of [this] kind is a blessing in disguise. God wants to try me through and through. I live in the faith that He will give me the strength too to pass through the ordeal.[73]

Desai, Kasturba, Patel, Harilal. Within days of Bajaj's death, an over-worked Mahadev, sent by Gandhi for a break in Nasik, collapsed *en route* at Wardha station, from where he was taken to hospital. A phone had by now been installed in Sevagram, where, on the evening of Sunday 27 February, an anxious Gandhi 'kept walking' to the phone booth to find out how Mahadev was faring in Wardha.

His weekly silence period having commenced, Gandhi scribbled questions to the aide in the booth. When, at night, Mahadev was brought back in a car to his hut, Gandhi 'came running', stroked Desai's head and asked, 'Mahadev, how do you feel now?' According to Narayan, Mahadev's son, this was 'the first time since his nephew Maganlal's death' that Gandhi had broken his weekly silence.[74]

Mahadev was soon back on his feet but now Kasturba took very ill. However, Gandhi had to leave for Calcutta to meet Chiang Kai-shek, who was visiting India. For the sake of China's defence against Japan, Chiang wanted an understanding between Indians and the British and wished to meet with Gandhi, Nehru and the Viceroy.

'I did not at all like leaving you,' Gandhi wrote from the train to Kasturba.[75] She recovered but remained weak; the Gandhi-Chiang meeting did not lead to much. Meanwhile, Patel sent word of *his* illness.

Early in April, when Gandhi visited Delhi, he saw Harilal, who was also in the capital, and found that his son had suffered a fracture of the hand. Gandhi arranged to send him to a hospital to get the fracture set. To Harilal's son Kanti, Gandhi wrote: 'He started talking about coming back to me, but that was only a ruse for getting money ... '[76]

Japan at the gate

Censoring *Harijan* was not attempted by the Raj, but Britain's reply to the Bardoli offer did not come until the end of March. Events in Asia induced it. On 15 February Singapore, Britain's 'strong and secure' Eastern bastion, was taken by Japanese forces, and on 7 March Rangoon fell.

So far, Churchill had resisted every suggestion for political advance in India, whether made by President Roosevelt or Generalissimo Chiang or anyone else, but the fall of Rangoon forced his hand. On 11 March he announced that his Cabinet colleague and the Leader of the House, Sir Stafford Cripps, would carry a proposal from the War Cabinet to India.

Belonging to the left wing of the Labour Party, a vegetarian, friendly with Nehru and a brilliant lawyer, Cripps had been ambassador to Moscow before Churchill invited him to join his War Cabinet. Arriving in Delhi on 22 March, Cripps described HMG's scheme.

Offering 'different items palatable to different tastes',[77] it contained three elements designed to satisfy the Congress. One, full dominion status for India after the war, with the right of secession from the Commonwealth. Two, a post-war Constituent Assembly (which the Congress had been demanding from the 1930s) for which provincial legislatures could elect members. And three, for the here and now, a national government composed of representatives of the leading political parties.

It had attractions for the princes too. They would have the right to send nominees to the Constituent Assembly and to decide the future of their states, a provision implying a right to declare independence.

And it had something for Jinnah. At the end of the war, even as India acquired the right to become a dominion, every province would have the right to stay out and become a separate dominion equal in status to the Indian dominion.

Invited to New Delhi to meet Cripps, Gandhi could not swallow the potential for balkanization, nomination by princes, or a clause in the scheme that placed India's defence during the war wholly in British hands. Confirmed in his belief that Churchill had resolved not to 'abandon [India] voluntarily',[78] he quickly returned to Sevagram, but not before using blunt language with Cripps: 'If this is your entire proposal to India, I would advise you to take the next plane home.'[79]

However, Azad, Nehru, Patel, C R and the rest of the Working Committee remained in New Delhi for talks with Cripps. Annoyed at Patel for 'stay[ing] on and on in the capital', Gandhi termed the talks an exercise in 'churning water to obtain butter'.[80]

Probed by Azad, Nehru and C R, Cripps at first agreed that in a national government the Viceroy would only be a constitutional head. However, after Linlithgow complained to Churchill, Cripps was obliged to say that the Viceregal veto would continue. A year later, Linlithgow would tell Wavell, his commander-in-chief in 1942 and successor as Viceroy:

> Cripps did not play straight over the question of the Viceroy's veto ... and did make some offer to Congress.[81]

The three Congress negotiators also objected to defence remaining with General Wavell. On this issue too Cripps tried to accommodate the Congress demand but was thwarted when Churchill cabled him to say that he would reject any arrangement over defence that did not have the full agreement, directly communicated to him, of Linlithgow and Wavell.

Not getting anything like the national government they had in mind, the Congress leaders formally turned down the scheme. While welcoming the secession clause as 'a recognition of Pakistan by implication', Jinnah, too, rejected the scheme because it only gave provinces and not what he called 'the Muslim nation' the right to separate.[82]

In rejecting the scheme's provisions for the secession of provinces or princely states, was the Congress asserting a right to coerce large populations? Answering the question, the Working Committee clarified that it 'cannot think in terms of compelling the people of any territorial unit to remain in an Indian Union against their declared and established will'. The Committee added that 'acceptance of this principle inevitably' ruled out any 'compulsion being exercised on other substantial groups within that area'.[83]

The first sentence conceded the possibility of secession by a people (not a party or a prince) after an Indian Union was formed. The second allowed parts or portions of a seceding unit to remain in the Union. These statements had the support of all in the Working Committee, including Azad, Patel and Nehru, and of Gandhi as well.

Before leaving India on 12 April, Cripps made a 'personal and private' appeal to Nehru, asking his friend to show 'the supreme courage of a great leader', that is, defy Gandhi and all his colleagues.[84] Jawaharlal demurred but was filled with doubt.[85]

Churchill was not sorry at Cripps's failure. 'When Mr Churchill learned of the breakdown of the Delhi negotiations he put on an act of sham tears and sorrow before his guests at Chequers, not troubling to conceal his own pleasure.'[86] Indians unable to agree was just the picture he wanted Roosevelt to get; in addition, an ambitious colleague had returned empty-handed.

Swept aside?

Post-war balkanization – an India in several parts, including one or two Muslim Indias and several princely Indias – was not Gandhi's only anxiety.

Until Pearl Harbor, Gandhi had thought that time was on his side. Whether or not Germany met with defeat, Britain was burning its resources. In a few years, assuming it retained a dominant profile, the Congress would non-violently inherit the Raj's power. These calculations were upset by Japan's conquests and America's entry into the war, even as Hitler's move had earlier destroyed the Congress's careful compact with the British. With America's wealth committed to the war, Britain's staying power had multiplied. As Gandhi observed, 'With America as her ally she has inexhaustible material resources and scientific skill.'[87]

Simultaneously, an aggressive Japan was at India's gate. Instead of a non-violent independence, India thus seemed more likely to obtain a war on its soil and seas – a no-holds-barred war between Japan and the Allies, fed as much on Indian lives and resources as on the combatants'.

From East Bengal he received reports of a scorched-earth policy to deny sustenance to Japanese invaders. Homesteads and boats had been destroyed. More destruction of homes and boats, of 'crops' and 'water-supply', of 'what belongs to or is of use to the masses'[88] seemed in store.

It was also possible, on the other hand, that the British would cut and run from India, even as they had evacuated Malaya, Singapore and Burma. As Gandhi put it:

India is not the home of the British people. If they are overwhelmed they will retire from India every man and woman and child, if they have facilities enough to carry them, even as they retired from Singapore, Malaya and Rangoon.[89]

Where would that leave the Indian population? 'Hundreds if not thousands' of Indians 'on their way from Burma [had] perished without food and drink', and 'wretched discrimination stared even these miserable people in the face'. There was 'one route for the whites, another for the blacks. Provision of food and shelter for the whites, none for the blacks. And discrimination even on their arrival in India.'[90] The Empire's first concern was for the British in India.

There was another cause for unease. Successive defeats that Asian Japan had inflicted on Western forces had made many Indians pro-Japanese and fiercely anti-British. These sentiments were strengthened by broadcasts from Berlin by Subhas Bose, heard from March 1942, 14 months after his escape from house arrest in Calcutta. For his bids for independence, Bose seemed willing to accept the aid of Hitler and the Japanese.

Gandhi heard reports that Bose's supporters would assist incoming Japanese forces, who it was thought might land in Orissa. Jawaharlal, on the other hand, was recommending a 'scorched-earth policy and guerrilla warfare' in the event of a Japanese invasion (82: 196), a position supported by the Indian Communist Party.

Would the Indian soil that recently offered the world an alternative to violence now witness a war between the Allies and the Axis powers *and* a violent clash between Indians?

The enlarged war was sweeping Gandhi, his life's work and his dream aside. It was threatening everything he had built or given birth to, or nourished or cherished – Swaraj, an Indian nation, Congress unity, non-violence, Hindu-Muslim friendship, Indo-British partnership ...

The response

It was Gandhi's biggest challenge yet, and he came up, as he had done so often before, with a simple response. This time it was 'Quit India!' He would ask the British to just leave his land and ask his people to repeat the call. Anything less bold or less simple would no longer work or even get heard.

With the call the initiative returned to him and the Congress; the lights came back to him and all he stood for, including Swaraj, an India for all, and non-violence. There would be some violence, surely, if he pressed the call – in the summer of 1942 Indians were angry. But he would risk a little violence for the survival of non-violence. When Hitler, Churchill and the Japanese spoke with gunboats and bombers, he could not remain silent.

A resourceful ally, Bajaj, was dead, and two crucial allies, Vallabhbhai and Mahadev, were unwell, as was Kasturba. He himself was nearly 73, and those trained in non-violence did not comprise a large number. Yet he could not wait. As he said on 28 May to about 100 members of the Rashtriya Yuvak Sangh ('National Youth Association') who called on him in Sevagram,

> I always thought that I would have to wait till the country was ready for a non-violent struggle. But my attitude has undergone a change. I feel that if I continue to wait I might have to wait till doomsday ... and in the meantime I may be enveloped and overwhelmed by the flames of violence that are spreading all around.[91]

Quit India. The two-word phrase was not his own and first used by him only on 3 August, in a letter to American friends.[92] But the idea behind it came to him in the middle of April.

'It was the Cripps fiasco that inspired the idea [of asking the British to go],' he told Louis Fischer, the American journalist, in June. 'Hardly had he gone when it seized hold of me.'[93]

British rule was 'unnatural' and had 'choked Indian life'.[94] The scheme that Cripps brought had 'divided Hindus from Muslims more than ever'.[95] Yes, 'anarchy' might reign for a while if the British left,[96] but India's conflicting forces would find their natural equilibrium. The Hindu-Muslim problem would become easier to resolve. If the British did not leave, the call would nonetheless proclaim that for Indians the first question was not Japan vs. Britain but Swaraj vs. slavery. When the call was given, most of India rallied behind him.

First move. He made his first move on or shortly before 24 April, sending a draft resolution to the Working Committee meeting later that month in Allahabad. He did not attend himself but authorized Mira to take his draft to the Committee.

The draft dealt with a likely Japanese attack on India's east coast. Wanting India to face the possibility of Britain's defeat or evacuation, Gandhi composed the following resolution:

> The Congress is of opinion that if the British withdrew from India, India would be able to defend herself in the event of Japanese or any aggressor attacking India. The A.I.C.C. is, therefore, of opinion that the British should withdraw from India ...
>
> This Committee desires to assure the Japanese Government and people that India bears no enmity either towards Japan or towards any other nation. But if Japan attacks India and Britain makes no response to its appeal the Committee would expect all those who look to Congress for guidance to offer complete non-violent non-cooperation to the Japanese forces and not render any assistance to them ...
>
> It is not difficult to understand the simple principle of non-violent non-cooperation: *1.* We may not bend the knee to the aggressor nor obey any of his orders.

2. We may not look to him for any favours nor fall to his bribes. But we may not bear him any malice nor wish him ill. *3.* If he wishes to take possession of our fields we will refuse to give them up even if we have to die in the effort to resist him.[97]

Nehru seems to have said to his Working Committee colleagues that the draft conveyed sympathy with Japan and the expectation that the Axis powers would win. Patel replied that the Bardoli resolution had 'made [it] clear that our sympathies were with the Allies' but added that the wording in Gandhi's draft could be changed to remove any unintended pro-fascist impression.[98]

Prasad edited Gandhi's draft accordingly but Nehru produced a resolution of his own. This too kept much of Gandhi's language while not asking the British, in so many words, 'to withdraw'. Nehru's draft rejected 'any schemes or proposals which retain, even in partial measure, British control and authority in India', and added: 'Not only the interests of India but also Britain's safety, and world peace and freedom, demand that Britain must abandon her hold on India.'[99]

When a vote was taken, six members and five invitees favoured the Gandhi-Prasad draft, while four members and two invitees preferred Nehru's. Azad, the president, did not vote, and Rajagopalachari, who was still in the Congress, opposed both. However, on Azad's urging, Prasad withdrew his version and asked for unanimous backing for Nehru's draft, which was reluctantly given.

Gandhi rebuked Patel for not fighting harder in Allahabad. Informed by Kripalani that Azad had secured the withdrawal of Prasad's draft by threatening to quit, Gandhi commented that the president should have been allowed to resign.[100] Yet he remarked also that Nehru's draft 'allowed him enough scope for work'.[101]

Simultaneously he increased the pressure. Encouraged by him, Patel and Prasad wrote to Azad that they and others were willing to resign from the Working Committee in view of 'fundamental differences'.[102] The resignations were not accepted. Azad knew, as did Nehru, that the public was with Gandhi, who said so in a letter to Azad: 'Sardar tells me that the public opinion is in favour of my resolution.'[103] Significantly, the Congress Socialists, close to Nehru in the 1930s, were entirely with Gandhi over Quit India.

On 24 April he had written to Nehru: 'The time has come when each of us must choose his own course.'[104] In July, when the Working Committee met in Wardha for nine days, Gandhi again said to Nehru and Azad that they were free to do as they pleased, and to resign if they must.[105]

The two yielded but also influenced Gandhi. At any rate Nehru did. Though Gandhi did not give in on Quit India, his language regarding Japan changed after Nehru questioned him. More importantly, Gandhi agreed to join to his Quit India call an expression of a freed India's willingness to host Allied troops, if needed, 'to prevent Japanese occupation'. Writing in *Harijan* on 28 June, Gandhi admitted that 'abrupt withdrawal of the Allied troops might result in Japan's occupation of India and China's sure fall'.[106]

Questions. From the start he had refused to see the Japanese as 'liberators', pointing to 'Chinese history' as proof of the opposite,[107] and he said he 'could only laugh at the suggestion' that he had 'turned pro-Japanese'.[108] On 26 April *Harijan* carried his comment that if 'the Nazis, the Fascists or the Japanese instead of leaving India alone choose to subjugate her, they will find that they have to hold more than they can in their iron hoop. They will find it much more difficult than Britain has. Their very rigidity will strangle them.'[109]

Yet it was a leader's duty to ready his people for any eventuality. On 7 June *Harijan* published his reaction to a story that Gandhi's 'present attitude towards England and Japan' was influenced by a belief that 'the Allies were going to be defeated':

> I have no hesitation in saying that it is not true. On the contrary I said only the other day in *Harijan* that the Britisher was hard to beat. He has not known what it is to be defeated. And with America as her ally she has inexhaustible material resources and scientific skill ... Thus I have no decisive opinion about the result of the War.[110]

To Mira, who had gone to Orissa to prepare the coastal population for a non-violent response to any Japanese attack, he wrote on 31 May:

> One thing they should never do – yield willing submission to the Japanese. That will be a cowardly act, and unworthy of freedom-loving people. They must not escape from one fire only to fall into another and probably more terrible.[111]

And in *Harijan* of 14 June he wrote:

> Neither food nor shelter is to be given nor are any dealings to be established with [the Japanese]. They should be made to feel that they are not wanted.[112]

On 5 June, after Nehru had convinced him about Allied troops, he told Fischer:

> Britain and America, and other countries too, can keep their armies here and use Indian territory as a base for military operations. I do not wish Japan to win the war. I do not want the Axis to win. Oh, [the Allies] could operate the railroads [as well]. They would also need order in the ports where they received their supplies ... I accept the proposition that there is a better chance if the democracies win.[113]

In *Harijan* of 14 June he said that the 'first act' of a free India 'would be to enter into a treaty with the United Nations for defensive operations against aggressive powers, it being common cause that India will have nothing to do with any of the Fascist powers and India would be morally bound to help the United Nations'. He added that Allied troops would be 'tolerat[ed] on the Indian soil under well-defined conditions'.[114]

Acknowledging that in the summer of 1942 Indians were nursing ill will against the British, Gandhi claimed that 'orderly British withdrawal will turn the hatred into affection',[115] which, he insisted, was still his goal. But he told Fischer that he had always known – from personal experience and from 'British history' – that Britons were 'impressed by action', and 'it is action that we must take now'.[116]

But would the British just pack up and leave? In June Rajagopalachari publicly objected to 'the fond expectation that the British will leave the country in simple response to a Congress slogan'.[117] And in July, in a letter to Gandhi, C R argued that Britain 'cannot add to her crimes the crowning offence of leaving the country in chaos to become a certain prey to foreign ambition'.[118]

C R resigns. From his east coast perspective, Gandhi's old friend and relative by marriage was convinced that Japan was India's principal foe. Keen on a Congress-League settlement that he hoped would lead to a national government in New Delhi, and eager to return as premier to defend the presidency of Madras, C R persuaded Congress members of the Madras legislature to pass two controversial resolutions on 24 April 1942.

By the first, the Madras legislators asked the AICC to concede the Muslim League's claim for the separation of 'certain areas' and ask for the League's support for 'a national administration at this hour of peril'. By their second resolution, the Madras legislators sought the AICC's permission for reviving a popular government in Madras (this time including members of the Muslim League) to prepare south Indians to face any Japanese attack.[119]

In defence of his moves, C R cited the 'non-coercion' resolution that the Working Committee had passed in April, shortly after the talks with Cripps, which disavowed 'compelling the people of any territorial unit to remain in an Indian Union against their declared and established will'.

Early in May, in Allahabad, the AICC heard Rajagopalachari but by an overwhelming majority turned down the requests from Madras. C R then took his case to the public, winning support in some quarters but losing that of his Working Committee colleagues and before long of most in the Congress. The bulk of the Madras legislators also deserted him.

While conceding that it was 'a noble thing to strive for Hindu-Muslim unity' and 'equally noble to strive to ward off the Japanese intrusion', Gandhi called C R's plan 'wholly unnatural',[120] and suggested that it would be 'most becoming' if he severed his connection with the Congress and then carried on his campaign with 'all the zeal and ability' he was capable of.[121]

Members could not be 'totally debarred from persuading Congressmen to alter their opinions,' C R argued, yet in July he resigned from the Congress, and also from the Madras legislature, 'in order to be absolutely free to carry on my campaign'.[122]

Passion and reason. On 9 June Fischer asked Gandhi whether he had 'any organization' with which to conduct his proposed struggle.

> *G*: The organization is the Congress Party. But if it fails me, I have my own organization, myself …
>
> *F*: If you look at this in its historic perspective, you are doing a novel and remarkable thing – you are ordaining the end of an empire.
>
> *G*: Even a child can do that. I will appeal to the people's instincts. I may arouse them …
>
> *F*: Do you expect drastic action when you launch the movement?
>
> *G*: Yes. I expect it any day. I am ready. I know I may be arrested.

Five days later, speaking to other American journalists, Gandhi again admitted the likelihood of quick arrests but added: 'Our arrests would work up the movement, they would stir everyone in India to do his little bit.'[123]

Fischer said to Desai that after listening carefully to Gandhi and studying his notes and 'wondering all the time what was the source of his hold on people', he had come 'to the tentative conclusion that it was his passion'.

> 'That is right,' Desai said.
>
> 'What is the root of his passion?' Fischer asked.
>
> 'This passion,' Desai explained, 'is the sublimation of all the passions that flesh is heir to.'
>
> 'Sex?'
>
> 'Sex and anger and personal ambition … Gandhi is under his own complete control. That generates tremendous energy and passion.'[124]

But the Quit India passion was not devoid of reason. Contrary to what Rajagopalachari suggested, there is no indication that Gandhi in fact expected the British to quit that summer or immediately thereafter. But he thought that apart from reminding the world of his vision, Quit India would strengthen the Congress in India.

Did he anticipate that Muslims generally might see Quit India as a bid to pre-empt Pakistan by replacing British control with that of the Congress? Or realize that suppression of the Congress could leave the field free for the Muslim League and its Pakistan call?

He did but felt helpless. Insisting, on 14 June, that he was not asking 'the British to hand over India to the Congress or to the Hindus', Gandhi added, 'Let them entrust India to God or in modern parlance to anarchy. Then all the parties will fight one another like dogs, or will, when real responsibility faces them, come to a reasonable agreement.'[125]

Talking with Cripps at the end of March, he had 'acknowledged the great influence of Jinnah and that the movement for Pakistan had grown tremendously in volume during the last two years'.[126] And in June and July, despite the sharp difference with Rajagopala-chari, he encouraged his friend to continue negotiating with Jinnah.[127] Yet he would not put off Quit India for a possible, but to him unlikely, agreement with Jinnah.

Did he have a plan or strategy for enlisting participation in Quit India? In a letter to Mira, written on 22 May, he gave an inkling of his expectations:

> I want to hasten slowly. I do not want to precipitate matters. Our steps must be firm but gradual so that people may understand them so far as it is possible. A time must come when the thing may become beyond control. We may not purposely let it go out of control.[128]

He does not wish to be arrested at once, yet he believes that once 'people understand' what he is getting at they will act on their own, even recklessly perhaps. Indeed 'a time must come' for that.

On 9 June (over a month before the Working Committee endorsed Quit India), Fischer asked Gandhi whether he was willing to listen to Chinese, Russia or American voices questioning his plan. When Gandhi said he was, Fischer asked, 'Have I your authority to say this to the Viceroy?' 'Yes, you have my permission,' Gandhi answered.

> F: Would you wish President Roosevelt to be informed about your attitude?
> G: Yes. I do not wish to appeal to anybody. But I would want Mr Roosevelt to know my plans, my views, and my readiness to compromise. Tell your President I wish to be dissuaded.[129]

Precautions. On 14 June Gandhi wrote to Chiang Kai-shek: 'To make it perfectly clear that we want to prevent in every way Japanese aggression, I would personally agree that the Allied Powers might, under treaty with us, keep their armed forces in India and use the country as a base for operations against the threatened Japanese attack.'[130] To Gandhi's disappointment, the Chinese leader expressed the fear that a Quit India campaign would hurt China's war effort.

On 21 June Gandhi publicly aired his views on the hopes of Subhas, who would reach Japan via German and Japanese submarines in the following year:

> I have no desire whatsoever to woo any power to help India in her endeavour to free herself from the foreign yoke. I have no desire to exchange the British for any other rule. Better the enemy I know than the one I do not ... There can therefore be no question of my approval of Subhas Babu's policy. The old difference of opinion between us persists. This does not mean that I doubt his sacrifice or his patriotism.[131]

A week later he defended C R's right to dissent and praised his colleague's deportment at a Bombay meeting where demonstrators had thrown tar at him:

> The report of hooliganism at Rajaji's meeting in Matunga makes painful reading. Has Rajaji lost every title to respect because he has taken what seems to be an unpopular view? ...
>
> Those who did not share his views might have abstained from attending the meeting ... They might have cross-questioned him. Those who tarred him and created a disturbance have disgraced themselves and have harmed their cause ...
>
> The calmness, good humour, presence of mind and determination that Rajaji showed at that trying time were worthy of him ... Rajaji has never lacked the qualities that go to make a hero.[132]

To Roosevelt. On 1 July Gandhi wrote a frank and prescient letter to President Roosevelt:

> Dear Friend: I twice missed coming to your great country. I have the privilege [of] having numerous friends there both known and unknown to me. Many of my countrymen have received and are still receiving higher education in America ... I have profited greatly by the writings of Thoreau and Emerson. I say this to tell you how much I am connected with your country.
>
> Of Great Britain I need say nothing beyond mentioning that in spite of my intense dislike of British rule, I have numerous personal friends in England whom I love as dearly as my own people. I had my legal education there. I have therefore nothing but good wishes for your country and Great Britain.
>
> You will therefore accept my word that my present proposal, that the British should unreservedly and ... immediately withdraw their rule, is prompted by the friendliest intention. I would like to turn into goodwill the ill will which, whatever

may be said to the contrary, exists in India towards Great Britain and thus enable the millions of India to play their part in the present war ...

Under foreign rule however we can make no effective contribution of any kind in this war, except as helots ... I venture to think that the Allied declaration that the Allies are fighting to make the world safe for freedom of the individual and for democracy sounds hollow so long as India and, for that matter, Africa are exploited by Great Britain and America has the Negro problem in her own home.

But ... in my proposal I have confined myself only to India. If India becomes free, the rest must follow, if it does not happen simultaneously.

In order to make my proposal foolproof, I have suggested that, if the Allies think it necessary, they may keep their troops at their own expense in India, not for keeping internal order but for preventing Japanese aggression and defending China ...

Mr Louis Fischer is carrying this letter to you ... I hope finally that you will not resent this letter as an intrusion but take it as an approach from a friend and well-wisher of the Allies. I remain, Yours sincerely, M.K. Gandhi[133]

Churchill persuaded Roosevelt not to respond to Gandhi, and British propaganda painted Gandhi in America as a pro-Axis defeatist. Found in documents seized by the Raj when the Congress office in Allahabad was raided, Nehru's comment in April on Gandhi's draft was used to support the allegation.

When, early in August, the Raj publicized these documents in India, Jawaharlal answered that the remarks quoted were no more than disjointed, unrevised, and out-of-context jottings by an assistant secretary.[134] Gandhi observed:

I have never even in the most unguarded moment expressed the opinion that Japan and Germany would win the war ... I have, therefore, nothing to withdraw and nothing to be ashamed of about the draft I had the privilege of sending to the Working Committee.[135]

On 17 July, well before the seizure of the supposedly damaging documents, Frederick Puckle, Director-General of Information, Government of India, had asked chief secretaries of all provincial governments to mobilize public opinion against the proposed campaign, and suggested the use of a cartoon showing 'Hitler, Mussolini, Tojo, each with microphones saying, "I vote for the Congress Resolution."'[136]

Communists aside, not many Indians were influenced by the Raj's propaganda. Criticisms of the Quit India call from the Muslim League, the princes, and other non-Congress elements stressed domestic, not international, considerations. Treating Muslims and not the British as the Hindus' principal foe, the Hindu Mahasabha and the RSS asked

Hindus to stay clear of Quit India and use Britain's war to gain expertise for a future clash with Muslims.

Working Committee decides. On 14 July, after a series of meetings in Wardha, the Working Committee resolved in favour of Quit India. Noting 'a rapid and widespread increase of ill will against Britain and a growing satisfaction at the success of Japanese arms', the Committee added:

> [A]ll aggression must be resisted, for any submission to it must mean the degrada-tion of the Indian people and the continuation of their subjection. The Congress is anxious to avoid the experience of Malaya, Singapore, and Burma and desires to build up resistance to any aggression on or invasion of India by the Japanese or any foreign power.
>
> The Congress would change the present ill will against Britain into goodwill ... This is only possible if India feels the glow of freedom.
>
> On the withdrawal of British rule in India, responsible men and women of the country will come together to form a provisional government.
>
> In making the proposal for the withdrawal of the British rule from India, the Congress has no desire whatsoever to embarrass Great Britain or the Allied powers in their prosecution of the war, or in any way to encourage aggression on India or increase pressure on China by the Japanese or any other power associated with the Axis group ...
>
> The Congress is, therefore, agreeable to the stationing of the armed forces of the Allies in India, should they so desire, in order to ward off and resist Japanese or other aggression and to protect and help China.
>
> Should, however, this appeal fail ... the Congress will then be reluctantly compelled to utilize all the non-violent strength it might have gathered since 1920 ... (83: 445–7).[137]

To ratify the resolution, the AICC was summoned for meetings in Bombay on 7 and 8 August. Meanwhile Gandhi asked Mira to inform the Viceroy that while he 'would do his very utmost to ensure non-violence', this time he 'would not feel justified in calling the movement off' if 'cases of violence occurred'.[138] Though Linlithgow refused to see her, Mira conveyed (on 17 July) Gandhi's message to Sir Gilbert Laithwaite, the Viceroy's secretary.

'To Every Japanese'. On 18 July 1942 Gandhi wrote a forthright letter 'To Every Japanese.' At least three newspapers in Japan reproduced the appeal:[139]

> Ever since I was a lad of eighteen studying in London ... I learnt ... to prize the many

excellent qualities of your nation. I was thrilled when in South Africa I learnt of your brilliant victory over Russian arms. After my return to India from South Africa in 1915, I came in close touch with Japanese monks who lived as members of our ashram from time to time ...

I grieve deeply as I contemplate what appears to me to be your unprovoked attack against China and, if reports are to be believed, your merciless devastation of that great and ancient land.

It was a worthy ambition of yours to take equal rank with the great powers of the world. Your aggression against China and your alliance with the Axis powers was surely an unwarranted excess of the ambition ...

You will be sadly disillusioned if you believe that you will receive a willing welcome from India. The end and aim of [our] movement for British withdrawal is to prepare India ... for resisting all militarist and imperialist ambition, whether it is called British Imperialism, German Nazism, or your pattern.

[Do not be] misled into feeling that you have but to step into the country that Britain has vacated ... [I]f you cherish any such idea and will carry it out, we will not fail in resisting you with all the might that our country can muster. I am, Your friend and well-wisher, M.K. Gandhi[140]

On the Hindu-Muslim question, Gandhi backed two proposals made by Azad, one proposing Congress-League talks and the other, addressed to Britain, suggesting that 'simultaneously with the declaration of independence' the British should hand over power either to the Congress or the Muslim League. Any party obtaining power would be obliged to share it with others, wrote Gandhi, for 'in free India government must depend wholly upon the willing consent of the people'.[141]

Action plan? Despite thinking over it for much of July, Gandhi could not prepare an action plan for Quit India satyagrahis. He knew that this time each participant would have to be a leader unto himself or herself, for all known leaders – Gandhi above all – would be behind bars before long. Gandhi hoped to delay arrests by asking, as in the past, to meet the Viceroy, but would Linlithgow really wait for an interview in the Viceroy's House where Gandhi formally asked the British to quit?

However, he presented a few ideas to the Working Committee in Wardha on 15 July.[142] One, those who believed in violence or hated the British or Indians of another faith should stay out of Quit India. Two, jail was not the goal this time: arrest cannot be sought from those you are asking to quit. Three, courageous students should leave government colleges and not return there until India was free. Four, there should be widespread stoppages of work and business. Five, the brave should withhold salt tax and land revenue and refuse orders to vacate a field or house. Six, government servants should resign rather than implement harsh orders. Seven, the defence of China and Russia should not be hampered.

But point seven seemed at odds with points four, five and six, and point one with point two. How was one to defy laws or bans and evade arrest without lying, concealing or using violence?

Between the Working Committee meetings that ended in Wardha on 14 July and the AICC sessions set for 7 and 8 August in Bombay, the leaders strove to prepare their regions. Though weary and ill (in June the Raj thought him to be near death[143]), Patel worked up Bombay and Gujarat. According to an intelligence report, this is what Patel said in Ahmedabad on 26 July:

> If all the leaders are arrested tomorrow and there is no time to meet again, [let me say to you], die but do not fall back. This time if a railway line is removed or an Englishman is murdered, the struggle will not be stopped ... Congressmen of course must act strictly within the limits of non-violence, even if Gandhiji and the other leaders are arrested before the AICC meeting.[144]

Whether on his own behalf or for the Working Committee and Gandhi as well, Patel also said in Gujarat:

> Let the railwaymen refuse to work on behalf of the railways. Let the post and telegraph men go on strike. Let Government servants give up their service. Let teachers and students keep away from schools and colleges and thus cooperate in bringing to a standstill the entire administrative machinery.[145]

On 2 August Patel addressed a mammoth meeting in Bombay and again asked for 'a complete standstill'. The next morning he received Gandhi, Kasturba, Mahadev and Pyarelal at Bombay's Dadar station. Gandhi and party went to Birla House; Patel was staying in his son's Marine Drive apartment.

From the 4th to the 8th the Working Committee met daily, and there were numerous smaller meetings. On 6 August Gandhi said in a public statement:

> I have definitely contemplated an interval between the passing of the Congress resolution and the starting of the struggle ... [A] letter will certainly go to the Viceroy, not as an ultimatum but as an earnest pleading for avoidance of a conflict. If there is a favourable response, then my letter can be the basis for negotiation (83: 180).

Bombay, 7–8 August 1942

There was an electric atmosphere and an immense throng at the Gowalia Tank grounds in central Bombay when, on 7 August, the AICC began its two-day session there. Azad presided, a converted Jawaharlal moved the Quit India resolution, and Patel seconded it. Vallabhbhai said:

> The object this time is to free India before the Japanese come and be ready to fight them if they come.
>
> They will round up the leaders, round up all. Then it will be the duty of every Indian to put forth his utmost effort – within non-violence. No source is to be left untapped, no weapon untried. This is going to be the opportunity of a lifetime.[146]

In his speech on 7 August, Gandhi spoke first of non-violence:

> I must tell you that there is no change in me. I stick to the principle of non-violence as I did before. If you are tired of it then you need not come with me.

He touched on the princely states, and sought to enlist rulers and subjects alike:

> Their number may be 600 or more ... Whatever the Princes may say, their people will acclaim that we have been asking for the very thing that they want. If we carry on this struggle in the way I want it, the Princes will get more through it than they can ever expect [from the British].

Power, he said, would come to Indians, not necessarily to the Congress or to Hindus:

> Our object is to achieve independence and whoever can take up the reins may do so. It may be, you decide to place it in the hands of Parsis ... Maybe that power may be given to those whose names had never been heard of in the Congress. It will be for the people to decide.

He addressed the issues of hate and violence:

> If there is the slightest communal taint in your minds, keep off the struggle. We must remove any hatred for the British from our hearts. At least in my heart there is no such hatred.
>
> At a time when I am about to launch the biggest fight in my life there can be no hatred for the British in my heart. The thought that because they are in difficulties

I should give them a push is totally absent from my mind. It never has been there
...

[I]n a moment of anger they might do things which might provoke you. Nevertheless you should not resort to violence and put non-violence to shame. When such
a thing happens ... [m]y blood will be on your head. If you don't understand this it
will be better if you reject this resolution.

I do not want to be the instrument of Russia's defeat nor of China's. If that
happens I would hate myself.

And he claimed there could be an Indian revolution greater than the French or the
Russian:

When I raised the slogan 'Quit India' the people in India who were then feeling
despondent felt I had placed before them a new thing. If you want real freedom you
will have to come together and ... create true democracy – democracy the like of
which has not been so far witnessed ...

I have read a good deal about the French revolution. Carlyle's works I read while
in jail. I have great admiration for the French people. Pandit Jawaharlal has told me
all about the Russian revolution. But I hold that though theirs was a fight for the
people it was not a fight for real democracy which I envisaged.

My democracy means every man is his own master. I have read sufficient history
and I did not see such an experiment on so large a scale for the establishment of
democracy by non-violence (83: 181–5).

At a dinner in London that night, Prime Minister Churchill and General Smuts from
South Africa were joined by Lord Moran, Churchill's physician. According to Moran,

Smuts spoke of Gandhi: 'He is a man of God. You and I are mundane people. Gandhi
has appealed to religious motives. You never have. That is where you have failed.' PM
(with a great grin): 'I have made more bishops than anyone since St Augustine.' But
Smuts did not smile. His face was very grave.[147]

On 8 August Gandhi took time to confirm to a friend of Jinnah's that if the Muslim
League joined in the Quit India call, Gandhi and the Congress would 'have no objection
to the British Government transferring all the powers it today exercises to the Muslim
League on behalf of the whole of India'.[148]

Later that day, before Gandhi was to leave Birla House for Gowalia Tank, Desai said
to Kalelkar: 'This evening's is the most important meeting of his life. He has decided to

pray before setting forth.' '*Vaishnava Jana*' was sung before a praying group of eight or ten persons, and Kalelkar thought that Gandhi's face during the singing 'shone with the pure radiance of trust in God, a firm resolve and gentleness'.[149] Ratifying the Working Committee's decision, the AICC authorized,

> for the vindication of India's inalienable right to freedom and independence, the starting of a mass struggle on non-violent lines on the widest possible scale, so that the country might utilize all the non-violent strength it has gathered during the last twenty-two years of peaceful struggle. Such a struggle must inevitably be under the leadership of Gandhiji and the Committee requests him to take the lead and guide the nation in the steps to be taken ...
>
> A time may come when it may not be possible to issue instructions or for instructions to reach our people, and when no Congress committees can function. When this happens, every man and woman who is participating in this movement must function for himself or herself within the four corners of the general instructions issued.
>
> Every Indian who desires freedom and strives for it must be his own guide urging him on along the hard road where there is no resting place and which leads ultimately to the independence and deliverance of India (83: 451–4).

A small group of 13, most of them Congressmen sympathetic to the Soviet Union, had voted against the ratification. Speaking twice after the voting, first in Hindi and then in English, Gandhi started with the dissenters:

> I congratulate the thirteen friends who voted against the resolution.

Turning to Muslims and the two-nation demand, he said:

> Time was when every Muslim claimed the whole of India as his motherland. During the years that the Ali Brothers were with me, the assumption underlying all their talks and discussions was that India belonged as much to the Muslims as to the Hindus.
>
> I can testify to the fact that this was their innermost conviction and not a mask; I lived with them for years. I spent days and nights in their company ...
>
> I believed even at [a] tender age that ... it did not matter if I made no special effort to cultivate friendship with Hindus, but I must make friends with at least a few Muslims. It was as counsel for a Muslim merchant that I went to South Africa. I made friends with other Muslims there, even with the opponents of my client, and gained a reputation for integrity and good faith ... I captured their hearts

and when I left finally for India, I left them sad and shedding tears of grief at the separation.

In India, too, I continued my efforts and left no stone unturned to achieve that unity. It was my life-long aspiration for it that made me offer my fullest co-operation to the Muslims in the Khilafat movement. Muslims throughout the country accepted me as their true friend.

Not a trace of suspicion lurked in anybody's heart. Where has all that dignity, that nobility of spirit, disappeared now?

I should ask all Muslims, including Quaid-e-Azam Jinnah, to recall those glorious days and to find out what has brought us to the present impasse. Quaid-e-Azam Jinnah himself was at one time a Congressman ... May God bless him with long life, but when I am gone, he will realize and admit that I had no designs on Muslims and that I had never betrayed their interests.

Where is the escape for me if I injure their cause or betray their interests? My life is entirely at their disposal. They are free to put an end to it, whenever they wish to do so. Assaults have been made on my life in the past, but God has spared me till now ...

But if someone were to shoot me in the belief that he was getting rid of a rascal, he would kill not the real Gandhi, but the one that appeared to him a rascal ... You may take it from me that one day you will regret the fact that you distrusted and killed one who was a true and devoted friend of yours.

He spoke of Hindu counterparts of Muslim separatists:

If the Hindus tyrannize over the Muslims, with what face will they talk of a world federation? Those Hindus who, like Dr Moonje and Shri Savarkar, believe in the doctrine of the sword may seek to keep the Muslims under Hindu domination.

I do not represent that section. I represent the Congress. You want to kill the Congress which is the goose that lays golden eggs. If you distrust the Congress, you may rest assured that there is to be a perpetual war between the Hindus and the Muslims.

But he could not wait for communal unity:

I ... want freedom immediately, this very night, before dawn, if it can be had. Freedom cannot now wait for the realization of communal unity ... [T]he Congress must win freedom or be wiped out in the effort. And forget not that the freedom which the Congress is struggling to achieve will not be for the Congressmen alone but for all the forty crores of the Indian people ...

In the coming revolution, Congressmen will sacrifice their lives in order to protect the Muslim against a Hindu's attack and vice versa.

After separately addressing journalists, government servants, soldiers, princes and students, Gandhi spoke again in personal terms:

I have travelled all over India as perhaps nobody in the present age has. The voiceless millions of the land saw in me their friend and representative, and I identified myself with them to the extent it was possible for a human being to do.

I saw trust in their eyes, which I now want to turn to good account in fighting this Empire upheld on untruth and violence. However gigantic the preparations that the Empire has made, we must get out of its clutches.

How can I remain silent at this supreme hour and hide my light under the bushel? Shall I ask the Japanese to tarry a while? If today I sit quiet and inactive, God will take me to task for not using up the treasure He had given me, in the midst of the conflagration that is enveloping the whole world ...

He outlined what lay ahead:

Nevertheless, the actual struggle does not commence this moment. You have only placed all your powers in my hands. I will now wait upon the Viceroy and plead with him for the acceptance of the Congress demand. That process is likely to take two or three weeks.

What would you do in the meanwhile? ... Every one of you should, from this moment onwards, consider yourself a free man or woman, and act as if you are free and are no longer under the heel of this imperialism ...

Here is a mantra, a short one, that I give you. You may imprint it on your hearts and let every breath of yours give expression to it. The mantra is: 'Do or Die.' We shall either free India or die in the attempt ...

Keep jails out of your consideration. If the Government keep me free, I will spare you the trouble of filling the jails ...

Take a pledge with God and your own conscience as witness, that you will no longer rest till freedom is achieved and will be prepared to lay down your lives in the attempt to achieve it. He who loses his life will gain it; he who will seek to save it shall lose it.

The cascading lava was Indian but also human and universal, so that Gandhi naturally used a biblical sentence and, a few sentences earlier, took his mantra from Tennyson's

Charge of the Light Brigade ('Theirs not to reason why, theirs but to do and die'). He said he was at last uttering the cry he had wanted to articulate from 1920, when non-cooperation was launched:

> For the last twenty-two years, I have controlled my speech and pen and have stored up my energy ... But today the occasion has come when I have to unburden my heart before you.

Perhaps the cry had lain even longer in the subconscious, from the moment half a century earlier when, in the Rajkot Residency, Charles Ollivant had asked Gandhi to quit. Now it was out.

> I have given you my message and through you I have delivered it to the whole of India (83: 186–200).

'It's done.' He had reached the finishing line, passed on the mantra to hundreds of thousands of hushed, stirred and anxious Indians. Now it wouldn't matter even if he was arrested the very next moment. But he was not. He continued in English:

> I have been called [the satyagrahis'] leader or, in military language, their commander. But I do not look at my position in that light. I have no weapon but love to wield my authority over anyone.
>
> I do sport a stick which you can break into bits without the slightest exertion. It is simply my staff with the help of which I walk. Such a cripple is not elated, when he is called upon to bear the greatest burden. You [would] share that burden only when I appear before you not as your commander but as a humble servant.

Once more he sought to woo Linlithgow:

> I have enjoyed the privilege of friendship ... with Lord Linlithgow. It is a friendship which has outgrown official relationship. Whether Lord Linlithgow will bear me out I do not know; but there has sprung up a personal bond between him and myself. He once introduced me to his daughter.
>
> His son-in-law, the ADC, was drawn towards me. He fell in love with Mahadev more than with me, and Lady Anne and he came to me. She is an obedient and favourite daughter. I take interest in their welfare ... It is a terrible job to have to offer resistance to a Viceroy with whom I enjoy such relations ...

The remarks in English were directed at Western correspondents:

> Then there is the sacred memory of Charlie Andrews which wells up within me at this
> moment. The spirit of Andrews hovers about me. For me he sums up the brightest
> tradition of English culture. I enjoyed closer relations with him than with most
> Indians. I enjoyed his confidence. There were no secrets between us. We exchanged
> our hearts every day ... He is unfortunately gone ...
>
> I know that the spirit of Andrews is listening to me ... [B]ut even for the friend-
> ship [of Western friends] or their love, I must not suppress the voice within, call it
> conscience ...
>
> That something in me which never deceives me tells me now: 'Forsake friends, wife,
> and all; but testify to that for which you have lived, and for which you have to die.'

Not that he wished to die. In fact he wanted to live long, seeing and enjoying the independence of India and of all colonies:

> Believe me, friends, I am not anxious to die. I want to live my full span of life.
> According to me, it is 120 years at least. By that time India will be free, the world
> will be free.

He spoke of 'the coloured races of the earth':

> Are England and America fighting for the liberty of these races today? You shall not
> limit my concept of freedom. The English and American teachers, their history and
> their magnificent poetry have not said you shall not broaden the interpretation of
> that freedom ...
>
> There are representatives of the foreign press assembled here today. Through them
> I wish to say to the world that [the] United Nations, who say that they have need for
> India, have the opportunity now to declare India free and prove their bona fides. If
> they miss it, they will be missing [the] opportunity of their lifetime.

Recalling that Britons had evacuated Malaya and Burma, he added:

> Where shall I go and where shall I take the forty crores of India? How is this vast
> mass of humanity to be aflame in the cause of world-deliverance? ... If lustre is to be
> put into their eyes, freedom has to come not tomorrow but today. I have, therefore,
> pledged the Congress and the Congress has pledged herself that she will do or die
> (83: 201–6).

Never before had he or his hearers been stirred like this.

Crackdown

Returning to Birla House, Gandhi talked with Patel, Desai and Birla. The last two were certain that Gandhi would be arrested before dawn, but Gandhi thought that Linlithgow would send for him, and that action would be withheld until then, or until he violated a law. He assured Kasturba that he would not be arrested 'unless I courted arrest myself'.[150]

He was mistaken. In consultation with Leopold Amery and Churchill, Linlithgow had planned an instant and tough response, including deporting Gandhi to Aden and the Working Committee to Nyasaland. Since the deportation idea seemed capable of enraging all Indians, including serving soldiers, it was abandoned, but plans were in place for arresting Gandhi and the Working Committee, suppressing defiance, breaking strikes, and unleashing propaganda.

In the pre-dawn hours of 9 August Gandhi, Mahadev and Mira were removed from Birla House and the Working Committee members and many local Congressmen from their lodgings in Bombay. Kasturba, who was shocked at her husband's arrest, and Pyarelal were told that they could either accompany Gandhi to jail or stay out. Desai's son Narayan has left an account of what followed:

> We all believed that this time in prison would be the final one. Miraben was pleased to be able to share it with Bapu. But Ba was perplexed. She said to Bapu, 'You tell me what to do.'
>
> Bapu said, 'Since you ask, I'd like you to get arrested separately by speaking in my place at the rally scheduled this for this evening. But if you want to come with me I won't object. If they arrest you separately they may keep you apart from me. You must consider all this and decide.'
>
> It was no easy choice. On the one hand was their life-long relationship. It was not certain that Bapu would survive this prison term. And even visiting Bapu might not be possible. On the other hand were Bapu's own wishes.
>
> Yet Ba made her decision in less time than it has taken to tell. She said resolutely, 'As for me, I would like to be with you in this hour. But even more, I want to fulfil your wishes. So I will stay.'
>
> I stared dazedly at her, at this example of sacrifice.

Adds Narayan:

> As Kaka ['Uncle', Narayan's word for his father] was about to get [inside the police car],
> I told him, 'We will meet again in free India.' In reply Kaka kissed my cheek.'[151]

Pyarelal too chose not to go with Gandhi. Prayers were recited before the three prisoners were driven off in a police car, and Gandhi dictated a message to Pyarelal:

> Let every non-violent soldier of freedom write out the slogan 'Do or Die' on a piece
> of paper or cloth and stick it on his clothes, so that in case he died in the course of
> satyagraha, he might be distinguished by that sign from other elements who do not
> subscribe to non-violence.[152]

Within hours the words 'Do or Die' – 'karenge ya marenge' in Hindi – would be on lips across India. Not knowing or caring, Churchill, who received word of the arrests on what in London was the night of 8 August, 'pouted' to Moran: 'We have clapped Gandhi into gaol.'[153]

In Bombay the arrested were all taken to Victoria Terminus station and put on a train. Azad and Patel entered the compartment where Gandhi was lodged but were ordered by the police to return to their seats. 'I don't think I will see you again,' Patel said to Gandhi and Desai before leaving.[154] He had sensed, or heard, that Gandhi and the Working Committee would be lodged in separate jails.

Gandhi asked Azad to demand a Congress president's rights in prison, but Azad, a reluctant convert to Quit India, was no longer eager for advice from one who had landed him and the Working Committee in an indefinite and probably long spell of imprisonment. Azad thought that Gandhi was taken by surprise by the prompt arrest and looked resentful.[155]

The train proceeded towards Poona. At Chinchwad station Gandhi, Mahadev, Sarojini Naidu and Mira were put in a car and taken to 'Aga Khan Palace', which the Raj had obtained from the Aga Khan, the head of the world's Ismaili or Khoja Muslims, for wartime use and had selected for Gandhi's detention. A group of Bombay Congressmen were herded into two lorries and taken to Yeravda jail. Some minutes later, at Kirkee station, another group of Bombay Congressmen, including the socialists Yusuf Meherally and Asoka Mehta, were taken off the train and sent to Yeravda jail. The Working Committee were taken beyond Poona to Ahmednagar station and thence to the 16th-century Ahmednagar fort, commandeered by the army, and known as 'the Keep'.

After Kasturba announced that she would address a meeting in the evening, she too was arrested, along with Sushila. Mercifully the two were sent to Aga Khan Palace, where Kasturba arrived violently sick. En route, at a railway station in Bombay, the two women detained in a waiting room observed that life went on even as critical events were overtaking many lives. Sushila would recall:

> Trains came and went, people came and went, the station officials passed by smoking and talking to each other, the coolies were heard haggling with the passengers. Ba had been watching this carefully. Suddenly she turned to me and said, 'Sushila, the world goes on as if nothing has happened. How will Bapuji win Swaraj?'[156]

The next morning (10 August) the Congress was banned, press censorship was tightened and all public meetings were prohibited. An official statement charged that the Congress had intended violence, was pro-Axis and aimed at totalitarian control over India.

India erupts

The scene at the railway station was misleading, however. The arrest of Gandhi and the Working Committee triggered a spontaneous, nationwide wave of fury. Town after town, and village after village, found heroes willing to defy, disrupt, and die. Six hundred were killed by the Raj's police in the first four days, and over 1,000, the House of Commons was informed, by the end of November. The actual figures were higher.

Areas in Bengal, Bihar, UP, Bombay, Karnataka and Orissa declared themselves free. Factories fell silent. In Bombay a clandestine radio station broadcast messages for three months. From Berlin, Subhas's voice encouraged the rebellion. Demonstrating Indians streamed out of bazaars, villages and colleges shouting 'Do or Die.' The Raj countered with arrests, beatings and bullets. In some places rebels were machine-gunned from the air. Over 100,000 Indian nationalists were jailed for indefinite terms, and the eruption was crushed by the end of August, but, in a letter to the King, Linlithgow called Quit India 'by far the most serious rebellion since that of 1857'.[157]

It was not peaceful. Bridges were blown up, telegraph and telephone wires cut, police and post offices burnt down, employees of the Raj killed. Some who believed in non-violence thought that on this occasion property could be destroyed as long as lives were not taken; stricter 'Gandhians' disagreed. Other rebels felt that freedom was the question, not non-violence.

Because all prominent Congress leaders were behind bars before the eruption occurred, it proved impossible for the Raj to connect any of them to the violence, though no effort was spared to find a link. The Raj supposed that a 'pre-concerted central plan' carried out through 'oral instructions', to use the words of Hallett, the UP governor,[158] had produced the rebellion, but Linlithgow would admit in January 1943, 'We have not yet got the link between the campaign of violence and the Working Committee.'[159] No link was found because none existed. In a fiercely anti-British climate, the arrests of Gandhi and the Working Committee sufficed to set off the violence.

In some places, underground governments functioned for a while: in Satara in Maharashtra, Midnapore in Bengal, Ballia in UP, and several Bihar areas. In its unplanned, undirected, explosive fury, Quit India was the complete opposite of the 1940–1 ICD, where Gandhi personally chose each satyagrahi and laid down a precise manner of law-breaking. In August 1942 each rebel, and mode of rebellion, was self-selected.

Escaping, in November 1942, from Bihar's Hazaribagh jail and conducting a secret campaign, Jayaprakash became a national hero. Aruna Asaf Ali, a Bengali Hindu whose Muslim husband was a member of the Working Committee and incarcerated in the Keep, was another underground leader of Quit India. The socialists Rammanohar Lohia and Achyut Patwardhan initiated several rebellious acts. Among the scores of women who provided leadership were Sucheta Kripalani, whose husband was also a prisoner in the Keep, and Usha Mehta, the organizer of Bombay's illegal broadcasts.

With the aid of Ramnath Goenka, who was publishing *Indian Express* from Madras, Devadas clandestinely produced *India Ravaged*, a book detailing British excesses. Businessmen provided funds to the rebels; Indian officials of the Raj gave warnings that enabled rebels to escape capture; some officials even hid rebels in their homes. As the Raj admitted, the public's 'general conspiracy of silence' prevented the capture of numerous rebels.[160]

Though Quit India had negative consequences as well, it decoupled the Indian people from their British rulers and fused them with the Congress. After August 1942 it became certain that the British would depart and the Congress take over; when, was the only question left.

Underscoring Gandhi as India's biggest player still, Quit India also proclaimed non-violence in the middle of the Second World War. The rebellion's violent aspects could not conceal Gandhi's salience or his message of non-violence.

Fighting from prison

The day after he was brought to Aga Khan Palace (AKP), Gandhi wrote a strong letter to Sir Roger Lumley, the governor of Bombay. Correctly terming the mansion, which was dusty and in disrepair, a 'temporary jail', he charged that at Chinchwad station he had witnessed 'an impatient English sergeant rough-handle' a Bombay Congressman 'and shove him into the lorry as if he was a log of wood', and asked that the unwell Patel, who was his 'patient', be brought to AKP, which was 'commodious enough'.[161]

Four days later, in a letter to the Viceroy, he directly accused the Raj. 'The Government of India were wrong in precipitating the crisis,' the letter began. The Raj 'should have waited at least till the time I inaugurated mass action', he said. There were several other assertions.

Firstly, 'violence was never contemplated [by the Congress] at any stage'. Secondly, 'the Congress was making every effort to identify India with the Allied cause'. Thirdly, the Congress's readiness to let the Muslim League form free India's first government disproved 'the charge of totalitarianism against the Congress'.

Fourthly, 'the living burial of the author of the [Quit India] demand has not resolved the deadlock, it has aggravated it.' Fifthly, the cause of the Allies did not require the arrests:

> The declared cause is common between the Government of India and us ... [I]t is the protection of the freedom of China and Russia. The Government of India think that the freedom of India is not necessary for winning the cause. I think exactly the opposite.
>
> I have taken Jawaharlal Nehru as my measuring rod. His personal contacts make him feel much more the misery of the impending ruin of China and Russia than I can – and may I say even you can ...
>
> He fought against my position with a passion which I have no words to describe. But the logic of facts overwhelmed him. He yielded when he saw clearly that without the freedom of India that of the other two was in great jeopardy. Surely you are wrong in having imprisoned such a powerful friend and ally.
>
> If notwithstanding the common cause, the Government's answer to the Congress demand is hasty repression, they will not wonder if I draw the inference that it was not so much the Allied cause that weighed with the British Government, as the unexpressed determination to cling to the possession of India as an indispensable part of the imperial policy.

Gandhi claimed, too, that 'Congress seeks to kill imperialism as much for the sake of the British people and humanity as for India' (83: 210–15).

Mahadev dies

Kasturba seemed to recover in Gandhi's company but on the morning of 15 August, the day after having typed and helped edit Gandhi's letter to Linlithgow, Mahadev suddenly collapsed and died, joining the ranks of several hundred Quit India martyrs. Kasturba sobbed that her husband had lost 'his left hand and his right hand'. When, weeks later, Patel heard the news in the Keep, he wrote to Gandhi:

With Mahadev Desai – 1938

For Mahadev to slip away suddenly and quickly like this, leaving everybody behind, shows God's wrath.[162]

Patel, softening, was willing to imply that Quit India had invited divine punishment, but not Gandhi, who had suffered perhaps one of his life's harshest blows. No matter who falls, a commander-in-chief may not question an ongoing battle. Yet Gandhi rushed to the lifeless body, took Mahadev's head in his lap, and cried, 'Mahadev! Mahadev!'[163] Later he sent a detailed telegram for Desai's wife and son, addressed to Chimanlal Shah, the manager of Sevagram ashram:

Mahadev died suddenly. Gave no indication. Slept well last night. Had breakfast. Walked with me, Sushila. Jail doctors did all they could but God had willed otherwise. Sushila and I bathed body. Body lying peacefully covered with flowers, incense burning. Sushila and I reciting Gita.

Mahadev has died yogi's and patriot's death. Tell Durga, Babla [Narayan] ... no sorrow allowed. Only joy over such noble death. Cremation taking place before me. Shall keep ashes. Advise Durga remain Ashram, but she may go to her people if she must. Hope Babla will be brave and prepare himself fill Mahadev's place worthily. Love. Bapu[164]

The telegram was delivered three weeks after it was sent. Meanwhile, and for the rest of his time in AKP, Gandhi walked twice a day to the spot where his 'son', cut down at 50, was cremated, to lay flowers there. To its credit, the Raj allowed Pyarelal to join Gandhi in AKP, in the place vacated by Mahadev's death.

In November Gandhi read in a newspaper allowed to him that a son of the former Viceroy, Irwin, now Lord Halifax, had been killed in the war. He wrote to Linlithgow: 'I have just read about the sad but heroic death of Hon'ble Peter Wood in action. Will you please convey to Lord Halifax my congratulations as well as condolences on the sad bereavement?'[165]

Unease and its remedy. But the Indian people's non-violent C-in-C was not at peace. The Raj had assiduously spread the line that Gandhi had condoned if not plotted violence and had pro-Axis leanings. In America in particular the propaganda had hurt his and the Congress's image. Muzzled, Gandhi could give no reply.

Another reason for unease had nothing to do with the Raj's distortions. Quit India had been launched (unavoidably, he thought) for India's identity, to answer the question, was India British or Indian? It had been launched, too, for the Congress's survival, and for non-violence's visibility.

Nevertheless it had caused violence. Though censored, newspapers conveyed this reality almost daily to Gandhi. He knew that his friends in England would be deeply saddened – people like Agatha Harrison, Horace Alexander, Muriel Lester, Henry Polak – and Gandhi was troubled in his own soul.

Reports of starvation from Bengal intensified the discomfort. As before, Gandhi turned to a fast for solace but also for a springboard. If he began a fast, he would be seen and heard. He prepared the ground with a letter to Linlithgow. Datelined 'Detention Camp, New Year's Eve', it said:

> Contrary to the biblical injunction, I have allowed many suns to set on a quarrel I have harboured against you, but I must not allow the old year to expire without disburdening myself of what is rankling in my breast against you. I had thought we were friends and should still love to think so. However what has happened since the 9th of August last makes me wonder ...
>
> If I have not ceased to be your friend, why did you not, before taking drastic action, send for me, tell me of your suspicions and make yourself sure of your facts? I am quite capable of seeing myself as others see me ...
>
> I find that all the statements made about me in Government quarters in this connection contain palpable departures from truth ...
>
> You know I returned to India from South Africa at the end of 1914 with a mission which came to me in 1906, namely, to spread truth and non-violence among mankind in the place of violence and falsehood in all walks of life.
>
> The law of satyagraha knows no defeat. Prison is one of the many ways of spreading the message, but it has its limits ... I had given myself six months. The period is drawing to a close, so is my patience. The law of satyagraha, as I know it, prescribes a remedy in such moments of trial. In a sentence it is: 'Crucify the flesh by fasting.' That same law forbids its use except as a last resort. I do not want to use it if I can avoid it.
>
> This is the way to avoid it: convince me of my error or errors, and I shall make ample amends. You can send for me or send someone who knows your mind and can carry conviction. There are many other ways, if you have the will. May I expect an early reply? May the New Year bring peace to us all.[166]

Though Linlithgow and his staff had fully expected Gandhi to threaten a fast, the letter produced anxious consultations between New Delhi and London. Understanding well that a fast would give Gandhi a voice again, the Raj knew, too, that India would be convulsed if he were to die. From the discussions emerged a reply in which Linlithgow said that in fact it was he who had been let down. The Viceroy then cited the killings and destruction that had occurred in Quit India's name. Gandhi rejoined:

[Y]ou throw in my face the facts of murders by persons reputed to be Congressmen. I see the fact of the murders as clearly, I hope, as you do. My answer is that the Government goaded the people to the point of madness. They started leonine violence in the shape of the arrests ...

Referring to starvation in Bengal, Gandhi again held British policy responsible:

Add to this tale of woe the privations of the poor millions due to India-wide scarcity which I cannot help thinking might have been largely mitigated, if not altogether prevented, had there been a bona-fide national government responsible to a popularly elected assembly.

He said he had to fast:

If then I cannot get soothing balm for my pain, I must resort to the law prescribed for satyagrahis, namely, a fast according to capacity. I must commence after the early morning breakfast of the 9th February, a fast for twenty-one days ending on the morning of the 2nd March.

Usually, during my fasts, I take water with the addition of salts. But nowadays my system refuses water. This time, therefore, I propose to add juices of citrus fruits to make water drinkable. For, my wish is not to fast unto death but to survive the ordeal, if God so wills.[167]

In a tough response, once more prepared after careful consultation, Linlithgow charged:

There is evidence that you and your friends expected this policy to lead to violence; and that you were prepared to condone it; and that the violence that ensued formed part of a concerted plan, conceived long before the arrest of Congress leaders.

The Viceroy proceeded to characterize the threatened fast as 'political blackmail', adding, in parentheses, 'Himsa', using the Hindi word for violence.[168] Worried, however, about consequences if Gandhi died in detention, he offered temporary release for the duration of the fast. The offer was declined.

On 10 February 1943 the fast began. Public opinion in India and the UK forced the Raj to issue regular communiqués on its prisoner's condition, to allow Bidhan Chandra Roy, the Bengal Congress leader who was also a leading physician, to monitor Gandhi's health and let another physician, M D D Gilder of Bombay, reside as a detainee in AKP, and to allow relatives to visit the prisoner.

On the 13th day he had difficulty swallowing water and it looked that he might die. With his permission, and in accordance with the latitude he had given himself beforehand, sweet lime juice was added to his water, and he survived. Yet he felt some guilt about imbibing the juice. To General Candy, the Raj's prison chief, he joked, 'Where is my fast now?' To Roy he said: 'To drink water with juice added and live, or die – this was the choice before me. I preferred to live.'[169] While Gandhi was 'nearly at death's door', Kasturba, scarcely fit herself, 'never cried or lost courage, but kept up other people's courage and prayed to God', her husband would later recall.[170]

The fast delivered a direct blow to the Raj. On 26 February three Indian members of the Viceroy's Council resigned their offices in sympathy with Gandhi: Sir Homi Mody, a Parsi, and two Hindus who had been in the Congress earlier, Nalini Ranjan Sarkar of Bengal and M S Aney of Maharashtra. Prison walls had once more been scaled.

C R's visit and proposal. As a relative, Rajagopalachari managed to see Gandhi on four successive days during the fast, after the crisis had passed. Having left the Congress before Quit India, C R was out of jail. The two talked 'both seriously and lightly', Rajagopalachari told the press,[171] including about Francis Thompson's poem, *The Hound of Heaven.* Their significant political discussion was about how to enlist the Muslim League.

First verbally and then in writing, C R presented his formula to Gandhi: the League should cooperate with the Congress in the formation of a provisional national government, and the Congress, on its part, should agree to abide by a post-independence plebiscite on Pakistan in contiguous Muslim-majority districts in the north-west and the east. In the event of separation, mutual agreements would cover common questions of defence, commerce and communications.

Gandhi said he could assent to such a pact. A month later, without disclosing his formula or Gandhi's endorsement of it, Rajagopalachari informed Jinnah that Gandhi was not inflexible over Pakistan, whereupon Jinnah publicly declared that he was open to an initiative from Gandhi. When Gandhi saw Jinnah's statement in *Dawn*, a newspaper founded by the League leader, he wrote to him:

To Jinnah, 4 May 1943: When some time after my incarceration the Government asked me for a list of newspapers I would like to have, I included the *Dawn* in my list ... Whenever it comes to me, I read it carefully ... I noted your invitation to me to write to you ...

I welcome your invitation. I suggest our meeting face to face rather than talking through correspondence. But I am in your hands.

I hope that this letter will be sent to you and, if you agree to my proposal, that the Government will let you visit me.[172]

The Raj did not allow the letter to reach Jinnah. A statement said:

> The Government of India have decided that this letter cannot be forwarded and have
> so informed Mr Gandhi and Mr Jinnah. They are not prepared to give facilities for
> political correspondence or contact to a person detained for promoting an illegal mass
> movement which he has not disavowed …[173]

Tussling. Aided by Pyarelal, Gandhi mounted attacks from his detention camp on the
Raj's distortions of Quit India before the Central Assembly in New Delhi and Parliament in London, and in *Congress Responsibility for the Disturbances, 1942–43,* an official
pamphlet issued shortly after Gandhi's fast had commenced. He was fortunately able to
rely on papers he or Pyarelal had brought: recent *Harijan* issues and Gandhi's notes for
the Quit India talks he had given on 7 and 8 August.

Some of Gandhi's refutations were not passed on. A long letter he addressed in May to
Lord Samuel, a Liberal peer, who had criticized Gandhi in the House of Lords on the basis
of the Raj's statements, was suppressed. But Gandhi's reply to Sir Reginald Maxwell, the
home member in New Delhi, who had said in the Central Assembly that 'the movement
initiated by the Congress has been decisively defeated', was delivered. 'I must combat
this statement,' Gandhi wrote to Maxwell, adding,

> Satyagraha knows no defeat. It flourishes on blows the hardest imaginable. But I
> need not go to that bower for comfort. I learnt in schools established by the British
> Government in India that 'freedom's battle once begun' is 'bequeathed from bleeding
> sire to son'. It is of little moment when the goal is reached …
>
> The dawn came with the establishment of the Congress sixty years ago. Sixth
> of April 1919, on which All-India satyagraha began, saw a spontaneous awakening
> from one end of India to the other. You can certainly derive comfort, if you like,
> from the fact that the immediate objective of the movement was not gained as some
> Congressmen had expected.
>
> But that is no criterion of 'decisive' or any 'defeat'. It ill becomes one belonging
> to a race which owns no defeat to deduce defeat of a popular movement from the
> suppression of popular exuberance – maybe not always wise – by a frightful exhibi-
> tion of power.[174]

Clearly the prisoner was enjoying his rhetorical tussles with the Raj, even though his
version was getting no press. In July he sent to the home department a comprehensive,
point-by-point rebuttal – well-argued, forceful, in places sparkling – of the *Congress
Responsibility* pamphlet, with Gilder and Pyarelal typing out his drafts.

Linlithgow leaves. In the autumn of 1943 Linlithgow's viceroyalty came to an end. There used to be warmth in Gandhi's relationship with him. Writing to Amery in February, Linlithgow had referred to Gandhi's 'very many likeable qualities' and added, 'My personal relations with him have always been very good.'[175] But the two had clashed bitterly over Quit India. When he read that Linlithgow was leaving, Gandhi wrote to him:

27 Sep. 1943: Dear Lord Linlithgow, On the eve of your departure from India, I would like to send you a word. Of all the high functionaries I have had the honour of knowing, none has been the cause of such deep sorrow to me as you have been. It has cut me to the quick to have to think of you as having countenanced untruth, and that regarding one whom, at one time, you considered as your friend. I hope and pray that God will some day put it into your heart to realize that you, a representative of a great nation, had been led into a grievous error. With good wishes, I still remain, Your friend, M.K. Gandhi

As much hurt by Quit India as Gandhi had been by the Raj's twisting of it, as loyal to Churchill and the Empire as Gandhi was to India and the Congress, Linlithgow threw the ball back into Gandhi's court:

7 Oct. 1943: Dear Mr Gandhi, I am indeed sorry that your feelings about any deeds and words of mine should be as you describe. But I must be allowed, as gently as I may, to make plain to you that I am quite unable to accept your interpretation of the events in question. As for the corrective virtues of time and reflection, evidently these are ubiquitous in their operation, and wisely to be ignored by no man. Yours sincerely, Linlithgow.[176]

Events outside. In November 1942, newspapers that Gandhi and the Working Committee read in their respective 'camps' quoted Churchill's remarks at the Lord Mayor's annual banquet in London:

I must say quite frankly that I hold it perfectly justifiable to deceive the enemy. (*cheers*) ... Let me make this clear. Let there be no mistake about it in any quarter. I have not become the King's First Minister in order to preside over the liquidation of the British Empire.[177]

The following month witnessed the death of the Punjab's premier, Sikandar Hyat Khan of the Unionist party. Commanding the allegiance of many of his province's Muslims,

Sikandar had criticized the idea of dividing India by religion. His departure further strengthened Jinnah, who had profited from the removal from the political scene of the Congress's ministries and leaders.

In 1942 the Muslim League formed (in alliance with other groups) a ministry in Sindh and another in the Muslim-minority province of Assam, where the Congress ministry had resigned in 1939. Helped by a British governor and defecting legislators, an additional League ministry took office in 1943. This was in the NWFP, where the former premier, Dr Khan Sahib, and his brother Ghaffar Khan were under arrest for Quit India. Governors and advisers controlled all the other provinces where the Congress had ruled.

In September 1943, after having organized clandestine resistance for nearly a year, Jayaprakash Narayan was arrested near Lahore. Despite Quit India, the British were still around, the League had spread itself, and the Congress was behind bars.

To shore up opposition to the Congress, two foes of Gandhi were included in the Viceroy's Executive Council in July 1942. Ambedkar was one. The other was N B Khare, a former Congressman who had joined the Hindu Mahasabha after he was removed for indiscipline from the Congress.

From time to time Rajagopalachari, identified with the Congress despite his resignation, pushed at the Raj's closed doors to see if they would yield, but neither Linlithgow nor his successor, Wavell, encouraged him. They saw no need to revive a Britain-Congress understanding: by the autumn of 1943, Japanese forces seemed halted well to the east of India. By this time, however, Bengal's rice shortage had reached its peak, and the province faced the subcontinent's worst famine since 1770.

In April 1944, fully 13 months after Gandhi had agreed to his formula, C R met Jinnah in Delhi and said that if the League joined the Congress in demanding a national government, Gandhi would ask the Congress to accept plebiscites over Pakistan. After studying Rajagopalachari's formula for a couple of minutes, Jinnah said to him, 'Your scheme does not satisfy me.' When Birla asked C R how his meeting with the League leader had gone, the reply was, 'Jinnah is too old.'[178]

Inside the Keep

For Azad, Nehru, Patel and nine other Working Committee members held in Ahmednagar Fort, there was no knowing how long they would remain confined. 'We saw no child or woman to break the monotony of our lives,' Kripalani would later recall,[179] and Nehru wrote from the Fort to his sister Krishna:

We have sight of [the planets and stars] and they never lose their freshness. But of the men we see the range is limited and I fear we grow less and less fresh to each other. And women? It struck me as an odd and arresting fact that for [a long time] I had not seen a woman even from a distance.[180]

Books were written: *Discovery of India* by Nehru; a study on Gandhi by Kripalani; a collection of unsent letters by Azad, who heard in the Keep that his wife Zuleikha had died; a history of his province by the Orissa leader, Hare Krishna Mahtab; a reconstruction by the UP socialist, Narendra Deva, of a lost Sanskrit text from its French translation; and *Feathers & Stones* by Andhra's Pattabhi Sitaramayya.

Gardening occupied some, notably Nehru and Patel. Badminton and bridge were other recreations: Pant, the former UP premier, Kripalani, Mahtab, and Prafulla Ghosh of Bengal were among the bridge enthusiasts, though the one keenest to win, and generally able to do so, was Patel, who was also the company's most voracious reader of books and of newspapers, which were allowed some weeks after the party found themselves in the Keep. It was agreed that as their president, Azad would see the papers first, followed by Patel and Nehru, in that order, and then the rest.

Shankarrao Deo of Maharashtra, Syed Mahmud of Bihar and Asaf Ali of Delhi completed the Keep's dozen. An important Working Committee member, Rajendra Prasad, had missed the Bombay meetings because of illness; he was arrested and confined in his province, Bihar. The fourteenth member, Sarojini Naidu, was detained in Poona's AKP. A 15th member, Bombay's Bhulabhai Desai, had resigned on health grounds in July 1942.

Relations among the 12 were correct, even cordial, but there was tension at times and a division into groups, one led by Nehru/Azad and the other by Patel, who at 67 was the Keep's oldest prisoner. Kripalani, Deo and Ghosh were seen as being in Patel's group, and Mahmud and Ali in the Nehru/Azad one. The remaining four (Pattabhi, Pant, Narendra Deva and Mahtab) were non-aligned.

When Lord Wavell, the new Viceroy, privately sent Nehru a copy of a book of poems, Jawaharlal informed Azad of the gesture but not Patel, thinking that Vallabhbhai 'would draw unwarranted conclusions'.[181] The Working Committee never met as such in the Keep, and common discussions were rare. Nehru walked out when, during one such discussion, Patel and Kripalani heatedly objected to Nehru's praise of Azad's intervention at the May 1942 Working Committee meeting that had induced Prasad to withdraw his draft in favour of Nehru's. Later, Nehru apologized.

What divided and made the dozen touchy was Quit India, which had brought imprisonment to them, suffering to thousands, and gains to the Muslim League. The question was never directly discussed, but Azad's disapproval of Quit India became quite obvious, and Nehru too seemed to question some of Gandhi's moves, though he was impressed, he wrote in his diary, by the running debate that a handicapped Gandhi was conducting with the Raj – Vallabhbhai had managed to obtain a cyclostyled copy of Gandhi's correspondence with the government and shown it to Nehru.

At least seven of the 12 (Patel, Kripalani, Pattabhi, Narendra Deva, Deo, Ghosh and Mahtab) continued to think that Quit India was necessary and unavoidable, while Azad, Asaf Ali and Mahmud thought it a blunder. Nehru and Pant seemed undecided. A possible approach to the Raj was proposed once by Azad and on another occasion by Pant, and Nehru seemed to lend his support, but Patel shot down the idea, saying that Gandhi would know what move to make and when.[182]

A momentous thought, however, had taken shape inside Patel's mind, and also inside the minds of Nehru, Azad and several others. Unexpressed in conversation or letters, it was a thought of independence from Gandhi. The path opened up by his instinct led to too many upheavals. The latest was a prolonged incarceration while the world changed outside and they grew older. *Next time around, they would think twice before obeying Gandhi's instinct.*[183]

Life in AKP. Isolated elsewhere in the same Marathi country, Gandhi was battling away. The prison officer supervising Gandhi's confinement in AKP, a titled Parsi called Khan Bahadur Ardeshir Eduljee Kateli, provided the following confidential report to his seniors, dated 15 December 1943:

> *1.* Mr Gandhi discusses political questions with other inmates, especially with Mr Pyarelal and Miss Slade; Miss Nayyar is always there. Very rarely with Dr Gilder. This takes place generally when they are reading newspapers.
>
> *2.* The daily routine of life of Mr Gandhi: He gets up about 6.30 a.m. and, after finishing morning ablution and breakfast, he reads books or newspapers. From 8.15 to 9.0 a.m. morning walk in the garden with Pyarelal and Misses Slade, Nayyar and Manu. While walking, they talk on political and other subjects. Doctors Gilder and Nayyar give him massage for about forty-five minutes and then bath upto 11.15. From 11.15 to 12 noon he takes his food, and Miss Slade talks or reads books to him.
>
> From 12 noon to 1.0 p.m. teaching Sanskrit to Miss Nayyar. 1.0 to 2.0 p.m. rest. From 2.0 to 3.0 p.m. Mr Pyarelal reads papers to him and discusses on several points arising from the papers, while he is either spinning or filing cuttings from the papers.
>
> From 3.0 to 4.0 p.m. teaching Miss Manu. From 4.0 to 5.30 p.m. indexing of newspaper cuttings on various subjects. He is assisted in this work by Pyarelal, Drs Gilder and Nayyar. They remove the selected and marked portions from the papers, paste them on slips of paper and give them to Mr Gandhi for indexing and filing.

From 5.30 to 6.30 p.m. Miss Slade reads papers to him and discusses on various political and other subjects. From 6.30 to 7.15 p.m. evening walk with other inmates in the garden.

From 7.30 p.m. to 8.15 p.m. spinning, while Pyarelal reads to him some books. From 8.15 to 9.0 p.m. prayer. From 9.0 to 10.0 p.m. reading and talking with Mr Pyarelal and Miss Nayyar.

He goes to bed at 10 p.m. He changes his time according to climatic conditions.

3. Mr Pyarelal does the typing work of Mr. Gandhi. When the big letter was sent to the Government of India regarding the reply to the *Congress Responsibility*, Dr Gilder typed the major part of the letter.

I have the honour to be, Sir, Your most obedient servant,
(Signed) OFFICER I/C, AGA KHAN'S PALACE[184]

Kateli's report omitted the dawn prayers that also were part of Gandhi's routine. The Miss Manu he mentions was Gandhi's 15-year-old grand-niece who had lost her mother in childhood. Her father was Jaisukhlal Gandhi, one of Ota Gandhi's numerous descendants. In May 1942 Gandhi had brought 'little' Manu, as he then called her, from Bombay to Sevagram, where, at the age of 14 or so, she helped Kasturba. On 30 July 1942, writing to her father from Sevagram, Gandhi had said:

Manu is a very sensible and smart girl. She serves Ba devotedly. She has become friendly with all. There is no complaint against her. She is quite good in her studies too. I see that she is happy. She comes every evening to massage my legs. Of course she also accompanies me in my walks. There is no need for you to worry about her.[185]

By March 1943 Manu was in AKP, after getting herself arrested for Quit India, and continuing to help Kasturba, who was unwell from the moment of her imprisonment and had specially asked for Manu.

By the end of 1943 Kasturba's illness was serious. Devadas was allowed to visit her and talk also with his father, though not on politics and only in the presence of Kateli, who reported:

Some talk took place about the Bengal famine, and Mr Devdas said that latterly some good arrangements were being made and the funds raised were used through public hands and not through Government.

Mr Devdas asked his father how he passed his time. Mr Gandhi replied that he taught Sanskrit to Dr Nayyar and Miss Manu, and the major part of his time was passed in preparing an index in all subjects from the various newspapers and filing the cuttings from the papers.

Mr Gandhi said that there was some correspondence between him and Government of India on *Congress Responsibility*, and he had asked the Government to release the correspondence but Government had refused.

The report (7 December) added that Gandhi had said to his son that he expected to 'be kept in custody for five years more' and that the persons about whose health Gandhi enquired included the prisoners Jayaprakash, Vallabhbhai and Yusuf Meherally.[186] Earlier, in his answer to *Congress Responsibility* sent in July 1943, Gandhi had defended Jayaprakash, for whose capture a large reward had been announced:

> [M]y differences [with Jayaprakash], great as they are, do not blind me to his indomitable courage and his sacrifice of all that a man holds dear for the love of his country. I have read his manifesto which is given as an appendix [in *Congress Responsibility*] ... [I]t breathes nothing but burning patriotism and his impatience of foreign domination. It is a virtue of which any country would be proud.[187]

Though reading, filing, indexing, thinking and writing for his contests with the Raj took much of his working day, Gandhi also sent repeated letters to officials regarding the health of Kasturba and of Mira, who suffered from acute pain in her back and arm, and the treatment they required, and about a baby left motherless in Delhi by the death of Shakuntala, the young sister-in-law of Pyarelal and Sushila.

Proposals. In October 1943 Gandhi made a pair of proposals to the government, both in the context of the Bengal famine. One related to the detained leaders and workers of the Congress:

> [I]f the Government think that it is only my evil influence that corrupts people, I submit that the members of the Working Committee and other detenus should be discharged. It is unthinkable that when India's millions are suffering from preventable starvation and thousands are dying of it, thousands of men and women should be kept in detention on mere suspicion, when their energy and the expense incurred in keeping them under duress could, at this critical time, be usefully employed in relieving distress.
>
> As I have said in my letter of 15th July last, Congressmen abundantly proved their administrative, creative and humanitarian worth at the time of the last terrible flood in Gujarat, and equally terrible earthquake in Bihar.[188]

The second proposal was that he should be moved from AKP to an ordinary prison:

> The huge place in which I am being detained with a large guard around me, I hold to be waste of public funds. I should be quite content to pass my days in any prison.[189]

In March 1944 he repeated the thought:

> Virtually the whole of this expense is, from my point of view, wholly unnecessary; and when people are dying of starvation, it is almost a crime against Indian humanity. I ask that my companions and I be removed to any regular prison Government may choose ...
>
> I cannot conceal from myself the sad thought that the whole expense of this comes from taxes collected from the dumb millions of India.[190]

A third proposal was conveyed earlier, to Linlithgow, in response to the Viceroy's demand that Gandhi should reconsider the Quit India resolution. Only the Working Committee could reassess one of its resolutions, said Gandhi (19 Jan. 1943). If a review was desired, 'put me among the members of the Working Committee'.[191] None of the proposals was accepted.

Engaging Wavell. The months of February, March and April 1944 saw correspondence between Gandhi and the new Viceroy. As with previous Viceroys, Gandhi tried to win Wavell over:

> *9 Mar. 1944*: Years ago, while teaching the boys and girls of Tolstoy Farm in South Africa, I happened to read to them Wordsworth's *Character of the Happy Warrior*. It recurs to me as I am writing to you. It will delight my heart to realize that warrior in you ...
>
> You are flying all over India. You have not hesitated to go among the skeletons of Bengal. May I suggest an interruption in your scheduled flights and a descent upon Ahmednagar and the Aga Khan's Palace in order to probe the hearts of your captives? We are all friends of the British, however much we may criticize the British Government and system in India. If you can but trust, you will find us to be the greatest helpers in the fight against Nazism, Fascism, Japanism and the like ...[192]

As Linlithgow too had done, Wavell asked Gandhi to withdraw the Quit India resolution if he wished to negotiate. Gandhi stuck to his ground and insisted in letters to the Viceroy that the Congress was far from being crushed:

9 Mar. 1944: Had Government stayed action till they had studied my speeches and those of the members of the Working Committee, history would have been written differently ...

   17 Feb. 1944: The spirit of India demands complete freedom from all foreign dominance ... The Congress represents that spirit in full measure. It has grown to be an institution whose roots have gone deep down into the Indian soil.

He cautioned Wavell against appearing to support the two-nation theory:

9 Mar. 1944: In the middle of page two, you speak of the welfare of 'the Indian peoples'. I have seen in some Viceregal pronouncements the inhabitants of India being referred to as the people of India. Are the two expressions synonymous? ...

Through the Viceroy, the Raj was reproved for its treatment of Mira:

9 Mar. 1944: I may be considered an impossible man – though altogether wrongly I would protest. But what about Shri Mirabai? As you know, she is the daughter of an Admiral and former Commander-in-Chief of these waters ...

   The only reason for burying her alive, so far as I can see, is that she has committed the crime of associating herself with me.

   I suggest your immediately releasing her, or your seeing her and then deciding. I may add that she is not yet free from the pain for the alleviation of which the Government sent Captain Simcox at my request ...[193]

Wavell's call for a change of heart by Gandhi was duly sent back to the Viceroy's court:

And unless there is a change of heart, view and policy on the part of the Government, I am quite content to remain your prisoner. Only I hope you will listen to the request made by me through the proper channels to remove me and my fellow-prisoners to some other prison where the cost of our detention need not be even one tenth of what it is today.[194]

Death of Kasturba

When, on one occasion, their fellow-detainee Gilder was allowed to receive some mangoes for his wedding anniversary, Kasturba asked Gandhi, 'How many years have we been married?' 'Why,' Gandhi replied, 'do you also want to celebrate your anniversary?' Kasturba, who was 74 in 1943, laughed along with the others,[195] but she found her time at AKP difficult. Shocked at what she thought was her husband's premature arrest, Kasturba was devastated soon thereafter by the sudden death of Mahadev, whom she loved.

On occasion she blamed her husband: 'Did I not tell you not to pick a quarrel with this government?' Or, 'Why do you ask the English to quit India? Our country is vast. We can all live here.' But she agreed with Gandhi that the British should stay as brothers, not as rulers, and was outraged when he asked if she wished an apology sent on her behalf.

'There is nothing to do now but to put up with the result of your doings,' she said. 'We will suffer with you. Mahadev has gone. Next it will be my turn.'[196] Indeed she felt certain that she was not going to see the world outside again. Coming on top of her unhappiness at Gandhi's detention, and their unending sorrow over Harilal, this sense of impending death greatly depressed her.

More than before, however, she enjoyed the lessons that Gandhi was now giving her daily: about the rivers of the Punjab, about the equator, longitudes and latitudes, with Gandhi using an orange for the earth, and so on. She successfully learnt (from him) two songs out of a Gujarati fifth-grade school reader, and while she had the strength husband and wife often 'sat down and sang the two songs together' at night, causing Sarojini Naidu to 'joke about the honey-mooning old couple'.[197]

Called Ammajaan (Mother) by Gandhi and the rest, Sarojini Naidu never missed a chance to tease a fellow-detainee. Mahadev received a dart from her while trimming his moustache on the morning of the day he would die. Keeping poorly throughout her detention, she was released on health grounds in early 1944.

During Gandhi's 21-day fast Kasturba's was a strengthening presence for him. She had left the others 'dumbfounded' by endorsing the fast.[198] But once it was over her condition steadily deteriorated, with mounting problems in the heart, lungs and kidneys. Fifteen-year-old Manu's company and nursing helped her, and during her husband's fast Kasturba was thrilled to see Ramdas and Devadas, but confinement without an end-date embittered her, and bitterness led to fretfulness.[199]

There was no question of her release being asked for, but Gandhi hoped that the Raj would offer to free her. Shortly after her death he would say:

Whilst it is true that no request was made by her or by me (as satyagrahi prisoners it would have been unbecoming), would it not have been in the fitness of things, if the Government had at least offered to her, me and her sons to release her? The mere offer of release would have produced a favourable psychological effect on her.[200]

In the circumstances, he found 'amazing' a report that Sir Girija Shankar Bajpai, agent in the USA of India's British government, had told the American public that 'at various times, the Government considered [Kasturba's] release for health reasons, but she wished to remain with her husband, and her wishes were respected'.[201]

In December Kasturba suffered three heart attacks. On the 29th Gandhi said in a letter to Agatha Harrison that she was 'oscillating between life and death'.[202] Eight days later he wrote to superintendent Kateli:

I must confess that the patient has got into very low spirits. She despairs of life, and is looking forward to death to deliver her. If she rallies on one day, more often than not, she is worse on the next. Her state is pitiful.[203]

Though refusing to apply for her release, Gandhi did not hesitate to ask for doctors and nurses, or for visits by relatives to offer bedside comfort. The Raj's response to repeated pleas was usually negative or tardy, though eventually Kanu Gandhi, a nephew of the late Maganlal, and Jayaprakash's wife, Prabhavati, who had been very close to Kasturba in Sabarmati and Sevagram, were let in. Prabhavati nursed Kasturba, and Kanu sought to soothe her with gentle bhajans.

After several letters from Gandhi, an ayurveda specialist, Pandit Shiv Sharma, and a nature cure expert, Dinshaw Mehta, were also permitted to see Kasturba. But when Devadas brought to AKP a new drug called penicillin that he had managed to import, Gandhi advised his son against using it on Kasturba. The drug was untested; injections would be hard for her to bear; her agony should not be increased. The son yielded.[204]

Twice during her illness Harilal came to see his mother. On the first occasion she was overjoyed. Ramdas and Devadas were also visiting at the same time, so she had three of her four sons with her: only Manilal, doing duty in South Africa, was missing. Sushila would record the 'great solace' that Kasturba derived, and Sushila also observed that 'Bapu came and stood by, watching the three brothers having [a] meal together.'[205] It was a sight he had not seen for decades, and his silence spoke of how moved he was. Sadly, Harilal was plainly drunk the second time he visited his sick mother, who beat her head in anguish.

At night she often sat up in bed, coughing, her head resting on a wooden stool. Gandhi was near her night and day, seeking to help or calm. On 22 February 1944, a day of the full moon, Shiva Ratri by the Hindu calendar, Kasturba died in her husband's arms. Devadas sobbed like a child on his dead mother's breast, and Sushila saw a tear well in Gandhi's eye.

He joined the women in bathing his wife's body, which was then wrapped, in accordance with Kasturba's wish, in a sari made of yarn spun by him. He parted her hair, combed it and put the kumkum tika on her forehead.[206] Round her wrists the women tied, as bangles, fresh yarn he had spun. He sat for hours near the body and later, while she was cremated in the grounds of AKP, near the pyre (which was lit by Devadas). And he appropriated the small stool on which her head had lain while she coughed, making it his dining table. Another intimate possession, a necklace of holy beads that Kasturba wore till the last, would be given, he decided, to Lakshmi, their Dalit 'daughter' whom Kasturba had grown to love dearly, after early hiccups.[207]

Wavell and his wife sent him their sympathy. In his reply to the Viceroy, Gandhi said:

> I send you and Lady Wavell my thanks for your kind condolences on the death of my wife. Though for her sake I have welcomed her death as bringing freedom from living agony, I feel the loss more than I had thought I should.
>
> We were a couple outside the ordinary. It was in 1906 that after mutual consent and after unconscious trials we definitely adopted self-restraint as a rule of life. To my great joy this knit us together as never before. We ceased to be two different entities. Without my wishing it, she chose to lose herself in me. The result was she became truly my *better* half.
>
> She was a woman always of very strong will which, in our early days, I used to mistake for obstinacy. But that strong will enabled her to become quite unwittingly my teacher in the art and practice of non-violent non-cooperation.[208]

Resisting first his sexuality and later his morality – his views on money, their children's education and caste – Kasturba had taught Gandhi the power of 'no'. But she also provided a lesson in 'yes', accepting the hardships and shocks of living with Gandhi, his changing circles of companions, his unusual practices. Through it all she looked after him, fed and nursed him, was his constant support and companion, and at least once (over his vow against milk) saved his life.

But other women also performed intimate chores for her husband. Sharing wifely tasks with them must have been as hard for the uneducated Kasturba as watching other women enter Gandhi's intellectual and political life in ways not open to her. Yet she somehow found it in her to get on with most of the women around her husband.

With some (Sushila and Prabhavati, for instance) she formed deep bonds, and was unhappy if she was deprived of their company, or Gandhi of their assistance. The wives of Chhaganlal and Maganlal and other women in the ashrams had given Kasturba friendship, and though Harilal was cause for boundless sorrow, she found joy in his children and grandchildren, and in her other sons and their families.

She was also, as we have seen, a fighter in her own right, courting imprisonment in South Africa and later during several battles in India, and was respected as such by large numbers. If Vallabhbhai, C R, Mahadev, Pyarelal and scores of other Indians who knew Kasturba entertained great warmth for her, the rest honoured her as Gandhi's faithful, sacrificing, courageous wife. Those knowing Kasturba also admired her caring, agility and neatness; her ease, despite handicaps, with women of rank; and her understanding of human nature.

Neither Mohandas nor Kastur gave everything the other desired; in some ways each disappointed the other; yet each was also fulfilled in the other. Despite his unusual ways, Kasturba's respect for Gandhi increased with the years. Despite her limitations, Gandhi's respect for her also grew. Each was obliged to find patience and tolerance, which grew into love, partnership and, from some perspectives, merger. India saw them as one, not merely inseparable.

'If I had to choose a companion for myself life after life, I would choose only Ba,' said Gandhi after she was gone.[209] In an earlier chapter we saw Harilal's remark to his father: '[A]ll the greatness you have achieved is because of Ba.' In June 1947 Gandhi would repeat the thought. 'It is because of her that I am today what I am.'[210]

Finding that stories of the trouble supposedly taken by the Raj over Kasturba's illness were being circulated in India, Britain and the USA, Gandhi reminded the Government of its reluctance and tardiness he had run into, and added:

> It is not pleasant or easy for me to write about such personal matters to the Government. But I do so in this case for the sake of the memory of one who was my faithful partner for over sixty-two years. I leave it to the Government to consider what could be the fate of other prisoners not so circumstanced as Shri Kasturba was.[211]

The other Gandhi

There was more to the AKP Gandhi than the unbowed, spirited and refreshing Empire-challenger we have seen. Depression often assailed him. The deaths, in fairly rapid succession, of Andrews, Bajaj, Mahadev and Kasturba had removed his trustiest sources of love and support; and politically the Raj had weathered his rebellion. In his low moments Gandhi was helped once more by the care of women, with Sushila, Prabhavati and young Manu (the latter two allowed in to nurse Kasturba) playing a role.

We get clues from two notes he jotted down on a Monday, his silence day, for Manu, whose mother had died. Written five days after Kasturba's death, the notes were preserved by Manu. The first note said:

> *27 Feb. 1944*: Chi. Manudi ('Blessed little Manu'), Did you sleep well? Yesterday I drafted a long letter about keeping you and Prabhavati here, but I kept thinking over the

matter the whole of last night and could get no sleep. In the end, I saw light. We cannot make such a request. Aren't we prisoners after all? We must endure our separation.

You are a sensible girl. Forget your sorrow. You want to do great service. Stop crying and live cheerfully. Learn what you can after leaving the jail. After all this service that you have given, you are bound to prosper no matter what happens. More after my silence ends. I am your mother. Am I not? It is enough, if you understand this much. Blessings from Bapu. P.S. Preserve this letter.

It seems plain that Manu and Prabhavati both wished to continue their stay in AKP. Kasturba's death had removed its reason, though from her death-bed she had evidently 'entrusted [Manu] to Gandhiji'.[212] Manu certainly, and perhaps Prabhavati also, cried about having to leave, but Gandhi too felt troubled by the impending separation – troubled enough to lie awake the whole night.

From the claim, 'I am your mother,' and the instruction to preserve the note bearing the claim, we may suspect that in AKP Gandhi thought of Manu as a future partner for developing his, and her, brahmacharya. The 'mother' remark asserts the contemplated experiment's innocent character. Whether Manu's apparent keenness to grow in brahmacharya was spontaneous or induced by him, it made her an ideal candidate, in his eyes, for the intimate circle.[213]

Gandhi's reliance on young Manu is made even clearer in the second note (translated from the Gujarati original), which also discloses admiration as well as concern for the 15-year-old who was evidently thinking of studying in Karachi:

27 Feb. 1944: I feel much worried about you. You are a class by yourself. You are good, simple-hearted and ever ready to help others. Service has become dharma with you. But you are still uneducated and silly also.

If you remain illiterate, you will regret it, and if I live long, I too will regret it. I will certainly miss you, but I do not like to keep you near me as that would be weakness and ignorant attachment.

I am quite sure that at present you should go to Rajkot. You will get there the benefit of the company of Narandas; such good company you will get nowhere else. You will learn there, besides music, the art of working methodically. You will learn Gujarati, too ...

If you go to Karachi or anywhere else you like after you have become more mature, you will get all that you want ... [Y]ou will get only education [in Karachi]. That also will be useful, of course. Living in the company of so many girls will also do you good. But what you will get in Rajkot you will get nowhere else. Blessings from Bapu[214]

We should mark that Gandhi allows a choice (Rajkot or Karachi) to Manu and also that he wishes her to get 'all that you want' in the future. To persons like Manu, Prabhavati and Sushila (who with Gandhi's approval had obtained an MD on top of her bachelor's degree in medicine), Gandhi offers both warmth and freedom.

These women are members of a privileged circle, counterparts, in Gandhi's private life, of key colleagues in his political life: men like Jawaharlal, Vallabhbhai and Rajagopalachari. If they are dependent on him, he is on them. His dealings with them are sensitive, often tender, at times plaintive, but at other times forthright.

Though not present in AKP, another young woman close to his private circle at this time was Abha, daughter of Amritlal Chatterjee, a Bengal Congressman. Older than Manu by about three years, Abha too had spent some time in Sevagram in 1942, and fallen in love with Kanu Gandhi, who was permitted inside AKP to lift Kasturba's morale. A photographer and one of Gandhi's associates and helpers in Sevagram, Kanu was the son of Maganlal's younger brother, Narandas.

Mira remained outside the circle. In AKP she was an important part of Gandhi's political team, Pyarelal being its other member.

Illness, darkness & release. After Kasturba's death Gandhi was listless and ill with malaria and dysentery. There was even a moment when his spirit seemed to fade. 'At one stage,' Pyarelal would write, 'the inner light which had sustained him all through life seemed to be on the point of going out. But it was momentary only.'[215] The faithful secretary recorded the darkness and its departure but did not elaborate on what clearly was a black night of the soul. In her account, Sushila would speak of Gandhi's 'delirium', 'depression' and high fever.[216]

In any case, on 4 May 1944 Wavell sent the following cable to Amery in London:

Latest reports show progressive deterioration in Gandhi's anaemia, blood-pressure and kidney functions, all of which in opinion of Dr. B. C. Roy, shared by Surgeon-General Candy, have tendency to produce coronary or cerebral thrombosis ... This is a case in which I consider we must be guided by medical opinion.

Deterioration in Gandhi's health appears such that his further participation in active politics is improbable and I have no doubt that death in custody would intensify feeling against Government ...

I am accordingly instructing Bombay Government to release Gandhi unconditionally at 8 a.m. on Saturday, 6th May, with announcement that release is entirely on medical grounds and am informing all Governors accordingly.[217]

On the evening of 5 May Gandhi was informed that he and his companions would be freed at eight the next morning. Kateli, the jailor, sought the prisoner's

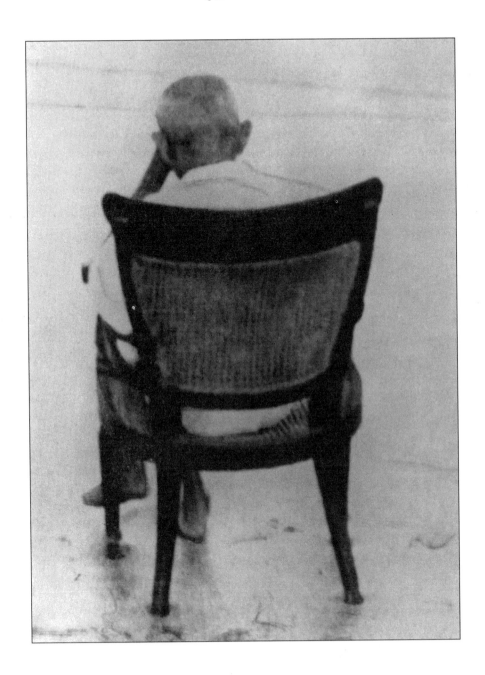

Shortly after Kasturba's death – 1944

blessings and quietly presented a purse of 75 rupees in anticipation of Gandhi's 75th birthday.

Despite a sleepless night Gandhi felt fresh in the morning, because, he told his companions, he had been repeating Ramanama all night, but also, we may suspect, because he was about to walk free. He added: 'I have felt so much at a loss ... I do not know what I shall do or speak. But He that has guided my footsteps so far will show me the path.'[218]

Before leaving the AKP Gandhi asked the government to ensure access for friends and relatives to the 'consecrated ground' where Kasturba and Mahadev had been cremated:

> *To the Home Secretary, Government of Bombay, 7.45 a.m., May 6, 1944*: Sir, I have been told by the Inspector-General of Prisons that the party of detenus in this camp is to be discharged at 8 a.m. today. I wish to put on record the fact that by reason of the cremation of the corpses of Shri Mahadev Desai and then my wife, the place of cremation which has been fenced off becomes consecrated ground ...
>
> I trust that the plot will be acquired by the Government with the right of way to it through H. H. the Aga Khan's grounds so as to enable those relatives and friends who wish to visit the cremation ground whenever they like. Subject to the permission of the Government, I would like to arrange for the upkeep of the sacred spot and daily prayers.[219]

The released prisoners stood in prayer at the cremation site before crossing the barbed-wire fence around AKP into freedom, and again three days later, before leaving Poona for Bombay.

In London, Churchill hated Wavell's decision to release Gandhi. Eight weeks later, as Gandhi seemed to improve, the Prime Minister sent Wavell, in the Viceroy's words, 'a peevish telegram to ask why Gandhi hadn't died yet'.[220]

14

Rejected

India, 1944–6

Twenty years earlier, released from Yeravda jail after an attack of appendicitis, Gandhi – a son of Porbandar – had gone to convalesce by the sea at Juhu in north Bombay. In May 1944 he turned once more to the Juhu beach, where he was again entertained by the Morarjee family. On 21 May he was persuaded to watch *Mission to Moscow*, a Hollywood movie made to popularize America's alliance with the Soviet Union, possibly the first talkie he had ever seen. It did not attract him to Stalin or Communism.

In the middle of June, after the monsoon had set in, Gandhi returned to Poona for a spell in Dinshaw Mehta's nature-cure clinic; the malaria had left him but worms and amoebae still troubled his stomach. From 5 July he spent nearly four weeks in Panchgani, the hill town to the south of Poona, where he much enjoyed Rajagopalachari's company, the sort of bracing fellowship, Pyarelal mused, that Gandhi had missed in AKP.[1] In the first week of August Gandhi returned to Sevagram.

❧

Soon after their release, Gandhi and Mira had clashed over her wish to marry a man she had known since the 1930s: Prithvi Singh, a revolutionary who had professed conversion to non-violence. Inclined to doubt the conversion and to believe critical reports about Singh, Gandhi questioned the proposed marriage. Saying she would have to leave Gandhi and start her own ashram in the Himalayan foothills (India's hot plains had always tormented her), Mira asked for the return of funds she had deposited at Sabarmati, to be used for her new venture.

Arranging to return the money, Gandhi cautioned Mira against being used by the

Communist party,[2] and added that he might have to publicly dissociate himself from her new venture. In two letters sent at this time, a piqued Gandhi called her 'Miss Slade' and signed himself 'M.K. Gandhi'. Continuing to sign herself, 'Ever your devoted daughter,' Mira wrote on 12 June:

> You have given me my freedom with one hand and taken it away with the other. To give me my money and freedom, and at the same time to say that as soon as I begin to use them you will publicly disapprove, is to sabotage anything I may try to do … My faith in God is my guide. My ideals have not changed in the last few days. I am the same person that I was when we used to talk happily together.[3]

The tiff soon ended, in part because Prithvi Singh did not wish to marry Mira. Prompted by Devadas, Gandhi reverted to calling her Mira and signing off as 'Bapu'. He also blessed the proposed new ashram near the Himalayas, where Mira hoped to rear cattle, and more or less asked to be forgiven:

> *18 Jul. 1944*: I am learning every day. I must not cause dear ones grief when it is avoidable … I know you forgave me long ago. But it is good to ask for forgiveness.[4]

Missing Kasturba, he was eager for letters from his sons. At the end of June he wrote to Ramdas and his wife Nirmala:

> Since Ba is not here, who is there gently to rebuke you for not writing at all? Every day I hope that I will see the handwriting of either of you … How are you all getting along?[5]

Gandhi had had a long and calm talk with Harilal during Kasturba's cremation, at which all their sons except Manilal were present. Early in 1945 Harilal went to the home in Mysore of his son Kanti, a doctor, and Kanti's wife from Kerala, Saraswati. There Harilal seemed to find some stability. In April 1945 Gandhi wrote to Saraswati:

> God will grant you success. The victory over Harilal which was denied to me has come to you two. You are correct in saying that if he can get rid of the two vices, he can be the best of all the brothers.[6]

Two months later he sent a warm letter to Harilal, urging him to continue in his son's home: 'How can you be a burden there? You may even help them while you are lounging about.'[7] But by August 1945 Harilal had left Mysore.

Learning in June 1944 that one of the Dandi Marchers, Anand Hingorani, had lost his wife Vidya, Gandhi wrote out for Anand a 'true thought,' as he called it, which was a consoling verse he had received, following Kasturba's death, from a Mrs Glen E Snyder of Grimes, Iowa: 'You cannot say, you must not say/ That she is dead. She is just away ...'[8] This was followed by Gandhi writing *each day* a thought for Anand, an exercise carried out, we may surmise, with Kasturba too in mind.

Answering a letter of sympathy from John Haynes Holmes, an old American admirer and Unitarian minister, he said of Kasturba: 'I remember only her great merits. Her limitations were reduced to ashes with the body.'[9] Gandhi agreed to chair a trust founded in his wife's name, which quickly received 75 lakh rupees, and asked that the trust limit itself to 'women and children in the villages', focusing on 'maternity, hygiene and the treatment of diseases, and [basic] education'.[10]

And in a letter to Kamaladevi Chattopadhyaya, a colleague from 1930, he said (18 July):

> My dream is to have India's women to lead the world of men who have led women up to now.[11]

Political tasks. In the summer of 1944, Hitler's defeat seemed not too far off, Japan's defeat also appeared inevitable, and Quit India, essentially crushed by end-1942, seemed only a memory. Nonetheless Gandhi felt certain that Indian independence was on its way, and that Quit India had bolstered the populace:

> 9 *Jul.* 1944: The heavy defeat of the Congress I do not feel at all. I have not a shadow of doubt that this passage through fire and suffering by thousands of Congressmen and Congress sympathizers has raised the status of India and the strength of the people. Victory, that is, independence of India as a whole, is a certainty.[12]

Two years earlier, with Japan at India's door, he had thought in now-or-never terms. In 1944 he felt time was again on his side. He gave himself two tasks: ensuring that the Congress received its due share of power when the British left, and finding Hindu-Muslim understanding.

On 17 June, writing from the Poona nature-cure clinic, he sought a meeting with the Viceroy as well as an opportunity to speak to the jailed Working Committee. Wavell replied that Gandhi should first reveal 'a definite and constructive policy'.[13] This Gandhi did between 4 and 6 July, when Stuart Gelder of England's *News Chronicle* interviewed him in Panchgani.

'I cannot take the country back to 1942,' acknowledged Gandhi. 'History can never be repeated.' He had 'no intention of offering civil disobedience today' but wanted a national government with 'full control of civil administration', to be chosen by 'elected members of the Central Assembly'. Only such a government could address 'the terrible progressive starvation of the people' from the Bengal famine.[14]

Provided India did not have to pay for them, Allied forces could carry on their operations on Indian soil for defeating Japan, Gandhi added. The Viceroy and the C-in-C could retain 'complete control' over war policy and over ports and the railways, but the national government should be entitled 'to offer advice and criticisms even in military matters'. Asked about his own role in such a national government, Gandhi replied:

> After independence [is] assured, I would probably cease to function as adviser to the Congress, and as an all-war resister I would have to stand aside; but I shall not offer any resistance against the national government or the Congress. My cooperation will be abstention from interfering with the even tenor of life in India.
>
> I shall work with the hope that my influence will always be felt to keep India peace-minded and [working for] brotherhood among all without the distinction of race and colour …

He saw India's independence as a prelude to the freedom of all of Asia and Africa:

> Freedom for India will bring hope to Asiatics and other exploited nations. Today there is no hope for the Negroes, but Indian freedom will fill them with hope.

'Will the Viceroy be there (in a national government)?' Gelder asked. 'Yes,' replied Gandhi, 'but he will be like the King of England guided by responsible ministers.'[15]

Speaking to other journalists a few days later, Gandhi said he felt awkward making proposals without consulting the Working Committee:

> If the indication of my mind affords any satisfaction to the authorities, they should open the gates of the prison, and let those who can speak with authority pronounce upon my proposal or at least let me confer with them. As it is, I do not know that I have not embarrassed them by my sharing my personal opinion with the public before first sharing it with them.[16]

Aside from the fact that along with Quit India his generalship in the Congress had expired, he correctly sensed that Nehru, Patel, Azad and company would henceforth want to act on their own. Still, in a letter sent on 27 July, Gandhi communicated his proposals directly to the Viceroy.

Subhas addresses Gandhi. Earlier, on 6 July, many Indians heard a broadcast that Subhas Bose made to India from 'somewhere in south-east Asia'. By this time his Indian National Army, operating alongside Japan's forces, had fought fierce, sacrificial and mostly losing battles around the India-Burma border. The broadcast conveyed selflessness and commitment:

> I can assure you, Mahatmaji, that I and all those who are working with me, regard ourselves as the servants of the Indian people. The only reward that we desire for our efforts, for our suffering and our sacrifice is the freedom of our motherland. There are many among us who would like to retire from the political field once India is free ...
>
> Nobody would be more happy than ourselves if, by any chance, our countrymen at home should succeed in liberating themselves by their own efforts, or if the British Government accept your Quit India resolution and give effect to it. We are however proceeding on the assumption that neither of the above is possible.

Addressed, as we see, to Gandhi, the broadcast called him the 'Father of the Nation'.[17] There is no evidence that Gandhi heard the broadcast but we must assume that he learnt of its contents and was moved.

Jinnah. A telegram went from Panchgani to another key player, Jinnah. It was sent by Rajagopalachari, who had consulted Gandhi. He was releasing his formula to the public, C R said in the telegram; would Jinnah mind if the League leader's rejection of the formula was also announced? He would indeed mind, Jinnah wired back. If Gandhi dealt directly with him, Jinnah added, he would convey the formula to the League.

Thereupon, on 17 July, Gandhi wrote from Panchgani to Jinnah – in Gujarati, with an attached Urdu translation – suggesting a meeting. Jinnah, also unwell, replied proposing a venue, his house in Bombay, to which Gandhi agreed, and the two decided to meet in September.

However, at the end of July Jinnah charged that the Rajagopalachari formula was 'a parody and a negation' of the League's Pakistan resolution and intended to 'torpedo' it. The Pakistan it offered, Jinnah added, was 'maimed, mutilated, and moth-eaten'.[18] The formula's 'mutual agreements' over defence etc. would cripple the new nation's independence, and limiting Pakistan to 'Muslim-majority districts' would shrink its size.

Another shot at the Gandhi-Jinnah talks, an indirect one, was fired by the Viceroy. Following instructions from the War Cabinet, Wavell replied to Gandhi that he saw no point in meeting him. Gandhi's national government proposal, the Viceroy added, was unacceptable even as a basis for discussion.

The true reason against a meeting between Gandhi and the Viceroy was that it would underline the prestige of the only recently released prisoner, and strengthen his hand for the encounter with Jinnah. During discussions in London, and between London and New Delhi, on the reply to be sent to Gandhi, Churchill had said to his War Cabinet:

> I hope the Cabinet will stand firm ... As a matter of fact, [the Viceroy] has no right to negotiate with Gandhi at all, considering he was responsible for passing to us the medical opinion on which we were told that he would never be able to take part in politics again ...

Churchill added that he objected to any impression 'of a great parley between the Viceroy and newly released invalid'.[19]

Other players. Ambedkar, from 1942 a member of the Viceroy's Executive Council, asked Gandhi at the end of July to address the 'communal problem between the Hindus and the untouchables' in addition to 'the Hindu-Muslim problem', and offered 'to formulate points on which a settlement is necessary'. Though Gandhi declined to be drawn into parallel negotiations with Ambedkar, his response revealed an interesting desire:

> *6 Aug. 1944:* [O]n broad politics of the country we see things from different angles. I would love to find a meeting ground between us ... I know your great ability and I would love to own you as a colleague and co-worker. But I must admit my failure to come nearer to you. If you can show me a way to a common meeting ground between us, I would like to see it. Meanwhile, I must reconcile myself to the present unfortunate difference.[20]

Master Tara Singh, the Akali leader, urged Gandhi to ensure that Sikh interests were not sacrificed at the altar of a Hindu-Muslim pact. To him Gandhi's response was: 'We shall come to no final terms. The smallest interest will have the same weight as the largest.'[21]

Churchill. From afar Churchill was continuing to exercise a powerful influence. As Gandhi told Gelder, the journalist: '[T]he common talk among us is that whatever the Viceroy may wish personally, he has no authority in the political sphere. Mr Churchill does not want any settlement.'[22]

While unaware that Churchill had expressed disappointment at his failure to die, Gandhi fully suspected the Premier's dislike of his release, and remembered Churchill's 1931 description of Gandhi as 'a half-naked fakir' whose ideas had to be 'grappled with and finally crushed'.[23] On 17 July (the day he also wrote to Jinnah), he dictated a letter to Churchill in which he asked to be trusted:

Dear Prime Minister, You are reported to have a desire to crush the simple 'naked fakir' as you are said to have described me. I have been long trying to be a fakir and that naked – a more difficult task. I, therefore, regard the expression as a compliment though unintended. I approach you then as such and ask you to trust and use me for the sake of your people and mine and through them those of the world. Your sincere friend, M.K. Gandhi[24]

Objecting that Gandhi was uncharitably recalling an old remark that Churchill probably regretted, Rajagopalachari advised against sending the letter. Convinced that without Churchill's approval the Viceroy would not move, Gandhi overruled the objection, and requested Wavell to forward his letter, which, however, did not reach Churchill for three months. All it then fetched was a line of acknowledgment via the Viceroy.

Underground leaders. Through a public statement Gandhi asked those still underground to present themselves to the police and claim rewards for their own capture. Some surrendered while others openly defied a law and courted arrest. Several, however, including the socialists Aruna Asaf Ali and Achyut Patwardhan, remained underground. From her hiding place Aruna conveyed her dissent to Gandhi, who replied:

> *30 Jun. 1944*: I consider myself to be incapable of asking anybody, much less you, of doing anything that would hurt your pride … This struggle has been full of romance and heroism. You are the central figure. I would love to see you since you are so near. Therefore come, if you at all can.
>
> Lest you cannot, this is my advice: I do not want you to surrender unless you feel that it is the better course … You must … be the best judge of what is proper …
>
> God be your sole guide and do as He bids you. This I promise: I will not judge you, no matter what you do. More if we meet. Much love from Bapu[25]

Aruna and Achyut did not come out until early 1946, after warrants against them were cancelled.

Savarkar and followers. No group disagreed more violently with Gandhi than the circle around Savarkar. At the end of August, after it was announced that Gandhi, by now back in Sevagram, would talk with Jinnah, two of Savarkar's followers, Nathuram Godse and an associate called L G Thatte, went from Poona to Sevagram with the announced aim of physically preventing Gandhi from leaving for Bombay. Accompanied by supporters, the pair arrived at the ashram entrance, where a police picket asked them to have their say and disperse.

On their refusal to leave, Godse and Thatte were arrested. A dagger was found on Thatte, who said that a martyr would kill Gandhi. When a policeman asked whether such matters should not be left to a leader like Savarkar, Thatte replied, 'That will be too great an honour for Gandhiji,' adding that his companion (Godse) 'will be quite enough for the purpose'. Without apparently naming the men, Wardha's police chief relayed the exchange to Pyarelal, who recorded it in a letter he was sending at the time to Sir Tej Bahadur Sapru, the Liberal leader.[26] That the two were Thatte and Godse would come to light later, after Gandhi's assassination.

Talks with Jinnah

Between 9 and 27 September 1944 – 29 years and eight months after Jinnah had welcomed Gandhi on his return from South Africa – Gandhi walked 14 times to talk with Jinnah in the latter's house on Mount Pleasant Road in Bombay's Malabar Hill. It was a short walk, for Gandhi too was staying on Mount Pleasant Road, in the house of the Birlas. A letter he wrote to Mira speaks of the family and team supporting him during the exercise, including Manilal, who was visiting from South Africa:

> *18 Sep. 1944*: My talks are dragging on. God alone knows the end of them. There is one good thing. I am bearing the strain well. I am keeping fit in spite of the two enemies within – the hookworm and the amoebae.
>
> It is good too that we [*Gandhi and Jinnah*] are within stone's throw of each other.
>
> Manilal is attending on me. He is my bed-fellow. Devadas too is here, so is Rajaji. Khurshedbehn [*a granddaughter of Dadabhai Naoroji*] is on the office staff and so is Mridula, I expect temporarily. They are all working full speed – not to mention Pyarelal, Sushila and Kanu. Pyarelal has a shorthand writer and typist. He is a rare man – silent and hard-working …
>
> Abha is here for medical examination. There is nothing wrong with her. Manu has come back from Karachi with her father. Pyarelal's mother and [infant niece] too are here. And they are all very happy.[27]

With the bed-fellow remark Gandhi was teasing Mira that women were not sharing his bed.

Jinnah was not blessed or burdened by anything like Gandhi's support team, and his illness was worse than Gandhi's: 'unresolved pneumonia in the base of his lungs' had just been diagnosed.[28] But he too had a stenographer and was in addition aided by a sharp mind, a steely spine and great popularity among the Muslims. In 1944 the League claimed two million members; 17 years earlier its membership had been less than 1,400.

With Muhammad Ali Jinnah – 1944

We saw that in the late 1930s Gandhi had found Jinnah 'a very tough customer' and despaired of a settlement with him. Yet from AKP he had made a bid for one, and now the two Gujaratis were face-to-face. In the Keep Azad told his colleagues that Gandhi was 'making a great mistake' by going to Jinnah.[29] The Viceroy, on the other hand, thought that 'the G-J meeting' would at the least 'result in a demand for the release of the Working Committee'.[30]

Journalists crowded Jinnah's lawns and those of Birla House. Indians saw pictures of the two leaders smiling and were encouraged by their repeated meetings. Gandhi sent to Jinnah his nature-cure doctor and, on Eid day, which fell during the talks, a supply of wheat-crackers.

But the talks failed. Gandhi said he was willing to ask the Congress to agree to a post-independence Pakistan along the lines of the Rajagopalachari formula. The offer was categorically rejected by Jinnah. However, when Gandhi asked him to 'give in writing what precisely on your part you would want me to put my signature to', Jinnah refused to do so.[31] He claimed nevertheless, when Gandhi probed him, that minorities would enjoy democratic rights in his Pakistan, including, if they wished, separate electorates.

Jinnah offered five grounds for rejecting Gandhi's Pakistan. One, it was not large enough: West Bengal and East Punjab were excluded from it. Two, it was not sovereign enough, for Gandhi envisaged bonds of alliance between the separated portions. To Gandhi 'utterly independent sovereignty, so that there is nothing in common between the two', seemed 'an impossible proposition' and a recipe for conflict.[32] Three, Gandhi's scheme gave all residents in Muslim-majority areas the right to vote on Pakistan, whereas Jinnah felt the right belonged to Muslims alone. Four, Gandhi wanted voting for separation to follow independence, whereas Jinnah wanted the British to divide India before quitting: he did not trust an independent India to arrange a plebiscite. Finally, though conceding the right of Muslim-majority areas to separate, Gandhi did not admit that Hindus and Muslims were two nations.

'Let us call in a third party or parties to guide or even arbitrate between us,' Gandhi suggested on 22 September.[33] Jinnah did not agree, and he also turned down Gandhi's request for a chance to present his scheme to the League's executive committee.

Gandhi said after the talks that Jinnah was 'a good man',[34] and Jinnah acknowledged that Gandhi had been 'very frank'.[35] Did the meetings produce anything? Only an increase in Jinnah's prestige, Azad (and others) thought. Gandhi was giving away parts of India, Savarkar charged.

Yet the talks had compelled Jinnah to be less vague. As long as it was not defined or delineated, 'Pakistan' enthused Muslims all across the land. After the Bombay talks, problems became apparent. His Pakistan, Jinnah had said, would include West Bengal and East Punjab. But if Hindu-majority areas could belong to Pakistan, why shouldn't

Muslim-majority areas remain in India? And if non-Muslims in Muslim-majority areas were denied a say, what were the prospects for Muslims in Hindu-majority areas?

Gandhi took away something else from the talks: a better understanding of Jinnah's mind. He saw that a passion had captured it; the secular Jinnah now spoke as a saviour of Islam. But Jinnah's refusal to draw a clear picture of Pakistan also conveyed a message.

This 'tough customer' seemed to want more than a large Pakistan area. Just what he wanted was not very clear to Gandhi or, at the time, even perhaps to Jinnah himself. Yet the talks produced a thought, filed in a corner of Gandhi's mind, that despite his advocacy of Pakistan Jinnah might, in some circumstances, accept a leading role for himself in India as a whole.

Troubled yet merry. When, soon after Gandhi's release, Malaviya expressed the hope that his friend would live for a hundred years, Gandhi complained that Malaviya had cut off 25 years. Yet for months Gandhi remained unwell and troubled, hearing mostly discouraging news. The Empire seemed heedless; he had failed with Jinnah; and friends like Kallenbach and Romain Rolland had died. A letter to Carl Heath, a Quaker from England, conveyed Gandhi's turmoil: 'Though in the midst of a raging storm, I often hum to myself, "Rock of Ages, cleft for me, let me hide myself in Thee".'[36] However, he took a little pleasure, some weeks later, in the wedding of Kanu and Abha.

On 2 October 1944, his 75th birthday, Gandhi planted a tulsi sapling in front of Kasturba's hut in Sevagram. Over 3,000 letters were waiting for the weary man in Sevagram, and any one of his numerous non-political concerns – spinning, village industries, basic education, the Kasturba Trust, a common language for all Indians, or whatever – could eat up all his time and strength.

Pressed by Rajagopalachari, Gandhi observed a 'work fast' and a 'speech fast'. Conversation between the two was often merry, as when Gandhi asked for more of the other man's company:

R: I may be able to come to Sevgram by the 30th.

G: So I shall look out for you ...

R: If you so desire.

G: What is the meaning of 'looking out for you'?

R: One looks out for dangers.

G: You may put it that way. I want that danger also. I have to compare notes about several things.

R: I hope both of us will have by then forgotten most of our notes ...

G: Then we shall laugh together and fatten.

Talk moved to a salt-free diet, to which Gandhi had recently returned.

R: When people are made to do without salt, they are likely to take to licking walls
...

G: The walls will be cleaner. This is the beginning of the laugh we shall abandon ourselves to ...

It was close to ten at night, past Gandhi's bedtime. He told C R: 'Now I am going to leave you if I am also to love you.'[37] Marking that Gandhi bubbled when someone like C R was around and could be downcast at other times, Pyarelal wrote in his diary (6 Dec. 1944):

There is something frightening in Bapu's utter spiritual isolation ... His role hereafter should not be that of an engine-driver but of a pointsman only. He should indicate the direction, give forth ideas, and radiate moral and spiritual influence.[38]

In January 1945 Gandhi did not hesitate to 'indicate the direction' when a political delegation from the NWFP arrived in Sevagram for his counsel. Their province's League ministry, installed in 1943, was highly unpopular, they said, and Dr Khan Sahib was in a position to come back as premier. Gandhi advised that he should try. On 12 March the League ministry lost its majority and Dr Khan Sahib was premier again. The release of his brother, Ghaffar Khan, quickly followed.

Working Committee released. If the isolated Gandhi felt certain of coming independence, that was also the Viceroy's reading. Telling Churchill in October 1944 that the wish to sever the British connection had large backing in India, Wavell, the former C-in-C, significantly added that British soldiers were unlikely to want to stay on in a post-war India.

While Gandhi was in detention, a British soldier serving in India and claiming to speak for 'many of us conscripted soldiers' had written to him of his support for Quit India and his regret at having 'to fight an imperialist war'.[39] Wavell was admitting that sentiments such as the ones expressed in this letter (which Gandhi saw only after his release) were not isolated.

To 'capture the Indian imagination' for salvaging British-Indian ties, the Viceroy asked for permission to release the Working Committee. Churchill sat on the proposal for eight months and agreed only after Wavell journeyed to England and, between March and June 1945, lobbied ministers, MPs and civil servants. On 29 March, when the Viceroy met Churchill, the Premier (according to Wavell's diary) 'launched into a long jeremiad about India which lasted for about forty minutes' and indicated his preference for 'partition into Pakistan, Hindustan, Princestan etc.'.[40] In May the war in Europe ended, and the general election was set for 5 July. But the Viceroy got the green light he wanted. Back in India, Wavell made his big radio announcement on 14 June: the Working Committee were being released and Indian leaders invited to talk with him in Simla about a new executive council.

'As soon as the jail gates were opened, we saw a new and surging life,' Kripalani would later write.[41] In the Keep the leaders had at times felt like non-persons. Now they saw that Quit India had turned them into heroes. Contradicting a rumour that his thinking had changed during detention, Patel said on 27 June:

> [Our] cause ... would have been lost for ever if the August 8 resolution had not been adopted ... Independence is approaching like the roaring flood.[42]

Thin, exhausted and ill but finally free, the leaders went to their homes, families and doctors and, in July, to Simla. They went in high hopes, for Wavell's announcement and telegrams of invitation had been couched in promising language. The Viceroy had invited Gandhi and Jinnah, other leaders of the Congress and the League, premiers and ex-premiers, and a few outside the two parties. But he had forgotten to invite Azad, who was still the Congress president.

Gandhi received his invitation in the hill town of Panchgani, where he had again gone to escape the summer. Reminding Wavell that he himself held no office in the party, Gandhi added that Azad would have to lead any Congress team. Rectifying the lapse over Azad, the Viceroy asked Gandhi to travel to Simla in any case.

Simla. This Gandhi did, travelling third-class across India's baking hinterland, but he did not join the formal talks. Evidently he too felt, like Pyarelal, that his days as the Congress's engine-driver had ended. After their time in the Keep, this was also the Working Committee's wish. They were keen to take over; he was ready to hand over.

Spending three weeks in the hill town (in 'Manor Ville', Rajkumari Amrit Kaur's house), Gandhi kept to the fringes of the conference, breathed the freshness that the monsoon's first rains bring to the Himalayas, and enjoyed, across Simla's mist, the view of distant snows.

But he was willing to criticize the Viceroy's proposal. This provided for a council with equal numbers of caste Hindus and Muslims, and equal numbers from the League and the Congress, plus a scheduled caste Hindu. Equating the Congress with caste Hindus predictably perturbed Gandhi. Cannily he advised the Working Committee to nominate only two or three caste Hindus, which, under the parity principle, would limit League Muslims to the same number. For remaining places the Congress should ask for talented and fair-minded persons (men *and* women, he insisted) from India's 'untouchable', Christian, Sikh, Parsi, Anglo-Indian and Jewish communities.

Anxious for a settlement, his colleagues disagreed. On behalf of the Congress, the

Working Committee accepted Wavell's proposal of a council with an equal number of caste Hindus and Muslims, all but one of the former from the Congress, all but one of the latter from the League, with a non-League, non-Congress Muslim filling the remaining Muslim place, one Scheduled Caste, and two or three from other minorities. The Working Committee also accepted Wavell's assurance that his viceregal veto should not be a problem.

When Jinnah asserted at the conference that the Congress represented none but Hindus, Dr Khan Sahib asked, 'What does he mean? I am a Congressman. Am I a Hindu or a Muslim?'[43] Jinnah, who refused in Simla to shake Azad's hand, offered no reply to Dr Khan Sahib. Also, he flatly turned down the Wavell proposal, saying that if he, as the League president, could not choose every Muslim name, the League would stay out. After Jinnah's 'no', Wavell, who had wanted to include the Punjab's Unionist premier Khizr Hyat Khan (the late Sikandar's successor but not a relative), abruptly announced the failure of his conference.

Some of his advisers, including governors, had suggested going ahead with the Congress list and a few others, keeping places vacant for the League, but Wavell and Churchill were firmly opposed to a Congress-dominated council. As the Viceroy admitted in a letter to the King, he 'could never rid [his] mind of' the damage that Quit India had caused to Britain's war effort in 1942, when he was C-in-C.[44] While fusing Indians with the Congress, Quit India had brought the Raj and the League closer together.

With London instructing him to refrain from blaming Jinnah,[45] Wavell accepted personal responsibility for Simla's failure. The result was a fresh shift in Muslim allegiance. Non-League leaders like Azad and Khizr lost support to Jinnah.

Patel's independence. In a letter to Gandhi, Patel remarked that Gandhi's talks with Jinnah ten months earlier had produced a similar effect.[46] 'I could not have done anything else,' Gandhi replied, adding that his had been a 'final' offer to Jinnah, beyond which he would not go, and that Patel should feel free to condemn 'from the housetops' Gandhi's approach to Jinnah.[47] This Patel did not do, but his independence was now obvious. Quit India had been necessary, he conceded. But obeying Gandhi, henceforth, was not.

Gandhi signified his acceptance of Patel's independence by calling him, from the middle of 1945, 'Chiranjiv' Vallabhbhai in his letters. Invoking blessings and long life, 'Chiranjiv' was a prefix for loved younger ones. Hitherto Gandhi's letters to Patel had begun with 'Bhai Vallabhbhai'. For years 'Chiranjiv' Jawaharlal had been a son to Gandhi, enjoying a son's independence and right to succession, and 'Bhai' Vallabhbhai, only six years younger than Gandhi, a trusty brother. Now Vallabhbhai too was a son with a mind of his own. In October 1945 Gandhi said, 'Sardar is as dear as a son to me.'[48] Two months later Gandhi again acknowledged Patel's new status, saying to him in a letter, 'You are after all the Sardar of Bardoli and, as it happens, of India.'[49]

Independence at 70 years of age was scarcely a shocking idea, but Vallabhbhai's determination to be his own guide was a new thing, produced by the Keep. Accepting his colleague's independence, Gandhi also supervised Patel's recovery in Dinshaw Mehta's nature-cure clinic in Poona clinic.

1945–6 elections. Doing what the now-dead Hitler had been unable to, British voters defeated Churchill in July 1945. The following month, after atom bombs were dropped on Hiroshima and Nagasaki, Japan surrendered. As for India, Clement Attlee, Churchill's successor as Premier, and Attlee's Labour colleagues agreed with Wavell that elections for the Central Assembly and provincial legislatures should be held in the winter of 1945–6.

Gandhi supported the Working Committee's decision to contest the elections. Following Patel's suggestion, Nehru drafted an election manifesto with Quit India as its basis.[50] As in 1937, Nehru was the Congress's ace campaigner and Patel the election 'in-charge'.

To know where his 'heir' stood, Gandhi, now 76, initiated a discussion with Nehru in the autumn of 1945. Since, wrote Gandhi (5 Oct. 1945), he was 'an old man' while Nehru was 'comparatively young', it was essential that 'I should at least understand my heir and my heir in turn should understand me.'

Some differences were of long standing: Nehru freely embraced modernity but was wary about religion, positions very different from Gandhi's. Nehru tended to use a language of class war that Gandhi disapproved of, and supported a state-dominated economy about which Gandhi was sceptical. We have seen that over Quit India Jawaharlal had been reluctant, and though Gandhi could not have known of Nehru's diary jottings in Ahmednagar in which Gandhi was often blamed, he was curious about Jawaharlal's latest thinking. Carried out through correspondence as well as face to face, the discussion did not reveal identical views.

Jawaharlal adhered to his objections to what he saw as *Hind Swaraj*'s anti-modern thrust and to Gandhi's emphasis on the village. 'I do not understand,' wrote Nehru, 'why a village should necessarily embody truth and non-violence. A village, normally speaking, is backward culturally and intellectually, and no progress can be made from a backward environment.'

Gandhi reiterated his belief that in India life had to be improved in the villages, where most of the population lived. Arguing that 'millions of people can never live in cities and palaces in comfort and peace', he added:

> In this village of my dreams the villager will not be dull – he will be all awareness. He will not live like an animal in filth and darkness. Men and women will live in freedom, prepared to face the whole world. There will be no plague, no cholera and no smallpox. Nobody will be allowed to be idle or to wallow in luxury ...

On the role of the state in the economy, and the relationship between the state and the individual, Gandhi said:

> The sum and substance of what I want to say is that the individual person should have control over the things that are necessary for the sustenance of life. If he cannot have such control the individual cannot survive. Ultimately, the world is made up only of individuals.

On several critical principles, however, they were in complete agreement, e.g. on equal rights and opportunities for all Indians. 'The talks ... have given me the impression that there is not much difference in our outlook or the way we understand things,' Gandhi wrote (13 Nov.). In sum he felt he could trust Jawaharlal to do the right thing. 'Our hearts will still remain one, for they are one,' he said (88: 118–20; 329–31).

He was called in to lower tensions between president Azad and Patel, who organized the Congress effort first from the Poona clinic and then from a small room in Bombay's Congress House. But Patel rejected Gandhi's advice against collecting funds from the rich.

To Azad he wrote, 'It must be understood between us that no seats should be lost for want of money.'[51] After the elections were over, Patel wrote to Gandhi: 'The Maulana and the Working Committee wanted me [to collect funds]. I did the work as I felt it was unavoidable. We would all have been blamed if it had not been done.'[52]

The elections showed a near-complete polarization, with the Congress winning the great bulk of non-Muslim seats and the Muslim League winning all 30 Muslim seats to the Central Assembly, and 427 of the 507 Muslim seats in provincial legislatures. The Congress formed eight provincial ministries and had a share in a ninth ministry: a Unionist-Akali-Congress coalition in the Punjab, headed by Khizr.

Though denied office in the Punjab, the Muslim League emerged as the largest party there, and it headed coalition ministries in Bengal and Sindh. For Gandhi and others saddened by the polarization, a silver lining was provided by the Muslim-majority NWFP, where the Khan brothers defeated the League in an election fought on the issue of Pakistan. Dr Khan Sahib again headed the ministry.

In Madras, C R, now back in the Congress, was willing to lead once more. He was publicly endorsed by Gandhi and Patel but – in another sign that Gandhi's word was no longer law – the province's Congress legislators punished Rajagopalachari for staying out of Quit India and chose T Prakasam as chief minister.

Bose's death. Reports reached India towards the end of August 1945, right after Japan's surrender, that Subhas Bose had been killed in a plane crash in Taiwan. 'It is just what would be given out if he meant to go underground,' Wavell wrote in his diary.[53] Gandhi too remained unconvinced of Subhas's death until the following year, when Colonel Habib-ur-Rahman, a Bose aide who survived the crash, gave him, in New Delhi, an eye-witness account of Bose's final, stoic moments.

Gandhi had last met Bose in 1940, a year after their big split and seven months before Subhas escaped from detention and went on to lead the Indian National Army (INA) alongside the forces, now defeated, of Imperial Japan. As we have seen, Quit India had brought the two closer to each other in their thoughts. Cripps (in 1942) and Azad (in 1942 and later) expressed surprise that Gandhi should laud the champion of a strategy conflicting sharply with his own, but Gandhi said that Bose should be judged no differently from heroes in other lands.

Naval mutiny

Unexpected angles to Gandhi's non-violence were revealed in his reaction to a brief mutiny in February 1946 in the Royal Indian Navy (RIN). The mutiny's initiators, a group of young naval ratings – Hindu and Muslim – had been thrilled by the INA's exploits and in particular by the release, prompted by the Raj's political calculations, of three INA officers earlier sentenced for life – a Hindu, a Muslim and a Sikh. The rebels rallied support around two issues: the discriminatory attitude of some white RIN officers and the quality of food issued to the ratings.

None of the large number of RIN's Indian officers joined the revolt but many ratings did. On 19 February a shore-based signal school in Bombay, HMIS *Talwar*, was captured and its Union Jack pulled down. A Naval Central Strike Committee (NCSC) was formed, shore-to-ship and ship-to-ship communications were set up, several ships taken over, and flags of the Congress and the Muslim League raised aboard them.

As one of the protagonists, B C Dutt, has related in *Mutiny of the Innocents*, the young rebels imagined that they were in a position to 'offer the Royal Indian Navy on a platter' to any Indian leaders willing to grab it.[54] Impressed by stories of her Quit India role, they went first to Aruna Asaf Ali, who was visiting Bombay. Her disappointing advice was that they should discuss their service demands with the naval authorities and their political dreams with Patel and Jinnah, both living in Bombay.

The next day the mutineers sent negotiators to Vice Admiral J H Godfrey, flag officer commanding the RIN, who wanted all ratings to surrender. This was unacceptable to the mutiny's leaders, and 21 February saw an exchange of fire between shore-based mutineers and loyal troops trying to confine them to barracks. Several ratings were killed. Angered by the troops' firing, Aruna, her socialist colleague Achyut Patwardhan and some Communist leaders in Bombay called upon Bombay's workers and students to strike in sympathy with the ratings. On 22 February many mill-hands and students took to the streets. Public buildings and railway stations were burnt and shops, including grain-shops, looted. There was 'a regular fury against Englishmen and English dress', and firing by the police and the troops.[55] The ports of Karachi and Calcutta also saw incidents.

That day Patel told mutineers calling on him that he agreed with the RIN chief that they should surrender. He would however press, Patel added, for the ratings' legitimate demands. Approached by Muslim ratings, Jinnah gave an identical response. On 23 February an exhausted NCSC, headed by a young Muslim called M S Khan, called off the mutiny, which along with related disturbances had resulted, over a four-day period, in 236 deaths and injuries to 1,156.

Before word of the end of the mutiny reached him, Gandhi commented on the disturbances in a statement from Poona. To compel 'a single person' to 'shout "Jai Hind"' was to drive a nail 'into the coffin of Swaraj in terms of the dumb millions of India'. The violence in the streets was 'unbecoming' and anti-poor, and the violence of the mutineers was thoughtless. 'For there is such a thing,' he added, 'as thoughtful violent action.'

Unimpressed that Hindus and Muslims had come together 'for the purpose of violent action', Gandhi in fact saw the combination as 'unholy' and 'probably ... a preparation for mutual violence'.[56] Criticizing Gandhi's statement, Aruna claimed that popular violence had helped the 1942 movement. As for the communal question, she said she would 'rather unite Hindus and Muslims at the barricade than on the constitutional front'.

When, on 26 February, Gandhi answered Aruna, whom he likened to a daughter, the end of the mutiny was known to all:

> I do not read the 1942 events as does the brave lady. It was good that the people rose spontaneously. It was bad that some or many resorted to violence ...
>
> India has become a pattern for all exploited races of the earth, because India's has been an open, unarmed effort which demands sacrifice from all without inflicting injury on the usurper. The millions in India would not have been awakened but for the open, unarmed struggle ...
>
> Aruna would 'rather unite Hindus and Muslims at the barricade than on the constitutional front'. Even in terms of violence, this is a misleading proposition ... Fighters do not always live at the barricade. They are too wise to commit suicide. The barricade life has always to be followed by the constitutional. That front is not taboo for ever ...
>
> It is a matter of great relief that the ratings have listened to Sardar Patel's advice to surrender. They have not surrendered their honour. So far as I can see, in resorting to mutiny they were badly advised. If it was for grievance, fancied, or real, they

should have waited for the guidance and intervention of political leaders of their choice.

If they mutinied for the freedom of India, they were doubly wrong. They could not do so without a call from a prepared revolutionary party ...

Aruna is entitled to say that the people 'are not interested in the ethics of violence or non-violence', but the people are very much interested in knowing the way which will bring freedom to the masses – violence or non-violence (90: 4–6).

Later, Dutt would acknowledge that the mutiny was 'immature' and 'a great futility'.[57] On his part, a Gandhi disapproving of violence was nonetheless ready, we have seen, to examine violence from the standpoint of its effectiveness – to distinguish between thoughtless and thoughtful violence, between foolhardiness and a mutiny that answered a 'call from a revolutionary party'.

'Britain will *quit.'* On 24 January 1946 – a month before the mutiny – a private telegram from London informed Wavell that three British ministers would visit in the near future to 'negotiate a settlement of the Indian problem'. On 19 February this was publicly announced, and on 15 March Premier Attlee told the House of Commons that Britain had indeed decided to quit. To figure out how, and to whom, the Empire would leave India, three ministers would arrive in New Delhi on 24 March. 'If India elects for independence,' said Attlee, 'she has a right to do so.'

Friends in England had indicated to Gandhi that a declaration like this was in the offing. It was what he had waited and worked for, but the Gandhi of early 1946 was older and less in command than the 1942 initiator of Quit India, not wholly clear on his role in negotiations with the British ministers, and not sure of how Nehru, Patel, Azad and company would deal with them. Also, he did not know how the British ministers would deal with Jinnah and his Pakistan demand.

On 10 February 1946, following a withdrawal of the ban against it, *Harijan* was able to resume publication. 'A newspaper man myself,' as he described himself in April, Gandhi was glad (90: 187). On 11 March he made his first public statement about the British ministers:

As brave people it is our duty to take at its face value the declaration of the British Ministers that they are coming to restore to India what is her due. If a debtor came to your house in contrition to repay his debt, would it not be your duty to welcome him? (90: 65)

The man. At 76 Gandhi was grappling with personal challenges also. For one thing, he was running into signs of a weakening memory.

To Maniben Nanavati, 2 Mar. 1946. Kishorelalbhai writes to tell me that I have not replied to your letter. If so, it is a matter of shame for me. It is, however, clear that I tend to forget (90: 25).

And in the first quarter of 1946 he seemed unclear about where he should be. By this time he had travelled to Bengal, Assam, Orissa and south India, making punishing journeys that reconnected him to his far-flung people.

A proposed visit to Bardoli was cancelled because Vallabhbhai, who had offered to take Gandhi there, was needed in Bombay to calm that city. In a letter written on 26 February, Gandhi had asked Vallabhbhai to make plans not with 'my convenience in view' but according to 'what the circumstances of the nation demanded of us' (90: 7).

He spent some weeks in Poona and a village south of Poona, Uruli-Kanchan, with nature-cure as his focus. For a while he thought that he and Dinshaw Mehta, the nature-cure expert, might establish a health centre in Poona. But Mehta seemed unable to impart his skills to others and in any case Poona was too big and far away for poor villagers. Others had earlier said as much, but Gandhi had not heeded them.

> It is plain to me as it has become to some of my friends that I am incorrigible. I can learn only by my mistakes. I do not know why I could not learn through objections or warnings from others. I can learn only when I stumble and fall and feel the pain (*Harijan*, 17 Mar. 1946; 90: 38).

He moved to a clinic at Uruli-Kanchan, where he practised nature-cure, prescribing treatment to numerous poor villagers. Surviving notes make it clear that 'Doctor' Gandhi was in his element while recommending (to women and men) hip-baths, mud-poultices, nude sunbathing 'in a solitary place' and fruit juices. Thus he said about a sick little boy brought to him at the village clinic:

> Can he see at the moment? If he takes a diet free from chillies, takes fruit, and hip-bath and friction-bath, he is likely to be all right. Does he pass stools? What is he fed? How come breast-feeding at this age? How old is he? How can a two-year-old child be allowed to suckle? He should be given only fruit-juice. He needs an enema, which can be done only here (90: 159).

For problems like cataract and hernia he prescribed surgery: 'Shripad: He must get himself admitted to the hospital. If he is willing and wants to have a note, he may go with one. There is no other remedy for hernia. A strap-belt can also be worn' (90: 158–9).

His time at Uruli-Kanchan, where he asked his Hindu patients to recite the word Rama, seemed to inject new life into Gandhi's old faith – first learnt from Rambha, his childhood nurse – in the sound of God's name:

Uruli-Kanchan, 23 Mar. 1946. Ramanama cannot perform the miracle of restoring to you a lost limb. But it can perform the still greater miracle of helping you to enjoy an ineffable peace in spite of the loss while you live and rob death of its sting and the grave its victory at the journey's end (90: 134).

Though having to work at his own health as well, Gandhi at times surprised callers by looking fitter than expected. Meeting Gandhi on 17 March 1946 in Poona, the British journalist Henry Brailsford thought he 'looked well and very much less than his age ... His manner was never solemn and often he relaxed in a humorous chuckle' (90: 99–100).

When Brailsford raised the Pakistan question, Gandhi said that in the absence of an agreed solution 'he was prepared to submit the whole issue to international arbitration' (90: 102). 'In a way hard to define,' wrote Brailsford, 'this man was speaking for India.' Some days earlier Gandhi had told a Gujarati caller: 'I want to live for 125 years and, if God fulfils my wish, I want to create a new world in India' (*Gujarat Samachar*, 10 Mar. 1946; 90: 54).

He hoped to be useful – in action. Urged to write a treatise on non-violence and satyagraha, Gandhi replied in *Harijan* (3 Mar. 1946): 'I am not built for academic writings. Action is my domain' (90: 1).

Companions. But with Kasturba and Mahadev gone for ever, Mira off to the Himalayan foothills, and Sushila needing to support a cousin in Quetta, Gandhi's in-house team had weakened. Pyarelal continued as a secretary and someone to bounce ideas off. While Amrit Kaur provided additional secretarial help, Abha Gandhi, the young Bengali wife of Gandhi's grand-nephew Kanu, and Sushila Pai of Poona attended to Gandhi's personal needs. But he missed Mahadev's sparkle and the stability that Kasturba used to bring.

Joining his father in Bengal and Assam at the end of 1945, Manilal, now 53, reminded Gandhi that he had failed 'to take care of his real family'. To another short-term companion, a young Bengali named Sudhir Ghosh, Gandhi said: 'Why don't you take Manilal to Shillong tomorrow for a trip? It is a pretty place ... [E]njoy yourselves. It must be boring for you to spend all your time with an old man.' Ghosh and Manilal went up for a day to the beautiful hill town where the Indian manager of a hotel told them that only white guests could be served. While Manilal commented to his father that South Africa was more enlightened than Shillong, Ghosh saw that 'Gandhiji looked sad ... because our fun was spoilt by some hotel manager.'[58]

Amtus Salaam from Rajpura in Patiala state was eager to be with him as he travelled but Gandhi asked her to be in Sevagram or near her mother in Rajpura. 'I have not been able to write to you, but I think of you every day,' he wrote to her on 20 March (90: 115).

When some women working for the Kasturba Trust met him in Uruli-Kanchan and said they wanted 'women alone to run the show', Gandhi assented but added: 'I am the only [male] whom you may find it hard to get rid of, for I have always counted myself as a woman. I believe I know your sex and your needs better than you do yourselves' (90: 155–6).

Earlier in 1945, in Sevagram, he had resumed the practice of letting women sleep right next to him. Shivering was once more part of the story, and no doubt he again relaxed amidst his sorority, but now he also clearly claimed that the exercise was integral to strengthening his brahmacharya and that of the women, who at different times may have included Amrit Kaur, Sushila, Prabhavati, Amtus Salaam, Manu, Abha and Kanchan (whose husband Munnalal Shah helped manage the ashram). Unhappiness was voiced by associates led by Kishorelal Mashruwala, and Gandhi halted the practice, but he insisted (March 1945) that it was only a postponement. He had not yielded, he said, when his stand against untouchability or for non-violence had been attacked; he would not permanently yield now over his brahmacharya exercise (86: 8–11).

Caste and communal hate. A new weapon against untouchability and caste was Gandhi's decision, expressed in a letter he wrote in April 1946, to bless a marriage 'only when one of the parties to the marriage is a Harijan'.[59] Just when he arrived at this decision is not clear: in April 1947 he would say it was 'long ago'.[60] With this decision Gandhi had taken an explicit position against caste and in favour of inter-caste marriages.

Shaken on being told, in early 1946, that 'in Gujarat only one well and one temple is shared with Harijans and this in Karadi (near Dandi),' Gandhi said he would seek henceforth to reside amidst the untouchables. So when a letter from Viceroy Wavell arrived in Uruli-Kanchan inviting Gandhi to meet the British ministers in New Delhi on 3 April, Gandhi asked friends in the capital, including Ghanshyamdas Birla and Brij Krishna, to arrange his stay in the sweepers' colony on Reading Road (now Mandir Marg), not far from a temple the Birlas had built, and right next to St Thomas's High School for Girls.

Uruli-Kanchan, 25 Mar. 1946. If I live apart from Harijans, what right have I to question the action of others who go further in their adherence to untouchability? … It goes without saying that I must not impose myself on Harijans anywhere (90: 138–9).

Reminding himself of the centrality of the Dalit question, Gandhi also smelt preparations for communal violence among Hindus and Muslims. Working in 'unholy combination', extremists from the two sides, he felt, were fuelling one another's fires. On 23 March a deeply perturbed Gandhi told an unnamed English friend: 'I would not want to live up to 125 to witness that consummation. I would rather perish in the flames' (90: 126).

Atom bomb. The revival of *Harijan* enabled him to comment on a range of issues. On Palestine he said that Jews had been 'cruelly wronged' in many places and their condition was 'a blot on the Christian world', but they had 'erred grievously in seeking to impose themselves on Palestine with the aid of America and Britain' and with the use of violence.[61]

Noting with regret that Russia, 'which stood for the people', had 'turned into an imperialist power' (*Harijan*, 29 Sep. 1946), he disputed the view that the atom bomb had helped the cause of peace:

Often does good come out of evil. But that is God's, not man's plan. Man knows that only evil can come out of evil, as good out of good.

Conceding that 'atomic energy, though harnessed by American scientists and army men for destructive purposes, may be utilized by other scientists for humanitarian purposes', he added:

So far as I can see, the atomic bomb has deadened the finest feeling that has sustained mankind for ages. There used to be the so-called laws of war which made it tolerable. Now we know the naked truth. War knows no law except that of might ...

Let no one run away with the idea that I wish to put in a defence of Japanese misdeeds in pursuance of Japan's unworthy ambition. The difference was only one of degree. I assume that Japan's greed was more unworthy. But the greater unworthiness conferred no right on the less unworthy of destroying without mercy men, women and children of Japan in a particular area (*Harijan*, 7 Jul. 1946; 91: 220–1).

Vision of free India. While at Panchgani he drew, in response to a reader's question, his picture of independent India. In his India, where 'the last is equal to the first or, in other words, no one is to be the first and none the last,'

Independence must begin at the bottom. Thus, every village will be a republic or panchayat having full powers ...

In this structure composed of innumerable villages, there will be ever-widening, never-ascending circles. Life will not be a pyramid with the apex sustained by the bottom. But it will be an oceanic circle whose centre will be the individual always ready to perish for the village, the latter ready to perish for the circle of villages, till at last the whole becomes one life composed of individuals, never aggressive in their arrogance but ever humble, sharing the majesty of the oceanic circle of which they are integral units.

Therefore the outermost circumference will not wield power to crush the inner circle but will give strength to all within and derive its own strength from it.

I may be taunted with the retort that this is all Utopian and, therefore, not worth a single thought. If Euclid's point, though incapable of being drawn by human agency, has an imperishable value, my picture has its own ... Let India live for this true picture, though never realizable in its completeness (*Harijan*, 28 Jul. 1946; 91: 325–7).

A new Congress president. 'I shall have to go,' Gandhi wrote to Patel, referring to Wavell's invitation for talks in Delhi (90: 123). Not he but the Working Committee or its nominees would represent the Congress at the negotiations, but he would be around to give counsel. After all, he knew the Empire better than the Working Committee did; and his understanding of the mind of Jinnah, who was bound to be a major factor in the talks, would also be useful.

Moreover, he had to sort out the urgent question of the Congress's next president. Struggles, bans and imprisonments had precluded any change since 1940, when Azad was chosen to the chair, but now there was scope for a new head who, if the British did part with power, would probably become India's Prime Minister.

Though Azad had been in the chair for six years, he had also been in jail for much of this time. He aspired for re-election. Recalling, among other credentials, Patel's Quit India exertions, several PCCs nominated him. Kripalani too was proposed. Gandhi concluded, however, that the position should go to Jawaharlal. When an Urdu newspaper reported that Azad was likely to be re-elected, Gandhi sent him a letter of frank advice, in Urdu:

20 Apr. 1946. Please go through the enclosed cutting ... I have not given my opinion to anyone. When one or two Working Committee members asked me, I said it would not be right for the current President to continue ...

If you are of the same opinion, it may be proper for you to issue a statement about the newspaper report and say that you have no intention to become president again.

In today's circumstances I would if asked prefer Jawaharlal. I have many reasons for this. Why go into them?[62]

As no PCC had proposed Nehru's name, Kripalani, acting, as he puts it, 'in deference to Gandhiji's wishes, sent a paper round, proposing the name of Jawaharlal'.[63] This was on 25 April, four days before the deadline for candidates. The Working Committee members signed the paper, including Azad and Patel, as also some Delhi Congressmen.

Nehru was now a proper candidate, but so were Vallabhbhai and Kripalani. At Gandhi's instance the latter two formally withdrew, and on the next day Azad issued a public statement asking for Nehru's election, which was unanimously achieved. Azad, however, suggested that his successor should not take over until the end of the year, but Gandhi again intervened, and it was agreed that Nehru's term would start in July.

Before long Gandhi publicly gave one of his reasons for preferring Nehru. 'He, a Harrow boy, a Cambridge graduate and a barrister is wanted to carry on the negotiations with Englishmen.'[64] If the talks were successful and led to a national government, Jawaharlal as the Congress president would lead it. This seemed appropriate to Gandhi, who for years had spoken of Nehru as his heir and India's future helmsman.

He was conscious, moreover, that Jawaharlal had links with Muslims that Patel, for one, lacked, a critical factor in the period of communal tension that had arrived. Nehru's capacity to 'make India play a role in international affairs' was another element weighing with Gandhi, who may have also reckoned that Patel was more likely than Nehru to be content in second place. 'They will be like two oxen yoked to the governmental cart,' said Gandhi, referring to Nehru and Patel. 'One will need the other and both will pull together.'[65] Another consideration, almost a decisive one, was Patel's poor health.

All the same, this was the third time that on Gandhi's word the dutiful Patel had stood down for Nehru, a repeat of 1929 and 1937. The newest sacrifice was hardly painless, yet a week after Nehru's nomination Patel was making everyone, including Gandhi, 'laugh a lot'.[66] He had had to make room for Nehru, but Patel was aware of his independence and strength in the Congress's inner circle.[67]

Sweepers' colony. It was in a room amidst the sweepers of Balmiki colony, though not exactly in a sweeper's home, that Gandhi lived in New Delhi.

Prayer-meeting remarks, 1 Apr. 1946. I ... do not delude myself with the belief that by staying here I am sharing the actual life with the Harijans ... I know too that this place has been brightened up. Indeed I feel embarrassed by the amenities that have been provided here by Seth Birla for me and my party. My coming to stay here, I hope, is my first step, not the last ... (90: 173–4)

In New Delhi, as at Uruli-Kanchan, he recommended the recitation of the name of God:

4 Apr. 1946. I laugh within myself, when someone objects that Rama or the chanting of Ramanama is for the Hindus only ... Is there one God for the Mussalmans and another for the Hindus, Parsis or Christians? No, there is only one omnipotent and omnipresent God. He is named variously, and we remember Him by the name which is most familiar to us.

My Rama, the Rama of our prayers, is not the historical Rama, the son of Dasaratha, the King of Ayodhya. He is the eternal, the unborn, the one without a second. Him alone I worship, His aid alone I seek, and so should you. He belongs equally to all. I, therefore, see no reason why a Mussalman or anybody should object to taking His name. But he is in no way bound to recognize God as [Rama]. He may utter to himself Allah or Khuda ... (90: 188).

The Cabinet Mission

Headed by the elderly Secretary of State for India, Frederick Pethick-Lawrence, whose Quaker wife Emmeline had collaborated with Gandhi in earlier years, the Cabinet Mission that arrived in India at the end of March 1946 included Sir Stafford Cripps, the brilliant lawyer, Labour party leader and president of the Board of Trade who had failed in his 1942 mission to India, and A V Alexander, who had risen from trade union ranks to become First Lord of the Admiralty. 'An imperialist disliking any idea of leaving India,' as Wavell described him, Alexander got on well with the Viceroy, who was the fourth member of the British negotiating team.[68]

This team had two goals: resolving the demand for Pakistan, and converting the Viceroy's Executive Council into an interim national government. For all of April, all of May and most of June the three ministers and Wavell conferred with Indian politicians – in New Delhi, Simla and New Delhi again. Never before had three Cabinet ministers from Britain spent three summer months together in India.

Pethick-Lawrence and Cripps broke some norms of Empire, calling on Gandhi in the Balmiki colony of the 'untouchables', attending some of his prayer meetings, and showing other courtesies that irritated Wavell, but Gandhi saw that despite its Labour background the Mission carried an imperial burden of 'fairness' that ruled out transferring power to the majority.

Gandhi was frankly told that the Mission would not recommend a transfer of power to the Congress, even though it enjoyed majority backing, since the Muslim League, supported by a majority of India's Muslims, was opposed; and also that the Mission would not right away say to Jinnah what it believed, which was that neither 'small' Pakistan (with the Punjab and Bengal divided) nor 'large' Pakistan (containing all of the Punjab and Bengal) was a solution.[69]

Unwilling to leave the future to Indians or pronounce their own clear opinion, the ministers said they wanted the Congress and the Muslim League to agree before they returned home. Going by his talks 19 months earlier with Jinnah, and by the more recent Simla conference, Gandhi thought this an impossible goal, humanly speaking. He said so to the Mission, and on 3 April he asked the large audience at his prayer meeting to pray:

> God alone can help us. Nobody else can help, neither you nor Englishmen. Let us
> pray to God to guide our talks and grant wisdom to all those participating in them
> ... (90: 183).

He however asked the Cabinet Mission for two things right away: the release of Jayaprakash Narayan, Rammanohar Lohia and other long-detained political prisoners, and the removal of the salt tax. While the first request was quickly granted, the second was turned down by the Viceroy. Abell, Wavell's secretary, told Amrit Kaur that Jinnah would be offended if the salt tax were abolished.[70]

Simla, forebodings & the 16 May Statement. At his first meeting with the Mission, Jinnah was asked if he would accept the 'small' Pakistan of the Rajagopalachari formula if it was entirely sovereign. He said no. He wanted, Jinnah said, 'all six provinces (Punjab, Sindh, the NWFP, Baluchistan, Bengal and Assam) and complete sovereignty'.[71] The Congress, on the other hand, made clear its opposition even to 'small' Pakistan if it was fully sovereign, if it preceded independence, and if the NWFP, where the Congress had recently defeated the League, was compelled to join it.

To square the circle the British conducted a series of negotiations, which were shifted after a month to Simla, where a four-member team represented the Congress: Azad, Nehru, Patel and Ghaffar Khan. Jinnah came to the mountain town with his League group. Both the Raj and the Working Committee asked Gandhi also to travel to Simla, which he did, but he did not sit at the negotiating table. Tantalizingly close to freedom and its rewards, including positions of prestige and power, Gandhi's colleagues were more eager than him to have issues 'settled'. During these negotiations they often felt closer to the British ministers than to their chief – their erstwhile chief, to be truer to the facts.

Their impatience troubled Gandhi as much as the Mission's insistence on a Congress-League accord; he sensed, in addition, that Hindu-Muslim relations were worsening at ground level. But he did not know what he should do. 'You do not know how uneasy I feel,' Gandhi wrote to Cripps on 29 April. 'Something is wrong.'[72]

'There is a crisis within a crisis,' he told Agatha Harrison, who had also come to Simla, 'a crisis within and a crisis without'.[73] His response to the unease was unexpected if also characteristic: he asked Pyarelal and others on his personal staff to leave Simla, where, along with Patel and Ghaffar Khan, he again stayed in 'Manor Ville', Rajkumari Amrit Kaur's home.

He must throw himself entirely on God, he told Pyarelal, and use 'the sharp axe of detachment', sending away aides who were also, or even more, his family, providing cushion, support and comfort. 'If you are surrounded by your family,' he explained, 'they divide your attention in however small or subtle a measure. I wish in this crisis to give my undivided self to God.'[74] He was acting in the spirit of Ralph Waldo Emerson's words written a century earlier: 'It is only as a man puts off all foreign support and stands alone that I see him to be strong and to prevail.'[75] Though pained and also worried for him, the aides were stoic. They left for Delhi.[76]

To Ghaffar Khan, who remained with him, Gandhi gave an unexpected assignment in Simla: the Badshah of the Pathans was to study the living conditions of the 'untouchables' of Simla. Their quarters were 'not fit for animals, much less for human beings', Ghaffar Khan reported, and Gandhi was 'filled with anger and grief'.[77]

The Simla talks centred around a scheme (thought up by Cripps) of a three-tiered India where Provinces would form the bottom tier, 'Hindu' and 'Muslim' Groups of provinces the middle tier, and a Union the top tier. On 6 May Jinnah said in Simla that he could agree to a nominal Union provided it enjoyed Hindu-Muslim parity and if the Muslim area was large enough.

Nehru said he could agree to Groups provided the Union had a legislature and Provinces were free to join or not join a Group. According to Wavell's diary, 'Patel's cold face of angry disapproval' when Nehru partially agreed with Jinnah 'was a study'.

Some minutes later Jinnah said that a Group should be able to secede after five years, at which Patel exclaimed, 'There, we have it now, what he has been after all the time.' Wavell wrote in his diary: 'The damage had been done in Patel's mind, and he had been given a handle for his contention that the League are not really in earnest about entering a Union and mean to get out as soon as possible.'[78]

That was the crux: mistrust. The Congress (not just Patel) thought that Jinnah would run off with six provinces, inclusive of Assam, East Punjab and West Bengal, where Muslims were in a minority, whereas Jinnah feared that the Congress would prevent any Muslim-majority area, howsoever small, from emerging.

Jinnah's parity demand was another obstacle. Consulted in the wings at Simla, Gandhi gave Cripps his opinion that parity between a Hindu majority and a Muslim minority was unreasonable and undemocratic and 'really worse than Pakistan'.[79] Once enjoined for the Union, Hindu-Muslim parity would become an India-wide demand at every level, from the village up.

At this stage, in an ideal world, the Mission should have said to the Congress that the

League had to be conceded a large area if it was to agree to a Union, and to the League that it had to unreservedly accept a Union if it wanted a large area. A sacrifice of territory had to match a sacrifice of sovereignty. Instead, the Mission chose to sacrifice clarity and consistency. Following the Simla talks, it drafted a document that the League could interpret one way, the Congress another, and both accept. This was the ingenious, brilliant and fatally ambiguous Statement of 16 May. Finally declaring (to the Congress's delight) that 'neither a larger nor a smaller sovereign state of Pakistan would be an acceptable solution', rejecting also the demand for parity in a Union legislature, and providing for a Union to deal with foreign affairs, defence and communications, the British Statement nonetheless outlined (in Para 15) a scheme permitting all the six provinces wanted by Jinnah to merge into two Muslim-majority Groups within an Indian Union, one in the west and the other in the east.

For preparing future constitutions for Provinces, Groups and the Union, 16 May spelt out (in Para 19) a procedure for creating a Constituent Assembly, or, rather, three Sections of a Constituent Assembly. Existing provincial legislatures would elect, and rulers of princely states nominate, representatives to a Constituent Assembly, which 'shall' meet in *three* Sections – members from Punjab, Sindh, the NWFP and Baluchistan assembling in one, those from Bengal and Assam in another, and the rest in a third. Meeting separately, the three Sections would first prepare their Group and Provincial constitutions. Then they would come together and jointly write the Union constitution.

While the Congress interpreted the scheme to mean that elected representatives from any or all of the six legislatures could *join or stay out* of a proposed 'Pakistan' or Muslim-majority Section (the word Pakistan was not used in the document) – thus enabling their province to join or stay out of a Group – the League not only insisted that all six provinces were *required* to amalgamate (four in the west and two, Bengal and Assam, in the east); it claimed a future right for the Pakistan Groups to secede from the Union.

The 16 May document used the expression 'should be free to' in one place (Para 15), and 'shall' elsewhere (Para 19). Cripps would explain to the House of Commons that the wording was kept 'purposely vague' so as to enable both sides to join the 16 May scheme.[80] The document also said that Union and Group constitutions could be reconsidered ten years after they were framed, a provision welcomed by the League as a door to secession. In short, while the League declared the *Union* in 16 May to be optional, the Congress said the *Groups* were.

On 24 May an aide to the Mission and a future British MP, Woodrow Wyatt, advised Jinnah that though Pakistan had been turned down in it, he could nonetheless accept 16 May 'as the first step on the road to Pakistan'.[81] On 6 June the League formally 'accepted' the 16 May plan, reiterating at the same time that 'complete sovereign Pakistan' remained 'its unalterable objective', claiming that 'the foundation of Pakistan' was 'inherent' in what it described as the plan's 'compulsory grouping', and asserting that 'by implication' 16 May gave the Muslim Groups 'the opportunity and the right of secession'.[82]

Explanations and assurances of an opposite kind were offered to the Congress. Relieved by its rejection of Pakistan and of parity, Gandhi welcomed 16 May, but he and the Working Committee asked for confirmation of a Province's right to stay out of a Group. At first the demand was turned down. In a statement on 25 May, the Mission said that Grouping was 'essential' to the scheme of 16 May and accorded with the Mission's 'intentions'. Gandhi and the Working Committee argued back that the text was more relevant than intentions, and that the wording of Para 15 ruled out compulsory grouping.

Interim government. The Working Committee, however, withheld a formal response to 16 May, preferring to look first at the outcome of negotiations for an interim government. These negotiations too troubled Gandhi. On 13 June he wrote a blunt letter to Wavell, telling the Viceroy what he also told the Working Committee, which was that a League-run interim government was preferable to an Empire-dictated coalition that compromised the Congress's national character:

> You are a great soldier – a daring soldier. Dare to do the right. You must make your choice of one horse or the other. So far as I can see you will never succeed in riding two at the same time. Choose the names submitted either by the Congress or the League. For God's sake do not make an incompatible mixture and in trying to do so produce a fearful explosion. Anyway, fix your time limit and tell us all to leave when that limit is over. I hope I have made my meaning clear (91: 156).

As Gandhi saw it, while the Congress had the credentials for leading a new government, even a minority government headed by the League and answerable to the Central Assembly would not damage India's future. But he would not agree to a 'solution' where the Congress was equated with Hindus, the League with Muslims, and both pressured to accept a distasteful 'compromise'. He sent a similarly frank letter the same day to Cripps:

> You are handling the most difficult task of your life. As I see it the Mission is playing with fire ... You will have to choose between the two – the Muslim League and the Congress, both your creations ...
>
> Coquetting now with the Congress, now with the League and again with the Congress, wearing yourself away, will not do. Either you swear by what is right or by what the exigencies of British policy may dictate.
>
> In either case bravery is required. Only stick ... to your dates even though the heavens may fall. Leave by the 16th whether you allow the Congress to form a coalition

or the League. If you think that the accumulated British wisdom must know better than these two creations of yours, I have nothing to add (91: 158).[83]

Only partially informed of the talks between the Congress and the Mission, Gandhi wanted the ministers, and especially their skilful draftsman, Cripps, to wind up the effort, but Cripps seemed determined to install a new government before returning home. In his reply to Gandhi, Cripps said: '[W]e want to temper ... courage with prudence. I still have great hopes that before we leave India, we may have helped towards a settlement of the problem' (91: 158). Actually, Cripps was once more competing with Gandhi for the minds of Nehru, Patel and company, and hoping to bring them round to support the Mission's plans, even if Gandhi disagreed.

On 16 June, Wavell's list for the interim government was announced. Six Congress Hindus (Nehru, Patel, C R, Prasad, Mahtab and the Dalit leader, Jagjivan Ram), five Muslims (Jinnah and four others from the League), a Sikh (Baldev Singh), a Christian (John Matthai), and a Parsi (N P Engineer) were invited to form a new council.

Though Azad, still the Congress president, was not included, four of the party's 'top five' had been, and it was a good guess that Baldev Singh and Matthai would support the Congress six in any division in the council. At last India would have a Congress-dominated council, with Nehru as its vice-president and *de facto* premier, even if the Viceroy continued to chair proceedings.

Yet there was a flaw: the list implied that the Congress represented only the Hindus, and that only the League represented Muslims. For the sake of a compromise – but perhaps also because he would not be leading the Congress team[84] – Azad was willing to accept an all-Hindu Congress list and its corollary: his exclusion. He even privately informed the Mission that the Working Committee 'would not stick out' on the question of a Congress Muslim.[85] When Gandhi suggested that Azad should replace one of the caste Hindus named, the latter 'absolutely refused'.[86]

Most in the Working Committee, including Nehru and Patel, seemed ready to go along with Azad, but they had reckoned without Gandhi, who on 19 June 'gave a final notice' that if they agreed to an all-Hindu Congress list 'he would have nothing to do with the whole business and leave Delhi'.[87] He would have nothing to do with a Congress that reduced itself to a Hindu body.

Gandhi might have been rejected by the Working Committee but for a letter from Wavell to Azad. Landing on 22 June, the letter asked the Congress not to press for a non-League Muslim. Rejecting Gandhi was conceivable for the Congress leadership in the summer of 1946, but submitting to a Viceregal diktat was not. When the Working Committee voted on the 16 June list, 'all except one were opposed'.[88]

Wavell and Jinnah were expecting the Congress to reject 16 June, and Jinnah thought he might lead a new government without the Congress. However, Cripps and Pethick-Lawrence were keen for the Congress too to come in. We can say in broad terms that Cripps and Pethick-Lawrence made up the pro-Congress (though not necessarily pro-Gandhi) half of the British team, with Alexander and Wavell constituting its pro-League half.

'The way out.' Cripps knew that prospects of the Congress coming in rested on clause 8 in the 16 June Statement. This clause said that if the 16 June list was unacceptable to the Congress or the League or both, then the Viceroy would 'proceed with the formation of an Interim Government which will be as representative as possible of those willing to accept the Statement of May 16th'.

According to Wavell's diary, clause 8 was put in at his behest to ensure that 'Mr Jinnah, who had accepted the Statement of May 16, should not be put at a disadvantage with the Congress, who had not.'[89] Under this clause Jinnah, if he wished, could renegotiate his party's representation in the new government, a right not available to those rejecting 16 May. But Cripps knew, and the Congress understood, that clause 8 entitled the Congress too to renegotiate its names – to include, for instance, a Muslim on its list – provided it accepted 16 May.

From the night of 22 June there were several direct and indirect contacts between Patel and Cripps/Pethick-Lawrence. It is not clear whether the initiative for these contacts was Patel's or of the Britons or of the man serving as a go-between, Sudhir Ghosh, a young Bengali who had studied at Cambridge and built links with the Labour Party. Ghosh has claimed that it was his:

> I told Cripps and Pethick-Lawrence that the only advice I could give them about salvaging something out of the wreckage was that they should have a private talk with Patel, who was the only man amongst the Congress leaders who was a practical statesman.[90]

Gandhi rejected. Whoever initiated them, the private talks resulted in the Congress accepting 16 May. What happened, and how it happened, constitutes a less than glorious episode in the final stages of India's freedom effort. It can be pieced together from three diaries (of Gandhi's secretary Pyarelal, Patel's daughter Maniben, and the British Viceroy, Wavell), the account supplied by Ghosh, and HMG's Transfer of Power volumes.

23 Jun. At New Delhi's Gole Post Office roundabout, Sudhir Ghosh, sitting with Pethick-Lawrence in the latter's car, stops, just before 8 a.m., the car in which Patel is returning to Birla House (his lodgings) after a visit to Gandhi in the sweepers' colony. Patel gets inside P-L's [Pethick-Lawrence's] car while Ghosh moves into Patel's. Both cars go a mile or so to 2 Willingdon Crescent (in the Viceroy's grounds), where P-L and Alexander are staying.

Patel and the three ministers talk from 8 a.m. for about half-an-hour. Though he has met them earlier as part of the Congress team, this is the first time that Patel meets them by himself. He tells them that the Congress will reject 16 June; P-L tells him that in that case, given clause 8, Jinnah would be invited to help form a government. Patel asks if the Congress too would be invited if it accepted 16 May. P-L and Cripps assure him that it would. Without authority yet with absolute certainty, Patel says that the Congress will accept 16 May.

23 Jun., 9:30 a.m. At the Viceroy's House, P-L startles Wavell, who was all set to call Jinnah, by telling him that the Congress will reject 16 June but accept 16 May. At Azad's residence, Vallabhbhai tells Azad, Nehru, C R and Prasad that acceptance of 16 May would bring the invitation from the British. Power beckons.

23 Jun., late afternoon. A crisis. Telegrams from Assam and Bombay inform Congress leaders that the form candidates for the Constituent Assembly had to fill required a commitment to Para 19. Learning of this, Gandhi says to the Working Committee that 16 May 'now stinks'.[91]

Still the same day, 23 Jun., 10:30 p.m. Ghosh brings to Patel an ingenious solution by Cripps. The form would be altered to read 'for the purposes of the declaration of May 16' instead of 'for the purposes of Para 19'. Patel is satisfied, but would Gandhi agree?

24 Jun., 7 a.m. Patel takes Gandhi to 2 Willingdon Crescent to meet the three ministers. P-L assures Gandhi and Patel that if the Congress accepted 16 May they would, thanks to clause 8, 'put themselves on the level with the Muslim League in respect of the interim government' and could send in new names.[92] Gandhi brings up the telegrams from Assam and Bombay. Cripps spells out his solution, but P-L intervenes and says, 'No, that presents difficulty.'[93] All agree to meet again at 8 p.m., with Wavell also present. Patel is irritated when Gandhi tells him that P-L's intervention troubled him.[94]

24 Jun., 8 p.m. By now Cripps has persuaded P-L to accept his solution regarding Para 19. Gandhi again asks about Para 19. P-L assures him that Congress candidates to the Constituent Assembly do not have to accept compulsory grouping. Wavell intervenes and says that grouping is essential but P-L, the leader of the British team, asks Wavell 'not to press the point'.[95]

'Are you satisfied?' Patel asks Gandhi after the interview. 'On the contrary,' replies Gandhi. 'My suspicion has deepened.'[96] A 'much disquieted' Wavell asks P-L and Cripps whether the assurance to Gandhi was sincere, but is 'out-talked' by them.[97] Late in the evening the Mission issues an elucidation that candidates to the Constituent Assembly are 'not bound down in terms of Para 19'.[98]

Patel and other Working Committee members rejoice. Four years earlier, in 1942, Cripps had come close to detaching Nehru from Gandhi. This time he has detached Patel, and through him the rest.

24 Jun., 10 p.m. Gandhi writes to Cripps that while his colleagues are now ready to enter the Constituent Assembly, he proposes 'to advise the Working Committee not to accept the long-term proposition … I must not act against my instinct.'[99]

25 June, 8 a.m. The Working Committee meets. At Gandhi's instance Pyarelal reads the note to Cripps. It is heard in uncomfortable silence. Gandhi says: 'I admit defeat. You are not bound to act upon my unsupported suspicion … I shall now leave with your permission.'

A hush falls over the gathering. Nobody speaks for some time. Then Azad, with (as Pyarelal would write) 'his unfailing alertness', asks the others: 'What do you desire? Is there any need to detain Bapu any longer?' Everybody is silent. The silence is a message. And the message is to Gandhi. He gets up and leaves.[100]

Wavell, Cripps & Gandhi. Later that day (25 June) the Working Committee formally rejected 16 June and, going against Gandhi's advice, formally accepted 16 May, with its 'own interpretation' of disputed clauses. The Viceroy was shocked at the Congress's acceptance of 16 May, which he attributed to Cripps's 'instigation', and felt that Cripps and Patel had 'outmanoeuvred' him.[101]

As soon as he heard of the Congress's acceptance of 16 May, Jinnah informed Wavell that the League, which had already agreed to 16 May, was accepting 16 June as well, demanded rejection of the Congress's 'insincere' acceptance, and readied himself for the Viceroy's invitation.

Though Wavell considered asking Jinnah 'to form a government' without inviting the Congress, he did 'not see how this could possibly be done'.[102] He had to recognize the Congress's acceptance of 16 May even as he had recognized the League's, which too was premised on an interpretation. But he could not reconcile himself to Cripps, whom he credited with the skill 'to make both black and white appear a neutral and acceptable grey'.[103] When at the end of June the Mission finally left India, Wavell and Cripps did not exchange goodbyes.

The Viceroy disliked Gandhi as well. In 1947 he would write of Gandhi as an implacable foe of Empire and the 'most formidable' of the opponents 'who have detached portions of the British Empire in recent years'.[104] Worse in Wavell's eyes was Gandhi's claim that he bore no ill-will towards the British. The Viceroy did not believe it.

Response to rejection. Being snubbed by his colleagues was not pleasant for Gandhi. Though it had happened before – in 1939, 1940 and 1941 – the 1946 rebuff, occurring on the threshold of Swaraj, was starker. It would lead his colleagues to high office and Gandhi, in old age, to the wilderness.

Being discarded was not pleasant, yet once again Gandhi's response was to back the Working Committee before the Raj and the world. Four years earlier, over Quit India, he had dared his colleagues to defy him and go their way, and they had followed him. Now he was older, weaker, without Kasturba and Mahadev, and without any significant allies or support. When he first presented Quit India, public opinion was with him even if several on the Working Committee were not. Now the public too desired a quick transfer of power, not a scrutiny of how or to whom it should be transferred.

Nehru, Patel, Azad, C R, Prasad and company were 'sons' who with his approval had taken over from Gandhi. The impatience of these sons was hurtful, but Gandhi lacked an alternative set of successors. Persons like Jayaprakash and Lohia might have provided the nucleus for such a set, but the two had only just been released. Moreover, they espoused a socialism that Gandhi thought divisive and was wary of.

The colleagues rejecting him were India's best and represented the Congress mind. He would support them despite his wounds, despite his knowledge that a game of double-speak was being played on all sides – by the British, the Congress and the League – and despite his sense of violence in the air.

Loyal to the Congress for more than 50 years – from 1894, when he started the Natal Indian Congress – he would strengthen the Congress's position in the transition to independence. Like Yudhishthira in the *Mahabharata*, who suppressed qualms of conscience while assisting the Pandavas, he would assist the Congress to the best of his ability.

When, therefore, the AICC met in Bombay (7 July) to pronounce on the Working Committee's acceptance of 16 May, Gandhi asked for ratification. With this meeting, Nehru took over from Azad as the Congress head. Jayaprakash and other Congress socialists argued that the Constituent Assembly would be a trap. Gandhi, who had welcomed the released Jayaprakash as 'an outstanding general in India's fight for freedom' (91: 194), admitted that 'the darkness' he had felt in respect of 16 May had not lifted. Yet, he added:

> The Working Committee [members] are your faithful and tried servants. You should not lightly reject their resolution. I am willing to admit that the proposed Constituent Assembly is not the Parliament of the people. It has many defects. But you are all seasoned and veteran fighters … If there are shortcomings in the proposed Constituent Assembly, it is for you to get them removed (91: 250).

By 204 votes to 51, the AICC ratified the decision.

Attempt on his life. After the AICC meeting Gandhi journeyed for the third successive summer to Panchgani in Maharashtra's Sahyadri hills, and stayed there for three weeks. Earlier, on the night of 28 June, the train in which Gandhi was travelling bumped against boulders deliberately placed on the rails, between Neral and Karjat, not far from Bombay. He slept right through the bump and through two clanging hours of repairs that followed, and learnt only the following morning of what probably was an attempt on his life.

That day, while on the train, he wrote this 'thought for the day' for Anand Hingorani: 'Man ever lives in the jaws of Death. He is said to be dead when Death closes its jaws.'[105] A few days later, when he was shown a photograph of himself sound asleep on the train while mechanics were fixing it, he laughed and said: 'I see here how I will look after my death.'[106]

Jinnah & direct action

Cheated of a great prize at the last minute, Jinnah accused Cripps and Pethick-Lawrence of treachery, Wavell of betrayal, and the Congress of dishonesty. He said that Cripps had 'debased his talents' and placed 'a fantastic and dishonest construction' on clause 8,[107] and that it was totally unjust that both the Congress and the League should be invited to send new names for an interim government.

Though clause 8 was clear, and its application to both the League and the Congress legitimate, Jinnah's wrath was understandable. Calling him 'a great Indian and the recognized leader of a great organization', Gandhi seems to have remarked at this time that Jinnah should have been treated better by the Mission.[108] But if the 'purposely vague' language of 16 May lay at the root of Jinnah's discomfiture, the Congress (like the League) had sought to take advantage of it, and, like Yudhisthira, Gandhi too had gone along.

The bitterness produced by the ambiguity of 16 May was sharpened by indiscreet remarks that Nehru made on 10 July. Jawaharlal told a press conference in Bombay that the Congress would be 'completely unfettered by agreements'; that the Union government was 'likely to be much stronger than what the Cabinet Mission envisaged'; that the western Muslim Group would 'collapse' because the NWFP would not join; and that Assam would not join the eastern Muslim Group 'under any circumstances whatever'.[109]

Jinnah, up in arms, claimed that Nehru's remarks constituted 'a complete repudiation' of 16 May and demanded that Britain should 'remove the impression' that the Congress had accepted 16 May.[110] Patel said privately that Nehru's statement was 'an act of emotional insanity',[111] and in a letter from Panchgani (17 July) Gandhi reproved his heir:

Your statement does not sound good. It must be admitted that we have to work within the limits of the State Paper [the 16 May document] ... If we do not admit even this much, we will be doing nothing and Jinnah Saheb's accusation will prove true (91: 297).

Passions spilled out onto the streets in some cities. On occasion it was bravely confronted. Two close friends who had taken part earlier in Gandhi-initiated satyagrahas, Vasantrao Hegishte, a 40-year-old Hindu, and Rajab Ali Lakhani, a 27-year-old Muslim, lost their lives on 1 July 1946 while together attempting to quell a mob in Ahmedabad.

When Jinnah's demand was not met by the Raj, the League revoked (on 29 July, in Bombay) its acceptance of 16 May, asked Muslims to return titles bestowed by the Raj, and announced 'Direct Action' to achieve Pakistan. 'Today we bid goodbye to constitutional methods,' said Jinnah. The Congress, he added, had always employed the weapon of mass struggle, and the British held 'authority and arms', but now 'we have also forged a pistol and are in a position to use it'.[112] August 16th was declared Direct Action Day.

Asked if Direct Action would be non-violent or violent, Jinnah replied, 'I am not going to discuss ethics.' Lesser leaders said that Muslims were 'not believers in Ahimsa'. A 'council of action' appointed by the League drew up a programme that used the language of jihad; leaflets, whether authorized by the League or not, spoke of clashes between Muslims and heathens; and the chief minister of Bengal, Hassan Shaheed Suhrawardy of the League, declared that if the Congress was put in power at the centre, Bengal would rebel.[113]

Direct Action triggered mayhem in Calcutta that the Suhrawardy ministry was unwilling or unable to prevent. On the first day, hundreds of Hindus were killed as thousands of youths armed with lathis and daggers and shouting slogans for Pakistan roamed the city. In the next three or four days, Hindus retaliated and an even larger number of Muslims were killed. *The Statesman*, British-owned, which had defended Jinnah in his dispute with Wavell, wrote of what became known as the Great Calcutta Killing:

20 Aug. 1946: The origin of the appalling carnage – we believe the worst communal riot in India's history – was a political demonstration by the Muslim League.

Gandhi's worst fears were coming true, but, back now in Sevagram, he did not know what he could do. In a statement (19 August) he called for refraining from retaliation, said that if the madness went on Calcutta 'will cease to be the City of Palaces, it will become the city of the dead', and added:

Would that the violence of Calcutta were sterilized and did not become a signal for its spread all over. It depends upon the leaders of the Muslim League of course, but the rest will not be free from responsibility (91: 45).

Once more airing forebodings of spreading violence, Gandhi, however, said that for ending riots Hindus and Muslims should turn to their own resources, not to 'the British authority' which, though weakening, was capable of extending its rule in the name of restoring peace.[114] Even for peace he would not embrace the Empire.

Confrontation with Wavell. On 24 August the composition of the interim government was announced. Seven of the twelve names were from the Congress: Nehru, Patel, C R, Prasad, Sarat Bose (Subhas's older brother), Jagjivan Ram, the Dalit leader from Bihar, and Asaf Ali, a Muslim. Two non-Congress Muslims (Ali Zaheer and Shafaat Ahmed Khan) and three others from outside the Congress, John Matthai (a Christian), Baldev Singh (a Sikh) and C H Bhabha (a Parsi) completed the list. Keeping Gandhi informed but not seeking his advice, Nehru and Patel had together chosen the team, and Wavell accepted it for the time being.

Three days later (27 Aug.), he invited Gandhi, who had returned to Delhi, and Nehru to talk with him at the Viceroy's House. The meeting was a disaster. The Viceroy showed Gandhi and Nehru a prepared statement that he wanted them to sign. The statement committed the Congress to accept the League's interpretation of 16 May, which the Viceroy said was also his and that of HMG.

He was a plain man and a soldier, not a lawyer, Wavell said, and did not wish to debate the intricacies of 16 May. If they signed the statement, the League too would be able to enter the interim government. If they did not sign, continued Wavell, riots would escalate. Also, he would not then convene the Constituent Assembly that 16 May had spelt out and initiated.

Gandhi and Nehru replied that the text of 16 May supported the Congress's reading. 'The argument went on for some time, and Nehru got very heated,' Wavell would note in his diary. According to Penderel Moon, the editor of the Viceroy's diary, 'Lord Wavell always used to say that on this occasion Gandhi thumped the table and said, "If India wants her bloodbath, she shall have it."' Wavell seems to have responded by saying that he was 'very shocked to hear such words' from Gandhi.[115]

The typed statement ready for signature and the threat of not convening the Assembly had clearly offended Gandhi, but even an unprovoked Gandhi would have rejected an Empire-imposed peace. The next morning, writing a letter to Wavell from his room in the sweepers' colony, Gandhi charged that Wavell had shown a 'minatory' attitude. For the Congress to let the Calcutta killings change its stand would only lead, he said, to 'an encouragement and repetition of such tragedies'. The letter added that Wavell should feel free to withdraw his invitation to Nehru and the rest to join his government – and should obtain for himself a legal aide. The last sentence read: 'You will please convey the whole of this letter to the British Cabinet' (92: 73).

Wavell did not implement his threats. The invitation to Nehru and company was not withdrawn: early in September the new ministers were sworn in, with Nehru taking the external affairs portfolio and Patel home. And the Constituent Assembly too was duly convened. But, with Nehru's consent, Wavell persisted in his bid to induct the League.

Before being sworn in at Viceroy's House on 2 September, Vallabhbhai, Sarat Bose, Rajendra Prasad and Jagjivan Ram called on Gandhi in the sweepers' colony for his blessing. Amrit Kaur garlanded them with yarn spun by Gandhi. It being his silent day, he scribbled out a message:

> Abolish salt tax, remember Dandi March, bring together Hindus and Muslims, remove untouchability, adopt khadi (92: 102).

A few days later, when a Christian missionary asked if an independent India would have a state religion, Gandhi gave this reply:

> If I were a dictator, religion and State would be separate. I swear by my religion. I will die for it. But it is my personal affair. The State has nothing to do with it. The State would look after your secular welfare, health, communications, foreign relations, currency and so on, but not your or my religion. That is everybody's personal concern (92: 190).

Noakhali & the Muslim League. On 15 October Gandhi was greatly troubled on hearing that Hindus in the district of Noakhali in East Bengal, a small minority amidst a large Muslim majority, were being attacked. That evening he said at his prayer meeting:

> Ever since I heard the news of Noakhali, indeed ever since the blood-bath of Calcutta, I have been wondering where my duty lies. God will show me the way. But I want to tell you and through you a wider public that it is the duty of every Hindu not to harbour any thoughts of revenge on Muslims in spite of ... Noakhali.[116]

The next day, he learnt that the Muslim League had agreed to enter the interim government – and that its five-member team would include a Hindu, an 'untouchable' leader from Bengal called Jogendra Nath Mandal. In the evening Gandhi said:

> I cannot sense any generosity in the nomination of a Harijan by the Muslim League in their quota of five seats especially when I read of what is happening in East Bengal.

A man like myself ought to be glad, you may say, that another seat has been given to a Harijan. But I would be deceiving myself and Mr Jinnah if I say so. Mr Jinnah has … been of the opinion that Muslims and Hindus are two nations. How then can [the League] nominate a Harijan to represent them?

I fear that the League's mode of entrance into the Cabinet has not been straight. I am therefore forced to wonder whether they have come into the Cabinet also to fight (92: 335–6).

A Hindu Leaguer – Jinnah's answer to Asaf Ali, the Congress Muslim – was not only a clever move; including a Hindu Harijan from Bengal in the League's quota could also strengthen a bid to claim all of Bengal for Pakistan.

Gandhi urged Nehru and Patel to make an issue of Mandal's nomination with the Viceroy, but they demurred. Their priority, they said, was to prevent Wavell from transferring the home portfolio to the League. Patel was able to retain home, but from its start the interim government became what Gandhi had feared, 'an incompatible mixture' and a house at war.

While the Congress ministers continued to challenge Groups, the League made clear its opposition to the Union envisaged by 16 May. Ghazanfar Ali Khan, one of the new ministers from the League, said frankly in Lahore: 'We are going into the interim government to get a foothold to fight for our cherished goal of Pakistan.'[117]

Liaqat Ali Khan headed the League team, for Jinnah, unwilling to be ranked below Nehru, had kept himself out. To make room for the League, Sarat Bose, Ali Zaheer and Shafaat Ahmed Khan left the government, which now had 14 ministers.

In January 1947 Azad replaced Asaf Ali in the council after Ali was named ambassador to Washington. Earlier, with Gandhi's concurrence, Kripalani had been elected Congress president to succeed Nehru, who resigned the party post on assuming governmental office.[118]

Departure for Noakhali. Conscious of his age, Gandhi planned each day in the sweepers' colony with care, giving precise thought to what he should eat, drink and do. As before, listening to visitors and writing to associates or for *Harijan* took up most of his time. To each conversation and chore he tried to give his best. 'You must watch my life,' he told a visiting missionary in September, 'how I live, eat, sit, talk, behave in general. The sum total … is my religion' (92: 190).

But he had little left to do in New Delhi, where his successors, about to be joined by the League, had taken over. He contemplated returning to Sevagram and/or to Uruli-Kanchan, but chose instead to go to Noakhali.

The League's strategy of uniting Muslims and 'untouchables' played a role in this decision: Gandhi wished to counter it by uniting Bengal's Hindus and Muslims. But he

On the way, in Simla, to see the Viceroy – 1945

was also influenced by the violence in Noakhali and the adjacent district of Tippera. He had heard of scores, perhaps hundreds, killed. There were reports, too, that 'women were being carried away, abducted and converted to Islam' (92: 344).

From February Gandhi had given expression to a sense of coming violence. In August, the Calcutta killings demanded an answer. Now, in October, Noakhali had occurred – in retaliation, it seemed, for the second phase of the Calcutta killings. How should he respond? Pyarelal thought that Gandhi was holding 'a silent court within himself'.[119]

He recalled the 1931 martyrdom for Hindu-Muslim unity of Ganesh Shankar Vidyarthi in Kanpur, the recent sacrificial deaths in Ahmedabad of Rajab Ali and Vasantrao, and, in Bombay, of another Hindu-Muslim duo, unnamed, who also braved the fury of a maddened crowd and (in Gandhi's description) 'went down together literally clasped in a fatal embrace but refused to desert each other' (92: 346).

'On or before 18 October' two associates from Bengal called on him, Satis Chandra Dasgupta, a scientist and inventor influenced by Gandhi who ran a khadi ashram near Calcutta, and Satin Sen. Both expressed willingness to go to Noakhali. In his remarks to them, Gandhi touched on 'Jesus's example' of 'perfect sacrifice':

A man who was completely innocent offered himself as a sacrifice for the good of others, including his enemies, and became the ransom of the world. It was a perfect act. 'It is finished' were the last words of Jesus, and we have the testimony of his four disciples as to its authenticity. But whether the Jesus tradition is historically true or not, I do not care. To me it is truer than history because I hold it to be possible and it enshrines an eternal law – the law of vicarious and innocent suffering taken in its true sense (92: 345–6).

'Go forth, therefore,' Gandhi said to the Bengali co-workers, who spoke of their readiness to die. 'Let there be no foolhardiness about it,' Gandhi added. 'You should go because you feel you must and not because I ask you to.' 'That goes without saying,' the two replied.[120]

On 17 October he expressed appreciation that Sarat Bose, though ill, was visiting his Bengal province, and that Kripalani, the new Congress president, and Kripalani's Bengali wife Sucheta were going to Noakhali 'to do what they could to stop the slaughter'. 'They were not going there to protect one party,' said Gandhi, 'but to stop the fratricidal warfare' (92: 344).

But he could not resist a call to go there himself. When 'a very esteemed friend' (which is how Pyarelal describes him, without giving his name) tried to persuade Gandhi not to travel at his age to a far, isolated and hazardous area, Gandhi explained his helplessness against 'the spontaneous urge which he felt within him to go to the people of Noakhali':

> I do not know what I shall be able to do there. All I know is that I won't be at peace with myself unless I go there.
>
> There are two kinds of thoughts – idle and active. There may be myriads of the former swarming in one's brain. They do not count. But one pure, active thought proceeding from the depth and endowed with all the undivided intensity of one's being, becomes dynamic and works like a fertilized ovum (Conversation 'on or before 28 October,' *Harijan*, 10 Nov. 1946; 92: 423).

Giving up the Sevagram/Uruli plan, he would also skip the Congress's annual session, scheduled for November in Meerut in western UP. This was not a minor decision, for he knew that much could hang on the lead the Congress gave. Yet Nehru or Patel or Kripalani, the new president, had not asked him to Meerut.

This may have been a factor, but what pulled him towards Noakhali was something much deeper. It was almost as if he suspected that all the journeys in his life so far – by ship, by train, on foot – were but a preparation for this journey to Noakhali.

Claiming that he was going 'as God's servant', not 'to pass judgement on anybody' but to 'wipe the tears' of Bengal's women and 'put heart into them if he could', Gandhi boarded a train for Calcutta on 28 October 1946.[121]

In Noakhali – 1946 (Original photo: G D Tendulkar)

15

Walk Alone ...

East Bengal, 1946–7

Swaraj seemed round the corner in October 1946. Leaders of popular parties had at last occupied governing positions in New Delhi. Yet the forebodings felt by Gandhi had touched others as well. In their anxious enthusiasm, many looked to Gandhi, who had just passed his 77th birthday.

At railway stations in UP and Bihar on his way to Calcutta, crowds converged onto Gandhi's train, clambered to the carriage-roof, blocked the windows, pulled the communication cord, and shouted, demanding his darshan. Gandhi plugged his ears with his fingers but turned down a suggestion to switch off the lights in the compartment: people should be able to see him if they wanted to, he said.[1] Despite the din, he managed to write a dozen or more letters and a few *Harijan* pieces on the train.

One of Gandhi's goals in Calcutta – his base for proceeding by train and boat to Noakhali – was to befriend Shaheed Suhrawardy (1892–1963), the Bengal premier who belonged to the Muslim League, and get him to do more to restore the security of Hindus in the eastern districts. During the Khilafat days young Suhrawardy had called Gandhi 'Bapu' (father); now, at the end of October 1946, he urged Gandhi to delay his departure for Noakhali. Calcutta, he said, also needed Gandhi's presence.

Assured by Suhrawardy that fresh attacks on Noakhali's Hindus would be prevented, Gandhi paused in Satis Dasgupta's khadi ashram in Sodepur on the outskirts of Calcutta. In the city he saw legacies of the August violence: entire streets of gutted shops and burnt-down houses, and high piles of garbage.

While waiting for the journey to Noakhali, Gandhi learnt of large-scale killings of Muslims in Bihar, a province to which he had been attached from the days of the 1917 Champaran satyagraha. Nehru flew to Bihar along with Patel and two League colleagues in the council, Liaqat Ali and Abdur Rab Nishtar; Rajendra Prasad and Jayaprakash made themselves active in their province; and a shaken Gandhi also wondered whether he should not go to Bihar instead of Noakhali. Though deciding to keep to his plan, he announced he would fast unto death if the Bihar violence, portrayed as avenging Noakhali, did not cease.

At this time Gandhi thought his end was not far off, and said as much in a number of letters he wrote between 3 and 6 November, addressed to or for his ashram associates (Mashruwala, Vinoba, Kalelkar and others), his political colleagues (Nehru, Patel, C R, Azad, Prasad), his 'sisters' and 'daughters' (including Amrit Kaur and Lilavati Asar), and his son Devadas.

They must remain where they were if he fasted, he wrote, and remain strong if he died. If some were not named in his letters, he explained, it was because he had no time, not because he had forgotten them. No one should worry over him; he was with a competent team.

However, he wanted one more person — someone in particular — to join him. To Jaisukhlal, the father of Manu, his 19-year-old grand-niece, Gandhi wrote (4 Nov.) of his hope that she would come to Noakhali, saying he needed her support (92: 440–51). He had been encouraged by a letter from Manu in October. We do not have its text, but in reply Gandhi had written (from Delhi):

11 Oct. 1946. Chi. Manudi, I have gone through your letter. I gave it to Sushila Pai, Kanu, Sushila (Dr) and Pyarelal to read. Here I shall tell you only this, that I liked your letter. Further, I shall be happy if you come over and have a talk with me. I do not wish to put any pressure on you. It is my earnest desire that you should remain a pure virgin till the end of your life and spend your life in service. I hope Umiya's son [*Umiya was Manu's older sister*] is doing well. Blessings to all from Bapu (92: 310).

He clearly wanted Manu near him, and said to colleagues that he wished to develop her and also explore Manu's possible marriage with Pyarelal, now 46, who was in love with her.[2] But there was another reason. Convincing himself of a link between chastity and non-violence, and of the power of the perfectly chaste to melt surrounding violence, Gandhi intended to strengthen his brahmacharya and that of his grand-niece, who also seemed resolved on it.

'To Bihar.' Reports that Bihar's Congress ministers had been indifferent or worse in face of the killings angered Gandhi and figured in an open letter from him that was published in the press and dropped by air in areas that had seen the violence:

'To Bihar', 6 Nov. 1946: You should not rest till every Muslim refugee has come back

to his home which you should undertake to rebuild and ask your Ministers to help you to do so. You do not know what critics have said to me about your Ministers.

What you have done is to degrade yourselves and drag down India ... I regard myself as a part of you. Your affection has compelled that loyalty in me ... I cannot rest till I have done some measure of penance...

I had put myself on the lowest diet possible soon after my reaching Calcutta. That diet now continues as a penance after the knowledge of the Bihar tragedy. The low diet will become a fast unto death, if the erring Biharis have not turned over a new leaf ...

No friend should run to me for assistance or to show sympathy. I am surrounded by loving friends ... Let no one be anxious for me, I am like all of us in God's keeping (92: 451–2).

The letter and its threat of a fast had an effect, as did the exertions of the central ministers camping in Bihar, and the killings ceased, but at least 7,000 Muslims had perished in Bihar.[3]

Noakhali. On 6 November a special train arranged by Suhrawardy took Gandhi and his party to Goalando in eastern Bengal. Also on the train were Shamsuddin, Bengal's minister for commerce, and Nasrullah Khan, the premier's parliamentary secretary. At Goalando, Gandhi and his party boarded the steamship *Kiwi* for an 80-mile river journey that brought them to Chandpur, a town at the western edge of the Tippera/Noakhali region.

Crisscrossed by waterways, Noakhali's green countryside was lush from recent rains. Trees, mostly coconut and areca-nut palms, shaded its winding paths, and the November weather was pleasant. However, London, New Delhi and Meerut, cities where India's independence was being designed, were far from Noakhali and seemed out of reach, as did even Calcutta; and the charming landscape was stained with violence.

Noakhali district had 1,800,000 Muslims and 400,000 Hindus. The latter were much better off, owning land and predominating in the professions but unmindful of grievances nursed around them. Anti-Hindu sentiment acquired a sharp edge in 1946, and when tales of violence against Calcutta's Muslims arrived in Noakhali, groups of local Muslims exploded in cruel attacks on the minority. They were encouraged by a few religious leaders in a region that seemed to specialize in Islamic theology: Noakhali sent out hundreds of teachers of Islam to all parts of the subcontinent.

Gandhi saw this part of Bengal (he called the province India's 'nerve centre')[4] as the right place for grappling afresh with a question dogging him right from boyhood: Hindu-Muslim relations at ground-level. For Swaraj he had crafted a sequence of brilliant if not always lasting political alliances between Hindus and Muslims, and more than once he had fasted for reconciliation in India's countless villages and towns. Yet Swaraj's compulsions had often pushed the latter goal to one side. Now, with Swaraj almost achieved but Hindus and Muslims trapped in mistrust, nothing was more vital than restoring relations on the ground. If this could be done in a province claimed for Pakistan, Indian unity too might be saved.

Muslims meeting Gandhi on the *Kiwi* in Chandpur told him that killings and forced conversions in Noakhali and Tippera did not add up to a large number and that only a small minority of the Muslim population had joined in the violence. Gandhi replied that a fence-sitting majority was as guilty as actual attackers, and even a single case of abduction, forcible conversion or forcible marriage was bad enough.

When Hindus talking separately to him on the boat complained that Muslims had not condemned the violence, Gandhi countered by asking if Hindu males had been manly enough:

> I have heard nothing but condemnation of these acts from Shaheed Suhrawardy downwards since I have come here. Words of condemnation may tickle your ears, but they are no consolation to the unfortunate women whose houses have been laid desolate or who have been abducted, forcibly converted and forcibly married. What a shame for Hindus, what a disgrace for Islam!
>
> No, I am not going to leave you in peace. Presently you will say to yourselves, 'When will this man leave us and go?' But this man will not go. He did not come on your invitation and he will go only on his own, but with your blessings, when his mission in East Bengal is fulfilled (93: 2).

So courage was going to be as much his contribution as solace. After a night on the boat at Chandpur, Gandhi and his party took a train for Chaumuhani, where, led by Charu Chowdhury, a team from the Sodepur ashram had arrived earlier to prepare the ground. Though the town of Chaumuhani had remained peaceful, villages around it had seen violence in October.

Frankness. Eighty per cent of the 15,000 or so attending Gandhi's prayer meeting in Chaumuhani on 7 November were Muslims. Gandhi's words to them were friendly but frank:

> I have not come to excite the Hindus to fight the Muslims. I have no enemies. I have fought the British all my life. Yet they are my friends. I have never wished them ill.
>
> I have heard of forcible conversions, forcible feeding of beef, abductions and forcible marriages, not to talk about murders, arson and loot. People have broken idols.

Muslims do not worship idols. Neither do I. But why should they interfere with those who wished to worship them? These incidents are a blot on the name of Islam.

I have studied the Koran. The very word Islam means peace. The Muslim greeting 'Salam Alaikum' is the same for all, whether Hindus or Muslims or any other. Nowhere does Islam allow such things as had happened in Noakhali and Tippera.

Shaheed Saheb and all the Ministers and League leaders who met me in Calcutta have condemned such acts unequivocally. The Muslims are in such overwhelming majority in East Bengal that I expect them to constitute themselves the guardians of the small Hindu minority. They should tell Hindu women that as long as they are there, no one dare cast an evil eye on them (93: 9–10).

At the start of the Noakhali mission Gandhi's party included, among others, Pyarelal, Sushila, Sucheta Kripalani, Amtus Salaam, Sushila Pai, Amritlal Thakkar, Kanu Gandhi, Abha, Nirmal Kumar Bose, an anthropology professor from Calcutta who translated for Gandhi, Parasuram from Kerala, who served as Gandhi's stenographer, and Prabhudas, an office assistant. Salaam was the only Muslim in the group.

After three nights in Chaumuhani, Gandhi shifted his camp to the village of Dattapara, where 6,000 Hindu refugees had taken shelter. It was a shame, he said there, that some human beings had caused fear, and others had given way to it. But he could not ask Hindus to return to their homes until at least one good Muslim and one good Hindu accompanied them and stood surety for them. To a prayer-meeting audience of Muslims and Hindus he said (10 Nov.):

I want you to forgive and forget what had happened. That does not mean that you should become cowards. But it serves no useful purpose to keep on recalling the unpleasant past.

I have not come here to fight Pakistan. If India is destined to be partitioned, I cannot prevent it. But I wish to tell you that Pakistan can't be established by force.[5]

Walking to the nearby village of Noakhala (11 Nov.), he saw the skulls and charred remains of the victims. The next day, in Nandigram, he looked at a desecrated temple, the ruins of hundreds of burnt-down homes, and the ashes of what had been the village school, a hostel and a hospital.

But he knew that Bihar was witnessing similar or worse inhumanities. To Rajendra Prasad he wrote (12 Nov.), 'If the Bihar fury does not abate, I do not wish to remain alive because my life would then be meaningless' (93: 23). And in a letter written the same day to Jayaprakash, who had toiled valiantly on behalf of Bihar's Muslims, he said, 'Will

With Abha Gandhi and Sushila Nayar – 1947

Bihar really become calm? ... Write to me frankly what is likely to happen now. Give me your unreserved opinion' (93: 22).

On 13 November Gandhi's party moved to Kazirkhil village, where Dasgupta's tireless workers had turned a devastated house into a habitable base. From here the party visited the village of Dasgharia, where Gandhi was met by Hindu women who had returned to their faith after being forced to become Muslims. To Gandhi's relief, the district magistrate, a Scot called McInerney, had ruled that forced conversions were illegal, but not all had the courage to return to their faith and families.

To Muslim audiences Gandhi quoted with appreciation a recent statement by Jinnah. Vengeance and retaliation, Jinnah had said, were against Islam and inimical to the hope of Pakistan. 'In the Pakistan areas,' Jinnah added, 'minorities will have fullest security of life, property, and honour just as the Muslims, nay even greater.'[6] But by now Muslims were being warned to stay away from Gandhi's meetings and prayers.

On Suhrawardy's instructions, guards from Bengal's police force accompanied Gandhi as he moved about – the premier did not want to risk an attack on his uninvited guest. Gandhi was unhappy about this security but helpless. Fear was at the root of Bengal's tragedy, he said. Even the greed of the attacker sprang from fear; and the best revenge was to do good to the one who harmed you.

'*Ekla Chalo Re*'. At Kazirkhil Gandhi announced a plan for giving courage to local Hindus. He would split up his group and send each of the party to a different village, to live there amidst a Muslim majority. If the person feared or disliked Muslims, he or she could go back, Gandhi said. The companions thus took on a village each, assisted where necessary by a Bengali-speaking worker from Sodepur.

Pyarelal took on Bhatialpur, his sister Sushila set up a clinic in Changirgaon, Amtus Salaam based herself in Sirandi, Sushila Pai in Karpara. Kanu went to Ramdevpur, his wife Bengali wife Abha, supported by Thakkar Bapa, to Haimchar. Prabhudas settled in Parkote. Accompanied by Bose and Parasuram, Gandhi himself would go to Srirampur. Since most of the adopted villages were close to one another and covered by the same police station (Ramganj), the dispersed workers could quite easily walk to one another and between them hope to impact an integrated block of 20 or so square miles.

After seven nights in Kazirkhil, Gandhi, Bose and Parasuram left (20 Nov.) for the village of Srirampur, a two-hour boat trip. They and their associates in the other villages would aim to impart fearlessness to the Hindus of Noakhali and remorse to its Muslims.

'If you want to know yourself, go forth alone.' This, Gandhi said, was his message to himself and his companions.[7] Cutting himself off from intimate companions was for him a hard step: we know that their company was Gandhi's security and delight.

But the victims' suffering called for the break-up; separation and isolation would throw him and his companions more fully into God's arms. East Bengal would now be the isolated Gandhi's home and workplace. He had become, he said, a Bengali. Even *Harijan* should not now expect regular articles from him or Pyarelal. Mashruwala, Vinoba, Kalelkar and Narhari Parikh were asked to edit the journal between them.

Srirampur. A cottage near palm trees had been found for Gandhi and his two aides in Srirampur, a village that had seen destruction. After making his bed on a wooden bedstead and arranging his books beside it, Gandhi held an evening prayer on open ground in which Hindus and Muslims joined. Within days Hindus from Srirampur and nearby villages began to move about freely, to chant their sacred words, even to sound their drums and cymbals. Dead souls were returning to life.

Thirty Hindus and Muslims of the Ramganj thana met in Srirampur with Gandhi and Shamsuddin, the commerce minister, and drew up a plan for restoring harmony that included peace committees in every village. On 23 November the plan was approved at a public meeting in Chandipur village at which Gandhi asked the Hindus to give the League ministry a chance to repair its image.

Every day Bose, whose aid Gandhi had specially solicited, gave Bengali lessons to the old man in Srirampur, his latest 'ashram'. Gandhi rose at or before four, read and wrote (on the bedstead) by the light of a kerosene lamp, did his spinning, conducted two prayer meetings a day, walked on dew-soaked paths to take his message to adjacent villages, added coconut to his diet, and practised nature-cure (mud packs on the forehead and abdomen, sunbaths) on himself and the villagers – Doctor Gandhi was once more enthusiastic about his practice.

But he also kept a steady if remote eye on the larger political picture, and pondered the next step in the Noakhali mission. This was soon clarified. Once the rice-fields were dry, Gandhi decided, he would walk from village to village across Noakhali and Tippera. Meanwhile, he said to Mira in a long letter (4 Dec. 1946), his work in Noakhali felt 'new, very pleasant, [and] equally taxing' (93: 98).

Chastity test

Another step, a personal one, had also clarified for Gandhi. Having heard from Manu and her father that she would be joining him, he resolved on a brahmacharya test in Noakhali, with Manu as his partner. He had discussed the idea with some (Pyarelal, Bose, Devadas, C R and possibly others) and would later discuss it with several more, but more to inform than to consult. Most thought the plan dangerous or crazy; all felt he was giving himself an avoidable burden; and many believed that valuable reputations were at risk: his own and his associates', and the reputations of their common undertakings.

Gandhi himself had no doubts. To address the violence around him he had to summon

With grandniece Manu in Calcutta – 15 August 1947

his chastity. This time it would be not an experiment but a 'yagna' (or 'yajna'), a sacrificial offering of his sexuality to God. He would feel equal to the Noakhali challenge, which was the challenge of violence in independence-eve India, if neither he nor Manu felt the sexual urge despite sharing the same bed. Rather than prove a distraction – a waste of time, thought and energy – the 'yagna', he claimed, would purify him, oblige him to pray more ardently, help him focus with all his being on the Noakhali task.

On 19 December, after he had been a month in Srirampur, Manu arrived. He asked her about the test he had in mind; she agreed to take part, adding that she was willing also to face death in Noakhali. The 'yagna' started right away, after midnight. A few hours later he wrote a note to her:

> Stick to your word. Don't hide even a single thought from me. Give a true answer to whatever I ask. The step that I took today was taken after careful thinking. Give me in writing what effect it had on your mind. I shall certainly reveal all my thoughts to you (93: 165).

Yet a chastity test was not the sole reason for wanting Manu near him. In letters to associates written on 26 December and 1 January, Gandhi admitted that it was 'attachment' – 'ignorant attachment' he called it in one of the letters – that kept Manu near him.[8] Though he wanted to face Noakhali (and himself) absolutely alone, though he had asked his associates to remain each on their own, he on his part not only had the support of Bose (to translate and teach Bengali) and Parasuram (to type), he also now had Manu, to cook and serve him and assist him in all his chores. (She also took down his remarks at interviews or meetings.)

He felt guilty about this attachment or dependence but did not shed it. The brave old man needed young Manu's company, touch and warmth, apart from the assistance she provided. With her, as before with other 'sisters', he relaxed, teased, allowed himself to be teased, laughed, and forgot his crushing load.

But as his partner in brahmacharya Manu also strengthened him to carry that load. So Gandhi claimed at any rate, and it is of some interest that the claim was endorsed by Pyarelal and Bose, who watched him constantly – Bose more than Pyarelal, who at this juncture seemed to divide his time between Bhatialpur and Srirampur. Pyarelal would later write extensively about Gandhi's brahmacharya in his biography, and Bose wrote frankly and critically of it in *My Days with Gandhi* (first published in 1953). Although Bose remained uneasy about the impact of Gandhi's experiments on the women who participated in them, he accepted Gandhi's linkage of brahmacharya with his battle for peace. And while not convinced of the soundness of Gandhi's step, Bose seemed satisfied as to its integrity. If it was a mask for lust, Bose would have been the first to know and the first to unmask Gandhi. Fortunately for Gandhi, it was the critical 46-year-old professor often disagreeing with him who recorded and analyzed the old man's unusual doings in Noakhali.

Though based now in different villages, Gandhi's 'party' knew of what was happening. The thin 'door' to his cottage-room was always open. On most nights, moreover, Gandhi's bedstead was used by a third person as well. Thus he wrote to Vallabhbhai on 25 December that his bedstead was large enough for three: Sucheta Kripalani, Gandhi added, lay asleep on one portion of it; he himself was lying down on another part but also dictating in a low voice; and Manu, presumably sitting on the bed, was taking down the letter (93: 186–7).

His close friends across the country also knew of his 'yagna'; Gandhi spoke of it to several of his visitors and wrote about it in many of his letters. The journalists covering him in Noakhali came to know, and we must assume that Suhrawardy and his police, as well as the British, now in the Empire's endgame, also knew.

There was an early casualty. Parasuram, whose efficient, silent service as a stenographer Gandhi had repeatedly praised, felt he could not continue his work unless Gandhi ceased the practice. We do not have the text of Parasuram's evidently long letter of protest, but after reading it between 3 and 4 a.m. on 2 January, Gandhi wrote to him:

> I cannot concede your demands ... Since such is my opinion and there is a conflict of ideals and you yourself wish to be relieved, you are at liberty to leave me today ... I like your frankness and boldness ...
>
> I shall always be interested in your future and shall be glad to hear from you when you feel like writing to me. Finally let me tell you that you are at liberty to publish whatever wrong you have noticed in me and my surroundings. Needless to say you can take what money you need to cover your expenses (93: 224–5).

Also upset following Manu's arrival in Noakhali was Sushila, who was shuttling between Changirgaon and Srirampur; in turn, as in the late 1930s, Gandhi became unhappy at Sushila's sadness. Early one morning Bose was startled to hear the sound of a slap coming from Gandhi's room. Running, he found that Gandhi had hit himself during an argument with Sushila.

But the distress of the two was short-lived, for Sushila had to focus on what she had taken on. To Gandhi's joy, her work won the confidence of Hindus and Muslims alike in Changirgaon and around, and some of the property looted from Changirgaon's Hindus was returned.

For all his keenness to 'understand' the 'yagna', Bose found himself unwilling to translate Gandhi's words into Bengali when, for the first time, he spoke publicly of it.

This was at a prayer meeting on 1 February 1947 in the village of Amishapara. Referring to 'small-talks, whispers and innuendos' going round, Gandhi said that he did not want his 'most innocent acts to be misunderstood and misrepresented'. Gandhi added:

> I have my granddaughter with me. She shares the same bed with me. The Prophet had discounted eunuchs who became such by an operation. But he welcomed eunuchs made such through prayer by God. This is my aspiration ...
>
> I know that my action has excited criticism even among friends. But a duty cannot be shirked even for the sake of the most intimate friends (93: 356).

Bose did not translate these sentences. Far away in Ahmedabad, Mashruwala and Narhari Parikh removed them from *Harijan*'s report of the speech. They were among the 'intimate friends' who hoped to persuade Gandhi to abandon the 'test'. Meanwhile they would put a lid on it.

In an indirect reference to his 'yagna', Gandhi recalled (27 Dec.) the ancient Hindu view, spelt out in one of Patanjali's sutras, that 'when ahimsa had been fully established, it would completely liquidate the forces of enmity and evil in the neighbourhood'. He said he had first come across this thought long ago, when he did not know Sanskrit, through a friend 'who used to carry Patanjali's *Yogasutra* constantly in his pocket'.

Though Gandhi did not name the friend, it was probably Rajchandra. Since, added Gandhi, his ahimsa had not dispelled the violence around him, he had to examine himself (93: 203). Bose one day overheard Gandhi saying to an associate about brahmacharya, 'If I can master this, I can still beat Jinnah.'[9]

In her diary Manu entered Gandhi's remarks in Noakhali about chastity. He told her that the life of one who kept his body as 'a holy temple for God' would speak as 'a poem of exquisite spiritual beauty,' and 'a full-blown flower of perfection' would banish communal hate.[10] Interestingly enough, the ascetic employs metaphors of poem, flower and beauty.

Here we must mark a resemblance between Gandhi's Noakhali trek and his march 40 years earlier in the Zulu country. Both occurred amidst memorable scenes, with Noakhali's network of rivers matching Zululand's hills and glens. Both brought Gandhi face to face with wounded humanity. As in the Zulu country, people in Noakhali turned to him with appealing eyes. He saw himself as a soldier in both terrains; and both exercises involved brahmacharya, embraced in Zululand and now daringly tested in East Bengal.

Mothering and being mothered. In February 1947 he said to Manu: 'Here I want to be tested to the fullest extent possible. If I fail the examination it will be under God. I want no testimony apart from God's. If there is any deceit, even if hidden from us, the world will come to know of it.'[11] The phrase 'fullest extent possible' hints at the drastic nature of the Noakhali 'yagna' where the two participants were at times naked together.[12]

But the man hoping with Manu's help to summon the power to reshape his surroundings was also (as both Pyarelal and Bose observe) a mother to her, helping with her study, food, rest and work. Strikingly, young Manu was in turn a mother to him. We see this clearly in her account of a short boat journey on 18 February, when Gandhi agreed to go from his camp in Aloonia village in Tippera district to the home of 'a very old man, not a leader or a prominent person but an ordinary man', who was 'desperately eager for Gandhi's darshan but unable to cross the river':

> After the evening prayer we crossed the Dakaria river ... The beautiful river flowed amid lush greenery. The sky was clear, it wasn't too cold, and the sun wasn't too strong. It was a journey of five to seven minutes. During those minutes Bapuji placed his head in my lap, closed his eyes, and took a nap ...
>
> Both banks were lined with human throngs and dense trees ... Right in the middle, the world's great figure lay asleep in my lap, while the boatman rowed his boat. My hand was on Bapuji's forehead ... Those moments of my life were blessed.[13]

So the nation's old father found warmth in the lap of a young 'mother'.

Disapproval and protest. We have noted that most of Gandhi's associates disagreed with the yagna. Shaken by it, Mashruwala and Parikh excused themselves from their *Harijan* duties. Swami Anand had a similar reaction. Devadas wrote to his father that he was on the wrong track. Vallabhbhai commented that Gandhi had left the path of dharma. Vinoba, however, refrained from offering an opinion. Prasad suggested that Kanu, Gandhi's grand-nephew, replace Manu as an aide. We do not know what Nehru or C R thought; it is unlikely that they approved.

Gandhi himself raised the subject with these and other friends, and also with Manilal and Ramdas. 'One day he wrote as many as twelve letters,' Pyarelal informs us.[14] He thought, for example, that Birla, who had helped Gandhi with funds, had the right to know and give his reaction. Likewise Kripalani, president of the Congress. He would not be hurt, Gandhi said, if associates responded by severing their links with him. They should follow their conscience, even as he claimed to be following his.

We do not have a record of Birla's reply but Kripalani gently recalled the *Gita*'s stress on conserving a society's values, equally gently asked whether Gandhi was not treating his female associates 'as means rather than as ends in themselves', but added that he knew that Gandhi had never exploited women. Kripalani continued:

> I can only say that I have the fullest faith in you. No sinful man can go about his

business the way you are doing ... I can never be disillusioned about you unless I find the marks of insanity and depravity in you. I do not find any such marks.[15]

A British Quaker, Horace Alexander, who called at Noakhali, was asked by Gandhi to give his reaction as a Christian even as Andrews would have done. Alexander said he thought the step was too extreme.[16] Nonetheless, Alexander noticed that Gandhi was working away

undaunted, showing the same courtesy, gentleness, firmness and sweetness to his endless visitors, helping all who came to him day by day to find things to laugh at, even when the world around was grim and overpowering.[17]

Another Christian caller was Stuart Nelson, the African-American dean of Howard University in Washington, who came with three others to meet Gandhi in his Srirampur cottage-room (1 or 2 January). The situation of African-Americans, not the yagna, was the topic discussed at this meeting – there is no evidence that Nelson had even heard of the yagna.

Nelson's record suggests that the yagna had not weakened Gandhi's capacities. His meeting with Gandhi, Nelson would write,

has proved one of my very great moments in India. The two hours in his retreat were packed with an inspiration which will abide with me ... The impression which I bore away ... derived from the extraordinary spiritual and intellectual qualities which he revealed even in so short a time ... Mr Gandhi has a complete mastery over the material demands upon his life ... The room could scarcely have been plainer. His mind met our problems most directly and constructively ... [18]

Pyarelal, who in the end married not Manu but a Hindu woman from Noakhali, would assert that Gandhi's expectation of Manu's growth in Noakhali 'was amply rewarded'. Pyarelal thought that in Gandhi's company Manu slept calmly, overcame fidgetiness and absent-mindedness, became clearer in thinking and firmer in speech, and seemed free from possessiveness.[19]

While holding that Gandhi did not fully consider the impact of his practice on Manu, Bose thought nonetheless that there was something noble about the Gandhi whom he watched and worked with in Noakhali during 'the greatest phase of Gandhi's great life', to use Bose's words.[20] Indeed, Gandhi's 'party' in Noakhali seemed a lot less troubled than associates far removed from him. Writing to Vinoba (10 Feb.) of his awareness that colleagues in 'Sevagram and elsewhere must be suffering' because of the 'yagna', Gandhi added, 'Here, on the contrary, everybody knows what is happening but I see no sign of its having any effect' (93: 391).

On 25 February one of his closest and oldest associates, Amritlal Thakkar – or Thakkar Bapa, as he was better known, and called 'my conscience-keeper' by Gandhi – talked to him on behalf of dissenting colleagues, stressing the risk of unscrupulous imitation. Gandhi answered that society would not allow it. In any case he had to give all of himself in Noakhali, and this included the yagna.

A few days later Thakkar – like Gandhi and his grand-niece a native of Kathiawar – told Manu that he was satisfied. He had watched her and Gandhi, he said, 'from day to day' and was persuaded by 'the sight of their perfectly innocent and undisturbed sleep' and by her 'single-minded and tireless' work. But he asked Manu for something in return for the change in his thinking: would she please ask Gandhi to suspend the yagna? Manu said she would, and Gandhi in turn agreed to the suspension – for the time being.[21]

Village to village on foot

On 2 January 1947, after spending six weeks in Srirampur, Gandhi, carrying a long bamboo staff, had left on foot to cover 'a village a day'. He had given up his latest ashram even as he had earlier renounced many of his companions. However, Manu, Bose, Parasuram (who would soon leave) and Ramachandran (also a stenographer) joined Gandhi on his latest journey.

Not far from Gandhi and his companions walked eight armed guards from the Bengal Police. Despite Gandhi pleading with them not to do so, about 100 villagers also trekked behind, and more, Hindus and Muslims, lined both sides of the narrow path on which he walked.

The ingenious Satis Dasgupta (who had carefully drawn up the itinerary, ensuring that Gandhi would not walk more than four miles on any one day) constructed a mobile hut and brought it before Gandhi. The hut was simple to take apart, carry, and put together. Gandhi was deeply touched but he declined the 'palace', as he called it.

Over the next two months he and his companions would halt overnight in forty-seven different villages in Noakhali and Tippera; their hosts were Hindus and Muslims, and included washermen, fishermen, cobblers and weavers. He did not find as many Muslim hosts as he had hoped but warmly thanked those that lodged him, including Maulvi Ibrahim, the host in Fatehpur village (8 Jan.) and Habibullah Patwari in Muraim (24 Jan.).

'They bathe us with love,' Manu wrote in her diary, referring to those who welcomed Gandhi and his party.[22]

A washerman, Rai Mohan Mali, hosted Gandhi in Dalta village (23 Jan.), and in

Palla (27 Jan.) Gandhi lived in a weaver's home. He said in Palla: 'The cottages of Bengal have become dearer to me than the prison-like solid walls of palaces. A house full of love, such as this one, is superior to a place where love does not reign.'[23]

Much of his time was spent with Hindu women stricken with fear. Bose noticed what he described as Gandhi's 'daily ministrations on behalf of love' and 'the extreme tenderness with which he regarded each individual' who related woes to him.[24] Sick children in the villages, Muslim and Hindu, also commanded Gandhi's attention. He sought to heal and to wipe away tears but said that courage rather than consolation was what he hoped to transmit. Thus Bose recorded that in the course of one meeting with bereaved women 'Gandhiji's face hardened, and he said that they must recover their courage.'[25]

With the caste Hindu women Gandhi was also frank about untouchability. Finding that the Namashudra 'untouchables' of East Bengal had been braver than caste Hindus in responding to attacks, he insisted that village peace committees should have Namashudra representation; and he warned caste Hindu women that if they continued to disown the 'untouchables', more sorrow would be in store. To women in Chandipur he proposed (3 Jan.) a radical step:

Invite a Harijan every day to dine with you. Or at least ask the Harijan to touch the food or the water before you consume it. Do penance for your sins.[26]

In Srirampur he had tried to prepare himself for the trek with exercise and a planned diet, but walking on East Bengal's slender bridges was not always easy. Gandhi provided both entertainment and anxiety when he negotiated these, but Bose or someone else was usually close enough to prevent a fall.

The poet and the poem. Renouncing his chappals, Gandhi walked barefoot. When Manu saw cuts on the soles of his feet and protested, Gandhi replied: 'We don't go to our temples, mosques or churches with shoes on ... We tread on holy ground where people have lost their loved ones ... How can I wear chappals there?'[27] But with a little exaggeration he also claimed (6 Feb., in Dharampur) that Noakhali's foot-paths were friendly:

The earth of Noakhali is like velvet and the green grass is a magnificent carpet to walk on. It reminds me of the soft grass I had noticed in England (93: 378).

In some villages Hindus would sing their welcome to him or walk with him to the next village, singing and beating their drums: their confidence was returning. Often the walk would commence with a prayer-song, *Vaishnava Jana* or Tagore's *'Ekla Chalo Re'* – 'Walk Alone'.

Gandhi sang himself. 'The pitch of his voice was low, but the tune was correct,' thought D G Tendulkar,[28] a future biographer of Gandhi drawn from Bombay to Noakhali by the old man's venture. Tagore was the author of the song but Gandhi, his purpose stronger than his feet, his message stronger than his voice, had become the song.

Half a dozen journalists, more at times, were also on the scene, capturing Gandhi's doings and what he said at his prayer meetings. Like Gandhi and his companions, the journalists stayed with the villagers, paying for their food.

Muslim response. The Muslim reaction varied from day to day, depending in part on how Gandhi's visit was portrayed at the local mosque. An evening prayer-meeting attended by thousands of Muslims could be followed by another drawing fewer than a dozen.

But he evoked wide admiration among educated Muslims across East Bengal, as was found on trains near Dhaka by a visiting Hindu from western India, Ramnarayan Chaudhary, who to prove to himself his fearlessness wore (not without trepidation) the white 'Gandhi' cap and found (to his relief) that the attention he received was usually of a welcoming kind. A Bengali Hindu told Chaudhary that as a result of Gandhi's stay 'the Hindus of Noakhali were slowly regaining the confidence they had lost, and the Muslims were undergoing a change of heart'.[29]

Noakhali's Muslims often asked Gandhi why he was not in Bihar; his answer was that his mention of a possible fast and the efforts of Nehru and others had brought that province under control. All in all, curiosity and warmth were the Muslims' strongest instincts towards Gandhi, and they noticed his regard for their sensitivities.

Thus he asked his followers not to carry the Congress flag; he asked local Hindus to cooperate in the League ministry's peace plan; he encouraged Manu to partake of vegetarian food offered to her by Muslim women; and at times he asked her and others singing of 'the good Vaishnava' to switch to 'the good Muslim' or 'the good Christian'.

However, some Muslims objected to a self-confessed Hindu like him reciting verses from the Koran or speaking of what their faith required of Muslims. One of them was Fazlul Huq (1873–1962), the mover in 1940 of the Muslim League's Pakistan resolution and Suhrawardy's rival in Bengal. He said he would push Gandhi into the water if he came to his district, Barisal. But when the visit occurred, in Haimchar, Huq called on Gandhi (27 Feb.) and said the remark was only a joke. Later, Huq said that spreading goodwill the way 'Mahatma Gandhi was doing' was his wish too.[30] Yet the earlier remark was indicative of the hostility towards Gandhi's visit in sections of East Bengal's Muslims.

At the prayers in Paniala village on 22 January 1947, Manu for the first time used a verse that would become familiar to millions of Hindus and Muslims in the years to come: '*Ishwar Allah Tere Naam*' – 'Ishwar and Allah [both] are Your Names.'

Manu told Gandhi that she had first heard the verse in a temple in Porbandar.

Observing that Paniala's Muslims, who had gathered in huge numbers, liked the verse, Gandhi asked Manu to sing the line 'daily from now on'. 'God Himself breathed it into your mind,' he added.[31]

On 31 January the Muslims of Navagram defended Gandhi's right to cite from the Koran, and in the village of Sadhurkhil, an influential Muslim, Salimulla Saheb, asked Gandhi (4 Feb.) to hold prayers on his grounds – in his *badi* – adding that he would not mind if the Hindu verse about Rama was chanted to the clapping of hands.[32]

'The Rama whom I adore,' Gandhi explained in Sadhurkhil, as he had done elsewhere, 'is God Himself', different from any historical Rama. 'He always was, is now and will be for ever,' a God who was 'Unborn and Uncreated' (93: 365).

His discourse. Two strapping Sikhs who had served with Subhas Bose's Indian National Army, Niranjan Singh Gill and Jivan Singh, joined Gandhi on his Noakhali trek, without carrying their kirpans. One of them occasioned a hearty laugh from Gandhi by slipping and falling on the treacherous ground. There was banter again when a group of British and Australian soldiers caught up with Gandhi, who teased one of the Australians about his country's White Australia policy.

But grimness and sadness were the more frequent notes. In Jagatpur (10 Jan.) Gandhi firmly told bereaved Hindu women weeping before him that 'tears won't bring back the dead'. However, after the women left he said to Manu that their faces would haunt him; all he could eat for dinner that evening was a lump of jaggery.[33] Two days later, in the village of Karpara ('adopted' by Sushila Pai), he stayed in what had been the home of Rai Saheb Rajendralal Chowdhury, who along with 29 relatives had perished in October.

His discourse was often a back-to-back mix of the religious and the secular. Hindus and Muslims, he said on 10 December, 'were nourished by food grown from the same soil, quenched their thirst from the waters of the same river and finally laid themselves to rest in the same earth. If they feared God they would fear no one else' (93: 127).

Insisting on the precise truth, and the removal of all exaggeration, in what complaining Hindus told him, he refused to congratulate Muslims who claimed that attacks on Hindus had been limited. 'If more mischief was not done' he said in Paniala (22 Jan.), 'God alone was to be thanked, not man'. However, he would concede that, 'be it said to their honour, there were Muslims who afforded protection to Hindus' (93: 313). He felt outraged when others were not outraged at the coercion of the weak. A maulvi remarking that those willing to convert had at least saved their lives was told by him: 'I am amazed that God has allowed someone with your views to become a scholar of Islam.'[34]

Asked about state schools and religious instruction after independence, Gandhi replied (21 Feb.) that he did not believe in a state religion even when the whole community followed one faith. 'State interference probably would always be unwelcome,' he said. Religion was a personal matter; he would be opposed even to partial state aid to religious bodies. But, he added, state schools could teach ethics, which were common to all religions.[35]

Four young Muslims in Sadhurkhil challenged Gandhi (4 Feb.) to say publicly that the number of deaths was smaller in Noakhali than in Bihar. Doing so, Gandhi announced his estimate that less than a thousand had died in Noakhali, and that 'the murders and brutalities in Bihar eclipsed those in Noakhali'.[36]

As during the salt march, he sought information about each village he visited, and got Manu to record its population, broken down by religion and caste. On occasion he talked rural economics. In Chandipur, close to the village that Sushila had taken on, Changirgaon, Gandhi said (4 Jan.):

> Bengal is a land full of verdure, with plenty of water and fertile soil. But through ignorance people are suffering from poverty and disease. You are content with betel-nut and coconut and a little agriculture. But with more knowledge you can increase productivity many times and convert villages into clean abodes of peace and prosperity (93: 238).

No matter how ascetic his own lifestyle, Gandhi wanted East Bengal's productivity multiplied 'many times'; he wished to see abodes of 'prosperity' and health. Two days later, still in Chandipur, he returned to the theme:

> I want to teach you ... how to get pure water in the villages, how to keep ourselves clean, how best to utilize the soil from which we have sprung, how to breathe in life's energy from the infinite sky above our head, how to draw fresh life from our surroundings and how best to use the sun's rays.
>
> Our country has become impoverished. I shall try and teach you so that you may, by making proper use of these resources, convert this [land] into a land of gold (93: 244).

To the American scholar and peace activist, A J Muste, who had asked about a free India's likely policies, Gandhi wrote (28 Feb.):

> I wish too that I could give you the assurance that India, when she has come to her own completely, will not join the race for the increase of armaments. I can only say that whatever I can do to prevent any such misfortune will not be left undone (94: 55).

Long hours, basic chores. Walking, spinning, writing, treating the sick and, most of all, listening until late in the evening or early in the morning, Gandhi did not usually sleep more than four hours at night. To Manu he said on 10 January:

> Just observe how God sustains me. Though I sleep at 10 or 11 p.m., rise at 2 or 2.30 a.m., do my work at high pressure and get no rest at all, I carry on somehow! That itself is a wonder.[37]

To Vallabhbhai, home member in the interim government, who was anxious about Gandhi's security in the East Bengal countryside, he wrote:

> There is the One ... above all of us who will look after me, and He is able enough.[38]

Manu cooked for Gandhi, washed his sore feet after stretches of barefoot walking, gave him an oil massage, and kept notes of his conversations and talks. But there were times in Noakhali when Gandhi did chores that for years others had performed, like cooking for himself, giving himself a rub and darning his clothes.

It was getting colder. One evening, burning some dry sticks, Manu heated water for Gandhi to wash his hands and face with before retiring. He was not pleased. 'Where people don't have twigs for baking their rotis,' he said, 'you want me to wash my face with warm water? I can understand heating water for bathing, but not for this.'[39]

A harder lesson had been given a few days earlier when Manu left behind Gandhi's scrubbing stone – given to him by Mira – in the village of Bhatialpur. Discovering the loss later in the day (15 Jan.) in Narayanpur, Gandhi asked Manu to walk back alone to Bhatialpur and retrieve the pumice stone. Though an old woman had thrown the stone away, Manu located it and hurried back.

Saying, 'Take your stone,' she threw the object before Gandhi, who laughed and said that Manu had passed a test. He added:

> If scoundrels had seized and killed you I would have danced with joy, but I would not have liked it a bit if you had run back out of fear ... I said to myself, 'This girl sings *'Ekla Chalo Re'* with enthusiasm but has she digested the message?' ... You can see how hard I can be ... I also realized it.[40]

The last two sentences suggest Gandhi's unease about his direction to Manu, which had been produced by a mix of reactions. Firstly, something he was used to had gone. As he admitted the next day to Manu, 'My nature dislikes any change in my routine.'[41]

Secondly, Manu had discarded a gift from someone he loved, Mira. Finally, there was a chance to test Manu.

The Gandhi ordering Manu to fetch the stone was hardly serene, but we can recognize his need to test her. She (and he) had to be willing to face what he was asking Noakhali's weak Hindus to face. The 'dancing with joy' phrase only means, as we have seen before, that though wanting a loved one to prefer death to surrender, he was praying every moment for her safety. Manu, who recorded the incident, also noted that Gandhi was anxious about her rest and nourishment after her return.

Earlier (10 Jan.), Gandhi had apologized to her after discovering that he had wrongly blamed her — we do not know for what. Manu recorded what he said:

I was absolutely wrong ... I am so much older than you. I am your grandfather. What pardon can I seek from you? Still there is nothing wrong in asking for it.

Gandhi added that while it was a wonder that God had kept him going, his end could come at any time; he wanted to make his confession before it came.[42]

Harilal & Kasturba. On 22 January he sent a letter to one he had sorrowed over for decades. Someone who had met Harilal had written to Gandhi that his 58-year-old son looked much older than his years. A pained father who had sent most aides away wished nevertheless to have the son with him in Noakhali, and sent Harilal a letter via the person who had met him.

It was only rarely that Gandhi knew how his son could be reached. However, in this letter of invitation Gandhi could not resist underlining Harilal's need to reform himself:

How delighted I shall be to find that you have turned over a new leaf! ... Mine is an arduous pilgrimage. I invite you to join in it if you can ... If you purify yourself, no matter where you are, you will have fully shared it ... [Y]ou will then also cease to look prematurely old ... (93: 307).

A month later, when he heard about Harilal from a correspondent who was seeing him in Madras, Gandhi wrote once more to his son, but what he said is not recorded (94: 20). We know that Harilal did not join his father.

February was the month of Kasturba's death, which had occurred on Shiva Ratri day. In 1947 Shiva Ratri fell on 19 February. At 7.35 p.m. that evening, in Birampur village, Gandhi wrote in his diary: 'On this day, and exactly at this time Ba quitted her mortal frame three years ago' (94: 13). Then he wrote to one of Manu's sisters informing her that earlier in the day Manu had recited the whole of the *Gita* in Kasturba's memory.

Added Gandhi:

> When, therefore, after the Eighth Chapter I stretched myself and dozed off a little, I felt as if Ba was lying with her head on my lap (94: 13).

Stars and dust. Observing him at close quarters, Bose concluded that it was Gandhi's 'questioning attitude towards his own perfection' that brought him close to ordinary men and women. It was a factor, Bose thought, in Gandhi's 'tenderness' which 'soothed' men and women and 'lifted them above their sorrows'.[43]

In Noakhali Gandhi once asked Bose (who among other things was compiling quotations from Gandhi) not to be misled by his sentences, which (said Gandhi) 'showed him at his best' and 'presented a picture of his aspirations, and not of his achievements'.

Bose answered by quoting Tagore, who had said that a man should be judged 'by the best moments of his life, by his loftiest creations, rather than by the smallnesses of everyday life'. To this Gandhi's response was quite stunning:

> Yes, that is true of the Poet, for he has to bring down the light of the stars upon the earth. But for men like me, you have to measure them not by the moments of greatness in their lives, but by the amount of dust they collect on their feet in the course of life's journey.[44]

Yet Gandhi could be poetic himself. On 18 December he said: 'Truth is greater than the sun; some day or the other it will come to light' (93: 159). And in a letter to Mira on 6 February (93: 375), he compressed several layers of meaning into a sentence of 14 short words, 12 of which needed only a single syllable:

> The way to truth is paved with skeletons over which we dare to walk.

The sentence is, firstly, a terse description of the Noakhali trek. Next it confesses a hurried, even insensitive, walk over or past grief. Thirdly, it accuses the living of concealing the full truth: only the skeletons know what really happened. Finally, Gandhi hints that India's path to freedom was paved with death and yet could not be abandoned.

'Adopted' villages. In their different villages Gandhi's associates achieved results that at times seemed 'astounding', to quote Pyarelal, who had taken on Bhatialpur. 'We were all of us men and women of ordinary clay,' Pyarelal would write, but with the strengths, he would add, of awareness 'of our shortcomings' and 'soldierly obedience' to Gandhi's instructions.[45]

Though full confession by perpetrators of violence in these villages was not forth-coming, remorse was ample, and Muslim elders were quick to punish anyone committing fresh acts of harassment or looting against Hindu neighbours. Hindus who had fled returned; chants and prayer-songs were heard again; conches were blown; Hindu women wore vermillion and bangles once more.

In Bhatialpur a committee of Muslims pledged that they would risk their lives to protect Hindus and do their utmost to get looted property and abducted women restored. In the presence of Muslims who had earlier broken it, an idol was restored in a Bhatialpur temple. Walking alongside Gandhi in Bhatialpur, 'a number of Muslim youths' assured him, according to the *Amrita Bazar Patrika* (19 Jan.), that 'they would stand guarantee' against a recurrence of attacks on Hindus (93: 278).

Sushila's ability to offer medical aid added to her effectiveness in Changirgaon. Looted goods were returned to Hindu homes there and in adjacent villages. In Karpara, where Sushila Pai was living, the local school was back on its feet, the weekly bazaar reopened, and Muslims 'even asked her to mediate in their disputes'.[46]

Kanu Gandhi organized group activities to break down barriers between Hindus and Muslims in Ramdevpur; in Haimchar his wife Abha used her artistic talents to the same end. Thakkar Bapa too was in Haimchar, staying in a Dalit home. In some adopted villages residents joined in tidying up common areas and digging trench-latrines. Elsewhere in Noakhali, Sucheta Kripalani helped locals fight destitution, and other 'elite' Bengali women like Renuka Roy, Ashoka Gupta and Sneharani Kanjilal also joined the relief effort, taking up residence in the affected countryside.

Amtus Salaam, who never missed a Ramzan fast and always slept with the Koran at her side, went on a fast in Sirandi when her call for a surrender of a sword used in attacks against Hindus was not heeded. While she fasted Gandhi wrote her a letter a day, sometimes two letters daily. After 25 days, though the sword was not returned, Gandhi persuaded her to end her fast (20 Jan.) and helped her sip some orange juice.

Eleven Muslims of Sirandi took the pledge, 'with God as witness', that they would defend the right of Hindus to practise their faith and continue to search for the missing sword. (The wording was drafted by Gandhi and bore some resemblance to the 1906 satyagraha pledge in Johannesburg.) Though the weapon was never found, 'things were altogether different in and around Sirandi after that fast', Pyarelal would write, adding that the fast 'blew away like a whiff of fresh air the musty charnel-house odours that had hung over the place since the riots'.[47]

In the village of Jayag (29 Jan.), the local zamindar, Barrister Hemanta Kumar Ghosh, donated his lands to Gandhi for setting up a charitable trust. Gandhi gave power of attorney to the Sodepur ashram's Charu Chowdhury, who established on Ghosh's lands a centre for Hindu-Muslim harmony and development that continues to this day, despite post-Partition trials that included Chowdhury's imprisonment.

Implementing advice given by Gandhi when they called on him in December, several women from Calcutta's elite families had based themselves in villages in Noakhali. One of them, Ashoka Gupta, who camped in Tumchar, would later write, referring to late February 1947: 'At that time the work in Noakhali to rehabilitate hundreds of families had gained momentum and was in full swing.'[48]

Politics. In the 'wilderness' of Noakhali, Gandhi's political antenna remained in good repair. The preparation of a free India's Constitution mattered to Gandhi: in a letter to Ghanshyamdas Birla (26 Nov.), he conveyed clear advice regarding the Constituent Assembly:

> I am not going into the Constituent Assembly; it is not quite necessary either. Jawaharlal, Sardar, Rajendra Babu, Rajaji, Maulana – any of these or all five can go – or Kripalani. Send them the message (93: 70).

That Gandhi had considered entering the Assembly himself before rejecting the idea is of some interest. On 11 December he wrote to Kripalani, the new Congress president, urging him to maintain good relations with Nehru, and added a comment on the question of questions:

> He [Nehru] is right also in his reflections on the Hindu-Muslim question. It is a terrible problem and a great responsibility rests upon the Congress now – therefore the greatest on you (93: 130–1).

At the end of December Gandhi once more offered clear political advice, after HMG had finally resolved – in the Muslim League's favour – the ambiguity in the Cabinet Mission Plan of 16 May. Following talks held in London in which Nehru (on behalf of the Congress), Jinnah and Liaqat Ali (for the League), and Wavell had taken part, HMG announced that Assam and the NWFP would *have* to join the Muslim Groups.

While Cripps and Pethick-Lawrence had argued in London for the Congress's interpretation, Wavell and Alexander defended that of the League. Prime Minister Attlee tipped the scale in the League's favour. The Congress was given the option of appealing to the Federal Court in New Delhi, but nobody expected this British-led court to defy HMG.

Patel wrote Cripps an angry letter, alleging betrayal. HMG's verdict meant, Patel said, that 'Bengal Muslims can draw up the constitution of Assam.' 'Do you think,' he added, 'that such a monstrous proposition can be accepted by the Hindus of Assam?'[49]

But Patel's indignation was also linked to his arguments with Gandhi over 16 May. Gandhi had expressed misgivings, but Patel had asked him not to be fussy.

In December 1946 Patel was in fact resigning himself to India's division and to a Pakistan that did not include East Punjab, West Bengal or Assam.[50] His experience of the interim government, where League ministers and several officials saw themselves as future Pakistanis rather than as Indians, had disillusioned Patel about trying to govern all of India alongside the League.

Once Pakistan was conceded, he reckoned, the League would lose its capacity to obstruct the Congress in the rest of India. For one thing, the Congress would feel free to abolish the separate Muslim electorate. And a strong central government, to Patel an imperative, seemed possible only in an India shorn of its Muslim-majority regions.

By now some others too were ready to concede Pakistan. On 18 December, Birla told Colville, who was acting as Viceroy while Wavell was in London, that 'he thought that some sort of Pakistan would come about'. On his part Jinnah at last seemed willing to accept Small Pakistan. He had told Wavell on 19 November that the Muslims had to have 'their own bit of country', adding, 'Let it be as small as you like. But it must be our own.'[51]

On 11 December the India Committee of the British Cabinet noted the 'pressure of events' that were 'leading to the establishment of some form of Pakistan',[52] and in a letter to Attlee on 1 January the Foreign Secretary Ernest Bevin, referred to 'handing over to established *governments* in India'.[53] (Italics added.) As prime minister and subsequently as the leader of the opposition, Churchill had favoured India's partition. Now it had become Britain's official if as yet private solution for India. From a longer perspective, it was also an almost inevitable outcome of Britain's unwillingness to let power flow to India's majority party, the Congress.

But conceding Pakistan was not yet Congress policy. Patel withheld his view from Nehru, Gandhi or Wavell, and he refrained from advocating rejection of the HMG verdict by the Congress, which would mean the exit of its ministers, himself included, from the interim government.

What was the Congress to do? Nehru and Kripalani, the Congress president, journeyed to Noakhali at the end of December and asked if Gandhi could suggest a way out. He replied that the latest British award had to be accepted by the Congress; after all it had signed on to 16 May. Moreover, rejecting 16 May meant giving up on a united India.

Yet, added Gandhi, Assam could stay out of the Muslim Group, if need be, by seceding from the Congress. This was also his advice to Assam's Congress leaders, who called on Gandhi on 15 December in Srirampur. He told them:

As soon as the time comes for the Constituent Assembly to go into Sections, you will say, 'Gentlemen, Assam retires' (93: 143).

The Congress adopted Gandhi's solution, but Wavell exploded at Gandhi's 'most mischievous' response, as it would be termed in the Viceroy's diary.[54] Calling Gandhi 'double-tongued' but 'single-minded' in his pursuit of independence, the Viceroy told the British Cabinet in December 1946 that Gandhi felt that his 'life work of driving the British from India' was 'almost accomplished'.[55] On his part the old man felt no qualms. He would not agree to Assam, or the NWFP, being coerced. So, in line with Krishna's tips to the Pandavas, he gave astute political counsel.

Accompanying Nehru to Noakhali, Mridula Sarabhai complained to Gandhi about some of Patel's public remarks, including a statement at the Congress's Meerut session that 'the sword will be met by the sword' if advocates of Pakistan departed from 'the method of peace and love'.[56] In a letter to Patel written at two in the morning of 30 December, Gandhi listed the accusations, adding, 'If we stray from the straight and narrow path we are done for.'[57]

In his answer, Vallabhbhai wrote, 'Mridula must have made these complaints ... She cannot stand it if anyone disagrees with Jawaharlal.' The Meerut remark, Patel added, had been 'torn out of a long passage and presented out of context'.[58]

At three in the morning of 30 December, after writing the letter to Patel, Gandhi scribbled a note for Jawaharlal, who was returning to Delhi. If Nehru wished to visit but could not, or if it was not 'seemly that you should often run to me', an emissary could be sent. 'Somehow or other,' Gandhi added, 'I feel that my judgement about the communal problems and the political situation is true. So I suggest frequent consultations with an old, tried servant of the nation' (93: 210–1).

The note thus breathed self-confidence, a sense of duty and a complaint that a seasoned general was being ignored.

Leaving Noakhali. Though constantly urged by Bengal's Muslims, including premier Suhrawardy, Fazlul Huq and others, to go to Bihar, Gandhi felt he was in the right place, and indeed able from Noakhali to influence Bihar. His certainty was disturbed, however, when Niranjan Singh Gill of the INA, sent by Gandhi to Bihar, reported on 21 February that the province's Congress ministry had been found wanting.

In letters to Shri Krishna Sinha, the Bihar premier, Gandhi complained that no one from Bihar had given him an account of what had happened, and he asked Sinha to hold an early inquiry into the killings (93: 170–1 & 94: 27–8).

On 28 February Gandhi made up his mind to go to Bihar, a decision clinched by a visit by Mujtaba, secretary to Syed Mahmud, a minister in Bihar and the province's leading Congress Muslim. When Mujtaba read aloud the letter he had brought from

Mahmud, 'his voice grew husky', women around Gandhi could not hold back their tears, and 'Bapu sank into deep thought'.[59]

❧

Fifty-three years later. Interviews conducted in Noakhali in April and November 2000 found residents retaining precise memories of Gandhi – his shaven head, pocket watch, vigorous walking, his drinking of goat's milk, and work as a doctor. Recollections always mentioned 'his granddaughters' as also his work for Hindu-Muslim peace.

The memory of him seemed to be fresh and near the top of people's minds, and many recalling him spontaneously recited or sang '*Raghupati Raghav Raja Ram ... Ishwar Allah Tere Naam*'. Though Gandhi's 1946–7 stay was seen as a special event, the remembrances were of an approachable and friendly man.

Abul Kalam Bhuiya, who looked around 70 and spoke some English, a farmer and son of Hyder Baksh Bhuiya, said in Srirampur:

> I attended his prayer meeting. He went to Muslim homes, offered them treatment. He took goat milk and a red leaf vegetable. Was punctual about his time, wore pocket watch at the waist, a dhoti that went down to his knee, advocated peace, love and brotherhood.

Also in Srirampur, Fazlul Huq Patwari, again around 70, a farmer and son of Jalauddin Patwari, recalled:

> I saw him. We sat together [*possibly at a prayer meeting*] ... He said, 'Let us live side by side [Hindus and Muslims].' He was a good man. He walked a lot and we were running behind him. He distributed toffees for the children. Muslims took and ate what he gave.

Most interviewees were in their teens at the time of Gandhi's visit. A day labourer, Aamir Husain Shaikh, 75 in 2000, said:

> When he came it was total chaos. He brought peace. I saw him many times. He wore khadi clothes.

Nepal Chandra Das, approaching 80, farmer and brother of Nimay Chandra Das, said, also in Srirampur:

My brother and I carried his mail to Chaumahini and Chandipur. We attended his prayer meetings in the school field.

Md. Akhtar uz Zaman of Srirampur, son of Maulana Abdul Majid (who may have been the imam of the Srirampur mosque in 1946–7), recalled:

He came to our home, showed my father the Koran, and asked where the holy book authorized wrongdoing.

Dr Ali Ahmed, around 70, a homeopathic doctor in Madhupur near Srirampur, son of a government official, said:

I attended many prayer meetings. He asked for Hindu-Muslim unity. He told the Hindus, 'No revenge.' He was first a pious man and then a politician. His name and fame will remain in this vicinity for ever, in every nook and corner.

Madhusudan Chakravarti, a 75-year-old grocer in Paniala, son of late Anada Charan Chakravarti, a priest, said:

I saw him. He stayed in Mazumdar badi … He got the whole village to sit together and have a meal – khichri – Hindus, Muslims, Harijans. This happened for the first time.

Sirajul Islam Majumdar of Kamalpur, in his late fifties, son of Dr Khaleelur Rahman Majumdar:

My father told us of [he sang] 'Raghupati Raghav Raja Ram, Ishwar Allah Tere Naam.' My grandfather protected Hindus on his roof.

Usha Rani Das, a widow, aged around 65, living in a house between Kamalpur and Bangsha:

There was a meeting in the fields. Hindus and Muslims all came. I was very young but married. He asked us to put on the bindi and the sindoor that we had taken off. We obeyed the advice and were not attacked.

In Chandipur, Ayub Ali, a day labourer in his late seventies who said he owned a little land, said:

His arms rested on the shoulders of two granddaughters. 'What has happened has happened,' he said. He came close to my house. He went to every house for peace, spoke to all. He spoke in Hindi, but there were translators. He knew the kalima. He was good. If he had not come troubles would have continued.

Abdul Khaleq, also in Chandipur: 'I helped grow vegetables for him.'[60]

🔬

'*Darkness*'. If his four months in Noakhali seemed the peak, so far, of Gandhi's lifelong effort to knit Indians together by serving them, they also saw a profound journey into his own soul, and included a daring test. He claimed he was stronger for the test, but we should also note his repeated references in Noakhali to a 'darkness' he felt around him. On 2 January he wrote in his diary:

Have been awake since 2 a.m. God's grace alone is sustaining me. I can see there is some grave defect in me somewhere which is the cause of all this. All around me is utter darkness. When will God take me out of this darkness into His light? (93: 227)

On 6 January he wrote to Patel: 'I am in complete darkness but my hope burns as bright as ever' (93: 242). The same day, in another letter, he said: 'The task here is a difficult one. I have to make my way through darkness. But "one step enough for me"' (93: 245).

On 9 January he told an interviewer in Fatehpur that he himself was in darkness and added, 'I hope I shall see light soon' (93: 256). The next day, in a letter to his son Ramdas, he wrote: 'I am still surrounded by darkness. I have no doubt whatever that it indicates a flaw somewhere in my method. Take it as though I had confined myself to this place to detect that flaw' (93: 259).

What Gandhi was saying, or admitting, was that he did not clearly see the lead he should give to prevent division and fresh violence in India. He was at a loss, or in the dark. A short-term answer for the dilemma in which the Congress found itself in December was hardly enough. India was hurtling towards partition and new rounds of killing, and he did not quite know the remedy to prescribe.

He had been in difficult situations before, but in the end light had always dawned, and he had known the 'one step' to recommend to the Congress and to his people, even if what lay beyond that step was often unclear. Confidence about finding a response had led him, in 1931, to make a large claim before Prime Minister MacDonald and others at the London RTC:

We have problems that would baffle any statesman. We have problems that other nations have not to tackle. But they do not baffle me (1 Dec. 1931; 54: 227).

This time, he felt, light was being greatly delayed, if not denied. Why? And, in any case, why the violence and ill will around him? Though nagged by such questions, Gandhi plodded away at the tasks of each day.

London announcement. On 20 February 1947, while Gandhi was making up his mind to leave Noakhali and go to Bihar, Prime Minister Attlee made a historic announcement in London. He said that Britain would leave India by June 1948, i.e. in 16 months or less, handing over 'to some form of central government or in some areas to the existing provincial governments' or 'in such other way as may seem most reasonable'. Attlee added that Wavell would be replaced as Viceroy by Lord Louis Mountbatten (1900–79), a 46-year-old admiral related to King George VI.

The statement set the stage for the final act of the India/Empire drama. It would be the final round also of one man's long struggle to lead his country to freedom in one piece, and his soul to God.

With Nehru at the AICC meeting – 1946

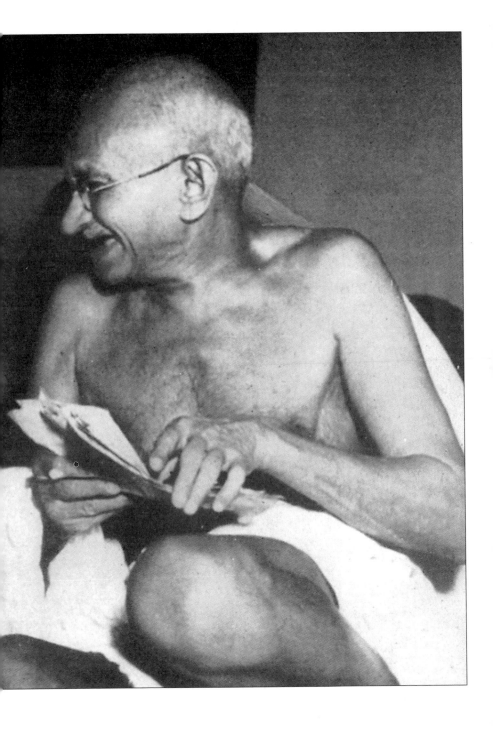

16

To Rama

1947–8

In a letter to Nehru from the village of Kazirkhil (24 Feb.), Gandhi highlighted the hint of partition that Attlee's announcement contained:

> I have read Attlee's speech ... This may lead to Pakistan for those provinces or portions which may want it ... (94: 33)

Since the League was in power in Bengal and Sindh and in a position to control Baluchistan, these provinces could emerge, in the light of 20 February, as Pakistan areas. However, a Unionist/Akali/Congress coalition led by Khizr governed the Punjab, and the Congress's Dr Khan Sahib was the premier in another Muslim-majority province, the NWFP. Would the Congress and its allies inherit the Punjab and the Frontier?

The League responded to Attlee's announcement by launching movements to remove the Punjab and NWFP ministries, as well as the Congress ministry in Assam, a province that Jinnah continued to claim for Pakistan, its non-Muslim majority notwithstanding. In Bengal, a response of an opposite kind was led by the Hindu Mahasabha's Shyama Prasad Mookerjee, who demanded a separate West Bengal, a Hindu-majority region that could stay out of any Pakistan.

On 28 February, Gandhi was asked in Haimchar whether Bengal's partition was not desirable. His answer, offered in a speech after prayers, was that he preferred a united India and a united Bengal, yet India's Hindu majority did not have the right 'to keep everyone united by means of compulsion', and Bengal's Muslim majority could not seek to compel the province's Hindu population or its western half. He was 'as much against forced partition as against forced unity' (94: 58).

Part of the darkness in his mind had lifted: 'non-coercion' was a principle he would go by. His four months in Noakhali had confirmed his faith in a people's right to choose their rulers and, if it came to that, their flag. The British flag, in any case, was on its way out:

> [W]hatever might have been the history of British rule in the past, there was no shadow of doubt that the British were going to quit India in the near future.

But neither Hindus nor Muslims could choose their neighbours, and all should be alert to a horrible possibility:

> It was time, therefore, that the Hindus and the Muslims should determine to live in peace and amity. The alternative was civil war which would only serve to tear the country to pieces (94: 58).

Despite his written plea to Nehru (30 Dec.) about 'frequent consultations with an old, tried servant of the nation', Gandhi was not consulted after the London announcement of 20 February. Nehru and Patel seemed to think that Gandhi was both out of touch and hard to reach, a view apparently shared by C R, Azad and Prasad, and also by the Congress president, Kripalani. Moreover, Nehru, Patel and company were under relentless pressure.

Events moved very fast in the Punjab, where the Congress was largely a Hindu party while the League was a Muslim organization and the Akali Dal a Sikh one. Representing well-off farmers of all three communities, the Unionist party was a declining force, suffering from a pro-British and pro-landlord image, and the Punjab Muslims' discontent with the Khizr cabinet, which included Congress and Akalis ministers, had grown.

Since Sikhs had governed the Punjab before British rule, and a large proportion of the province's traders were Hindus or Sikhs, ending domination by the non-Muslim minority had long been a rallying cry. In 1900, agitation by the Punjab's Muslim farmers had secured from the Raj a law against alienation of land to traders; and communal bitterness had been reinforced by campaigns for and against the Arya Samaj, founded by the Hindu reformer Dayanand Saraswati (1824–83), who made remarks critical of both Islam and Sikhism.

For three years, 1919–22, there was an unexpected Hindu-Muslim-Sikh alliance. After that disintegrated, several Muslim, Hindu and Sikh newspapers disseminated hate.

And following violence in eastern India in the second half of 1946, armed bands of Muslims, Sikhs and Hindus were formed in the Punjab.

In February 1947, the League's call to prevent Muslim-majority Punjab from being taken over by Hindus and Sikhs drew a fervent response. Defying restrictions, crowds of Muslims, including women and students, picketed government buildings, hoisted the League's flag over them, and stopped the movement of trains. Attacked as a betrayer of Islam, Khizr caved in, resigning on 2 March.

When, the next day, Governor Evan Jenkins asked the League leader in the legislature, the Khan of Mamdot, to form a government, Master Tara Singh, the Akali leader, emerged sword in hand and declared that the Sikhs would not be cowed down. An 'Anti-Pakistan Day' was announced by Sikh and Hindu leaders, provoking a fierce counter-reaction. Within a couple of days at least 1,000 were killed in different places in the province. Rawalpindi was the worst-hit city, and Sikhs and Hindus the main victims there.

Patel reacted by asking for a division of the Punjab, thereby conceding Pakistan. To Jinnah's close Hindu friend, Kanji Dwarkadas, he wrote (4 Mar.): 'If the League insists on Pakistan, the only alternative is the division of the Punjab and Bengal.'[1]

On 5 March the Mamdot ministry was dismissed, governor's rule promulgated, and the military asked to enforce peace, but the Punjab's unity had died during the two days of carnage. As Patel had done, the province's Hindu and Sikh leaders demanded a separate East Punjab province where non-Muslims would enjoy a majority. Nehru, Kripalani, Azad, C R and Prasad fell in, and on 8 March, only 16 days after the London announcement, the Congress Working Committee formally asked for a division of the Punjab. Though Bengal was not directly mentioned, the resolution clearly implied that province's partition as well.

In the Frontier Province, the Khan brothers and the Congress ministry would hold out for some months more, but by 9 March when, alongside the Working Committee resolution, the *Hindustan Times* published maps showing two Punjabs and two Bengals, the division of India had been sealed.

Future observers might say that the Empire – its overlords in London and guardians in India, including the Viceroy in New Delhi and the governor in Lahore – had been negligent, indifferent or inept regarding the consequences in the Punjab of the Attlee announcement. As the interim government's two leading figures, Nehru and Patel (who held the home portfolio) would also be assigned some responsibility. But perspectives were hazier in March 1947, when neither the Raj nor the Congress was as energetic as the Punjab's bands of killers and arsonists. Moreover, the interim government at the centre was a house divided among itself, with Liaqat Ali Khan and his League colleagues refusing to accept Nehru as their chief. As finance minister, Liaqat had announced taxes aimed at the Congress's backers.

On 9 March Gandhi saw the Working Committee resolution in newspapers in Bihar, where he had arrived four days earlier. He had not been informed of any plan to ask for a division of the Punjab. Kripalani, the Congress president, had indeed sent Gandhi a telegram on 3 March: 'We all consider your presence here next Working Committee meeting sixth essential. Kindly postpone Bihar programme till ninth.' To this Gandhi, who was in Calcutta by now, on his way to Bihar, answered the same day: 'Your wire. Regret inability. Send messenger Bihar. Bapu' (94: 67).

But no emissary was sent to brief Gandhi or obtain his views. The Working Committee's momentous decision on partitioning the Punjab (and Bengal) was thus taken without his knowledge or input. He realized, of course, that events had forced his colleagues' decision, and it was not until 20 March that he wrote to Jawaharlal about it. The letter also referred to the censorship imposed on reports from the Punjab:

> I would like you ... to tell me what you can about the Punjab tragedy. I know nothing about it save what is allowed to appear in the Press ... Nor am I in sympathy with what may be termed by the old expression of 'hush hush policy'. It is amazing how the country is adopting almost the very measures which it criticized during the British administration ...
>
> I have long intended to write to you asking you about the Working Committee resolution on the possible partition of the Punjab. I would like to know the reason behind it ...

Invoking his 'non-coercion' criterion, Gandhi added in this letter that he was against any partition based on 'compulsion' or on 'the two-nation theory'. While he could think of a 'willing consent' to partitioning a province following 'an appeal to reason and heart', the Working Committee resolution seemed a submission to violence (94: 153–4). On 11 March he had said:

> Jinnah Saheb is my friend. I have gone to his house many a time. If Jinnah Saheb says to me: 'Concede Pakistan or I will kill you,' I will reply: 'You may kill me if you like; but if you want Pakistan, you should first explain it to me. If you convince me that Pakistan is a worthy ideal and Hindus are maligning it for no reason, I shall proclaim to the Hindus from the house-tops that you should get Pakistan' (94: 99).

Non-coercion was the prescription also of his friend Ghaffar Khan, who had joined Gandhi in Bihar. On 16 March, the Frontier leader said:

The Muslim League wants Pakistan. They can have it only through love and willing consent. Pakistan established through force will prove a doubtful boon.[2]

On 22 March Gandhi wrote to Vallabhbhai: 'If you can, please explain your resolution about the Punjab' (94: 168). He received the following replies:

From Jawaharlal, 25 Mar.: I feel convinced and so did most of the members of the Working Committee that we must press for this immediate division so that reality might be brought into the picture. Indeed this is the only answer to partition as demanded by Jinnah. I found people in the Punjab agreeable to this proposal except Muslims as a rule (94: 154).

From Patel, 24 Mar.: It is difficult to explain to you the resolution about the Punjab. It was adopted after the deepest deliberation ... Nothing has been done in a hurry or without full thought ... The situation in the Punjab is far worse than in Bihar. The military has taken over control. As a result, on the surface things seem to have quietened down somewhat. But no one can say when there may be a flare-up again. If that happens, I am afraid even Delhi will not remain unaffected. But here of course we shall be able to deal with it (94: 168).

Patel was hinting that a Gandhi camping in Bihar or Noakhali could not understand the realities that he and Nehru were grappling with in Delhi and the Punjab. Having removed himself to the periphery, could Gandhi really appreciate what they faced in Delhi?

Well, he thought he could. In fact he came up with a possible response to the violence that in seven months had leapt from Calcutta to Noakhali to Bihar to the Punjab and was threatening to spread further and escalate. The 'darkness' he had been speaking of seemed to leave his mind, and he knew what action to propose. Before looking at his solution, however, we will take in Gandhi's encounter with Bihar.

Bihar, March 1947. Almost four months had passed after the killing and destruction of early November, yet Bihar's Muslims, comprising less than 13 per cent of the population, continued to feel frightened and bitter. Around 7,000 of their number had been killed and nearly 10,000 homes destroyed in the violence that had gripped six districts – Saran, Monghyr, Bhagalpur, Santhal Parganas, Patna and Gaya.[3] Apart from a few places where attackers were subdued, the state police merely looked on.

Women and children were brutally killed, wells were stuffed with bodies, villages were burnt down. More than 100,000 Muslims migrated to Bengal, and tens of thousands fled their villages to refugee camps in Patna and other cities in Bihar. Many sold their property for a song.

In several places Hindu neighbours indeed protected defenceless Muslims, and there were stories like that of the headmaster in Gaya district, Sakal Babu, who, supported by students and friends, took all the Muslims of Daulatpur, Nagama and Rasalpur villages to safety in the town of Jehanabad.[4] And leaders were not devoid of sympathy. Gandhi's host in Bihar, minister Syed Mahmud, had noticed that Premier S K Sinha wept at his helplessness when from their plane the two saw women and children waving frantically at them from rooftops, while their homes were surrounded by a thousands-strong hostile mob.

Yet, as Jayaprakash confirmed to Gandhi,[5] the overall record of the state government was appallingly inadequate. No passion to control the violence descended down from Bihar's ministers to officials and the police. The province still had several British officers, but their willingness to act was eroded both by the attitude of the ministers and by the officers' memory of Quit India.

Some in Bihar justified the November violence as a means of saving Hindus across India, including in Bihar, from attacks of the kind perpetrated in Noakhali. A pamphlet issued by the provincial Hindu Mahasabha claimed that Bihar's Muslims had planned surprise attacks on the Hindus but the latter had 'wisely taken time by the forelock', preempting the supposed plan.[6] Told by Prasad that many Biharis thought 'they had done well', Gandhi replied that 'it was to save them from that sin that he had come'.[7] He knew that the real impact of the Bihar violence had been to sway Muslims across the subcontinent in favour of Pakistan. A report (1 Dec. 1946) by the Bihar Muslim League had alleged 'genocide' and spoken of the 'fascism' of the 'Hindu Congress'; and from November 1946 onwards pictures of the Bihar killings were displayed in the Punjab and the NWFP as proof that Muslims would be unsafe in Hindu-majority India.[8]

Telling Premier Sinha that the Bihar killings were 'like the Jallianwala massacre',[9] Gandhi spoke with similar bluntness to officials, Congress committees and the public. To Congress workers in Bir he said (19 Mar.):

Is it or isn't it a fact that quite a large number of Congressmen took part in the disturbances? ... How many of the 132 members of your Committee were involved? ... I have also worked in the Congress. Today I am not even a four-anna member. But there was a time when I was ... all in all. Hence I know the Congress inside out ... I wish to ask you, how could you live to see an old woman of 110 years being butchered before your eyes? ... I will not rest nor let others rest. I [will] wander all over on foot and ask the skeletons [what] happened. There is such a fire raging in me that I [will] know no peace till I have found a solution for all this ...

If I find that my comrades are deceiving me, I will be furious and I shall walk barefoot on and on through hail or storm. I would throw away the soft seat and other amenities which you have offered me (94: 147–8).

There was, he said on 5 March, a way out for Bihar:

> The Hindus of Bihar have committed a grave sin. They will raise the head of Bihar much higher if they do honest reparations, greater in magnitude than their crimes. There is an English saying: 'The greater the sin, the greater the saint' (94: 75–6).

Abducted women, stolen goods and illegal arms should be returned, Gandhi said, to the police – or, he added, to him, Rajendra Prasad or Syed Mahmud. Or to Ghaffar Khan, who was also in Bihar to assist. If Bihar wanted its fame back, 'rebuild what you have destroyed,' he said.[10] The government on its part should catch culprits and award due punishment (94: 114).

> *Khusropur, 14 Mar.*: I want a genuine feeling of repentance and an honest atonement for the atrocities committed by thousands of Hindus on a handful of Muslims ... Hindus, Muslims and Sikhs are all engaged in a bitter feud in the Punjab ... If you sincerely think that the way of the Punjab is the proper answer to the challenge of the times, you are free to follow it. I plead with you in all earnestness to tell me frankly that you do not approve of my way. I will not be hurt by your honesty.
>
> I shall not say that Bihar has ignored my past services. I do not want you to do anything for my sake. I want you to work in the name of God, our Father. Confess your sins and atone for them with God alone as witness (94: 111–13).

Bihar being the land of Sita and of the Buddha, Gandhi's utterances invoked the *Ramayana* and the Buddha's life. Large numbers attended his prayer meetings, where he collected funds for Muslim refugees. When a beggar gave four annas, Gandhi exclaimed: 'This is true charity! These are the people of Bihar!' (94: 80) On 11 March he cast himself in a beggar's role while explaining the dynamics of retaliation:

> If I am starving and you feed me, the contentment in my eyes will brighten your face too ... Suppose I am starving and demand food from you by abusing you. You will drive me away, saying: 'Go and starve yourself to death.' My abuses will not get me food. They will, however, make me feel that I am a brave man. Again, if you ask your gate-keeper to beat me up for my abuses, that will sow the seeds of hatred against you in my heart ... The next day I shall gather a few friends and retaliate. Or, if you manage to kill me, it will create among my relations and friends a feeling of revenge against you ... (94: 99)

Gandhi was in Bihar for most of March, half of April and about a third of May. Most of

his nights in the province were spent in Mahmud's home on the bank of the Ganga, but he managed to visit several villages and towns, at times on foot. But it was summer and Bihar's roads were dusty, making walking more difficult than it had been in Noakhali.

Within days of his arrival there were signs of remorse in Bihar's Hindus, and Gandhi was given confessional letters, stolen goods and arms by some of the November attackers. Pyarelal recorded a scene from the village of Masaurhi, where fearful destruction had occurred:

> After the prayer address, Gandhiji stayed on to collect money for the Muslim relief fund. There was a stampede as everybody pushed forward to be the first to put his or her copper into the Mahatma's hands. As he bent forward with outstretched hands, he read in those faces, aquiver with emotion, the unmistakable evidence that repentance had at last crept into their hearts.[11]

Relieved by Gandhi's arrival, Bihar's Muslims slowly regained their confidence, but the provincial Muslim League was critical of his disapproval of its demands for 'Muslim pockets' and a Muslim police in Bihar. In the end Gandhi agreed to Muslim refugees settling in villages with ample Muslim populations instead of returning to the scenes of their suffering, but he would not concede that only Muslim police could protect Muslim citizens. That would be accepting the two-nation theory.

However, even though premier Sinha disliked the idea, he would insist on an inquiry into the Bihar violence and the ministry's handling of it. The Muslim League had also asked for such an inquiry. On Gandhi's urging, a one-man commission under Justice Reuben of the Patna High Court was announced, but it was denied resources or help.

The government of Bihar – 'his' Congress ministry in 'his' Bihar – was no keener on justice than Bengal's League ministry, and not more enthusiastic about their 'guest'. Not only was Mahmud criticized by his colleagues for pressing Gandhi to come to Bihar; before long the relief portfolio was taken away from him.

From the Punjab, meanwhile, Gandhi was receiving serious news. On 23 March he told his prayer audience:

> A friend has written that a semblance of peace appears to have been established in the Punjab. But this peace and tranquillity has come through military occupation. Everyone is preparing openly for a fight and is busy collecting arms (94: 176).

The resignation of Khizr, the only Muslim leader in the Punjab trusted by Hindus and Sikhs, had led to complete polarization in the province. Once the Congress resolution of 8 March spoke of two Punjabs, militant Muslim groups made up their minds to push out West Punjab's Hindus and Sikhs, while their Sikh and Hindu counterparts in East Punjab nursed a parallel resolve regarding Muslims.

Gandhi's solution

'I would know no peace till I have found a solution for all this' – we saw that he said this on 19 March. Before the month ended he knew what he should ask for. As with all inspired solutions, his looks self-evident in hindsight, but at the time it was far from obvious. It took shape as he contemplated the realities around him.

The Punjab was waiting to explode again. Bihar too was viciously polarized, as was much of India. So was the interim government in Delhi. As for the long term, Jinnah hated the division of the Punjab and Bengal as much as the Congress hated India's division.

Weighing up these realities, Gandhi saw that a Jinnah-led Muslim League government in Delhi, if installed with the Congress's agreement, could address all of them. Remedying polarization across the subcontinent, a Congress-supported Jinnah government could preserve the unity not only of the Punjab and Bengal but also of India as a whole.

Reckoning that the Congress majority in the Central Assembly would prevent a Jinnah ministry from going too far, Gandhi also recalled something from his 1944 talks with the League leader. Refusing then to draw a clear picture of Pakistan, Jinnah had indirectly conveyed an interest in a role in India as a whole. Gandhi thought the League leader might accept his offer.

If he did, peace and unity could return to an India about to be free. Here was an answer at the top that might simultaneously bring mutual confidence at ground level and enable the winding down of private militias. Among the many breathing more freely would be his companion Ghaffar Khan, who, as Gandhi daily saw, was weighed down by two spectres: Hindu-Muslim violence and the subjugation, in any Pakistan, of his Frontier Province. The Frontier leader agreed at once with the idea.

Gandhi fleshed out five key components of his proposal: One, let Jinnah head an interim government of his choice, comprising League members alone or including others as well. Two, unless an impartial umpire, e.g. the Viceroy, were to rule that a League measure was against the national interest, the Congress would back the League government and its measures in the Central Assembly.

Three, private militias should be disbanded. Four, Muslim Groups could be formed in India, but without Assam, the Frontier Province, East Punjab and West Bengal, unless, as a result of the League's persuasion (as distinct from coercion) any or all of these areas also opted to join the Muslim Groups. The fifth and final item in the plan was that if Jinnah and the League were not willing, under these terms, to form a cohesive government, Nehru and the Congress should be given the same opportunity.[12] (94: 209–10 and 228–9)

The date when he hit upon his 'Jinnah card' is not precisely known, but it was certainly before 1 April, for on that day he revealed it to Mountbatten, the new Viceroy, who had invited Gandhi to meet him in Delhi. Nehru too had urged Gandhi to come to Delhi – to speak to a conference of Asian leaders he had convened, where the Mahatma was certain to be a great draw.

Arriving in Delhi by train on 31 March, Gandhi had a 90-minute interview with Mountbatten that day. At another long meeting, on 1 April, Gandhi presented his Jinnah proposal to the Viceroy. Notes by Pyarelal and Mountbatten inform us of what happened at the 1 April interview. Apparently the Viceroy began by remarking, in truth or flattery or both, that Gandhi's 'non-violence had won' and that the British 'had decided to quit as a result of India's non-violent struggle'.[13] Gandhi proposed the dissolution of the interim government and spelt out his five points. A 'staggered' Mountbatten obtained Gandhi's permission 'to discuss the matter with Pandit Nehru and Maulana Azad, in strict confidence, the next time they came to see me'.[14] Since Vallabhbhai's 'opposition to any such plan was well-known', he was excluded.[15] Patel had convinced himself that the only alternative to partition was civil war.[16]

Patel met Gandhi off the train on 31 March and it was he who dropped Gandhi at Viceroy's House for the 1 April interview. His certainty that partition was the best way out contributed to the pessimism in Gandhi's remarks at his prayer meeting on the evening of 1 April:

Whatever the Congress decides will be done; nothing will be according to what I say. My writ runs no more. If it did, the tragedies in the Punjab, Bihar and Noakhali would not have happened. No one listens to me any more. (94: 216–17)

The next day, however, Gandhi again met the Viceroy and reiterated his proposal. At this meeting (2 Apr.) Mountbatten accused Gandhi of proposing a League government but designing a Congress one, for surely he expected Jinnah to reject the offer?

However, the Viceroy (to quote his words) became convinced of his caller's 'burning sincerity' when Gandhi offered all his services to the Viceroy to 'get the Jinnah government through, first by exercising his influence with Congress to accept it and secondly by touring the length and breadth of the country getting all the people of India to accept the decision'.[17]

Half an hour after Gandhi had left him, Azad met the Viceroy, who recorded his discussion with the Congress's leading Muslim figure:

I told [Azad] straightaway of Gandhi's plan, of which he already knew from Gandhi that morning. He staggered me by saying that in his opinion it was perfectly feasible of being carried out, since Gandhi could unquestionably influence the whole of Congress to accept it and work it loyally. He further thought that there was a chance that I might get Jinnah to accept it, and he thought that such a plan would be the quickest way to stop bloodshed.[18]

The Viceroy, however, secured Azad's assent to the view that other solutions might be more practical.[19] For though assuring Gandhi that he would examine the scheme and privately admitting to his staff that 'it would not be very easy for Mr Jinnah to refuse Mr Gandhi's offer' and that 'basically Mr Gandhi's objective was to retain the unity of India and basically he was right in this',[20] Mountbatten in fact was hostile to the scheme.

This dashing Admiral, whose real dream was to command the Royal Navy, had taken on the New Delhi assignment to see if, pulling off a personal coup, *he* could resolve 'the India question', not to share any glory with Gandhi or Jinnah or to sign, in Irwin's footsteps, anything like a 'Gandhi-Jinnah-Mountbatten Pact'.

Troubled by the possibility of the Congress Working Committee endorsing the scheme, Mountbatten sought ideas from his staff to scuttle it. After a staff meeting on 5 April, his papers tell us, Mountbatten 'decided to talk to Pandit Nehru that afternoon about Mr Gandhi's scheme'.[21] One of Nehru's close friends, V K Krishna Menon, was also encouraged to work on him. 'Krishna Menon and Ismay (the Viceroy's chief of staff), at Mountbatten's request, had a prolonged talk about Gandhi's proposals',[22] and the Viceroy had Krishna Menon to lunch on his own as well.

A vital role was also played by V P Menon, the Viceroy's talented reforms secretary, who had cultivated close relations with Patel. Though Patel was supposed at this stage to be excluded from discussions, V P Menon met him from day to day. We must assume that the Jinnah idea was discussed at these meetings, for it was V P Menon who wrote for Mountbatten and his team a paper entitled 'Tactics to be adopted with Gandhi as regards his scheme'.

We do not have details of the various talks in the first part of April involving Mountbatten, Nehru, Patel, Ismay, Krishna Menon and V P Menon. But the record conveys both anxiety and activity regarding the Gandhi scheme, and there is evidence of Mountbatten's effort to keep Patel detached from Gandhi.

On 1 April, after Gandhi had first outlined his proposal to Mountbatten, the Viceroy told Patel of his opposition to an inquiry in Bihar.[23] The next day, when Gandhi brought up the inquiry, Mountbatten told him that he, Patel and the Bihar governor were all against it. According to Mountbatten's account, Gandhi 'flatly disagreed'[24] with their reasoning; but the Viceroy's ability to count on Patel's support is noteworthy. Aware, however, of Gandhi's earlier hold over his Congress colleagues, Mountbatten feared a revival of the old magic. And during a three-hour meeting with Jinnah on 9 April, when Mountbatten tested the waters, he saw that the offer was likely to tempt Jinnah.

As Mountbatten recalled right after the talk, he began the interview by saying that 'it was a daydream of mine to be able to put the Central Government under the Prime Ministership of Mr Jinnah himself'. Thereafter, Jinnah 'once more appealed' against 'a moth-eaten Pakistan'. Continues Mountbatten's record:

> Some thirty-five minutes later, Mr Jinnah, who had not referred previously to my personal remark about him, suddenly made a reference out of the blue to the fact that I had wanted him to be the Prime Minister. There is no doubt that it had greatly tickled his vanity, and that he had kept turning over the proposition in his mind. Mr Gandhi's famous scheme may yet go through on the pure vanity of Mr Jinnah![25]

Defeat

But in two days the Viceroy's anxieties were over. Gandhi's Congress colleagues rejected his proposal, which was therefore never put to Jinnah. On the morning of 11 April Gandhi wrote a letter to Mountbatten, admitting defeat:

> I had several short talks with Pandit Nehru, and an hour's talk with him alone, and then with several members of the Working Committee last night about the formula I had sketched before you, and which I had filled in for them with all the implications. I am sorry to say that I failed to carry any of them with me except Badshah Khan ...
>
> I felt sorry that I could not convince them of the correctness of my plan from every point of view. Nor could they dislodge me from my position although I had not closed my mind against every argument. Thus I have to ask you to omit me from your consideration. Congressmen who are in the Interim Government are stalwarts, seasoned servants of the nation and, therefore, so far as the Congress point of view is concerned, they will be complete advisers (94: 283–4).

The 'several members of the Working Committee' with whom Gandhi talked are not all identified. If Azad was one of them, his rejection of the Gandhi scheme would have been inconsistent with his saying to Mountbatten that the scheme offered the best hope of stopping bloodshed.

Nor do we know what passed between Gandhi and Nehru in their 'several short talks' or in their hour between themselves, when the 'heir' was in effect asked to agree to someone else becoming India's first Prime Minister. But we can assume that the discussion was not about personalities or positions; it would have been about what was wise and feasible. The Congress leaders on their part had little doubt. A diary entry by C R tells us that 'Gandhiji's ill-conceived plan of solving the present difficulties' was 'objected to by everybody and scotched'.[26]

Yet the 'ill-conceived' plan was perhaps the last chance for peace and unity in India. It could have helped undo the division conceded by the 8 March resolution of the Working Committee. Gandhi understood what its 'scotching' meant. The next day (11 Apr.), when two leaders of South Africa's Indians, Yusuf Dadoo and G M Naicker, called on Gandhi, he said to them that India no doubt stood

> on the threshold of independence. But this is not the independence I want. To my mind it will be no independence if India is partitioned and the minorities do not enjoy security, protection and equal treatment ... If what is happening today is an earnest of things to come after independence, it bodes no good for the future.

'I therefore feel ill at ease,' Gandhi added. 'But I am content to leave the future in God's good hands' (94: 286). And he was content to leave for Bihar.

On 12 April a 'leading paper with a large circulation' reported that Gandhi was leaving Delhi because he had 'fallen out' with the Working Committee. In the evening the man who had been comprehensively rejected called the report 'sheer nonsense' and pointed out that Azad, C R, Patel, Nehru and Kripalani had seen him during the day. 'We have our differences,' Gandhi admitted, but he added he would be back 'the moment [he] heard [Patel's] summons' (94: 294).

The sharpest difference in the world would not break his bond with his colleagues, whom he thought of as sons, or cause him to undermine their standing. Equally, however, his fullest loyalty would not hide the fact that in April 1947 – as in the summer of the previous year – his 'sons' felt closer to the Empire's guardians than to him.

At least one of Jinnah's biographers, Stanley Wolpert, would later offer the view that Gandhi's plan 'might just have worked'. 'Surely,' Wolpert added, 'this was a King Solomon solution.'[27] That Jinnah's acceptance was not to be wholly ruled out is suggested by his response in 1942 to a similar proposal:

> If the British government accepts the solemn declaration of Mr Gandhi and by an arrangement hands over the government of the country to the Muslim League, I am sure that under Muslim rule non-Muslims would be treated fairly, justly, nay generously ...[28]

On 12 April, just before he left for Bihar, Gandhi signed with Jinnah not the 'solution' he had envisaged but a joint appeal for peace proposed by Mountbatten:

> We deeply deplore the recent acts of lawlessness and violence that have brought the utmost disgrace on the fair name of India ... We denounce for all time the use of force to achieve political ends, and we call upon all the communities of India, to whatever persuasion they may belong, not only to refrain from all acts of violence and disorder, but also to avoid both in speech and writing any words which might be construed as an incitement to such acts (94: 290).

Gandhi had wanted Kripalani, the Congress president, to sign this appeal instead of or in addition to himself, but Jinnah said he would sign only with Gandhi. Yielding, Gandhi signed in Hindi, English and Urdu – his way of signalling his right to reach Muslims as well as Hindus. Also, whereas the draft shown to him had referred to 'peoples of India', Gandhi altered the phrase to 'communities of India'. Even in defeat Gandhi was not accepting the two-nation theory.

On 6 May, when on Nehru's invitation he found himself again in Delhi, Gandhi spent, as he would say to Mountbatten, 'a very pleasant two hours and three-quarters' with Jinnah in the Lutyens-designed house the League leader had acquired on Aurangzeb Road (95: 46). Patel and others had tried to prevent the meeting but Gandhi said he would go to Jinnah 'seventy times seven' if necessary.

After the meeting Gandhi reported that he and Jinnah had agreed that 'what we talk should remain between us' (95: 42). But we know that Gandhi reiterated his opposition to partition. In a statement issued by Jinnah with Gandhi's concurrence, the League leader said their discussions had covered

> the question of division of India into Pakistan and Hindustan and Mr Gandhi does not accept the principle of division. He thinks division is not inevitable, whereas, in my opinion, not only is Pakistan inevitable but this is the only practical solution of India's political problem (95: 411).

In his prayer-meeting talk the next day, Gandhi said:

> I claim to have [Jinnah's] friendship. After all he also belongs to India. Whatever happens, I have to spend my life with him (95: 43).

At the sweepers' colony on Delhi's Reading Road, where Gandhi and Ghaffar Khan again stayed during the 1947 summer, there was occasional objection to the recitation of verses from the Koran in the prayers conducted by Gandhi. If that reading was to go, he replied, the Hindu texts too would be left out. It was a chance to teach tolerance, but the climate was not calm.

He was urged to visit the Punjab. When the call came he would go, Gandhi replied. Meanwhile he would hope to affect the Punjab from wherever he was. He asked the Punjab's Muslim leaders to protect Hindus and Sikhs in their areas:

> 7 Apr.: No matter how provocative had been the language of Hindus and Sikhs in the Punjab, that was no excuse for the barbarity and cruelty perpetrated on non-Muslims by Muslims in the areas where they were in a majority (94: 256).

But he did not make public his 'Jinnah card' or the Working Committee's opposition to it. As in the past, he would champion the Working Committee even when it went against him; he knew of no nucleus of leaders who could steer India better than Nehru, Patel and company. He acknowledged Nehru's role in assembling Asian leaders in New Delhi and conveyed to the gathering his understanding of Asia's message:

> 1 Apr.: All the Asian representatives have come together. Is it in order to wage a war against Europe, against America or against non-Asiatics? I say most emphatically 'No'. This is not India's mission (94: 212).
>
> 2 Apr.: The first of [Asia's] wise men was Zoroaster. He belonged to the East. He was followed by the Buddha who belonged to the East – India. Who followed the Buddha? Jesus, who came from the East. Before Jesus was Moses who belonged to Palestine though he was born in Egypt. After Jesus came Mohammed ... I do not know of a single person in the world to match these men of Asia. And then what happened? Christianity became disfigured when it went to the West.
>
> [T]he message of Asia ... is not to be learnt through Western spectacles or by imitating the atom bomb. If you want to give a message to the West, it must be the message of love and the message of truth. I want you to go away with the thought that Asia has to conquer the West through love and truth.
>
> Of course, I believe in 'one world'. How can I possibly do otherwise, when I became an inheritor of the message of love that these great unconquerable teachers left for us?
>
> In this age of democracy, in this age of awakening of the poorest of the poor, you can redeliver this message with the greatest emphasis. You will complete the conquest of the West not through vengeance because you have been exploited,

but with real understanding ... This conquest will be loved by the West itself (94: 222–3).

The visitors were aware of the violence in India in the autumn of 1946 and in March 1947, and Gandhi expressed his shame at it. Yet the visitors seemed thrilled about India's coming freedom. Someone brought lines written by the Arab poet, Mikhail Noema:

> The spindle in Gandhi's hand became sharper than the sword; the simple white sheet wrapping Gandhi's thin body was an armour-plate which guns from the fleets of the master of the seas could not pierce; and the goat of Gandhi became stronger than the British Lion.[29]

3 June partition plan

On 20 April 1947 Nehru publicly conceded Pakistan: 'The Muslim League can have Pakistan, if they wish to have it, but on the condition that they do not take away other parts of India that do not wish to join Pakistan.'[30] Nine days later, Prasad, who chaired the Constituent Assembly, spoke to it of the likelihood of 'not only a division of India but a division of some provinces'.[31]

Unwilling as yet to declare it in public, Patel conveyed his acceptance of Pakistan to Mountbatten.[32] 'I for one cannot agree to Pakistan on any account,' said Gandhi on 7 May, but it was also clear that his dissent would take the form of dissociation, not defiance. 'When I say that I cannot bear it,' explained Gandhi, 'I mean that I do not wish to be a party to it' (95: 42–3). And though Jinnah called partitioning Bengal and the Punjab a 'sinister' idea,[33] he could advance no argument against it that did not also undermine his case for Pakistan.

'Small Pakistan' thus became, in April and May, the acceptable basis for negotiations involving the Congress, the League and the Raj that produced the independence-cum-partition plan of 3 June 1947. Unveiled simultaneously in New Delhi and London, the plan provided for a commission to demarcate borders for dividing Bengal and the Punjab, and for a referendum between India and Pakistan in the Frontier Province (and in Assam's Muslim-majority district, Sylhet). Their link with the British Crown ending, rulers of princely states were asked to enter into a relationship or 'particular political arrangements' with India or Pakistan or both.[34]

Invited to sessions of the Working Committee held on 31 May and 1 and 2 June to consider the plan (its elements were known to the Congress negotiators), Gandhi told the Committee that he 'disagreed' with it 'but would not stand in the way' (95: 192).

Ghaffar Khan, Jayaprakash Narayan and Rammanohar Lohia also expressed unhappiness, but everyone else was in favour, and the plan was approved.

The Frontier Province. However, Gandhi and Ghaffar Khan asked for a modification of the proposal for a referendum in the NWFP. Launched on 20 February, the League's agitation against Dr Khan Sahib's Congress ministry had acquired great intensity after the premier ordered the arrest of thousands of Muslims on rioting charges. 'Islam in danger' was the League's battle-cry, people were 'reminded of Bihar' (95: 304), and Ghaffar Khan and his older brother were portrayed as pro-Hindu traitors.

The Viceroy and his team were sympathetic to the League's demand for Dr Khan Sahib's removal and fresh elections. A Congress ministry running a Muslim-majority province was viewed as a 'bastard situation' by Lord Ismay, who headed the Viceroy's staff.[35] Though opposing new elections, Vallabhbhai, who had privately concluded that the NWFP 'would have to be written off',[36] and Jawaharlal accepted the referendum.

In the summer of 1947 the question of India or Pakistan in the Frontier Province would be a choice between Hinduism and Islam and lead only to one result. As between Pathan identity and submergence in a Pakistan, however, the Frontier was capable of choosing the former. Ghaffar Khan and Gandhi therefore asked the Working Committee to 'find out if the proposed plebiscite … could include the alternative of independence alongside the choice of India or Pakistan'.[37]

The Working Committee declined to do this. Gandhi continued to press Nehru, but Jawaharlal's hands were tied.[38] He wrote to Gandhi:

> *8 Jun.*: The British Government and the Viceroy are definitely committed to the referendum, and some of us are more or less committed. The question of the referendum is therefore a settled one, and it is not clear how we can get out of it.[39]

The truth was that by proposing the division of the Punjab and Bengal and again by killing the 'Jinnah card', the Working Committee had accepted the two-nation theory in all but name and prepared the ground for abandoning the faithful Khan brothers.

The brothers' response was to boycott the referendum. Apart from the certainty of losing to 'Islam', they were also alert to the violence that a contest was likely to provoke. Backing their choice, Gandhi sought to strengthen the brothers' hands for a revised objective: Pathan autonomy within a federal Pakistan, which would come into being on 14 August. India would be free on 15 August.

Agony & resilience

Dividing the summer between Bihar and Delhi, thinking about the Punjab and in May making a trip to Calcutta, Gandhi was often in agony. He felt that partition would lead to more violence, not less, but his Working Committee and ministerial allies thought the opposite. He felt that details of the division should be settled between the Congress and the League, without the mediation of the Raj; they disagreed. Having 'scotched' his Jinnah card, they seemed set also on a large army for India and on large-scale industrialization. The charkha had been forgotten.

He had been rejected on several fronts. 'I feel as if I was thrown into a fire-pit and my heart is burning,' he said from his prayer meeting in Delhi on 5 June. 'God alone knows why I continue to live in spite of this.' But he had no intention to die of self-immolation 'to prove that I alone was right'.

'I have a very big job to do,' he claimed (95: 214–15). And he felt that he was being led, that his insights were of value. In the pre-dawn hours of 1 June, having woken up earlier than usual, he mused on his isolation. Manu recorded his words:

Today I find myself all alone. [Even the Sardar and Jawaharlal] think that my reading of the situation is wrong and peace is sure to return if partition is agreed upon … They did not like my telling the Viceroy that even if there was to be partition, it should not be through British intervention or under the British rule. They wonder if I have not deteriorated with age …

But somehow in spite of my being all alone, in my thoughts, I am experiencing an ineffable inner joy and freshness of mind. I feel as if God himself was lighting my path before me. And it is perhaps the reason why I am able to fight on single-handed.

People now ask me to retire to Kashi or go to the Himalayas. I laugh and tell them that the Himalayas of my penance are where there is misery to be alleviated, oppression to be relieved.

There can be no rest for me so long as there is a single person in India whether man or woman, young or old, lacking the necessaries of life, by which I mean a sense of security, a life style worthy of human beings, i.e., clothing, education, food and shelter of a decent standard …

But maybe all of them are right and I alone am floundering in darkness (95: 182–3).

The last sentence was a dig at colleagues, not a confession of confusion.

Last-minute fight? 'I am after all a gambler,' he said to himself on 4 June (95: 206). Prepared not to 'worry about anarchy', he looked for likely allies and any groundswell of support for a possible fight against the 3 June plan. But no promising signs appeared.

Some socialists were indeed willing to stand up, as were Hindu nationalists like Purshot-tamdas Tandon in the UP, Hindu politicians in Sindh, and a few Muslim leaders in north India who for years had opposed the League.

These elements did not add up to a strong force. Moreover, they had little in common with one another, and some of them differed sharply from Gandhi. 'How can love and enmity go together?' he asked on 9 June (95: 245). Gandhi thought of the inhabitants of the Pakistan-to-be as part of 'his' people and did not want to lose them. The Hindu nationalists' opposition, on the other hand, was to the loss of territory, not to the exit of Muslim inhabitants.

A group of leading politicians in Bengal including Suhrawardy and Sarat Bose sought a united and independent Bengal. Nehru, Patel and the Working Committee rejected the idea, as did many in the Bengal Congress and the Hindu Mahasabha's Shyama Prasad Mookerjee, but Gandhi was willing to explore it.

In May he visited Bengal, held long discussions with Suhrawardy and his colleagues, and made a remarkable offer in writing to the premier:

> 13 May: I recognize the seriousness of the position in Bengal in the matter of the partition. If you are absolutely sincere in your professions and would disabuse me of all the suspicion against you and if you would retain Bengal for the Bengalis – Hindus or Muslims ... I am quite willing to act as your honorary private secretary and live under your roof till Hindus and Muslims begin to live as [the] brothers that they are.

Terming it a 'mad offer', Suhrawardy ignored it. Thereafter Gandhi viewed the plan for an independent Bengal with caution. Remembering the League's nomination of Mandal to the interim government, Gandhi also seemed to fear a possible deal between the Muslim League and some of the province's Dalit leaders that might take all of Bengal into Pakistan. Nursing an opposite fear, Jinnah thought that a united Bengal might join India. With no support from the Congress, Gandhi or Jinnah, and with only modest backing from within Bengal, the project petered out.

Many Hindu critics attacked Gandhi for not fasting to death against partition, not because they expected such a fast to prevent Pakistan, but because seven years earlier (in September 1940) Gandhi had said, 'Cut me to pieces first and then divide India.' Since Pakistan was to appear, they wished Gandhi to disappear. At his 9 June prayer meeting Gandhi addressed the sentiment:

> Lately I have been receiving a large number of letters attacking me. A friend points out how ineffective were my words when I said that vivisection of the country would

be the vivisection of my own body ... When I said that the country should not be divided, I was confident that I had the support of the masses. But when the popular view is contrary to mine, should I force my own view on the people? ... I must step aside and stay back (95: 245).

In 1947, the League's demand for a Muslim homeland was joined by demands for a non-Muslim space by the Hindus and Sikhs of the Punjab and by many of Bengal's Hindus. Gandhi was unwilling to oppose the widespread preference for separation with a fast unto death.

AICC endorses. Aware that Gandhi's bond with India's masses was strong enough even if nowhere near its earlier levels, the Congress leadership wanted Gandhi's acquiescence to be formally and publicly declared. Nehru and president Kripalani therefore urged him to attend the 14–15 June AICC meeting called to ratify the Working Committee's acceptance of the 3 June plan. At this meeting Gandhi asked the Committee's critics whether they had the strength to defy the leaders:

No one could be as much hurt by the division of the country as I am. And I don't think that anyone can be as unhappy today as I am ...

[I]f you feel that the Working Committee is in the wrong you should remove it, you should revolt and assume all power. You have a perfect right to do so, if you feel that you have the strength. But I do not find that strength in us today. If you had it I would also be with you and if I felt strong enough myself I would, alone, take up the flag of revolt. But today I do not see the conditions for doing so ...

Would Gandhi have revised his stance of non-defiance if at this point delegates had cried, 'We are ready to revolt', or 'Give us a lead, and we will fight'? There was no such cry, nor did Gandhi expect it. He added:

When now the responsibility of Government has devolved on us we have gladly accepted it and we have detailed some of our best workers for the job. There they have to grapple with some very intricate problems. They have to attend to the affairs of the millions of our countrymen.

I criticize them, of course, but afterwards what? Shall I assume the burdens that they are carrying? Shall I become a Nehru or a Sardar or a Rajendra Prasad? ...

He brought up the *Ramayana* story as a reminder that good could come out of evil, but he was, in addition, suggesting that he too had been 'exiled' – and that from his 'exile' he would fight the Ravana of ill will and cruelty:

[Rama's] father went mad and his mother became foolish and Rama was exiled. The people of Ayodhya were grieved but it all led to something glorious coming out at the end ... It was [not the ten-headed Ravana] but ... the Ravana that was adharma ... that Rama killed during his exile and saved dharma. This is what we have to do today ...

I am not the one to be upset by defeat. From my childhood up I have spent my life fighting and my struggle has been to extract good from evil ... We should draw out gold and diamonds even from mud.

He expressed awareness that for all their statements against Pakistan some Hindu nationalists were secretly happy that large Muslim populations were being detached from India:

If, therefore, the Hindus present at this meeting claim that India is their country and in it Hindus will have a superior status, then it will mean that the Congress has not made a mistake and that the Working Committee has only done what you secretly wanted ...

In this speech of less than ten minutes, more forward-looking than the utterances of younger colleagues, the old man underlined three challenges that a free if truncated India would immediately face: Hindu-Muslim relations, the caste and ethnic divide, and the question of the princely states:

In the three-quarters of the country that has fallen to our share Hinduism is going to be tested. If you show the generosity of true Hinduism, you will pass in the eyes of the world. If not you will have proved Mr. Jinnah's thesis that Muslims and Hindus are two separate nations ...

And what about the 'untouchables'? ... If you say that 'untouchables' are nothing, the Adivasis are nothing, then you are not going to survive yourselves. But if you do away with the distinction of savarna and avarna, if you treat the Shudras, the 'untouchables' and the Adivasis as equals then something good will have come out of a bad thing ...

[T]hat some States should [want to] secede from India ... is a very serious thing ... [The princes] must recognize the paramountcy of the people as they recognized the paramountcy of the British Government ... (95: 286–7)

Apart from feeling that Nehru, Patel and company comprised 'our best workers', there was also, of course, a personal bond, built up during three decades of shared efforts, imprisonments, joys and sorrows. 'I have to do many things out of the love that binds me to Jawahar and Sardar,' he would say on 22 July. 'They have tied me up with the chains of their love' (96: 106). Thanks to his call, these two and others had made large sacrifices. To foreign visitors calling on him he would say (also on 22 July):

> Jawahar and his colleagues appear old. The struggles of satyagraha and frequent incarcerations have reduced their expectation of life by twenty to twenty-five years (96: 111).

Aware that desire for power had influenced their acceptance of Partition, he yet refused to obstruct his 'sons' while they collected crowns or medals for their faithful toil of three decades, and he knew that the trophies were thorny.

At the AICC meeting, Nehru, Patel, Azad, Pant and president Kripalani defended their acceptance of the 3 June plan. Resisting the temptation to point out that he had proposed an identical plan in 1942, C R remained silent. Tandon opposed the resolution endorsing the Working Committee decision, as did Choithram Gidwani of Sindh, whose remark on the 'ultimate sacrifice' of Hindus in Muslim-majority areas reduced many to tears.[40] Maulana Hifzur Rahman and Dr Saifuddin Kitchlew spoke of a surrender to communalism.

The resolution was carried by 157 votes to 27, with 32 absentions. Yet a delegate, N V Gadgil, noted, 'It was the only resolution other than a condolence resolution approved in total silence during my forty years in Congress.'[41]

New tasks

How he should tackle 'the very big job' before him, or where he should base himself, was not quite clear. While not always relishing his advice, Nehru and Patel urged him to remain in Delhi. Reluctant to defy their wishes, Gandhi was nonetheless wary of making Delhi his home.

He gave many of the summer's weeks to Bihar and Calcutta. On 15 May, in Patna, he wore a surgical mask and watched an operation on Manu for appendicitis – 23 years earlier, similar surgery had been performed on him. Manu quickly regained strength and resumed taking down letters that Gandhi dictated in Hindi or Gujarati, as well as his public utterances.

With Bose returning to Calcutta from Bihar and Pyarelal remaining in Noakhali for most of the time, her secretarial role was crucial. Dev Prakash Nayar (Pyarelal's cousin) assisted with Gandhi's English letters. For part of this time Sushila too was on Gandhi's personal staff, as was, from July, Abha, and, joining a little later, Shivbalak Bisen, sent by Kaka Kalelkar.

Earlier, in the middle of March, two men arrived in Patna to speak to Gandhi on behalf of all colleagues troubled by his yagna, which had been suspended at the end of February: Kedar Nath Kulkarni, or Nathji, as he was known, who was Mashruwala's guru, and Swami Anand, one of Gandhi's earliest and closest associates in Sabarmati. Despite long talks with Kulkarni and Anand, Gandhi did not concede any error. He said to them:

> I am not so lost as you seem to think. You do not seem to regard a lapse in respect of truth, non-violence, non-stealing etc. to be so serious a matter. But a fancied breach in respect of brahmacharya ... upsets you completely. I regard this conception of brahmacharya as narrow, hidebound and retrograde. To me truth, ahimsa and brahmacharya are all ideals of equal importance (94: 121).

Disappointed and saddened, the two returned whence they came. On 29 April Gandhi said to Manu:

> I do feel that I have come nearer to God and Truth. It has cost me quite a few of my old friends but I do not regret it. To me it is a sign of my having come nearer to God. That is why I can write and speak frankly to everyone. I have successfully practised the eleven vows undertaken by me. This is the culmination of my striving for the last sixty years. You have become an instrument in this (94: 412).

Translatable as 'the way of greatness', brahmacharya was, apart from anything else, Gandhi's bid to recover the innocence of childhood and a renunciation of sexuality in line with Christ's call for eunuchs for the sake of the kingdom of heaven. It was also a response to, and in Gandhi's hopes a weapon against, the unmerited suffering he saw around him.[42] Noting that Gandhi's renunciations were 'unsettling' but also 'effective', a European scholar, J C Heesterman, has written of Gandhi as 'the archetypal dissenter [who] disturbs the settled order ... Yet it is precisely the disturbing quality that is the outward sign of the ultimate value he stands for.'[43]

Later in the summer – in June or July, it would seem – Gandhi resumed the practice he had suspended, with Manu alone as his partner.[44]

On 8 June Manu jotted down Gandhi's remarks about Kasturba, made to an unidentified 'relative visiting from South Africa', possibly Sita, Manilal's daughter:

> Ba was in no way weaker than I; in fact she was stronger. If I had not had her cooperation, I would have been sunk. It was that illiterate woman who helped me to observe all my vows with the utmost strictness and kept me ever vigilant.

Similarly in politics also she displayed great courage and took part in all the campaigns ...

She was a devout Vaishnavi, used to worship the tulsi, religiously observed sacred days and continued to wear the necklace of holy beads right up to her death. I have given that necklace to [Lakshmi]. But she loved [this] Harijan girl as much as she loved Manu or Devadas's Tara.

She was a living image of the virtues of a Vaishnava described by Narasinha Mehta in his bhajan. It is because of her that I am today what I am ... In the fast of 1943 ... I was nearly at death's door, but she never cried or lost courage but on the contrary kept up other people's courage and prayed to God. I can see her face vividly even today (95: 233–4).

Dalit head of state. On the Dalit question Gandhi proposed a strong symbolic move: appointing a Dalit woman or man as free India's first President. His objective was to pre-empt a polarization over caste as destructive as the polarization over religion.

The proposal was sparked off by the death, at the end of May, of Chakrayya, a talented young Andhra Dalit who had been with the Sevagram ashram from its inception. Gandhi had nursed high hopes for Chakrayya. 'I feel like crying over his death,' he said, 'but I cannot cry. For whom should I cry and for whom should I refrain from crying?' (95: 179) On 2 June he said at his prayer meeting:

[T]he time is fast approaching when India will have to elect the first President of the Republic. I would have proposed the name of Chakrayya, had he been alive (95: 193).

On 6 June he repeated the idea in a conversation with Rajendra Prasad, suggesting at the same time that some prominent leaders should stay out of the government:

If all the leaders join the Cabinet, it will be very difficult to maintain contact with the people at large ... That is why I suggested even in my prayer speech that a Harijan like Chakrayya or a Harijan girl should be made the nation's first President and Jawaharlal should become the Prime Minister ... [S]imilar arrangements [can be] made in the provinces too ... (95: 217)

Three weeks later he returned to the subject:

27 Jun.: [I]f I have my way the President of the Indian Republic will be a chaste and brave Bhangi girl. If an English girl of seventeen could become the British Queen and later even Empress of India, there is no reason why a Bhangi girl of robust love of her people and unimpeachable integrity of character should not become the first President of the Indian Republic ...

By electing a Harijan girl to that office we shall ... show to the world that in India there is no one high and no one low ... She should be chaste as Sita and her eyes should radiate light ... We shall all salute her and set a new example before the world. After all she does not have to concern herself with running the Government of India. She will have a cabinet of ministers and she will act on its advice. She will merely have to sign papers.

If such a girl of my dreams becomes President, I shall be her servant and I shall not expect from the Government even my upkeep. I shall make Jawaharlal, Sardar Patel and Rajendra Babu her ministers and therefore her servants (95: 417–18).

In identifying chastity as a key quality and selecting from different Dalit groups the 'Bhangi' or 'cleaning' jati, Gandhi revealed long-held predispositions, and we should note that once again (as over Suhrawardy) Gandhi expresses willingness to be a servant.

His radical suggestion of a Dalit head of state was not considered because Nehru, Patel and company wished to retain Mountbatten as Governor-General. (The Congress had decided, with Gandhi's agreement, that after independence India would remain in the British Commonwealth, and Jinnah had decided similarly for Pakistan.) Nehru and Patel thought that the princely states would be more likely to opt for India if the King's cousin continued as Governor-General. Gandhi agreed on Mountbatten staying on – 'because we have to negotiate with the Princes' – but added that 'when democratic rule is firmly established then it will be possible' to have an 'untouchable' head of state (96: 174).

His plea that some of the best-known leaders should remain out of the Cabinet was also turned down, but Nehru and Patel accepted an earlier suggestion from Gandhi regarding Ambedkar, who had been a member of the Viceroy's Executive Council in the mid-1940s.[45]

One of Ambedkar's biographers, C B Khairmode, refers to a conversation in December 1946 between Ambedkar and Muriel Lester, Gandhi's friend and his hostess during the Round Table Conference in London, when Gandhi and Ambedkar had clashed sharply. Lester evidently informed Ambedkar that 'Gandhi was keen that the Congress should include Ambedkar in the central Cabinet and use his learning and leadership ...'

According to Khairmode, Ambedkar gave an encouraging response, which Lester conveyed to Gandhi, who then asked Nehru and Patel to invite Ambedkar to join free India's first cabinet.[46] Nehru and Patel extended the invitation at the end of July 1947. Accepting it, Ambedkar became India's law minister, chaired the committee that drafted the Constitution, and piloted the Constitution Bill into law. The invitation and acceptance were gestures of wisdom and magnanimity.

On 26 July, Gandhi spoke, in a conversation with Syed Mahmud, of the folly of rejecting talented people merely because they had worked for the Raj:

> They have not become our enemies because they served the British Government ...
> Please remember that they are at heart patriots ... If we seek the advice of such ...
> persons, they will show their genius (96: 147–8).

While final decisions were made by Nehru and Patel, Gandhi's suggestions influenced the remarkably diverse composition of free India's first Cabinet. Apart from Nehru, who would be Prime Minister, and Patel, who would be styled deputy prime minister (Gandhi may have been behind this innovation), the Cabinet of 14 included

A woman (Rajkumari Amrit Kaur),

two Muslims (Azad plus Jawaharlal's associate from the UP, Rafi Ahmed Kidwai),

two 'untouchables' (Ambedkar and Jagjivan Ram),

two Christians (John Matthai and Amrit Kaur),

two former (and future) foes of the Congress (Ambedkar and Shyama Prasad
    Mookerjee of the Hindu Mahasabha),

a Sikh (Baldev Singh),

a Parsi (C H Bhabha),

one former Raj loyalist (R K Shanmukham Chetty), and

altogether seven (including Amrit Kaur) from outside the Congress.

Rajendra Prasad was retained in the Cabinet but C R was asked to move to Calcutta as governor of West Bengal.

Princely states. From 8 April 1947, when he first said that the question of the princely states could turn India into 'a battleground' (94: 261), Gandhi cast a steady eye on it. His consistent position, expressed publicly and in talks with the Viceroy, was that the end of British paramountcy should lead to the people's sovereignty, that the ruler could not have the ultimate say.

> *31 May, New Delhi*: Any Prince, just because he is a Muslim, would not be entitled
> to say that he would join Pakistan. Nor can a Hindu ruler, because he is a Hindu, say
> that he would be with the Congress. Either would have to follow the wishes of the
> people (95: 179).

Referring specifically to the Nizam of Hyderabad, the Nawab of Junagadh and the Maharaja of Kashmir, he said in April and June that not these rulers but the people of these and all other states had the right to choose their future (94: 261; 95: 178–9).

In Muslim-majority Kashmir, the Hindu ruler, Hari Singh, saw a possibility of independence in the conflict between the state's popular pro-India leader, Sheikh Abdullah, and elements favouring Pakistan. When Abdullah, with whom Nehru had close links, was jailed by Hari Singh, Jawaharlal declared he would go to Kashmir, the land of his forebears.

Since a visit by Nehru was likely to generate friction, Gandhi offered to go in his place and made, between 31 July and 6 August, his first-ever trip to Kashmir. To a friend he wrote (30 Jul.):

> I am going to Kashmir … to see for myself the condition of the people. In any case I shall have a glimpse of the Himalayas. Who knows if I am going there for the first and the last time? (96: 176)

Before leaving for Kashmir he said (29 Jul.):

> I am not going to suggest to the Maharaja to accede to India and not to Pakistan. This is not my intention … The people of Kashmir should be asked whether they want to join Pakistan or India. Let them do as they want (96: 173–4).

The trip enabled stops in the Punjab – in Lahore and Rawalpindi and in Wah, where Hindu and Sikh refugees were camped out – as well as a visit to the Punja Sahib Gurdwara. In Kashmir, where huge crowds came to his prayer meetings, Gandhi met Hari Singh and his wife, Hari Singh's premier, Ramchandra Kak, and Begum Abdullah, the detained leader's wife. From the maharaja Gandhi elicited the admission that the wishes of the people should prevail.

On his way back, Gandhi said in Wah (where Sushila was asked to stay on to assist the refugees) that Kashmir 'had the greatest strategic value, perhaps, in all India' (96: 192). And in a note (6 Aug.) to Nehru and Patel he quoted the assessment of Abdullah's colleague, Bakshi Ghulam Mohammad, that if Abdullah and his co-prisoners were released, all bans removed, and premier Kak replaced, 'the result of the free vote of the people … would be in favour of Kashmir joining India' (96: 194).

When a delegation of Nagas led by A Z Phizo met him on 19 July and spoke of Naga independence, Gandhi said that complete isolation was not possible. He added:

> I was independent when the whole of India was under the British heel … Personally,

I believe you all belong to me, to India. But if you say you don't, no one can force you (96: 84–5).

Aung San, the Burmese leader, and several of his colleagues were assassinated on 19 July. Observing that Aung San had 'brought Burma to the gates of freedom', Gandhi expressed grief at killings in a Buddhist land. The news reminded him of conversations with Indian militants who 'did not accept my advice' and, like the killers of Aung San, regarded their 'victims as criminals' but 'never regarded themselves as criminals' (96: 102).

Hindu/Muslim, India/Pakistan. The Hindu-Muslim question, an inescapable part of his 'very big job', had morphed, with the acceptance of Partition, into two questions: Hindu-Muslim relations inside each new nation, and the India-Pakistan equation.

Gandhi grappled with the questions in several ways. One, he urged the Congress and the League to *make the division an Indian rather than an imperial affair.* Thus on 7 July 1947 he asked 'ten representatives of either party' to 'sit together in a mud hut and resolve that they will not leave the hut till they have arrived at an understanding' (96: 9).

Two, he *refused to limit himself to one* of the two new countries. 'Both India and Pakistan are my country,' he said on 2 July. 'I am not going to take out a passport for going to Pakistan' (95: 388–9). Three, he *acknowledged Jinnah's feat.* 'Mr. Jinnah is doing something very big,' he said on 11 June. 'Nobody had ever dreamt that in this day and age Pakistan would become a possibility' (95: 260).

Four, he *challenged Jinnah,* urging him (7 Jun.) 'to build a Pakistan where the Gita could be recited side by side with the Koran, and the temple and the gurdwara would be given the same respect as the mosque, so that those who had been opposing Pakistan till now would be sorry for their mistake and would only sing praises of Pakistan' (95: 229). On 5 July he said:

> But the real test of Pakistan will be the way it treats the nationalist Muslims, Christians, Sikhs and Hindus in Pakistan. Then Muslims themselves have various sects; there are Shias and Sunnis and various others. It is to be seen how these various sects are treated (95: 404).

Five, he *championed Hindustani,* written either in Nagari or Urdu, as *the subcontinent's common language.* In the bitter 1947 summer, this bid too was unsuccessful, and a common language spoken by large numbers of Hindus and Muslims was sought to be split into two, a Sanskritized Hindi for India and an Urdu loaded with Arabic and Farsi words for Pakistan. Yet overthrowing habit and convenience would not prove easy, and a great many in India and Pakistan would continue to speak the language that Gandhi had espoused.

Six, he *reprimanded* those like S K Patil, the Bombay Congress leader, who, according to press reports, had spoken of reprisals after 15 August by the Congress in India if Hindus were harmed in Pakistan.

> *12 Jul.*: You are enunciating the doctrine of an eye for an eye and a tooth for a tooth. Only you will wait till the 15th August ... Who will be responsible for the incalculable harm that will have overtaken the people of India as well as Pakistan in the meantime? Who can control the people if they go mad and launch on a course of retaliation? (96: 32)

Warning against an arms race, he said on 6 July:

> The Pakistanis will say that they must increase their armed forces to defend themselves against India. India will repeat the argument. The result will be war ... [S]hall we spend our resources on the education of our children or on gunpowder and guns? (95: 408–9)

Seven, he asked himself and everyone else, including refugees, to *put disappointment to use*:

> *24 Jun.*: If, therefore, we learn a lesson from the misery that has overtaken us and make our lives successful, then that misery is not misery but happiness ... Had Rama been crowned a king, he would have spent his days in luxury and comfort and the world would hardly have heard of him. But the day he was to be crowned, he had to put on bark clothing and go into exile. Isn't it the limit of unhappiness? But Rama and Sita turned that sorrow into joy ... (95: 328)

Eight, he insisted on *the unity of Divinity*:

> *13 Jun.*: When God is here, there and everywhere God must be one ... That is why I [ask] whether those calling God Rahim would have to leave [India] and whether in the part described as Pakistan Rama as the name of God would be forbidden. Would someone who called God Krishna be turned out of Pakistan? Whatever be the case there, this cannot be permitted here. We shall worship God both as Krishna and Karim and show the world that we refuse to go mad (95: 270).

Finally, he *dealt directly*, in his daily prayer-talks, *with hate, anger and revenge*. Thanks to Patel, who held the information and broadcasting portfolio as well as home, these talks were now being relayed over All India Radio. On 28 May Gandhi answered 'somebody [who] asked what we should do with a mad dog, whether we should not kill it'. Saying that the questioner really wanted to know 'what should be done when a man went mad', Gandhi related an incident from his boyhood:

> I remember when I was about ten, a brother of mine had gone mad. Afterwards he was cured. He is no more ... In a fit of madness he would rush out and strike everyone. But what could I do to him? Could I beat him? Or could my mother or father beat him? ... A vaidya was called in and he was asked to treat my brother in every possible manner except by beating him. He was my blood-brother. But now I make no such distinctions. Now all of you are like my blood-brothers. If all of you lose your sanity and I happen to have an army at my disposal, do you think I should have you shot? (95: 161–2)

His utterances were in Hindi and in a voice that seemed constructed in the heart, not in the throat. The pitch was never raised, he did not stress his words, and yet the voice could penetrate listeners with its earnestness. 'We almost wept,' Erik Erikson would later write (referring to his wife Joan and himself), 'when Pyarelal and his sister Sushila arranged for us to listen (in 1963) to Gandhi's own voice and diction on recordings.'[47]

Violence & serenity. For 30 years he had taught non-violence to India. Yet Calcutta, Noakhali, Bihar and the Punjab had erupted in violence. His explanation (24 Jul.) was that

> Outwardly we followed truth and non-violence. But inwardly there was violence in us. We practised hypocrisy and as a result we have to suffer the pain of mutual strife. Even today we are nurturing attitudes that will result in war and if this drift is not stopped we shall find ourselves in a conflict much more sanguinary than the Mutiny of 1857 (96: 129).

Three days earlier, in a response to Swami Sivananda of Rishikesh, who asked about the violence, Gandhi had said: 'There was violence in the name of non-violence and now we are tasting its bitter fruit' (96: 99). The twin components of Gandhi's non-violence, 'fear not' and 'hate not', were both difficult, but the first found wider acceptance than the second. And it was a short step from hating one lot of people (the British) to hating another lot (Hindus or Muslims). On 16 June he said:

> No one at the time [*during the battles for Swaraj*] showed us how to make an atom bomb. Had we known how to make it we would have considered annihilating the English with it (95: 289).

Because a violent alternative was not visible, Gandhi added, 'my advice was accepted'. Each time violence occurred during a Swaraj campaign Gandhi had offered a similar diagnosis, but although he frequently suspended a campaign because of violence, a resumption or a new campaign always followed.

Despite his pain and shame at the violence, the fact that 'a great power had to leave the country' was noteworthy, he said (8 Jul.; 96: 13). But, he warned, if the violence continued, 'England, Russia, America or China – any of these countries' could intervene (25 Jul.; 96: 130).

A letter he dictated to Manu on 10 June conveys agony but also a sense of peace and a sense of achievement. The unidentified addressee was obviously someone close to Gandhi:

> I have passed through many an ordeal in my life. But perhaps this is to be the hardest … I am dictating these letters [to Manu] early in the morning … I know I make her work beyond her capacity. But God seems to sustain her in spite of it all …
>
> Still another sign of His grace is the way in which He is keeping up my physical strength, enabling me to maintain my serenity in the midst of daily shocks and turmoil. I remain happy and cheerful.
>
> For sixty years we have been in the thick of the fight, and now we have ushered the goddess of liberty into our courtyard (95: 247–8).

Gandhi sounded ready, however, to be killed:

> *25 May*: I would die smiling with the name of Rama on my lips (95: 140).
> *16 Jun.*: I shall consider myself brave if I am killed and if I still pray to God for my assassin (95: 290).

Bitter 'refinement'. In July the Congress and the Constituent Assembly selected a refined Congress flag as India's national flag. Not agreeing that it was 'haughty' on the part of the Congress to propose its banner as the national flag, Gandhi pointed out that all over India freedom's battles had been waged under the tricolour with the charkha in the middle.

But he was hurt when told that 'instead of the charkha there is only a wheel on the flag'. Though he said (22 Jul.) that it was 'all the same to me whether they keep or do not keep the charkha,' adding, 'Even if they cast it away, I will still have it in my hand and in my heart' (96: 112), his pain was apparent. Since the original design was largely his, the change was a personal rebuff. Moreover, the charkha symbolized non-violence, and its removal from the flag seemed an explicit rejection of non-violence.

At the wheel – 1946

Defending the 'refinement', Nehru argued that the charkha was represented by the Asoka chakra or wheel replacing it, but it was obvious that he thought the wheel more artistic than the charkha. This Gandhi was unwilling to concede, but he underlined Emperor Asoka's pluralism and non-violence[*]:

> 24 Jul.: There is not much difference between the new and the old flag except that the old one was a little more elegant (96: 129).
> 27 Jul.: Looking at the wheel some may recall that prince of peace, King Asoka, ruler of an empire, who renounced power. He represented all faiths; he was an embodiment of compassion. Seeing the charkha in his chakra adds to the glory of the charkha. Asoka's chakra represents [the] eternally revolving divine law of ahimsa (96: 152–3).

Independence day

Remarks Gandhi made in a talk in Delhi on 8 July 1947 with Aruna Asaf Ali and Sushila Nayar reveal his uncertainty about where he should be as India approached independence:

> At one time I feel that Bihar is calling me, at another time I hear the call from Noakhali where I succeeded to some extent in establishing peace. When I came here from Patna a month ago, I imagined that I would be back at my work in a week. But in the course of this one month so many changes have taken place in the country that a family wouldn't have seen … in a generation. I am rotting in Delhi. However, I have not at all given up Noakhali and Bihar work. I am very keen to go to the Punjab also (96: 11).

On 10 June he had said:

> [I]f I go to the Punjab I shall live there regarding it as my home and if I am killed I shall accept death (95: 252).

Well aware, as we have seen, of preparations for renewed violence in the Punjab, and urged by many to go there, he however felt the absence of 'a call from within' (96: 199). Fearing that Gandhi might be killed in the Punjab, Nehru and Patel opposed his going there.

In the first week of August he found clarity. After completing his Kashmir foray, he

---

[*] Asoka = 3rd-century BC Indian emperor who embraced Buddhism.

entrained in Lahore on 6 August for Patna: he would rather be in Bihar and Bengal than in New Delhi, and plan to reach Noakhali before mid-August.

Choosing to spend independence day in Noakhali, and thus in Pakistan, he had also concluded that the day called for appropriate celebration. On the eve of his Kashmir trip he had said in Delhi (29 Jul.):

> [W]e should fast and pray on August 15. I may say that I do not intend to mourn. But it is a matter of grief that we have no food and no clothes. Human beings kill human beings. In Lahore, people cannot leave their houses for fear that they will be killed. These are not the conditions in which we can rejoice and feast. I shall, therefore, say that we must celebrate the day but by fasting, praying and spinning. Yes, we should not mourn (Delhi, 29 Jul.; 96: 174–5).

Nine days earlier he had said:

> *20 Jul.*: Unfortunately the kind of freedom we have got today contains also the seeds of future conflict between India and Pakistan. How can we therefore light the lamps? (96: 92)

While on the train to Patna he again acknowledged, in a note for *Harijan*, the possibility of being killed. But that would not be the end of the story:

> *7 Aug.*: I shall be alive in the grave and, what is more, speaking from it (96: 202).

On arrival in Patna (8 Aug.) he said he 'wanted to live both in Hindustan and Pakistan and both were his homelands. Similar was the case with Jinnah Saheb. Muslims had got Pakistan. Now it was incumbent on the people of both Hindustan and Pakistan to live like good human beings and bring peace to the country' (96: 204–5).

The next day he said he 'must reach Noakhali two or three days before August 15 as the people there were extremely nervous' (96: 204). On 9 August, *en route* to Noakhali, he arrived in Calcutta, where Muslim and Hindu friends urged him to 'to tarry in Calcutta'. Suhrawardy was on his way out as premier, and Prafulla Chandra Ghosh of the Congress was about to take over as the chief minister of West Bengal. 'Muslim police and officials were almost withdrawn and replaced by Hindus, and the Hindus had begun to believe that they were now free to do what they liked, as the Muslims were reported to have done under the League Ministry.'

Many Muslims were living in terror, Gandhi was told, and he was urged, 'before he went up to Noakhali', to spend some days in Calcutta to 'pour a pot of water over the raging fire' that was burning the city (96: 206). On 10 August Gandhi said (in Satis Dasgupta's Sodepur ashram, where he had stopped over) that he had 'decided to stay to see if he could contribute his share in the return of sanity in the premier city of India' (96: 208).

This point of time, when Gandhi again feels obliged to change his plans, is a good place to note the contrast between the Gandhi who once executed his strategies by the calendar and the map – a Gandhi who knew precisely when and where he and his forces would march – and the more uncertain Gandhi we now see, one forced again and again to alter his plans. And if the sure general of earlier years provoked our admiration, perhaps we should also note the older man's responsiveness to rapidly changing situations. He retains his equanimity when things do not go his way, even as he had resisted excessive elation when they did, and when a schedule he has patiently prepared for has to be abruptly abandoned.

Four days before freedom, the BBC asked for a message from the Empire's chief foe. The moment of triumph was also one of grief, and Gandhi felt he had nothing to say. The BBC pleaded: his message would be broadcast in several languages, Gandhi was told. Through Nirmal Kumar Bose, who had rejoined him in Calcutta, Gandhi conveyed a firm answer:

I must not yield to the temptation. They must forget that I know English (96: 209).

Later that day (11 Aug.), when Suhrawardy said that Calcutta needed Gandhi for a while, Gandhi answered that he would put off his Noakhali visit provided 'you and I are prepared to live together': he was repeating his 'mad offer' of May. Added Gandhi:

We shall have to work till every Hindu and Mussalman in Calcutta safely returns to the place where he was before. We shall continue in our effort till our last breath. I do not want you to come to a decision immediately. You should go back home and consult your daughter ... [T]he old Suhrawardy will have to die and accept the garb of a fakir (96: 214).

This time the offer was accepted. At his 12 August prayer meeting in Sodepur, Gandhi said that he had been warned by some Hindus that Suhrawardy was 'not to be relied upon'. But then some Muslims imagined him (Gandhi) 'to be a consummate hypocrite' and an enemy of Muslims. 'God alone knew men's hearts,' Gandhi added. He would trust Suhrawardy even as he hoped to be trusted himself.

Both would live under the same roof, and have no secrets from each other. They would together see all the visitors. People should have the courage to speak out the truth under all circumstances and in the presence of those against whom it had to be said (96: 216–17).

On the morning of 13 August Gandhi left the Sodepur ashram, Suhrawardy left his house in the city, and Hydari Manzil, 'an old abandoned Muslim house' in Beliaghata, a run-down Hindu-majority locality, became his latest base or ashram, with Suhrawardy as his latest ashram-mate, and Abha, Manu and Bisen as his aides. But among the Hindus of Beliaghata 'young blood [was] boiling', as Gandhi wrote to Pyarelal within hours of moving into Hydari Manzil (96: 222).

Accusing Gandhi of pro-Muslim bias, a band of angry young Hindus asked him to leave Beliaghata. He had two sessions with the group, including one in Suhrawardy's presence. If Beliaghata's Hindus invited their Muslim neighbours to return, he said to them, he and Suhrawardy would move to a predominantly Muslim area until Hindus were invited to return there. The young men were 'completely won over' by this offer,[48] and another irate group was pacified when Suhrawardy boldly admitted responsibility for the Great Calcutta Killings a year earlier (96: 230).

The next day, 14 August, was so different that it even became possible for Calcutta's residents to imagine that 'there never had been bad blood between the Hindus and the Muslims'. A grateful Gandhi wrote:

In their thousands they began to embrace one another and they began to pass freely through places which were considered to be points of danger by one party or the other. Indeed, Hindus were taken to their masjids by their Muslim brethren and the latter were taken by their Hindu brethren to the mandirs. Both with one voice shouted 'Jai Hind' or 'Hindus-Muslims! Be one'.[49]

India was independent before morning, and Gandhi once more opened his eyes in a Muslim house in one of the poorest corners of Calcutta. Three hours or so earlier, at midnight in New Delhi, speaking inside a magnificent circle of sandstone built by the Raj, Jawaharlal Nehru had made one of his greatest speeches, on India's 'tryst with destiny'.

Content where he was, Gandhi recited his pre-dawn prayers, plied his charkha, remembered Mahadev Desai, whose birthday it was, and said he would consume only fruit juice during the day. Though he had not felt like lighting lamps, fireworks had lit up Calcutta for all of the previous night. The day saw a stream of visitors to Hydari Manzil: the new ministry, led by Prafulla Ghosh, Rajagopalachari (the governor), students, Communists, and others, including 'numberless Hindus and Muslims'.[50]

Gandhi's advice to the new ministers was offered in short sentences: 'Be humble. Be forbearing … [N]ow you will be tested through and through. Beware of power; power corrupts. Do not let yourselves be entrapped by its pomp and pageantry. Remember, you are in office to serve the poor in India's villages' (96: 233).

He wrote the day's quota of letters. One was addressed to his Quaker friend in England, Agatha Harrison:

> My dear Agatha, This letter I am dictating whilst I am spinning. You know, my way of celebrating great events, such as today's, is to thank God for it and, therefore, to pray. This prayer must be accompanied by a fast, if the taking of fruit juices may be so described. And then as a mark of identification with the poor and dedication there must be [extra] spinning … My love to all our friends (96: 230–1).

So the Empire's principal foe sent his love to Britons on independence day. In the afternoon he conducted a prayer meeting on an open ground in Beliaghata. Thousands of Muslims and Hindus attended. There, and earlier in the day, Gandhi felt that 'the joy of fraternization [was] leaping up from hour to hour'.[51]

In a short prayer talk, Gandhi expressed joy at the turn of events in Calcutta and concern over the news coming in of 'madness' in Lahore and of flooding in the Chittagong area, now part of Pakistan. He ended the talk by asking Calcutta's residents to 'treat the Europeans who stayed in India with the same regard as they would expect for themselves' – Gandhi had heard of some Europeans being compelled to utter independence cries (96: 232).

Making an unusual request, he then asked to be driven anonymously round the city. He wanted to take in more of Calcutta's joy and also to probe whether it was 'Miracle or Accident?', his title for a piece he wrote the next day for *Harijan*:

> 16 Aug.: By whatever name [the change in Calcutta] may be described, it is quite clear that all the credit that is being given to me from all sides is quite undeserved; nor can it be said to be deserved by Shaheed Saheb [Suhrawardy]. This sudden upheaval is not the work of one or two men. We are toys in the hands of God. He makes us dance to His tune … In the present exuberance one hears also the cry of 'Long Live Hindustan and Pakistan' from the joint throats of the Hindus and the Muslims. I think it is quite proper (96: 236–7).

Eid day fell on 18 August. Half a million Hindus and Muslims attended Gandhi's prayer meeting, held on the grounds of the Mohammedan Sporting Football Club. 'I will never be able to forget the scene I have witnessed today,' Gandhi said (96: 247).

His secret. Someone in Calcutta asked Gandhi for an answer to doubt. Gandhi's reply appears as a plate opposite page 89 in the final volume of Tendulkar's eight-volume biography of Gandhi, with Gandhi's signatures in Hindi and Bengali below the text, which is in English. But Tendulkar does not name the questioner, who may have been the reticent Tendulkar himself, and he does not give a precise date. But he implies that it was in August 1947:

> I will give you a talisman. Whenever you are in doubt, or when the self becomes too much with you, apply the following test. Recall the face of the poorest and the weakest man whom you may have seen, and ask yourself if the step you contemplate is going to be of any use to him. Will he gain anything by it? Will it restore him to a control over his own life and destiny? In other words, will it lead to swaraj for the hungry and spiritually starving millions? Then you will find your doubts and yourself melting away.

A man of God who was definitely not a godman,* Gandhi appealed to believers and also to agnostics, of whom Tendulkar was one. In this famous text, Gandhi characteristically defines Swaraj in terms of empowering the weak.

Jehangir Patel and Marjorie Sykes would write that Gandhi's distinctive offering was 'the gift of the fight', and Rammanohar Lohia would say: 'This enabling the individual to resist oppression by himself and without any support is to my mind the greatest quality of Mahatma Gandhi's action and life.'[52]

Endorsing the thought, Upton Close would write: 'What was his secret? I think my wife discovered it. She said: "In his presence I felt a new capability and power in myself rather than a consciousness of his power. I felt equal, good for anything – an assurance I had never known before, as if some consciousness within me had newly awakened."'[53]

Punjab. By independence day, however, terrifying cries were being uttered in the Punjab. On 2 August Evan Jenkins, the governor, had told Mountbatten that roughly 1,200 Muslims and 3,800 Sikhs and Hindus had been killed in the province since 4 March. In his final days as Viceroy, Mountbatten was urged by Jinnah, Nehru and Patel alike to be ruthless in suppressing rioters, if need be by imposing martial law, but Jenkins and senior military commanders argued against the step, and Mountbatten agreed with them.[54]

The Empire quitting India was not going to risk many British lives to keep the peace in the Punjab. As for the Raj's Indian soldiers, they were not thought capable of shooting rioters from their community. The Empire would, however, allow 'a few hundred British civilian and military officers' to remain in the province through independence day.

---

* Godman = a charismatic person with supposed supernatural powers.

From 1 August a newly created Punjab Boundary Force (PBF) under the command of a British officer, Major-General T W Rees, was placed along the likely 'border' that Sir Cyril Radcliffe's Boundary Commission was to delineate by the middle of the month. Though the PBF's officers comprised whites as well as Hindus, Muslims and Sikhs, its 55,000 men did not include a single Briton.

The numbers worked out to little more than one soldier per square mile. As independence day approached and the border was delineated, it proved easy for murderous bands in the Punjab to bypass the PBF; and for minorities the option of moving across the border became a compulsion to leave.

In the Frontier Province (and in Assam's Sylhet district), the referendum went in Pakistan's favour as expected. A week after Pakistan's emergence Dr Khan Sahib's ministry was dismissed, and the vilification of Badshah Khan and his Khudai Khidmatgars continued.

Gandhi's reaction to the Punjab news was to offer to go there, but Nehru and Patel persisted in their opposition to the idea, while urging him to come to Delhi. Meanwhile Governor-General Mountbatten wrote to Gandhi (26 Aug.):

In the Punjab we have 55,000 soldiers and large-scale rioting on our hands. In Bengal our forces consist of one man, and there is no rioting. As a serving officer, as well as an administrator, may I be allowed to pay my tribute to the One-man Boundary Force, not forgetting his Second in Command, Mr Suhrawardy (96: 303).

Writing back (30 Aug.) to Mountbatten that credit should probably go instead to 'suitable conditions' in Bengal (96: 303), Gandhi told Nirmal Kumar Bose that his gift lay not in 'creating a new situation' but in sensing and 'giving shape' to 'what is stirring in the heart of the masses'.[55] The claim of insight and craftsmanship was thus joined to an admission of dependence on his people.

Gandhi asked Mountbatten too about going to the Punjab (96: 303). In a letter written the same day to Nehru, he said:

About my going to the Punjab, I won't move without your and Vallabhbhai's wish. I want to say, however, that every day pressure is being put upon me to rush to the Punjab before it is too late …

If I am not going to the Punjab, would I be of much use in Delhi as an adviser or consultant? I fancy I am not built that way. My advice has value only when I am actually working at a particular thing. I can only disturb when I give academic advice as on food, clothing, the use of the military …

Left to myself I would probably rush to the Punjab and if necessary break myself in the attempt to stop the warring elements from committing suicide (96: 304).

And to Patel, Gandhi wrote, also on 30 August:

May God give all of you the strength and the wisdom the situation demands. Did you ever think that you would have to face such a difficult situation so soon? His will be done (96: 304).

Plans made & unmade

The next day Gandhi decided that, accompanied by Suhrawardy, he should after all go, as earlier planned, to Noakhali – to Pakistan, that is. Having played a valiant part in Hydari Manzil, Suhrawardy left for his home to get ready for Noakhali. However, a hostile demonstration at Hydari Manzil on the night of 31 August caused yet another change in Gandhi's plans.

At about 10 p.m. a crowd of angry Hindus smashed the house's windows, doors and ceiling fans. Gandhi, Abha, Manu and Bisen came out to meet the demonstrators. Bricks and a lathi were thrown at Gandhi, at an unidentified Muslim who was present, and at Bisen, whom the crowd took for a Muslim. Only the unknown Muslim was hit and no one was hurt, but it was a close call. Abha and Manu, 'two very brave girls', as Gandhi called them, did not leave his side and held on to him throughout the disturbance (96: 315). Instructing the Muslims in the house and the two policemen present to remain calm, he folded his hands, in the Hindu fashion, towards the demonstrators while firmly asking them to disperse, but they did so only after the police superintendent arrived.

Going to sleep at 12.30 a.m., Gandhi was up again in three hours. One of his first acts thereafter was to write to Vallabhbhai, describing the incident. He also mentioned urgings to visit the Punjab, referred to Nehru, and added, 'I feel totally lost. I pin my hopes on you two' (96: 313). Soon he learnt of killings elsewhere in the city during the night. He went to some affected areas, saw 'two dead bodies of very poor Muslims' (96: 317), and wondered about Calcutta's peace.

In the afternoon, however, a telegram arrived from Nehru suggesting a visit to the Punjab 'as early as possible',[56] whereupon Gandhi thought he should do that the next day (2 Sep.), giving up Noakhali (96: 321). The decision in favour of the Punjab was made in the teeth of Patel's view (27 Aug.): 'You will not be able to put out the conflagration in Punjab.'[57]

But after visitors brought more news of Calcutta's violence – around 50 had been killed during the night of 31 August and the day of 1 September – he was clear about something else. At about 8 p.m. on 1 September he decided he would go neither to Noakhali nor to the Punjab: he would stay put in Hydari Manzil *and fast* until peace returned to Calcutta.

'If the fury (in Calcutta) did not abate, my going to the Punjab would be of no avail,' he wrote to Jawaharlal (96: 321). And if Calcutta responded positively to his fast, he could go with confidence to the Punjab.

Running to Hydari Manzil from the mansion once designed for the Empire's chief functionary in India, governor Rajagopalachari asked Gandhi: 'Can you fast against the goondas?' Gandhi's reply was that his fast could touch 'the hearts of those behind the goondas', without whose 'sympathy and passive support the goondas would have no legs to stand on' (96: 318).

Announced at 8.15 p.m. on 1 September, the fast had an immediate impact. Violence died down. Hindus and Muslims marched jointly for peace. About 500 members of the north Calcutta police force, including a few Britons and Anglo-Indians, themselves went on a 24-hour sympathy fast while remaining on duty. A professor would later recall:

> Some [university students] even gathered weapons from streets and homes at great personal risk and returned them to Gandhiji. Men would come back from their offices in the evening and find food prepared by their family ready for them; but soon it would be revealed that the women of the home had not eaten during the whole day … They could not understand how they could go on when Gandhiji was dying for their own crimes.[58]

Rammanohar Lohia, the Socialist leader, brought to Gandhi a group of young Hindus who admitted complicity in violence and handed over a small arsenal of arms. Inspecting the surrendered weapons, Gandhi remarked that he was seeing a Sten gun for the first time (96: 342). When (4 Sep.) members of another gang turned up, asking for 'any penalty' and pleading, 'Only you should now end your fast,' Gandhi said they should go 'immediately among the Muslims and assure them full protection' (96: 337).

Not forgetting Noakhali, Gandhi sent (4 Sep.) a letter via Pyarelal to Khwaja Nazimuddin, the new chief minister of Pakistan's East Bengal province, informing him that he was being asked to visit 'both parts of the Punjab', which had gone 'utterly mad', and asking Nazimuddin 'to tell me all about Noakhali' (96: 333).

At 6 p.m. on 4 September a deputation of Mahasabha, Sikh and Muslim League leaders, headed by Suhrawardy, went up to Gandhi's bedside in Hydari Manzil and asked for the fast to end. Gandhi asked them if they would risk their lives to prevent a recurrence of the events of 31 August and 1 September. After withdrawing to another room, the leaders returned with a pledge. Gandhi reminded them that 'above all, there is God, our witness' and agreed to break his fast, which had lasted for 73 hours.

On 1 September a young Hindu, Sachin Mitra, had been killed in Calcutta while defending Muslims, and on 3 September, another young Hindu, Smritish Banerjee, lost his life while guarding a peace march. During the fast, 'processions of young women and girls of both communities … walked across the city to Gandhi's lodging and brought peace'. According to Martin Green, the Calcutta of September 1947 demonstrated the power of 'the saint, the martyr and the virgin, [working] together …'[59]

'Gandhiji has achieved many things,' C R observed on 5 September, 'but in my considered opinion there has been nothing, not even independence, which is so truly wonderful as his victory over evil in Calcutta.'[60]

During the fast a British journalist asked Gandhi about his ability 'to maintain a spirit of detachment in such a surprising manner'. Gandhi answered that 'it was not true that he was never off his balance. Such occasions were rare, yet the long exercise of self-restraint enabled him, through God's grace, to keep his irritation within very narrow bounds' (96: 329).

From the fast the Shanti Sena (Peace Brigade) emerged on 5 September, a body of young people prepared to intervene non-violently in any clash. And when Devtosh Das Gupta, the Shanti Sena secretary, asked Gandhi for a message, he received a short sentence written in Bengali:

My life is my message (96: 342).

Two years earlier, when Denton Brooks Jr. of the *Chicago Defender* had asked for a message for Americans, Gandhi had given a similar reply:

My life is its own message. If it is not, then nothing I can now write will fulfil the purpose (87: 8).

The Calcutta miracle notwithstanding, the man at whose call India's prisons used to be filled, and streets emptied, was now often short of help and living an uncertain life. To Jivanji Desai, *Harijan*'s manager in Ahmedabad, Gandhi wrote:

20 Aug.: I am very sorry to learn that you got the articles on Wednesday … I take the utmost care to see that you get all the material on Monday evening. With that aim, I send the material by air-mail from Calcutta on Sunday. But …

I have no paid employee ... Do you send anybody to the airport on Mondays? (96: 254–5)

His situation at this time and also his businesslike approach come across from a piece inviting the honest opinion of *Harijan*'s readers:

Harijan, 31 Aug. 1947: My life has become, if possible, more tempestuous than before. Nor can I at present claim any place as a permanent habitation. The columns are predominantly filled by my after-prayer speeches. In the original I contribute, on an average, only one and a half columns per week. This is hardly satisfactory. I would like, therefore, the readers ... to give me their frank opinion as to whether they really need their *Harijan* weekly to satisfy their political or spiritual hunger.

They should send their answers to the Editor of the *Harijan*, Ahmedabad ... In the left hand upper corner of the envelope containing the answer, the writer should state: 'About *Harijan*' (96: 270–1).

Man proposes

His way to the Punjab cleared, Gandhi thanked Calcutta, emphasised the martyrdom of Mitra and Banerjee, and on the night of 7 September boarded a train for Delhi – *en route*, he informed Nehru in a telegram, to the Punjab (96: 345).

After mid-August that province was covered in blood. A foul wind touched down in scores of places in the Punjab and set off frenzied attacks. Major-General Rees of the Punjab Boundary Force would record that he witnessed 'pre-medieval savagery'.

Neither sex nor age was spared. Mothers with babes in their arms were cut down, speared or shot, and Sikhs cried 'Rawalpindi' as they struck home. Both sides were equally merciless.[61]

Gandhi had recognized 'the savagery of the Punjab' (1 Sep., 96: 316), but as his train rattled across West Bengal, Bihar, and UP to Delhi he did not know that by the end of September killings in the Punjab would amount to a quarter of a million or more, with equal numbers of Muslims and non-Muslims falling victim, or that a large number of women would be raped or abducted.

Nor did he know that the two-way flow that had started in August – eastward of Hindus and Sikhs, westward of Muslims – would continue until the summer of 1948 and enter history as the Great Migration, with about five-and-a-half million Hindus and Sikhs moving to India and a similar number of Muslims to Pakistan, many of them trudging with bullock-carts in long convoys, and others packed in trains, several of which delivered only dead bodies at their destinations.

Yet what was known by 7 September was horrific enough. Gandhi was aware that on 3 September Premier Nehru and deputy premier Patel had flown to Lahore to discuss the Punjab violence with Jinnah, who had taken over as Pakistan's Governor-General, and Liaqat Ali Khan, the new country's first Premier. On his train journey of two nights Gandhi must have wondered how he would grapple with a province – now two provinces – where neighbours had turned into killers. He had not faced a greater challenge in all his life.

Gandhi bore a minor grievance as well, for he had been informed that before proceeding to the Punjab he might be put up in Delhi not with his Harijans on Reading Road but in Birla House on Albuquerque Road (now 30 January Marg), not far from the houses of Nehru (York Road, now Motilal Nehru Marg) and Patel (on Aurangzeb Road).[62]

He had been told, moreover, to get off his train at Shahdara, before Delhi's main station, for the situation was tense even in the capital. Although Gandhi 'knew nothing about the sad state of things in Delhi when [he] left Calcutta',[63] violence had broken out there on the morning of 5 September, hundreds had since been killed, 'localities like Karol Bagh, Sabzimandi and Paharganj were being emptied of Muslims', the city was under curfew, and people's rations were exhausted.[64]

Meeting Gandhi at Shahdara station at dawn on 9 September, Patel confirmed that he was being taken to Birla House, for it would be hard to protect him in the sweepers' colony and hard also for visitors to meet him there; moreover, refugees were living in the colony. A disappointed Gandhi was troubled even more by Patel's sombre countenance. In their long association, this was the first encounter where Vallabhbhai did not crack a joke. The police officers accompanying him also looked worried.

In the car Patel gave Gandhi Delhi's troubling details. Off quickly to work, Gandhi called that day at a camp near Humayun's Tomb where Muslim Meos from Alwar and Bharatpur had taken refuge, at the Jamia Millia, where many Delhi Muslims had huddled together, and at three camps (Diwan Hall, Wavell Canteen and Kingsway) filled with Hindu and Sikh refugees from West Punjab.

For a 'whole day long' he listened 'to the tale of woe that is Delhi today' (96: 352). Zakir Husain spoke at the Jamia of his escape on a train a few days earlier: had a Sikh army captain and a Hindu railway official not helped, Husain, who had believed all his life in a single India, would have been killed. Gandhi heard, too, that Saifuddin Kitchlew, from 1919 a national-level leader of the Congress, had been forced to flee from his Delhi home for Kashmir, the land of his forebears.

Hindu and Sikh refugees from Pakistan told Gandhi that while they had not forgotten his services to the Punjab, he 'had not undergone the hardships that they did … not lost

[his] kith and kin ... [and] not been compelled to beg at every door' (96: 357). And his hosts at Birla House said that the city was in such disarray that even they, belonging to one of India's richest families, had not been able to obtain fruits and vegetables (96: 356). In a conversation during the day with P C Joshi, a Communist leader, Gandhi said: 'I do not remember an occasion in my life ... when I have felt [as] baffled as I am today' (96: 353).

Yet, at the end of the day, Gandhi found clarity: he would not go to the Punjab but remain in Delhi until the capital 'regained its former self' (96: 352). 'Man proposes, God disposes', Gandhi said that night while announcing the latest change in his plans (96: 342).

The next morning a Sikh taxi driver told Brij Krishna, Gandhi's aide in Delhi from the 1920s: 'If Gandhiji had waited some more days before coming to Delhi, all the Muslims here would have been eliminated.'[65] In the inflamed climate of August/ September 1947, when refugees brought ghastly accounts from Pakistan, turning Delhi into a solely Hindu city was not altogether a fantasy. An angry section of the populace would have supported such a bid, and quite a few civil and police officials would have winked at it.

Anti-Muslim elements in Delhi had in fact hoped for word to spread that home minister Patel was secretly on their side. Very human and very Hindu, Patel was undoubtedly more disturbed by a report of Hindus or Sikhs having been killed than by similar news about Muslims. Yet the home minister's hand was ruled not by his heart but by the law. As far back as March, after violence had first hit the Punjab, Patel had assured Gandhi that 'here (in Delhi) of course we shall be able to deal with it' (94: 168); and on 8 September the *Hindustan Times* published Patel's warning that partisan officials would be punished.

With Gandhi present in Delhi, and Patel plainly ready to do his bidding, it became impossible for anyone high or low in the police or the bureaucracy, or indeed for anyone in the public, to separate Patel from Gandhi or from Nehru, or to claim that Vallabhbhai would condone anti-Muslim violence. The bid to expel or eliminate all the Muslims of Delhi was aborted.

Agonizing at what was happening in the two Punjabs, in the Frontier Province, and in Delhi, Gandhi was nonetheless at peace. He had found 'a particular thing' to 'work at' in Delhi. In the days to follow he would speak frequently of the city's significance:

13 Sep.: It is said that in the *Mahabharata* period the Pandavas used to stay in this Purana Quila. Whether you call it Indraprastha or Delhi, the Hindus and the Muslims have grown here together. It was the capital of the Mughals. Now it is the capital of India ... The Mughals came from outside. They identified themselves with the manners and customs of Delhi ... In such a Delhi of yours the Hindus and the Muslims used to live together peacefully. They ... would fight for a short while and then be united again ... This is your Delhi (96: 368–9).

25 Sep.: If peace is not established here, the whole of Hindustan will be on fire (96: 424).

3 Nov.: Ultimately Delhi will decide the destiny of the whole country (97: 221).

18 Nov.: I have to do or die here. If heart unity is not restored in Delhi, I can see flames raging all over India (97: 343).

Remembering his own links with Dehli, he recalled friends who were no more: Swami Shraddhanand, Hakim Ajmal Khan, Mukhtar Ahmed Ansari, Charlie Andrews, who had taught at St Stephen's College, Sushil Kumar Rudra, the St Stephen's principal in whose home Gandhi had composed his non-cooperation challenge to the Viceroy, and others.

He had indeed seen Delhi change and grow and add New Delhi to itself. Delhi was where, in 1918, he had addressed the Raj in Hindustani and in 1931 signed his pact with Irwin. It was also where, in 1924 in Muhammad Ali's home, he had fasted for 21 days for Hindu-Muslim unity. And Delhi was where his grandson – Harilal's young son Rasik – had died in 1929, and where his youngest son, Devadas, editor of the *Hindustan Times*, was living with his family.

In and from this Delhi – in such teamwork as became possible with his people and with his political 'sons' – he would serve his newly freed but also wounded and traumatized India, and also Pakistan, which too he saw as his. He would serve by standing up to hate.

Strategy against hate

Three days after arriving in Delhi, Gandhi confronted the RSS chief, M S Golwalkar, with reports of the RSS's role in the Delhi violence. Denying the allegations, Golwalkar also said, in answer to a question from Gandhi, that the RSS did not stand for the killing of Muslims. Gandhi asked him to say so publicly. Golwalkar said Gandhi could quote him. This Gandhi did in his prayer talk that evening, but he told Golwalkar that the statement ought to come from him. Afterwards, Gandhi said to Nehru that he did not find Golwalkar convincing.[66]

On 16 September, at Gandhi's instance, a number of RSS activists called on him. He told them that while he had been impressed years earlier by the discipline, simplicity and absence of untouchability he had noticed in an RSS camp, 'sacrifice without purity of motive and true knowledge has been known to prove ruinous to society'. Their 'strength could be used in the interest of India or against it', the RSS men were told.

Asked by one of them if Hinduism did not permit killing an evildoer, Gandhi answered: 'How could a sinner claim the right to judge or execute another sinner?' Only a properly constituted government was entitled to punish an evildoer. To chasten any in the group hoping to play Patel against Nehru, Gandhi said, '[The two] have been colleagues for years and have the same aim,' and added:

> Both the Sardar and Pandit Nehru will be rendered powerless if you become judge and executioner in one ... Do not sabotage their efforts by taking the law into your own hands (96: 382).[67]

Not taking the law into their own hands – rather than absolute non-violence – was what he was also prescribing to the people at large, who were hearing of attacks on Hindus and Sikhs in Pakistan, even as the public in Pakistan heard of attacks on Muslims in India.

In September and thereafter, Gandhi's team and staff in Birla House consisted of Abha, Manu, Brij Krishna, Bisen, Kalyanam (a stenographer) and, when they were in Delhi, Pyarelal and his sister Sushila, though Pyarelal was more in Noakhali than in Delhi, while Sushila was often in the Punjab. All in the team, including Gandhi, slept on thin mats on the floor in one room and/or its verandah at the western end of the house. At three in the morning Bisen roused everyone else, including Gandhi, but at times this chore was performed by Gandhi.

The room was also where, sitting on a thin mat covered with white khadi, Gandhi wrote, span, received callers and ate his meals, and where he and the others prayed before dawn each morning. At five in the evening Gandhi and his companions walked past a lawn for multi-faith prayers held in the open at the southern end of the Birla House grounds. Anyone who wanted could attend the prayers and hear Gandhi's post-prayer remarks: usually a few hundred did.

Refugees from West Pakistan and Muslims feeling insecure in India constituted the majority of his callers at Birla House. Nehru and Patel frequently dropped in, as did others including Amrit Kaur, now India's health minister, and Devadas and his family, and, occasionally, Mira, visiting from her ashram in the foothills of western UP.

Delivered in simple Hindi (or Hindustani, as he preferred to call it), his prayer talks were relayed live on national radio and carried by the newspapers. He prepared these talks with care, writing out, for the sake of the press, a draft in English. The remarks of 12 September, when he spoke of the pointlessness of tit for tat and of what would enable him to go to the two Punjabs, provide an example:

The very first thing I want to tell you is that I have received disturbing news from the Frontier Province ... What I think to myself I may as well convey to you, that is, we should not get angry. We can, of course, feel the pain ... It is natural to feel, 'Why not kill the Muslims because our brothers have been killed.' But I for one cannot kill even the actual murderers of my brothers. Should I then prepare myself to kill other innocent people? ...

I have seen the terrible plight of the Hindus and Sikhs of Pakistan. I have lived in Lahore. Do you think I am not pained? I claim that my pain is no less than that of any Punjabi. If any Hindu or Sikh from the Punjab comes and tells me that his anguish is greater than mine because he has lost his brother or daughter or father, I would say that his brother is my brother, his mother is my mother, and I have the same anguish in my heart as he has.

I am also a human being and feel enraged but I swallow my anger. That gives me strength. What revenge can I take with that strength? How should I take revenge so that they feel repentant for their crimes and admit that they have committed grave crimes?

I had gone to the Jama Masjid today. I met the [Muslim] residents of that area. I also met their womenfolk. Some of the women wept before me and some brought their children to indicate their sad plight. Should I narrate to them the plight of the Hindus and Sikhs in West Punjab and in the Frontier Province? Will it mitigate the sorrow of the Hindus and Sikhs of the Punjab in any way?

The people of Pakistan resorted to ways of barbarism, and so did the Hindus and Sikhs [in India]. He who does good to one who has been good to him is a mere Bania and a pseudo-Bania at that. I say that I am a Bania myself; and I am a true Bania. May you not become pseudo-Banias. [The] true human being ... does a good turn for evil. I learnt this in my childhood. I still believe in the rightness of this. I would like you to return evil with good.

The Government needs arms, what has the citizen got to do with them? None of the city people should possess arms. I would like the Muslims to surrender all the arms in their possession to the Government. The Hindus too should surrender all their arms ...

The same thing happened in Calcutta and the Hindus and the Muslims have started living like brothers ... You must soon create such a situation in Delhi that I can immediately go to the Punjab and tell the people there that the Muslims of Delhi are living in peace. I would ask for its reward there. I would ask for that reward from the Nawab of Mamdot (the West Punjab chief minister). I would go to East Punjab as well ... (96: 361–5)

But the situation in the Punjab was getting worse. In the middle of September the governments of India and Pakistan agreed that in the two new Punjabs 'priority should be given to the transfer of refugees rather than the maintenance of law and order'.[68] On 17 September Sushila wrote to Pyarelal in Noakhali:

> Bapu is going to have a hard time of it here [Delhi]. Yesterday he was saying that he would not be surprised if some of us might have to go the way of the leaders of the French Revolution. The exchange of population is actually taking place however much we may dislike it. Will there be a mass exodus of Hindus from East Pakistan after the manner of West Pakistan? Bapu says it would be a catastrophe (96: 382).

Stirred by news of Hindu and Sikh women in Pakistan preferring death to dishonour, Gandhi said on 18 September:

> [T]hey have gone with courage. They have not sold away their honour. Not that their lives were not dear to them, but they felt it was better to die with courage rather than be forcibly converted to Islam by the Muslims and allow them to assault their bodies. And so those women died. They were not just a handful, but quite a few (96: 388–9).

We may note other remarks by him in September:

> *18 Sep.*: When I go to Pakistan I will not spare them. I shall die for the Hindus and the Sikhs there. I shall be really glad to die there. I shall be glad to die here too ...

> *20 Sep.*: This is the time to remember Khuda, Allah, Ishwar and Rama ... [T]he blood of these three communities [Hindus, Muslims and Sikhs] is one. I would do everything possible to prove this. I would cry myself hoarse and shed tears before God in order to attain this. I do not shed tears before man, but I can do so before God (96: 395–6).

> *23 Sep.*: I want to go to Lahore. I want to go to Rawalpindi ... If you avoid fighting in Delhi I will take it that God has granted my prayer. Then with the grace of God, I will go to the Punjab. Let me tell you that once peace descends on Delhi, I shall not stay here even a day longer (96: 412).

> *24 Sep.*: I have just a handful of bones in my body. But my heart belongs to me. So do your hearts belong to you ...

The trains coming from Pakistan these days do not bring the Muslims. The Hindus and the Sikhs are brought in those trains. Some get killed in the train. And the people who go from here are Muslims who are killed on the way. I am told that I should count the figures. What figures should I count? ... And what will I do knowing the figures? (96: 418–19)

Exchange with Churchill. In a speech in London on 27 September 1947, Winston Churchill, now in opposition, underscored Gandhi's shame:

The fearful massacres which are occurring in India are no surprise to me. We are, of course, only at the beginning of these horrors and butcheries, perpetrated upon one another, with the ferocity of cannibals, by the races gifted with capacities for the highest culture, and who had for generations dwelt, side by side, in general peace, under the broad, tolerant and impartial rule of the British Crown and Parliament. I cannot but doubt, that the future will witness a vast abridgment of the [subcontinent's] population.[69]

To these formidable phrases from his old foe, Gandhi offered an immediate and also impressive response the next day. After translating Churchill's sentences for his prayer-meeting audience, he called the former Premier 'a great man', acknowledged that that there was 'no doubt' that Churchill, who 'took the helm when Great Britain was in great danger', had 'saved the British Empire' in the Second World War, and admitted that 'a few lakhs in India had taken to the path of barbarism'.

At the same time he took Churchill to task for describing the killings in India with, as Gandhi put it, 'such relish and gross exaggeration', and asked Churchill 'to take the trouble' of thinking about Britain's responsibility in the tragedy. Though not referring to Churchill's personal wish for India's partition, Gandhi added that by dividing India before quitting, Britain had 'unwittingly invited the two parts of the country to fight each other', a step 'the future may or may not justify'. He concluded by saying to his people:

Many of you have given grounds to Mr Churchill for making such remarks. You still have sufficient time to ... prove Mr. Churchill's prediction wrong (97: 6–8).

Lahore never left Gandhi's thoughts.

1 Oct.: All those who have their properties in Lahore should get them back ... What wonderful buildings I have seen there! And what about all those educational institutions for girls? ... The people of the Punjab come of a sturdy stock. They are business-minded and produce wealth. There are great bankers there who know how to spend money as well as earn it. I have seen all that with my own eyes. They have built all those buildings, all those colleges for men and women, and then all those grand hospitals (97: 25).

He scented continuing ill will in Delhi and spoke about it:

1 Oct.: I do not quite know who they are, but they are definitely there, and are working to carry out preplanned murders, arson and forcible occupation of buildings (97: 24).

Birthday. On the morning of his 78th birthday he emerged from his bath to find that Mira had laid out flowers on the floor to form three symbols: the word Rama (in Hindi), the sacred syllable Om, and a Cross. Nehru and Patel, Ghanshyamdas Birla and several from the Birla family, Lady Mountbatten, and many others turned up to greet him. Many touched his feet.

'Bapuji', an unidentified visitor remarked, 'on our birthdays it is we who touch the feet of other people and take their blessings but in your case it is other way about. Is this fair?' Laughing, Gandhi answered: 'The ways of Mahatmas are different! It is not my fault. You made me Mahatma, maybe a bogus one; so you must pay the penalty!'

But the merry note quickly vanished. Repeating a thought he had been expressing for weeks, he requested those present to pray that 'either the present conflagration should end or He should take me away. I do not wish another birthday to overtake me in an India still in flames.'

Patel's daughter Maniben wrote later that day in her diary: 'His anguish was unbearable. We had gone to him in elation; we returned home with a heavy heart.'[70] But Gandhi must have been moved by a letter he received for his birthday from Sonja Schlesin, his talented secretary four decades earlier in Johannesburg:

Far from losing your desire to live until you are 125, increasing knowledge of the world's lovelessness and consequent misery should cause you rather to determine to live longer still ... You said in a letter to me some time ago that everyone ought to wish to attain the age of 125, you can't go back on that (97: 204).

Arguing that the violence in India was 'the final attempt of the forces of evil' to foil a 'divine plan' of India leading the world to non-violence, and warning Gandhi against feeling depressed, a well-wisher asked him to remember that he was 'the only instrument to further the divine purpose'. *Harijan* (12 Oct.) carried the well-wisher's letter as well as Gandhi's reply:

> I am not vain enough to think that the divine purpose can only be fulfilled through me. It is as likely as not that a fitter instrument will be used to carry it out and that I was good enough to represent a weak nation, not a strong one. May it not be that a man purer, more courageous, more farseeing is wanted for the final purpose? (97: 39)

Purity, courage and farsightedness are thus the three qualities Gandhi deems necessary in one wanting to change history. Added Gandhi:

> If I had the impertinence openly to declare my wish to live 125 years, I must have the humility under changed circumstances openly to shed that wish ... This has not been done in a spirit of depression. The more apt term perhaps is helplessness. In that state I invoke the aid of the all-embracing Power to take me away from this 'vale of tears' rather than make me a helpless witness of the butchery by man become savage ... Yet I cry – 'Not my will but Thine alone shall prevail' (97: 39–40).

Warned by a *Harijan* reader against sheltering 'frozen Muslim snakes' which would bite on revival, Gandhi allowed himself some fun in his reply:

> 3 Oct.: To liken a human being, however degraded he may be, to a snake to justify inhuman treatment is surely a degrading performance ... I have known rabidly fanatical Muslims to use the very analogy in respect of Hindus ... Lastly, let me, for the sake of snake-kind, correct a common error [and point out] that eighty snakes out of every hundred are perfectly harmless and they render useful service in nature (97: 30).

Shuttling between Delhi and Karachi, the capital of Pakistan, Suhrawardy carried messages from Gandhi to Jinnah and back. Gandhi wished to know (25 Oct.) 'what Pakistan really wants to do – whether they want the Hindus to stay there or not'. He added that he was aware of what was 'happening to the minorities in the Punjab, in Sindh and in the Frontier province' (97: 169).

But East Punjab's minority too had been pushed out. On 16 October Gandhi wrote to Amtus Salaam, who was continuing to serve in Noakhali, that the Patiala of old, to which Amtus Salaam belonged, was 'now but a dream'. Her relatives were all safe (he had helped arrange their departure for Pakistan) but, bemoaned Gandhi, 'they had to leave Patiala for good!' (97: 93).

To acquaint him with developing events, a small group of Delhi's Muslim leaders met with Gandhi every day. On 26 October, which was Eid day, Gandhi asked them to help him cultivate the right attitude towards his likely assassin:

> Jesus Christ prayed to God from the Cross to forgive those who had crucified him. It is my constant prayer to God that He may give me the strength to intercede even for my assassin. And it should be your prayer too that your faithful servant may be given that strength to forgive (97: 163).

Sikhs. Following a visit he had made to Karachi, Jamnadas Dwarkadas of Bombay conveyed to Gandhi (20 Sep.) a remark by Ghazanfar Ali Khan, a minister in Pakistan: 'If Sikhs can be kept aside they would be perfectly happy to let the Hindus stay.' 'Separating Sikhs from Hindus – I can never accept that,' said Gandhi.[71]

After others returning from Karachi repeated the hint of a Hindu-Muslim pact minus the Sikhs, Gandhi made a public comment:

> *Harijan, 7 Dec. 1947*: I know the vicious suggestion that the Hindus would be all right if they would sacrifice the Sikhs who would never be tolerated in Pakistan. I can never be a party to any such fratricidal bargain. There can be no rest for this unhappy land unless every Hindu and Sikh returns with honour and in safety to West Punjab and every Muslim refugee to the Union, barring of course those who do not choose to do so for reasons of their own (97: 384).

But a Gandhi critical of cruelty at Muslim and Hindu hands spoke also of Sikh excesses and of the misuse of the kirpan. Warned by a Sikh politician that he 'should be cautious about what he says about the Sikhs', Gandhi refused to yield:

> I speak freely and frankly because I am [the Sikhs'] true friend. I make bold to say that many a time the Sikh situation was saved because the Sikhs in general chose to follow my advice … A sacred thing has to be used on sacred and lawful occasions. A kirpan is undoubtedly a symbol of strength, which adorns the possessor only if he exercises amazing restraint over himself and uses it against enormous odds … (97: 383–4)

Kashmir & Junagadh. The subcontinent's 'yellow' pockets were disappearing. While almost all princely states had joined India or Pakistan, three presented problems: Hyderabad and Junagadh, which had Muslim rulers and preponderantly Hindu populations, and Kashmir, where a Hindu ruled over a Muslim majority, and where Gandhi had spent five days on the eve of independence.

While the Nizam of Hyderabad and Kashmir's Maharaja dallied, each hoping to emerge as an independent ruler, the Nawab of Junagadh acceded to Pakistan on 15 August, sparking off protests in his coastal territory in Kathiawar, adjacent to Porbandar. Nonetheless, Junagadh's accession was accepted (on 13 September) by Jinnah, who was applying to princely states not the two-nation theory but the principle of the ruler's wish. In response, Patel, who assumed charge of New Delhi's relationship with the princely states, declared that neither he nor the people of the region would allow Junagadh to become part of Pakistan.

Not to let Kashmir join India was, on the other hand, the goal of influential elements in Pakistan, including Abdul Qayyum Khan, the new chief minister of the Frontier Province, and Major-General Akbar Khan of the Pakistan army. Fearing that Hari Singh, the Hindu Maharaja, might after all accede to India, these elements sponsored, on 22 October, a raid into Kashmir by thousands of Afridi tribesmen.

When the raiders neared Srinagar, Kashmir's capital, Hari Singh as well as Sheikh Abdullah, the state's popular leader (who had been released by the Maharaja at the end of September), pleaded for India's help. Discussions involving Nehru, Patel, Hari Singh and Abdullah produced three immediate outcomes. The ruler acceded to India; Indian troops were flown to Srinagar to defend Kashmir; and Abdullah was empowered as Kashmir's *de facto* premier. In addition, it was declared that following the restoration of peace the people of Kashmir would decide their state's future.

Kept fully in the picture by Patel, Nehru and Abdullah, Gandhi gave, in his own phrase, 'tacit consent' to the dispatch of Indian forces to Kashmir (98: 319). On 29 October he even said, publicly, that 'the job of armed soldiers is to march ahead and repel the attacking enemy' (97: 185).

This amounted to blessing a violent exercise. Yet the fact that Abdullah, 'the lion of Kashmir', sought to represent 'not only the Muslims but the entire masses in Kashmir' (97: 285–6) made all the difference to Gandhi. He thought that Kashmir, where Hindus and Sikhs stood at Abdullah's side (97: 383–4), might provide an antidote for the subcontinent's Hindu-Muslim divide:

> 29 *Oct.*: After all, Kashmir cannot be saved by the Maharaja. If anyone can save Kashmir, it is only the Muslims, the Kashmiri Pandits, the Rajputs and the Sikhs who [live there]. Sheikh Abdullah has affectionate and friendly relations with all of them ...
>
> The poison which has spread amongst us should never have spread. Through Kashmir that poison might be removed from us (97: 185–6).

After the raiders were repulsed, Gandhi continued, 'Kashmir would belong to the

Kashmiris' (97: 185). In Kashmir, as in Hyderabad and Junagadh, the will of the people should prevail.

> *11 Nov.:* The dispute as to which Union Junagadh would finally accede to can be resolved only by taking public opinion, that is, by referendum … Whatever I have said about Junagadh equally applies to Kashmir and Hyderabad.
>
> Neither the Maharaja of Kashmir nor the Nizam of Hyderabad has any authority to accede to either Union without the consent of his people … If it had been only the Maharaja who had wanted to accede to the Indian Union, I could never support such an act. The Union Government agreed to the accession for the time being because both the Maharaja and Sheikh Abdullah, who is the representative of the people of Jammu and Kashmir, wanted it. Sheikh Abdullah came forward because he claims to represent not only the Muslims but the entire masses in Kashmir (97: 285–6).

The Nawab of Junagadh fled to Pakistan after Gandhi's nephew Samaldas (Laxmidas's son) led a popular movement in the state and Vallabhbhai sent Indian soldiers to Junagadh's borders. In a referendum held in February 1948, Junagadh's population voted overwhelmingly for India.

In Kashmir the pro-Pakistan forces were pushed back though they retained control over part of the state. Later in the year the Indian government referred the Kashmir question to the United Nations. Said Gandhi:

> *25 Dec.:* I shall advise Pakistan and India to sit together and decide the matter. If the two are interested in the settlement of the dispute, where is the need for an arbitrator? (98: 114)
>
> *4 Jan. 1948*: Mistakes were made on both sides. Of this I have no doubt … Therefore the two Dominions should come together with God as witness and find a settlement. The matter is now before the United Nations Organization. It cannot be withdrawn from there. But if India and Pakistan come to a settlement the big powers in the U.N.O. will have to endorse that settlement (98: 171).

Body & spirit

Asked by an Indonesian visitor about his apparent cheerfulness, Gandhi replied (7 Nov.):

> I look after my health with care … I have decided to live cheerfully even in this atmosphere of darkness and inhumanity. Moreover, I consider no one as my enemy

... I also resort to certain outward remedies. You see that even while guests such as you are visiting here I lie with a mud-pack on me. Do please forgive me my lack of manners (97: 251).

A Czech writer, Jiri Nehnevasja, shook Gandhi's hand and later described it:

My hand rests in his for a while. It is a small wrinkled hand with a white palm and pale fingers. The handshake is firm, manlike.[72]

In December one of these fingers was crushed when Brij Krishna slammed the door of the car in which they had gone to a meeting. To an anxious Ramdas his father wrote (22 Dec.):

It is true that I crushed my finger ... It was nothing to worry about. The pain subsided in a minute or two and I addressed the meeting ... I am no doubt careful but even a careful person does meet with such accidents (98: 96).

Though his listening, writing and counselling tasks in Delhi seemed 'endless', and he said he got 'utterly exhausted by the end of the day' (9 Nov.; 97: 268), he was usually able to start all over again the next morning, and unfailingly took his morning and evening walks.

He was letting the subcontinent's shame, sorrow and guilt flow into his heart and hoping that his listeners too would be affected:

1 Oct.: I do not wish to be a witness to these things. I do not wish to see such a downfall. My only prayer to God is that He should take me away before that happens ... I tried to sacrifice my life for India's freedom. I did not lose my life; but freedom came. But what is the point of remaining alive to see this happening in the wake of freedom? So I pray to God day and night that He should take me away. Or He should give me the power to extinguish this fire (97: 25).

1 Nov.: There are countless women at [the] Kurukshetra [refugee camp] who are still wearing the same clothes with which they had arrived. I cannot even bear to hear about these things – who knows what will happen if I have to see these things? (97: 211)

Aware, as Delhi's winter approached and advanced, of uprooted and unprotected ones – Hindu, Sikh and Muslim – shivering in Delhi's camps, he shivered himself. People pursued unto their hospital rooms and killed there, a train passenger stabbed and thrown into a river, a man killed while opening the little shop where he repaired spectacles, train-loads of refugees blocked and butchered, all because they belonged to the wrong religion and none because of any wrong committed, all before approving or silent onlookers – such were the incidents related to, and then by, Gandhi:

> 9 Nov.: There is a constant stream of visitors. How can I refuse to listen to their sorrows? Very often my own grief becomes overwhelming (97: 268).

> 29 Nov.: But when someone commits a crime anywhere I feel I am the culprit. You too should feel the same (97: 420).

An impression of hardness is conveyed by the record of some of his interviews with Hindu leaders arriving from Pakistan. Gandhi appears to rebuke them for escaping instead of fighting and for abandoning poorer Hindus who could not leave. Thus he said to Lalji Mehrotra, who had fled Karachi:

> 21 Oct.: The leaders were able to come so easily with their families and belongings but the poor, helpless villagers are in a sad plight. If even one of you had died there I would have danced for joy ... [But] I attach no blame to you (97: 129–30).

While reflecting Gandhi's sadness at the damage to his vision of Hindu-Muslim co-existence as well as his concern for those continuing in insecurity, such words conceal the warmth in Gandhi's eyes and arms as he welcomed men like Mehrotra. A young Punjabi judge, Gopal Das Khosla, a refugee himself from Lahore, noticed this warmth when he went to Gandhi for advice regarding evacuee property, for which he had been assigned responsibility:

> I began to tell him of my assignment, and the difficulties I had encountered. It was a long story and Gandhiji listened patiently without interrupting me ... There was no mysterious or hypnotic force to which I was being subjected ... He spoke in a calm matter of fact way. What I heard was not a command but a simple statement of truth ... He did not digress into a high-falutin' moral discourse but kept to the practical problem I had put before him. Realization came to me that this man had only one sentiment in his heart and that was the sentiment of love ... When he looked at me I noticed a softness in his eyes and I felt ashamed.[73]

The tenderness was also observed by Dilip Kumar Roy, the poet and musician who sang at Gandhi's prayer meeting on 1 November:

After the meeting I made my last obeisance on the lawn. He looked at me tenderly with his gentle sad eyes and said, 'It was good, that song.' *'I know you had a special liking for that song.'* He sighed: 'When do I hear you next? Tomorrow?' *'I must fly tomorrow for Calcutta.'* He smiled. 'Well, well! If you must, you must, and there's an end of it. But I will miss you tomorrow.' When I left him my eyes were moist with tears. I was moved by him as never before.[74]

Two days later, in a letter to someone not named in the record but obviously close to him, Gandhi likened his condition to that of Draupadi in the *Mahabharata* when the Kauravas tried to disrobe her:

3 Nov.: I saw your letter only now, after listening to the sweet and sad bhajan containing Draupadi's prayer ... Draupadi had mighty Bhima and Arjuna and the truthful Yudhishthira as husbands; she was the daughter-in-law of men like Dronacharya, Bhishma and Vidura, and yet amidst an assembly of people it appeared she was in a terrible plight. At that hour, she did not lose faith and prayed to God from her heart. And God did protect her honour ... Today I also am seated in a 'palatial' house, surrounded by loving friends. Still, I am in a sad plight. Yet there is God's help, as I find each day (97: 221).

Though living in Birla House and protected by Nehru, Patel and others in power, Gandhi too felt helpless – and yet aided. Giving of his best, he tried to recognize his imperfections. To Mathuradas Trikamji he wrote (15 Nov.):

I cannot be a witness to [the] pride, impatience, etc., [that] I may be having ... [O]nly outsiders can ... witness them (97: 314).

Dictating a letter to another friend (not identified in the record), Gandhi said (18 Nov.) that he had just given Manu (who was taking down the dictation) 'a long lecture' in answer to a question she had asked. Added Gandhi: 'Has it not become my profession to lecture people?' Referring to Manu's ability to make 'notes and summaries of my interviews with visitors', he said, 'It occurs to me how dense I was at the age of eighteen' (97: 343–4).

Some tasks afforded pleasure or satisfaction. For the wedding of Britain's Princess Elizabeth to Prince Philip (to whom the Viceroy was related), Gandhi sent a small tablecloth made from thread he had drawn on his charkha. It was taken to London by the Mountbattens.

9 Nov.: Dear Lord Mountbatten, This little thing is made out of doubled yarn of my own spinning. The knitting was done by a Punjabi girl who was trained by Abha's husband, my grandson. Lady Mountbatten knows Abha. Please give the bride and the bridegroom this with my blessings, with the wish that they would have a long and happy life of service of men. Yours sincerely, M.K. Gandhi (97: 265)

For the three weeks that Mountbatten was away, Rajagopalachari, coming from Calcutta to serve as acting Governor-General, lived in the Lutyens-designed palace that was called Viceroy's House until independence, when it was renamed Government House.

When one of C R's house guests, Sarojini Naidu (who had become the UP governor), fell ill, Gandhi called at the palace to see her and also to see C R in his new 'home'. C R and his widowed daughter Namagiri, who functioned as first lady, welcomed Gandhi in the north court of Government House with rose petals, and C R asked if Gandhi would care for an idli. 'Idli?' Gandhi exclaimed. 'In Gujarat a samdhi [daughter-in-law's father] offers sweets.'

Kasturba featured in his remarks. 'Don't you know that I was a barrister and Ba was almost illiterate?' he said in a letter (6 Nov.) to someone who had expressed unhappiness with his partner, adding, 'And, yet, whatever progress I have been able to make in my life today is all due to my wife' (97: 242). When a Bombay artist wishing to portray Kasturba asked for a photograph and details, Gandhi said he did not have any photographs. Naming someone else who was likely to have them, he did, however, provide a few particulars:

To Bapsy Pavry, 2 Dec.: The ground of Kasturba's sari always used to be white. Occasionally it had lines or dots in colour. The hem and the borders used to be coloured. There was no particular choice in the colours (97: 438).

He made faces at his youngest grandchild, Devadas's son Gopu, who was two-and-a-half at the end of 1947, and enjoyed Gopu's mimicking of grandfather's prayer-meeting call: 'Bhaiyo aur behno, aap shaant ho jaiye' ('Brothers and sisters, please be silent').[75] He missed Gopu when they did not show up, Gandhi told Devadas, who with his wife and children frequently visited his father, usually just before 9 p.m.

For his body, mind and soul, he seemed to turn even more than before to God and the utterance of God's name, for which, as we know, Gandhi's preference was Raam, as he pronounced it.

27 Sep.: My physician today, in my thought, speech and action, is Raam, Ishwar, Rahim (97: 3).

Conversation, 8 Nov.: [I]t is my hope that when I die I shall die with Ramanama in my heart. This faith becomes stronger in me each day. You see there was a time when even my opponents took my guidance. Today, let alone my being assailed by my opponents, even my co-workers, friends and close relatives who are like sons to me, do not see eye to eye with me. Still, I am mentally in such excellent health that it surprises me that with the flames raging around me I remain untouched by their heat or sparks. The reason for this is that God is filling me with strength and I am sustained by Ramanama (97: 257).

18 Nov.: My Raam is not a man with two hands and two feet. But if I am perfectly fit it is due to Raam's grace (97: 343).

State of the Congress

Having achieved power after decades of struggle, many in the Congress seemed absorbed in extracting all they could from it. Disappointed by pleas from freedom fighters for posts in the new India, Gandhi remarked, 'If someone has been to jail, has he done a favour to India?' (96: 34) On 4 November he spoke of 'Congress leaders [who] have completely isolated themselves from the refugees' (97: 230).

Divisions within the Congress bothered him. 'For instance,' he wrote to a friend on 14 November, 'Jayaprakash has immense energy. But he does not come forward because of party considerations' (97: 310). Making Jayaprakash – or his older socialist colleague, Narendra Deva – the Congress president was one remedy Gandhi thought of in November.

The incumbent head, Kripalani, was not clicking with Nehru or Patel and had said he wished to resign before his term ended. Gandhi agreed that he should, and so did Nehru and Patel, but the two were not willing to accept Jayaprakash or Deva. In the event Rajendra Prasad, resigning from the Cabinet, took over from Kripalani.

Appointing Jayaprakash as Congress chairman would have thrilled India's youth and paved the way for an interesting succession in the future, but this was another of Gandhi's ideas that Nehru and Patel jointly and successfully resisted.

Yet in November Gandhi managed to persuade first the Working Committee and then the AICC to recommit the party to 'a democratic secular State where all citizens enjoy full rights and are equally entitled to the protection of the State, irrespective of the religion to which they belong' (97: 476–7). In the bitter climate of late 1947, such a reaffirmation was both necessary and difficult, and Gandhi had to work hard to obtain it.

To a friend (not identified), 15 Nov.: The more I look within the more I feel that God is with me. [I]t is He who is giving me strength. These days the Working Committee meeting is going on and I am doing some plain speaking with them. We shall perish if we become cowards, that is, the Congress will die (97: 317).

To an unnamed associate, 17 Nov.: I am pulling on somehow. These days we are busy with the A.I.C.C. meeting. There is great pressure of work. I hardly have time to breathe. Letters have heaped up ... Everything here is quite uncertain at the moment. But God will certainly show a way out (97: 338).

To Pyarelal in Noakhali, 1 Dec.: I see my battle has to be fought and won in Delhi itself. There is a lot for me to do here ... The ... resolutions of the All-India Congress Committee this time were practically mine ... It now remains to be seen how they are implemented (97: 433).

Though coming together to defeat some of Gandhi's solutions, Nehru and Patel were often in conflict. At the end of September Gandhi had thought that for the sake of unity one or the other should leave the government,[76] but on 2 December he said at a public meeting, referring to Nehru and Patel: 'The two make an inseparable pair. Neither can do without the other' (97: 445).

While often speaking of Nehru and Patel in the same breath, and working to preserve their partnership, Gandhi strove also to protect Nehru's superior position in it, above all because Nehru was identified with secularism in a way that Patel was not. At the AICC meeting (15 Nov.), Gandhi warned the Congress against 'part[ing] company with Jawaharlal' and added:

Even those who have fabulous wealth, vast armies and the atom bomb respect the moral worth of Jawaharlal's leadership. We in India ought to have due appreciation for it (97: 317–23).

Attacking calls for the ousting of India's Muslims, Gandhi said:

I know what some people are saying. 'The Congress has surrendered its soul to the Muslims. Gandhi? Let him rave as he will. He is a wash out. Jawaharlal is no better. As regards Sardar Patel there is something in him. A portion of him is sound Hindu, but he too is after all a Congressman.'

Such talk will not help us. Where is an alternative leadership? Violent rowdyism will not save either Hinduism or Sikhism ... Hinduism cannot be saved by orgies of murder.

Fighting for the soul of Congress, he told the delegates:

> You represent the vast ocean of Indian humanity ... [T]here are many places today
> where a Muslim cannot live in security. There are miscreants who will kill him or
> throw him out of a running train for no reason other than that he is a Muslim ...
>
> [S]uch things should never happen in India. We have to recognize that India does
> not belong to Hindus alone, nor does Pakistan to Muslims ...
>
> Hinduism teaches us to return good for evil. The wicked sink under the weight
> of their own evil. Must we also sink with them? It is the basic creed of the Congress
> that India is the home of Muslims no less than of Hindus ...
>
> [I]f you maintain the civilized way, whatever Pakistan may do now, sooner or later
> she will be obliged by the pressure of world opinion to conform (97: 317–23).

Pressed by Gandhi, the AICC resolved also in favour of 'the ultimate return' to their
homes of refugees from Pakistan and India. Those who had not left their homes were
'encouraged to stay there unless they themselves desire to migrate' (97: 477–8). To the
AICC, Gandhi spoke, too, of reports that the Meos of Alwar and Bharatpur were being
coerced to leave for Pakistan. At one time designated as 'criminal tribes', these Meos
were Muslims.

> I understand that 1,500,000 Muslims are about to be sent to Pakistan ... If there are
> criminal tribes in India, whose fault is it? We are to blame for not having reformed
> them. They were here during the British regime. Was there any talk of deporting
> them then? ... How shameful it is for us that we should force them to trudge 300
> miles on foot! (97: 317–23)

Gandhi's intervention put paid to the plan. It was no longer possible for anyone to ask
openly for the Meos' expulsion, or for the government to allow it.

Yet Gandhi's concern regarding the Congress was not allayed. By rejecting his
proposal regarding Jayaprakash or Narendra Deva, Nehru and Patel had shown their
attachment to the status quo. And Congress members affected by the communal virus
had openly resented Gandhi's call for the ultimate return of refugees to their homes.
After the AICC session, Gandhi gave private expression to a radical thought:

> I am convinced that no patchwork treatment can save the Congress. It will only
> prolong the agony. The best thing for the Congress would be to dissolve itself before
> the rot sets in further. Its voluntary liquidation will brace up and purify the political
> climate of the country. But I can see that I can carry nobody with me in this.[77]

The Nehru-Patel relationship suffered severe strains in December. Patel felt offended on two scores. One, Nehru had asked a civil servant to reassess a situation in Ajmer in central India on which Patel had already given an opinion. Then, and this was more hurtful to Patel, Nehru wanted Kashmir removed from Patel's charge and placed in the hands of another Cabinet member, N. Gopalaswami Ayyangar.

Patel and Nehru both offered to resign. In separate letters to Gandhi they communicated the offers as well as their conflicting perspectives on the two issues. At the end of December Gandhi returned to an earlier thought and said to Patel: 'Either you should run things or Jawaharlal should.' Replying that he lacked the physical strength, Patel said he would support the younger man from outside the government.[78] 'Umpire' Gandhi asked for time to give his verdict.

Failure in Panipat. He had failed, meanwhile, in a bid to persuade Muslims in Panipat, 60 miles north of Delhi, not to migrate to Pakistan. Visiting the town on 10 November, Gandhi met with its Muslims, including several lying in hospital with injuries received in communal attacks. 'Nurse' Gandhi 'spent a few minutes with every patient, occasionally covering a patient properly with the sheet' (97: 275). He also met with Hindu and Sikh refugees from West Punjab, who had come into Panipat in thousands and made their homes on the railway platform, where deaths and births took place.

Though belonging to eastern Punjab, Panipat was far from Lahore and linked to Delhi by trade and proximity. Despite their fears (and notwithstanding the agreement for a two-way transfer of the Punjab's minorities), the town's Muslims told Gandhi that they would stay on if assured protection. Promises were offered by East Punjab's chief minister, Gopichand Bhargava, and by local officials.

On 22 November Gandhi thought he should shift to Panipat to encourage its Muslims, but Nehru advised against the move (97: 366). By the time Gandhi visited Panipat again (2 Dec.), the Muslims had made up their minds to leave. They did not feel safe in Panipat, their leaders told Gandhi. Deeply disappointed, he said to them:

> If … you want to go of your own will, no one can stop you. But you will never hear Gandhi utter the words that you should leave India. Gandhi can only tell you that you should stay, for India is your home. And if your brethren should kill you, you should bravely meet death …
>
> The Ministers have assured you that they will protect you even at the risk of their own lives. Still if you are resolved to go and do not place any trust in their word there is nothing further I can say to you. What can I do to reassure you? If I should die tomorrow you would again have to flee … You have to decide for yourselves …
>
> But today, having heard you and seen you, my heart weeps. Do as God guides you (97: 443–4).

Returning to New Delhi, Gandhi reported his failure to the Birla House prayer audience. He also described an encounter with a Hindu or Sikh boy in Panipat:

2 Dec.: Today a small boy confronted me. He was wearing a sweater. He took it off and stood glaring at me as if he would eat me up ... 'You say that you have come to protect us', he said, 'but my father has been killed. Get me my father back.' ... I can imagine that if I had been of his age and in his position, perhaps I would have done the same (97: 449).

Excerpts indicate the range of his concerns in November and December:

21 Nov.: I am told that the Roman Catholics are being harassed near Gurgaon ... in a village called Kanhai which is twenty-five miles away from Delhi ... the Roman Catholics were threatened that they would have to suffer if they did not leave the village ... The freedom we have achieved does not imply the rule of Hindus in the Indian Union or that of Muslims in Pakistan (97: 364).

23 Nov.: It is a matter of shame for us that there are ... Jats and perhaps Ahirs too [who] felt that the Harijans were their slaves ... They may be given water and food but they can get nothing by right ... We feel that we can even intimidate a judge if we are brought before him ... The result is that the Harijans are ruined (97: 378).

Welcoming a resolve at Lahore to recover women abducted in the two Punjabs, Gandhi said (26 Dec.):

The number could be in hundreds or even thousands ... Muslims have abducted Hindu and Sikh girls ... I have [also] received a long list of [Muslim] girls abducted from Patiala. Some of them come from very well-to-do Muslim families. When they are recovered it will not be difficult for them to be returned to their parents. As regards Hindu girls it is still doubtful whether they will be accepted by their families.

This is very bad ... Even if the girl has been forced into marriage by a Muslim, even if she has been violated, I would still take her back with respect ... If my daughter has been violated by a rascal and made pregnant, must I cast her and her child away? ... (98: 117–18)

Looking from September for a ripe moment to visit Pakistan, he cultivated different channels. These included the shuttling Suhrawardy, who was in touch with Jinnah; Parsi friends with Karachi links such as Bombay's Jehangir Patel and Poona's Dinshaw Mehta; and Lahore's Mian Iftikharuddin and his wife Ismat. Until 1946, when he joined the League, Iftikharuddin had been in the Congress and headed its Punjab unit for a term. Learning that Iftikharuddin's wife Ismat had been ill, Gandhi wrote to her:

> 9 Dec.: I was sorry that you were so ill and glad to hear that you were better. You should get quite well quickly, so as to do the very necessary work of reclaiming the poor abducted women in both the parts of the Punjab. Tell Iftikhar it was naughty of him to cease to write to me after his transfer of loyalty (98: 16).

Yet reports of continuing attacks on Pakistan's minorities made him ask (30 Dec.) whether the new country had 'become Islamistan where no non-Muslim may live or where he can only live as a slave' (98: 141).

Sending letters to 'sisters' and 'daughters' remained part of his life. To Lilavati Asar, who had spoken of a demanding professor supervising her medical studies, he wrote (21 Dec.):

> You should not be put out by his severity. You should welcome it and benefit from it … If a doctor makes a mistake, the patient has to pay for it – at times with his life. One should therefore look for a teacher who does not condone mistakes … Ponder and digest what you read. The student who is given to cramming is considered a fool of the first water (98: 90).

When Sharda Chokhawala, daughter of Chimanlal Shah (manager of the Sevagram ashram), wrote that she was seriously ill and might die, Gandhi wrote back (23 Dec.): 'But how can you die before I do? The very thought is unbearable to me' (98: 101). He wrote to Sharda again on 30 December, 31 December and 12 January.

More to offer

In the middle of December 1947 Pyarelal rejoined him. Though he had valued Pyarelal's work in Noakhali, Gandhi was glad to have his company again.

'I am taking Pyarelal home for dinner,' Devadas said to Gandhi one evening. 'Do you ever think of inviting me?' answered Gandhi with a great laugh that sizzled with the energy of 60 years of self-denial.[79] It was true that Devadas had never asked his father over to his second-floor apartment on Connaught Circus – he had assumed that Gandhi would not have the time or the inclination. On his visits to Delhi Gandhi had put up at the sweepers' colony or at Birla House, not at Devadas's. In fact the only son with whom Gandhi ever stayed was Harilal, who had hosted his father in Calcutta in 1920.

As a new year commenced, Gandhi recognized his restiveness. His most earnest – and most careful – toil had not made much of a difference. When a Thai visitor complimented him on independence, Gandhi remarked (1 Jan.): 'Today not everybody can move about freely in the capital. Indian fears his brother Indian. Is this independence?'[80]

He longed to visit Pakistan, where faithful friends like Ghaffar Khan and his older brother Dr Khan Sahib faced persecution, and Hindus and Sikhs lived in fear. On 6 January 120 Sikhs were killed in Karachi in a gurdwara where they had sought shelter. Yet could he go and counsel Pakistanis when Delhi's Muslims felt threatened?

Another disturbance was caused by a Cabinet decision to withhold the transfer of Pakistan's share (55 crore rupees) of the 'sterling balance' that undivided India held at independence. The conflict in Kashmir was cited as the reason: Patel said (either on 3 or 4 January) that India could not give money to Pakistan 'for making bullets to be shot at us'.[81] But Gandhi was not convinced that a violent dispute entitled India to keep Pakistan's money.

On 11 January he was shaken afresh when a group of Delhi's 'nationalist' Muslims asked him to arrange their 'passage to England' as they felt unsafe in India but were opposed to Pakistan and did not wish to go there.[82]

That Swaraj felt like a curse was the message also of a letter arriving at this time from Konda Venkatappayya of the Telugu country, a veteran freedom fighter whom Gandhi called an 'aged friend'. Saying that he was 'old, decrepit, with a broken leg, slowly limping on crutches within the walls of my house', Venkatappayya referred to the moral degradation of Congress legislators who made money by protecting criminals. His last sentence was: 'The people have begun to say that the British government was much better.' Gandhi found the letter 'too shocking for words' (98: 213–21).

He had to do, or give, more. But what, and how? On the morning of 12 January he found complete peace. Every unease, sense of shame, and feeling of inadequacy left Gandhi as the 'conclusion flashed upon' him that he must fast and not resume eating until and unless firm steps were taken. That afternoon, while 'sitting out on the sun-drenched spacious Birla House lawn',[83] Gandhi wrote out a statement announcing and explaining the fast. Sushila translated it into Hindustani and read it out at the 5 p.m. prayer meeting: Gandhi could not speak himself as it was Monday, his 'silent' day.

Having made the strategic decision to fast, Gandhi also gave thought to his tactics. In 1932, after resolving to fast against separate electorates for Dalits, he had told his jail companions, Patel and Desai, that he wanted the news to 'come upon everybody suddenly', that he wanted 'to give a shock'. It was the same this time. Nehru and Patel separately called on him on 12 January, but Gandhi gave no inkling of his plan to either. Like the rest of India, they received a shock that night from Gandhi's statement:

> *12 Jan. 1948*: Though the voice within has been beckoning for a long time, I have been shutting my ears to it lest it might be the voice of Satan ... I never like to feel resourceless; a satyagrahi never should. Fasting is his last resort in the place of the sword ... I ask you all to bless the effort and to pray for me and with me.
>
> The fast begins from the first meal tomorrow (Tuesday 13 January). The period is indefinite and I may drink water with or without salts and sour limes. It will end when and if I am satisfied that there is a reunion of hearts of all communities brought about without any outside pressure, but from an awakened sense of duty.
>
> The reward will be the regaining of India's dwindling prestige ... I flatter myself with the belief that the loss of her soul by India will mean the loss of the hope of the aching, storm-tossed and hungry world ...
>
> If the whole of India responds or at least Delhi does, the fast might be soon ended. But whether it ends soon or late or never, let there be no softness in dealing with what may be termed as a crisis.
>
> Death for me would be a glorious deliverance rather than that I should be a helpless witness of the destruction of India, Hinduism, Sikhism and Islam. That destruction is certain if Pakistan does not ensure equality of status and security of life and property for all professing the various faiths of the world and if India copies her. Only then Islam dies in the two Indias, not in the world. But Hinduism and Sikhism have no world outside India ...
>
> I would beg of all friends not to rush to Birla House nor try to dissuade me or be anxious for me. I am in God's hands. Rather they should turn the searchlight inwards ... (98: 218–20)

In another tactical move, Gandhi went to Mountbatten immediately after the prayer-meeting and asked for the Governor-General's support for his step. Accepting Gandhi's decision, Mountbatten said that if things in India were rectified as a result of the fast, improvement in Pakistan would inevitably follow. He added that he agreed with Gandhi's view on the 55 crore.[84]

Writing to his father late at night on 12 January, Devadas pleaded against the fast:

> You have surrendered to impatience ... Your patient labour has saved thousands of lives ... By your death you will not be able to achieve what you can by living. I would therefore beseech you to pay heed to my entreaty and give up your decision to fast.[85]

Admitting that his son's final sentence had touched him, Gandhi, however, asked Devadas to join in the prayer that 'the temptation to live may not lead me into a hasty or premature termination of the fast' (98: 231–2). Others also sought to dissuade Gandhi. One who did not was C R, who said in Calcutta:

> I have wrangled with Gandhiji on several occasions in the past. But this time I confess I am not inclined to wrangle. The only sane man today is Gandhiji.

Also expressing support, Arthur Moore, former editor of *The Statesman,* started a fast of his own on the 13th. Informing Gandhi of his gesture, the Briton wrote: 'You did much in Calcutta. But far more is needed here; you are the only hope.'[86]

On 13 January a 'very much upset'[87] Vallabhbhai repeated his offer to resign and thought that his departure might end the fast, but by now Gandhi had returned to the view that Patel and Nehru had to stay together. However, Gandhi raised the question of the 55 crore rupees with Patel. On the afternoon of 14 January the Cabinet met and decided to release the money, but not before Patel broke down and wept.

Gandhi likened this revocation by the Indian Cabinet to the change he had secured in 1932, in prison, from HMG (98: 246). Referring again to Delhi's significance, he also recalled a boyhood dream:

> *14 Jan.*: Delhi is the capital of India … It is this city which was Indraprastha, which was Hastinapur … It is the heart of India … All Hindus, Muslims, Sikhs, Parsis, Christians and Jews who people this country from Kanyakumari to Kashmir and from Karachi to Dibrugarh in Assam … have an equal right to it … Therefore, anyone who seeks to drive out the Muslims is Delhi's enemy number one and therefore India's enemy number one …
>
> When I was young I never even read the newspapers. I could read English with difficulty and my Gujarati was not satisfactory. I have had the dream ever since then that if the Hindus, Sikhs, Parsis, Christians and Muslims could live in amity not only in Rajkot but in the whole of India, they would all have a very happy life. If that dream could be realized even now when I am an old man on the verge of death, my heart would dance. Children would then frolic in joy … (98: 229–35)

At this juncture, while our fasting subject of 78 years hopes for a melting of the fears and hatreds around him, we may reflect on his connection to those fears and hates. Since Gandhi more than any others had led the Indian people over the preceding thirty years, the historian must ask whether or not his impulses and strategies contributed to the wounds of 1946–8.

The criticism that Gandhi put Muslims off by frequently invoking a Hindu vocabulary (Rama, God, Ahimsa) and Hindu-sounding phrases (satyagraha, Ram Rajya) is balanced, and perhaps cancelled, by another charge that he was not Hindu enough, that he appeased Muslims. There is also the more serious complaint that he injured India's climate by bringing religion into politics.

A striking criticism of Gandhi's use of religious metaphors comes from Arundhati Roy, who says that Gandhi 'rubbed the magic lamp and invited Ram and Rahim to partake of human politics and India's war of independence against the British'. The result, according to Roy, was not only 'a sophisticated, magnificent, imaginative struggle' that won freedom, but also 'the carnage of Partition'. In 'the hands of lesser statesmen,' she adds, 'it has won us the Hindu Nuclear Bomb'.[88]

We know, however, that the India that Gandhi returned to in 1915, and soon thereafter led, was hardly indifferent over religion. Ram and Rahim were not Gandhi's gifts to India. Occurring before he was born, the chilling events of 1857 had much to do with both Hinduism and Islam, and also with Christianity. About 39 years later, Sayyid Ahmad Khan's charge that reforms sought by the Indian National Congress (created in 1885) would benefit Hindus and harm Muslims showed that religion and politics were already intertwined.

By the end of the 19th century, at least three crucial provinces, the Punjab, Bengal and Bombay, were sharply communal. We have touched already on the Punjab's history. In Maharashtra, Muslims felt frightened in the 1890s when Tilak mobilized Hindus around religious festivals. In 1905, when Bengal was partitioned into Muslim-majority and Hindu-majority portions, and again in 1911, when this division was annulled, politics in that province bore a fiercely religious face. In between, in 1909, the Muslim League (founded in 1906) had obtained the promise of a separate electorate for Muslims in any elections the Raj might conduct.

Between a politics that pretended that religion was absent from India and a politics that squarely faced religion's hold, Gandhi chose the latter, and tried to remind all concerned that true Hinduism taught goodwill, and that true Islam, Sikhism and Christianity did the same. Our survey suggests that he made the right choice, and also that without him intolerance would have been even stronger in both Hindu India and Muslim India.

Nobody could banish religion from India's polity, let alone from Indian society, but thanks to Gandhi's effort religion was invested – or reinvested – with the task of spreading goodwill between Hindus and Muslims, even though other hands used it to foment hate, and would so use it in the future. India's tragedy in 1946–8 was not that

Gandhi had brought religion into politics; it was that despite every effort he failed to overcome the hate and fear that many an Indian nursed and spread at the time.

If not to blame for the religious tensions of 1946–8, did he not pave the way for violence through his disobedience campaigns? Wasn't lawlessness the other side of his satyagraha coin? Yet the choice for Gandhi's India was not simply between a 'constitutional' path and disobedience. A third route was on offer: insurrection. If the first path was unpromising at best, the third tempted many Indians. Yet it was capable of inviting devastation, as it had done in 1857. By providing non-violent alternatives, Gandhi may have prevented an unknown number of disastrous eruptions, even if incidents of violence occurred while he was at the helm, including a few linked directly to his campaigns.

More to the point, we have seen no evidence that a purely 'lawful' struggle for independence would have removed the fear of a Hindu majority on which the Muslim League built its successful campaign for Partition. After all Sayyid Ahmad Khan opposed a 'constitutionalist' Congress three decades before Gandhian satyagraha showed its face.

The carnage of 1947 was produced not by Ram or Rahim or satyagraha but by a failure of trust between Hindus and Muslims, or, more specifically, between the Congress and the League. Since there was no Congress-League understanding that might have prevented Partition, or made it orderly and peaceful, Gandhi, the Congress's undisputed leader between 1919 and 1945, has to take some responsibility.

We have seen that the British did not help him, and at times his close colleagues let him down. Over the Jinnah idea, as we saw, his colleagues and the British worked together against him. A bitter and in fact impossible dilemma faced Gandhi. His heart, and his people, wanted to oust the British, but only this enemy could prevent Partition. You wanted someone you were ousting to hand you all the keys. The one being ousted naturally preferred to give some of the keys to your rival (Jinnah), and to prevent any deal between you and the rival.

Though he tried his best with Jinnah, with the British and with his colleagues, Gandhi could not square the circle, or straighten out the triangle. It was a failure all would regret in the end – Hindus, Muslims and the British.

At least in the short term, there was an incurable contradiction in Gandhi's great goals. As long as Indians harboured rage at the British, Swaraj and non-violence were bound to clash. As long as Hindus and Muslims distrusted one another, Swaraj and Indian unity would clash.

The pertinent question is about Gandhi's success in managing the contradictions, and in setting the stage for their eventual resolution. We have to conclude that this success was remarkable.

Repudiating stories that his fast was aimed at Patel, Gandhi said (15 Jan.) that Vallabhbhai's critics were wrong to isolate him, 'a lifelong and faithful comrade', from 'Pandit Nehru and me, whom they gratuitously raise to the sky'. Added Gandhi: 'The Sardar has a bluntness of speech which sometimes unintentionally hurts, though his heart is expansive enough to accommodate all' (98: 237). Earlier, on 18 September, Gandhi had told Delhi's Muslims that whatever his biases Patel did not 'let his suspicion colour his actions' (96: 385).

For all his grievance about the fast and the reversal of the 55-crore decision, Patel said on 15 January: 'Let it not be said that we did not deserve the leadership of the greatest man in the world.' The next day, in a public talk in Bombay, Patel remarked, 'We take a short-range view while he takes a long-range one.'[89]

Asked what he wanted Delhi to do, Gandhi gave precise answers. Muslims should be allowed to hold their annual fair at the mausoleum of Khwaja Qutbuddin. Mosques converted into temples and gurdwaras should be returned. Muslims should be ensured safety in their homes and on trains. The economic boycott imposed against them should be lifted.

Hosting hundreds of thousands of refugees who carried bitter memories, Delhi was a tougher prospect than Calcutta, yet here too a tide of concern about the fasting Gandhi lifted people beyond their usual selves. The Sikh ruler of Patiala, which had seen large-scale attacks on Muslims, asked Delhi's Sikhs to help end Gandhi's fast. Some of the city's Hindus and Sikhs invited a group of Muslims who had left for Karachi to return to Delhi. Prasad, the Congress president, and Azad, India's leading Muslim politician, strove to mobilize Delhi's citizens, officials and organizations to meet Gandhi's terms.

Activity in Delhi was matched by an unexpected response in Pakistan, where 'in the twinkling of an eye the Muslim League's enemy number one of pre-partition days was transformed into their "greatest friend"'.[90] From West Punjab, Mridula Sarabhai (who was trying to recover abducted Hindu and Sikh women) wired that Pakistanis were asking how they could help. They too should turn the searchlight inwards, Gandhi replied.

Prayers were offered in public and 'by Muslim women in the seclusion of their purda'.[91] In Karachi minister Ghazanfar Ali Khan said that Gandhi had applied 'a drastic remedy', and in Lahore West Punjab's chief minister, the Khan of Mamdot, finance minister Mumtaz Daulatana and League leader Firoz Khan Noon offered their 'deep admiration and sincere appreciation' for Gandhi's step, with Noon saying, 'Religious founders apart, no country has produced a greater man than Mahatma Gandhi.'[92]

Through Sri Prakasa, the Indian high commissioner in Karachi, and Zahid Husain, Pakistan's high commissioner in New Delhi, Jinnah sent a message urging Gandhi to 'live and work for the cause of Hindu-Muslim unity in the two dominions'.[93] It was an indirect appeal for ending the fast. However, a vicious attack on a refugee train at West Punjab's Gujrat station on 13 January killed or maimed hundreds of Hindus and Sikhs from Bannu in the Frontier Province. Gandhi reacted frankly:

> *14 Jan.*: [If] this kind of thing continues in Pakistan, how long will the people in India tolerate it? Even if 100 men like me fasted they would not be able to stop the tragedy that may follow.

Then Gandhi challenged his people, Pakistanis and Indians, by reminding them of a well-known verse:

> The poet says, 'If there is paradise it is here, it is here.' He had said it about a garden. I read it ages ago when I was a child … But paradise is not so easily secured. If Hindus, Muslims and Sikhs became decent, became brothers, then that verse could be inscribed on every door. But that will be only when Pakistan has become pure … If that happens in Pakistan, we in India shall not be behind them …
>
> Society is made up of individuals. It is we that make society … If one man takes the initiative others will follow and one can become many; if there is not even one there is nothing (98: 234–5).

In sympathy with Gandhi, many Hindu and Sikh refugees in Delhi cut down on their meals. Muslims were welcomed in Subzimandi and other areas where a boycott had earlier been in force. Peace processions marched across the city, and about 200,000 signatures were secured to a commitment to assure Muslim rights.

Though he lost weight and doctors worried about acetone levels in his body, Gandhi was enduring the deprivation remarkably well, putting in plenty of work and walking when it was thought he would have to be carried.

Writing to Mira in her ashram in the Himalayan foothills, Gandhi said (16 Jan.) he thought he was on his 'greatest fast'. Other lines in this letter show Gandhi's attempt to draw amusement from the self-imposed ordeal:

> I am dictating this immediately after the 3.30 a.m. prayer and while I am taking my meal … The food consists of eight oz of hot water sipped with difficulty … It revives me whenever I take it. Strange to say, this time I am able to take about eight meals [a day] of this poison-tasting but nectar-like meal. Yet I claim to be fasting and credulous people accept it (98: 240).

On 18 January, the sixth day of the fast, a delegation of over 100 persons representing

different communities and bodies called on a shrivelled Gandhi at Birla House, and
Rajendra Prasad read from a declaration all had signed:

> We take the pledge that we shall protect the life, property and faith of the Muslims
> and that the incidents which have taken place in Delhi will not happen again.
>
> We want to assure Gandhiji that the annual fair at Khwaja Qutbuddin Mazar will
> be held this year as in the previous years.
>
> Muslims will be able to move about in Subzimandi, Karol Bagh, Paharganj and
> other localities just as they could in the past. The mosques which ... now are in the
> possession of Hindus and Sikhs will be returned.
>
> We shall not object to the return to Delhi of the Muslims who have migrated
> from here if they choose to come back and Muslims shall be able to carry on their
> business as before.
>
> We assure that all these things will be done by our personal effort and not with
> the help of the police or military (98: 253).

Appeals for ending the fast were then made by Prasad, Azad, Zahid Husain (the Pakistani
high commissioner), Ganesh Dutt, who said he spoke for the Hindu Mahasabha and the
RSS, Harbans Singh, in the name of the Sikhs, and Khurshid and M S Randhawa for the
Delhi administration.[94]

Acceding, Gandhi added that he would not 'shirk another fast' if he found that he
had been deceived. Brij Krishna thought that Gandhi's shrunken and lined face looked
radiant.[95] After prayers from five faiths were sung, there was complete silence as Azad
handed a glass of orange juice to Gandhi, who extended a long thin hand to grasp it.
There were shouts of delight when he sipped. Then he asked everyone present to partake
of fruit. Among those in tears was Jawaharlal, who told Gandhi that he had been secretly
fasting from the previous day.

As for Patel, with Gandhi's full approval he had gone on a mission to integrate
Kathiawar's princely states, including Porbandar, Rajkot and Bhavnagar, into Union
territory.

Nehru having left Birla House, Gandhi scribbled a note for him: 'Break your fast ...
May you live for many long years and continue to be India's Jawahar [jewel].' Asking
Pyarelal to deliver the note right away to Nehru, Gandhi remembered Arthur Moore
as well. Sushila was told to 'phone Moore at once' with the news and to advise him on
sensible ways of breaking a fast. When reached, Moore said he had heard the good news
and already broken his fast – with a cup of coffee and a cigar.[96]

Gandhi had energy enough to compose a statement for the prayer meeting on the
evening of the 18th:

They have assured me that from now on Hindus, Sikhs and Muslims will live as brothers and under no conditions and on no provocation will the residents of Delhi, including the refugees, become enemies of each other. This is not a small thing ...

[W]e must pledge that once we have turned our face towards God we shall never turn away. When that happens India and Pakistan will unitedly be able to serve the world and make the world nobler. I do not wish to live for any other purpose.

In lines quoted often in the future, Gandhi proceeded to explain why instead of 'God' he spoke at times of 'Truth':

I embarked on the fast in the name of Truth whose familiar name is God ... In the name of God we have indulged in lies, massacres of people, without caring whether they were innocent or guilty, men or women, children or infants. We have indulged in abductions, forcible conversions and we have done all this shamelessly. I am not aware if anybody has done these things in the name of Truth. With that same name on my lips I have broken the fast (98: 260–1).

Conspiracy. Others, meanwhile, were embarked on a conspiracy to kill Gandhi. They included Nathuram Godse, who edited a Marathi journal in Poona called *Hindu Rashtra*; Narayan Apte, the journal's manager; Nathuram's brother Gopal Godse; Digambar Badge, who ran an arms shop in Poona; Badge's servant Shankar Kistayya; Vishnu Karkare of Ahmednagar; and Madanlal Pahwa, a refugee from Pakistan who worked as Karkare's assistant.

Several in the group were Chitpavan Brahmins from Maharashtra, as was their hero, Savarkar, who was alleged though not proved to be part of the conspiracy. Gandhi's political mentor, Gokhale, and close associate, Vinoba Bhave, were Chitpavan Brahmins too. So was Tilak, India's most popular leader before Gandhi.

In August 1947, Nathuram Godse and Apte had flown with Savarkar from Bombay to Delhi and back, and in January 1948 Godse and Apte seem to have had two meetings with Savarkar.[97] According to Savarkar's biographer, Dhananjay Keer, Godse was 'a staunch Savarkarite, and was fairly known as the vanguard and lieutenant of Savarkar'.[98]

The date when killing Gandhi was first considered in this circle is not certain, though we saw that Nathuram Godse had turned up in Sevagram in 1944 with hostile intentions. There are suggestions that earlier that summer he had gone with a similar urge to Panchgani, while Gandhi was there.[99] According to Badge's later testimony, Nathuram Godse and Apte asked him to supply two slabs of gun-cotton, five hand grenades and two revolvers on 10 January 1948, but the plan may have been conceived earlier.

A member at different times of the Hindu Mahasabha and the RSS, Nathuram Godse would say afterwards that he hated non-violence and the charkha, and that Gandhi had weakened Hindu society and India. Gandhi's sympathy for Muslims offended him and the other conspirators, but perhaps there also was a grudge at Gandhi's stature as India's leader, a position rightfully belonging, in the view of men such as Nathuram Godse, to Savarkar.

Seven members of the conspiracy were in Delhi by the night of 19 January: the Godse brothers and Apte, Badge and Kistayya, Karkare and Pahwa. They had the gun-cotton slabs, grenades and revolvers. On the morning of 20 January, three of them went to Birla House where, from outside the compound, they surveyed the site of Gandhi's prayer-meeting.

A plan of action was worked out at a meeting in a New Delhi hotel room that quickly followed. First Pahwa would explode an explosive charge beside a wall not far from where Gandhi sat. Immediately thereafter, in the expected confusion, Apte and Godse would give signals and the rest would attack. Badge and Kistayya would fire revolvers at Gandhi, and these two as well as Karkare, Gopal Godse and Pahwa would throw grenades at Gandhi.

All seven reached Birla House in the evening. After prayers had been recited and Gandhi had commenced speaking, Pahwa detonated his charge, causing an explosion about 75 feet from where Gandhi was seated. But the rest of the plan was not carried through: for one thing, Badge's courage failed him. In any case all except Pahwa slipped away to a waiting taxi. As for Pahwa, he was spotted by a woman, Sulochana Devi, appre-hended by others present, and handed over to the police.

Later in the evening Gandhi heard that a man had been arrested for the explosion. At the time of the explosion, he did not realize what had caused it. The audience seemed to panic, but Gandhi said in a firm voice recorded by All India Radio: 'Listen! Listen! Listen! Nothing has happened.' Order was restored and Gandhi resumed speaking. Later that night and the following day he received numerous messages praising him for his poise. He also heard that Madanlal Pahwa had been defiant in custody. In his post-prayer remarks of 21 January, Gandhi's outlook came across, as also his battle for the Hindu mind, his certainty about his role, and his intuition that Pahwa was not acting on his own:

Let me first deal with the bomb incident of yesterday. People have been sending me wires congratulating me and praising me. In fact I deserve no congratulations. I displayed no bravery. I thought it was part of army practice somewhere. I only came to know later that it was a bomb and that it might have killed me if God had not willed it that I should live …

You should not have any kind of hate against the person who was responsible for this. He had taken it for granted that I am an enemy of Hinduism. Is it not said in

Chapter Four of the Gita that whenever the wicked become too powerful and harm dharma God sends someone to destroy them? The man who exploded the bomb obviously thinks that he has been sent by God to destroy me. I have not seen him. But I am told that is what he said when questioned by the police. He was well dressed too.

But ... if we do not like a man, does it mean that he is wicked? ... If then someone kills me, taking me for a wicked man, will he not have to answer before God? ... When he says he was doing the bidding of God he is only making God an accomplice in a wicked deed ...

Those who are behind him or whose tool he is, should know that this sort of thing will not save Hinduism. If Hinduism has to be saved it will be saved through such work as I am doing. I have been imbibing Hindu dharma right from my childhood. My nurse, who literally brought me up, taught me to invoke Rama whenever I had any fears ...

[H]aving passed all the tests I am as staunch a Hindu today as intuitively I was at the age of five or six ... Do you want to annihilate Hindu dharma by killing a devout Hindu like me? Some Sikhs came to me and asked me if I suspected that a Sikh was implicated in the deed. I know he was not a Sikh. But what even if he was? What does it matter if he was a Hindu or a Muslim? May God bless him with good sense ...

Yesterday an illiterate woman displayed courage in having the culprit arrested. I admire her courage (98: 281–4).

Reading in the papers that one Madanlal Pahwa was in custody for exploding a device at Gandhi's prayer-meeting, Jagdish Chandra Jain of Bombay, a professor at Ruia College, realized that this was the young refugee he had been trying to help. More importantly, Jain remembered that Pahwa had talked of a conspiracy to assassinate Gandhi. Contacting Kher, the chief minister of Bombay, and Morarji Desai, the home minister, Jain conveyed what he had heard, including the names of some other co-conspirators. The Bombay government passed on the information to Patel, who spoke to Gandhi and had a police officer also speak to Gandhi. Though Gandhi 'absolutely refused' to have the police present at his prayer meetings,[100] a few plainclothesmen were posted at Birla House.

But leads supplied were not followed up with energy in Bombay or Delhi, and no one other than Pahwa was arrested. Gandhi was not part of the Establishment, which looked after its own – ministers, generals, police chiefs or secretaries to government – with zeal, but was less thorough over others, even over someone spoken of as the father of the nation. Moreover, the season's heart-hardening poison had 'permeated many branches of the services, not excluding the police'.[101]

'To Pakistan'. Following the fast, Gandhi's prestige was at its apex, nationally and globally. *The Times* of London, the *Post* of Washington, and other newspapers had commented on its impact, *The Times* saying that Gandhi's 'courageous idealism has never before been more plainly vindicated'.[102] A young British cleric opposing racism in South Africa, Rev. Michael Scott, sent Gandhi a tribute to satyagraha, adding, '[Y]our invincible spirit will always inspire mankind.' Scott signed himself 'Your grateful pupil Michael'.[103]

Pyarelal has given a description of the Gandhi of January 1948. At times betraying 'signs of flagging memory', his mind was 'razor sharp', his judgement 'uncannily sure' and 'the intuitions, if anything, more unerring than ever'. Despite his age and the fast, he 'could put in an amazing amount of physical and ... mental work'.[104] Yet the fast had damaged both his kidneys and his liver. Gandhi blamed his 'inadequate' faith in God.

Having done his duty by Delhi, he was free to go to Pakistan. After Mian Iftikharuddin from Lahore called on him, Gandhi wrote to the visitor's wife:

22 Jan.: My dear Ismat, I was disappointed when Iftikhar appeared without you and was sorry when I learnt that the cause was your illness. Your services are required much more than ever before. Therefore be up and doing. I assure you I am eager to go to Lahore as soon as my convalescence is finished and the way is open for me to go to Lahore (98: 284–5).

Returning from a visit to Karachi, Gandhi's Parsi friends Jehangir Patel and Dinshaw Mehta, who were accompanied by a third Parsi, the khadi-wearing Karachi-based helper of refugees, Jamshed Mehta, informed him that Pakistan would welcome him, on two conditions: he should not ask for reunion, and he should accept protection by Pakistani police.

At first resisting the second condition, Gandhi yielded when Jamshed Mehta pressed him. By 27 January the three Parsis were back in Karachi. In talks with Pakistan's leaders, Gandhi's arrival in Pakistan was tentatively set for 8 or 9 February.[105]

He thought he would go to Karachi first, then to the Frontier Province to be with the Khan brothers, and finally to the Punjab. Sent by him to aid insecure Hindus and Sikhs in Bahawalpur, Sushila was already in Pakistan. She would help prepare the ground.

Without giving us his name, Pyarelal writes of 'a Muslim leader from Pakistan' who at this time told Gandhi that he 'looked forward to witnessing a fifty-mile-long procession of Hindus and Sikhs returning to Pakistan with Gandhiji at its head'. Whoever visualized the unlikely scene, Gandhi, it seems, was 'thrilled' at the thought.[106]

But before Pakistan he would go to Wardha and Sevagram: among other things, institutions started there by him needed attention. He thought he should leave for Wardha on 2 February.

21–29 January 1948. 'Afflicted men cannot be balanced men. Everybody cannot be a Mahatma Gandhi,' said Giani Kartar Singh, an influential Akali leader. He was speaking to Gandhi on 21 January, after listening to Gandhi's praise of the Sikhs for signing the Delhi commitment. Kartar Singh received this reply: 'Mahatma Gandhi is neither an angel nor a devil. He is a man like you' (98: 280).

On 23 January Gandhi remembered Subhas, whose birthday it was, and also Harilal, for that day he wrote to Kanti, Harilal's son. Answering a letter from Kanti, the grandfather said, 'Your letter is beautiful' (98: 292).

The next day he thought of Mahadev while writing about Manu's progress to her father, Jaisukhlal:

> She has made great progress in writing the diary. She takes great interest in writing notes and when I see them Mahadev's face appears before my eyes …
>
> Manu is enjoying herself. If you have some magic for making her fat you should let me know (98: 296–7).

Three days later he made it a point to attend the annual fair at the 12th-century tomb in Mehrauli, south of Delhi, of the Muslim mystic, Khwaja Qutbuddin. Held year after year for centuries, the fair was set to be abandoned after the recent violence, but his fast had saved it. He asked for 'a vow at this holy place' by Hindus, Muslims and Sikhs that strife would not be allowed again (98: 309).

Though back on a gruelling schedule, he found time for journalists from afar. On 27 January Kingsley Martin of the *New Statesman & Nation* questioned Gandhi about the violence he had condoned in Kashmir, and on 29 January he was interviewed by Margaret Bourke-White, photographer for *Life* magazine. After a talk with him on 27 January, Vincent Sheean, an American reporter, asked for another appointment, which Gandhi provisionally scheduled. Writes Sheean: '[Gandhi] added very gently, in a voice that would have melted the heart of an enemy (and I was no enemy), "If there is no time, you will understand."' At Sheean's request, Gandhi spelt out his understanding of the Gita and the Sermon on the Mount, and he also translated for Sheean the *Isho-panishad* verse always recited in his evening prayer: 'Renounce the world and receive it back as God's gift. And then covet not.' Gandhi explained that the last four words were crucial, for a renouncer was often tempted, after surrender and acceptance, to covet again. Sheean thought that Gandhi's words reached out 'from the depths to the depths'.[107]

Among the letters he sent on 29 January was one (written at 4.30 a.m.) to Vijaya Walji Sodawala, a Harijan girl taking her medical finals in Bombay, assuring a scholarship. Another was a warm note to Kishorelal Mashruwala, the former *Harijan* editor who had withdrawn in the context of Gandhi's chastity experiments. The two anticipated a reunion during Gandhi's Wardha's visit.

On 29 January about 40 Hindus from Bannu in the NWFP called on Gandhi. They carried wounds on their bodies and in their spirits (perhaps incurred on the 13 January attack on the train at Gujrat station), and took out some of their unhappiness on Gandhi. In the prayer-meeting talk that evening, he supplied a gist of the conversation:

> One of them … said I had done enough harm already and that I should stop and disappear from the scene. He did not care whether I was a mahatma. I asked him where he wanted me to go. He said that I might go to the Himalayas … I asked why I should go to the Himalayas merely because he wished it… I can only do as God bids …
>
> God is the help of the afflicted. But an afflicted person is not God … I cannot run away because anyone wants me to run away … God will do what He wills. He may take me away … My Himalayas are here (98: 331).

Later in the evening, however, he said to Brij Krishna: 'You should take that as notice served on me … We should accept curses from a sorrow-laden heart like that as the voice of God.'[108]

In this prayer talk he also spoke of his hope that a farmer, or one 'who produced food-grain out of the earth, becomes our chief, our Prime Minister' (98: 332). After dark he began to put down in writing his radical ideas regarding the Congress's future. He was lying down in his bed on the floor when, at about 9.30 p.m., Devadas and his wife Lakshmi arrived.

'What news?' Gandhi exclaimed; it was his usual greeting for the editor-son. Saying he had nothing important to impart, Devadas asked, 'How does the ship of state fare?' The question was about the Nehru-Patel relationship. Replied Gandhi: 'I am sure the little differences will vanish. But things may have to await my return from Wardha. That won't be long. I am sure they must hold together.'

After some more conversation, Devadas said, preparing to leave, 'Bapu, will you sleep now?'

'No, there is no hurry … Talk some more,' the father said.[109]

Friday 30 January began like any other day. Up at 3.30 a.m., Gandhi and his companions recited the morning prayers, including these lines:

Forgive, O Merciful and Loving God of Gods, all my sins, of hand or foot, body or speech, eye or ear, of commission or omission … I ask neither for a kingdom nor for heaven nor for liberation but only for an end to the pain of the suffering ones …

Elsewhere in the city, in a retiring room at Delhi station, Nathuram Godse, Narayan Apte and Vishnu Karkare were still asleep. They had returned to the capital with a new plan and with weapons, including a pistol procured in Gwalior.

Fortified by a hot drink of lemon-and-honey and a glass of sweet lime juice prepared by Manu and Abha, Gandhi worked until six a.m. on his Congress draft. Its role completed with India's political independence, the Congress, the draft said, should be willing to dissolve itself and 'flower into' an association for gaining 'social, moral and economic independence'.

The new body (for which Gandhi had thought of a name, Lok Sevak Sangh, or People's Servants' Association) would tackle illiteracy, ill-health, unemployment, untouchability and communal intolerance in every village in India. Parties from the left to the right, including new ones, would fill the political vacuum left by the Congress's departure and accommodate those in the Congress unable to live without politics.

Handing the draft to Pyarelal, Gandhi asked him to 'fill in any gaps'. 'I wrote it under a heavy strain,' added Gandhi. At eight Brij Krishna gave Gandhi an oil massage. After a bath Gandhi had a brunch of goat's milk, boiled vegetables, tomato, radish and orange juice. Over the meal he encouraged Pyarelal to return to Noakhali. He needed Pyarelal's assistance in Delhi, Gandhi said, yet the work in East Pakistan should have priority.

After an old associate from Durban, Rustom Sorabji, called with his family, Gandhi took a short nap. Nourished by another drink of lemon-and-honey, he had his daily talk with Delhi's Muslim leaders. 'I can't go away to Wardha without your consent,' he told them. Supporting his going, they said: 'We will find out what Delhi is like in your absence.'[110]

Sudhir Ghosh, who was in town, and Pyarelal asked Gandhi about a comment in the London *Times* on the friction between Nehru and Patel. Gandhi said he would raise the matter with Patel, who was coming at four, and with Nehru, due in at seven in the evening, and also in his prayer talk.

In the early afternoon he stretched out under the sun, first listening to P B Chandwani of Sindh, who read from the day's newspapers, and then receiving visitors to whom Brij Krishna had given time. These included Jat leaders from East Punjab (Gandhi asked them about the condition of Dalits in their areas); Hindu refugees from Sindh; Sri Lanka's de Silva, who came with his daughter; the historian, Radha Kumud Mookerjee, bringing a book he had written; a French photographer; a delegation from former princely states joining the Punjab; and another of Sikhs wanting to organize a large meeting in Delhi.

To the Hindus from Sindh, Gandhi spoke in what Chandwani felt was 'an exceedingly tender voice'. While 'outwardly he seemed light and happy', he said, his 'heart was smitten with grief'. He told them what the Bannu refugee had said the previous day. Chuckling, Gandhi added that by going to the Himalayas he would become a double Mahatma and attract bigger crowds. But he preferred to face 'the prevailing darkness and misery' (98: 340).

An arm resting on Brij Krishna's shoulder, at 4 p.m. he walked back to his room. Brij Krishna was told to arrange the journey to Wardha 'in consultation with Patel'. 'Ask Bisen to pack Professor Mookerjee's book with my things,' Gandhi added.

By now Vallabhbhai had arrived, accompanied by his daughter Maniben. Gandhi and he talked beyond prayer time (5 p.m.). During the conversation Gandhi plied his charkha and ate his evening meal (served by Abha) of goat's milk, raw carrots, boiled vegetables and three oranges.

Acknowledging that earlier he had thought that either Patel or Nehru should withdraw from the Cabinet, Gandhi told Patel that he had now 'come to the firm conclusion that the presence there of both of them was indispensable'.[111] Any breach in their ranks at this stage would be disastrous. Gandhi added that he would underline this right away in his prayer-speech, and also to Nehru, who was coming at seven. Tomorrow, said Gandhi, 'the three of us' should have a joint talk.[112]

There was much that Patel wanted to say. Aware that Gandhi hated being late for the prayer-meeting, Abha fidgeted. But Patel was India's strong man, and she did not dare interrupt. However, she picked up Gandhi's pocket watch and held it up in front of him. But Gandhi was focused on his old comrade. Eventually, Maniben intervened, but it was ten minutes past five when Gandhi got up.

Quickly getting into his chappals, Gandhi started walking to the prayer site, his left arm on Manu's shoulder, his right on Abha's. Brij Krishna and a few others followed behind. 'You gave me cattle fare,' he teased Abha as they walked, referring to the carrots. 'Ba called it horse fare,' said Abha. 'Isn't it grand of me,' said Gandhi, 'to relish what no one else cares for?'

Abha laughed but complained: 'Bapu, your watch must have felt neglected.' 'But I have time-keepers,' Gandhi replied. 'Why should I look at my watch?' 'You would not look at the time-keepers either,' Abha rejoined. This drew a comment on Abha's hesitation in Patel's presence:

It is your fault that I am ten minutes late. It is the duty of nurses to carry on their work even if God himself should be present there. If it is time to give medicine to a patient and one feels hesitant about it, the poor patient will die. So it is with prayers. It irks me if I am late for prayers even by a minute.

By the end of this remark he and the girls had come to the five gentle steps leading up to the prayer site, and they and those behind them turned completely silent. It was understood that small talk and laughter had to cease before they set their feet on the prayer site. Behind them, as they cleared the easy steps, the winter sun was setting. Ahead, about 30 yards to the right, was the khadi-covered platform where they would sit for the prayers. The path to that platform was lined on either side by scores of women and men joining their hands in reverential, but also warm, greeting to Gandhi.

Removing his hands from the girls' shoulders, Gandhi brought them together to return the greetings. From the side to his left, Nathuram Godse thrust his way towards him and appeared to be bending down. Manu, who was carrying Gandhi's rosary and the book of ashram songs, thought he wanted to touch Gandhi's feet. She said they were late already; Gandhi should not be detained. But Godse had got very close. Manu tried to shove his hand away. She was violently pushed aside by Godse. The rosary and the book fell. As Manu knelt down to pick up the objects, Godse planted himself in front of Gandhi, pulled out a pistol, and fired three shots in quick succession, one into Gandhi's stomach and two into his chest.

'Raam, Raa …m,' Gandhi uttered[113] as crimson spread across his white clothes, and gun-smoke billowed in the air he was breathing. The hands raised in the gesture of greeting which was a sign also of prayer and goodwill flopped down, and the limp body sank towards the ground, where dew had started to form. As he fell, his right arm landed on Abha's left shoulder. She caught the falling Gandhi's head in her hands, and sat down with it.

Following behind Gandhi, Brij Krishna had run forward on hearing the shots and seen Gandhi first standing, blood streaming down his body, and then collapsing into Abha's lap.

'Handled by us with a tenderness greater than we would extend to flowers,' Brij Krishna would write, 'prepared to be trampled under it rather than see it bruised in any way, we saw that gentle body of his lying lifeless on the grass and moist mud.'[114]

Five centuries earlier, the weaver-poet Kabir had likened the human body to a handspun and hand-woven 'chadariya', or length of cloth, which the soul has to keep in good repair but ultimately shed. But the body too needed a covering. For the sake principally of his poor compatriots, Gandhi had always underlined the value of his hand-made khadi (crimson now, but otherwise always white, and never longer than necessary), and he had always done his best to keep it spotless.

For the sake of India's liberty and honour, he had also taken good care of the body his khadi covered. This inner chadariya, his frame and limbs and heart, had enveloped many, and especially the weak, with a sheltering love. As with Draupadi's garment, its capacity to extend itself had been multiplied by a bountiful providence, so that an unbelievable number felt Gandhi's warmth. Old and frayed, the chadariya at times needed a supporting sheet of cloth, but like Gandhi's outer khadi it remained unsoiled.

For 40 or more years, first in South Africa and then in India, this chadariya had fluttered confidently at the head of columns of unarmed women and men marching for dignity. At times it waved alone, proclaiming a hard truth. Even from afar other chadariyas drew strength from it. But this precious chadariya, his human body, so loved by Brij Krishna, Abha, Manu, Pyarelal, Sushila, Mira, Amtus Salaam, Devadas, and many others, was only an outer garment for the real Gandhi.

That Gandhi, the spirit that wanted to bless and forgive his assassin, even as it wanted to bless and forgive all the grudge-bearing residents of India, Pakistan, and the world — the spirit that brought the chadariya's hands together and wanted to take the name of God at the moment of death, that Gandhi the bullets did not kill. They only released that Gandhi for the ages and the continents.

Postscript

The world grieved. Albert Deutsch, a columnist from New York, wrote that there was still hope for a world that had 'reacted as reverently as it did to the death of Gandhi'. From London King George VI said that mankind, and not India alone, had suffered an irreparable loss. In the USA, Mary McLeod Bethune, daughter of slaves, said that 'a great warm light had been extinguished'. A former Premier of France, Leon Blum, remarked that though he had never seen Gandhi or set foot in India, he felt 'as if [he] had lost someone near and dear'.[1]

In Pakistan, Jinnah referred to Gandhi's 'noble death', and Mian Iftikharuddin said: 'Each one of us who has raised his hand against innocent men, women and children during the past months, who has publicly or secretly entertained sympathy for such acts, is a collaborator in the murder of Mahatma Gandhi.'[2] After hearing the news on the evening of 30 January, many in Pakistan skipped their meal that night.[3]

In New Delhi, rushing to Gandhi's still-warm body in Birla House, Nehru cried like a child and buried his head in the lap of a stoic Patel, who had got there earlier. Then the two embraced each other, and Patel told Nehru of what Gandhi had said to him. Shortly afterwards, the two addressed India over the radio. Speaking first in Hindi and then in English, Nehru said:

> The light has gone out of our lives and there is darkness everywhere. I do not know what to tell you or how to say it. Our beloved leader, Bapu as we called him, the Father of the Nation, is no more ...
>
> The light has gone out, I said, and yet I was wrong. For the light that shone in this country was no ordinary light. The light that illumined this country for these

many, many years will illumine this country for many more years, and a thousand years later, that light will still be seen in this country, and the world will see it, and it will give solace to innumerable hearts ...

Patel spoke in Hindi:

Just now my dear brother Pandit Jawaharlal Nehru has spoken to you. My heart is aching. What shall I say to you? My tongue is tied. This is a day of sorrow, shame and agony for India ...

The mad youth who killed him was wrong if he thought that thereby he was destroying his noble mission. Perhaps God wanted Gandhiji's mission to fulfil and prosper through his death.[4]

In Calcutta, Rajagopalachari said:

Bharat Mata* is writhing in anguish and pain over the loss. No man loved Bharat Mata and Indians more than Mahatma Gandhi ...

No one could die a more glorious death than Mahatma Gandhi. He was going to the seat of his prayer to speak to his Rama. He did not die in bed calling for hot water, doctors or nurses. He did not die after mumbling incoherent words ... He died standing, not even sitting down.

Patel's hunch that the assassination would advance Gandhi's goals proved correct. On 31 January 1948 vast numbers of mourning Indians followed Gandhi's body to Rajghat, where it was cremated. As the pyre was about to be lit, Manu placed her 'face in the Sardar's lap and wept and wept'. Looking up, she noticed that Patel had suddenly aged.[5]

A special train carrying Gandhi's ashes from Delhi to Allahabad was mobbed by tens of thousands at every station *en route*. On 12 February, Allahabad's river banks were packed by a concourse of humanity witnessing the immersion of the ashes. All across the land Indians expressed their grief, and it became clear that Gandhi's killers had discredited themselves, their associates and the idea of Hindu supremacy.

India's sorrow led to bans on the RSS and the arrests of many of its members. One of Gandhi's worst fears, the communalization of the Congress – a fear contributing to his proposal for its dissolution – was averted. Nehru's position in the Congress was strengthened, as was the body's commitment to protect minorities. India's Hindu extremists would remain marginalized for the next 40 years.

---

* Bharat Mata = Mother India.

Speaking to Congress MPs on 4 February 1948, Vallabhbhai for the first time referred to Nehru as 'my leader', and added:

> I am one with the Prime Minister on all national issues. For over a quarter of a century, both of us sat at the feet of our master and struggled together for the freedom of India. It is unthinkable today, when the Mahatma is no more, that we would quarrel.[6]

Though Patel rejected a charge (levelled by Jayaprakash among others) that as home minister he had failed to protect Gandhi, he was not free from self-reproach. On 5 March he suffered a heart attack. After three hours of drug-induced sleep, his first words were, 'I had to go with Bapu. He has gone alone.'[7] Patel was recalling his 1932 compact with Gandhi.

But he recovered, and he and Nehru governed India as a duumvirate until Patel's death in December 1950. Unbroken, though not without friction, the bond between the two assisted India's democratic governance at the start of independence, and aided renewal after the upheaval of August and September 1947.

Ten weeks before his death, Vallabhbhai spoke of Gandhi, Kasturba and Nehru:

> Today I see before me the whole picture of life ever since I joined Bapu's army. The love which Ba bore me I never experienced from my own mother. Whatever parental love fell to my lot, I got from Bapu and Ba ...
>
> We were all soldiers in their camp. I have been referred to as the Deputy Prime Minister. I never think of myself in those terms. Jawaharlal Nehru is our leader. Bapu appointed him as his successor ...
>
> It is the duty of all Bapu's soldiers to carry out his bequest. Whoever does not do so from the heart ... will be a sinner before God. I am not a disloyal soldier. I never think of the place that I am occupying. I know only this much, and am satisfied, that I still am where Bapu posted me.[8]

As for Jawaharlal, he led the Congress, which was not dissolved, to victory in elections in 1952, 1957 and 1962, and he continued as India's Prime Minister until his death in 1964. Shortly before his death he authorized Kashmir's leader, Sheikh Abdullah, to visit Pakistan to explore an India-Pakistan rapprochement and a settlement of the Kashmir dispute. Talks between Abdullah and General Ayub Khan, Pakistan's military ruler, went well, but Nehru's death in May 1964 cut short the reconciliation effort.

Eighteen months later, after a brief Indo-Pakistan war, Prime Minister Lal Bahadur Shastri and General Ayub Khan signed an agreement in Tashkent, then part of the Soviet Union. Remembering Gandhi and believing that 'peace and good relations with

Pakistan were essential if India was to preserve her soul',[9] Shastri accepted Ayub's invitation to visit Pakistan before returning to India, but he died of heart failure while still in Tashkent.

In 1971–2 India and Pakistan fought a third war that resulted in East Pakistan emerging as the independent nation of Bangladesh. The year 1999 saw a fourth conflict, in Kargil in Kashmir, but on 1 January 2001 Prime Minister Atal Bihari Vajpayee said: 'In our search for a lasting solution to the Kashmir problem ... we shall not traverse solely on the beaten track of the past. Rather, we shall be bold and innovative designers of a future architecture of peace and prosperity for the entire South Asian region.'[10]

The sentiment has been repeated since by Prime Minister Manmohan Singh and by Pakistan's President, General Pervez Musharraf, but the subcontinent still awaits the peace that Gandhi wanted to secure by visiting Pakistan in February 1948, an exercise prevented by the assassination.

And after the suicide attacks in New York and Washington on 11 September 2001, and the American attacks that followed in Afghanistan and Iraq, the whole world awaits the reconciliation between Muslims and non-Muslims for which Gandhi gave his life.

The sons. When, in Bombay, he heard of the assassination, Harilal said: 'I will not spare the man who killed a saint, the Mahatma of the world, who was my father.'[11] Three or four days afterwards, he turned up at Devadas's home in New Delhi, wanting to share his grief with his youngest brother. Less than six months later, on 18 June 1948, Harilal died in a Bombay hospital, in the presence of his daughters Rami Parikh and Manu Mashruwala. He was 60.

Editing *Indian Opinion,* Manilal challenged South Africa's racism, inviting imprisonment. He fought, too, for non-violence in the South African struggle. Under his care, Phoenix and its gardens grew and its multiracial character was strengthened. He died there in 1956, at the age of 64.

The youngest, Devadas, the only son living in Delhi, had reached Birla House within minutes of the killing and pleaded into his father's ear, 'Speak, Bapu, speak.' He continued to edit and look after the *Hindustan Times* until 1957 when, at the age of 57, he succumbed to a heart attack in Bombay.

The third son, Ramdas, was the one to light his father's pyre in Rajghat. Until 1951, he managed a branch office of Tata Oil Mills in Nagpur, the big city closest to Sevagram/Wardha; his home provided hospitality to visitors from the ashram. Outliving his brothers, Ramdas died in Bombay in 1969, at the age of 71.

Two of the sons, Manilal and Ramdas, pleaded for the death sentence awarded to Godse and Apte to be commuted, as did the parents of Godse. However, Nehru, Patel and the Governor-General, Rajagopalachari, turned down the requests, and the sentences were carried out in 1949.

Harilal

Manilal

Ramdas

Devadas

We may note here what happened to some others featuring in our story. **Winston Churchill** regained Britain's Premiership in 1951, resigned it in 1955, and died in 1965. **Linlithgow**, the Viceroy who faced Quit India, died in 1952, and Viceroy **Wavell** in 1950. The Viceroy who signed the pact with Gandhi, Lord **Irwin**, later known as Lord Halifax, lived until 1959.

Fulfilling his ambition, **Mountbatten**, the last Viceroy, became Britain's First Sea Lord in 1955. He lived until 1979, when he was killed in Ireland by a bomb planted by the Provisional IRA.

Seven months after Gandhi's assassination, **Jinnah**, founder of Pakistan and its first Governor-General, died of illness in Karachi. He was 72.

A prisoner of the British for 12 years, **Abdul Ghaffar Khan** spent another 15 years, in different spells, in Pakistani jails. Never swerving from his faith in Muslim-Hindu friendship, in non-violence, in a reconciling Islam, and in Pakhtun autonomy, he died in 1988, at the age of 98.

After chairing the Constituent Assembly that produced India's Constitution, **Rajendra Prasad** served until 1962 as India's President. He died in 1963.

Succeeding Mountbatten as Governor-General in the summer of 1948, **C. Rajagopalachari** became home minister after Patel's death in 1950. Parting company with Nehru in the late 1950s, C R launched the Swatantra party to oppose the state's increasing role in the economy. He died in 1972, aged 94.

Until his death in 1958, **Abul Kalam Azad** served as India's education minister, interpreter of Islam, and a symbol and defender of India's pluralism.

The principal craftsman of the Constitution, **Bhimrao Ambedkar**, resigned from Nehru's Cabinet in 1951 after complaining about the slow pace of legislation for reforming Hindu personal laws. In 1956 he renounced Hinduism and embraced Buddhism, along with hundreds of thousands of his Dalit followers in Maharashtra. He died in December of that year.

Accused of complicity in the assassination and taken into custody, **Vinayak D Savarkar** denied the charge but offered to refrain from political activity 'for any period the Government may require' if he was released.[12] His offer was turned down but for want of corroborative evidence Savarkar was acquitted by the courts. He lived until 1966. In 2003, when the Bharatiya Janata Party led the government in New Delhi, Savarkar's portrait was installed in the Central Hall of Parliament House.

Jayaprakash Narayan led nationwide if controversial campaigns for Gandhian and democratic values in the 1960s and 1970s. The struggle against India's 1975–7 Emergency was waged under his banner, but he was ill when, in 1977, India seemed to turn to him. He died in 1979, six years after the death from cancer of his wife **Prabhavati.**

Of the 'Gandhian' team of political leaders, **Jivatram Kripalani** survived the longest. He died in 1982, at the age of 94. Uncomfortable with the Nehru-Patel duumvirate, he opposed the Congress from the early 1950s.

The non-political 'Gandhians' accepted **Vinoba Bhave** as their leader after Gandhi's death. Covering all of India on foot, Bhave persuaded landowners to give hundreds of thousands of acres for the landless. He died in his ashram in Paunar near Wardha in 1982, leaving behind a large corpus of writings and talks.

Continuing to innovate for the common Indian, **Satis Dasgupta** helped farmers conserve water and produced a popular writing ink, among other services. Living to the age of 99, he died in 1979.

Kishorelal Mashruwala edited *Harijan* after Gandhi's death, helped with the publication of Manu Gandhi's diaries and wrote a valuable little book, *Gandhi vs. Marx.* He died in 1952.

His writings on literary, religious and political topics attracting a wide readership, **Dattatreya** or 'Kaka' **Kalelkar** lived until 1981, when he was 96.

After spending some time in Noakhali, **Pyarelal** wrote a multi-volume biography of Gandhi and other books, including a study of Ghaffar Khan, whom he had gone to meet in Kabul. He died in 1982.

Mira Behn (Madeleine Slade) worked in the Himalayan foothills until the late 1950s, when she went to Austria to be close to the spirit of Beethoven. Her book about her association with Gandhi, *The Spirit's Pilgrimage,* was published in 1960. She was 90 when she died in 1982.

Though critical of Quit India, **Henry Polak** helped interpret Gandhi in Britain, where he died in 1959.

Sushila Nayar assisted refugees, obtained advanced medical degrees in the USA, served as India's health minister, ran a medical college in Wardha in Gandhi's name, filled gaps left in her brother's massive biography of Gandhi and died in 2001 at the age of 86.

Amtus Salaam helped recover abducted Hindu and Sikh women from West Punjab, bringing many of them to Rajpura, her town in the former princely state of Patiala, where she founded several institutions, including one named after Kasturba. She died in 1985.

Manu, who remained single, wrote accounts of Gandhi's final months in Noakhali, Bihar and Delhi. A radiant disseminator of Gandhi's message to different parts of India, she was not yet 40 when illness ended her life in New Delhi in 1969, the centenary of Gandhi's birth.[13]

Abha and her husband **Kanu Gandhi** directed for years a rural centre (in Kasturba's name) in Tramba near Rajkot. Abha was 68 when she died in 1995. Kanu had died in 1986.

Nirmal Kumar Bose published an account of his months at Gandhi's side and other studies, lectured on Gandhi in the USA and Japan, and served as director of the Anthropological Survey of India and India's commissioner of Scheduled Tribes and Scheduled Castes. He was the president of the Asiatic Society when, at the age of 71, he died of cancer in 1972.

Mahadev Desai's son **Narayan,** 81 in 2006, works from Vedchhi in Gujarat for peace and justice, and narrates Gandhi-Katha (the Gandhi story) to live audiences. His works include a four-volume biography of Gandhi.

Because of their efforts for freedom without violence, or for reconciliation after violence, or for empowering the weak, individuals from different countries would later get linked to Gandhi, including a man in the American south named Martin Luther King, Jr., the Dalai Lama of Tibet, Nelson Mandela of South Africa, a woman in Burma called Aung San Suu Kyi, Benigno Aquino of the Philippines, and Ibrahim Rugova of Kosovo, and numerous others, whether famous or not.

When great non-violent changes occurred in east Europe in the late 1980s and in South Africa in the early 1990s, observers or participants remembered Gandhi. Persons striving in the century's closing decades to protect the earth's environment also thought of Gandhi.

But all that is another story.

Notes

Chapter 1: Boyhood

1. M K Gandhi, *My Experiments with Truth* (Ahmedabad: Navajivan, 1930). Edition by Dover Publications, New York, 1983, p 28.

2. Prabhudas Gandhi, *Jeevan Prabhat* (New Delhi: Sasta Sahitya Mandal, 1967), p 68.

3. J M Upadhyaya, *Mahatma Gandhi – A Teacher's Discovery* (Ahmedabad: Navajivan, 1969), p 7.

4. Pyarelal, *Mahatma Gandhi: The Early Phase* (Ahmedabad: Navajivan, 1965), p 188.

5. M K Gandhi, *Collected Works of Mahatma Gandhi* (New Delhi: Publications Division), vol. 94, p 111, or 94: 111. All references in this study are to volumes in the digitized edition of the *Collected Works*, which have appeared in more than one version.

6. Mukul Kalarthi, *Ba and Bapu* (Ahmedabad: Navajivan, 1962), p 108.

7. Gandhi's remarks to Vallabhbhai Patel quoted in Chandrashanker Shukla, *Gandhi's View of Life* (Bombay: Bhavan, 1968), p 147.

8. Martin Green, *Gandhi: Voice of a New Age Revolution* (New York: Continuum, 1993), p 65.

9. See also Green, *Gandhi*, p 66.

10. Green, *Gandhi*, p 65.

11. Prabhudas Gandhi, *Jeevan Prabhat*, p 62.

12. D B 'Kaka' Kalelkar, *Bapu ki Jhankian* (Ahmedabad: Navajivan, 1948), p 99.

13. Interview (in May or June 1891) to *The Vegetarian* of London, 13 Jun. 1891; 1: 42.

14. Letter of 21 May 1943 from detention to Reginald Maxwell, Home Secretary, 83: 311.
15. Interview (in May or June 1891) to *The Vegetarian* of London, 13 June 1891; 1: 44.
16. Quoted in Ainslee Embree, *India's Search for National Identity* (Delhi: Chanakya, 1988), p 1.
17. Interviews in *The Vegetarian*, London, March and April 1891; 1: 30–9.
18. Mazmudar actually called it 'divine strength'.
19. Letter quoting Mazmudar from Narhari Parikh to Mahadev Desai, 1919, Gandhi Sangrahalaya, New Delhi.

Chapter 2: London and Identity

1. Pyarelal, *Mahatma Gandhi: The Early Phase* (Ahmedabad: Navajivan, 1965), p 232.
2. See article by A J Parel in B R Nanda (ed.), *Mahatma Gandhi: 125 Years* (New Delhi: Indian Council for Cultural Relations, 1995), p 238.
3. James D Hunt, *Gandhi in London* (Delhi: Promilla, 1978), p 10.
4. Pyarelal, *Mahatma Gandhi: The Early Phase*, p 211.
5. B R Nanda, *Mahatma Gandhi: A Biography* (New Delhi: Allied, 1968), p 28.
6. M K Gandhi, *Guide to London*, 1: 105; Hunt, *Gandhi in London*, p 17.
7. M K Gandhi, *Guide to London*, 1: 106.
8. Hunt, *Gandhi in London*, p 18.
9. D B Kalelkar, *Bapu ki Jhankian*, p 22.
10. Hunt, *Gandhi in London*, p 232.
11. Hunt, *Gandhi in London*, p 33.
12. Pyarelal, *Mahatma Gandhi: The Early Phase*, p 232.
13. Hunt, *Gandhi in London*, p 27.
14. Hunt, *Gandhi in London*, p 27.
15. 'My Friend Gandhi', by Josiah Oldfield in Chandrashanker Shukla (ed.), *Reminiscences of Gandhiji* (Bombay: Vora, 1951), p 188.
16. Pyarelal, *Mahatma Gandhi: The Early Phase*, p 258.
17. Hunt, *Gandhi in London*, p 13.
18. D G Tendulkar, *Gandhi in Champaran* (New Delhi: Publications Division, 1994; first edition 1957), p 27.
19. 'I had evidence of [Pan-Islamism] even while I was a student in England many years ago.' Remark to Muslim leaders in Bengal in May 1947, 87: 442–3.
20. Green, *Gandhi*, p 95.

21. 'My Friend Gandhi,' by Josiah Oldfield in Shukla (ed.), *Reminiscences of Gandhiji*, p 188.
22. Green, *Gandhi*, p 97.
23. See, for instance, the evidence in Pyarelal, *Mahatma Gandhi: The Early Phase*, p 266; and *The Vegetarian*, 13 June 1891.
24. Hunt, *Gandhi in London*, p 231.
25. Pyarelal, *Mahatma Gandhi: The Early Phase*, p 268.
26. Quoted in Green, *Gandhi*, p 113.

Chapter 3: South Africa and a Purpose

1. M K Gandhi, *Satyagraha in South Africa* (Ahmedabad: Navajivan, 1928, 1993 edition), p 37.
2. A, p 93.
3. See also Green, *Gandhi*, p 122, citing 48: 171 (first *Collected Works* version).
4. P Mani, *The Secret of Mahatma Gandhi* (New Delhi: Arnold, 1989), p 35.
5. Green, *Gandhi*, p 123.
6. James D Hunt, *Gandhi and the Nonconformists: Encounters in South Africa* (Columbia, Missouri: South Asia Books, 1986), p 32.
7. Hunt, *Gandhi and the Nonconformists*, p 34.
8. Green, *Gandhi*, p 101.
9. Hunt, *Gandhi and the Nonconformists*, p 42.
10. Green, *Gandhi*, p 103, citing 37: 261 (first version).
11. Joseph J Doke, *M. K. Gandhi: An Indian Patriot in South Africa* (London: Indian Chronicle Press, 1909), p 45.
12. Green, *Gandhi*, p 130.
13. Green, *Gandhi*, p 131.
14. See Gandhi's remarks in London in September 1931, 53: 364–5.
15. Quoted in Chandran Devanesen, *The Making of the Mahatma* (New Delhi: Orient Longmans, 1969), p 316.
16. See A 177.
17. D G Tendulkar, *Mahatma*, 7: 429.
18. Quoted in C F Andrews, *Mahatma Gandhi's Ideas* (London: Allen & Unwin, 1929), 1949 edition, p 364.
19. Green, *Gandhi*, p 139.
20. As related by Gandhi to Pyarelal, in Pyarelal, *Mahatma Gandhi: Volume 2* (Bombay: Sevak, 1980), pp 282–3.
21. Erik Erikson, *Gandhi's Truth* (New York: W W Norton, 1969), p 316.

Chapter 4: Satyagraha

1. Quoted in Mukul Kalarthi, *Ba and Bapu*, pp 44–5.
2. Pyarelal, *Mahatma Gandhi: Volume 3* (Ahmedabad: Navajivan, 1986), p 359.
3. Pyarelal, *Mahatma Gandhi: Volume 3*, p 26.
4. *Indian Opinion*, 30 April 1904.
5. Pyarelal, *Mahatma Gandhi: Volume 3*, p 78.
6. Pyarelal, *Mahatma Gandhi: Volume 3*, p 79.
7. Pyarelal, *Mahatma Gandhi: Volume 3*, p 86.
8. Pyarelal, *Mahatma Gandhi: Volume 3*, p 432.
9. Letter of 12 May 1905 quoted in Pyarelal, *Mahatma Gandhi: Volume 3*, pp 361–8.
10. Nilam Parikh, *Gandhiji's Lost Jewel: Harilal Gandhi* (New Delhi: National Gandhi Museum, 2001), pp 114–15.
11. The Gujarati word '*kalo*', translated as 'coloured' in the *Collected Works* (English), has been retranslated here as 'black'.
12. Dube's remark quoted from Andre Odendaal, *Vukani Bantu* (1984), p 70, in E S Reddy, *Gandhiji: Vision of a Free South Africa* (New Delhi: Sanchar, 1995), p 21.
13. Erikson, *Gandhi's Truth*, p 194.
14. Green, *Gandhi*, p 160.
15. Mani, *The Secret of Mahatma Gandhi*, p 58.
16. Letter of 31 Dec. 1942 to Linlithgow; 83: 274–6
17. Speech in Birmingham, England, 18 Oct. 1931; *Young India*, 5 Nov. 1931; 54: 47.
18. From the title of the book by Marjorie Sykes and Jehangir Patel, *Gandhi: His Gift of the Fight* (Rasulia, MP: Friends Rural Centre, 1987).
19. Jonathan Schell, *The Unconquerable World: Power, Nonviolence, and the Will of the People* (New York: Metropolitan, 2003), pp 114–15.
20. Pyarelal, *Mahatma Gandhi: Volume 3*, p 483.
21. Pyarelal, *Mahatma Gandhi: Volume 3*, p 498.
22. See article by George Hendrick, quoting the American journalist Webb Miller, who cites Gandhi's comment to him, in G Ramachandran and T K Mahadevan (eds.), *Quest for Gandhi* (Bombay: Bhavan, 1970), p 174.
23. Ramachandran and Mahadevan (eds.), *Quest for Gandhi*, pp 175–6.
24. Pyarelal, *Mahatma Gandhi: Volume 3*, p 511. See also C F Andrews, *Mahatma Gandhi At Work* (London: Allen & Unwin, 1931), p 8.

Chapter 5: Hind Swaraj

1. Letter from Gandhi to Ghanshyam Das Birla in 1935 cited in M M Juneja, *The Mahatma and the Millionaire* (Hissar, Haryana: Modern, 1993), pp 201–3.

2. Winston Churchill, *My African Journey* (London: The Holland Press, 1962), pp 33–7.

3. Letter, probably written in 1907, in Parikh, *Gandhiji's Lost Jewel*, p 130.

4. Quoted in B R Nanda, *In Search of Gandhi* (New Delhi: OUP, 2002), p 36.

5. With minor editing, this is the exact conversation as recalled by Gandhi in *Satyagraha*, pp 148–50.

6. Doke's account quoted in Andrews, *Mahatma Gandhi At Work*, pp 378–9.

7. Parikh, *Gandhiji's Lost Jewel*, p 18.

8. Maureen Swan, *Gandhi: The South African Experience* (Johannesburg: Ravan, 1988), p 171; Gandhi to Smuts, 14 August 1908, 9: 62.

9. Swan, *Gandhi: The South African Experience*, p 136.

10. 9: 256.

11. 9: 270.

12. Nelson Mandela in Nanda (ed.), *Mahatma Gandhi: 125 Years*, p 17.

13. Parikh, *Gandhiji's Lost Jewel*, p 131.

14. From undated letters, probably written in 1908, in Parikh, *Gandhiji's Lost Jewel*, pp 121–2.

15. Parikh, *Gandhiji's Lost Jewel*, pp 21–2. (Also 9: 150, 175–6, 200.)

16. Undated letters in Parikh, *Gandhiji's Lost Jewel*, pp 123–5.

17. Undated letter, probably written in 1909, Parikh, *Gandhiji's Lost Jewel*, p 139.

18. Letter of 14 May 1908 to Meghjibhai and Khushalchand Gandhi in Prabhudas Gandhi, *Jeevan Prabhat*, p 103.

19. Prabhudas Gandhi, *Jeevan Prabhat*, p 148.

20. Letter of 25 Mar. 1909 in Uma Dhupelia Mesthrie, *Gandhi's Prisoner? The Life of Gandhi's Son Manilal* (New Delhi: Permanent Black, 2005), p 80.

21. Letter of 25 Mar. 1909; 9: 318.

22. Letters of 17 Sept. and 22 Oct. 1909 quoted in Mesthrie, *Gandhi's Prisoner?*, p 81.

23. Devadas quoted in Pyarelal and Sushila Nayar, *In Gandhiji's Mirror* (New Delhi: OUP, 1991), p 117.

24. Prabhudas Gandhi, *Jeevan Prabhat*, p 153.

25. See Swan, *Gandhi: The South African Experience*, pp 163–4.

26. Prabhudas Gandhi, *Jeevan Prabhat*, p 99.

27. M K Gandhi, *From Yeravda Mandir* (Ahmedabad: Navajivan, 1932), p 25.

28. Prabhudas Gandhi, *Jeevan Prabhat*, p 148.

29. Albert West quoted in Mesthrie, *Gandhi's Prisoner?*, p 72.

30. Prabhudas Gandhi, *Jeevan Prabhat*, p 105.

31. *Indian Opinion*, 30 Dec. 1905 and 17 Mar. 1906.

32. See also Doke, *M. K. Gandhi*, pp 101–2.

33. *Young India*, 28 March 1929. See also his speech in Bombay, 26 June 1939; 76: 66.

34. Letter of 1909 in Parikh, *Gandhiji's Lost Jewel*, p 130.

35. See Gandhi's letter of 29 Oct. to Polak, 10: 195.

36. Ali and Rajan in Shukla (ed.), *Reminiscences of Gandhiji*, p 17 and pp 259–61.

37. Preface to 1921 edition reprinted in M K Gandhi, *Hind Swaraj* (Ahmedabad: Navajivan, 1938), p xxv.

38. Martin Green, *Tolstoy & Gandhi* (New Delhi: HarperCollins, 1998), p 90.

39. Gandhi's remarks of 21 Feb. 1940, 77: 357.

40. *Indian Opinion*, 8 Jan. 1910; 10: 107–10.

41. Anthony J Parel (ed.), *Hind Swaraj* (Oxford: 1997), p xv.

42. Prabhudas Gandhi, *Jeevan Prabhat*, p 87.

43. Parel (ed.), *Hind Swaraj*, pp xiv–xv.

44. Parel (ed.), *Hind Swaraj*, p 6 and p 42.

45. Parel (ed.), *Hind Swaraj*, p 6.

46. Parel (ed.), *Hind Swaraj*, p 1.

47. *Indian Opinion*, 25 Dec. 1909; 10: 244.

48. See also Green, *Gandhi*, pp 198–9, and Andrews, *Mahatma Gandhi's Ideas*, p 197.

49. See Parel (ed.), *Hind Swaraj*, p lviii.

50. Prabhudas Gandhi, *Jeevan Prabhat*, pp 197–8.

51. Speech in Lahore, 1909, quoted in Karve and Ambedkar (ed.), *Speeches and Writings of G.K. Gokhale* (Bombay: Asia, 1966), vol. 2, p 420.

Chapter 6: A Great March

1. See Gandhi's (undated) letter to Harilal, clearly sent immediately after his son's disappearance, in Parikh, *Gandhiji's Lost Jewel*, pp 132–3.

2. Devadas Gandhi quoted in Parikh, *Gandhiji's Lost Jewel*, p 152.

3. Devadas Gandhi quoted in Parikh, *Gandhiji's Lost Jewel*, pp 151–2.

4. Mesthrie, *Gandhi's Prisoner?*, p 82.

5. Quoted in Parikh, *Gandhiji's Lost Jewel*, p 33.

6. Parikh, *Gandhiji's Lost Jewel*, p 128.

7. Parikh, *Gandhiji's Lost Jewel*, p 37.

8. Parikh, *Gandhiji's Lost Jewel*, p 120 and p 125.

9. Quoted in Martin Green, *Gandhi*, p 296.

10. Green, *Gandhi*, p 152.

11. Green, *Gandhi*, p 178.

12. Green, *Gandhi*, p 153.

13. Quoted in Nirmal Kumar Bose, *Lectures on Gandhism* (Ahmedabad: Navajivan, 1971), pp 61–2.

14. Quoted in Green, *Gandhi*, p 177.

15. *Indian Opinion*, 2 Apr. 1910.

16. Swan, *Gandhi: The South African Experience*, pp 230–1.

17. See also Swan, *Gandhi: The South African Experience*, p 235.

18. From Colonial Office records cited in Swan, *Gandhi: The South African Experience*, p 260.

19. See also Swan, *Gandhi: The South African Experience*, p 240.

20. Swan, *Gandhi: The South African Experience*, p 240.

21. Swan, *Gandhi: The South African Experience*, p 247.

22. Swan, *Gandhi: The South African Experience*, p 242.

23. Swan, *Gandhi: The South African Experience*, p 247.

24. Green, *Gandhi*, pp 207–8.

25. Swan, *Gandhi: The South African Experience*, p 251.

26. Smuts quoted in Swan, *Gandhi: The South African Experience*, p 250.

27. See also 24: 45–6.

28. From article by E S Reddy, 'First Martyrs of Satyagraha', *Mainstream*, New Delhi, 14 August 1993.

29. See Swan, *Gandhi: The South African Experience*, p 254, and M K Gandhi, *Satyagraha*, p 286.

30. Green, *Gandhi*, p 185.

31. Smuts quoted in K P Goswami (ed.), *Mahatma Gandhi: A Chronology* (New Delhi: Publications Division, 1971), p 58.

32. Quoted in Mesthrie, *Gandhi's Prisoner?*, pp 107–8.

33. Letter of 20 Sep. 1932 to Srinivasa Sastri, 57: 80.

34. Goswami (ed.), *Mahatma Gandhi: A Chronology*, p 58.

35. From Goswami (ed.), *Mahatma Gandhi: A Chronology*, p 58.

36. Robert A Huttenback, *Gandhi in South Africa* (Ithaca, NY: Cornell University Press, 1971), p 330.

37. Pearson's account quoted in Ravjibhai Patel, *The Making of the Mahatma* (Ahmedabad: Navajivan, 1989), pp 216–17.

38. Quoted in Swan, *Gandhi: The South African Experience*, p 133.

39. Smuts quoted in Sushila Nayar, *Mahatma Gandhi* (Ahmedabad: Navajivan, 1989), vol. 4, p 168.

40. Recalled by Gandhi in letter to Lord Chelmsford, 22 Jun. 1920, 20: 413–16.

41. Speech in London, 8 Aug. 1914; 14: 282.

Chapter 7: Engaging India

1. C L R Fletcher and Rudyard Kipling, *A History of England* (Oxford: 1911, 1930 edition), p 241.

2. Fletcher and Kipling, *A History of England*, p 243.

3. Mani, *The Secret of Mahatma Gandhi*, pp 97–8.

4. From Andrews, *Mahatma Gandhi's Ideas* , p 5.

5. See Choudhary Khaliquzzaman, *Pathway to Pakistan* (Lahore: Pakistan Longman, 1961), p 33.

6. Letter to Srinivasa Sastri, 23 Sep. 1915; 15: 46.

7. See Erikson, *Gandhi's Truth*, p 299.

8. Indulal Yagnik, *Gandhi As I Knew Him* (New Delhi: Danish Mahal, 1943), pp 9–10.

9. Quoted in Parikh, *Gandhiji's Lost Jewel*, pp 44–5. See also p 152.

10. Parikh, *Gandhiji's Lost Jewel*, p 153.

11. Parikh, *Gandhiji's Lost Jewel*, pp 47–9.

12. Mesthrie, *Gandhi's Prisoner?*, p 140.

13. Naidu's foreword to a 1917 publication of Gandhi's writings and speeches, quoted in B R Nanda, *Gandhi: Pan-Islamism, Imperialism and Nationalism in India* (New Delhi: OUP, 2002), p 170.

14. Erikson, *Gandhi's Truth*, p 283.

15. William L Shirer, *Gandhi: A Memoir* (New Delhi: Rupa, 1993), p 64.

16. David Hardiman, *Gandhi: In His Time and Ours* (New Delhi: Permanent Black, 2003), p 125.

17. Quoted in Michael Brecher, *Nehru* (London: Oxford University Press, 1959), p 60.

18. Mavlankar quoted in Francis Watson, *The Trial of Mr. Gandhi* (London: Macmillan, 1969), pp 71–2.

19. Quoted in Tendulkar, *Gandhi in Champaran*, p 103.

20. Quoted in Tendulkar, *Gandhi in Champaran*, pp 112–13.

21. Edwin S Montagu, *An Indian Diary* (London: Heinemann, 1930), pp 57–67.

22. David Hardiman, *Peasant Nationalists of Gujarat* (New Delhi: Oxford, 1981), p 84 .

23. Hardiman, *Peasant Nationalists of Gujarat*, p 89.

24. See note dictated by Gandhi to Jagadish Munshi, August 1944, reproduced in K M Munshi, *Pilgrimage to Freedom* (Bombay: Bhavan, 1967), p 439.

25. Quoted in B R Ambedkar, *Writings and Speeches*, vol. 2 (Bombay: Education Department, 1982), p 446.

26. Narhari Parikh, *Sardar Vallabhbhai Patel* (Ahmedabad: Navajivan, 1971 edition), vol. 1, p 55.

27. Rajmohan Gandhi, *Patel: A Life* (Ahmedabad: Navajivan, 1990), pp 46–7.

28. Parikh, *Sardar Vallabhbhai Patel*, 1: 68.

29. Mahadev Desai, *Day-to-day with Gandhi* (Varanasi: Sarva Seva Sangh), vol. 1, pp 92–3.

30. From Kripalani's foreword in K L Panjabi, *The Indomitable Sardar* (Bombay: Bhavan, 1962), pp viii–ix.

31. Rajmohan Gandhi, *Patel*, p 60.

32. Parikh, *Sardar Vallabhbhai Patel*, 1: 84.

33. Erikson, *Gandhi's Truth*, p 361.

34. Quoted in Erikson, *Gandhi's Truth*, p 391.

35. Mahadev Desai, *Day-to-day with Gandhi*, 1: 56–7 & p 182.

36. Mahadev Desai, *Day-to-day with Gandhi*, 1: 108–12.

37. Mahadev Desai, *Day-to-day with Gandhi*, 1: 148.

38. Mahadev Desai, *Day-to-day with Gandhi*, 1: 183 & 237–8.

39. Mahadev Desai, *Day-to-day with Gandhi*, 1: 157.

40. Quoted in Erikson, *Gandhi's Truth*, pp 372–4.

41. Quoted in Green, *Gandhi*, p 14.

42. See Rajendra Prasad, *Autobiography* (Bombay: Asia, 1957), p 104.

43. Quoted in Mahadev Desai, *Day-to-day with Gandhi* , 1: 56–7.

44. Mahadev Desai, *Day-to-day with Gandhi*, 1: 2–3.

45. Mahadev Desai, *Day-to-day with Gandhi*, 1: 264.

46. Mahadev Desai, *Day-to-day with Gandhi*, 1: 293–4.

47. Millie Polak, *Mr. Gandhi: The Man* (London: Allen & Unwin, 1931), p 142.

48. Gandhi recalling the incident in *Harijan*, 29 Dec. 1946.

49. Remark to the Press. Mahadev Desai, *Day-to-day with Gandhi*, 1: 303.

50. Remark to the Press. Mahadev Desai, *Day-to-day with Gandhi*, 1: 303.

51. Mahadev Desai, *Day-to-day with Gandhi*, 1: 298–9.

52. Quoted in G M Nandurkar (ed.), *Sardar Vallabhbhai Patel Centenary Volumes* (Ahmedabad: 1974–8), vol. 1, p 488.

53. Secret File 271 of 1919, Tamil Nadu Archives, Chennai.

54. Mahadev Desai, *Day-to-day with Gandhi*, 2: 323–6.

55. Cable of 19 Sep. 1919 to Chelmsford in Home (Pol.), B Series, National Archives, New Delhi.

56. Willingdon to Montagu, 9 Jun. 1919, Willingdon Papers, India Office Library, London.

57. Geoffrey Ashe, *Gandhi: A Study in Revolution* (Bombay: Asia, 1968), p 189.

58. Quoted in Pyarelal and Sushila Nayar, *In Gandhiji's Mirror*, pp 5–7.

59. Mahadev Desai, *Day-to-day with Gandhi*, 2: 67.

60. Pyarelal and Nayar, *In Gandhiji's Mirror*, pp 5–7.

61. Green, *Gandhi*, p 143.

62. Green, *Gandhi*, p 226 and p 275.

63. Letter to Kallenbach, 10 Aug. 1920; 21: 131.

64. Green, *Gandhi*, p 284.

65. Green, *Gandhi*, pp 274–84.

66. Green, *Gandhi*, p 279.

67. Rajagopalachari Papers.

68. Letter of 16 Jun. 1920 from Madras, with Gopal Gandhi, Kolkata.

69. Devadas Gandhi, *Ba, Bapu aur Bhai* (New Delhi: Sasta Sahitya Mandal, 1956), p 16.

70. Mahadev Desai, *Day-to-day with Gandhi*, 2: 217.

71. Erikson, *Gandhi's Truth*, p 392.

72. Quoted in A H Merriam, *Gandhi vs. Jinnah* (Calcutta: Minerva, 1980), p 45.

73. Munshi, *Pilgrimage to Freedom*, pp 16–17.

74. Pyarelal and Nayar, *In Gandhiji's Mirror*, pp 5–7.

75. Quoted in Mahadev Desai, *Day-to-day with Gandhi*, 2: 54–5 fn.

76. Munshi, *Pilgrimage to Freedom*, pp 16–17.

Chapter 8: The Empire Challenged

1. Quoted in Afzal Iqbal, *Mohamed Ali* (Delhi: Idarah-i-Adabiyat, 1978), p 199.

2. Letter to Razmia, 27 Mar. 1920; 20: 185.

3. Viceroy quoted in 20: 338.

4. Parikh, *Gandhiji's Lost Jewel*, p 62.

5. Pyarelal and Nayar, *In Gandhiji's Mirror*, p 13.

6. Quoted in Dhananjay Keer, *Mahatma Gandhi* (Bombay: Popular Prakashan, 1973), p 324.

7. Parikh, *Sardar Vallabhbhai Patel*, 1: 115.

8. Hector Bolitho, *Jinnah: Creator of Pakistan* (Westport, Conn.: Greenwood Press, n.d.), pp 83–5.

9. Judith Brown, *Gandhi's Rise to Power* (Cambridge: University Press, 1992), p 297.

10. Quoted in D G Tendulkar, *Mahatma*, vol.2, p 38.

11. Quoted in S M Ikram, *Modern Muslim India and the Birth of Pakistan* (Lahore: Institute of Islamic Culture), p 160.

12. Allan and Wendy Scarfe, *J.P.: His Biography* (New Delhi: Orient Longman, 1975), p 44

13. Quoted in Iqbal, *Mohamed Ali*, p 280.

14. Iqbal, *Mohamed Ali*, p 267.

15. Quoted in *Navajivan*, 5 Dec. 1920; 22: 57.

16. Remark quoted by Gandhi in *Young India*, 23 Apr. and 4 May 1921; 23: 46–7.

17. See David Hardiman, *Gandhi: In His Time and Ours*, pp 136–55.

18. Andrews, *Mahatma Gandhi's Ideas*, pp 276–7.

19. Quoted by V V Ramana Murti in Ramachandran and Mahadevan (eds.), *Quest for Gandhi*, p 287.

20. Iqbal, *Mohamed Ali*, p 394.

21. Iqbal, *Mohamed Ali*, p 267.

22. Ikram, *Modern Muslim India and the Birth of Pakistan*, p 160.

23. Quoted in Iqbal, *Mohamed Ali*, p 294.

24. Quoted in Iqbal, *Mohamed Ali*, p 256.

25. Quoted in Ashe, *Gandhi: A Study in Revolution*, p 218.

26. Hardiman, *Gandhi: In His Time and Ours*, p 139.

27. Tendulkar, *Mahatma*, 2: 89.

28. Letter in Sep. 1921 to Reading, Willingdon Papers, India Office Library, London.

29. Krishnadas, *Seven Months with Mahatma Gandhi* (Ahmedabad: Navajivan, 1951), p 90, hereafter K.

30. Nanda, *Gandhi: Pan-Islamism, Imperialism and Nationalism in India*, p 354.

31. Tendulkar, *Mahatma*, 2: 106.

32. Nanda, *Gandhi: Pan-Islamism, Imperialism and Nationalism in India*, pp 352–3.

33. Nanda, *Gandhi: Pan-Islamism, Imperialism and Nationalism in India*, pp 352–6 and p 405.

34. Nanda, *Gandhi: Pan-Islamism, Imperialism and Nationalism in India*, p 355.

35. Quoted in Rajmohan Gandhi, *Rajaji: A Life* (New Delhi: Penguin, 1997), p 67.

36. Quoted in Parikh, *Sardar Vallabhbhai Patel*, 1: 166–7.

37. Quoted in Nanda, *Gandhi: Pan-Islamism, Imperialism and Nationalism in India*, p 401, from V C Joshi (ed.), *Writings of Lajpat Rai* (Delhi: 1966), vol. 2, p 89.

38. Remark of Dec. 1924 quoted in Nanda, *Gandhi: Pan-Islamism, Imperialism and Nationalism in India*, p 408.

39. Quoted in Parikh, *Sardar Vallabhbhai Patel*, 1: 165.

40. See Nanda, *Gandhi: Pan-Islamism, Imperialism and Nationalism in India*, pp 403–5.

41. See Krishnadas, *Seven Months with Mahatma Gandhi*, pp 220–1, and Ramnarayan Chaudhary, *Bapu As I Saw Him* (Ahmedabad: Navajivan, 1959), pp 24–8.

42. Quoted in Nanda, *Gandhi: Pan-Islamism, Imperialism and Nationalism in India*, p 406.

43. Iqbal, *Mohamed Ali*, p 285 and p 394.

44. Ashe, *Gandhi: A Study in Revolution*, p 230.

45. Nanda, *Gandhi: Pan-Islamism, Imperialism and Nationalism in India*, p 406.

Chapter 9: Building Anew

1. Gandhi's preface dated 2 Apr. 1924 in *Satyagraha in South Africa* (Ahmedabad: Navajivan, 1968 edition), p xiii.

2. Yagnik, *Gandhi As I Knew Him*, p 303.

3. *Indian Opinion*, 7 July 1922, cited in Mesthrie, *Gandhi's Prisoner?*, p 167.

4. Letter of 16 April 1923 from Patel to his daughter Maniben in G M Nandurkar (ed.), *Sardarshri na Patro* (Ahmedabad: 1975–8), vol. 3, p 5.

5. Rajmohan Gandhi, *Patel: A Life*, p 111.

6. Tendulkar, *Mahatma*, 2: 172.

7. Diary entry dated 17 Feb. 1924 quoted in Iqbal, *Mohamed Ali*, pp 314–15.

8. See Hardiman, *Gandhi: In His Time and Ours*, p 175; and Jyotirmaya Sharma, *Hindutva* (New Delhi: Penguin, 2003), pp 136–48.

9. Hardiman, *Gandhi: In His Time and Ours*, p 165.

10. Iqbal, *Mohamed Ali*, pp 312–13.

11. Andrews, *Mahatma Gandhi's Ideas*, p xi.

12. Quoted in Virendra Prakash, *Hindutva Demystified* (Delhi: Virgo, 2002), p 41.

13. Quoted in Prakash, *Hindutva Demystified*, p 41.

14. Quoted in Juneja, *The Mahatma and the Millionaire*, pp 76–7.

15. G D Birla, *A Talk on Bapu* (Calcutta: Sangeet Kala Mandir, 1981).

16. Andrews, *Mahatma Gandhi's Ideas* (London: Allen & Unwin, 1929, 1949 edition), pp 113–16.

17. Sushila Nayar in Savita Singh (ed.), *Kasturba* (New Delhi: Gandhi Smriti, 1994), p 49.

18. Prabhavati Narayan quoted in http://www.gandhi-manibhavan.org/gandhicomesalive/chap06.htm

19. Mesthrie, *Gandhi's Prisoner?*, p 177.

20. Mesthrie, *Gandhi's Prisoner?*, p 185 and p 176.

21. Tendulkar, *Mahatma*, 2: 405.

22. Parikh, *Gandhiji's Lost Jewel*, p 67.

23. D B Kalelkar, *Gandhi Charitra Kirtan* (Ahmedabad: Navajivan, 1970), pp 50–1.

24. Geoffrey Moorhouse, *To the Frontier* (London: Phoenix, 1998), pp 222–3.

25. From Hindi, *Hindi Navajivan*, 4 Jul. 1929; 46: 240–1.

26. From Gujarati. *Navajivan*, 28 Jul. 1929; 46: 318–21.

27. Narayan Desai, *Bliss Was It To Be Young – With Gandhi* (Bombay: Bhavan, 1988), p 2.

28. Narayan Desai, *Bliss Was It To Be Young – With Gandhi*, p 22.

29. Mira Behn to author, Vienna, 1978.

30. Quoted in Francis Watson and Maurice Brown, *Talking of Gandhiji* (Calcutta: Orient Longmans, 1957), p 47

31. According to Raihana Tyabji as quoted in Watson and Brown, *Talking of Gandhiji*, p 48.

32. Letter of 23 Apr. 1926; 35: 123.

33. Letter of 23 Jan. 1928 quoted in S Gopal, *Nehru* (New Delhi: Oxford) vol.1, p 112.

34. Mahadev Desai, *Day-to-day with Gandhi*, 5: 224.

35. Quoted in Rajmohan Gandhi, *Patel*, p 171.

36. Tendulkar, *Mahatma*, 2: 441.

37. Quoted in Khaliquzzaman, *Pathway to Pakistan*, p 37.

38. From note of Afzal Haque, who was present, quoted in G A Allana, *Jinnah* (Lahore: Ferozsons, 1967), p 213.

39. Bolitho, *Jinnah: Creator of Pakistan*, pp 94–5.

40. Subhas Bose, *The Indian Struggle* (Bombay: Asia, 1964), p 169.

41. Brecher, *Nehru*, p 137.

42. A Parikh, *Sardar Vallabhbhai Patel*, 1: 411.

43. Pattabhi Sitaramayya, *The History of the Indian National Congress 1935–1947* (Bombay: Padma, 1947), p 600.

Chapter 10: Assault – with Salt

1. Thomas Weber, *On the Salt March* (New Delhi: HarperCollins, 1997), p 59.

2. Gandhi in *Harijan*, 14 May 1938; 73: 155; see also Weber, *On the Salt March*, p 88.

3. *Young India*, 27 Feb. 1930; 48: 349–50.

4. Weber, *On the Salt March*, p 89.

5. Weber, *On the Salt March*, p 103.

6. Weber, *On the Salt March*, p 85.

7. Quoted in Weber, *On the Salt March*, p 90.

8. Narayan Desai, *Bliss Was It To Be Young – With Gandhi*, p 22.

9. Quoted in Weber, *On the Salt March*, p 101.

10. Weber, *On the Salt March*, p 112.

11. Weber, *On the Salt March*, pp 490–6.

12. Weber, *On the Salt March*, p 139.

13. Weber, *On the Salt March*, p 288.

14. Erikson, *Gandhi's Truth*, p 446.

15. Weber, *On the Salt March*, p 209.

16. Weber, *On the Salt March*, p 165.

17. Weber, *On the Salt March*, p 207.

18. Weber, *On the Salt March*, p 210.

19. Weber, *On the Salt March*, pp 272–4.

20. Letter of 7 Apr. 1930 from Irwin to Benn, Secretary of State for India, in Weber, *On the Salt March*, p 415.

21. Weber, *On the Salt March*, p 333.

22. Weber, *On the Salt March*, p 478.

23. Weber, *On the Salt March*, p 405.

24. Weber, *On the Salt March*, p 405.

25. Quoted in Rajmohan Gandhi, *Rajaji: A Life*, p 123.

26. Irwin's letter to the Secretary of State quoted in Brecher, *Nehru*, p 153.

27. Letter of 15 Apr. in Weber, *On the Salt March*, p 378.

28. Weber, *On the Salt March*, p 427.

29. In October 1988, before the author.

30. Thomas Weber, after interviewing surviving marchers in 1983. See Weber, *On the Salt March*, pp 479–80.

31. Weber, *On the Salt March*, p 428.

32. Weber, *On the Salt March*, pp 443–7.

33. Quoted in Weber, *On the Salt March*, p 454.

34. Weber, *On the Salt March*, p 407.

35. Quoted from Brailsford, *Rebel India*, in Weber, *On the Salt March*, p 498.

36. Note of 13 Jul. 1930, Home Pol 257/V and KW 1930, quoted in Weber, *On the Salt March*, p 408.

37. Rajmohan Gandhi, *Rajaji: A Life*, p 124.

38. Narhari Parikh, *Sardar Vallabhbhai Patel*, 2: 35.

39. Quoted in Madhu Limaye, *Prime Movers* (New Delhi: Radiant, 1985), p 34.

40. Quoted in Weber, *On the Salt March*, p 405.

41. Letter of 28 Jul. quoted in Weber, *On the Salt March*, p 479.

42. See Parikh, *Sardar Vallabhbai Patel*, 2: 31–2.

43. Kalelkar, *Bapu ki Jhankian*, p 130.

44. See 50: 140.

45. Quoted in Tendulkar, *Mahatma*, 3: 60–2.

46. Martin Gilbert, *Winston Churchill*, vol. 5, p 390, quoted in Hardiman, *Gandhi: In His Time and Ours*, p 238.

47. See 84: 147, where the 'crushed' remark is quoted, taken from R K Prabhu, *This Was Bapu* (Ahmedabad: Navajivan, 1954), p 139.

48. Sitaramayya, *History of the Indian National Congress*, p 786.

49. Sitaramayya, *History of the Indian National Congress*, p 737.

50. Quoted by Paresh Vaidya in *Frontline*, Cheenai, 14–27 April 2001.

51. Tendulkar, *Mahatma*, 3: 81–2.

52. Irwin (Halifax) in *Fulness of Days* (London: Collins, 1957), pp 146–51.

53. Quoted in Limaye, *Prime Movers*, p 34.

54. Sitaramayya, *History of the Indian National Congress*, pp 755–63.

55. Shirer, *Gandhi: A Memoir*, p 60.

56. Shirer, *Gandhi: A Memoir*, p 57.

57. Shirer, *Gandhi: A Memoir*, p 103.

58. 51: 330.

59. Parikh, *Sardar Vallabhbhai Patel*, 2: 57.

60. Shirer, *Gandhi: A Memoir*, pp 130–1.

61. Tendulkar, *Mahatma*, 3: 138.

62. Parikh, *Sardar Vallabhbhai Patel*, 2: 72.

63. Mira Behn, *The Spirit's Pilgrimage* (London: Longmans Green, 1960), p 131.

64. Related to author by Devadas Gandhi, present at the conversation.

65. Quoted by Akhtarul Wasey in N N Vohra (ed.), *History, Culture and Society in India and West Asia* (Delhi: Shipra, 2003), p 281.

66. 54: 224.

67. Shirer, *Gandhi: A Memoir*, p 141.

68. Lester quoted in Watson and Brown, *Talking of Gandhiji*, pp 73–5.

69. Watson and Brown, *Talking of Gandhiji*, p 72.

70. Albert Docker quoted in Watson and Brown, *Talking of Gandhiji*, p 75.

71. Shirer, *Gandhi: A Memoir*, p 152.

72. Quoted in Mira Behn, *The Spirit's Pilgrimage*, p 143.

73. Viscount Templewood (Lord Samuel Hoare), *Nine Troubled Years* (London: Collins, 1954), pp 59–60. See also Pyarelal and Nayar, *In Gandhiji's Mirror*, p 22.

74. Sheridan quoted in Watson and Brown, *Talking of Gandhiji*, pp 70–85.

75. Quoted in Green, *Gandhi*, p 322.

76. Horrabin in Chandrashanker Shukla (ed.), *Incidents in Gandhiji's Life* (Bombay: Vora, 1949), pp 84–5.

77. Shirer, *Gandhi: A Memoir*, p 162.

78. Templewood, *Nine Troubled Years*, p 58.

79. Comment to *Bristol Evening News* quoted in Goswami (ed.), *Mahatma Gandhi: A Chronology*, p 134.

80. Lester quoted in Watson and Brown, *Talking of Gandhiji*, p 92.

81. Quoted in Green, *Gandhi*, p 322.

82. See Narayan Desai, *Agnikundma Ugelun Gulab* (Ahmedabad: Navajivan, 1992), pp 392–5.

83. Sitaramayya, *History of the Indian National Congress*.

84. Entry dated 10 Apr. 1932 in Mahadev Desai, *The Diary of Mahadev Desai* (Ahmedabad: Navajivan, 1953), vol. 1, p 66.

85. Parikh, *Gandhiji's Lost Jewel*, p 72.

86. Parikh, *Gandhiji's Lost Jewel*, p 72.

87. Parikh, *Sardar Vallabhbhai Patel*, 2: 91–2.

88. Parikh, *Sardar Vallabhbhai Patel*, 2: 136.

89. Pyarelal, *The Epic Fast* (Ahmedabad: Navajivan, 1932), p 49.

90. Pyarelal, *The Epic Fast*, p 59.

91. Pyarelal, *The Epic Fast*, p 89 and p 93.

92. Pyarelal, *The Epic Fast*, p 59.

Chapter 11: Negotiating Repression

1. *Harijan Sevak*, 28 Apr. 1933; 61: 16.

2. Quoted in Parikh, *Gandhiji's Lost Jewel*, p 74.

3. Andrews's letter quoted in David M Gracie (ed.), *Gandhi & Charlie* (Cambridge, Mass.: Cowley, 1989), p 155.

4. See letter of 14 Sep. 1933 to Jawaharlal, 61: 396.

5. Nehru's telegram to Gandhi, 26 Sep. 1932; 57: 113.

6. Letter of 14 Sep. 1933 to Nehru, 61: 396.

7. Remark to ashram colleagues, Patna, 22 Mar. 1934; 63: 305.

8. Talk to ashram inmates, Patna, 22 Mar. 1934; 63: 300–6.

9. S Gopal (ed.), *Selected Works of Jawaharlal Nehru* (New Delhi: Orient Longman, 1974), vol. 6, p 248.

10. Patel quoted back by Gandhi in M K Gandhi, *Letters to Sardar Vallabhbhai Patel* (Ahmedabad: Navajivan, 1957), pp 57–9.

11. Letter of 30 Aug. 1934, Devadas Gandhi Papers.

12. Letters of 13 and 28 Sep. 1934, Devadas Gandhi Papers.

13. Letter to S B Rath, 10 Nov. 1931, Ashram File 20, Rajagopalachari Papers.

14. 65: 212–13 and 65: 229–30.

15. To Pandit Narayan M Khare, 22 Sep. 1934; 65: 58.

16. Parikh, *Gandhiji's Lost Jewel*, p 76.

17. Parikh, *Gandhiji's Lost Jewel*, p xii.

18. Parikh, *Gandhiji's Lost Jewel*, pp 172–3.

19. Parikh, *Gandhiji's Lost Jewel*, pp 149–55.

20. Narayan Desai, *Bliss Was It To Be Young – With Gandhi*, p 73.

21. Parikh, *Gandhiji's Lost Jewel*, p 85.

22. Narayan Desai, *Bliss Was It To Be Young – With Gandhi*, pp 73–4.

23. Dhananjay Keer, *Dr. Ambedkar* (Bombay: Popular Prakashan, 1962), p 258.

24. Jagjivan Ram to author, New Delhi, 1980.

25. Letter of 13 Sep. 1935 in M K Gandhi, *Letters to Sardar Vallabhbhai Patel*, p 112.

26. Munshi, *Pilgrimage to Freedom*, p 28.

27. Patwardhan quoted in S Gopal, *Nehru*, vol. 1, p 210.

28. See letter from Prasad to Nehru quoted in Brecher, *Nehru*, p 224; Patel to Prasad, 29 May 1936, in *Rajendra Prasad's Correspondence* (New Delhi: Allied, n.d.), vol. 1, p 17; and new 69: 198.

29. Letter of 8 Jul. 1936, 69: 198–9.

30. S Gopal, *Nehru*, vol. 1, p 215.

31. Letter of 15 Nov. 1936 in G M Nandurkar (ed.), *Bapu, Sardar ane Mahadevbhai* (Ahmedabad), p 237.

32. Letter of 15 Nov. 1936 in Nandurkar (ed.), *Bapu, Sardar ane Mahadevbhai*, p 237.

33. See Parikh, *Sardar Vallabhbhai Patel*, 2: 218.

34. J B Kripalani, *Autobiography* (typescript), pp 390–1.

35. Parikh, *Sardar Vallabhbhai Patel*, 2: 220.

36. Green, *Gandhi*, p 349.

37. Quoted in Parikh, *Sardar Vallabhbhai Patel*, 2: 220.

38. Brecher, *Nehru*, p 227.

Chapter 12: Dream under Fire

1. Quoted in J Ahmad, *Middle Phase of the Muslim Political Movement* (Lahore: Publishers United, 1969), p 170.

2. Parikh, *Sardar Vallabhbhai Patel*, 2: 224.

3. Parikh, *Sardar Vallabhbhai Patel*, 2: 289.

4. For differing accounts of the UP talks see Abul Kalam Azad, *India Wins Freedom* (Calcutta: Orient Longmans, 1959); Khaliquzzaman, *Pathway to Pakistan*; Gopal, *Nehru* (vol. 1), pp 225–8; and the papers by B R Nanda and S R Mehrotra in C H Philips and M D Wainwright (eds.), *The Partition of India* (London: Allen & Unwin, 1970).

5. Letters quoted in Rajmohan Gandhi, *India Wins Errors* (New Delhi: Radiant, 1989), pp 22–3.

6. Rajmohan Gandhi, *India Wins Errors*, pp 22–3.

7. See letters from Gandhi to Nehru of 1 and 22 Jul. 1937; 72: 9 & 72: 56.

8. Quoted by A G Noorani, *Frontline*, Chennai, 15–28 Mar. 2003.

9. *The Hindu*, Madras, 10 Jan. 1938.

10. Parikh, *Sardar Vallabhbhai Patel*, 2: 271.

11. M K Gandhi, *Letters to Sardar Patel*, p 129

12. Parikh, *Sardar Vallabhbhai Patel*, 2: 260.

13. On 16 Feb. 1938. 72: 468.

14. M K Gandhi, *Letters to Sardar Patel*, p 130.

15. See Narayan Desai, *Bliss Was It To Be Young – With Gandhi*, p 44.

16. On 26 Mar. 1938; 73: 46.

17. 73: 454; 3 Mar. 1938.

18. Letter to Amrit Kaur, 18 May 1938; 73: 171.

19. Letter to Amrit Kaur, 22 May 1938; 73: 190.

20. Letter to Amrit Kaur, 18 May 1938; 73: 171.

21. Mahadev Desai, *Two Servants of God* (New Delhi: Hindustan Times, 1935), pp 61–2.

22. On 4 May 1938; 73: 143–5.

23. 74: 158.

24. D G Tendulkar, *Abdul Gaffar Khan: Faith is a Battle* (Bombay: Popular Prakashan,1967), p 244.

25. On 31 Oct. 1938; 74: 180.

26. On 16 Oct. in Hoti Mardan; 74: 115.

27. On 31 Oct. 1938; 74: 180.

28. 74: 147.

29. Tendulkar, *Faith is a Battle*, p 291.

30. Tendulkar, *Faith is a Battle*, p 244.

31. Tendulkar, *Faith is a Battle*, pp 253–4.

32. Tendulkar, *Faith is a Battle*, p 285.

33. Tendulkar, *Faith is a Battle*, p 238.

34. Relayed by Halifax to Anthony Eden, quoted in Earl of Avon, *The Eden Memoirs* (London: Cassell, 1962), p 516.

35. Munshi, *Pilgrimage to Freedom*, p 53.

36. See A C Guha, *India's Struggle, 1921–1946* (New Delhi: Publications Division, 1982), Part 1, p 425.

37. Sitaramayya, *History of the Indian National Congress*, p 105.

38. Parikh, *Sardar Vallabhbhai Patel*, 2: 390.

39. Parikh, *Sardar Vallabhbhai Patel*, 2: 390–2.

40. *Indian Review*, Madras, Apr. 1939.

41. Letter of 23 Nov. 1939; 77: 125.

42. Green, *Gandhi*, p 284.

43. Sudarshan Kapur, *Raising up a Prophet: The African-American Encounter with Gandhi* (Boston: Beacon Press, 1992), p 13.

44. Thurman quoted in Kapur, *Raising up a Prophet*, p 88.

45. Quoted in Kapur, *Raising up a Prophet*, p 100.

46. E Stanley Jones, *Gandhi* (Nashville: Abingdon, 1948), pp 33–4.

47. Prabhavati quoted in http://www.gandhi-manibhavan.org/gandhicomesalive/chap06.htm.

48. Sushila Nayar in Savita Singh (ed.), *Kasturba* (New Delhi: Gandhi Smriti, 1994), pp 50–1.

49. Sushila Nayar in Singh (ed.), *Kasturba*, p 51.

50. Shirer, *Gandhi: A Memoir*, p 198.

51. *Harijan*, 22 Apr. 1939; 75: 475.

52. See also Chandran Devanesen, *The Making of the Mahatma* (New Delhi: Orient Longmans, 1969), p 314.

53. See Shirer, *Gandhi: A Memoir*, pp 196–7, where he discusses Ved Mehta's interviews with Abha Gandhi and Sushila Nayar.

54. Quoted in Parikh, *Gandhiji's Lost Jewel*, p 93; see also 94: 96.

55. See Gandhi's letter to Pyarelal, 23 May 1938; 73: 192.

56. Kasturba quoted in Gandhi's letter to her, 18 Feb. 1939; 75: 90.

57. Green, *Gandhi*, p 346.

58. Green, *Gandhi*, p 346.

59. Green, *Gandhi*, p 346.

60. Green, *Gandhi*, p 346.

61. Green, *Gandhi*, p 346.

62. Green, *Gandhi*, p 346.

63. Kalelkar, *Bapu ki Jhankian*, p 22.

64. Remark of 1931 quoted in Raghavan Iyer, *The Moral and Political Thought of Mahatma Gandhi* (New Delhi: OUP, 1973), p 395.

65. Remark of March 1940 quoted in Iyer, *The Moral and Political Thought of Mahatma Gandhi*, p 12.

66. Parikh, *Sardar Vallabhbhai Patel*, 1: 336.

67. Parikh, *Sardar Vallabhbhai Patel*, 1: 329.

68. Patel recalling the episode is quoted in *The Hindustan Times*, New Delhi, 14 Nov. 1947.

69. Desai, *Day-to-day with Gandhi*, 8: 310.

70. 75: 27.

71. *Harijan*, 8 Apr. 1939.

72. Kalelkar, writing on 16 Mar. 1946, in Shukla (ed.), *Incidents in Gandhiji's Life* , pp 99–100.

73. *Harijan*, 22 Apr. 1939; 75: 475.

74. Kalelkar, writing on 16 Mar. 1946, in Shukla (ed.), *Incidents in Gandhiji's Life*, pp 99–100.

75. Pritam Pal Singh, a host in Abbottabad, to author, Pune, 2003.

76. Buber quoted by Avner Falk in Ramachandran and Mahadevan (eds.), *Quest for Gandhi*, pp 140–54.

77. S Gopal (ed.), *Selected Works of Jawaharlal Nehru* (New Delhi), vol. 9, p 300.

78. S Gopal (ed.), *Selected Works of Jawaharlal Nehru*, vol. 10, p 117.

79. Munshi, *Pilgrimage to Freedom*, p 55.

Chapter 13: 'Quit India!'

1. Entry dated 9 Sep. 1939, Diary of Maniben Patel, Patel Papers, Ahmedabad.

2. *The Hindu*, 4 Sep. 1939.

3. Prasad to B Shiva Rao, as related by Rao to author, 1973.

4. Brecher, *Nehru*, p 262.

5. Quoted in Rajula Jain, *Patel's Role in the Congress, 1934–39* (unpublished study, 1985), p 192.

6. See Penderel Moon, *Divide and Quit* (Berkeley: University of California Press, 1962), pp 24–8.

7. Parikh, *Sardar Vallabhbhai Patel*, 2: 409.

8. Linlithgow to George VI, 19 Oct. 1939, Linlithgow Papers, India Office Library, London.

9. Letter of 18 November 1939 from Linlithgow to Zetland quoted in Gopal, *Nehru*, vol. 1, p 258.

10. To Louis Fischer, 4–9 Jun. 1942; 82: 403.

11. Conversation on 11 Aug. 1950 between Patel and Narhari Parikh, recorded in the Diary of Maniben Patel, entry dated 11 Aug. 1950.

12. Parikh, *Sardar Vallabhbhai Patel*, 2: 411.

13. *Harijan*, 4 Feb. 1939; 75: 478.

14. Letter from Rajagopalachari to J B L Munro, 25 Dec. 1939, Munro Papers.

15. *The Hindu*, 18 Oct. 1939.

16. Narayan Desai, *Bliss Was It To Be Young – With Gandhi*, pp 68–71.

17. Narayan Desai, *Bliss Was It To Be Young – With Gandhi*, pp 68–71.

18. Quoted in Prakash, '*Hindutva*' *Demystified*, p 72.

19. See letter from Gandhi to Hyat Khan, 1 Nov. 1939, 77:72; and telegram from Gandhi to Hyat Khan, 25 May 1940, 78: 246.

20. Merriam, *Gandhi vs. Jinnah*, pp 64–5.

21. John Glendevon, *The Viceroy at Bay* (London: Collins, 1971), p 119.

22. Merriam, *Gandhi vs. Jinnah*, pp 67.

23. Quoted in C M Naim (ed.), *Iqbal, Jinnah and Pakistan* (Syracuse: Syracuse University, 1979), p 186.

24. Arsh Malsian, *Abul Kalam Azad* (New Delhi: Publications Division, 1976).

25. Merriam, *Gandhi vs. Jinnah*, p 66.

26. H V Hodson, *The Great Divide* (London: Hutchinson, 1969), p 89.

27. Telegram from Jinnah, 12 July 1942, in S S Peerzada (ed.), *Leaders' Correspondence with Mr. Jinnah* (Bombay: Taj Office, 1944), p 213.

28. 15 March, Ramgarh; 78: 59.

29. Article by G D Birla in Shukla (ed.), *Incidents in Gandhiji's Life*, pp 26–30.

30. Article by G D Birla in Shukla (ed.), *Incidents in Gandhiji's Life*, pp 26–30.

31. *The Hindu*, 9 Jun. 1940.

32. Discussion in Delhi, 3–7 Jul. 1940; 78: 403.

33. Discussion in Delhi, 3–7 Jul. 1940; 78: 393.

34. Discussion in Delhi, 3–7 Jul. 1940; 78: 393.

35. Discussion in Delhi, 3–7 Jul. 1940; 78: 395.

36. *Harijan*, 28 Jul. 1940; 79: 33.

37. Discussion in Delhi, 3–7 Jul. 1940; 78: 403.

38. 22 Jun. 1940; 78: 343–5.

39. Discussion in Delhi, 3–7 Jul. 1940; 78: 394.

40. Discussion in Delhi, 3–7 Jul. 1940; 78: 401.
41. Quoted by Pyarelal in Pyarelal and Nayar, *In Gandhiji's Mirror*, p 30.
42. *Harijan*, 4 Aug. 1940; 79: 58.
43. *Harijan*, 4 Aug. 1940; 79: 58.
44. *Harijan*, 13 Jul. 1940; 78: 416.
45. See cable of 13 Aug. 1940, *Harijan*, 18 Aug. 1940; 79: 117.
46. *The Hindu*, 12 Aug. 1940.
47. Parikh, *Sardar Vallabhbhai Patel*, 2: 434–6.
48. Quoted in Pyarelal, *Mahatma Gandhi: The Last Phase*, 2 vols. (Ahmedabad: Navajivan, 1956), 1: 476.
49. Speech of 15 Sep. 1940; 79: 221.
50. Speech in Bombay, 15 Sep. 1940; 79: 221.
51. AICC resolution passed on 16 Sep. 1940; 79: 207.
52. 79: 360–1.
53. Manohar Diwan.
54. *Harijan*, 20 Oct. 1940; 79: 307–8.
55. *Harijan*, 20 Oct. 1940: 79: 310.
56. Azad, *India Wins Freedom*, p 41.
57. *Harijan*, 13 Jul. 1940; old 72: 259–60.
58. *The Hindu*, 23 Oct. 1941; 81: 219.
59. Speech in Bombay, 16 Sep. 1940; 79: 226–7.
60. Statement to the press, 6 Jul. 1941; 80: 348.
61. Letter of 16 Oct. 1941; 81: 205.
62. M K Gandhi, *Letters to Sardar Patel*, p 158.
63. Linlithgow to Hope, 8 May 1941, Linlithgow Papers, India Office Library, London; and B Shiva Rao, New Delhi correspondent of *The Hindu* and the intermediary between Hyat Khan and Srinivasan, to author, New Delhi, 1974.
64. 81: 334.
65. Remark of 4 Dec. 1941; 81: 334.
66. To Working Committee, Bardoli, on or before 30 Dec. 1941; 81: 396.
67. *Harijan*, 25 Jan. 1942; 81: 433–4.
68. *Harijan*, 25 Jan. 1942; 81: 430.
69. Devadas Gandhi Papers.
70. *Harijan*, 25 Jan. 1942; 81: 432–3.
71. Chaudhary, *Bapu As I Saw Him*, p 217.
72. *Harijan*, 25 Jan. 1942; 81: 432–4.
73. *Harijan*, 15 Feb. 1942, and *Harijan Sevak*, 22 Feb. 1942; 82: 7, 26.
74. Narayan Desai, *Bliss Was It To Be Young – With Gandhi*, p 85.

75. Letter of 14 Mar. 1942; 82: 54.

76. Letter of 6 Apr. 1942; 82: 173.

77. Sitaramayya, *History of the Indian National Congress*, vol. 2, p 315.

78. Article by Birla in Shukla (ed.), *Incidents in Gandhiji's Life*, pp 26–7.

79. As recalled by Gandhi to Louis Fischer, 4 Jun. 1942; 82: 395.

80. See Gandhi's letter to Patel, 13 Apr. 1942, in M K Gandhi, *Letters to Sardar Patel*, p 164, and Parikh, *Sardar Vallabhbhai Patel*, 2: 459.

81. Penderel Moon (ed.), *Wavell: A Viceroy's Journal* (London: Oxford University Press, 1973), p 33.

82. Merriam, *Gandhi vs. Jinnah*, p 77.

83. Quoted in Philips and Wainwright (eds.), *The Partition of India*, p 214.

84. Gopal, *Nehru*, vol. 1, p 284.

85. See Gopal, *Nehru*, vol. 1, p 288; Azad, *India Wins Freedom*, pp 64–7; and Rammanohar Lohia, *Guilty Men of India's Partition* (Allahabad: Kitabistan, 1960), pp 24–6.

86. Hodson, *The Great Divide*, p 103.

87. *Harijan*, 7 Jun. 1942; 82: 401.

88. From Gandhi's draft resolution for Working Committee sent 'before 24 April' 1942; 82: 233.

89. *Harijan*, 7 Jun. 1942; 82: 345.

90. *Harijan*, 14 Jun. 1942; 82: 377.

91. 82: 338.

92. Letter of 3 Aug. 1942; 83: 163.

93. Talks with Fischer, 4–9 Jun. 1942; 82: 420.

94. Article in *Harijan*, 3 May 1942; 82: 236.

95. Talks with Fischer, 4–9 Jun. 1942; 82: 403.

96. *Harijan*, 14 May 1942; 82: 279.

97. 82: 231–2.

98. N Mansergh and E W R Lumby (eds.), *The Transfer of Power*, 12 vols. (London: Her Majesty's Stationery Office, 1970–83), vol. 2, p 162.

99. Working Committee resolution of 1 May 1942; 82: 393.

100. J B Kripalani, *Gandhi: His Life and Thought* (New Delhi: Publications Division, 1970), p 201fn.

101. Parikh, *Sardar Vallabhbhai Patel*, 2: 467.

102. Letter of 3 May 1942 in Nandurkar (ed.), *Sardarshri ke Patra* (Ahmedabad: 1981), vol. 2, p 301.

103. Letter of 5 May 1942; 82: 260–1.

104. Letter of 24 April 1942: 82: 234.

105. See Desai to Patel, 15 Jul. 1942, in Nandurkar (ed.), *Bapu, Sardar, and Mahadevbhai*, pp 255–8, and letter from Gandhi to Nehru, 13 Jul. 1942; 82: 97–8.
106. *Harijan*, 28 Jun. 1942; 83: 42–3.
107. Interview with Congressmen, 15 May 1942; 82: 284.
108. Interview with *The Hindu*, 28 May 1942: 82: 341.
109. 82: 216.
110. 82: 347.
111. 82: 353.
112. 82: 360.
113. 82: 399–400.
114. 82: 367.
115. *Harijan*, 31 May 1942; 82: 316.
116. 82: 414.
117. *The Hindu*, 16 Jun. 1942.
118. Letter of Jul. 1942 quoted in Reginald Coupland, *The Indian Problem* (Oxford: 1942), p 337.
119. *The Hindu*, 25 Apr. 1942.
120. *The Hindu*, 31 May 1942.
121. Letter of 5 Jul. 1942, Rajagopalachari Papers.
122. *The Hindu*, 10 Jul. 1942.
123. 82: 374.
124. Quoted in Narayan Desai, *Bliss Was It To Be Young – With Gandhi*, p v.
125. *Harijan*, 14 Jun. 1942; 82: 378.
126. 82: 385.
127. See letter to Rajagopalachari, 20 Jul. 1942, and telegram to Rajagopalachari, 7 Aug. 1942; 83: 125–6 & 180–1.
128. Letter of 22 May 1942; 82: 313.
129. 82: 421–2.
130. 83: 27.
131. *Harijan*, 21 Jun. 1942; 83: 18–19.
132. Article of 28 Jun. in *Harijan*, 5 Jul. 1942; 83: 58.
133. 83: 67–8.
134. Statement of 5 Aug. 1942; 83: 450–1.
135. Statement to the press, 5 Aug. 1942; 83: 174–6.
136. 83: 178.
137. 83: 445–7.
138. 83: 128.

139. *Nichi Nichi*, *Yomiuri*, and *Miyako*. See 83: 114.

140. Article written on 18 Jul. 1942 in *Harijan*, 26 Jul. 1942; 83: 114–16.

141. *Harijan*, 2 Aug. 1942; 83: 145.

142. See entry dated 15 Jul. 1942 in Maniben Patel, *Diary of Maniben Patel*, Patel Papers, Ahmedabad.

143. Mansergh and Lumby (eds.), *The Transfer of Power*, 2: 186.

144. P N Chopra (ed.), *Quit India Movement: British Secret Report* (Faridabad: Thomson Press, 1976), pp 196–8.

145. Parikh, *Sardar Vallabhbhai Patel*, 2: 474–7.

146. Rajmohan Gandhi, *Patel*, p 316.

147. Lord Moran, *Winston Churchill* (London: Constable, 1966), p 52.

148. 83: 187.

149. Kalelkar, *Gandhi Charitra Kirtan*, p 42.

150. See Gandhi's letter to Wavell, 9 Mar. 1944; 84: 25–6.

151. Narayan Desai, *Bliss Was It To Be Young – With Gandhi*, pp 88–9.

152. Tendulkar, *Mahatma*, 6: 216.

153. Lord Moran, *Winston Churchill*, p 52.

154. Patel's recollection in a speech in Bombay on 27 Jun. 1945 published in *Hindustan Times*, 2 Jul. 1945.

155. Abul Kalam Azad, *India Wins Freedom* (Calcutta: Orient Longmans, 1959, 1988 edition), pp 88–9.

156. Sushila Nayar in Savita Singh (ed.), *Kasturba* (New Delhi: Gandhi Smriti, 1994), p 54.

157. Linlithgow to Churchill, 31 Aug. 1942. Linlithgow Papers, F 125/58, India Office Library, London.

158. Quoted in S Gopal, *Nehru*, 1: 300.

159. Quoted in S Gopal, *Nehru*, 1: 301.

160. Unnamed Raj official quoted in Brecher, *Nehru*, p 290.

161. Letter of 10 Aug. 1942; 83: 208–10.

162. Letter of 12 Sep. 1942 in G M Nandurkar (ed.), *Bapu, Sardar and Mahadevbhai* (Ahmedabad), p 363.

163. Pyarelal and Nayar, *In Gandhiji's Mirror*, p 60.

164. Telegram of 15 Aug. 1942; 83: 215.

165. Letter of 5 Nov. 1942; 83: 222.

166. Letter of 31 Dec. 1942; 83: 274–6.

167. Letter of 29 Jan. 1943; 83: 279–81.

168. Letter of 5 Feb. 1943; Mansergh and Lumby (ed.), *The Transfer of Power*, 3: 588.

169. Sushila Nayar, *Bapu ki Karavaas Kahani* (New Delhi: Sasta Sahitya Mandal, 1950), p 316.

170. Remarks on 8 Jun. 1947, from Manu Gandhi's diary; 95: 234.

171. *The Hindu*, 4 Mar. 1943.

172. 83: 299–300.

173. 83: 301.

174. Letter of 21 May 1943; 83: 311–12.

175. Letter of 8 Feb. 1943; Mansergh and Lumby (eds.), *The Transfer of Power,* 3: 639.

176. Mansergh and Lumby (eds.), *The Transfer of Power*, 4: 381.

177. Quoted by Pattabhi Sitaramayya, a Working Committee member held in the Keep, in his *Feathers and Stones* (Bombay: 1946), p 44.

178. Letter of 14 Apr. 1944 from Birla to Devadas Gandhi, Devadas Gandhi Papers. See also J Ahmad (ed.), *Speeches & Writings of Mr. Jinnah* (Lahore: Ashraf, 1947), vol. 2, and S S Peerzada (ed.), *Leaders' Correspondence with Mr. Jinnah* (Bombay: Taj Office, 1944).

179. Kripalani, *Autobiography* (typescript).

180. Letter of 3 Oct. 1944 quoted in Gopal, *Nehru*, 1: 297.

181. Gopal (ed.), *Selected Works of Jawaharlal Nehru*, vol. 13, p 511.

182. See Rajmohan Gandhi, *Patel*, pp 329–32.

183. See Rajmohan Gandhi, *Patel*, pp 336–7.

184. Chief Commissioner's Office, Bombay, File No. 46, Secret, Home Department, Special Branch (6), 1943–4; 83: 472–4.

185. 83: 50.

186. 83: 435–5.

187. Letter of 15 Jul. 1943 to Additional Home Secretary, Government of India; 83: 381–2.

188. Letter of 26 Oct. 1943 to Additional Home Secretary; 83: 426–8.

189. Letter of 26 Oct. 1943 to Additional Home Secretary; 83: 426–8.

190. Letter of 4 Mar. 1944; 84: 21–2.

191. Letter of 19 Jan. 1943; 83: 276.

192. 84: 25–31.

193. 84: 13–4 and 25–31.

194. 84: 40–1.

195. Mukul Kalarthi, *Ba and Bapu*, p 49.

196. Sushila Nayar in Singh (ed.), *Kasturba*, p 58.

197. Sushila Nayar in Singh (ed.), *Kasturba*, p 56.

198. Sushila Nayar in Singh (ed.), *Kasturba*, p 59.

199. Letter of Gandhi to Wavell, 9 Mar. 1944; 84: 25–6.

200. Letter of 4 Mar. 1944 from Gandhi to Additional Home Secretary; 84: 22–4.
201. 84: 22–4.
202. 83: 439.
203. Letter of 6 Jan. 1943; 83: 439–40.
204. Devadas Gandhi, *Ba, Bapu aur Bhai*, pp 8–9.
205. Sushila in Pyarelal and Nayar, *In Gandhiji's Mirror*, p 75.
206. 'She was "Ba"' by Prabhavati, quoted in www.gandhimanibhavan.org/
     gandhicomesalive/chap06.htm.
207. 95: 233–4.
208. Letter of 9 Mar. 1944; 84: 25–6.
209. Kalarthi, *Ba and Bapu*, p 118.
210. Remarks on 8 Jun. 1947, from Manu Gandhi's diary; 95: 234.
211. Letter of 1 Apr. 1944 to Additional Home Secretary; 84: 36–7.
212. Pyarelal, *Mahatma Gandhi: The Last Phase*, vol. 1, p 575.
213. Gopi Krishna, *Mahatma Gandhi and the Kundalini Process*, http://www.icrcanada.
     org/gandhi.html
214. 84: 20–21.
215. Pyarelal, *Mahatma Gandhi: The Last Phase*, 1: 12.
216. Sushila Nayar, *Mahatma Gandhi's Last Imprisonment* (New Delhi: Har-Anand,
     1996), pp 385–91.
217. 84: 44.
218. Pyarelal, *Mahatma Gandhi: The Last Phase*, 1: 14.
219. 84: 44–5.
220. Moon (ed.), *Wavell*, p 78.

Chapter 14: Rejected

1. Pyarelal, *Mahatma Gandhi: The Last Phase*, vol. 1, p 104.
2. See letter from Gandhi to Mira, 11 Jun. 1944; 84: 101.
3. 84: 442–3.
4. 84: 206.
5. 84: 141.
6. Parikh, *Gandhiji's Lost Jewel*, p 92.
7. Parikh, *Gandhiji's Lost Jewel*, p 93.
8. Anand Hingorani, *Bapu ke Ashirvad* (New Delhi: Publications Division, 2000),
   p xvi.
9. Letter of 6 Jul. 1944; 84: 153–4.
10. 84: 142.

11. 84: 207.

12. Remark of 9 Jul. 1944 in Panchgani; 84: 215.

13. 84: 112.

14. 84: 215.

15. 84: 147–51.

16. Remarks of 15 Jul. 1944; 84: 192.

17. Sitanshu Das, *Subhas: A Political Biography* (New Delhi: Rupa, 2000), pp 574–5.

18. Merriam, *Gandhi vs. Jinnah*, pp 92–107.

19. 84: 454, referring to Mansergh and Lumby (eds.), *The Transfer of Power*, 4: 1138–91.

20. 84: 272.

21. Letter of 15 Aug. 1944; 84: 296.

22. 84: 147.

23. See 84: 147.

24. 84: 197.

25. 84: 139–40.

26. Pyarelal, *Mahatma Gandhi: The Last Phase*, 1: 86. See also Hardiman, *Gandhi In His Time and Ours*, pp 176–7.

27. 84: 392–3.

28. Bolitho, *Jinnah*, p 148.

29. Azad, *India Wins Freedom*, p 93.

30. Moon (ed.), *Wavell*, p 87.

31. Letter of 23 Sep. 1944 to Jinnah; 84: 406.

32. Press interview, 28 Sep. 1944; 84: 422.

33. 84: 404.

34. 84: 425.

35. Bolitho, *Jinnah*, p 152.

36. Letter of 13 Nov. 1944; 85: 153.

37. Pyarelal, *Mahatma Gandhi: The Last Phase*, 1: 67.

38. Pyarelal, *Mahatma Gandhi: The Last Phase*, 1: 104–5.

39. Quoted in Pyarelal, *Mahatma Gandhi: The Last Phase*, 1: 11.

40. Moon (ed.), *Wavell*, p 120.

41. J B Kripalani, *Fateful Year* (Bombay: Vora, 1948).

42. *Hindustan Times*, 2 Jul. 1945.

43. Pyarelal, *Mahatma Gandhi: The Last Phase*, 1: 132.

44. Letter of 8 Jul. 1946 in Moon (ed.), *Wavell*, p 494.

45. See A I Singh, *The Origins of the Partition of India* (New Delhi: Oxford, 1987), pp 121–3.

46. See letter of 12 Aug. 1945 in M K Gandhi, *Letters to Sardar Patel*, p 172

47. See letter of 12 Aug. 1945 in M K Gandhi, *Letters to Sardar Patel*, p 172.

48. *Bombay Chronicle*, 1 Nov. 1945

49. Letter of 3 Jan. 1946 in M K Gandhi, *Letters to Sardar Patel*, p 175.

50. See Durga Das (ed.), *Sardar Patel's Correspondence*, vol. 2 (Ahmedabad: Navajivan), pp 1–9.

51. Letter of 27 Nov. 1945 in G M Nandurkar (ed.), *Sardar Patel Centenary Volumes*, vol. 4, p 16

52. Letters in Jul. 1946 in M K Gandhi, *Letters to Sardar Patel*, p 184.

53. On 24 August 1945. Moon (ed.), *Wavell*, p 164.

54. B C Dutt, *Mutiny of the Innocents* (Bombay: Sindhu, 1971), p 137.

55. See letter of 24 Feb. 1946 from Patel to Gandhi in Nandurkar (ed.), *Bapu, Sardar ane Mahadevbhai*, p 309.

56. 89: 441

57. Dutt, *Mutiny of the Innocents*, pp 177–84.

58. Sudhir Ghosh, *Gandhi's Emissary* (Bombay: Rupa, 1967), pp 68–9.

59. Letter written before 24 Apr. 1946 to Munnalal Shah; 90: 304

60. Remark in Bihar on 24 Apr. 1947; old 87: 350

61. *Harijan*, 21 Jul. 1946; 91: 272–3.

62. File 4/33, Pyarelal Papers.

63. J B Kripalani, *Gandhi: His Life and Thought* (New Delhi: Publications Division, 1970), pp 248–50.

64. Statement of 1 Jun. 1947 in Tendulkar, *Mahatma*, 8: 3.

65. See remarks by Maniben Patel in Das (ed.), *Sardar Patel's Correspondence*, vol. 10, p xxxviii, and Durga Das, *India from Curzon to Nehru* (London: Collins, 1969), p 230.

66. See entry dated 3 May 1946, Diary of Maniben Patel.

67. See letter of 29 Jul. 1946 from Patel to D P Mishra in Das (ed.), *Sardar Patel's Correspondence*, 3: 153–4.

68. Moon (ed.), *Wavell*, p 269.

69. See Pyarelal, *Mahatma Gandhi: The Last Phase*, 1: 201–2.

70. Pyarelal, *Mahatma Gandhi: The Last Phase*, 1: 210.

71. Moon (ed.), *Wavell*, p 246.

72. Pyarelal, *Mahatma Gandhi: The Last Phase*, 1: 204.

73. Pyarelal, *Mahatma Gandhi: The Last Phase*, 1: 204.

74. Tendulkar, *Mahatma*, 7: 129.

75. Ralph Waldo Emerson, *Self-Reliance* (Mount Vernon, NY: Peter Pauper, 1967), p 58.

76. Pyarelal, *Mahatma Gandhi: The Last Phase*, 1: 204–5.

77. Tendulkar, *Abdul Ghaffar Khan: Faith is a Battle*, pp 370–1.

78. Moon (ed.), *Wavell*, pp 258–9.

79. Mansergh and Lumby, *The Transfer of Power*, 7: 465–6.

80. House of Commons Debates, 8 June 1946, quoted by S R Mehrotra in Philips and Wainwright (ed.), *The Partition of India* , p 218.

81. Mansergh and Lumby (eds.), *The Transfer of Power* 6: 684–7.

82. J Ahmad (ed.), *Historic Documents of the Muslim Freedom Movement* (Lahore: Publishers United), pp 522–3.

83. See also Pyarelal, *Mahatma Gandhi: The Last Phase*, 1: 225–6.

84. See Pyarelal, *Mahatma Gandhi: The Last Phase*, 1: 228–35; and Rajmohan Gandhi, *Patel*, pp 363–7.

85. Mansergh and Lumby, *The Transfer of Power*, 7: 990.

86. Pyarelal, *Mahatma Gandhi: The Last Phase*, 1: 232.

87. Pyarelal, *Mahatma Gandhi: The Last Phase*, 1: 232.

88. Pyarelal, *Mahatma Gandhi: The Last Phase*, 1: 232.

89. Moon (ed.), *Wavell*, p 304.

90. Ghosh, *Gandhi's Emissary*, p 167.

91. Pyarelal, *Mahatma Gandhi: The Last Phase*, 1: 235.

92. Moon (ed.), *Wavell*, p 302.

93. Pyarelal, *Mahatma Gandhi: The Last Phase*, 1: 236.

94. Pyarelal, *Mahatma Gandhi: The Last Phase*, 1: 236.

95. Moon (ed.), *Wavell*, p 303.

96. Pyarelal, *Mahatma Gandhi: The Last Phase*, 1: 238.

97. Moon (ed.), *Wavell*, pp 303–4, and p 491.

98. Pyarelal, *Mahatma Gandhi: The Last Phase*, 1: 238.

99. Pyarelal, *Mahatma Gandhi: The Last Phase*, 1: 238–9.

100. Pyarelal, *Mahatma Gandhi: The Last Phase*, 1: 239.

101. Moon (ed.), *Wavell*, pp 304–5.

102. Moon (ed.), *Wavell*, pp 303–4.

103. Moon (ed.), *Wavell*, p 310.

104. Moon (ed.), *Wavell*, p 439.

105. Hingorani, *Bapu ke Ashirvad*, p 585.

106. Photograph and caption in Tendulkar, *Mahatma*, 7: between p 176 & p 177.

107. J Ahmad, *Creation of Pakistan* (Lahore: Publishers United, 1976), p 274.

108. Pyarelal, *Mahatma Gandhi: The Last Phase*, 1: 251.

109. Taken from Brecher, *Nehru* , p 316, and V P Menon, *The Transfer of Power in India* (Calcutta: Orient Longmans, 1957), p 281.

110. V P Menon, *The Transfer of Power in India*, p 281.
111. Letter to Dwarka Prasad Mishra, 29 Jul. 1946, in Das (ed.), *Sardar Patel's Correspondence*, 3: 153–4.
112. J Ahmad, *Creation of Pakistan*, p 278.
113. Quotes in this para from Pyarelal, *Mahatma Gandhi: The Last Phase*, 1: 251–3.
114. Pyarelal, *Mahatma Gandhi: The Last Phase*, 1: 256–7.
115. Moon (ed.), *Wavell*, pp 340–1.
116. From *Hindustan Times*, 16 Oct. 1946. 92: 328–9. The newspaper's indirect version has been altered here to direct speech.
117. Pyarelal, *Mahatma Gandhi: The Last Phase*, 1: 283.
118. See Gandhi's letter of 11 Dec. 1946 to Kripalani, 93: 130–1.
119. Pyarelal, *Mahatma Gandhi: The Last Phase*, 1: 347.
120. Pyarelal, *Mahatma Gandhi: The Last Phase*, 1: 320.
121. Pyarelal, *Mahatma Gandhi: The Last Phase*, 1: 353; and 92: 419.

Chapter 15: Walk Alone …

1. Pyarelal, *Mahatma Gandhi: The Last Phase*, 1: 353–4.
2. See Gandhi's letters of 30 Dec. 1946 and 6 Jan. 1947 to Pyarelal, 93: 214 and 240–1.
3. Sir Francis Tuker, *While Memory Serves* (London: Cassell, 1950), pp 195–202.
4. Letter of 5 Dec. 1946 to Agatha Harrison, 93: 110.
5. Tendulkar, *Mahatma*, 7: 310–11.
6. Tendulkar, *Mahatma*, 7: 316.
7. On 20 Nov. Tendulkar, *Mahatma*, 7: 326.
8. Letters of 25 Dec. to Balvant Sinha and 1 Jan. 1947 to Amtus Salaam, 93: 195 and 222 .
9. Quoted in Erikson, *Gandhi's Truth*, p 401.
10. Manu Gandhi, *The Lonely Pilgrim* (Ahmedabad: Navajivan, 1964), p 45 and p 93.
11. Manu Gandhi, *Ekla Chalo Re* (Ahmedabad: Navajivan, 1957), pp 143–4.
12. See Gandhi's letter of 30 Dec. 1946 to Pyarelal, 93: 213; and Green, *Gandhi*, p 11.
13. Manu Gandhi, *Ekla Chalo Re*, p 160.
14. Pyarelal, *Mahatma Gandhi: The Last Phase*, 1: 581.
15. Pyarelal, *Mahatma Gandhi: The Last Phase*, 1: 582–3.
16. Pyarelal, *Mahatma Gandhi: The Last Phase*, 1: 580.
17. Alexander's preface in Andrews, *Mahatma Gandhi's Ideas* , pp 20–1.

18. Nelson quoted in Kapur, *Raising up a Prophet: The African-American Encounter with Gandhi*, p 135.

19. Pyarelal, *Mahatma Gandhi: The Last Phase*, 1: 576–7.

20. N K Bose, *My Days With Gandhi* (Calcutta: Nishana, 1953), p 8.

21. Pyarelal, *Mahatma Gandhi: The Last Phase*, 1: 585–7.

22. Manu Gandhi, *Ekla Chalo Re*, p 108.

23. Tendulkar, *Mahatma*, 7: 373.

24. N K Bose, *My Days with Gandhi*, p 8, and N K Bose, *Lectures on Gandhism*, p 65.

25. N K Bose, *Lectures on Gandhism*, p 106.

26. Tendulkar, *Mahatma*, 7: 350; also 93: 229.

27. Manu Gandhi, *Ekla Chalo Re*, p 54.

28. Tendulkar, *Mahatma*, 7: 355.

29. Chaudhary, *Bapu As I Saw Him*, pp 226–7.

30. Pyarelal, *Mahatma Gandhi: The Last Phase*, 1: 614.

31. Manu Gandhi, *Ekla Chalo Re*, pp 91–2.

32. Tendulkar, *Mahatma*, 7: 382.

33. Manu Gandhi, *Ekla Chalo Re*, p 69.

34. N K Bose, *My Days with Gandhi*, pp 149–50.

35. Tendulkar, *Mahatma*, 7: 399.

36. Tendulkar, *Mahatma*, 7: 383.

37. Manu Gandhi, *Ekla Chalo Re*, pp 89–90.

38. Manu Gandhi, *Ekla Chalo Re*, p 55.

39. Manu Gandhi, *Ekla Chalo Re*, pp 111–12.

40. Manu Gandhi, *Ekla Chalo Re*, pp 75–7.

41. Manu Gandhi, *Ekla Chalo Re*, pp 75–7.

42. Manu Gandhi, *Ekla Chalo Re*, p 65.

43. N K Bose, *Lectures on Gandhism*, p 63.

44. N K Bose, *Lectures on Gandhism*, pp 105–6.

45. Pyarelal, *Mahatma Gandhi: The Last Phase*, 1: 445.

46. Pyarelal, *Mahatma Gandhi: The Last Phase*, 1: 453.

47. Pyarelal, *Mahatma Gandhi: The Last Phase*, 1: 515.

48. Ashoka Gupta, 'Those days in Noakhali...', www.india-seminar.com/2002/510.

49. Letter of 15 Dec. 1946 in Durgadas (ed.), *Sardar Patel's Correspondence*, vol. 3, pp 313–25.

50. See Rajmohan Gandhi, *Patel*, pp 384–8.

51. Moon (ed.), *Wavell*, p 378.

52. Mansergh and Lumby (eds.), *The Transfer of Power*, 9: 358.

53. Mansergh and Lumby (eds.), *The Transfer of Power*, 9: 431–3.

54. Moon (ed.), *Wavell*, p 409.
55. Moon (ed.), *Wavell*, p 387 and p 495.
56. Patel quoted in Mansergh and Lumby (eds.), *The Transfer of Power*, 9: 381.
57. Letter of 30 Dec. 1946 quoted in Pyarelal, *Mahatma Gandhi: The Last Phase*, 1: 488–9.
58. Letter of 7 Jan. 1947 in Nandurkar (ed.), *Bapu, Sardar and Mahadevbhai*, pp 336–7.
59. Pyarelal, *Mahatma Gandhi: The Last Phase*, 1: 615.
60. Interviews by author in April and November 2000.

Chapter 16: To Rama

1. Quoted in Kanji Dwarkadas, *Ten Years to Freedom* (Bombay: Popular Prakashan, 1968), pp 207–8.
2. Tendulkar, *Faith is a Battle*, p 404.
3. Pyarelal, *Mahatma Gandhi: The Last Phase*, 1: 641.
4. Pyarelal, *Mahatma Gandhi: The Last Phase*, 1: 669.
5. Pyarelal, *Mahatma Gandhi: The Last Phase*, 1: 624.
6. Pyarelal, *Mahatma Gandhi: The Last Phase*, 1: 633.
7. Pyarelal, *Mahatma Gandhi: The Last Phase*, 1: 622.
8. Pyarelal, *Mahatma Gandhi: The Last Phase*, 1: 641–2.
9. Pyarelal, *Mahatma Gandhi: The Last Phase*, 1: 622.
10. Pyarelal, *Mahatma Gandhi: The Last Phase*, 1: 666.
11. Pyarelal, *Mahatma Gandhi: The Last Phase*, 1: 661.
12. For the text of his scheme that Gandhi left for the Viceroy on 4 April, see 94: 229.
13. 94: 209.
14. Mansergh and Lumby (eds.), *The Transfer of Power*, 10: 69.
15. Pyarelal, *Mahatma Gandhi: The Last Phase*, 2: 80.
16. See Rajmohan Gandhi, *Patel*, p 401.
17. Mansergh and Lumby (eds.), *The Transfer of Power*, 10: 84.
18. Mansergh and Lumby (eds.), *The Transfer of Power*, 10: 86.
19. Mansergh and Lumby (eds.), *The Transfer of Power*, 10: 86.
20. Mansergh and Lumby (eds.), *The Transfer of Power*, 10: 84.
21. Mansergh and Lumby (eds.), *The Transfer of Power*, 10: 128.
22. Alan Campbell-Johnson, *Mission with Mountbatten* (London: Robert Hale, 1962 edition), p 57.
23. Mansergh and Lumby (eds.), *The Transfer of Power*, 10: 73.

24. Mansergh and Lumby (eds.), *The Transfer of Power*, 10: 83.

25. Mansergh and Lumby (eds.), *The Transfer of Power*, 10: 104.

26. Entry dated 13 Apr. 1947. Rajagopalachari Papers.

27. Stanley Wolpert, *Jinnah* (New York: Oxford, 1984), p 317.

28. Quoted in Philips and Wainwright (eds.), *The Partition of India*, p 185.

29. Edited from quotation by Omar el-Haqqaq in Nanda (ed.), *Mahatma Gandhi: 125 Years* , p 80.

30. Quoted in Menon, *The Transfer of Power in India*, p 354.

31. Menon, *The Transfer of Power in India*, p 355.

32. See Rajmohan Gandhi, *Patel*, pp 396–8.

33. Quoted in Menon, *The Transfer of Power in India*, 10: 778.

34. Memorandum of 12 May 1947 embodying, according to HMG's Statement of 3 June 1947, Britain's policy towards the States, quoted in Menon, *The Transfer of Power in India*, p 498.

35. Tendulkar, *Faith is a Battle*, p 427.

36. Pyarelal, *Mahatma Gandhi: The Last Phase*, 2: 257.

37. Ghaffar Khan quoted by Lohia, who was present, Lohia, *Guilty Men of India's Partition*, p 21.

38. See Hodson, *The Great Divide* , pp 284–5; Gopal, *Nehru*, vol. 1, p 352; and Pyarelal, *Mahatma Gandhi: The Last Phase*, 2: 270.

39. Quoted in Tendulkar, *Faith is a Battle*, p 430.

40. Gidwani quoted in Brecher, *Nehru*, p 349.

41. N V Gadgil, *Government from Inside* (Meerut: Meenakshi, 1968), p 40.

42. See Ramchandra Gandhi's comments in T N Madan (ed.), *Way of Life: King, Householder, Renouncer* (Delhi: Motilal Banarsidass, 1988), pp 220–1.

43. Heesterman in Madan (ed.), *Way of Life: King, Householder, Renouncer*, p 252.

44. Pyarelal, *Mahatma Gandhi: The Last Phase*, 1: 598. See also letter from Gandhi of 3 Jan. 1948, 98: 163.

45. But apparently only after Gandhi insisted on Ambedkar's inclusion as an essential part of the 'atonement' due to India's 'untouchables'. See G Ramachandran, *Thoughts and Talks* (Madurai: 1964), p 179.

46. Khairmode quoted in M S Gore, *The Social Context of an Ideology: Ambedkar's Political and Social Thought* (New Delhi: Sage, 1993), pp 180–1.

47. Erikson, *Gandhi's Truth*, p 92.

48. Pyarelal, *Mahatma Gandhi: The Last Phase*, 2: 367–8.

49. From article of 16 Aug. by Gandhi in *Harijan*, 24 Aug. 1947; 96: 236–7.

50. From article of 16 Aug. by Gandhi in *Harijan*, 24 Aug. 1947; 96: 236–7.

51. From article of 16 Aug. by Gandhi in *Harijan*, 24 Aug. 1947; 96: 236–7.

52. Rammanohar Lohia, *Marx, Gandhi and Socialism* (Hyderabad: Lohia Samata Vidyalaya Nyasa, 1963), p 122, as quoted in Hardiman, *Gandhi In His Time and Ours*, p 57.

53. Quote in Gene Sharp, *Gandhi Wields the Weapon of Moral Power* (Ahmedabad: Navajivan, 1960), p 226.

54. For an account of the Empire's effort against violence in the Punjab, see Hodson, *The Great Divide*, pp 337–45.

55. N K Bose, *Lectures on Gandhism*, p 112.

56. 96: 321fn.

57. Letter to Gandhi of 27 Aug. 1947 quoted in Nandurkar (ed.), *Bapu, Sardar ane Mahadevbhai*, p 348.

58. Amiya Chakravarty quoted in Sharp, *Gandhi Wields the Weapon of Moral Power*, pp 259–60.

59. Green, *Gandhi*, p 240.

60. *The Statesman*, Calcutta, 6 Sep. 1947.

61. Hodson, *The Great Divide*, pp 344–5.

62. See letter of 7 Sep. 1947 to Maniben Patel, 96: 345.

63. Gandhi's statement to the press, 9 Sep. 1947, 96: 352.

64. Brij Krishna, *Gandhiji ki Dilli Diary* (Delhi: 1970), vol. 3, p 278.

65. Brij Krishna, *Gandhiji ki Dilli Diary*, vol. 3, p 382.

66. See Brij Krishna, *Gandhiji ki Dilli Diary*, 3: 287, and letter of 27 Oct. 1948 from Nehru to Patel in Das (ed.), *Sardar Patel's Correspondence*, vol. 7, p 672.

67. See also Brij Krishna, *Gandhiji ki Dilli Diary*, 3: 294–7.

68. Hodson, *The Great Divide*, pp 410–11.

69. Quote in 97: 6.

70. Pyarelal, *Mahatma Gandhi: The Last Phase*, 2: 456–8.

71. Brij Krishna, *Gandhiji ki Dilli Diary*, 3: 304–5.

72. Quoted by Miloslav Krasa in Nanda (ed.), *Mahatma Gandhi: 125 Years*, p 104.

73. G D Khosla, *A Taste of India* (Bombay: Jaico, 1970), pp 21–2.

74. Dilip Kumar Roy, *Among the Great* (Bombay: Jaico, 1950), p 110.

75. Pyarelal, *Mahatma Gandhi: The Last Phase*, 2: 241.

76. See letter to Nehru of 29 Sep. 1947, 97: 14.

77. Pyarelal, *Mahatma Gandhi: The Last Phase*, 2: 675–6.

78. For details and references see Rajmohan Gandhi, *Patel*, p 458.

79. From Devadas Gandhi, *Ba, Bapu aur Bhai*.

80. Pyarelal, *Mahatma Gandhi: The Last Phase*, 2: 697.

81. Nandurkar (ed.), *Sardar Patel Centenary Volumes*, vol. 2, p 19.

82. Pyarelal, *Mahatma Gandhi: The Last Phase*, 2: 700–1.

83. Pyarelal, *Mahatma Gandhi: The Last Phase*, 2: 701.

84. Pyarelal, *Mahatma Gandhi: The Last Phase*, 2: 703. See also Hodson, *The Great Divide*, p 505.

85. Pyarelal, *Mahatma Gandhi: The Last Phase*, 2: 704.

86. Pyarelal, *Mahatma Gandhi: The Last Phase*, 2: 725.

87. Entry of 12 Jan. 1948 in Maniben Patel, *Diary*.

88. *Frontline*, Chennai, 14 Aug. 1998.

89. *Hindustan Times*, 16 and 17 Jan. 1948.

90. Pyarelal, *Mahatma Gandhi: The Last Phase*, 2: 713.

91. Pyarelal, *Mahatma Gandhi: The Last Phase*, 2: 713.

92. Pyarelal, *Mahatma Gandhi: The Last Phase*, 2: 714.

93. Jehangir Patel and Marjorie Sykes, *Gandhi: His Gift of the Fight* (Rasulia: Madhya Pradesh, 1987), p 188.

94. 98: 253–7.

95. Brij Krishna, *Gandhiji ki Dilli Diary*, 3: 576–81.

96. Pyarelal, *Mahatma Gandhi: The Last Phase*, 2: 731.

97. See Report of the Justice Kapur Commission on the assassination quoted in A G Noorani, *Savarkar and Hindutva* (New Delhi: Left Word, 2002), pp 130–1.

98. Keer quoted in Noorani, *Savarkar and Hindutva*, p 106.

99. See Hardiman, *Gandhi In His Time and Ours* , p 176.

100. Pyarelal, *Mahatma Gandhi: The Last Phase*, 2: 756.

101. Pyarelal, *Mahatma Gandhi: The Last Phase*, 2: 756.

102. Pyarelal, *Mahatma Gandhi: The Last Phase*, 2: 735.

103. Pyarelal, *Mahatma Gandhi: The Last Phase*, 2: 735.

104. Pyarelal, *Mahatma Gandhi: The Last Phase*, 2: 747.

105. Pyarelal, *Mahatma Gandhi: The Last Phase*, 2: 758–9; and Patel and Sykes, *Gandhi: His Gift of the Fight*, p 191.

106. Pyarelal, *Mahatma Gandhi: The Last Phase*, 2: 759.

107. Vincent Sheean, *Lead Kindly Light* (New York: Random House, 1949), pp 190–3.

108. Brij Krishna, *Gandhiji ki Dilli Diary*, 3: 571.

109. From Devadas Gandhi, *Ba, Bapu aur Bhai*.

110. Pyarelal, *Mahatma Gandhi: The Last Phase*, 2: 770.

111. Pyarelal, *Mahatma Gandhi: The Last Phase*, 2: 771.

112. Letter of 5 Feb. 1948 from Patel to Nehru quoted in 98: 341.

113. 'After a most careful and exhaustive inquiry from first witnesses on the spot that I made at the time, I am convinced that the words that issued from Gandhiji's mouth as he lost consciousness were not "Hey Rama!" but "Rama, Rama" – not an invocation but simple remembrance of the Name.' – Pyarelal, who was out on

an errand until a few minutes after the shooting, in *Mahatma Gandhi: The Last Phase*, 2: 861. We know that Gandhi pronounced Rama as Raam. According to Vishnu Karkare, one of the conspirators present at the killing, only 'a guttural rasp, "Aagh"', emanated from Gandhi. (Quoted in Green, *Gandhi*, p 386.) It is possible that Karkare did not hear, or want to remember, the starting and closing consonants. See also Abha's account in Kanu and Abha Gandhi, *Bapu ke Saath* (New Delhi: Publications Division, 1990), pp 50–1; Manu Gandhi, *Last Glimpses of Bapu* (Agra: Shiva Lal Agarwala, 1962), pp 308–9; Manu Gandhi, *Dillimaan Gandhiji* (Ahmedabad: Navajivan, 1966), pp 426–7; and Brij Krishna, *Gandhiji ki Dilli Diary*, 3: 576–81.

114. Brij Krishna, *Gandhiji ki Dilli Diary*, 3: 576–81

Postscript

1. Pyarelal, *Mahatma Gandhi: The Last Phase*, 2: 786–7.
2. Quoted in *Homage* (New Delhi: Publications Division, 1949), p 27.
3. 'Kitchen fires were not lit that night in many homes in Pakistan.' – Raza Kasim, in Lahore, to the author, 1994.
4. *Hindustan Times*, 31 Jan. 1948.
5. Manu Gandhi, *End of an Epoch* (Ahmedabad: Navajivan, 1962), p 61.
6. Quoted in Nandurkar (ed.), *Sardar Patel Centenary Volumes*, vol. 2, pp 221–2.
7. Entry of 5 March 1948 in Maniben Patel, *Diary*, Patel Papers, Ahmedabad.
8. Speech of 2 Oct. 1950 quoted in V Shankar, *My Reminiscences of Sardar Vallabhbhai Patel* (New Delhi: Macmillan, 1975), vol. 2, pp 236–7.
9. Shastri's remark in Tashkent quoted by L P Singh, who heard it, in Singh, *Portrait of Lal Bahadur Shastri* (New Delhi: Ravi Dayal, 1996), p 96.
10. http://www.indianembassy.org/special/cabinet/Primeminister/pm_january_01_2001.htm.
11. Remark in an unidentified Bombay daily quoted in Parikh, *Gandhiji's Lost Jewel*, p xii.
12. Noorani, *Savarkar and Hindutva*, p 96.
13. Manu's radiance was apparent in 1969 when the author visited her in hospital in New Delhi.

Further Reading

Ali, Chaudhari Muhammad, *The Emergence of Pakistan* (New York: Columbia, 1967).

Ambedkar, B R, *Thoughts on Pakistan* (Bombay: Thacker, 1941).

———, *What Congress and Gandhi have done to the Untouchables* (Bombay: Thacker, 1945).

———, *Writings and Speeches* (Bombay: Education Department, 1982).

Andrews, C F, *Mahatma Gandhi at Work* (London: Allen & Unwin, 1931).

———, *Mahatma Gandhi: His Own Story* (London: Allen & Unwin, 1930).

———, *Mahatma Gandhi's Ideas* (London: Allen & Unwin, 1929).

Ashe, Geoffrey, *Gandhi: A Study in Revolution* (Bombay: Asia, 1968).

Azad, Abul Kalam, *India Wins Freedom* (Calcutta: Orient Longmans, 1959).

Behn, Mira, *The Spirit's Pilgrimage* (London: Longmans Green, 1960).

Bhattacharya, Bhabani, *Mahatma Gandhi* (New Delhi: Arnold Heinemann, 1977).

Bhattacharya, Sabyasachi (ed.), *The Mahatma and the Poet* (New Delhi: National Book Trust, 1997).

Birla, G D, *A Talk on Bapu* (Calcutta: Sangeet Kala Mandir, 1981).

———, *In the Shadow of the Mahatma* (Bombay: Vakils, 1968).

Bolitho, Hector, *Jinnah: Creator of Pakistan* (Westport, Conn.: Greenwood Press, n.d.).

Bondurant, Joan, *Conquest of Violence: The Gandhian Philosophy of Conflict* (Princeton, NJ: Princeton University, 1958).

Bose, Nirmal Kumar, *Lectures on Gandhism* (Ahmedabad: Navajivan, 1971).

———, *My Days with Gandhi* (Calcutta: Nishana, 1953).

Bose, Subhas, *The Indian Struggle* (Bombay: Asia, 1964).

Brecher, Michael, *Nehru* (London: Oxford University Press, 1959).

Brown, Judith, *Gandhi: Prisoner of Hope* (Delhi: Oxford, 1990).

Campbell-Johnson, Alan, *Mission with Mountbatten* (London: Robert Hale, 1972).

Chandra, Bipan, *Communalism in Modern India* (New Delhi: Vikas, 1984).

Chatterjee, Margaret, *Gandhi and his Jewish Friends* (London, Macmillan, 1992).

——, *Gandhi's Religious Thought* (New Delhi: Macmillan, 1983).

Chaudhari, K K, *Quit India Revolution: The Ethos of the Central Direction* (Mumbai: Popular, 1996).

Chaudhary, Ramnarayan, *Bapu As I Saw Him* (Ahmedabad: Navajivan, 1959).

Chopra, P N (ed.), *Quit India Movement: British Secret Report* (Faridabad: Thomson Press, 1976).

Choudhari, Manmohan, *Exploring Gandhi* (New Delhi: Gandhi Peace Foundation, 1989).

Choudhary, Valmiki, *Dr. Rajendra Prasad: Correspondence & Documents,* 20 vols. (New Delhi: Allied).

Churchill, Winston, *My African Journey* (London: The Holland Press, 1962).

Dalal, Chandulal B (ed.), *Gandhijini Dinwari (1915–1948),* (Gandhinagar: Information Department, 1970).

—— (comp.), *Gandhijini Dinwari (1869–1915)* (Ahmedabad: Sabarmati Ashram Trust, 1976).

Das, Durga (ed.), *Sardar Patel's Correspondence,* 10 vols. (Ahmedabad: Navajivan).

Desai, Mahadev, *Day-to-day with Gandhi,* several vols. (Varanasai: Sarva Seva Sangh).

——, *The Diary of Mahadev Desai,* 2 vols. (Ahmedabad: Navajivan).

Desai, Narayan, *Agnikundma Ugelun Gulab* (Ahmedabad: Navajivan, 1992).

——, *Bliss Was It To Be Young – With Gandhi* (Bombay: Bhavan, 1988).

Devanesen, Chandran, *The Making of the Mahatma* (New Delhi: Orient Longmans, 1969).

Doke, Joseph J, *M. K. Gandhi: An Indian Patriot in South Africa* (New Delhi: Publications Division, 1967).

Dutt, B C, *Mutiny of the Innocents* (Bombay: Sindhu, 1977).

Erikson, Erik H, *Gandhi's Truth* (New York: Norton, 1969).

Fischer, Frederick B, *That Strange Little Brown Man Gandhi* (New Delhi: Orient Longmans, 1970).

Fischer, Louis, *The Life of Mahatma Gandhi* (New York: Harper, 1950).

Gandhi, Devadas, *Ba, Bapu aur Bhai* (New Delhi: Sasta Sahitya Mandal, 1956).

Gandhi, Kanu and Abha, *Bapu ke Sath* (New Delhi: Publications Division, 1990).

Gandhi, Manu, *Bapu ki Ye Baaten* (Ahmedabad: Navajivan, 1969).

——, *Biharni Komi Aagmaan* (Ahmedabad: Navajivan, 1956).

——, *Dillimaan Gandhiji,* 2 vols. (Ahmedabad: Navajivan, 1966).

——, *Ekla Chalo Re* (Ahmedabad: Navajivan, 1957).

——, *Last Glimpses of Bapu* (Agra: Shiva Lal Agarwala, 1962).

——, *The Lonely Pilgrim* (Ahmedabad: Navajivan, 1964).

Gandhi, Mohandas K, *Autobiography* (New York: Dover, 1983).

——, *Collected Works of Mahatma Gandhi,* 100 vols. (New Delhi: Publications Division).

——, *Hind Swaraj* (Ahmedabad: Navajivan).

——, *Letters to Sardar Patel* (Ahmedabad: Navajivan, 1957).

——, *My Experiments with Truth* (Ahmedabad: Navajivan, 1930).

——, *Satyagraha in South Africa* (Ahmedabad: Navajivan, 1928).

——, *Speeches and Writings* (Madras: Ganesan, 1922).

——, *Unto This Last: A Paraphrase* (Ahmedabad: Navajivan, 1956).

Gandhi, Prabhudas, *Jeevan Prabhat* (New Delhi: Sasta Sahitya Mandal, 1967).

Gandhi, Rajmohan, *India Wins Errors* (New Delhi: Radiant, 1989).

——, *Patel: A Life* (Ahmedabad: Navajivan, 1990).

——, *Rajaji: A Life* (New Delhi: Penguin, 1997).

——, *The Good Boatman* (New Delhi: Penguin, 1995).

——, *Understanding the Muslim Mind* (New Delhi: Penguin, 1987).

Ghosh, Sudhir, *Gandhi's Emissary* (Bombay: Rupa, 1967).

Glendevon, John, *The Viceroy at Bay* (London: Collins, 1971).

Gopal, S, *Nehru,* 3 vols. (New Delhi: Oxford).

Gore, M S, *The Social Context of an Ideology: Ambedkar's Political and Social Thought* (New Delhi: Sage, 1993).

Goswami, K P (ed.), *Mahatma Gandhi: A Chronology* (New Delhi: Publications Division, 1971).

Gracie, David M (ed.), *Gandhi & Charlie* (Cambridge, Mass.: Cowley, 1989).

Green, Martin, *Gandhi: Voice of a New Age Revolution* (New York: Continuum, 1993).

Hardiman, David, *Gandhi: In His Time and Ours* (New Delhi: Permanent Black, 2003).

Hasan, Mushirul (ed.), *India's Partition* (New Delhi: OUP, 1993).

Hingorani, Anand (ed.), *God is Truth* (Bombay: Bhavan, 1971).

—— (ed.), *On Myself* (Bombay: Bhavan, 1972).

Hodson, H V, *The Great Divide* (London: Hutchinson, 1969).

Hunt, James D, *Gandhi and the Nonconformists; Encounters in South Africa* (New Delhi: Promilla, 1986).

——, *Gandhi in London* (New Delhi: Promilla, 1978).

Hutchins, Francis G, *Spontaneous Revolution: The Quit India Movement* (New Delhi: Manohar, 1971).

Huttenback, Robert A, *Gandhi in South Africa* (Ithaca, NY: Cornell University Press, 1971).

Iqbal, Afzal, *Mohamed Ali* (Delhi: Idarah-i-Adabiyat, 1978).

Irwin (Halifax), *Fulness of Days* (London: Collins, 1957).

Iyer, Raghavan, *The Essential Writings of Mahatma Gandhi* (New Delhi: OUP, 1991).

——, *The Moral and Political Thought of Mahatma Gandhi* (New Delhi: OUP, 1973).

Jones, E Stanley, *Gandhi* (Nashville: Abingdon, 1948).

Juneja, M M, *The Mahatma and the Millionaire* (Hissar, Haryana: Modern, 1993).

Kalarthi, Mukul, *Ba and Bapu* (Ahmedabad: Navajivan, 1962).

Kalelkar, D B, *Bapu ki Jhankian* (Ahmedabad: Navajivan, 1948).

——, *Gandhi Charitra Kirtan* (Ahmedabad: Navajivan, 1970).

Kapur, Sudarshan, *Raising up a Prophet: The African-American Encounter with Gandhi* (Boston: Beacon, 1992).

Khaliquzzaman, Choudhary, *Pathway to Pakistan* (Lahore: Pakistan Longman, 1961).

Khosla, G D, *A Taste of India* (Bombay: Jaico, 1970).

Kripalani, J B, *Autobiography* (typescript), Kripalani Papers, New Delhi.

——, *Gandhi: His Life and Thought* (New Delhi: Publications Division, 1970).

Krishna, Brij, *Gandhiji ki Dilli Diary*, 3 vols. (Delhi, 1970).

Krishnadas, *Seven Months with Mahatma Gandhi* (Ahmedabad: Navajivan, 1961).

Kulkarni, Sumitra, *Anmol Virasat*, 3 vols. (Delhi: Prabhat Prakashan, 1988).

Limaye, Madhu, *Prime Movers* (New Delhi: Radiant, 1985).

Lohia, Rammanohar, *Guilty Men of India's Partition* (Allahabad: Kitabistan, 1960).

Mani, P, *The Secret of Mahatma Gandhi* (New Delhi: Arnold, 1989).

Mansergh, N, and Lumby, E W R (eds.), *The Transfer of Power*, 12 vols. (London: Her Majesty's Stationery Office, 1970–83).

Mashruwala, K G, *In Quest of Truth* (Ahmedabad: Shravana, 1983).

Menon, V P, *The Transfer of Power in India* (Calcutta: Orient Longmans, 1957).

Merriam, A H, *Gandhi vs. Jinnah* (Calcutta: Minerva, 1980).

Mesthrie, Uma Dhupelia, *Gandhi's Prisoner? The Life of Gandhi's Son Manilal* (New Delhi: Permanent Black, 2005).

Moon, Penderel (ed.), *Wavell: A Viceroy's Journal* (London: OUP, 1973).

Moran, Lord, *Winston Churchill* (London: Constable, 1966).

Munshi, K M, *Pilgrimage to Freedom* (Bombay: Bhavan, 1967).

Nanda, B R (ed.), *Mahatma Gandhi: 125 Years* (New Delhi: Indian Council for Cultural Relations, 1995).

——, *Gandhi: Pan-Islamism, Imperialism and Nationalism in India* (New Delhi: OUP, 1989).

——, *In Search of Gandhi* (New Delhi: OUP, 2002).

——, *Mahatma Gandhi: A Biography* (New Delhi: OUP, 1996).

Nandurkar, G M (ed.), *Sardar Vallabhbhai Patel Centenary Volumes,* 5 vols. (Ahmedabad: 1974–8).

—— (ed.), *Sardar's Letters: Post-centenary Series,* 3 vols. (Ahmedabad: 1980–3).

—— (ed.), *Sardarshri na Patro,* 5 vols. (Ahmedabad: 1975–8).

—— (ed.), *Sardarshri ke Patra,* 2 vols. (Ahmedabad: 1981).

Nayar, Sushila, *Mahatma Gandhi,* vols. 4 & 5 (Ahmedabad: Navajivan, 1989, 1994).

Noorani, A G, *Savarkar and Hindutva* (New Delhi: LeftWord, 2002).

Parekh, Bhikhu, *Colonialism, Tradition, and Reform* (New Delhi: Sage, 1989).

Parel, Anthony J (ed.), *Gandhi:* Hind Swaraj *and Other Writings* (Cambridge: Cambridge University Press, 1997).

Parikh, Narhari, *Sardar Vallabhbhai Patel,* 2 vols. (Ahmedabad: Navajivan, 1971).

Parikh, Nilam, *Gandhiji's Lost Jewel: Harilal Gandhi* (New Delhi: National Gandhi Museum, 2001).

Patel, C N, *Mahatma Gandhi in his Gujarati Writings* (New Delhi: Sahitya Akademi, 1981).

Patel, Maniben, *Diary of Maniben Patel,* Patel Papers, Ahmedabad.

Patel, Ravjibhai, *The Making of the Mahatma* (Ahmedabad: Navajivan, 1989).

Philips, C H, and Wainwright, M D (eds.), *The Partition of India* (London: Allen & Unwin, 1970).

Prasad, Rajendra, *Autobiography* (Bombay: Asia, 1957).

Pyarelal, *Mahatma Gandhi: The Early Phase* (Ahmedabad: Navajivan, 1965).

——, *Mahatma Gandhi: The Last Phase,* 2 vols. (Ahmedabad: Navajivan, 1956).

——, *Mahatma Gandhi: Volume 2* (Bombay: Sevak, 1980).

——, *Mahatma Gandhi: Volume 3* (Ahmedabad, Navajivan, 1986).

——, *The Epic Fast* (Ahmedabad: Navajivan, 1932).

—— & Sushila Nayar, *In Gandhiji's Mirror* (New Delhi: OUP, 1991).

Ramachandran, G, *Thoughts and Talks* (Madurai, Tamil Nadu: 1964).

——, and Mahadevan, T K (eds.), *Quest for Gandhi* (Bombay: Bhavan, 1970).

Rao, B Shiva, *India's Freedom Movement* (Madras: Orient Longmans, 1960).

Rau, Chalapati, *Gandhi and Nehru* (New Delhi: Allied, 1967).

Reddy, E S, and Gandhi, Gopalkrishna (eds.), *Gandhi and South Africa* (Ahmedabad: Navajivan, 1993).

Roy, Dilip Kumar, *Among the Great* (Bombay: Jaico, 1950).

Rudolph, Susanne Hoeber and Lloyd I, *Gandhi: The Traditional Roots of Charisma* (Hyderabad: Orient Longman, 1987).

Sharp, Gene, *Gandhi Wields the Weapon of Moral Power* (Ahmedabad: Navajivan, 1960).

Sheean, Vincent, *Lead Kindly Light* (New York: Random House, 1949).

Shirer, William L, *Gandhi: A Memoir* (New Delhi: Rupa, 1993).

Shukla, Chandrashanker (ed.), *Reminiscences of Gandhiji* (Bombay: Vora, 1951).

——, *Gandhi's View of Life* (Bombay: Bhavan, 1968).

—— (ed.), *Incidents in Gandhiji's Life* (Bombay: Vora, 1949).

Sitaramayya, Pattabhi, *The History of the Indian National Congress, 1935–47* (Bombay: Padma, 1947).

Swan, Maureen, *Gandhi: The South African Experience* (Johannesburg: Ravan, 1985).

Templewood, Lord, *Nine Troubled Years* (London: Collins, 1954).

Tendulkar, D G, *Gandhi in Champaran* (New Delhi: Publications Division, 1994).

——, *Mahatma,* 8 vols. (Bombay).

Watson, Francis, and Maurice Brown, *Talking of Gandhiji* (Calcutta: Orient Longmans, 1957).

Weber, Thomas, *On the Salt March* (New Delhi: HarperCollins, 1997).

Wolpert, Stanley, *Jinnah* (New York: Oxford, 1984).

Yagnik, Indulal, *Gandhi As I Knew Him* (New Delhi: Danish Mahal, 1943).

Glossary

adharma	against dharma or righteousness
adivasis	India's indigenous people
ahimsa	non-violence
Ahmadi	member of Muslim sect, heterodox to some and heretical to others
Akalis	reformist Sikh group, later a political party
Antyajas	'the last people', a phrase for the untouchables
anna	16 annas made a rupee
aparigraha	non-possessiveness
Arya Samaj	reformist Hindu sect
Ashram	Retreat or centre (spiritual or political)
avarna	not from a high caste
Ayurveda/ic	ancient Indian school of medicine/ of that school
Ba	Gujarati expression meaning mother but used for his wife Kastur (or Kasturba) by Gandhi and others
Bania (or Vania)	trader or merchant; belonging to the 'third' category of Hindu high castes, after Brahmins (priests or teachers) and Kshatriyas (warriors)
Bapu	Father; word used for Gandhi by many Indians and by his wife and sons
begar	forced labour
bhagwa	saffron flag of Hindu warriors
bhajan	devotional or prayer song

bidi	handmade cigarette
brahmacharya	celibacy, chastity
Brahmin	member of highest Hindu caste of priests and teachers
caste (system)	The caste system separates people into castes (varnas) and sub-castes (jatis), and grades castes and sub-castes from high to low. One born into a particular jati is expected to marry within that jati.
chadariya	sheet or length of cloth
chamar	belonging to an 'untouchable' group working with hides
chappal	loose sandals
charkha	spinning wheel
crore	10 million
dal	lentil
Dalit	suppressed or down-trodden; belonging to an 'untouchable' group
darshan	merit-conferring sight or view of virtuous person
dehat	village
dharma	righteousness, duty, religion
dharmashala	inn (usually crowded) costing travellers little or nothing
dhoti	loose lower garment for males
Divali	annual Hindu festival of lights
diwan	chief minister
durbar	court
fatwa	authoritative opinion, edict
goondas	criminals
gurdwara	Sikh shrine
hareli	lit. 'an enclosed place' in Persian; used by the Vaishnava sect to refer to their temples in Gujerat
Harijan	literally, person of God; expression popularized by Gandhi for 'untouchables'
hartal	suspension of business
hijrat	emigration (of Muslims) from an unholy land to a virtuous one
Holi	springtime Hindu festival
idli	popular South Indian savoury cake of lentil and rice-flour
jaggery	unrefined sugar
Jain, a	follower of the Jain or Jaina religion
Jalebi	Indian sweet
jati	sub-caste or group into which one is born

Kaka	Gujarati for father's brother
kalima	Islamic credo
kameez	shirt
karmayogi	dedicated to action
karmabhoomi	land or space for one's work or struggle
khadi	handspun and hand-woven cloth
Khilafat	Caliphate; Muslim sovereignty over Islam's holy sites
kirpan	small dagger or sword that Sikh males must carry
kranti	revolution
lakh	100,000
lathi	stick, staff or baton
Lok Sevak Sangh	People's Servants' Association
Mahatma	Great soul
malish	oil massage
mamlatdar	administrative head of a taluka (q.v.), a 'collector' or 'deputy commissioner' being the head of a district comprising several talukas
mandirs	temples
masjids	mosques
maulvi	Islamic scholar
namaaz	formal Islamic prayer
panchayat	group or committee of village leaders
Purna Swaraj	Complete Independence
quam	Muslim community
Rashtriya Swayamsevak Sangh	literally, National Volunteer Association; body formed in 1925 'to protect Hindu culture'
Rashtriya Yuvak Sangh	National Youth Association
Sabha	Assembly
sadagraha	firmness for the good
sadhu	renunciate or recluse
salwar	lower garment
sanatan or sanatana ('sanatanist')	literally, eternal; defenders of Hindu orthodoxy called themselves 'sanatanists'
sangathan	organization
sarvodaya	literally, the rise of all, which Gandhi said was to be preferred to 'the greatest good of the highest number'

satyagraha	literally, firmness for the truth; non-violent struggle
savarna	member of a high caste
shakti	force or strength
shanti	peace
shastra	scriptural text
Sheth	rich man
shikha	hair-knot kept by high-caste Hindu males
shuddhi	purification
sindoor	red powder applied to the hair of a Hindu woman to show she is married
sowar	Indian cavalry trooper
Swami	literally, Lord; title accorded to spiritually exceptional Hindu male
Swaraj (or Swarajya)	Self-rule; independence
Swarajya Sabha	Self-rule Assembly or Association
swadeshi	of one's nation
tabligh	Arabic for 'delivering [the message]'
takli	hand-held spindle
talati	village revenue collector reporting to the mamlatdar (q.v.)
taluka	administrative unit comprising many villages and constituting a portion of a district
tanpura	drone instrument
tanzim	Arabic for organization
thakore	lord or ruler
thana	police station
tilak	auspicious forehead mark
tinkathia	compelling peasants to plant indigo
tulsi (beads)	beads made from stem of tulsi (basil) plant, sacred to many Hindus
vaidya	doctor
vakil	pleader or lawyer
varna	caste
veth	extortion of free services for government functionaries
yajna/yagna	sacrificial rite or practice
zamindar	landlord

Abbreviations

AICC	=	All India Congress Committee
AKP	=	Aga Khan's Palace
AMU	=	Aligarh Muslim University
ANC	=	African National Congress
BIA	=	see TBIA
CP	=	'Central Provinces' (unit of British India)
CPB	=	Congress Parliamentary Board
ENO	=	Europeans and Nominated members and Officials
GPCC	=	Gujarat Provincial Congress Committee
HMG	=	His Majesty's Government
HMIS	=	His Majesty's Indian Ship
ICD	=	individual civil disobedience
IEA	=	Indian Educational Association
INA	=	Indian National Army
KK	=	Khudai Khidmtagars
KPP	=	Krishak Praja Party
LVS	=	London Vegetarian Society
MLA	=	Member Legislative Assembly
NCSC	=	Naval Central Strike Committee
NIA	=	Natal Indian Association
NIC	=	Natal Indian Congress
NWFP	=	North-West Frontier Province
OFS	=	Orange Free State
PA	=	political agent
PBF	=	Punjab Boundary Force
PCC	=	provincial Congress committee
RIN	=	Royal Indian Navy
RSS	=	Rashtriya Swayamsevak Sangh
RTC	=	Round Table Conference
SABIC	=	South African British Indian Committee
TARA	=	Transvaal Asiatic Registration Act
(T)BIA	=	(Transvaal) British Indian Association
TIRA	=	Transvaal Immigrants Restriction Act
UP	=	'United Provinces' (unit of British India, now the Indian state of Uttar Pradesh)
YMCA	=	Young Men's Christian Association

Index